FEATURES AND BENEFITS

Essentials for Algebra, Concepts and Skills

All important **prealgebra concepts and skills** are presented to thoroughly prepare students for success in Algebra. See pp. 1, 159, 241, 292.

Many lessons open with motivating, **realistic problems** that set the stage for the skill being taught. See pp. 53, 145, 173, 265.

Worked-out examples followed by **Your Turn** aid understanding and allow students to immediately test that understanding. See pp. 24, 90, 155, 265.

Numerous graded exercises, often followed by word problems, provide an abundance of practice and also provide for differences in individual students. See pp. 55, 188, 214, 384–385.

Enrichment Lessons and **Challenges** accommodate the more capable student. See pp. 204, 321.

Algebra Practice lessons at the end of each chapter constantly reinforce the skills students need to succeed in Algebra. See pp. 27, 63, . . .

Self-Tests, Chapter Reviews, Chapter Tests, and **Cumulative Reviews** provide opportunities to reinforce skills and check understanding. See pp. 126, 131–133.

Problem Solving Lessons present students with a variety of problem-solving methods in the context of consumer and career related topics. See pp. 64–65, 222–223, 234–235.

Optional **Using the Calculator** and **Using the Computer** activities apply new technology in a meaningful way. See pp. 258, 261.

Programming in BASIC is an optional chapter that teaches simple programming and reviews skills and concepts learned throughout the year. This chapter can be completed without access to a computer. See Chapter 14.

Lesson Commentary, Extra Chapter Tests, and an **Assignment Guide** provide comprehensive teaching support. See pp. T14, T45, T36.

Practice Masters and **Tests,** both on duplicating masters without overprinted answers, are available to provide additional support for reinforcement and evaluation.

Essentials for Algebra
Concepts and Skills

AUTHORS
Robert E. Willcutt
Patricia R. Fraze
Francis J. Gardella

EDITORIAL ADVISER
Charles E. Allen

TEACHER CONSULTANTS
Dotty J. Garrett   Adrienne A. Kapisak   Patricia C. McNeil
Tommy Tomlinson   Marvin Weingarden

Houghton Mifflin Company · Boston

Atlanta   Dallas   Geneva, Ill.   Lawrenceville, N.J.   Palo Alto   Toronto

Authors

Robert E. Willcutt
Associate Professor, Science-Mathematics
Education Department, School of Education, Boston University

Patricia R. Fraze
Chairman, Mathematics Department
Ann Arbor Huron (Michigan) High School

Francis J. Gardella
Mathematics Supervisor
East Brunswick Public Schools, New Jersey

Editorial Adviser

Charles E. Allen
Instructional Specialist, Secondary Mathematics
Los Angeles City Schools, California

Teacher Consultants

Dotty J. Garrett
Mabry Middle School
Marietta, Georgia

Adrienne A. Kapisak
Gateway Senior High School
Monroeville, Pennsylvania

Patricia C. McNeil
Parkland Junior High School
Rockville, Maryland

Tommy Tomlinson
T. K. Gorman High School
Tyler, Texas

Marvin Weingarden
Detroit Public Schools
Michigan

ISBN: 0-395-37881-8

BCDEFGHIJ-D-943210/89876

Table of Contents

ESSENTIALS FOR ALGEBRA

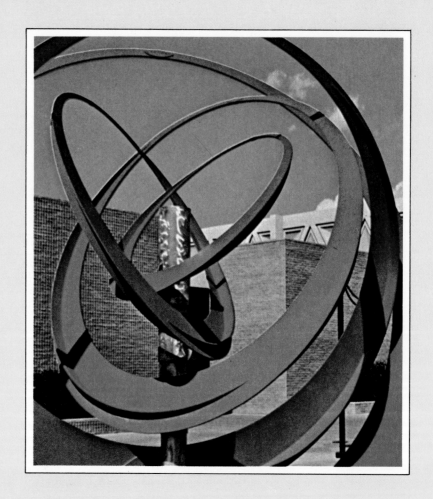

The pre-algebra course written
especially for high-school students
...and it's everything you'd expect
from the #1 algebra publisher.

Houghton Mifflin

*Complete algebra preparation.
Your students will learn all the essential skills and concepts they'll need to succeed in first-year algebra.

*Written especially for high-school students.
Development is always careful and clear so your students will learn gradually and confidently.

*Plentiful and timely problem solving.
Numerous applications and problem-solving strategies prepare your students for life inside and outside the classroom.

*The most teachable program you'll find anywhere.
Learners and teachers alike will find this course logical and complete. Success is the natural conclusion.

Let us show you how ▶

Your students will learn all the essential skills and concepts they'll need to succeed in first-year algebra.

Using variables

As they review computation skills, your students will learn the concept of a variable — essential for writing equations to solve problems.

Writing algebraic expressions

Beginning with very simple expressions in Chapter 1, your students will get plenty of practice in writing equations.

1-1 Variables

It costs $4 per hour to rent a canoe at the Bantam Boatyard. The total cost of any rental varies with the amount of time spent canoeing. If you let n equal the number of hours spent canoeing, then $4 \times n$ stands for the cost of the rental. We call n a **variable** and $4 \times n$ an **expression**.

Here are some other ways you can show multiplication.

$$4 \cdot n \qquad (4)(n) \qquad 4n$$

To evaluate the expression $4n$, replace n with different numbers.

Example 1 Evaluate $4n$ when $n = 6$, when $n = 10$

Solution
$4n = (4)(6) \qquad 4n = (4)(10)$
$\quad = 24 \qquad\qquad = 40$

Your Turn Evaluate the expression.
- $3x$, when $x = 8$
- $12 + (2a)$ when $a = 12$ ⟵ *Work inside the parentheses first.*

You can often write expressions for word phrases.

Example 2 Write an expression for the phrase.
a number n added to 45

Solution $n + 45$ or $45 + n$ ⟵ *Either order*

1

urday. How many packages does he deliver in all?
- Monica sells 40 lb of fish on Wednesday and 39 on Thursday. How many pounds does she sell in all?
- Gavin pumps 256 gal of gasoline on Tuesday and 460 on Wednesday. How many gallons are pumped in all?

The following properties can be used to make addition easier.

Commutative Property of Addition

Changing the order of the addends doesn't change the sum.

In Arithmetic	In Algebra
$5 + 6 = 6 + 5$	$a + b = b + a$

Associative Property of Addition

Changing the grouping of the addends doesn't change the sum.

In Arithmetic	In Algebra
$(5 + 6) + 7 = 5 + (6 + 7)$	$(a + b) + c = a + (b + c)$

You can combine the commutative and associative properties to make addition easier.

Example 3 Use the commutative and associative properties to add $(26 + 8) + 4$.

Solution Think: $(26 + 8) + 4 = 26 + 4 + 8$ ⟵ *To add in your head look for sums of 10, 20, 30, etc. to add first.*
$\qquad = 30 + 8$
$\qquad = 38$

Reading and using generalizations

Properties and relationships essential to understanding algebra are explained in simple language . . . and shown in <u>both</u> arithmetic and algebraic terms.

5-3 Using Division

A pair of running shoes weighs 800 g. How much does each shoe weigh?

Of course you can solve this problem by dividing 800 by 2. We can also show how to solve it by writing an equation with a variable.

Let s represent the weight of one shoe. Then $2s$ represents the weight of the pair. So $2s$ equals 800.

To solve the equation $2s = 800$, you can divide each side of the equation by 2. Then s equals 400. Each shoe weighs 400 g.

$$2s = 800$$
$$\frac{2s}{2} = \frac{800}{2}$$
$$s = 400$$

Some equations can be solved by dividing each side by the same non-zero number. Division by a non-zero number "undoes" multiplication by that number.

Example 1   Solve $24 = 4y$.

Solution
$$24 = 4y$$
$$\frac{24}{4} = \frac{4y}{4} \longleftarrow \text{\textit{To "undo" multiplication by 4, divide by 4.}}$$
$$6 = 1y$$
$$6 = y$$

140

Solving equations
Your students will balance equations — first through inspection of simple equations and then by using more formal rules.

Graphing equations
They'll learn to graph solution sets of equations. Developing solution sets for linear equations will also reinforce their understanding of variables.

Class Exercises

What sum is shown on the number line?

Exercises

Use a number line to find the sum.

A
1. $8 + {}^-2$ 2. $^-5 + 4$ 3. $^-8 + 6$ 4. $^-4 + 5$
5. $9 + {}^-9$ 6. $12 + {}^-8$ 7. $4 + {}^-7$ 8. $^-6 + 9$

Find the sum.

B
9. $^-2 + 3$ 10. $^-6 + 1$ 11. $2 + {}^-7$ 12. $8 + {}^-10$
13. $^-12 + 12$ 14. $13 + {}^-4$ 15. $12 + {}^-10$ 16. $^-9 + 18$
17. $^-11 + 7$ 18. $3 + {}^-20$ 19. $^-14 + 16$ 20. $9 + {}^-21$

Solve the equation.

21. $x = 15 + {}^-4$ 22. $b = {}^-6 + 13$ 23. $14 + {}^-19 = t$
24. $d = {}^-2 + 18$ 25. $g = 23 + {}^-8$ 26. $^-28 + 16 = m$
27. $c = {}^-5 + 32$ 28. $56 + {}^-18 = y$ 29. $x = 84 + {}^-92$
30. $g = {}^-37 + 67$ 31. $n = 41 + {}^-37$ 32. $33 + {}^-53 = p$

Combine like terms.

33. $3a + {}^-2a$ 34. $^-d + 5d$ 35. $7y + {}^-8y$ 36. $^-4n + 4n$
37. $^-8x + 12x$ 38. $10g + {}^-16g$ 39. $14m + {}^-8m$ 40. $^-k + {}^-16k$

Using integers
After extending their knowledge of positive and negative numbers, your students will use variables with integers and positive and negative rationals. To help students visualize relationships with integers, the familiar number line is used throughout.

Development is always careful and clear so your students will learn gradually and confidently.

Introductions

Lessons open with motivating, realistic problems that set the stage for the skill being taught.

Examples and Solutions

Completely worked-out examples — with reminders — aid understanding.

Your Turn

Problems similar to the worked-out examples let your students test their understanding so they can proceed with confidence to the exercise sets. (Answers to Your Turn are in the back of the book.)

7-4 Percent of a Number

To approve of a new camera at least 40% of the people in a survey must respond favorably. If there are 300 people in the survey, how many favorable responses are needed?

You can write and solve an equation to answer the question "What number is 40% of 300?"

Let n = the number of favorable responses needed

Then n is 40% of 300 ⟵ *In percent problems, "of" means multiply.*
$n = 0.40 \times 300$ ⟵ *Write the percent as a decimal and solve.*
$n = 120$

At least 120 people must give favorable responses.

When you compute sales tax and interest you're finding a percent of a number.

Example 1 The Wilcox family bought camping gear that cost $439.98. If the sales tax rate is 5%, how much was the sales tax? What was the price including tax?

Solution Let n = the amount of the sales tax
Then n = 5% of $439.98
$n = 0.05 \times 439.98$
$n = \$21.999$ ⟵ *Round to the nearest cent.*
$\$439.98 + \$22 = \$461.98$ ⟵ *Add the tax to the total cost.*
The sales tax was $22 and the price including tax was $461.98.

Your Turn • Riverdale High chartered a bus for a class trip. The cost of the charter was $178.45 plus 4% sales tax. What was the amount of the tax?

219

Class Exercises

You are to solve for *x*. By what number would you divide each side of the equation?

1. $5x = 35$ 2. $24 = 3x$ 3. $7x = 14$ 4. $4x = 48$
5. $27 = 9x$ 6. $80 = 8x$ 7. $13x = 13$ 8. $30 = 2x$

Exercises

Use division to solve. Check the solution.

A 1. $2b = 6$ 2. $18 = 9c$ 3. $8d = 48$ 4. $5e = 15$
5. $72 = 8f$ 6. $3g = 12$ 7. $2h = 8$ 8. $5j = 35$
9. $3k = 21$ 10. $20 = 4m$ 11. $10n = 65$ 12. $8p = 12$

Solve. Check the solution.

B 13. $9a = 270$ 14. $186 = 6b$ 15. $15c = 75$ 16. $11d = 913$
17. $244 = 4e$ 18. $93 = 31f$ 19. $14g = 420$ 20. $9h = 972$
21. $25j = 175$ 22. $640 = 16k$ 23. $960 = 30m$ 24. $40n = 1600$
25. $65p = 130$ 26. $75q = 600$ 27. $360 = 18r$ 28. $19s = 76$

These equations have fractions or decimals. Solve and check.

29. $6a = 7.2$ 30. $4.5 = 15w$ 31. $0.6m = 120$ 32. $1.2q = 36$
33. $1.8 = 0.2x$ 34. $0.01y = 2$ 35. $1.4d = 28$ 36. $15 = 0.5r$

Exercises

After working through the Class Exercises as a group, your students will be prepared for independent work with graded Exercises. **Problems,** which frequently follow the exercises, combine a variety of previously learned skills.

Enrichment

At the end of each chapter there's a full page of Enrichment for students who have mastered the chapter material. Short **Challenge** features engage students who finish their assignment early.

Fibonacci Numbers

The Fibonacci Sequence consists of a series of numbers in which each term is the sum of the preceding two terms.

1, 1, 2, 3, 5, 8, 13, ...

This sequence can be noted in many natural phenomena. The centers of most sunflowers have 21 spirals in one direction and 34 spirals in the other. The stalks of many plants have new leaves growing in a pattern such that starting at the base of the stalk and counting upward, each new leaf growing directly above another leaf is in a position corresponding to a Fibonacci number. If the first leaf is 1 the next leaf directly above it will be 8 and the next 13, etc.

1. Write the first 20 terms of the Fibonacci Sequence.
2. Find the sum of the first five terms of the sequence. (to the seventh term. Repeat this for the sum of the fi and the first seven terms. What do you discover?
3. Use the results of Exercise 2 to write the sums of the terms, ten terms, and fifteen terms without actually d tion.
4. It will take two months for a newborn pair of rabbits their first pair of rabbits. After that they produce one month. If you start with one pair of rabbits producing this pattern and each succeeding pair of rabbits prod to the same pattern, how many pairs of rabbits will y end of each of the next twelve months?

30

Formulas

Algebra Practice

Write an equation. Solve.

1. The product of 355 and 982 is r.
2. The sum of 16.74, 39.1, and 26.492 is m.
3. 0.0861 divided by 0.07 is equal to x.
4. The difference between $5\frac{1}{2}$ and $2\frac{4}{9}$ is d.
5. $\frac{1}{8}$ of $4\frac{4}{5}$ is equal to q.

Chapter Review

Match.

1. perimeter of a rectangle
2. $A = \pi r^2$
3. perimeter of a square
4. $P = a + b + c$

a. area of a circle
b. area of a square
c. lines that are the same distance apart
d. $P = 2l + 2w$

Cumulative Review (Chapters 1–6)

Solve the equation.

704 − 96   2. $0.4 \times 36 = x$ 3. $6.2 \times 10 = n$

4.2 = t   5. $\frac{3}{4} \cdot 284 = s$ 6. $\frac{4}{5} = \frac{x}{10}$

2) − 6 =   8. $10 \cdot 10 \cdot 10 = $ 9. $A = (6.2)(5)$

Review and Testing

elf-Tests, Algebra Practice, Chapter Reviews, and Cumulative Reviews ffer you plenty of opportunities to heck your students' understanding... nd to provide reteaching when necessary. Chapter Tests in the student book re paralleled by Extra Chapter Tests in he Teacher's Edition.

Chapter Test

Which number is a solution of the equation?

1. $7a = 364$ 52 or 92?   2. $16 + b$

Solve the equation.

3. $c + 8 = 17$ 4. $6 + h = 21$
6. $5e = 45$ 7. $132 = 6p$
9. $d - 4 = 11$ 10. $49 = n - 3$
12. $\frac{1}{2}f = 7$ 13. $\frac{g}{3} = 4$
15. $8a + 4 = 28$ 16. $6x - 1 = 17$

Self Test 1

Answer *Yes* or *No*.

1. Is 26 a solution of $x + 27 = 53$?   5-1
2. Is 36 a solution of $73 = 2y + 1$?

Solve the equation.

3. $a + 13 = 71$ 4. $32 = b + 7$ 5. $51 + c = 69$ 5-2
6. $7d = 91$ 7. $400 = 8e$ 8. $3f = 693$ 5-3
9. $g - 17 = 74$ 10. $102 = h - 21$ 11. $j - 43 = 12$ 5-4

Numerous applications and problem-solving strategies prepare your students for life inside and outside the classroom.

Problem Solving on the Job
Problem Solving for the Consumer

Special lessons show your students the kinds of problems people face as workers and consumers. This real-world exposure demonstrates why we study math.

Problem Solving for the Consumer

Buying a Car

The amount of money a dealer pays a factory for a car is called the dealer cost. To make a profit a dealer must charge a customer more than the dealer cost. To give you an idea of a fair price for that charge, consumer magazines will estimate a cost factor. This cost factor is often expressed as a decimal. To determine dealer cost, just multiply the list price the dealer tells you by the cost factor.

Complete the chart to find the approximate dealer cost.

	Model	List Price	Cost Factor	Dealer Cost
1.	Fire fly	$10,370	0.88	?
2.	Cruiser	$ 7095	0.86	?
3.	Wanderer	$ 6714	0.90	?
4.	Stallion	$ 8979	0.84	?

Options are not included in the basic price of a car, so you have to add those extra charges onto the cost. Here's a list of some options on one car model and the list prices. Answer the questions.

5. What's the total cost of these options?
6. Which options total $881?

OPTIONS	LIST PRICE
POWER BRAKES	100.00
POWER STEERING	315.95

Basic Car			Options			(a) Total List Price	(b) Total Dealer Cost	Difference (a − b)
List Price	Cost Factor	Dealer Cost	List Price	Cost Factor	Dealer Cost			
8. $6278	0.88	?	$1375	0.85	?	?	?	?
9. $7762	0.93	?	$ 495	0.84	?	?	?	?
10. $8449	0.87	?	$1036	0.87	?	?	?	?

It's smart to compare the gas mileage ratings of cars. The average driver might drive 12,000 mi per year. Suppose gas costs $1.08 a gallon. Complete the chart. Round the answers to the nearest hundredth.

	Model	Miles Per Gallon (Highway driving)	Number of Gallons Per Year	Cost of Gas Per Year
11.	Darter	42.6	281.69	?
12.	XM-Hawk	33.4	?	?
13.	Winslow	25.7	?	?

Solve.

14. A Cobra gets 39 mi per gallon. When air conditioning is running it gets 4.2 fewer miles per gallon. How many gallons of gas would be used for running the air conditioner constantly on a 420-mile trip?

15. Suppose you have the following options, but you decide to buy only two of them. How many different combinations of two options do you have?
    automatic transmission   air conditioning   power brakes
    stereo with AM-FM system   fog lights

65

3-5 Problem Solving

Finding and using a pattern can be the key to solving certain kinds of problems.

Example 1   A city planner needs to know the number of street intersections before ordering new traffic lights. If there are 20 North-South streets intersecting with 20 East-West streets, how many intersections are there?

Solution   First we'll find how many intersections there are if there are fewer streets in each direction. We draw diagrams and count to determine the number of intersections if there are 1, 2, 3, or 4 streets in each direction.

Problem-Solving Strategies

Because no one strategy is right for solving every problem, your students will learn a variety of problem-solving methods. When faced with a new problem, they'll be equipped with options for solving it.

20. For any right triangle ABC with the right angle at C, is it true that $\tan A \cdot \tan B = 1$? Show how you discovered this.

Using the Calculator

Find the value of the symbol in the table on page 470, use a calculate to evaluate the expression, and round to the nearest whole number.

1. $\sqrt{3} \cdot \sqrt{3}$ **2.** $\sqrt{7} \cdot \sqrt{7}$ **3.** $\sqrt{15} \cdot \sqrt{15}$ **4.** $\sqrt{23} \cdot \sqrt{23}$ **5.**

6. Is the following statement true? $\sqrt{n} \cdot \sqrt{n} = n$

Using the Computer

You can use something called the random number function to simulate a coin tossing experiment on a computer. The following program may need to be adjusted for use on your computer to provide different results on every RUN. RUN the program several times for N = 20.

```
  5  REM: SIMULATING TOSSING A COIN
 10  PRINT "HOW MANY TOSSES";
 20  INPUT N
 30  FOR I=1 TO N
 40  LET A=RND(1)  ◄─── To get different tosses on every RUN,
 50  IF A<.5 THEN 90      you may need to alter line 40. Check the
 60  LET T=T+1            manual for your computer.
 70  PRINT "  T"
 80  GOTO 110
 90  LET H=H+1
100  PRINT "H"
110  NEXT I
120  PRINT "H =";H,"T =";T,"H/N =";H/N
130  END
```

Using the Calculator

Through interesting problems students gain facility with calculators . . . and learn their value in doing tedious calculations.

Using the Computer

Using chapter content as a springboard, your students will keyboard programs . . . and see how fast the computer can provide answers.

Programming in BASIC

Designed to be used <u>without</u> a computer, this optional chapter introduces your students to the principles of programming in BASIC.

And that's not all! Since this chapter reviews many of the skills and concepts learned throughout the textbook, it becomes a motivating vehicle for year-end review.

14-2 REM, LET, and PRINT

You can use a REMARK (REM) statement to state what a program or part of a program is supposed to do. These statements are numbered within the program and are printed only when the program is listed. They do not interfere with or have any effect on the execution of the program. LET statements are used to assign a value to a variable.

Example 1 Write a program to calculate the circumference of a circle with a radius of 2.75.

Solution
```
10  REM CALCULATE THE CIRCUMFERENCE OF A CIRCLE
15  REM FORMULA FOR CIRCUMFERENCE IS C=2*PI*R
20  LET P = 3.14  ◄─── P stands for π.
30  LET R = 2.75  ◄─── R stands for radius.
40  PRINT 2*P*R
50  END
```

You may use any letter to stand for a variable. Always be sure that the assigned value of a variable is on the right of the equal sign. The statement LET A + B = C is not valid, but LET C = A + B is.

You can use quotation marks around any group of words, numbers, or symbols that you want printed exactly as they appear.

Example 2 Write the output for the program.
```
10  REM CALCULATE THE AREA OF A RECTANGLE
20  LET L = 12.5
30  LET W = 5.7
40  LET A = L*W
50  PRINT "THE AREA OF THE RECTANGLE IS" A
60  END
```
The computer prints

If a program contains an error or "bug" the computer cannot complete execution. Some type of error message will be printed to tell you at which line and why execution was halted.

Example 3 Debug the program.
```
10  REM CALCULATE INTEREST
20  LET P = 100
30  LET R = 0.15
40  LET 2 = T
50  PRINT "INTEREST IS $" P*R*T
60  END
```

Solution Line 40 is incorrect. It should read
```
40  LET T = 2
```

Your Turn Write the output for the program.
```
 5  REM AREA OF A SQUARE
10  LET S = 8.4
20  LET A = S↑2
30  PRINT "THE AREA IS" A
40  END
```

Debug the program.
```
10  LET 50 = A
20  LET B = 65
30  LET 35 = C
40  PRINT A+B+C
50  END
```

Use a comma or a semicolon to separate variables in a PRINT statement when you want more than one calculation printed on the same line.

Example 4 Write the output for the program.
```
 5  REM CIRCUMFERENCE AND AREA OF A CIRCLE
10  LET P = 3.14
20  LET R = 7.2
30  LET C = 2*P*R
40  LET A = P*R↑2
50  PRINT C, A
60  END
```

The most teachable program you'll find anywhere gives you all the support you'd ever need.

Teacher's Edition
So you can concentrate on teaching, we save you time in planning.

*complete annotations for all answers
*teaching suggestions to get each lesson
 started
*an assignment guide to help you set the
 pace for different groups of students
*extra chapter tests to parallel those in the
 student book

Practice Masters
Extra learning help when it's needed.

*skills practice
*problem-solving practice
*cumulative reviews
*end-of-year review
*record-keeping form

Test Masters
Another timesaver for you.

*quizzes
*chapter tests
*cumulative tests
*mid-year and final exams
*record-keeping form

Solution Key
Complete solutions for every textbook exercise.

ESSENTIALS FOR ALGEBRA

CONCEPTS AND SKILLS

from America's first family of mathematics books

Houghton Mifflin

1 Whole Numbers and Variables

1-1 Variables

Objective: Evaluate algebraic expressions.

In *Essentials for Algebra,* variables are introduced early and repeated frequently. In this way students become both familiar and comfortable with the concept of a letter standing for a number. Reinforce the idea that the choice of variable has no bearing on the value of the variable. Remember that in having your students write expressions, you are preparing them to deal with problem solving and algebraic equations. To develop an awareness for problem solving, ask students for problem situations. Discuss possible algebraic expressions for these. Remind students that the variable must be assigned to the unknown value at the beginning of the problem.

1-2 Addition

Objective: Use equations to review addition of whole numbers.

Before you start this section, review addition of whole numbers. Use the Class Exercises to diagnose student weaknesses in this area. As you start to review student responses, begin to incorporate the use of variables to stand for sums. Then, have students reverse the addends in the exercises or rearrange addends to introduce the commutative and associative properties. While reviewing these exercises, have students relate problem situations from which these examples could arise. Have your students write word problems for these exercises.

1-3 Subtraction

Objective: Use equations to review subtraction of whole numbers.

As in section 1-2, use the Class Exercises to diagnose student weaknesses. As you begin to review the exercises, incorporate the use of variables to stand for differences.

1-4 Problem Solving

Objective: Learn a sequence of steps for problem solving.

Problem solving is the main emphasis of the study of Algebra, and as a result is a major focus of *Essentials for Algebra.* Before you approach the text, give your students a problem to solve. Discuss the different approaches the students take. List the various steps on the chalkboard. Take these ideas and relate them to the problem solving steps in the text. Lead the class to decide upon steps for problem solving. Give each student an index card. Have your students copy these steps down on the card. Have each student keep this card in the text book. Make sure to refer to the card as you solve problems throughout the course, and have students refer to it as they solve problems.

1-5 Multiplication

Objective: Review multiplication of whole numbers.

Use the Class Exercises to diagnose student weaknesses in multiplication. Use an approach similar to that used with addition to introduce the properties. Use the one-digit times two-digit exercises to introduce the distributive property.

1-6 Division

Objective: Review division of whole numbers.

Use the Class Exercises to diagnose student weaknesses in division. Watch closely for those students who have particular difficulties with the specific forms of division, such as

$$6)\overline{24}, \quad 24 \div 6 = 4, \text{ and } \frac{24}{6} = 4.$$

As you review the exercises, introduce the relationship between multiplication and division, and show how multiplication can help check division. Emphasize the place the remainder plays in checking division by multiplication.

1-7 Identity Properties

Objective: Know and use special properties of 0 and 1.

Students have seen the arithmetic use of the properties addressed in this section. As you explain these, make sure to carry the idea from the arithmetic to the algebraic. Introduce the identity for addition first. Make sure your students are comfortable with this before going to the identity for multiplication. If you introduce them together, students could confuse them. Confusion here could carry over into the use of these properties in the solution of equations.

Make sure your lesson includes a discussion of why division by zero is impossible.

1-8 Order of Operations

Objective: Use order of operations.
Combine like terms.

Start the lesson in a problem situation that shows students the need for the order of operations. Ask your students to create examples where a calculation can have different answers.

Example: $3 + 4 \times 6$ and $(3 + 4) \times 6$

Ask students which is correct. Introduce Example 1 in the text to derive the actual order.

Introduce like terms by having each term represent a real object. For example, 7 tables, 3 chairs, and 2 tables is 9 tables and 3 chairs. So, $7t + 3c + 2t = 9t + 3c$.

Have students create their own real examples. Have students then transform their examples into algebraic expressions and combine like terms.

2 Decimals

2-1 Reading and Writing Decimals

Objective: Read and write decimals to millionths.

To review the concept of decimal place value draw a place value chart on the chalkboard. Write various decimal numbers in the chart and have students read the decimals. Next have students write decimals in the table as you read them. Emphasize the fact that decimals are read differently than whole numbers. For example 642 is read "six hundred forty-two," while 0.642 is read "six hundred forty-two thousandths" (not hundredths).

2-2 Ordering Decimals

Objective: Order a group of decimals from least to greatest or greatest to least.

You may want to review the symbols for "less than" and "greater than." Help students think of ways to make it easier to remember what each symbol stands for. For instance the arrow always points to the lesser number as in $75 > 65$ and $65 < 75$.

When comparing two decimals it may be helpful to write the numbers vertically and align the decimal points. In this way it is easy to see the comparison of each numeral in the same place value position.

Example: Compare 54.0642 and 5.40642.

When written vertically the comparison is easier to see.

$$54.0642$$
$$5.4062$$

Since $54 > 5$, $54.0642 > 5.4062$

2-3 The Rounding Process

Objective: Round a decimal to a specific place value amount.

Since place values are a critical part of rounding

decimals, you may want to show the place-values between millions and millionths. The number line offers students a visual understanding of the rounding process. Students may find it interesting that we often round numbers when dealing with very large amounts (national debts, budgets, populations) and when working with very small amounts (measurements, laboratory data).

2-4 Adding Decimals

Objective: Review addition of decimals.

When adding decimals it's important to align the decimal points. Students should understand that alignment is by place value. Review estimation skills. Remind students that it's a good idea to estimate before computing in order to check the placement of the decimal point.

2-5 Subtracting Decimals

Objective: Review subtraction of decimals.

Some students may need practice with the regrouping aspects of subtraction. Estimation is again included in this lesson to help students catch careless mistakes.

2-6 Problem Solving

Objective: To solve word problems involving limits.

This lesson helps students realize that many problems don't have numerical answers but require some manipulation of numbers before a satisfactory answer can be reached. Though the problems may look difficult at first, students should be encouraged to look for a starting point and then compare their first attempts with what is being asked. For instance in Exercise 1 students may randomly add numbers and compare sums. However after thinking about the problem they will realize that they must first locate the greatest numbers and then add these to attain the greatest sum.

2-7 Multiplying Decimals

Objective: Review multiplication of decimals.

If students have mastered the skill of multiplying whole numbers, they can transfer that knowledge to multiplying decimals. Remind your students that digits and not decimal points are aligned when multiplying decimals. You may wish to show multiplication as repeated addition and compare the sum to the product in a related multiplication problem.

$$
\begin{array}{r}
3.72 \\
3.72 \\
+3.72 \\
\hline
11.16
\end{array} \longleftarrow \text{2 decimal places}
$$

$$
\begin{array}{rl}
3.72 & \longleftarrow \quad \text{2 decimal places} \\
\times 3 & \longleftarrow \quad +0 \text{ decimal places} \\
\hline
11.16 & \longleftarrow \quad \text{2 decimal places}
\end{array}
$$

2-8 Dividing Decimals

Objective: Review division of decimals.

Use the Class Exercises to check students' understanding. Remind students that when dividing by a whole number they can write the decimal point in the quotient at any time.

To help students understand why it's possible to multiply both dividend and divisor by the same power of ten, without changing the quotient, use real life examples. Ask which driver was going faster, Ed who traveled 110 miles in 2 hours or Mary Lou who traveled 1100 miles in 20 hours?

2-9 Metric System

Objective: Review the metric system.

The metric system gives students a realistic opportunity to work with powers of ten, both in multiplication and division. This section gives students a chance to see how efficient the entire system can be once we become familiar with the different prefixes. Students may need a good deal of exposure to the terminology if they have had little previous experience. When comparing two amounts as in the C section, students may want to convert the given amounts to the same basic unit of measurement before attempting to compare the two amounts.

3 Number Theory

3-1 Divisibility Tests

Objective: Determine divisibility using the divisibility rules for 2, 3, 4, 5, 6, 8, 9, and 10.

Remind students that using the divisibility rules can allow them to do many divisions in their head. Divisibility rules are particularly useful when you are only interested in whether or not a certain division will produce a remainder.

3-2 Factors and Prime Numbers

Objective: Write the prime factorization of a number.

Suggest that students use the divisibility rules when looking for factor pairs to begin a factor tree. Remind students that if a number is even, they can always choose 2 for a factor, if the ones digit is 0, 10 will be a factor, etc. Review the meaning of exponents if necessary before writing prime factorizations with exponents.

3-3 The Greatest Common Factor

Objective: Find the Greatest Common Factor for two numbers.

In this lesson, students get to apply their skill in prime factoring to find the G.C.F. When students have mastered working with two numbers, they may want to find the G.C.F. of three or more numbers. That is, find the G.C.F. of 60, 75, and 80. For students who find visual explanations helpful, the G.C.F. can be expressed as:

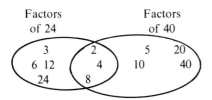

Greatest Common Factor

3-4 Factoring in Algebra

Objective: To factor an algebraic expression.

A common factoring error occurs when students forget that 1 is a factor of every number. When students are just learning to factor, it's helpful to write out all the factors of each term, identify the common factors, and then group the remaining factors.

Factor $4a^3 + 2a$.

factors of $4a^3$ **factors of $2a$**

$②· 2 ·②· a · a \; + \; 1 ·②·②$

$(2 · a · a + 1)$

$2a(2a^2 + 1)$

Students may also gain a better understanding of factoring if they are encouraged to check their factored expressions by multiplication.

3-5 Problem Solving

Objective: To solve word problems by looking for patterns.

Looking for patterns in problems can be both challenging and rewarding. Students should be encouraged to look for patterns as a means of making their work easier. Students can be asked to look for patterns in such everyday places as telephone rate tables, mailing rate tables, and price lists.

3-6 The Least Common Multiple

Objective: Determine the least common multiple of two or more numbers.

Be sure students can explain the difference between factors and multiples. Students may find it helpful to remember a phrase such as "factors are few but multiples are many." Students may wish to look for short cuts for finding the LCM of two numbers. Students could list a few multiples of one number and then check to see if any of these are also multiples of the second number. The first such common multiple is the LCM.

3-7 Scientific Notation

Objective: Write a number in scientific notation and write the standard form for a number in scientific notation.

Write the following list of numbers on the chalkboard and ask students to insert decimal points to make the numbers between 1 and 10. 85, 6432,

T17

7008, 40,369, 30,072, 14,785,691. After the numbers are written as decimals, ask the students to write them using scientific notation. Make sure students understand how moving the decimal point is related to succeeding powers of 10.

To write numbers between 0 and 1 in scientific notation requires the use of negative exponents. For students who are familiar with negative numbers you might use the following pattern to introduce them to negative exponents.

Call to their attention this pattern for powers of 10 that have *positive* exponents:

$$\begin{array}{lll} \text{Exponents} & 10^4 = 10{,}000 & \text{Powers are} \\ \text{decrease} & 10^3 = 1{,}000 & \text{divided} \\ \text{by 1} & 10^2 = 100 & \text{by 10} \\ & 10^1 = 10 & \end{array}$$

If we continue this pattern using exponents of 0, $^-1$, $^-2$, and so on, we assign values to powers of 10 as follows:

$$10^0 = 1$$
$$10^{-1} = 0.1$$
$$10^{-2} = 0.01$$
$$10^{-3} = 0.001$$

This use of 0 and negative exponents is useful in writing numbers between 0 and 1 in scientific notation. For example,

$$0.26 = 2.6 \times 0.1 = 2.6 \times 10^{-1}$$

$$0.085 = 8.5 \times 0.01 = 8.5 \times 10^{-2}$$

$$0.00432 = 4.32 \times 0.001 = 4.32 \times 10^{-3}$$

4 Fractions

4-1 Fraction Concept

Objective: Read and write fractions.

Fractions are presented in this lesson as coordinates of points on a number line. Emphasize that a fraction corresponds to a point to the left of 1, at 1, or the right of 1, depending on whether its numerator is less than, equal to, or greater than its denominator. Remind students that a denominator cannot be zero since division by zero is undefined. Stress the meaning of mixed numbers as the sum of a whole number and a fraction. Discuss the use of fractions in familiar situations such as recipes, shopping for meats, fruits, and vegetables.

For Example 2, explain that we want to find the number of $\frac{1}{5}$'s in $3\frac{4}{5}$. $3\frac{4}{5} = 3 + \frac{4}{5}$. To find the number of $\frac{1}{5}$'s in 3, we multiply, $5 \times 3 = 15$. Thus $3 = \frac{15}{5}$. So $3\frac{4}{5} = \frac{15}{5} + \frac{4}{5} = \frac{15+4}{5} = \frac{19}{5}$.

4-2 Renaming Fractions

Objective: Write equal fractions and write fractions in lowest terms.

For Examples 1 and 2, explain that when you multiply or divide the numerator and denominator of a fraction by the same nonzero number, you are really multiplying or dividing the fraction itself by

1. Since 1 is the identity number for multiplication (p. 21), the product or quotient is the same as the original fraction. For example,

$$\frac{7}{10} = \frac{7 \times 3}{10 \times 3} \text{ since}$$

$$\frac{7 \times 3}{10 \times 3} = \frac{7}{10} \times \frac{3}{3} = \frac{7}{10} \times 1 = \frac{7}{10}.$$

Watch for these two common student errors:

1. $\dfrac{a}{2a} = 2$, instead of $\dfrac{1}{2}$. Stress the need to write the quotient each time a number or a variable is divided by another: $\dfrac{1\overset{1}{\cancel{a}}}{2\underset{1}{\cancel{a}}} = \dfrac{1}{2}$.

2. $\dfrac{\overset{1}{\cancel{5}}a + 10}{\underset{1}{\cancel{5}}} = a + 10$, instead of

$\dfrac{\overset{1}{\cancel{5}}(a + 2)}{\underset{1}{\cancel{5}}} = a + 2$. Emphasize the importance of dividing the entire numerator and denominator, not just a term, by the same number.

4-3 Adding Fractions

Objective: Add fractions and mixed numbers with like or unlike denominators.

For Example 1, use a number line, as follows, to show why we add the numerators:

Review LCM with your students. Find the LCM of **1.** 5, 6 and **2.** 4, 6, 10. Then discuss the LCD of

1. $\frac{3}{5}$, $\frac{5}{6}$ and **2.** $\frac{1}{4}$, $\frac{5}{6}$, $\frac{7}{10}$. Emphasize that when we rewrite $\frac{3}{5}$ as $\frac{18}{30}$, we multiply both 3 and 5 to obtain an equal fraction with the desired denominator. Note that any common denominator is acceptable but using the LCD simplifies writing the sum in lowest terms.

4-4 Subtracting Fractions

Objective: Subtract fractions and mixed numbers with like or unlike denominators.

Point out to your students the occasional necessity of regrouping when subtracting mixed numbers. For example to subtract $3\frac{2}{5}$ from $7\frac{1}{5}$, first rewrite $7\frac{1}{5}$ as $6\frac{6}{5}$, then subtract:

$$
\begin{array}{r}
7\frac{1}{5} = 6\frac{6}{5} \\
-3\frac{2}{5} = -3\frac{2}{5} \\
\hline
3\frac{4}{5}.
\end{array}
$$

Remind students that any regrouping is done after the fractions are written with a common denominator.

4-5 Multiplying Fractions

Objective: Multiply fractions and mixed numbers.

Point out to your students that multiplying a fraction and a whole number is a shortcut to repeated addition. For example, $4 \times \frac{2}{3}$ or $\frac{2}{3} \times 4$ means $\frac{2}{3} + \frac{2}{3} + \frac{2}{3} + \frac{2}{3} = \frac{8}{3}$. When multiplying by whole numbers, students may find it easier to write the whole number over a denominator of 1. When this is done the familiar procedures of multiplying numerators and multiplying denominators can be followed.

You can use a diagram to show that, for example, $\frac{1}{3} \times \frac{1}{2} = \frac{1}{6}$.

In Example 2, you can show that multiplying the numerators and multiplying the denominators works by using the commutative and associative properties.

$$
\frac{2}{3} \times \frac{7}{8} = \left(2 \times \frac{1}{3}\right) \times \left(7 \times \frac{1}{8}\right)
$$
$$
= (2 \times 7) \times \left(\frac{1}{3} \times \frac{1}{8}\right)
$$
$$
= 14 \times \frac{1}{24} = \frac{14}{24} = \frac{7}{12}.
$$

Students usually enjoy cancelling factors to simplify writing a product in lowest terms. They should be encouraged to write the quotient for each division and to look for common factors in all numerators and denominators. An example such as the following will demonstrate how cancelling can change a long tedious problem into a rather simple computation.

$$
\frac{\cancel{4}}{\cancel{11}} \times \frac{1}{\cancel{2}} \times \frac{\cancel{33}}{\cancel{16}} \times \frac{\cancel{8}}{\cancel{15}} = \frac{1}{1} \times \frac{1}{1} \times \frac{1}{1} \times \frac{1}{5} = \frac{1}{5}
$$

4-6 Dividing Fractions

Objective: Divide fractions and mixed numbers.

Expand the discussion of reciprocals to include:

1. 5 and $\frac{1}{5}$ are reciprocals since $5 \times \frac{1}{5} = \frac{5}{5} = 1$.

2. $\frac{2}{3}$ and $\frac{3}{2}$ are reciprocals since $\frac{\cancel{2}}{\cancel{3}} \times \frac{\cancel{3}}{\cancel{2}} = 1$.

3. Ask your students to state the reciprocal of

    a. 9   **b.** $\frac{1}{3}$ **c.** $\frac{5}{7}$ **d.** $2\frac{3}{5}$

You can use the diagram below to illustrate that $\frac{2}{3} \div 4 = \frac{2}{3} \times \frac{1}{4}$, that is, that multiplying by $\frac{1}{4}$ is the same as dividing by 4.

4-7 Problem Solving

Objective: To solve word problems by working backwards.

Working backwards is a strategy students often use without realizing it. Discuss some real life examples such as the following: **1.** A person wants to buy a car. Knowing the cost of the car, insurance, taxes and registration, the person could work backwards to compute the monthly cost and decide whether the purchase was affordable. **2.** A person has a project to complete by a specified date. Knowing the amount of free time available before the deadline, the person can plan the best use of time in order to meet the deadline.

Students can be asked to think of situations where they have worked backwards to solve a problem.

4-8 Fractions and Decimals

Objective: Write a fraction as a terminating or repeating decimal, and a terminating decimal as a fraction.

Converting fractions to decimals provides your students with an opportunity to practice interpreting $\frac{x}{y}$ as $x \div y$, $y \neq 0$. Point out to your students that most terminating decimals greater than 1 can be written as a fraction or as a mixed number. For example:

$$2.33 = 2 + 0.33 = 2 + \frac{33}{100} = 2\frac{33}{100} = \frac{233}{100}$$

This section also provides ample opportunity for your students to use a calculator to convert fractions to decimals, which can promote learning common equivalences such as $0.\overline{3} = \frac{1}{3}$.

5 Solving Equations

5-1 Equations

Objective: Solve equations by inspection.

Draw a balance beam on the chalkboard and build an equation to illustrate the concept of treating both sides of an equation in the same way. Start with $x = 5$. Next add 3 to both sides and elicit from students that the scales remain in balance. Next subtract 2 from one side and ask students what should be done to maintain the balance. Continue to explore ways of changing one side of the balance and discussing what must be done to maintain a balanced situation.

5-2 Using Subtraction

Objective: To solve equations of the form $x + a = b$ where a and b are constants.

Introduce the lesson by referring to a balance scale example in which a place holder box is used to represent the variable.

Refer to the variable as the unknown quantity or weight. Elicit from students that if 7 is removed from one side of the balance it must also be removed from the other. Translate the balance scale example to an algebraic example. Repeat with other examples having the class solve the balance scale example and an individual student translating the example into algebraic form.

5-3 Using Division

Objective: To solve equations of the form $ax = b$ where a and b are constants.

Begin the lesson by discussing problems with respect to the balance scale. When students begin to work well with these, introduce the equation and how each action with the balance scale can be shown in the equation. Reinforce the need for your students to check their work.

5-4 Using Addition

Objective: To solve equations of the form $x - a = b$ where a and b are constants.

Review the solving of equations using subtraction. Emphasize the inverse relation of addition and subtraction by writing several related equations such as $3 + 5 = 8$, $8 - 5 = 3$, $8 - 3 = 5$. Give students practice writing related equations with numbers and then with variables.

Encourage students to use substitution to check the results of their solutions. This will provide immediate feedback and help identify students who do not understand the concept.

5-5 Using Multiplication

Objective: To solve equations of the form $\frac{x}{a} = b$, where a and b are constants, and $a \neq 0$.

Begin the lesson by emphasizing the solution of the equation $4n = 24$, and the use of the inverse operation, division, to solve it. Once your students have mastered this concept introduce the equation $\frac{n}{4} = 24$.

Make sure your students realize that $\frac{n}{4}$ is a division expression. Then ask for the inverse operation. Use it to solve the equation.

Before you introduce equations such as $\frac{3}{4}n = 12$, make sure that your students know what a reciprocal is, and how it is used to transform $\frac{3}{4}n$ into $1n$.

5-6 Using Two Steps

Objective: To solve equations of the form $ax \pm b = c$, where a, b, and c are constants.

Begin the class by having students give you a value for the variable a, say 6.
Write $a = 6$.
Ask for a factor by which to multiply both sides, say 3.
Write $3a = 3 \times 6$
$\qquad 3a = 18$
Ask for an addend, say 7.
Write $3a + 7 = 18 + 7$
$\qquad 3a + 7 = 25$.
List what was done.
Step 1: Multiply by 3.
Step 2: Add 7.
Then start with $3a + 7 = 25$, and ask students how

you can get back to $a = 6$.
REVERSE THE STEPS.
Step 1: Subtract 7
Step 2: Divide by 3.
Follow these steps to show that this does lead back to $a = 6$.

5-7 Equations With More Steps

Objective: To solve equations of the form $ax + b = cx + d$, where a, b, c, and d are constants.

Begin the lesson with the balance scale:

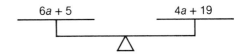

Ask students for suggestions of how to solve this balance problem. Here are two possible first steps. **a.** Subtract 5 from both sides, or **b.** Subtract $4a$ from both sides.
If **(a)** is the first step, then **(b)** is the second.
If **(b)** is the first step, then **(a)** is the second.

When the balance is solved, review it using the equation $6a + 5 = 4a + 19$. After steps **a** and **b** are used, you will have $2a = 14$. Recall procedures from section 5-3 to solve this.

After this, have students work with equations which have various patterns of signs, such as $3x - 4 = x + 4$, and $3x + 4 = 8 - x$.

5-8 Writing Algebraic Expressions

Objective: Write an algebraic expression for a verbal problem.

Quickly review the steps to problem solving listed in section 1-4. Give your students the following example. The Jog Shop received a shipment of running shoes on Monday. On Friday they received a shipment that contained 55 fewer pairs of running shoes. Discuss the unknown quantity to be found. Although your students do not know the value of the variable, they can express increases (additions and multiplications), decreases (subtractions), and distributions (divisions). Have your students write expressions for several types of problems. Then, give your students expressions for which to write verbal problems.

5-9 Writing Equations

Objective: To translate sentences into equations.

Introduce the lesson by using newspaper clippings of sports events. Omit some of the statistics and have students write equations based on the information in the clippings.

Example: The Crows won 15 more games than they lost. Let n = the number of games they lost. Then $n + 15$ = the number of games they won. The equation $n + 15 = 35$ will yield the number of games lost.

Bush League		
	Won	Lost
Crows	35	?
Beagles	?	28
Frogs	19	35
Penguins	25	30

5-10 Problem Solving

Objective: Solve verbal problems using equations.

Give students the following sentence. Mary has 8 more books than Sally. Have students write an expression for this.

Let c = number of books Sally has
Then $c + 8$ = number of books Mary has

Then, on the chalkboard, write "Mary has 10 books." Have the students write an equation using the expression they just wrote. Finally, write "How many books does Sally have?" Discuss where in the equation $c + 8 = 10$ they can find the number of books Sally has. Have the class solve the equation.

Do several simple problems of this type. Then, have your students each write a verbal problem. Review some of these and have your students solve them using the model above.

6 Formulas

6-1 Perimeter

Objective: To find the perimeter of a figure.

Review the concept of perimeter being the distance around a figure. Tell students that using the formulas is a shortcut that can be used for certain figures. Suggest some realistic examples when people might need to find a perimeter such as fencing in a yard, trimming a blanket, or framing a picture. Ask students to think of other examples including some with irregular shapes.

6-2 Circumference

Objective: To find the circumference of a figure.

Introduce the lesson by letting students measure the circumference and diameter of several circular objects. (juice cans, flower pots, hockey pucks, phonograph records, plates or saucers) Make a chart on the chalkboard and record the measurements of each object. If available, use a calculator to compute the ratio $C \div d$. Students will see that though each ratio is slightly different, they are all approximately the same number which is symbolized by the Greek letter π. Explain that because this ratio is true for all circles, we can use the formula $C = \pi d$ to compute the circumference of any circle.

6-3 Angle Measurement

Objective: To classify angles as acute, obtuse, right, or straight.

Draw several pairs of intersecting lines on the chalkboard. Ask students whether the angles formed appear to be less than or greater than 90°. Use an object with a corner, such as this book, to "test" the angle. Ask students to draw examples of acute and obtuse angles and again use a corner to show that the angle is indeed less than or greater than a right angle.

6-4 Area of Polygons

Objective: To use formulas to find the areas of various polygons.

Introduce the lesson by suggesting realistic examples of items being measured in square units. If possible have real items available such as a box of grass seed, a paint can, or an ad for carpeting to demonstrate the practical use of area.

Ask students to estimate and then measure the area of the classroom floor. Discuss how the resulting measurement could be used to determine the amount of carpeting or vinyl flooring needed to cover the floor.

6-5 Area of Circles

Objective: To use the area formula to find the area of a circle.

Introduce the lesson by cutting a cardboard circle into pie shaped sections. Label the radius of the circle on one of the wedges. With the class watching, rearrange the wedges to approximate a parallelogram. Develop the area formula by noting that the base of the parallelogram is about as long as $\frac{1}{2}$ the circumference of the circle. Work through the substitution step-by-step until you're sure students understand how the formula is derived. Make actual measurements of the radius of the circle and the length and height of the parallelogram. Find the area of each using the proper formula and compare the results.

6-6 Problem Solving

Objective: To solve word problems using formulas.

Introduce the lesson by explaining that formulas are ways of recognizing patterns among certain variables. Once a pattern, such as the relationship between the distance an object falls and the time it takes to fall, is observed a formula can be used to simplify further calculations of those values.

Ask students for realistic examples of patterns that can be translated into formulas such as the price of gas per gallon $\times$ number of gallons = total cost.

6-7 Volume of Prisms and Pyramids

Objective: To use formulas to find the volume of prisms and pyramids.

Introduce the lesson by using blocks to build pyramids and prisms. Emphasize the three-dimensional aspects of the volume concept and use the blocks to demonstrate the concept of cubic units.

If possible use cardboard models of pyramids and prisms with similar dimensions and show that it takes three times as much sand to fill the prism as the pyramid.

6-8 Volume of Cylinders and Cones

Objective: To use formulas to find the volume of cylinders and cones.

Introduce the lesson by reminding students that the volume of a prism is found by multipying the area of the base by the height. Tell students that the same relationship holds for the volume of a cylinder and elicit that since the base of a cylinder is a circle, the formula for volume involves multiplying the area of the circular base by the height. Review the formula for area of a circle and work through the Class Exercises with the class.

6-9 Surface Area

Objective: To combine various formulas to find the surface area for different figures.

Introduce the lesson by cutting apart a small box and flattening the pieces. Show students that the combined areas of the pieces make up the surface area. Repeat using an oatmeal box to demonstrate the parallel case for cylinders. Use the circular base of the oatmeal box as a trundle wheel to demonstrate the fact that the length of the base of the flattened rectangle is the same as the circumference of the circular base.

7 Ratio, Proportion, Percent

7-1 Ratio

Objective: Compare quantities using ratios.

Begin the lesson by taking a survey in your class. The topic may be the favorite singing group, color, movie, or sport team. Use the results of the survey to compare different responses. Introduce the concept of ratio in this way. When your students have discussed the comparisons then begin to call each of these a ratio. Begin to write the ratios using the three forms. Emphasize that each form names the same ratio. Relate ratios in lowest terms to fractions in lowest terms. Work through the Class Exercises with your students.

7-2 Proportions

Objective: Solve problems using proportions.

Use the results of the survey from section 7-1 to project the probable relationship to groups larger than your class. For example, if there are 25 students in your class and seven said blue was their favorite color, ask, "How many would you expect to choose blue if there were 50 in the class?" Establish the variable to stand for the unknown. Set up the ratio for the situation in your class, $\frac{7}{25}$. Then ask your students for the ratio using the variable, $\frac{n}{50}$. Set up the proportion and explain why these two ratios are equal.

7-3 Percents

Objective: Use ratios to find the percent of a number.

The stress of the lesson is to introduce percent as a ratio whose denominator is 100. Emphasize that a percent is the numerator when the denominator is 100. The key is to compare ratios to a ratio out of 100. Use newspaper ads to show realistic applications of percent. Have students look for interest rates, discount rates, sales tax rates, and down payment rates and then write these percents as decimals and ratios with denominators of 100.

7-4 Percent of a number

Objective: Find the percent of a number.

Begin by writing on the chalkboard "This week only. All records one-half off." Ask students how much the savings would be for a $12.00 record. Elicit from students the method they used to compute their answer. Suggest that either multiplying by $\frac{1}{2}$ or by 0.5 gives the same results. Next show that $\frac{1}{2}$ and 0.5 are the same as 50%. Emphasize that students can use either a decimal or fraction to compute the answer, but that sometimes a decimal is easier. Demonstrate this by using the example of finding one-half off of a $13.98 record.

7-5 Problem Solving

Objective: Use charts in problem solving.

Use newspaper advertisements for various cars to make a chart comparing prices with and without various options, such as radio, power steering, and air conditioning.

Have students find the most expensive and least expensive way to buy a car. Tell students they have a certain amount of money. Have them choose a car and options they can afford using the amount given.

7-6 More Percents

Objective: Use percents less than 1 or greater than 100 to solve problems.

Give your students a situation where they must find 2% of 400. Ask them to find 1% of 400. Make a chart of the results

Total	%	Result
400	2%	8
400	1%	4

Emphasize that as the percent is cut in half, so is the result. Ask students to think about $\frac{1}{2}$% of 400. Add this line to the chart:

$$400 \qquad \frac{1}{2}\% \qquad ?$$

Discuss possible answers. Then introduce the method for changing the fractional percent to a decimal. Introduce percents greater than 100 in the same manner.

7-7 Finding the Base

Objective: Solve problems to find the base of a percent.

Review exercises finding 10% of 60 and 20% of 80, by setting up the equations:

$$n = 10\% \times 60 \qquad k = 20\% \times 80$$
$$n = 6 \qquad\qquad k = 16$$

Emphasize the format *Percent of the Number = % × base*. Give students the same problems with the variable as the base number.

$$6 = 10\% \times y \qquad 16 = 20\% \times z$$

Work through the problems step-by-step and

T24

then proceed to do several problems where students must set up the equation for a word problem such as John saved $16 by buying a tennis racket at a 25% off sale. What was the original price of the racket? Make sure students can both set up and solve this type of equation.

7-8 Percent of Increase or Decrease

Objective: Find the percent of increase or decrease between two numbers.

Introduce the lesson by telling students that the price of a first class stamp was $.02 in 1885 and $.20 in 1981. Ask them first what was the amount of increase and next what was the percent of increase? ($.18, 900%) Next give the example of a hand-held calculator that cost about $168 in 1970 and about $25 in 1981. Ask again for the amount of decrease and the percent of decrease. Emphasize that percent of change problems always involve the following steps:

1. finding the amount of change;
2. writing the amount of change as a percent of the original amount.

8 Integers and Rational Numbers

8-1 Integers on the Number Line

Objective: To recognize the order of positive and negative numbers on the number line.

Introduce the lesson by referring to a thermometer. Ask students to name the temperature when the temperature starts at 0° and goes up 5°. Next ask for the temperature if the thermometer reads 8° and the temperature goes down 6°. Finally, ask for the new temperature when the thermometer reads 3° and the temperature drops 3°, 4°, 6°. Use other realistic examples to help students grasp the concept of positive and negative numbers.

Remind students that a number line can be horizontal or vertical and that negative numbers are to the left of zero on a horizontal number line, and below zero on a vertical number line.

8-2 Adding Negative Integers

Objective: To add negative integers.

Draw a number line on the chalkboard. To show $^-6 + {}^-3$, demonstrate the movement from 0 to $^-6$ and then from $^-6$ another 3 units to the left.

$$^-6 + {}^-3 = {}^-9$$

Next, use the number line to show the solution of an equation with negative integers. Ask a student for the solution of the equation $x = {}^-3 + {}^-2$. Encourage the use of the number line until students are comfortable with both the negative numbers and the variables.

8-3 Adding Integers of Opposite Sign

Objective: To add positive and negative integers.

Draw a number line on the chalkboard. Demonstrate addition of positive and negative numbers with the following problems:

1. Bill has $5 in his checking account. He writes a check for $9. How much is left in his account?

2. At 4:00 P.M. on Tuesday the temperature was $^-4$°. By 9:00 P.M. on Tuesday, the temperature had risen 6°. What was the 9:00 P.M. temperature?

3. Mary has a balance of $3a$ dollars in her checking account. She writes a check for $3a$ dollars. What is her new balance?

After students have had sufficient exposure to concrete examples, go over the examples in the text applying the rules given.

8-4 Subtracting Integers

Objective: To subtract positive and negative integers.

Use a number line to demonstrate the fact that subtracting an integer yields the same result as adding its opposite. Give students the following examples and make sure they understand how to apply the rule for adding an opposite.

1. $^-5 - 3 = x$ **2.** $5 - ^-3 = y$ **3.** $^-5 - ^-3 = a$

4. $^-10 - ^-9 = b$ **5.** $10 - ^-9 = z$ **6.** $^-10 - 9 = w$

8-5 Multiplying Integers

Objective: To multiply positive and negative integers.

Use a number line to demonstrate that multiplying a positive integer by a negative integer is a repeated addition and therefore the product is negative.

To show that multiplying two negative integers results in a positive integer, you might try this application of the distributive property.

$$^-8 \times ^-5 = ^-8(1 - 6) =$$
$$^-8 - (^-8 \times 6) = ^-8 - ^-48 =$$
$$^-8 + 48 = 40$$

8-6 Dividing Integers

Objective: To divide positive and negative integers.

Review the inverse relationship of multiplication and division. Tell students that the same relationship holds for integers as for whole numbers. After showing students several examples, write a multiplication equation using integers on the chalkboard. Ask a student to give a related division equation. Check the signs to make sure students understand how the equations are related.

8-7 Adding/Subtracting Rationals

Objective: To add and subtract rational numbers.

Review the rules for adding and subtracting integers. Go over several examples on a number line to show the similarities between adding and subtracting integers and adding and subtracting positive and negative rationals.

8-8 Multiplying/Dividing Rationals

Objective: To multiply and divide rational numbers.

Review the rules for multiplying and dividing integers. Write the following equations on the chalkboard and ask students to write related equations showing the inverse relationship of multiplication and division.

1. $a = (^-7.3)(4.2)$ **2.** $x = 2.7 \div ^-0.3$

3. $y = (0.5)(^-0.5)$ **4.** $b = \left(\frac{1}{4}\right)\left(\frac{^-3}{8}\right)$

5. $w = \frac{^-3}{4} \div \frac{^-1}{2}$ **6.** $m = ^-1\frac{1}{8} \div 2\frac{1}{3}$

Work through the Class Exercises and be sure students understand how the signs of the factors determine the sign of the product or quotient.

8-9 Problem Solving

Objective: To solve word problems by drawing a diagram.

Drawing a diagram can help clarify the most mundane problems. Tell students that engineers, scientists, and mathematicians often draw models or diagrams to depict problem information in a logical way before using numbers to generate a solution. Work through the following problem. Suppose you set your watch at 10:15. At 2:15 you notice that your watch is 4 minutes slow. If your watch continues to lose time at the same rate, how many minutes will it lose by 10:15 the next day? Show how the problem can be simulated on a clock face and then write a ratio to solve the problem numerically.

8-10 Equations with Rationals

Objective: To solve equations using rational numbers.

Review the process for solving equations when only positive numbers are used. Remind students that it's necessary to add, subtract, multiply, or divide the same amount on both sides of an equal sign to maintain balance. Work through the Class Exercises with students to make sure they don't confuse the sign of the operation with the sign of the rational.

8-11 Inequalities

Objective: To solve inequalities.

Introduce the lesson by drawing a number line on the chalkboard and reviewing inequalities involving positive and negative numbers. Read the following inequalities aloud and have students write them in symbols.

1. 6 is less than 8

2. ⁻4 is greater than ⁻9

3. ⁻12 is greater than or equal to x

4. 7 is less than or equal to y

Check students' papers to make sure the concept is understood. Go over the rules for solving inequalities and use them to work through the given examples.

9 Graphing in the Coordinate Plane

9-1 Collecting Data

Objective: To find a given term in a sequence when a general expression for the sequence is known.

Introduce the lesson by writing the following expressions on the chalkboard.

1. $3n + 1$ **2.** $4x + 2$ **3.** $5n + 7$

Ask students to evaluate the expressions using values ranging from 0 to 10 for the variable. Make a table showing the results of the computation and ask students to look for a pattern. Tell students that finding any given term in a sequence is the same as substituting that number in the general expression for the sequence. For instance, to find the 26th term in the sequence $2x + 7$, substitute 26 for x in the general expression for the sequence.

9-2 Finding Expressions for Data

Objective: To write the general expression for any term in a sequence.

Work through the Class Exercises for this section. Use the following sequences to further clarify the process by which a general expression is generated.

1. 11, 17, 23, 29, 35, . . . $(6n + 5)$

2. 10, 15, 20, 25, 30, . . . $(5n + 5)$

3. 13, 16, 19, 22, 25, . . . $(3n + 10)$

4. 13, 21, 29, 37, 45, . . . $(8n + 5)$

9-3 The Coordinate Plane

Objective: To graph ordered pairs on a coordinate plane.

Introduce the lesson by showing students a street map of their town. Review the process for locating a particular street and give students a chance to demonstrate understanding by locating their own street or some unfamiliar street. Tell students that a similar process is used to locate points in a coordinate plane. Review the terms horizontal and vertical and then draw a coordinate plane on the chalkboard. Give students opportunities to both plot points and name the coordinates of given points before working through the Class Exercises.

9-4 Graphing Data

Objective: To graph lines on a coordinate plane.

Draw a coordinate plane on the chalkboard. Work through the Class Exercises. After predicting the required term in the first quadrant, ask students to predict the next two or three terms in the opposite direction. Tell students that errors in plotting points can be easily detected if connecting the points doesn't produce a straight line.

9-5 Equation of a Line

Objective: To graph the solution set for a linear equation.

Use the following examples to give students practice in forming a solution set for a linear equation. Tell students it's a good idea to get into the habit of setting up a table to show ordered pairs.

1. $y = x - 2$ **2.** $y = 5 - 2x$ **3.** $y = x + 4$

Point out that there are an infinite number of ordered pairs that can be elements of the solution set, but that only two are needed to determine the line.

9-6 Slope and Intercept

Objective: To find the slope and y-intercept of a line, given a linear equation.

Draw a coordinate plane on the chalkboard. Graph the equation $y = 4x + 8$. Tell students that the slope is a ratio that measures the steepness of a line. For every unit change in x there is a corresponding constant change in y. For example, in the equation $y = 2x + 5$, for every change of 1 unit in x, there is a change of 2 units in y.

9-7 Linear Inequalities

Objective: To graph the solution set of a linear inequality in two variables.

10 Statistics

You can use the chalkboard or the overhead projector to teach your students how to graph linear inequalities. For example, to graph $y > 3x + 2$, you first graph $y = 3x + 2$, using a dashed line to indicate that the graph of $y = 3x + 2$ is *not* included in the graph. (You would use a solid line if you were graphing $y \geq 3x + 2$.) Since y is *greater* than $3x + 2$, you shade the region *above* the dashed line to show the graph of $y > 3x + 2$.

To check that you have shaded the correct region, test the coordinates of a point above the dashed line by substituting them in $y > 3x + 2$. If a true statement results, the point belongs to the graph of $y > 3x + 2$. For example, the point whose coordinates are $(^-2, 1)$ is above the dashed line $y = 3x + 2$. Substituting $(^-2, 1)$ in $y > 3x + 2$, you obtain $1 > ^-6 + 2$, or $1 > ^-4$, a true statement. Thus, $(^-2, 1)$ is on the graph of $y > 3x + 2$.

To double-check, you can test a point below the line $y = 3x + 2$. For example, try $(0, ^-1)$. Substituting in $y > 3x + 2$, you obtain $^-1 > 2$, a false statement. Thus, $(0, ^-1)$ is not on the graph of $y > 3x + 2$.

10-1 Introduction to Statistics

Objective: To find the mean, median, mode, and range of a data set.

Point out to your students the differences among the three "measures of central tendency" of a data set: the mean, the median, and the mode. It is instructive to show how much the addition of one very large number can affect the mean. You might find and compare all three measures for a set of data such as your students' ages or heights in inches. Be sure that students are listing each data item, including repeats, when rearranging data to find the median.

Discuss with your students the statistics encountered in daily information on economics, sports, and opinion polls.

10-2 Circle Graphs

Objective: Interpret data from a circle graph.

Stress to your students that the circle represents an entire quantity of data, and the size of each section represents the fraction of the data having a common characteristic. Also, the total amount represented by the circle is needed to gain specific information about the amount in each section.

Your students might profit from constructing a circle graph of the distribution of birthdays of class members. Each section should represent the percent of students having birthdays in the same month with a section for each month in which a birthday is recorded. Point out that the largest section corresponds to the mode of the data set, since it contains the largest number of data items.

10-3 Pictographs

Objective: Interpret data from a pictograph.

Point out to your students that a key to interpreting a pictograph is knowing the quantity represented by each symbol. A pictograph can be used instead of a circle graph, but it can also be used to compare data over time. Your class might discuss how to convert one of the circle graphs in section 10-2 into a pictograph, and one of the pictographs in this section into a circle graph. You may need to review rounding to a specific place value, a concept used in constructing pictographs.

10-4 Bar Graphs

Objective: Interpret data from a bar graph.

A bar graph compares data in a manner similar to a pictograph, but the length of the bar, rather than the number of symbols, is the measure of the amount of data in each category. Your class could construct a bar graph indicating preference for one of several sports or TV shows. Graph paper can be of assistance here. You could also construct a multiple bar graph by counting preferences of males and females separately.

10-5 Line Graphs

Objective: Interpret data from a multiple line graph.

Point out to your students that the purpose of a line graph is to show changes in data over a period of time. A multiple line graph is used to compare changes in more complex data over a period of time. From the list of topics below, have the students identify those topics which would best be presented on a bar graph and those topics which would best be presented on a line graph.

1. the height of students in the class (*bar graph*)

2. the inflation rate during the past 10 years (*line graph*)

3. the population increase in a city from 1975 to 1980 (*line graph*)

4. the popularity of 4 television stations (*bar graph*)

5. the decrease in the average price of calculators from 1972 to 1982 (*line graph*)

6. the average monthly high and low temperatures for a given city (*line graph*)

7. a comparison of money spent and saved over a period of 12 months (*bar graph*)

8. the attendance at various performances of a movie (*bar graph*)

10-6 Problem Solving

Objective: To identify needed information in order to formulate a problem.

Ask students how they decide what to have for lunch everyday. For most students the decision will be based on the quality and cost of the food available in the cafeteria. In this instance students face and solve a problem everyday. Ask students for a list of questions needed to solve the problems suggested by the following situations:

1. painting a room

2. planning a trip

3. buying a calculator

4. choosing a meal from various menu items

5. looking for a part time job

Emphasize that many problem solving situations involve questions and answers that are not numerical. For example when painting a room, the choice of color is as much a part of the problem solving process as estimating the amount of paint to buy.

10-7 Histograms

Objective: Interpret data from a histogram and from a frequency polygon.

An instructive class activity would be the construction of a frequency distribution and a histogram for the heights in inches of the students. You could then accumulate the data in a cumulative histogram. After collecting the height data, discuss with your students the appropriate height intervals to use for grouping the data (this will depend on the range of the data).

10-8 Scattergrams

Objective: To interpret data from a scattergram and a trend line.

Scattergrams are used to display the relationship between two types of data. Computer programs exist to find the trend line, or regression line, that best represents the tendency of the scattered points. Point out that the trend line is then used to predict one quantity from the other. Your students can plot the height in inches vs. the age of class members to see whether a positive or negative relationship exists, perhaps separating the information by sex.

11 Special Triangles

11-1 Similar Triangles

Objective: Understand the meaning of similar triangles.

Point out to your students that either angle measures or side measures can be used to determine whether two triangles are similar:

1. If three angles of one triangle are equal to three angles of a second triangle, then the triangles are similar.

2. If three sides of one triangle are proportional to three sides of a second triangle, then the triangles are similar.

Emphasize that corresponding sides are sides of two similar triangles that are opposite equal angles. It is essential that corresponding sides be consistently paired when writing a proportion.

Discuss examples of similar objects such as photo enlargements and scale models of buildings, ships, trains, automobiles, etc.

Calculators are useful in performing many of the calculations in the chapter.

11-2 Similar Right Triangles

Objective: Solve problems using right triangles.

Point out to your students that the sun is so far from the earth that its rays strike all vertical objects in one location at the same angle. Similar triangles are formed, so that the lengths of the shadows of these vertical objects will be proportional to the lengths of the objects.

Students should practice writing the three known lengths in this proportion, using a variable for the fourth length, and then cross multiplying, to solve for the variable.

11-3 Pythagorean Theorem

Objective: Learn to use the Pythagorean Theorem and to interpret square roots.

Emphasize to your students that the *hypotenuse* of a right triangle is always the side opposite the right angle and is always the longest side. Its length is always represented by c in $c^2 = a^2 + b^2$, the Pythagorean Theorem. Also point out that the Pythagorean Theorem is used to determine whether a triangle is a right triangle by replacing the variables with the lengths of the sides.

When finding the length of the hypotenuse, c, from the lengths of the legs, a and b, it is essential that the calculations be done in this order:

1. compute a^2 and b^2

2. add a^2 and b^2 to get c^2

3. find c using the square root table.

11-4 Tangent of an Angle

Objective: Compute the tangent of an acute angle.

Discuss the meanings of opposite and adjacent and the locations of the opposite leg and the adjacent leg for acute angles in various right triangles. Point out that before computing the tangent it may be necessary to use the Pythagorean Theorem to determine the length of one of the legs.

11-5 Sine and Cosine of an Angle

Objective: Compute the sine and cosine of an acute angle.

Review the terms opposite, adjacent, and hypotenuse. Draw several right triangles on the chalkboard and ask students to name the sides opposite or adjacent to several angles. Work through the Class Exercises for the section. Remind students that the Pythagorean Theorem must be used to find the length of a missing side if all lengths are not given.

11-6 Using Trigonometry Tables

Objective: Use a trigonometry table.

Your students will need to practice reading the tables two ways: **1.** given the measure of an angle, find its sine, cosine, or tangent; and **2.** find the angle measure having the given value of sine, co-sine, or tangent.

Emphasize that when only the length of one side and the measure of an acute angle A of a right triangle are known, a trigonometric ratio from the table can be used to find the length of another side as shown in the following table.

Known side length	Desired length	Ratio to use
leg opposite A	adjacent leg	tan A
leg opposite A	hypotenuse	sin A
leg adjacent to A	hypotenuse	cos A
leg adjacent to A	opposite leg	tan A
hypotenuse	opposite leg	sin A
hypotenuse	adjacent leg	cos A

Remind students to use multiplication to solve equations such as $0.5774 = \dfrac{XE}{5}$.

11-7 Finding Angle Measures

Objective: Use trigonometry tables to find the measure of an angle in a right triangle when the lengths of two sides are given.

The key to finding the unknown acute angle measure in a right triangle is knowing which trigonometric ratio to use.

If the known side lengths are:	use the ratio:
opposite leg and hypotenuse	sine
adjacent leg and hypotenuse	cosine
opposite leg and adjacent leg	tangent

Discuss with your students how to determine to which of two table readings a number is nearest by computing or estimating the difference between the number and each of the table readings.

12 Probability

Try to include hands on classroom experiments in this chapter, to give students a more concrete understanding of probability.

12-1 Probability

Objective: Write the probability of an event composed of one or more equally likely outcomes.

Discuss the concept of equally likely outcomes and point out that each outcome has the same probability. Stress that probabilities may be written as ratios, decimals, or percents. Practice counting the total number of outcomes and the number of favorable outcomes in a variety of situations. Also discuss the probabilities of impossible and certain events.

12-2 Sample Spaces

Objective: Make tree diagrams to tabulate sample spaces.

Discuss with your students how a tree diagram is constructed and how the possible outcomes are thereby obtained from the branches. Students will need to practice using this technique and computing the probabilities of events composed of the outcomes.

12-3 Counting Principle

Objective: Find the number of outcomes for an activity of two or more stages.

Build on your students' work with tree diagrams to explain the counting principle. Emphasize the advantages of using the counting principle to replace making a tree diagram when the number of branches is large. Practice finding the total number of outcomes and computing probabilities of events.

Emphasize the necessity of counting the number of possible outcomes first.

12-4 Independent Events

Objective: Find the probability of two or more independent events.

You can motivate the rule $P(A, B) = P(A) \cdot P(B)$ for independent events A and B with specific examples such as tossing a coin three times: **1.** list the sample space; **2.** compute $P(HHT)$ directly from the sample space; **3.** show that $P(HHT) = P(H) \cdot P(H) \cdot P(T)$

$$
\left.\begin{array}{ll} HHH & HTT \\ HHT & THT \\ HTH & TTH \\ THH & TTT \end{array}\right\} \; P(HHT) = \frac{1}{8}, \text{ and}
$$

$$
P(H) \cdot P(H) \cdot P(T) = \frac{1}{2} \cdot \frac{1}{2} \cdot \frac{1}{2} = \frac{1}{8}
$$

Point out the advantage of multiplying the individual probabilities rather than listing the entire sample space.

12-5 Dependent Events

Objective: Find the probability of two or more dependent events.

Emphasize that although we multiply probabilities to compute the probability of two or more dependent events, the probabilities must be computed in the order in which the events occur. This is because the probability of the second outcome is dependent on the first outcome, the third on the second, etc. It is helpful to model dependent probabilities with marbles, cubes, or names on slips of paper, so students can see how the probabilities change according to prior outcomes.

12-6 Odds

Objective: Find the odds in favor and the odds against an event.

Point out that the odds in favor of an event are the ratio $\dfrac{number\ of\ favorable\ outcomes}{number\ of\ unfavorable\ outcomes}$. The reciprocal ratio gives the odds against the event. Modeling with objects helps students understand the concept of odds.

12-7 Experimental Probability

Objective: Understand and compute experimental probabilities.

Discuss with your students how experimental probabilities are computed as the ratio of the number of favorable outcomes to the total number of experiments. A class experiment can help students understand the convergence of an experimental probability as the number of experiments increases. For example, have each student flip a coin or a thumbtack 20 or 30 times, recording each outcome. Have each student compute an experimental probability. Then combine results for 5 students, 10, and the entire class to find experimental probabilities. Compare the results as the number of experiments increases.

12-8 Using Samples

Objective: Draw conclusions about a population from a random sample.

Emphasize to your students the two characteristics of a random sample:

1. Each outcome is as likely to occur as any other outcome.

2. The number of items in the sample is large enough to reflect the entire sample space.

To reinforce these characteristics, give students the following situations and ask whether the sample is random.

1. A quality control engineer tests every tenth part that comes off the assembly line.

2. A soap manufacturer concludes that a new product is a success because several favorable letters have been received about the product.

3. You can't decide where to go for your summer vacation so you write the names of ten possibilities on slips of paper. You then shake them in a bag and draw one without looking.

Your class might plan a real or imaginary survey of a random sample of students in your school to determine their favorite TV program or movie or recording artist. Discuss how the group could select a random sample and use it to predict results for all students. Also discuss how one could purposely bias the results by not selecting the sample randomly and what those results might be.

13 Geometry

13-1 Points, Lines, and Planes

Objective: To recognize and name points, lines, and planes.

Discuss the concepts of point, line, and plane and make sure students understand the notation associated with each.

The concept of a plane may be more readily understood if actual objects such as blocks or boxes are used to supplement the text.

Draw several sets of intersecting lines on the chalkboard. Point to different lines and have students tell whether or not the line is a transversal. Have students give a reason for their answer. Next draw pairs of lines cut by a transversal some of which appear to be parallel and others that do not. Ask students to identify the alternate interior angles and the corresponding angles. Again ask for reasons to substantiate choices. Emphasize that alternate interior and corresponding angles are formed only when a transversal cuts parallel lines.

13-2 Polygons

Objective: To identify and classify polygons.

Review the polygons shown in the table. Remind students that the prefix associated with each figure is a clue to the number of sides. Go over the definitions of vertex and diagonal and be sure they are understood by students.

Work through the development of the formula for determining the sum of the angles of a polygon. It may be helpful to draw several different quadrilaterals, sketch in the diagonals and from there show that all quadrilaterals have angles that add up to 360°.

13-3 Similar, Congruent Polygons

Objective: To use proportions to find missing parts of similar polygons and to identify congruent triangles.

In Chapter 11 students were introduced to the concept of similar triangles. That concept is expanded here to include polygons. Go over the definitions of similarity and congruence and make sure students

understand the difference. Ask students to explain why all congruent figures are similar but not all similar figures are congruent.

Emphasize the importance of naming corresponding parts in order. Give students practice in naming corresponding parts of figures that are in the same relative position and those that have been rotated into a different position. Work through the Class Exercises making sure students understand how the proportions were set up.

13-4 Problem Solving

Objective: To solve word problems using a simpler model.

Tell students that many textbook word problems appear to be more difficult than they really are. The inclusion of decimals, fractions, negative integers, or numbers raised to a power may be intimidating as students try to recall how to deal with the numbers rather than the problem. It may help students to block out the numbers completely when first reading a problem or to substitute small, whole numbers for those in the problem. Asking students to rewrite problems in their own words is also helpful. If students misunderstand a problem it should be obvious from the wording of their mini-problems.

13-5 Triangles

Objective: To identify and classify triangles.

Work through the Class Exercises to make sure students understand the implications of each definition. Draw several triangles on the chalkboard. Ask students to classify the triangles and give a reason for their answer.

Review the definition of perimeter and discuss the examples given in the text.

13-6 Quadrilaterals

Objective: To identify and classify quadrilaterals.

Discuss the concept of formal proof. Tell students that though many steps seem obvious, they are included to form a logical sequence. In more advanced courses students will learn to apply the same principles to more difficult and less obvious proofs.

Work through the Class Exercises. Ask students to give reasons for choosing true or false for each exercise and ask for examples to support answers.

14 Programming in BASIC

This chapter offers students a unique introduction to a programming language. Many of the algebraic concepts learned throughout the course are reinforced in a new and highly motivating way. All exercises can and should be completed with paper and pencil. If computers are available, students should be encouraged to try running the programs and comparing their answers with the computer output. Students should also be encouraged to experiment with a variety of changes in the programs just to see what happens.

Variations in BASIC make it advisable to check the manual for your machine before attempting to run any of the programs in the chapter. Minor changes in syntax may be necessary to avoid the frustrating experience of getting repeated error messages after carefully entering a program exactly as it appears.

14-1 Symbols and Line Numbers

Objective: Learn BASIC operation symbols, order of operations, and one use of the PRINT instruction.

Point out that the PRINT statement is used to make the computer perform a calculation and to display the answer on a screen or on paper. Emphasize the use of positive integer line numbers to show the computer the order in which instructions are to be performed.

Discuss the example programs in detail including what goes on in computer memory and what we see, if anything, as each statement is performed.

Writing expressions in BASIC symbols and writing output for BASIC programs reinforces the order in which mathematical operations are performed. Throughout the chapter, encourage students to look back at previous examples and exercises for ideas.

14-2 REM, LET, and PRINT

Objective: Learn the REM, LET, and other uses of PRINT statements.

Mention to your students that REM statements are used, particularly in lengthy programs, to remind the programmer what the program is doing next.

Emphasize that a LET statement tells the computer to save certain data in memory under the name given after the word LET. Nothing appears on the screen or on paper when a LET statement is executed; only computer memory is affected.

Point out the difference between two statements such as 10 PRINT 15 * 22 and 10 PRINT "15*22". Such statements can be combined to produce a more pleasing result: 10 PRINT "15 * 22 =" 15*22 Note that when printing more than one calculation on a line, using a comma to separate the variables spaces numbers rather far apart, while a semicolon prints numbers very close together. This is one of the few times that punctuation marks are used in BASIC statements.

14-3 FOR—NEXT

Objective: Learn the paired statements FOR and NEXT.

Emphasize that FOR and NEXT are paired instructions: they must always appear together with FOR executed first. FOR and NEXT can be used to merely count the number of times a procedure is performed, or the FOR variable can actually be used in the loop procedure. For example, all three programs below print the first 10 multiples of 7:

```
10  LET N=7            10  FOR X=1 TO 10
20  FOR X=1 TO 10      20  PRINT X*7
30  PRINT N            30  NEXT X
40  LET N=N+7          40  END
50  NEXT X
60  END


10  FOR X=7 TO 70 STEP 7
20  PRINT X
30  NEXT X
40  END
```

14-4 Problem Solving

Objective: To draw flowcharts for various problem solving situations.

Introduce the lesson by asking students to list the steps involved in completing the following activities:

1. choosing a birthday gift for their mother
2. making a meatloaf
3. taking a weekend trip

Lists should include some questions such as "Does the store have what I want?" "Is it the right color? price? size?" Tell students that breaking a problem down into small, manageable segments is the essence of flowcharting. Also tell students that though this method of conceptualizing a problem is favored by programmers, it is also applicable and useful in solving many everyday problems.

Work through the Class Exercises to help students develop a logical plan of attack.

14-5 READ . . . DATA, GOTO

Objective: Learn the READ, DATA, and GOTO statements.

Emphasize the paired relationship between the READ and DATA instructions. One cannot appear without the other, although more than one DATA statement can appear with a READ statement. Frequently, the DATA lines appear near the end of the program, so they are easily seen when the program is listed, and therefore easily modified if new data or additional data is desired before the program is run again. Discuss what goes on in computer memory and what appears on the screen, if anything, as the computer executes each line of the example programs.

Also discuss how to rewrite a program so that it uses READ . . . DATA to assign values to variables.

```
Example:  10  LET X=14
          20  LET Y=23
          30  LET Z=41
          40  PRINT "AVERAGE="(X+Y+Z)/3
          50  END
```

$\left(\begin{array}{l}\textit{Replace lines 10, 20, and 30 with } 10 \text{ READ X, Y, Z,} \\ \textit{and add a line } 45 \text{ DATA 14, 23, 41}\end{array}\right)$

14-6 More READ . . . DATA, GOTO

Objective: Learn more uses of READ . . . DATA and GOTO

Review with your students how to find a percent (P) of a given number (N), by multiplying N by $\frac{P}{100}$. Again, trace through the example line by line, discussing what goes on in the computer memory and/or on the screen. Note the use of quotes only as needed in the PRINT statement. The variables whose values are to be printed are left out of the quotes.

14-7 Branching: IF . . . THEN

Objective: Learn the IF . . . THEN statement.

With your students, trace through the Example and Your Turn programs line by line, noting especially what happens when an IF . . . THEN statement is encountered. Note the outcome as each data item is processed. Review the meanings of $\leq$ and $\geq$ and $\neq$, and note how these symbols are written in BASIC.

14-8 More Uses of IF . . . THEN

Objective: Reinforce understanding of the IF . . . THEN statement.

Discuss the occasional need for a repeated GOTO in a program with an IF . . . THEN statement. Also mention that a program may include many IF . . . THEN statements, to account for various situations.

The following schedule suggests time frames and assignments for completing the course. It is intended to provide an overview of teaching and testing which we hope will make your planning easier.

For your convenience, the schedule has been divided into both a semester and trimester program. This schedule also suggests the number of days you might spend on each chapter, but of course you should be guided by the needs of your students.

The assignment guide outlines a suggested sequence of assignments for minimum, average, and maximum course coverage. Each successive level provides more in-depth coverage and somewhat less drill than its predecessor. The assignment guide also suggests appropriate times to include review, testing, and ancillary material.

	←———Semester 1———→							←———Semester 2———→							
Chapter	1	2	3	4	5	6	7	8	9	10	11	12	13	14	
Number of Days	11	13	11	11	14	15	13	17	15	13	11	13	10	13	Total 180
	←———Trimester 1———→				←——Trimester 2——→				←———Trimester 3———→						

T E A C H I N G				**Support Material**
Section	**Minimum**	**Average**	**Maximum**	
1-1	1–15, odd or even; 19–24	6–18, odd or even; 21–31; Problems 1, 2	7–36, odd or even Problems 1, 2	
1-2	1–6; 7–19, odd or even; 22–24; 28, 29	7–32, odd or even; 33	13–32, odd or even; 33, 34	
1-3	1–4; 9–12; 18–27, odd or even	9–35, odd or even; 36, 37	18–35, odd or even, 36, 37	Self Test 1 p. 10 Practice Master 1 Quiz p. 1
1-4	1–8	3–10	5–14	
1-5	1–10; 18–30, odd or even Problem 1	9–34, odd or even; Problems 1, 2	15–34, odd or even Problems 1–3	
1-6	1–29, odd or even	9–32, odd or even; 33, 34 Problem 1	15–32, odd or even; 33, 34 Problems 1, 2	

■ Practice Masters   ■ Tests

	T E A C H I N G			Support Material
Section	**Minimum**	**Average**	**Maximum**	
1-7	1–28, odd or even	13–36, odd or even; 37	13–36, odd or even; 37	
1-8	1–23, odd or even	7–43, odd or even	15–43, odd or even	Self Test 2 p. 26 Practice Master 2 Practice Master 3
REVIEW	Algebra Practice p. 27 Chapter Review p. 31 Cumulative Review p. 33			Chapter Test p. 32 Extra Test p. T49 Chapter Test p. 2
2-1	1–24, odd or even	6–28, odd or even; 31–34	11–37, odd or even	
2-2	1–21, odd or even Problems 1, 2	10–31, odd or even; Problems 1–4	14–37, odd or even; Problems 5–10	
2-3	1–5; 6–40, odd or even	4–45, odd or even; 46, 47	11–51, odd or even	Self Test 1 p. 44 Quiz p. 3
2-4	1–4; 10–13; 19–30, odd or even	16–36, odd or even; Problems 1–10, odd or even	25–45, odd or even Problems 1–14, odd or even	
2-5	1–3; 10–12; 19–21; 31–33; 40–43	16–43, odd or even; 48, 49; Problems 1–10 odd or even	25–51, odd or even; Problems 1–10, odd or even	Practice Master 4
2-6	1–6	1–8	1–8	
2-7	1–30, odd or even; 31, 32, 37, 38, 43, 44	16–45, odd or even; 49–51 Problems 1–14, odd or even	27–54, odd or even; Problems 1–17, odd or even	
2-8	1–4; 13–43, odd or even Problems 1, 2	21–44, odd or even; 50–52; Problems 1–3, 10, 11	21–46, odd or even; 50–55, odd or even; Problems 1–14, odd or even	
2-9	1–15, odd or even	7–21, odd or even	10–24, odd or even	Self Test 2 p. 62 Practice Master 5 Practice Master 6
REVIEW	Algebra Practice p. 63 Chapter Review p. 67 Cumulative Review p. 69			Chapter Test p. 68 Extra Test p. T50 Chapter Test p. 4

	T E A C H I N G			**Support Material**
Section	**Minimum**	**Average**	**Maximum**	
3-1	1–41, odd or even Problem 1	17–52, odd or even; Problems 1, 2	32–55, odd or even; Problems 1–4	
3-2	1–22, odd or even; Problem 1	3–29, odd or even; Problems 1, 2	13–29, odd or even; Problems 1, 2	
3-3	1–10; 13–24, odd or even	10–34, odd or even	13–36, odd or even	
3-4	1–26, odd or even	9–29, odd or even	15–35, odd or even	Self Test 1 p. 83 Practice Master 7 Quiz p. 5
3-5	1–4	1–5	1–6	
3-6	1–28, odd or even	13–42, odd or even	25–45, odd or even	
3-7	1–20, odd or even	9–26, odd or even	13–26, odd or even	Self Test 2 p. 92 Practice Master 8 Practice Master 9
REVIEW	Algebra Practice p. 93 Chapter Review p. 97 Cumulative Review p. 99			Chapter Test p. 98 Extra Test p. T51 Chapter Test p. 6
4-1	1–27, odd or even; 33–52, odd or even	28–56, odd or even; Problems 1–3	31–47, odd or even; 57–62, odd or even; Problems 4–9	
4-2	1–28, odd or even	7–40, odd or even	17–48, odd or even	
4-3	1–17, odd or even; Problems 1, 2	7–21, odd or even; Problems 1–5, odd or even	8–21, odd or even; Problems 1–5 odd or even	
4-4	1–28, odd or even Problems 1, 4	11–39, odd or even Problems 1–4	17–32, odd or even; 37–42; Problems 3–6	Self Test 1 p. 114 Practice Master 10 Quiz p. 7
4-5	1–20, odd or even; Problems 1, 2	9–29, odd or even Problems 1–4	17–29, odd or even Problems 2–5	
4-6	1–20, odd or even Problems 1, 4	9–28, odd or even Problems 2–5	17–32, odd or even; Problems 1–8, odd or even	Practice Master 11
4-7	1–5	3–7	5–9	
4-8	1–5; 16–20; 31–35	21–42, odd or even	26–45, odd or even	Self Test 2 p. 126 Practice Master 12 Practice Master 13

TEACHING				Support Material
Section	Minimum	Average	Maximum	
REVIEW	Algebra Practice p. 127 Chapter Review p. 131 Cumulative Review p. 133 Practice Master 14 Cumulative Review			Chapter Test p. 132 Extra Test p. T52 Chapter Test pp. 8–9 Cumulative Test pp. 10–11
5-1	1–31, odd or even	7–43, odd or even	22–51, odd or even	
5-2	1–35, odd or even	9–38, odd or even	17–41, odd or even; 42	
5-3	1–32, odd or even; 41–43	9–45, odd or even; 49, 50	21–54, odd or even	
5-4	1–24; odd or even	17–40, odd or even; Problems 1–5	25–48, odd or even; Problems 1–5	
5-5	1–28, odd or even	9–36, odd or even	25–52, odd or even	Self Test 1 p. 148 Practice Master 15 Quiz p. 12
5-6	1–24, odd or even; 37–42	5–32, odd or even; 46–54, odd or even	29–57, odd or even	
5-7	1–25, odd or even	5–34, odd or even	13–43, odd or even	Practice Master 16
5-8	1–15	1–19	1–23	
5-9	1–8	1–11	1–13	Practice Master 17
5-10	1–6	1–9	1–12	Self Test 2 p. 164 Practice Master 18
REVIEW	Algebra Practice p. 165 Chapter Review p. 169 Cumulative Review p. 171			Chapter Test p. 170 Extra Test p. T53 Chapter Test pp. 13–14
6-1	1–9	4–12	7–13	
6-2	1–10	4–15; Problem 1	4–15; Problems 1, 2	
6-3	1–18, odd or even	5–22, odd or even; 23	7–25, odd or even	Self Test 1 p. 182 Practice Master 19 Quiz p. 15
6-4	1–6	1–9; Problems 1–3	4–9; Problems 3–6	
6-5	1–14, odd or even	3–18, odd or even; 19	8–20, odd or even	Practice Master 20
6-6	1–8	4–10	4–10	Self Test 2 p. 191 Quiz p. 16

Section	TEACHING Minimum	Average	Maximum	Support Material
6-7	1-8	5-13; Problems 1-4	5-13; Problems 1-7, odd or even	
6-8	1-6	4-10; 11	7-12	
6-9	1-6	3-9	4-9	Self Test 3 p. 200 Practice Master 21 Practice Master 22
REVIEW	Algebra Practice p. 201 Chapter Review p. 205 Cumulative Review p. 207			Chapter Test p. 206 Extra Test p. T54 Chapter Test pp. 17-18 Mid-Year Exam pp. 19-22
7-1	1-20, odd or even	5-20, odd or even; Problem 1	15-20; odd or even; Problems 1-3	
7-2	1-14, odd or even; Problems 1, 2	1-18, odd or even; 19; Problems 1-4	5-20, odd or even; Problems 4-8	
7-3	1-30, odd or even; 38, 39	7-41, odd or even	18-43, odd or even	
7-4	1-5; 13-22 odd or even	7-24; odd or even; Problem 1	9-24; odd or even; Problems 1, 2	Practice Master 23
7-5	1-3	1-4	3-5	Self Test 1 p. 224 Quiz p. 23
7-6	1-18, odd or even; Problem 1	8-21; odd or even Problems 1, 2	11-21, odd or even Problems 1-3	Practice Master 24
7-7	1-10	3-12 Problems 1-3	5-14 Problems 1-3	
7-8	1-15, odd or even Problem 1	10-21, odd or even; 28 Problems 1-3	16-28, odd or even; Problems 1-3	Self Test 2 p. 232 Practice Master 25 Practice Master 26
REVIEW	Algebra Practice p. 233 Chapter Review p. 237 Cumulative Review p. 239			Chapter Test p. 238 Extra Test p. T55 Chapter Test pp. 24-25
8-1	1-15	6-20	8-27	
8-2	1-28, odd or even	9-36, odd or even	17-40, odd or even	
8-3	1-36, odd or even	15-46, odd or even	21-50, odd or even	
8-4	1-30, odd or even	7-37, odd or even	10-45, odd or even	Practice Master 27
8-5	1-34, odd or even	17-43, odd or even	29-52, odd or even	

| Section | T E A C H I N G | | | Support Material |
	Minimum	Average	Maximum	
8-6	1–34, odd or even Problem 1	25–48, odd or even Problems 1, 2	29–52, odd or even Problems 1–3	Self Test 1 p. 255 Practice Master 28 Quiz p. 26
8-7	1–26, odd or even	9–32, odd or even	15–34, odd or even	
8-8	1–34, odd or even	17–34, odd or even	23–37, odd or even	
8-9	1–5	2–7	5–10	
8-10	1–28, odd or even	17–40, odd or even	23–43, odd or even	
8-11	1–34, odd or even	9–36, odd or even	13–39, odd or even	Self Test 2 p. 270 Practice Master 29 Practice Master 30
REVIEW	Algebra Practice p. 271 Chapter Review p. 275 Cumulative Review p. 277 Practice Master 31 Cumulative Review			Chapter Test p. 276 Extra Test p. T56 Chapter Test pp. 27–28 Cumulative Test pp. 29–30
9-1	1–10	1–16	5–18	
9-2	1–12	1–18; Problems 1–8 odd or even	7–22; Problems 1–10 odd or even	
9-3	1–18, odd or even	9–28, odd or even	13–28, odd or even	
9-4	1–12, odd or even	5–16, odd or even; Problem 1	5–16, odd or even; Problems 1, 2	Self Test 1 p. 291 Practice Master 32 Quiz p. 31
9-5	1–14, odd or even	3–22, odd or even	9–23, odd or even	
9-6	1–11	1–14; Problem 1	10–18 Problems 1, 2	Practice Master 33
9-7	1–10	1–16	5–18	Self Test 2 p. 300 Practice Master 34
REVIEW	Algebra Practice p. 301 Chapter Review p. 305 Cumulative Review p. 307			Chapter Test p. 306 Extra Test p. T57 Chapter Test pp. 32–33
10-1	1–7 Problem 1	7–9; Problems 1, 2	7–9; Problems 2–4	
10-2	1–5	4–9	4–9	
10-3	1–10	5–12	9–16	Self Test 1 p. 317 Practice Master 35 Quiz p. 34
10-4	1–6	3–9 Problem 1	7–15 Problems 1, 2	

	T E A C H I N G			Support Material
Section	Minimum	Average	Maximum	
10-5	1–7	6–12 Problem 1	9–15 Problem 1	Self Test 2 p. 325 Practice Master 36 Quiz p. 35
10-6	1–4	3–7	3–8	
10-7	1–5	2–10	6–13	
10-8	1–6	4–9 Problems 1, 2	5–11 Problems 1, 2	Self Test 3 p. 336 Practice Master 37 Practice Master 38
REVIEW	Algebra Practice p. 337 Chapter Review p. 341 Cumulative Review p. 343			Chapter Test p. 342 Extra Test p. T58 Chapter Test pp. 36–37
11-1	1–5	1–7	1–10	
11-2	1–4 Problem 1	1–6; Problems 1, 2	1–6 Problems 3, 4	Practice Master 39
11-3	1–16; Problems 1, 2	11–22; Problems 2, 3	15–28; Problems 3–5	Self Test 1 p. 354 Practice Master 40 Quiz p. 38
11-4	1–9	7–17	10–20	
11-5	1–14, odd or even	5–22, odd or even	7–27, odd or even	Practice Master 41
11-6	1–6; Problems 1, 2	1–9; Problems 2, 3	1–9; Problems 3, 4	
11-7	1–16, odd or even	7–21, odd or even; Problem 1	7–21, odd or even; Problems 1, 2	Self Test 2 p. 366 Practice Master 42
REVIEW	Algebra Practice p. 367 Chapter Review p. 371 Cumulative Review p. 373			Chapter Test p. 372 Extra Test p. T59 Chapter Test pp. 39–40
12-1	1–20, odd or even; Problems 1, 2	9–26, odd or even; Problems 1–3	21–29; Problems 1–4	
12-2	1–12	5–21; Problem 1	7–25; Problems 1, 2	
12-3	1–14 Problems 1, 2	1–20, odd or even; Problems 1–3	9–23, odd or even; Problems 3–6	
12-4	1–14	7–19; Problem 1	7–21; Problems 1, 2	Self Test 1 p. 389 Practice Master 43 Quiz p. 41
12-5	1–20, odd or even	4–23, odd or even; Problems 1–3	7–26, odd or even; Problems 3–6	

Section	T E A C H I N G			Support Material
	Minimum	Average	Maximum	
12–6	1–20, odd or even	11–31, odd or even	15–36, odd or even	Practice Master 44
12–7	1–12; Problems 1–3	1–17; Problems 1–3	6–20; Problems 1–3	
12–8	1–10	4–12	7–15	Self Test 2 p. 402 Practice Master 45
REVIEW	Algebra Practice p. 403 Chapter Review p. 407 Cumulative Review p. 409			Chapter Test p. 408 Extra Test p. T60 Chapter Test pp. 42–43
13–1	1–18, odd or even	1–20, odd or even	11–23, odd or even	
13–2	1–10	1–13	1–15	
13–3	1–13, odd or even	4–20, odd or even	4–20, odd or even	Practice Master 46
13–4	1–4	1–4	1–4	Self Test 1 p. 424 Quiz p. 44
13–5	1–12, odd or even	1–14, odd or even	1–14, odd or even	
13–6	1–12	1–12	1–12	Self Test 2 p. 430 Practice Master 47 Practice Master 48
REVIEW	Algebra Practice p. 431 Chapter Review p. 435 Cumulative Review p. 436 Practice Master 49 Cumulative Review			Chapter Test p. 436 Extra Test p. T61 Chapter Test pp. 45–46 Cumulative Test pp. 47–49
14–1	1–12	7–14	9–15	
14–2	1–7, 9	5–12	6–14	
14–3	1–7	3–9	4–11	Practice Master 50
14–4	1–5	3–8	5–9	Self Test 1 p. 451 Quiz p. 50
14–5	1–5	3–6	4–7	
14–6	1–4	3–6	3–7	
14–7	1–3	1–4	1–4	
14–8	1, 2	1–3	1–4	Self Test 2 p. 462 Practice Master 51 Practice Master 52
REVIEW	Algebra Practice p. 463 Chapter Review p. 467 Cumulative Review p. 469 Practice Master 53 Cumulative Review			Chapter Test p. 468 Extra Test p. T62 Chapter Test pp. 51–52 Final Exam pp. 53–56

Notes

ANSWERS

Chapter 1. **1.** 35 **2.** 16 **3.** 60 **4.** 5
5. 4 **6.** 36 **7.** 140 **8.** 25 **9.** 412
10. 2159 **11.** 1237 **12.** 9335 **13.** 871
14. 5477 **15.** 574 **16.** 1226 **17.** 1203
18. 4797 **19.** 5218 **20.** 5719 **21.** yes;
total cost $490 **22.** 595 **23.** 9000
24. 80,766 **25.** 151,320 **26.** 117,105
27. 266,161 **28.** 275 **29.** 121 **30.** 87
31. 358 **32.** 489 **33.** 134 **34.** 12,301
35. 9567 **36.** 3572 **37.** 2008 **38.** 21,352
39. 2853 **40.** 100 **41.** 14
42. $8a + 2b$ **43.** $3x + 3y$ **44.** $8a + 5b + 5c$
45. $3x + 2xy + 5y$

Chapter 2. **1.** 13.05 **2.** 635.0028 **3.** 300.015
4. 40.003017 **5.** 3.55, 3.57, 3.75, 3.77
6. 5.6, 5.64, 5.641, 5.6417 **7.** 9.1, 9.15, 9.51,
95.1 **8.** 23.2, 23.23, 23.232, 23.32 **9.** 7.3
10. 0.5 **11.** 18.0 **12.** 280.1 **13.** 18.09
14. 0.36 **15.** 2.59 **16.** 12.40 **17.** 13.13
18. 388.99 **19.** 37.8257 **20.** 7.41
21. 33.43 **22.** 8.105 **23.** $136.50; $59.50
24. 32.452 **25.** 37 **26.** 0.43 **27.** 6.25
28. 0.1632 **29.** 50 **30.** 0.72 **31.** 450
32. 75

Chapter 3. **1.** No **2.** Yes **3.** Yes
4. Yes **5.** Yes **6.** No **7.** No **8.** Yes
9. Yes **10.** $3 \times 7 \times 11$ **11.** $2^2 \times 3^3 \times 5$
12. $2^2 \times 5 \times 29$ **13.** 2^9 **14.** $3^2 \times 5^2 \times 7$
15. $2^4 \times 3^3$ **16.** 1 **17.** 6 **18.** 3
19. 3 **20.** x **21.** xy **22.** $9(2y + 1)$
23. $2b(b - 2)$ **24.** $3(x^2 - 2x + 3)$
25. $a(1 + 5)$ **26.** $2z(2z + 1)$
27. $3n(n^2 + 3n + 2)$ **28.** $2b(3b + 4 + a)$
29. $x(x + 2)$ **30.** $y(7y + 14y + 1)$
31. 10 cans **32.** 30 **33.** 126 **34.** $60a^2$
35. 7.0×10^7 **36.** 2.2×10^4 **37.** 5.34×10^6
38. 350 **39.** 7,200,000 **40.** 31,900,000

Chapter 4. **1.** $\frac{13}{3}$ **2.** $\frac{34}{5}$ **3.** $\frac{43}{8}$ **4.** $\frac{95}{12}$
5. $1\frac{3}{4}$ **6.** 3 **7.** $4\frac{7}{10}$ **8.** 3 **9.** $\frac{3a}{5}$
10. $3x^2$ **11.** $\frac{4c}{3}$ **12.** $\frac{2x}{3y}$ **13.** $\frac{9x}{8}$ **14.** $\frac{10}{g}$
15. y **16.** $12\frac{1}{2}$ **17.** $7\frac{5}{24}$ **18.** $\frac{9x}{a}$
19. $\frac{2s}{15}$ **20.** $2\frac{31}{40}$ **21.** $3x$ **22.** $\frac{3}{2y}$
23. $\frac{x}{8}$ **24.** $\frac{2}{3r}$ **25.** $\frac{4}{15b}$ **26.** $\frac{1}{48}$
27. 150 calories **28.** 0.625 **29.** $0.2\overline{8}$
30. 0.9375

Chapter 5. **1.** 132 **2.** 6 **3.** 32 **4.** 11
5. 51 **6.** 12 **7.** 16 **8.** 21 **9.** 30
10. 102 **11.** 57 **12.** 24 **13.** 20 **14.** 75
15. 3 **16.** 8 **17.** 8 **18.** 17 **19.** 8
20. 3 **21. a.** $x + 6$, **b.** $x - 6$, **c.** $6x + 2$
d. $4 + a - 3y$ **22. a.** $2b$ **b.** $2b + 3$
23. $3h = 36$; 12 hours **24.** $x - 7 = 43$; $50
25. $x + x + 7 = 63$; 28 years

Chapter 6. **1.** 12.98 ft **2.** 37.8 m **3.** 43.96 ft
4. 50.24 in. **5.** 144.44 m **6.** F **7.** F
8. 1369 ft^2 **9.** 391 yd^2 **10.** 1133.54 cm^2
11. 24.6176 ft^2 **12.** 78,386.96 yd^2 **13.** 143 lb
14. 180 in.^{3} **15.** 98.4 cm^3 **16.** 1808.64 ft^3
17. 593.46 m^3 **18.** 220 m^2 **19.** 972.144 cm^2

Chapter 7. **1.** $\frac{1}{4}$; $\frac{2}{15}$; $\frac{17}{180}$; $\frac{3}{10}$; $\frac{2}{9}$ **2.** 27; 14; 10;
32; 24 **3.** 36% **4.** 60% **5.** 15%
6. 38% **7.** 58% **8.** $130.38 **9.** $567.10
10. $7287.50

No. of copies	85	132	215
Cost	$8.50	$12.56	$18.90

12. 0.6 **13.** 69.3 **14.** 4.02 **15.** 76
16. 1200 **17.** 66.7% **18.** 21.9% **19.** 42.9%

Chapter 8. 1. $2 > {}^-7$ 2. $14 > {}^-5$ 3. ${}^-8 > {}^-12$ 4. ${}^-5 > {}^-31$ 5. ${}^-19$ 6. ${}^-12$ 7. ${}^-22$ 8. ${}^-5$ 9. ${}^-12$ 10. ${}^-34$ 11. ${}^-4$ 12. 4 13. 17 14. ${}^-1$ 15. 13 16. 74 17. 5 18. ${}^-15$ 19. 15 20. 31 21. ${}^-8$ 22. ${}^-52$ 23. ${}^-56$ 24. 45 25. ${}^-60$ 26. ${}^-18$ 27. 60 28. ${}^-220$ 29. 3 30. ${}^-8$ 31. ${}^-3$ 32. ${}^-3$ 33. ${}^-27$ 34. 3 35. 13.5 36. ${}^-5.4$ 37. ${}^-16.3$ 38. 6.3 39. ${}^-32.7$ 40. 0.4 41. ${}^-49.2$ 42. 31.5 43. ${}^-0.8$ 44. ${}^-5.46$ 45. ${}^-0.3$ 46. ${}^-12$ 47. 50 ft × 50 ft 48. ${}^-24$ 49. ${}^-4.7$ 50. ${}^-2.1$ 51. 8.6 52. ${}^-3$ 53. 73.5 54. $x < {}^-4$ 55. $x > {}^-12$ 56. $x > 9$ 57. $y < 26$ 58. $d < 9$ 59. $k < {}^-3$

Chapter 9. 1. ${}^-4, {}^-3, {}^-2, {}^-1, 0$ 2. 2, 7, 12, 17, 22 3. 1, 4, 7, 10, 13 4. 3, 2, 1, 0, ${}^-1$ 5. $3x - 1$; 44, 89 6. $5x - 4$; 71, 146 7. $2x + 5$; 35, 65 8. $3x + 8$; 53, 98 9-14. Check students' graphs. 15-17. Answers will vary. 18. 2; 1 19. 1; 3 20. $\frac{1}{3}$; 0 21. Yes 22. No 23. No

Chapter 10. 1. 43 2. 117.2 3. $294 4. 110 5. Game 2 6. A 7. Answers will vary. 8. 10–19 9. positive

Chapter 11. 1. 20.4 2. 1.5 3. 15 ft 4. 13.5 m 5. $b = 5$ 6. $c = 8.5$ 7. $a = 9.7$ 8. 1.75 9. 0.75 10. 2.4 11. $\frac{10}{16}$ 12. $\frac{12}{16}$ 13. $\frac{10}{16}$ 14. $\frac{12}{16}$ 15. 15.6 16. 17.7 17. 8.5 18. $\angle A = 37°, \angle B = 53°$ 19. $\angle A = 45°, \angle B = 45°$ 20. $\angle A = 40°, \angle B = 50°$

Chapter 12. 1. $\frac{1}{5}$ 2. $\frac{3}{5}$ 3. 0 4-5. Check students' diagrams. 6. 24 7. 72 8. $\frac{1}{20}$ 9. $\frac{1}{10}$ 10. $\frac{1}{10}$ 11. $\frac{1}{20}$ 12. $\frac{3}{20}$ 13. 1 to 5 14. 2 to 1 15. $\frac{7}{20}$ 16. $\frac{9}{20}$ 17. $\frac{1}{5}$ 18. $\frac{7}{10}$ 19. $\frac{3}{10}$ 20. 4200

Chapter 13. 1. $\angle 6$ and $\angle 4$; $\angle 5$ and $\angle 3$ 2. 70°, 70° 3. 110°, 110° 4. 180°, 43° 5. 360°, 55° 6. $x = 8.75$ 7. $x = 1.5, y = 1.25$ 8. 41% 9. 15, 36, 39 10. 23, 23, 37 11. 37, 49, 58 12. $\triangle SWI$ 13. HS

Chapter 14. 1. $(5 * X + 4)/3$ 2. $5 * A \uparrow 2 + 9$ 3. $(B + 7) \uparrow 2/5$ 4. 7 cubed = 343 5. Cost is $401. 6. Check students' programs. 7. Check students' flowcharts. 8. THE VOLUME OF A PRISM IS 120; THE VOLUME OF A PRISM IS 510; THE VOLUME OF A PRISM IS 225 9-10. Check students' programs. 11. 28 17 IS WITHIN BUDGET; 35 35 IS WITHIN BUDGET; 42 45 PRODUCES A DEFICIT

Chapter 1 Test

Let $x = 4$, $y = 15$, and $z = 20$. Evaluate the expression.

1. $y + z$
2. $z - x$
3. $y \cdot x$
4. $z \div x$ 1-1

5. $3z \div y$
6. $2z - x$
7. $3z + 4z$
8. $3y - 5x$

Solve the equation.

9. $x = 87 + 325$
10. $956 + 1203 = h$
11. $57 + 1180 = v$ 1-2

12. $y = 9008 + 327$
13. $500 + 371 = q$
14. $4387 + 1090 = r$

15. $a = 582 - 8$
16. $1321 - 95 = k$
17. $x = 1278 - 75$ 1-3

18. $n = 7322 - 2525$
19. $6070 - 852 = m$
20. $y = 6000 - 281$

Solve.

21. The Spring Dance Committee plans to spend \$235 for a band, \$172   1-4
    for refreshments, and \$83 for decorations. Will a \$500 budget cover
    all the costs?

Solve the equation.

22. $35 \cdot 17 = a$
23. $y = (25)(360)$
24. $g = 1923 \cdot 42$ 1-5

25. $(6305)(24) = x$
26. $n = 555 \cdot 211$
27. $f = (809)(329)$

28. $2475 \div 9 = y$
29. $k = 4114 \div 34$
30. $7221 \div 83 = y$ 1-6

31. $9666 \div 27 = b$
32. $t = 45{,}477 \div 93$
33. $11{,}524 \div 86 = n$

34. $d = 12{,}301 + 0$
35. $9567 \times 1 = p$
36. $p = 0 + 3572$ 1-7

37. $r = (1)(2008)$
38. $21{,}352 + 0 = x$
39. $a = 2853 \cdot 1$

40. $t = 12 + (8 \cdot 11)$
41. $8 + 3 \cdot 16 \div 8 = k$ 1-8

Combine like terms.

42. $a + 7a + 2b$
43. $4x - 2x + 3y + x$

44. $6b + 7a + 5c + a - b$
45. $y + 4y - x + 4x + 2xy$

Chapter 2 Test

Write the decimal.

1. 13 and 5 hundredths   **2.** 635 and 28 ten-thousandths   **2-1**

3. three hundred and fifteen thousandths

4. forty and three thousand seventeen millionths

Write the decimals in order from least to greatest.

5. 3.75, 3.77, 3.57, 3.55   **6.** 5.641, 5.6, 5.6417, 5.64   **2-2**

7. 9.51, 95.1, 9.15, 9.1   **8.** 23.23, 23.2, 23.232, 23.32

Round to the nearest tenth.

9. 7.31   **10.** 0.542   **11.** 17.9631   **12.** 280.074   **2-3**

Round to the nearest hundredth.

13. 18.087   **14.** 0.3642   **15.** 2.5949   **16.** 12.3972

Solve the equation.

17. $3.62 + 9.51 = x$ **18.** $380.2 + 8.79 = y$ **19.** $9.3257 + 28.5 = z$ **2-4**

Solve the equation.

20. $16.13 - 8.72 = a$ **21.** $35.6 - 2.17 = w$ **22.** $27.04 - 18.935 = b$ **2-5**

Solve.

23. Tickets to Ballet on Ice range in price from $8.50 to $19.50 de-   **2-6**
pending on the day and time of the performance. What is the most
you could pay for 7 tickets? the least?

Solve the equation.

24. $5.32 \times 6.1 = k$ **25.** $100 \times 0.37 = g$ **26.** $21.5 \times 0.02 = p$ **2-7**

Solve the equation.

27. $143.75 \div 23 = d$ **28.** $16.32 \div 100 = n$ **29.** $8.5 \div 0.17 = m$ **2-8**

Complete.

30. $72 \text{ cm} = \underline{\ ?\ } \text{ m}$ **31.** $0.45 \text{ kg} = \underline{\ ?\ } \text{ g}$ **32.** $0.75 \text{ daL} = \underline{\ ?\ } \text{ dL}$ **2-9**

Chapter 3 Test

Is the first number divisible by the second number? Answer *Yes* **or** *No.*

3-1

1. 749 by 3   **2.** 1628 by 4   **3.** 920 by 5

4. 450 by 6   **5.** 738 by 9   **6.** 515 by 10

7. 2371 by 3   **8.** 468,505 by 5   **9.** 10,016 by 4

Use exponents to write the prime factorization of each number.

3-2

10. 231   **11.** 540   **12.** 580

13. 512   **14.** 1575   **15.** 432

Write the GCF of each set of expressions.

3-3

16. 7 and 18   **17.** 24 and 42   **18.** 12, 18, and 81

3-4

19. $3x$ and 9   **20.** x^2 and $4x$ **21.** $3xy^2$, $2x^2y$, and x^2y^2

Use the distributive property to factor each expression.

22. $18y + 9$ **23.** $2b^2 - 4b$ **24.** $3x^2 - 6x + 9$

25. $a + 5a$ **26.** $4z^2 + 2z$ **27.** $3n^3 + 9n^2 + 6n$

28. $6b^2 + 8b + 2ab$ **29.** $x^2 + 2x$ **30.** $7y^2 + 14y^2 + y$

Solve.

3-5

31. There are 16 entrants in a tennis tournament. When players lose a match they are out of the tournament. A new can of balls is used for every other match. How many cans are needed for the tournament?

Write the LCM of each set of expressions.

3-6

32. 6 and 10   **33.** 18 and 42   **34.** 5, $12a^2$, and $6a$

Write the number in scientific notation.

3-7

35. 70,000,000   **36.** 22,000   **37.** 5,340,000

Write the number in standard form.

38. 3.5×10^2 **39.** 7.2×10^6 **40.** 3.19×10^7

Chapter 4 Test

Write a fraction for the variable.

1. $4\dfrac{1}{3} = x$ **2.** $6\dfrac{4}{5} = y$ **3.** $5\dfrac{3}{8} = z$ **4.** $7\dfrac{11}{12} = m$ **4-1**

Write a mixed number or a whole number for the variable.

5. $a = \dfrac{7}{4}$ **6.** $b = \dfrac{15}{5}$ **7.** $c = \dfrac{47}{10}$ **8.** $d = \dfrac{39}{13}$

Write the fraction in lowest terms.

9. $\dfrac{6ab}{10b}$ **10.** $\dfrac{12x^2y}{4y}$ **11.** $\dfrac{24c^2x}{18cx}$ **12.** $\dfrac{14x}{21y}$ **4-2**

Find the sum.

13. $\dfrac{3x}{8} + \dfrac{x}{8} + \dfrac{5x}{8}$ **14.** $\dfrac{7}{g} + \dfrac{3}{g}$ **15.** $\dfrac{4y}{7} + \dfrac{2y}{7} + \dfrac{y}{7}$ **4-3**

Simplify the expression using the given value for the variable.

16. $3\dfrac{4}{5} + x; \; x = 8\dfrac{7}{10}$ **17.** $4\dfrac{5}{8} + y; \; y = 2\dfrac{7}{12}$

Write the difference in lowest terms.

18. $\dfrac{12x}{a} - \dfrac{3x}{a}$ **19.** $\dfrac{4s}{5} - \dfrac{2s}{3}$ **20.** $7\dfrac{3}{8} - 4\dfrac{3}{5}$ **4-4**

Write the product in lowest terms.

21. $12 \cdot \dfrac{x}{4}$ **22.** $\dfrac{2x}{5} \cdot \dfrac{15}{4xy}$ **23.** $2\dfrac{3}{4} \cdot \dfrac{x}{22}$ **4-5**

Write the quotient in lowest terms.

24. $\dfrac{7}{4r} \div 2\dfrac{5}{8}$ **25.** $\dfrac{10}{9b} \div 4\dfrac{1}{6}$ **26.** $\dfrac{3}{8}x \div 18x$ **4-6**

Work backwards to find the answer.

27. Randall makes a batch of oatmeal that has 800 calories. If the batch contains $5\frac{1}{3}$ cups of oatmeal, how many calories are in one cup of oatmeal? **4-7**

Write a terminating or repeating decimal for the variable.

28. $\dfrac{5}{8} = n$ **29.** $\dfrac{13}{45} = x$ **30.** $\dfrac{15}{16} = y$ **4-8**

Chapter 5 Test

Which number is a solution of the equation?

1. $x - 33 = 99$ 66 or 132?

2. $2y - 1 = 11$ 5 or 6?

5-1

Solve the equation.

3. $x + 7 = 39$

4. $29 = 18 + q$

5. $72 = h + 21$

5-2

6. $4e = 48$

7. $7r = 112$

8. $252 = 12s$

5-3

9. $23 = x - 7$

10. $y - 12 = 90$

11. $25 = w - 32$

5-4

5-5

12. $8 = \frac{1}{3}h$

13. $\frac{3}{4}z = 15$

14. $\frac{2}{3}n = 50$

15. $7x + 3 = 24$

16. $36 = 5y - 4$

17. $9b - 7 = 65$

5-6

18. $4n - 5 = 3n + 12$

19. $6m + 3 = 4m + 19$

20. $5b - 10 = 8 - b$

5-7

Complete by writing an algebraic expression.

21. a. 6 more than $x = $ ___?___

5-8

   b. x decreased by 6 $= $ ___?___

   c. 6 times x increased by 2 $= $ ___?___

   d. 4 plus a minus 3 times $y = $ ___?___

22. Susan is twice as old as Brian. Let $b = $ Brian's age.

   a. Susan's age $= $ ___?___

   b. Juan is 3 years older than Susan. Juan's age $= $ ___?___

Write an equation. Solve the problem.

23. Freida worked three times as many hours as Angela did.

5-9

   Freida worked 36 hours.

   How many hours did Angela work?

   (Let $h = $ the number of hours Angela worked.)

24. Ruth has 7 dollars less than Fred.

   Ruth has $43.

   How much money does Fred have?

25. Arlene is 7 years older than Sarah. The total of their ages is 63. How old is Sarah?

5-10

Chapter 6 Test

Find the perimeter of the figure described.

6-1

1. triangle
    sides = 3.60 ft, 4.20 ft, 5.18 ft

2. rectangle
    $l = 13.7$ m, $w = 5.2$ m

Find the circumference of the circle. Use $\pi \approx 3.14$.

3. $d = 14$ ft   **4.** $r = 8$ in.   **5.** $r = 23$ m   6-2

True or false? Write T or F. Use the diagram shown at the right.

6. $\overleftrightarrow{AB}$ is perpendicular to $\overleftrightarrow{CD}$.   6-3

7. $\angle 1$ is an acute angle.

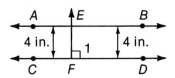

What is the area of the polygon described?

8. square
    $s = 37$ ft

9. rectangle
    $b = 17$ yd, $h = 23$ yd

6-4

What is the area of the circle? Use $\pi \approx 3.14$.

10. $r = 19$ cm   **11.** $r = 2.8$ ft   **12.** $d = 316$ yd   6-5

6-6

The formula $w = \dfrac{11(h - 40)}{2}$ where $w =$ normal weight in pounds and $h =$ height in inches, relates weight and height for teenagers. Use the formula to solve the problem.

13. Clara is 5 ft 6 in. tall. About how much should she weigh?

Find the volume of the figure described. Use $\pi \approx 3.14$.

14. triangular prism
    $B = 12$ in.², $h = 15$ in.

15. square pyramid
    $B = 36$ cm², $h = 8.2$ cm

6-7

16. cylinder
    $r = 8$ ft, $h = 9$ ft

17. cone
    $r = 9$ m, $h = 7$ m

6-8

What is the surface area of the figure shown? Use $\pi \approx 3.14$.

18.

19.

6-9

Chapter 7 Test

1. Use the table to write a ratio in lowest terms to compare the number of signatures for each day to the total signatures for the week.

7-1

Petition Signatures					
Day	Mon.	Tues.	Wed.	Thurs.	Fri.
Signatures	45	24	17	54	40

2. Three out of 5 people signing the petition were female. Use the table above to find out how many females signed each day.

7-2

Write as a percent. Round to the nearest hundredth.

3. $\dfrac{9}{25}$ 4. $\dfrac{45}{75}$ 5. $\dfrac{12}{80}$ 6. $\dfrac{3}{8}$ 7. $\dfrac{7}{12}$ 7-3

If state sales tax is 6%, what will be the total cost, including tax, of the following?

8. coat-$123   9. refrigerator-$535   10. car-$6875   7-4

Solve.

11. At a copying service, the first 100 copies are 10¢ apiece, the second 100 copies are 8¢ apiece, and all additional copies are 6¢ apiece. Make a chart showing the cost for the following: 85 copies, 132 copies, and 215 copies.

7-5

Find the number. Round to the nearest hundredth.

12. $\dfrac{3}{4}$% of 80 is x 13. 165% of 42 is y 14. $5\dfrac{1}{2}$% of 73 is m 7-6

Write and solve an equation to find the base.

15. 19 is 25% of what number?   16. 84 is 7% of what number?   7-7

Find the percent of increase or decrease to the nearest tenth of a percent.

17. from 18 to 30   18. from 128 to 100   19. from 7 to 4   7-8

Chapter 8 Test

Write a number sentence using > to show which number is greater.

1. $^-7$ or 2   **2.** $^-5$ or 14   **3.** $^-8$ or $^-12$ **4.** $^-31$ or $^-5$ **8-1**

Solve the equation.

5. $a = ^-7 + ^-12$ **6.** $x = ^-3 + ^-9$ **7.** $h = ^-17 + ^-5$ **8-2**

8. $b = ^-3 + ^-2$ **9.** $q = ^-7 + ^-5$ **10.** $f = ^-22 + ^-12$

11. $g = ^-9 + 5$ **12.** $f = 15 + ^-11$ **13.** $h = ^-6 + 23$ **8-3**

14. $a = ^-5 + 4$ **15.** $x = 45 + ^-32$ **16.** $d = 79 + ^-5$

17. $x = ^-3 - ^-8$ **18.** $y = ^-8 - 7$ **19.** $d = 5 - ^-10$ **8-4**

20. $y = 19 - ^-12$ **21.** $t = ^-13 - ^-5$ **22.** $m = ^-38 - 14$

23. $x = 7(^-8)$ **24.** $b = ^-5(^-9)$ **25.** $y = ^-6(10)$ **8-5**

26. $r = 6(^-3)$ **27.** $z = ^-12(^-5)$ **28.** $k = ^-10(22)$

29. $g = ^-24 \div ^-8$ **30.** $a = 16 \div ^-2$ **31.** $f = ^-21 \div 7$ **8-6**

32. $x = ^-75 \div 25$ **33.** $y = 54 \div ^-2$ **34.** $g = ^-39 \div ^-13$

35. $h = 7.2 - ^-6.3$ **36.** $k = ^-9.5 + 4.1$ **37.** $b = ^-7.8 - 8.5$ **8-7**

38. $b = 9.5 + ^-3.2$ **39.** $h = ^-31.8 - 0.9$ **40.** $j = ^-5.9 + 6.3$

41. $n = 6(^-8.2)$ **42.** $m = ^-3.5(^-9)$ **43.** $y = 5.6 \div ^-7$ **8-8**

44. $a = 4.2(^-1.3)$ **45.** $r = 2.7 \div ^-9$ **46.** $p = 14.4 \div ^-1.2$

Draw a diagram to help you solve the problem.

47. A farmer has twenty 10 ft fence sections. What are the dimensions   **8-9**
of the four-sided pen with the largest area that can be constructed
using whole fence sections?

Solve the equation.

48. $\dfrac{^-3}{4}t = 18$ **49.** $n + 8.2 = 3.5$ **50.** $^-6m = 12.6$ **8-10**

51. $6.3 + x = 14.9$ **52.** $^-4.1 g = 12.3$ **53.** $^-21.9 + b = 51.6$

Solve the inequality.

54. $x - 3 < ^-7$ **55.** $x + 7 > ^-5$ **56.** $^-5x < ^-45$ **8-11**

57. $y + 7 < 33$ **58.** $d - 15 < ^-6$ **59.** $^-12k > 36$

Chapter 9 Test

Find the first five terms of the sequence of numbers produced by the given expression.

1. $y - 5$ **2.** $5x - 3$ **3.** $3n - 2$ **4.** $^-x + 4$ **9-1**

Write an expression for any term of the sequence, then find the 15th and 30th terms.

5. 2, 5, 8, 11, 14, . . .   **6.** 1, 6, 11, 16, 21, . . .   **9-2**

7. 7, 9, 11, 13, 15, . . .   **8.** 11, 14, 17, 20, 23, . . .

Graph the ordered pair on a coordinate plane.

9. (4, 1)   **10.** ($^-2$, 4)   **11.** (3, $^-2$)   **12.** (0, $^-4$)   **9-3**

Graph the following data. Use your graph to find the 8th term.

13.   **9-4**

No. of term	1	2	3	4	5
Sequence	$^-3$	$^-1$	1	3	5

14.

No. of term	1	2	3	4	5
Sequence	7	4	1	$^-2$	$^-5$

Find three ordered pairs that are solutions of the given equation; then graph them and draw the line for the equation.

15. $y = 3x + 2$ **16.** $y = 2x - 4$ **17.** $y = ^-2x + 5$ **9-5**

What is the slope and y-intercept of the graph of the equation? Graph the equation.

18. $y = 2x + 1$ **19.** $y = ^-x + 3$ **20.** $y = \frac{1}{3}x$ **9-6**

Is the ordered pair a solution of the linear inequality?

21. (2, 4), $y > 3x - 5$ **22.** (1, 4) $y \leq ^-2x + 3$ **9-7**

23. (7, 2), $y > x - 5$

Find the mean of the given data.

1. 40, 37, 42, 53, 40, 46

2. 145, 68, 37, 225, 111

10-1

Use the corresponding graph to answer the following questions.

Garden Fair

Total Sales: $1400

Library Use

9 A.M.–noon

noon–5 P.M.

5 P.M.–9 P.M.

⚇ = 20 People

3. About how much money was spent on seeds?

4. About how many people use the library from noon to 5 P.M.?

10-2, 3

5. At which game were the most apples sold?

6. Which cinema had the greater attendance on Friday?

10-4, 5

Write a question and solve the problem.

7. A coat usually sells for $135. It is on sale for 20% off. There is a 5% sales tax. Your budget is $115.

10-6

Use the graph to answer the question.

8. Which range of commuting distances has the greatest number of people?

9. Does this scattergram show a positive or negative association?

10-7, 8

Chapter 11 Test

For each pair of similar triangles, find x.

1.

2.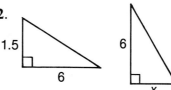

11-1

Use the similar right triangles to find the height marked h.

3.

4.

11-2

A right triangle has sides of lengths a, b, and c, with c the length of the hypotenuse. Find the length of the missing side to the nearest tenth.

5. $a = 12$, $c = 13$ 6. $a = 6$, $b = 6$ 7. $b = 7$, $c = 12$ 11-3

Find the value of $\tan A$.

8.

9.

10.

11-4

In $\triangle ABC$, $\angle C = 90$, $CB = 10$, $AB = 16$, and $AC = 12$. Find the value of the ratio.

11. $\sin A$ 12. $\sin B$ 13. $\cos B$ 14. $\cos A$ 11-5

Use the table on page 471 to find the length of x to the nearest tenth.

15.

16.

17.

11-6

Find the measure of $\angle A$ and $\angle B$ to the nearest degree.

18.

19.

20.

11-7

Chapter 12 Test

A game cube has faces painted red, yellow, green, blue, white, and black. A bag contains marbles numbered 1, 2, 3, 4, 5. Use the game cube, the marbles, and the spinner shown to do the exercises on this page.

One marble is chosen from the bag. What is the probability, written as a ratio, that it will be the following?

1. $P(3)$ 　　　　　　**2.** P(odd number) 　　　　　**3.** $P(6)$ 　　　**12-1**

Draw a tree diagram to list the outcomes.

4. Roll the game cube; then toss a coin.

5. Spin the spinner; then choose a marble.

12-2, 3

How many outcomes are there for each set of activities?

6. Roll the game cube; then spin the spinner.

7. Roll the game cube twice; then toss a coin.

Suppose you choose a marble, then spin the spinner. What is the probability of the outcome?

8. $P(5, Z)$ 　　　　**9.** P(even number, Q) 　　　　**10.** $P(4,$ vowel$)$ 　　**12-4**

Suppose you choose two marbles, one after the other, without replacement. What is the probability of the outcome?

11. $P(1,$ then $4)$ 　　　　　　**12.** $P(2,$ then a number $> 2)$ 　　　**12-5**

What are the odds for each event?

13. Odds in favor of rolling red on the game cube 　　　　　　　**12-6**

14. Odds against rolling green or white on the game cube

Suppose you drop a fork 20 times. It lands pointing up 7 times, pointing down 9 times, and pointing to the side 4 times. What is the experimental probability of the outcome?

15. P(up) 　　　　　**16.** P(down) 　　　　　　　**17.** P(side) 　　**12-7**

A survey of 150 students shows that 105 buy their lunches and 45 bring lunches from home. What is the probability?

18. P(buy) 　　　　　　**19.** P(not buy) 　　　　　　　　**12-8**

20. If there are 6000 students in the school system, about how many can be expected to buy lunch?

12-9

Chapter 13 Test

For Exercises 1–3 refer to the figure on the right. $AB \parallel CD$.

1. Name two pairs of alternate interior angles.

2. $\angle 7 = 70°$, so $\angle 3 = \underline{\ ?\ }$ and $\angle 5 = \underline{\ ?\ }$.

3. $\angle 4 = 110°$, so $\angle 6 = \underline{\ ?\ }$ and $\angle 1 = \underline{\ ?\ }$.

13-1

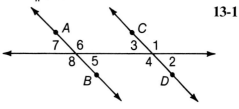

For Exercises 4 and 5 find the sum of the angles in the polygon and the measure of $\angle x$.

4.

5.

13-2

In Exercises 6 and 7 the polygons are similar. Find the lengths of the missing sides.

6.

7.

13-3

Solve.

8. In one year the price of a share of MBA stock fell from $87.78 to $51.79. What was the percent of decrease?

13-4

Find the lengths of the sides of the triangle.

9.

$5x$ $13x$ $12x$

perimeter: 90.

10.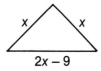

x x $2x - 9$

perimeter: 83.

11.

x $x + 12$ $2x - 16$

perimeter: 144.

13-5

Exercises 12–13 refer to parallelogram *WISH*.

12. $\triangle WSH \simeq \triangle \underline{\ ?\ }$

13. $\overline{WI} \parallel \underline{\ ?\ }$

13-6

Chapter 14 Test

Write the expression using BASIC symbols.

1. $(5x + 4) \div 3$ **2.** $5a^2 + 9$ **3.** $(b + 7)^2 \div 5$ **14-1**

Write the output for the program.

4.
```
10  LET B = 7
20  PRINT B "CUBED = "B↑3
30  END
```
   14-2

5.
```
20  LET M = 234
30  LET L = 167
40  LET C = M+L
50  PRINT "COST IS $" C
60  END
```

6. Change the program in Exercise 4 to print the cubes of the first six multiples of 3.   **14-3**

7. Make a flow chart to show the steps involved in solving a problem to calculate the perimeter of a rectangle.   **14-4**

Write the output for the program.

8.
```
10  READ B,H
20  LET V = B*H
30  PRINT "THE VOLUME OF A PRISM IS" V
40  GOTO 10
50  DATA 10,12,17,30,25,9
60  END
```
   14-5

9. Change the program in Exercise 8 to calculate the volume of a pyramid.   **14-6**

10. Change the program in Exercise 8 to include an IF-THEN statement. Have it print "THE VOLUME IS TOO SMALL" if V is less than 40.   **14-7**

Write the output for the program.

11.
```
10  READ R,E
20  IF R>=E THEN 50
30  PRINT R,E "PRODUCES A DEFICIT"
40  GOTO 10
50  PRINT R,E "IS WITHIN BUDGET"
60  GOTO 10
70  DATA 28,17,35,35,42,45
80  END
```
   14-8

Now that you have used Essentials for Algebra, Concepts and Skills in your classroom, we at Houghton Mifflin would like to hear from you so that we may share your ideas with our authors and editors and consider your suggestions when we publish future editions and related materials. Please ☑ all the choices that apply, complete as many blanks as possible in the letter below, and send it to us.

TO   School Mathematics Department
        Houghton Mifflin Company
        One Beacon Street
        Boston, MA 02108

FROM _____
        name

       _____
        school or district

       _____
        address

       _____
        city   state   zip

About my School and Myself

I've been teaching for_____year(s). The general ability of my students is ☐ above average/ ☐ average/ ☐ below average. I teach the following course(s)_____

_____.

I have a ☐ B.A./ ☐ M.A. degree in_____. In the past I have taught the following courses._____

_____.

Our school includes grade_____to grade_____. It's located in a(n) ☐ urban/ ☐ suburban/ ☐ rural area. We have approximately_____students enrolled. My students ☐ may/ ☐ may not use calculators in the classroom. My school ☐ does/ ☐ does not have a computer that students may use. My training in the use of computers has been_____

_____

_____.

I think the number one problem I face as a teacher is_____

_____

_____.

After they've finished this course my students might take a course in ☐ Algebra/

☐ Geometry/ ☐ Consumer Mathematics/ ☐ Business Mathematics/ ☐ other_____

_____.

About Essentials for Algebra, Concepts and Skills

In your book, I'd like to see more emphasis placed on_____

_____, and less emphasis on_____

_____. The feature of your book that I like best is_____.

For my students the level of difficulty of the book is ☐ too easy/ ☐ appropriate/ ☐ too

difficult. We used Chapters_____through_____. My opinion of the Problem

Solving lessons is_____.

We used the Special features ☐ in class/ ☐ as homework/ ☐ not at all. One thing that I

believe would greatly improve the program is_____.

Besides the textbook and the Teacher's Edition, my school has also acquired the ☐ Test

Masters/ ☐ Practice Masters/ ☐ Solution Key. My opinion of these materials is_____

_____. I wish you'd publish other materials such as_____

_____

_____.

P.S. Here's something else I'd like you to know:_____

_____

_____

_____.

Essentials for Algebra
Concepts and Skills

AUTHORS

Robert E. Willcutt
Patricia R. Fraze
Francis J. Gardella

EDITORIAL ADVISER

Charles E. Allen

TEACHER CONSULTANTS

Dotty J. Garrett   Adrienne A. Kapisak   Patricia C. McNeil
Tommy Tomlinson   Marvin Weingarden

Houghton Mifflin Company · Boston

Atlanta   Dallas   Geneva, Ill.   Lawrenceville, N.J.   Palo Alto   Toronto

Authors

Robert E. Willcutt
Associate Professor, Science-Mathematics
Education Department, School of Education, Boston University

Patricia R. Fraze
Chairman, Mathematics Department
Ann Arbor Huron (Michigan) High School

Francis J. Gardella
Mathematics Supervisor
East Brunswick Public Schools, New Jersey

Editorial Adviser

Charles E. Allen
Instructional Specialist, Secondary Mathematics
Los Angeles City Schools, California

Teacher Consultants

Dotty J. Garrett
Mabry Middle School
Marietta, Georgia

Adrienne A. Kapisak
Gateway Senior High School
Monroeville, Pennsylvania

Patricia C. McNeil
Parkland Junior High School
Rockville, Maryland

Tommy Tomlinson
T. K. Gorman High School
Tyler, Texas

Marvin Weingarden
Detroit Public Schools
Michigan

Printed in U.S.A.

ISBN: 0-395-37880-X

DEFGHIJ-D-943210-89876

Table of Contents

7 *Ratio, Proportion, Percent*

8 *Integers and Rational Numbers*

9 *Graphing in the Coordinate Plane*

10 Statistics

11 Special Triangles

12 Probability

13 Geometry

14 Programming in BASIC

1
Whole Numbers and Variables

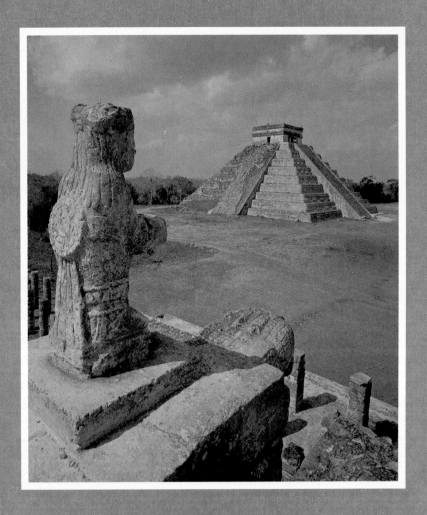

How old is algebra? Older than the hills! When the ancient Mayan city of Chichén Itzá was settled around A.D. 530 the study of algebra was already about 2300 years old.

1-1 Variables

It costs $4 per hour to rent a canoe at the Bantam Boatyard. The total cost of any rental varies with the amount of time spent canoeing. If you let n equal the number of hours spent canoeing, then $4 \times n$ stands for the cost of the rental. We call n a **variable** and $4 \times n$ an **expression.**

Here are some other ways you can show multiplication.

$$4 \cdot n \qquad (4)(n) \qquad 4n$$

To evaluate the expression $4n$, replace n with different numbers.

Example 1   Evaluate $4n$ when $n = 6$, when $n = 10$

Solution
$$
\begin{aligned}
4n &= (4)(6) \\
&= 24
\end{aligned}
\qquad
\begin{aligned}
4n &= (4)(10) \\
&= 40
\end{aligned}
$$

Your Turn   Evaluate the expression.
- $3x$, when $x = 8$ 24
- $12 + (2a)$ when $a = 12$ 36 ⟵ *Work inside the parentheses first.*

You can often write expressions for word phrases.

Example 2   Write an expression for the phrase.
a number n added to 45

Solution $n + 45$ or $45 + n$ ⟵ *Either order*

1

Example 3   Write an expression to show that Alison's new salary is $10 more per week than her old salary.

Solution   Let x = Alison's old salary.
Then $x + 10$ = her new salary.

Example 4   Write an expression to show that the distance from Boston to Springfield is 15 miles less than the distance from Boston to Northampton.

Solution   Let d = the distance from Boston to Northampton. So, you should subtract 15 from d to find the distance from Boston to Springfield. The expression is $d - 15$.

Your Turn   Complete.
- Ron is 7 years older than Nan.
  Let a = Nan's age.
  Then __?__ = Ron's age. $a + 7$
- The attendance at the evening performance was 3 times as great as at the matinee.
  Let n = the number of people at the evening performance.
  Then __?__ = the number of people at the matinee. $n \div 3$

Class Exercises

What is the variable in the expression?

1. $4a + 7$ a

2. $32 + 3x$ x

3. $57b \div 2$ b

4. $37 + w$ w

5. $(20)(b) - 3$ b

6. $a + 72$ a

7. $68 \div p$ p

8. $175 - 3y$ y

Let $n = 9$. Evaluate the expression.

9. $6 + n$ 15

10. $22 - n$ 13

11. $n - 5$ 4

12. $n + n$ 18

13. $12 - n$ 3

14. $54 \div n$ 6

15. $n + 37$ 46

16. $81 \div n$ 9

Exercises

Evaluate the expression using the given value for the variable.

A **1.** $(4n) + 6$; $n = 3$ 18

2. $n + 7$; $n = 12$ 19

3. $x \div 3$; $x = \overset{11}{33}$

4. $9 + (3a)$; $a = 8$ 33

5. $75 - (5b)$; $b = 5$ 50

6. $38 - (2n)$; $n = \overset{8}{15}$

7. $48 \div y$; $y = 6$ 8

8. $16 - (2z)$; $z = 7$ 2

9. $x - 15$; $x = \overset{6}{21}$

Let $x = 5$, $y = 6$, and $z = 15$. Evaluate the expression.

B **10.** $8x$ 40

11. $x + y$ 11

12. $y + 2$ 8

13. $(2x) + y$ 16

14. $z \div x$ 3

15. $(xy) - z$ 15

16. $x + y + z$ 26

17. $(2y) + (3z)$ 57

18. $(5y) \div z$ 2

Write an expression for the phrase.

19. 15 added to x $\qquad$ $x + 15$ **20.** 47 times n $\qquad$ $47n$

21. y minus 65 $\qquad$ $y - 65$ **22.** a plus 155 $\qquad$ $a + 155$

23. r divided by 26 . $\qquad$ $r \div 26$ **24.** z times 79 $\qquad$ $z \cdot 79$

25. the number of hours in n days $24n$ **26.** the numbers of eggs in n dozen $\overset{12n}{}$

27. the quotient of s divided by 8 $s \div 8$ **28.** the product of y and 37 $y \cdot 37$

29. n increased by 52 $\qquad$ $n + 52$ **30.** 84 less a number x $\qquad$ $84 - x$

31. 8 more than y $\qquad$ $y + 8$ **32.** z decreased by 12 $\qquad$ $z - 12$

33. 125 decreased by t $\qquad$ $125 - t$ **34.** 85 greater than b $\qquad$ $b + 85$

35. the cost of one gallon of gas if n gallons cost \$19.35 $19.35 \div n$ **36.** The cost of b plants if one plant costs \$4.98 $(\$4.98)(b)$

Problems

Complete.

1. A grasshopper can jump a distance that is 20 times its body length.
   Let b = body length.
   Then ___?___ = the jumping distance. $20b$

2. Charlie slept 4 fewer hours on Sunday than on Saturday.
   Let h = the hours slept on Saturday.
   Then ___?___ = the hours slept on Sunday. $h - 4$

1-2 *Addition*

Numerical sentences containing the equality symbol, =, are called
equations.

Example 1   Write and solve an equation to show that n is the sum
of 897 and 675.

Solution   Let $n =$ the sum
Then, $n = 897 + 675$ ◄───
$n = 1572$

Remember how to add whole numbers.

$$\begin{array}{r} {}^{1\ 1}\\ 897 \\ +675 \\ \hline 1572 \end{array}$$

Your Turn   Write an equation for the sentence. Solve the equation.
• The sum of 482 and 59 is x. $482 + 59 = x; \; x = 541$
• 1535 plus 496 equals b. $1535 + 496 = b; \; b = 2031$

   Though some problems may be easy to solve without writing equations, they offer practice that will help you write and solve more difficult problems later.

Example 2   Sales are booming at Computers, Etc. Last month 659
personal computers were sold. The month before 398
were sold. How many computers were sold in the two
months?

Solution   Let $n =$ the total number sold
Then, $n = 659 + 398$
$n = 1057$
A total of 1057 computers were sold.

Your Turn Write an equation using n for the variable. Solve the equation.

- Harry delivers 35 packages on Friday, and 37 on Saturday. How many packages does he deliver in all? $35 + 37 = n$; $n = 72$
- Monica sells 40 lb of fish on Wednesday and 39 on Thursday. How many pounds does she sell in all? $40 + 39 = n$; $n = 79$
- Gavin pumps 256 gal of gasoline on Tuesday and 460 on Wednesday. How many gallons are pumped in all? $256 + 460 = n$; $n = 716$

The following properties can be used to make addition easier.

Commutative Property of Addition

Changing the order of the addends doesn't change the sum.

In Arithmetic   In Algebra
$5 + 6 = 6 + 5$ $a + b = b + a$

Associative Property of Addition

Changing the grouping of the addends doesn't change the sum.

In Arithmetic   In Algebra
$(5 + 6) + 7 = 5 + (6 + 7)$ $(a + b) + c = a + (b + c)$

You can combine the commutative and associative properties to make addition easier.

Example 3 Use the commutative and associative properties to add $(26 + 8) + 4$.

Solution Think: $(26 + 8) + 4 = 26 + 4 + 8$ ⟵ *To add in your head look for sums of 10, 20, 30, etc. to add first.*
$= 30 + 8$
$= 38$

Your Turn Use the commutative and associative properties to add.

- $(99 + 47) + 1$ 147
- $(88 + 66) + 12$ 166
- $(187 + 136) + 73$ 396

5

You can also use the properties to make column addition easier.

Example 4   Add: $6 + 8 + 4 + 8$.

Solution

$$
\begin{array}{r}
6 \\
8 \\
4 \\
+8 \\
\hline
26
\end{array}
$$

$10 = 6 + 4$
$16 = 8 + 8$

First look for sums of 10 to make the addition easier.

Class Exercises

Find the sum.

1. 56	**2.** 855	**3.** 1391	**4.** 99	**5.** 67,481
+44	+ 76	+ 900	+199	+ 3,892
100	931	2291	298	71,373
6. 175	**7.** 27	**8.** 89	**9.** 6734	**10.** 991
82	336	15	266	1158
376	424	+111	842	769
+198	+ 82	215	+1746	+4442
831	869		9588	7360

Exercises

Use the commutative and associative properties to do the addition in your head.

A **1.** $(33 + 15) + 7$ 55

2. $(45 + 39) + 5$ 89

3. $(96 + 89) + 4$ 189

4. $186 + 57 + 14$ 257

5. $381 + 56 + 19$ 456

6. $597 + 398 + 103$ 1098

Solve the equation.

B **7.** $n = 326 + 263$ 589

8. $a = 465 + 132$ 597

9. $465 + 932 = b$ 1397

10. $375 + 975 = a$ 1350

11. $563 + 999 = m$ 1562

12. $r = 9642 + 8659$ 18,301

13. $t = 1235 + 427$ 1662

14. $9003 + 75 = z$ 9078

15. $3992 + 793 = b$ 4785

Write an equation for the sentence. Solve the equation.

16. The sum of 4862 and 57 is *n*.
$4862 + 57 = n; \ 4919$

17. 63 added to 598 is *x*.
$598 + 63 = x; \ 661$

18. The total of 60,845 and 72 is *b*.
$60,845 + 72 = b; \ 60,917$

19. The numbers 886 and 749 add to a sum of *y*.
$886 + 749 = y; \ 1635$

20. 64 increased by 93 is *y*.
$64 + 93 = y; \ 157$

21. 158 plus 6839 is *z*.
$158 + 6839 = z; \ 6997$

Use the commutative and associative properties to solve the equation.

22. $a = (47 + 59) + 3$ — 109

23. $46 + (39 + 4) = x$ — 89

24. $n = (14 + 49) + 36$ — 99

25. $y = (56 + 192) + 8$ — 256

26. $b = 137 + (15 + 13)$ — 165

27. $n = 999 + (881 + 1)$ — 1881

Use the map below. Write and solve an equation for the exercise.

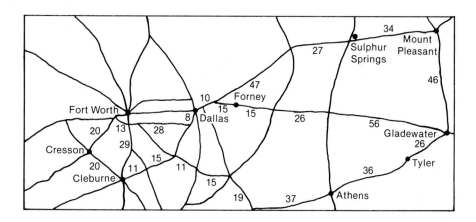

Find the total distance.

28. from Ft. Worth to Cleburne to Athens.
$29 + 11 + 15 + 11 + 15 + 19 + 37 = d; \ d = 137$

29. from Forney to Gladewater to Mount Pleasant.
$15 + 26 + 56 + 46 = d; \ d = 143$

30. from Mount Pleasant to Sulphur Springs to Dallas.
$34 + 27 + 47 + 10 = d; \ d = 118$

31. from Gladewater to Forney to Dallas.
$56 + 26 + 15 + 15 + 10 = d; \ d = 122$

32. from Cleburne to Cresson to Dallas.
$20 + 20 + 13 + 28 + 8 = d; \ d = 89$

Solve.

C 33. How many miles are covered in a round trip from Athens to Cleburne to Ft. Worth? 274

34. You can travel to Mount Pleasant from Dallas by way of Sulphur Springs or Gladewater. Which is the shorter route? Sulphur Springs

7

1-3 *Subtraction*

There are 1547 seats in the opera hall of the Sydney Opera House in Australia. At a recent performance 1459 seats were filled. How many seats were empty?

You can subtract to solve the problem.

$$\begin{array}{r} \overset{4}{1}\overset{13}{\cancel{5}}\overset{17}{\cancel{4}}7 \\ -\ 1459 \\ \hline 88 \end{array}$$

There were 88 empty seats.

Addition and subtraction are opposite operations.

In Arithmetic

If $8 + 11 = 19$, then $19 - 11 = 8$.

In Algebra

If $a + b = c$, then
$c - b = a$.

You can use addition to check subtraction. Since $1459 + 88 = 1547$ the answer above is correct.

Example Write an equation to show that n is the difference between 687 and 29. Solve and check.

Solution $n = 687 - 29 \longleftarrow$

$$\begin{array}{r} \overset{7}{6}\overset{17}{\cancel{8}}\cancel{7} \\ -\ \ 29 \\ \hline 658 \end{array}$$

$n = 658$

Check: $658 + 29 = 687$

Your Turn   Write and solve an equation for the sentence.
- The difference 1500 minus 685 is *y*. $1500 - 685 = y$; 815
- The number of days in a year minus 87 equals *n*.
  $365 - 87 = n$; 278

Class Exercises

Subtract.

1. $\begin{array}{r} 76 \\ -35 \\ \hline \end{array}$ 41	**2.** $\begin{array}{r} 186 \\ -56 \\ \hline \end{array}$ 130	**3.** $\begin{array}{r} 59 \\ -49 \\ \hline \end{array}$ 10	**4.** $\begin{array}{r} 168 \\ -29 \\ \hline \end{array}$ 139
5. $\begin{array}{r} 3000 \\ -241 \\ \hline \end{array}$ 2759	**6.** $\begin{array}{r} 4001 \\ -1392 \\ \hline \end{array}$ 2609	**7.** $\begin{array}{r} 5050 \\ -62 \\ \hline \end{array}$ 4988	**8.** $\begin{array}{r} 7777 \\ -499 \\ \hline \end{array}$ 7278
9. $\begin{array}{r} 30{,}048 \\ -6{,}829 \\ \hline \end{array}$ 23,219	**10.** $\begin{array}{r} 100{,}064 \\ -29{,}833 \\ \hline \end{array}$ 70,231	**11.** $\begin{array}{r} \$684.00 \\ -27.59 \\ \hline \end{array}$ \$656.41	**12.** $\begin{array}{r} \$847.00 \\ -199.99 \\ \hline \end{array}$ \$647.01

Exercises

Subtract. Use addition to check your answer.

A
1. $6384 - 4695$ 1689
2. $7635 - 3746$ 3889
3. $4000 - 2998$ 1002
4. $\$29.00 - 16.98$ \$12.02
5. $\$30.00 - 26.59$ \$3.41
6. $\$85.00 - 25.55$ \$59.45
7. $30{,}060 - 7912$ 22,148
8. $104{,}600 - 75{,}633$ 28,967

Solve.

B
9. $n = 417 - 325$ 92
10. $g = 387 - 211$ 176
11. $m = 1529 - 299$ 1230
12. $7006 - 378 = r$ 6628
13. $682 - 293 = m$ 389
14. $769 - 590 = x$ 179
15. $k = 3652 - 937$ 2715
16. $p = 4300 - 411$ 3889
17. $r = 6340 - 798$ 5542

Write an addition or subtraction equation for the sentence.

18. 16 greater than 30 is *x*. $30 + 16 = x$

19. The difference between 4080 and 67 is *x*. $4080 - 67 = x$

20. The sum of 278 and 439 is *y*. $278 + 439 = y$

21. *x* is equal to 6000 minus 87. $x = 6000 - 87$

22. *n* is 239 more than 18. $n = 18 + 239$

23. *a* is 75 plus 46. $a = 75 + 46$

9

Evaluate the expression using the given value of the variable.

24. $x - 358$; $x = 1500$ 1142   **25.** $n - 27$; $n = 45$ 18   **26.** $a - 986$; $a = 2000$ $\overset{1014}{}$

27. $472 - y$; $y = 98$ 374   **28.** $6000 - b$; $b = 571$ 5429   **29.** $1003 - z$; $z = 744$ $\overset{259}{}$

30. $8006 - d$; $d = 322$ 7684   **31.** $b - 403$; $b = 500$ 97   **32.** $n - 59$; $n = 208$ $\overset{149}{}$

The table shows the attendance at various performances during a Summer Arts Festival that toured several cities.

	City						
Activity	**Orleans**	**Newark**	**Joplin**	**Adelphi**	**Chester**	**Nichols**	**York**
Rock Concert	1351	625	2600	1758	4000	901	2177
Play	649	1400	399	637	768	539	426
Symphony	327	598	406	482	888	603	749
Circus	703	255	–	897	1006	591	986

Write and solve an equation to show the difference in attendance for the performance.

33. circus attendance in Adelphi and Newark $897 - 255 = n$; 642

34. rock concert attendance in Chester and Orleans $4000 - 1351 = n$; 2649

35. play attendance in Joplin and York $426 - 399 = n$; 27

Solve.

C **36.** Is subtraction commutative? Give examples to support your answer.   no; $5 - 3 \neq 3 - 5$

37. Is subtraction associative? Give examples to support your answer.   no; $(6 - 4) - 2 \neq 6 - (4 - 2)$

Self Test 1

Evaluate the expression using the given value of the variable.

1. $6a$; $a = 7$ 42   **2.** $(15x) + 3$; $x = 2$ 33   **3.** $18 - (2y)$; $y = 8$ 2   **1-1**

Solve the equation.

4. $n = 18 + 35$ 53   **5.** $75 + 103 = b$ 178   **6.** $y = 96 + (12 + 4)$ 112   **1-2**

7. $4001 - 376 = x$ 3625   **8.** $b = 339 - 276$ 63   **9.** $160 - 98 = a$ 62   **1-3**

1-4 *Problem Solving*

The problem solving process can be broken down into several steps. Though the solutions to some problems may be obvious, others will be more easily seen if you take the problem apart.

Example 1 Harold had $68 in a savings account. When he decided to close the account and take out his money he received $97. How much interest had the money earned?

Solution Break the problem down into smaller segments.
1. What do you know and what do you want to know? Harold had $68. He received $97. How much interest?
2. Make a plan. Write a subtraction equation to show that the interest is the difference between $97 and $68.
3. Use the plan.
   Let i = the interest earned
   Then $i = 97 - 68$
   $i = 29$
4. Show your answer and check to see that it is reasonable and answers the question.
   The money earned $29 interest.

Your Turn Use the problem solving process to solve the problem.
- In June, Seth weighed 75 kg. By the time soccer practice began in September he was down to 69 kg. How much weight did he lose?
   $75 - 69 = w$; 6; lost 6 kg

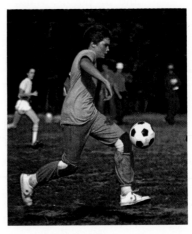

Class Exercises

A ░ **covers the numbers in the problems below. Match each problem to an equation and solve the equation.**

1. Mary has 2 stamp albums. One contains ▓ stamps, the other ▓. How many stamps does she have in all?

   d. $376 + 978 = n$; 1354

2. A sports arena has seating for ▓ people. At a recent concert, ▓ seats were occupied. How many seats were empty?

   a. $y = 10{,}937 - 7465$; 3472

3. Olivia earns ▓ each week as a computer programmer. Weekly taxes amount to ▓. How much does Olivia receive in her paycheck?

   b. $p = 527 - 149$; 378

a. $y = 10{,}937 - 7465$
b. $p = 527 - 149$
c. $400 + 0 = p$
d. $376 + 978 = n$
e. $a = 47 - 15$

Exercises

Write an equation. Solve.

A 1. There are 480 freshmen, 521 sophomores, 511 juniors, and 609 seniors at Watson High School. What is the school's total enrollment?
   $480 + 521 + 511 + 609 = t$; 2121 students

2. During a recent football game, the Benson High team scored 16, 27, 13, and 37 points. What was the team's total score for the game?
   $16 + 27 + 13 + 37 = p$; 93 points

3. Wally won the 400 m race with a time of 72 seconds. Harley, the second place finisher, completed the race in 94 seconds. How much better was Wally's time than Harley's?
   $94 - 72 = t$; 22 seconds

4. "I drove 579 mi last week," said Estelle, "and 623 mi the week before." How many more miles did Estelle drive the first week?
   $623 - 579 = m$; 44 miles

B 5. Regal Repair received payments of $350 for repair of a computer terminal and $158 for repair of a video disk player. From the total, an assistant's salary of $198 was deducted. How much money was left?
   $(350 + 158) - 198 = m$; $310

6. Miriam took two rolls of film at a class picnic. One roll contained 36 shots and the other contained 24. Of the photos taken, 17 did not come out. Should Miriam buy an album that holds 50 photos or one that holds 70?
   $(36 + 24) - 17 = p$; 43 photos came out; An album for 50 photos.

7. On Tuesday, John had a balance of $475 in his checking account. He paid a bill for $298 and then deposited a check for $965. What is John's new balance? $(475 - 298) + 965 = b$; $1142

8.

> Memorandum   ABC Industries
>
> To: Cashier   From: Evelyn Clanden
>
> Subject: Travel Expenses
>
> Enclosed is an itemized report of expenses for my recent business trips. The total for the Washington trip was $789. The total for the Chicago trip was $367. I received a cash advance of $1500.

$1500 - (789 + 367) = m$; $344; ABC Industries
How much money is owed? To whom is the money owed?

Use the information in the phrases to write and solve a problem. Answers will vary.

c **9.** Air fare—$479.82
  Hotel—$688.50
  Meals—$285.79

10. Food Bills
  Jan.—$365.47
  Feb.—$308.51
  Mar.—$386.32

11. Earned—$1508.17
  Spent— $68.37
  Saved— $150.00

12. Trip distance—1407 mi
  Drove—528 mi

13. Stamp Collection
  Have—478
  Sold— 99
  Bought— 35

14. Car Sales
  On hand—72
  Sold—13
  New shipment— 9

1-5 *Multiplication*

The Waukegan Widget Company produces 3542 widgets per day. At this rate how many widgets will they produce in 21 days? You can use a multiplication equation to solve the problem.

Let $n = 3542 \times 21$ ◄————

Then, $n = 74,382$

In 21 days 74,382 widgets will be produced.

> *Remember how to multiply whole numbers.*
>
> $$\begin{array}{r} 3542 \\ \times 21 \\ \hline 3542 \\ 70840 \\ \hline 74,382 \end{array}$$

Like addition, multiplication has a commutative and associative property.

Commutative Property of Multiplication

Changing the order of the factors does not change the product.

In Arithmetic
$3 \cdot 8 = 8 \cdot 3$

In Algebra
$ab = ba$

Associative Property of Multiplication

Changing the grouping of the factors does not change the product.

In Arithmetic
$(6 \cdot 4)5 = 6(4 \cdot 5)$

In Algebra
$(ab)c = a(bc)$

Multiplication also has another special property.

The Distributive Property of Multiplication over Addition and Subtraction

In Arithmetic
$6(5 + 3) = 6 \cdot 5 + 6 \cdot 3$
$3(4 - 2) = 3 \cdot 4 - 3 \cdot 2$

In Algebra
$a(b + c) = ab + ac$
$a(b - c) = ab - ac$

You can check to see if the distributive property is true.

$$6(5 + 3) \overset{?}{=} 6 \cdot 5 + 6 \cdot 3$$

$6 \cdot 8$	$30 + 18$
48	48

We read $a \overset{?}{=} b$ as "is a equal to b?"

$48 = 48$, so $6(5 + 3)$ is equal to $6 \cdot 5 + 6 \cdot 3$.

Using the properties of multiplication can make it easier to do some multiplication.

Example 1   Solve.
$n = (25 \cdot 6)2$

Solution $n = (25 \cdot 6)2$
$= (25 \cdot 2)6$ ⟵ *Associative and commutative properties*
$= 50 \cdot 6$
$= 300$

Your Turn   Use the properties of multiplication to help make the multiplication easier.
- $x = (2 \cdot 97)5$ 970
- $y = (25 \cdot 86)4$ 8600
- $n = 50(2 \cdot 77)$ 7700
- $a = 6(50 + 7)$ 342

When a factor is multiplied by itself it is raised to a **power.** A raised number called an **exponent** is used to indicate the number of times the factor is used.

Example 2   Write $3 \cdot 3 \cdot 3 \cdot 3$ using an exponent.

Solution 3^4 ⟵ *The exponent tells you that the factor 3 will be multiplied by itself 4 times.*

Example 3   Write $a \cdot a \cdot a \cdot a \cdot a$ using an exponent.

Solution $a^5 \longleftarrow$ *The factor a is multiplied by itself 5 times.*

Example 4   What is the value of $2x^3$ if $x = 3$?

Solution $2x^3 = 2(3^3) \longleftarrow$ *Do all exponentiations first.*
$= 2(27)$
$= 54$

Your Turn   Write the product.
- $y \cdot y \cdot y \cdot y \cdot y$ y^5
- 4^2 16
- $3y^2$ when $y = 4$ 48

Class Exercises

Multiply.

1. 14	**2.** 75	**3.** 37	**4.** 432	**5.** 1006
$\times 3$	$\times 9$	$\times 6$	$\times 25$	$\times 328$
42	675	222	10,800	329,968

Exercises

Multiply.

A

1. 38	**2.** 47	**3.** 671	**4.** 587	**5.** 3316
$\times 26$	$\times 19$	$\times 39$	$\times 75$	$\times 919$
988	893	26,169	44,025	3,047,404

Solve.

B   **6.** $n = 36 \cdot 9$ 324

7. $z = 12^3$ 1728

8. $p = 59 \cdot 9$ 531

9. $x = 3^2$ 9

10. $w = 20^4$ 160,000

11. $r = (77 \cdot 31)3$ 7161

12. $p = 4^5$ 1024

13. $x = 128(95 \cdot 2)$ 24,320

14. $d = 6^6$ 46,656

15. $d = 6(7 + 9)$ 54

16. $y = 25(7 + 10)$ 425

17. $m = 14(8 + 9)$ 238

Evaluate the expression using the given value of the variable.

18. $m \cdot 27$; $m = 10$ 270   **19.** $58a$; $a = 7$ 406   **20.** $17y$; $y = 58$ 986

21. x^3; $x = 7$ 343   **22.** $w \cdot 63$; $w = 40$ 2520   **23.** $10m^2$; $m = 6$ 360

24. $35p^2$; $p = 2$ 140   **25.** $5 + y^2$; $y = 9$ 86   **26.** $a^5 - 10$; $a = 2$ 22

Write an addition, subtraction, or multiplication expression.

27. 5086 multiplied by b $5086b$ **28.** the sum of x and 4075 $x + 4075$

29. r increased by 3000 $r + 3000$ **30.** the product of t and 375 $t \cdot 375$

31. 7215 more than a $a + 7215$ **32.** y used as a factor 6 times y^6

33. A parking garage has 9 levels. Let n = the number of spaces on each level. Then ___?___ = the number of spaces in the garage. $9n$

34. A contractor ordered 88 spools of wire. Let f = the number of feet of wire on each spool. Then ___?___ = the total amount of wire ordered. $88f$

Problems

Use the table to answer the questions.

Ticket Prices for Strings'n'Things			
	Sun.–Thurs.	Fri.–Sat.	Matinee (Sun., Wed.)
Orchestra	$20	$22	$18
1st Balcony	$19	$20	$17
2nd Balcony	$17	$18	$15

1. Selma is buying 6 orchestra tickets for Saturday night. How much will they cost? $132

2. The Thespian Club bought 7 tickets for 1st balcony on Sunday evening and 5 tickets for the 1st balcony for the Sunday matinee. How much did they spend? $218

3. Suppose you received a $50 gift certificate for theater tickets. What is the greatest number of tickets you could buy? What seats and what days would they be good for? How much money would you have left? 3 tickets; 2nd balcony matinee; $5

17

1-6 Division

There are several different ways to show division. In the divisions below, the 6 is the **divisor,** the 24 is the **dividend,** and the 4 is the **quotient.**

$$6)\overline{24} \qquad 24 \div 6 = 4 \qquad \frac{24}{6} = 4$$

Multiplication and division are inverse operations.

In Arithmetic   In Algebra

If $4 \cdot 3 = 12$, then $12 \div 3 = 4$ If $ab = c$, then $c \div b = a$, $b \neq 0$

Example 1   Write a related equation: $3 \times 37 = 111$.

Solution $111 \div 37 = 3$

Your Turn   Write a related equation.

- $3 \times 92 = 276$
  $276 \div 3 = 92$ or $276 \div 92 = 3$
- $696 \div 8 = 87$
  $87 \times 8 = 696$
- $679 \times 9 = 6111$
  $6111 \div 9 = 679$
  or $6111 \div 679 = 9$

Since multiplication and division are opposites, you can use multiplication to check division.

Example 2   Solve the equation $n = \dfrac{45}{3}$. Use multiplication to check your quotient.

Solution $n = \dfrac{45}{3}$ ⟵

$n = 15$

Check: $15 \times 3 = 45$

Remember how to divide whole numbers.

$$3)\overline{\begin{array}{r} 15 \\ 45 \\ -3 \\ \hline 15 \\ -15 \end{array}}$$

Your Turn Write and solve an equation for the problem. Check your answer.
- The quotient 68 divided by 5 is *n*. $68 \div 5 = n$; $n = 13R3$
- Mark traveled 160 mi on 12 gal of gas. How many miles per gallon does he get? $160 \div 12 = g$; $g = 13R4$

Class Exercises

Divide.

1. $3\overline{)39}$ 13   **2.** $4\overline{)57}$ 14R1   **3.** $4\overline{)577}$ 144R1   **4.** $7\overline{)928}$ 132R4

5. $72 \div 9$ 8   **6.** $60 \div 12$ 5   **7.** $221 \div 17$ 13   **8.** $777 \div 37$ 21

9. $\dfrac{56}{7}$ 8   **10.** $\dfrac{121}{11}$ 11   **11.** $\dfrac{48}{6}$ 8   **12.** $\dfrac{182}{26}$ 7

Exercises

Divide.

A   **1.** $8\overline{)96}$ 12   **2.** $6\overline{)768}$ 128   **3.** $7\overline{)896}$ 128   **4.** $6\overline{)942}$ 157

    5. $3\overline{)4678}$ 1559R1   **6.** $15\overline{)6380}$ 425R5   **7.** $35\overline{)3254}$ 92R34   **8.** $72\overline{)7609}$ 105R49

Solve.

B   **9.** $a = 64 \div 4$ 16   **10.** $b = \dfrac{88}{4}$ 22   **11.** $m = 81 \div 9$ 9

    12. $1102 \div 29 = x$ 38   **13.** $12{,}750 \div 35 = m$ 364R10   **14.** $585 \div 9 = t$ 65

    15. $p = \dfrac{121}{11}$ 11   **16.** $r = 144 \div 12$ 12   **17.** $w = \dfrac{225}{15}$ 15

Evaluate the expression using the given value of the variable.

18. $\dfrac{x}{7}$; $x = 49$ 7   **19.** $121 \div a$; $a = 11$ 11   **20.** $\dfrac{986}{y}$; $y = 17$ 58

21. $m \div 50$; $m = 750$ 15   **22.** $\dfrac{b}{78}$; $b = 632$ 8R8   **23.** $5162 \div d$; $d = 89$ 58

19

Write a variable expression for the phrase.

24. The quotient of 1335 and *n*. $1335 \div n$

25. 468 divided by *x* $468 \div x$

26. *d* divided by 782 $d \div 782$

27. 76 more than the number *r* $r + 76$

28. *n* increased by 1580 $n + 1580$

29. the quotient of *w* and 339 $w \div 339$

Complete.

30. George took 120 pictures on his vacation.
Let *r* = the number of pictures on one roll of film.
Then __?__ = the number of rolls of film used. $120 \div r$

31. Rhonda has 21 oz of cheese to divide among friends.
Let *n* = the number of friends.
Then __?__ = the amount of cheese for each friend. $21 \div n$

C 32. The pups in a new litter registered the following weights:

Butch 15 oz	Sundance 17 oz	Foxy 14 oz
Wishbone 14 oz	Redeye 18 oz	

What is the average weight of a new pup from the litter? 15.6 oz

33. Is division commutative? Give examples to explain your answer. no; $6 \div 3 \neq 3 \div 6$

34. Is division associative? Give examples to explain your answer. no; $(8 \div 4) \div 2 \neq 8 \div (4 \div 2)$

Problems

Solve.

1. When the Masons had telephone service installed in their new house, they were charged for the following services: Service order charge—$5.00, Home visit charge—$5.50, Telephone handling charge—$5.00 per phone. If 3 phones were installed, what was the total bill? $25.50

2. It takes about 8 to 10 oranges to make a quart of freshly squeezed orange juice. About how many oranges are needed for 5 quarts? 40 to 50 oranges

1-7 *Identity Properties*

The numbers 0 and 1 have some special properties. When 0 is added to any number the resulting sum is **identical** to the original number.

Identity Number for Addition
The identity number for addition is zero.
In Arithmetic   In Algebra
$0 + 7 = 7$ $0 + a = a$

When 1 is multiplied by any number, the resulting product is **identical** to the original number.

Identity Number for Multiplication
The identity number for multiplication is one.
In Arithmetic   In Algebra
$1 \cdot 3 = 3$ $a \cdot 1 = a$

Division by zero is impossible. To see why this is true consider the inverse relationship of multiplication and division.

$$\text{If } 8 \div 0 = n \text{ then } n \cdot 0 = 8$$

Since 0 multiplied by any number is 0, there is no value of n that will be a solution for the equation $n \cdot 0 = 8$.

Class Exercises

Add or multiply.

1. $6 + 0$ 6   **2.** $84 \cdot 1$ 84   **3.** $6842 + 0$ 6842   **4.** $398 \cdot 1$ 398

5. $1 \cdot 9306$ 9306   **6.** $0 + 438$ 438   **7.** $278 \cdot 1$ 278   **8.** $4775 + 0$ 4775

21

Exercises

Add or multiply.

A **1.** $0 + 1$ 1   **2.** $10 + 0$ 10   **3.** $23 + 0$ 23   **4.** $0 + 125$ 125

    5. $1 \cdot 76$ 76   **6.** $478 \cdot 1$ 478   **7.** $0 + 0 + 0$ 0   **8.** $999 \cdot 1$ 999

    9. $0 + 9865$ 9865   **10.** $0 + 125$ 125   **11.** $675 \cdot 1$ 675   **12.** $1 \cdot 1$ 1

Solve.

B **13.** $a = 96 \cdot 1$ 96   **14.** $k = 36 + 0$ 36   **15.** $p = 0 + 9$ 9   **16.** $b = 58 \div 0$ impossible

    17. $z = 49 + 0 + 1$ 50   **18.** $y = 19 \cdot 1$ 19   **19.** $m = 0 + 999 + 1$ 1000   **20.** $y = 417 \cdot 1$ 417

    21. $36 = 36 + m$ 0   **22.** $46p = 46$ 1   **23.** $56 + r = 56$ 0   **24.** $n + 9 = 9$ 0

    25. $9r = 9$ 1   **26.** $p \cdot 46 = 46$ 1   **27.** $(a)(102) = 102$ 1   **28.** $n + 68 = 68$ 0

What is the value of n?

C **29.** $na = a$ 1   **30.** $n + b = b$ 0   **31.** $n(3a) = 3a$ 1   **32.** $n + 2b = 2b$ 0

Solve the equation in your head.

    33. $x = 37(468 - 467)$ 37   **34.** $n = 725 + (95 - 95)$ 725

    35. $(229 - 228)76 = y$ 76   **36.** $a = 400 + (637 - 637)$ 400

Solve.

    37. Is there an identity number for subtraction? Show why or why not. yes, 0; $n - 0 = n$

Using the Calculator

Use your calculator to evaluate the following expressions for the given value of the variable.

1. $375x - 52$, if $x = 1953$ 732,323   **2.** $4287n + 3781$, if $n = 274$ 1,178,419

3. $11,597 - 13b$, if $b = 372$ 6761   **4.** $\dfrac{a}{359} + 23,281$, if $a = 1,447,488$ 27,313

5. $\dfrac{162n}{156}$, if $n = 21,918$ 22,761   **6.** $\dfrac{(328)(1404)}{y}$, if $y = 108$ 4264

1-8 *Order of Operations*

If you put on your shoes before your socks you'll achieve a different result than if you perform the activities in the reverse order. When you calculate mathematical expressions that have more than one operation the order of the operations also makes a difference.

Example 1 Morgan earns $15 per day. During one week he earned a $2 bonus for the week. During another week he earned a $2 bonus each day. How much did he earn for each 5-day week?

Solution

Week 1
$$(5)(15) + 2 = n$$
$$75 + 2 = n$$
$$77 = n$$
Morgan earned $77.

Week 2
$$5(15 + 2) = y$$
$$(5)(17) = y$$
$$85 = y$$
Morgan earned $85.

As you can see, computing with the same numbers can lead to different answers. Use the following rules to insure the correct order of operations.

1. Do all work in parentheses first.
2. When there are no parentheses, do all multiplications and divisions first, working from left to right. Next do all additions and subtractions working from left to right.

Example 2 Solve the equation $a = 3(5 + 2)4$.

Solution

$a = 3(5 + 2)4$ ⟵ *Work inside the parentheses first.*
$a = 3 \cdot 7 \cdot 4$
$a = 84$

Example 3 Solve the equation $a = 3^2 \cdot 5 + 2 \cdot 4$.

Solution $a = 3^2 \cdot 5 + 2 \cdot 4$ ⟵ *First raise 3 to the second power.*
$a = 9 \cdot 5 + 2 \cdot 4$ ⟵ *Do the multiplications next.*
$a = 45 + 8$
$a = 53$

Your Turn Solve the equation.
- $a = 3 \cdot 4 + 2$ 14 $b = 3(4 + 2)$ 18
- $m = 5^2 \cdot 6 - 2$ 148 $n = (6 - 2)5^2$ 100

The expression $7f + 9s + 2f$ contains three **terms,** $7f$, $9s$ and $2f$. The numbers 7, 9, and 2 are called the **coefficients** of the terms. When the variables in more than one term of an expression are the same, they are called **like terms.** You can combine like terms by addition or subtraction.

Example 4 Combine the like terms in the expression.
$6a + 4b + a$ ⟵─────────── | *The expression $6a + a$ is the same as $6a + 1a$. When the terms are combined, the result is $7a$.*

Solution $6a + 4b + a = 7a + 4b$

Your Turn Add or subtract to combine the like terms.
                                                          $6z + y$
- $7a + 3a$ 10a   • $13n + 9n + 2x$ 22n + 2x   • $14z - 8z + y$

Class Exercises

Solve the equation.

1. $6 + 2 \cdot 3 = a$ 12   **2.** $(6 + 2)3 = b$ 24   **3.** $14 \div 2 + 5 = x$ 12

4. $14 \div (2 + 5) = y$ 2   **5.** $4 + 3 \cdot 14 = m$ 46   **6.** $(4 + 3)14 = n$ 98

7. $4 \div 2 - 1 = a$ 1

8. $4 \div (2 - 1) = b$ 4

9. $4 \cdot 4 + 4 = q$ 20

10. $4(4 + 4) = r$ 32

11. $0 \cdot 1 + 1 = w$ 1

12. $0(1 + 1) = z$ 0

Exercises

Solve the equation.

A **1. a.** $4 + 9 \cdot 2 = a$ 22
b. $(4 + 9)2 = r$ 26

2. a. $5 \cdot 3^2 + 6 = y$ 51
b. $5(3^2 + 6) = w$ 75

3. a. $8 + 6 \cdot 3 = t$ 26
b. $(8 + 6)3 = b$ 42

4. a. $14 \cdot 3 + 9 = q$ 51
b. $14(3 + 9) = d$ 168

5. a. $15 + 4 \cdot 6 = m$ 39
b. $(15 + 4)6 = s$ 114

6. a. $19 - 1 \cdot 8 = n$ 11
b. $(19 - 1)8 = d$ 144

7. a. $3 + 6 \cdot 4 + 4 = x$ 31
b. $(3 + 6)(4 + 4) = g$ 72

8. a. $17 - 8 \div 4 - 1 = k$ 14
b. $(17 - 8) \div (4 - 1) = y$ 3

9. a. $4^3 \cdot 3 + 6 \cdot 3 = h$ 210
b. $4^3(6 + 3)3 = j$ 1728

Name the coefficients and the variables in the expression.

B **10.** $3a$ 3; a

11. $4b$ 4; b

12. $16n$ 16; n

13. $87c$ 87; c

14. $47x$ 47; x

15. $963z$ 963; z

16. $6n + 7m$ 6, 7; n, m

17. $4p + 7q$ 4, 7; p, q

18. $18g + 9g$ 18, 9; g

Combine like terms.

19. $n + 3n$ $4n$

20. $1n + 3n$ $4n$

21. $15x + x$ $16x$

22. $13z + 17z + 4a$ $30z + 4a$

23. $66r - 19r - 17x$ $47r - 17x$

24. $75t + 92t - 6r$ $167t - 6r$

25. $46s - 16s - 5t$ $30s - 5t$

26. $19j + 17k + j$ $20j + 17k$

27. $27e - 27b - 16e$ $11e - 27b$

Let $a = 2$, $b = 8$, and $c = 6$. Evaluate the expression.

C **28.** $a + bc$ 50

29. $(a + b)c$ 60

30. $3a + 8c$ 54

31. $a(a + b)$ 20

32. $4 + 6b$ 52

33. $(b - c) \div a$ 1

34. $ab - ac$ 4

35. $a(b - a)c$ 72

36. $a + b \div a + 4$ 10

37. $\dfrac{(a + c)}{(c - a)}$ 2

38. $a^3 + ab$ 24

39. $2c^3 + 6$ 438

Combine like terms.

40. $14x + 12y + 3x - 8y$ $17x + 4y$

41. $33a - 14a + 16b - 10b$ $19a + 6b$

42. $48 + 3n - 4 + n$ $4n + 44$

43. $63 - 4y + 12 + 6b$ $6b - 4y + 75$

25

Using the Computer

This program demonstrates that a computer using BASIC follows the rules for the Order of Operations. After trying this program, you may wish to try some examples of your own.

```
  5  REM: ORDER OF OPERATIONS
 10  PRINT "3*4+5*2 =";
 20  PRINT 3*4+5*2
 30  PRINT "3+4*5+2 =";
 40  PRINT 3+4*5+2
 50  PRINT "(3+4)*(5+2) =";
 60  PRINT (3+4)*(5+2)
 70  PRINT "6+8/2 =";
 80  PRINT 6+8/2
 90  PRINT "(6+8)/2 =";
100  PRINT (6+8)/2
110  PRINT "2↑3+5 =";
120  PRINT 2↑3+5
130  PRINT "2↑(3+5) =";
140  PRINT 2↑(3+5)
150  PRINT "4+2↑3 =";
160  PRINT 4+2↑3
170  PRINT "(4+2)↑3 =";
180  PRINT (4+2)↑3
190  END
```

$3 * 4 + 5 * 2 = 22$
$3 + 4 * 5 + 2 = 25$
$(3 + 4) * (5 + 2) = 49$
$6 + 8/2 = 10$
$(6 + 8)/2 = 7$
$2 ↑ 3 + 5 = 13$
$2 ↑ (3 + 5) = 256$
$4 + 2 ↑ 3 = 12$
$(4 + 2) ↑ 3 = 216$

Self Test 2

Solve.

1. Mr. Rice drove 360 mi on 25 gal of gas. How many miles did he travel per gallon of gas? 14.4 miles per gallon   **1-4**

2. $n = 17 \cdot 84$ 1428   3. $46 \cdot 55 = x$ 2530   4. $a = 27 \cdot 15$ 405   **1-5**

5. $x = \dfrac{325}{25}$ 13   6. $1248 \div 16 = a$ 78   7. $y = \dfrac{1053}{39}$ 27   **1-6**

8. $r = 872 \cdot 1$ 872   9. $q = 475 + 0$ 475   10. $z = 1006 + 0$ 1006 60   **1-7**

11. $3 + 7 \cdot 6 = n$ 45   12. $(14 \cdot 2) + 6 = a$ 34   13. $4 \cdot 3 + 6 \cdot 8 = n$ **1-8**

Algebra Practice

Evaluate the expression using the given value for the variable.

1. $(3w) + 2$; $w = 4$ 14
2. $64 - (4y)$; $y = 7$ 36
3. $r \div 5$; $r = 45$ 9
4. $16 + (3b)$; $b = 2$ 22
5. $100 - (10g)$; $g = 4$ 60
6. $42 \div j$; $j = 6$ 7

Write an equation for the sentence. Solve the equation.

7. The total of 406 and 97 is *s*. $406 + 97 = s$; 503
8. The difference between 2001 and 1906 is *a*. $2001 - 1906 = a$; 95
9. 89 increased by 19 is *l*. $89 + 19 = l$; 108
10. 84,013 minus 47,219 is *w*. $84{,}013 - 47{,}219 = w$; 36,794
11. The numbers 623 and 94 add to a sum of *f*. $623 + 94 = f$; 717
12. 19 greater than 28 is *p*. $28 + 19 = p$; 47

Write a variable expression for the phrase.

13. the product of *h* and 42 $h \cdot 42$
14. 89 divided by *x* $89 \div x$
15. the quotient of 6273 and *n* $6273 \div n$
16. *j* used as a factor 5 times j^5
17. *c* increased by 50 $c + 50$
18. the quotient of *d* and 12 $d \div 12$

Solve.

19. $b = 42 + 0$ 42
20. $r = 17 \cdot 1$ 17
21. $p = 0 + 683$ 683
22. $71 = 71 + n$ 0
23. $29c = 29$ 1
24. $(65)(a) = 65$ 1
25. $q = 14 \div 2 - 3$ 4
26. $k = 8 \times 2 - 4 \div 2$ 14
27. $3 + (3 \times 3) \div 3 = e$ 6

Let $x = 4$, $y = 5$, $z = 1$. Evaluate the expression.

28. $x + y - z$ 8
29. $(x + z)y$ 25
30. $(2z + 4y)x$ 88
31. $x(y - z)$ 16
32. $2x(y + z)$ 48
33. $y - z - x$ 0
34. $4z - x + y$ 5
35. $y(x - 4z)$ 0
36. $z(y - x)$ 1

Combine like terms.

37. $3n - 2n + n$ 2n
38. $4f - 3f + 1$ $f + 1$
39. $4s + s + t$ $5s + t$
40. $2a - 3b - a$ $a - 3b$
41. $4x + y + 4x$ $8x + y$
42. $6p - 7 + 4p$ $10p - 7$
43. $5a + 6a - a + 8$ $10a + 8$
44. $3t + 7 + 8t - 1$ $11t + 6$
45. $4x + 2y - y - x$ $3x + y$

27

Problem Solving on the Job

Construction Careers

Most construction jobs require the services of carpenters to transform wood into parts of a building.

```
CARPENTER

DESCRIPTION: Work on construction
projects. Measure and mark room
layouts.

QUALIFICATIONS: 4-5 years on-the-
job training as an apprentice plus
about 144 h per year of classroom
work.

JOB OUTLOOK: Openings expected to
be as good as other occupations;
Outlook may change in response to
reduced building activity.
```

	Year	Rate	Hours Worked	Total Pay
1.	1	$ 6.00	38	? $228.00
2.	1	? $6.00	35	$210.00
3.	1	$ 7.00	? 42	$294.00
4.	2	$ 8.50	40	? $340.00
5.	2	? $8.75	37	$323.75
6.	2	$ 9.35	? 41	$383.35

At various stages of a training program, an apprentice earns different rates of pay.

Complete the table.

Solve.

7. Molly is in the first year of her apprenticeship. She earns $6.00 per hour for the first 40 hours and time and a half for anything over 40 hours. How much will she earn in a week if she works 45 hours? $285.00

8. Ned is an apprentice earning $9.35 per hour. He earns double pay if he works on holidays. How much will he earn in a week that he works 38 regular hours and 7 holiday hours? $486.20

A contractor is building a housing development that will include 15 new houses.

9. Each new house will have a brick front. The bricklayer estimates that each house will require 500 bricks. How many bricks should be purchased for all the houses? 7500 bricks

10. Each new house will need 8 doors for rooms, 5 doors for large closets, and 3 doors for small closets. How many doors of each size will be needed for the entire development? 120 for rooms; 75 for large closets; 45 for small closets

11. The contractor estimates it will take 2 plumbers 4 days to do the major pipe installation in each house. If each plumber works 7 hours per day and earns $17 per hour, how much should the contractor estimate for the entire plumbing costs? $14,280

12. To wallpaper the living room of each new house requires 24 rolls of wallpaper. Each roll costs $9. How much will be spent for living room wallpaper for all the houses in the development? $3240

13. Each house has a master bedroom 23 yd² in size. Wall-to-wall carpeting that costs $12 per yd² is being used for the master bedrooms for all the houses. How much will it cost? $4140

14. Nine of the houses have patios 24 yd² in size. The size of the patios for the other 6 houses is 21 yd². Indoor-outdoor carpeting that costs $14 per yd² is being used to cover all the patios. How much will it cost? $4788

15. The landscaping for each lot of the development includes the following trees and shrubs.

> 1 tree at $25
> 5 juniper bushes at $16 each
> 6 rose bushes at $13 each

How much will be spent on trees and shrubs for all the lots in the development? $2745

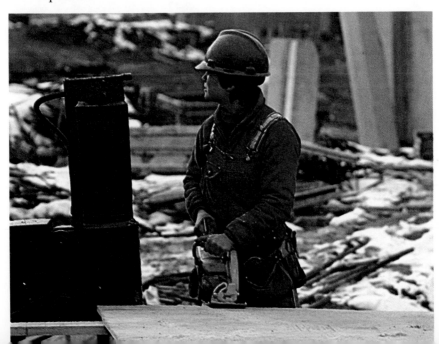

Enrichment

Fibonacci Numbers

The Fibonacci Sequence consists of a series of numbers in which each term is the sum of the preceding two terms.

$$1, 1, 2, 3, 5, 8, 13, \ldots$$

1, 1, 2, 3, 5, 8, 13, 21, 34, 55, 89, 144, 233, 377, 610, 987, 1597, 2584, 4181, 6765

This sequence can be noted in many natural phenomena. The centers of most sunflowers have 21 spirals in one direction and 34 spirals in the other. The stalks of many plants have new leaves growing in a pattern such that starting at the base of the stalk and counting upward, each new leaf growing directly above another leaf is in a position corresponding to a Fibonacci number. If the first leaf is 1 the next leaf directly above it will be 8 and the next 13, etc.

1. Write the first 20 terms of the Fibonacci Sequence.
2. Find the sum of the first five terms of the sequence. Compare this to the seventh term. Repeat this for the sum of the first six terms and the first seven terms. What do you discover? The sum is 1 less.
3. Use the results of Exercise 2 to write the sums of the first eight terms, ten terms, and fifteen terms without actually doing the addition. 54; 143; 1596
4. It will take two months for a newborn pair of rabbits to produce their first pair of rabbits. After that they produce one new pair each month. If you start with one pair of rabbits producing according to this pattern and each succeeding pair of rabbits produces according to the same pattern, how many pairs of rabbits will you have at the end of each of the next twelve months? 1 pair, 2 pairs, 3 pairs, 5 pairs, 8 pairs, 13 pairs, 21 pairs, 34 pairs, 55 pairs, 89 pairs, 144 pairs, 233 pairs

Chapter Review

Match the word phrase to the expression.

1. n decreased by 56   c   **a.** $n + 56$
2. the product of 56 and n f   **b.** $n \div 56$
3. the sum of n and 56   a   **c.** $n - 56$
4. a number n divided by 56   b   **d.** $56 - n$
5. 56 reduced by a number n d   **e.** $56 \div n$
                                                 f. $56n$

Choose the correct answer. Write a, b, or c.

6. $479 + 378 = n$ b   **a.** $n = 101$
                          b. $n = 857$
                          c. $n = 747$

7. $y = 3000 - 55$ c   **a.** $y = 3055$
                          b. $y = 2955$
                          c. $y = 2945$

8. $t = 680 \cdot 79$ a   **a.** $t = 53,720$
                          b. $t = 48,020$
                          c. $t = 43,720$

9. $14{,}874 \div 6 = x$ a   **a.** $x = 2479$
                          b. $x = 2110$
                          c. $x = 3479$

10. $4 \cdot 8 + 6 = y$ c   **a.** $y = 18$
                          b. $y = 56$
                          c. $y = 38$

11. $(33 \div 11) + (7 \cdot 6) = v$ a   **a.** $v = 45$
                                           b. $v = 136$
                                           c. $v = 3$

12. $3(7 + 6) - 4 = j$ c   **a.** $j = 23$
                          b. $j = 27$
                          c. $j = 35$

13. $(5 + 7)(10 - 2) = w$ b   **a.** $w = 73$
                                    b. $w = 96$
                                    c. $w = 61$

True or false? Write *T* or *F*.

14. $12n + 5n = 17n$ T   15. $3b + 4a + b = 4b + 4a$ T

16. $16 + 3a = 19a$ F   17. $39y - 12 - 6y = 33y - 12$ T

18. $100a + 100b = 100ab$ F   19. $46x - 10x + 3 = 39x$ F

20. $45x - 3 - 10x = 35x - 3$ T   21. $6n + 2n - 5n = 3$ F

22. $16 + 4a + 3a = 7a - 16$ F   23. $5x + 2y + 3x + y = 8x + 3y$ T

24. $x + 4y - x - 4y = 2x + 8y$ F   25. $n + 8m + 20n = 21n + 8m$ T

26. $8a + 6b - 2a = 6a + 6b$ T   27. $50n - 49n = n$ T

28. $65r - 8r + 17r - 2 = 72r$ F   29. $25t - 15t - 10t = 0$ T

Chapter Test

Let $a = 5$, $b = 10$, and $c = 25$. Evaluate the expression.

1. $a + b$ 15   **2.** ab 50   **3.** $c - a$ 20   **4.** $b \div a$ 2   **1-1**

5. $3a + c$ 40   **6.** $5b \div c$ 2   **7.** $2a + 2c$ 60   **8.** $10b - 4c$ 0

Solve the equation.

9. $n = 6872 + 439$ 7311   **10.** $6759 + 775 = y$ 7534   **11.** $d = 766 + 389$ 1155   **1-2**

12. $a = 600 + 251$ 851   **13.** $4007 + 398 = b$ 4405   **14.** $r = 773 + 86$ 859

15. $h = 761 - 7$ 754   **16.** $1256 - 87 = c$ 1169   **17.** $5306 - 93 = k$ 5213   **1-3**

18. $y = 5002 - 111$ 4891   **19.** $4533 - 2779 = q$ 1754   **20.** $9000 - 625 = v$ 8375

Solve.

21. In June, Gordon's Fishcake Company spent $6215 for a TV ad,   **1-4**
$488 for a newspaper ad, and $2715 for a direct-mail ad. What is
the difference between the most and least expensive types of advertising purchased in June? $5727

Solve the equation.

22. $(43)(16) = y$ 688   **23.** $r = 750 \cdot 27$ 20,250   **24.** $(7093)(86) = t$ 609,998   **1-5**

25. $3891 \cdot 54 = m$ 210,114   **26.** $a = (973)(355)$ 345,415   **27.** $466 \cdot 784 = n$ 365,344

28. $1585 \div 5 = x$ 317   **29.** $y = 6750 \div 27$ 250   **30.** $d = 3036 \div 138$ 22   **1-6**

31. $5676 \div 22 = d$ 258   **32.** $17{,}136 \div 48 = p$ 357   **33.** $f = 3397 \div 79$ 43

34. $r = 4862 \times 1$ 4862   **35.** $76{,}842 + 0 = n$ 76,842   **36.** $q = 0 + 88{,}615$ 88,615   **1-7**

37. $t = 3541 \cdot 1$ 3541   **38.** $m = 0 + 15{,}987$ 15,987   **39.** $(1)(3422) = k$ 3422

40. $b = 17 + (4 \cdot 8)$ 49   **41.** $9 \cdot 8 + 18 \div 6 = a$ 75   **1-8**

42. $f = (16 + 4)(4 - 2)$ 40   **43.** $(11 - 5) \div (2 \cdot 3) = n$ 1

Combine like terms.

44. $2a - a + b$ $a + b$ **45.** $3x + 2y - 2x - x$ $2y$

46. $m + 8m + 4t - 4t$ $9m$ **47.** $16x + 9y + 2x - x - y$ $17x + 8y$

32

Cumulative Review (Chapter 1)

Add, subtract, multiply, or divide.

1. $470 + 18 - 2$ 486   **2.** $356 - 24 - 6$ 326 **3.** $7305 - 38$ 7267 **4.** $4000 - 458$
   3542

5. $(279)(8)$ 2232 **6.** $(56)(18)$ 1008 **7.** $(56 \div 8) \cdot 5$ 35 **8.** $(11{,}028)(0)$ 0

9. $16 \cdot 5$ 80 **10.** $230 + 7 - 49$ 188 **11.** $(17 \cdot 8) - 3$ 133 **12.** $6 + (8 \cdot 6)$ 54

13. $45 - 5 \cdot 6$ 15 **14.** $16 + 5 \cdot 8$ 56 **15.** $36 \div 9 \cdot 4$ 1 **16.** $25 - 4 \cdot 6$ 1

Evaluate the expression.

17. $a + b$; $a = 2$, $b = 7$ 9 **18.** $4x - 1$; $x = 12$ 47 **19.** $x \div y$; $x = 80$, $y = 5$ 16

20. $5n - 2x$; $n = 6$, $x = 1$ 28 **21.** $7 + 3k$; $k = 12$ 43 **22.** $2p + 4t$; $p = 1$, $t = 2$ 10

23. $10m^2$; $m = 2$ 40 **24.** $5y^2$; $y = 9$ 405 **25.** $2 - 3x^2$; $x = 0$ 2

26. $a^2 - 6$; $a = 4$ 10 **27.** $4 - x^2$; $x = 1$ 3 **28.** $(2m)^2$; $m = 4$ 64

Simplify.

29. $4(x + 1)$ $4x + 4$ **30.** $a(6 - a)$ $6a - a^2$ **31.** $5x + 2x$ $7x$

32. $7a - a$ $6a$ **33.** $4y - 2y - y$ y **34.** $3(a - b)$ $3a - 3b$

35. $12p + 6 - 6p$ $6p + 6$ **36.** $9n - 4n - 1$ $5n - 1$ **37.** $a + 7b - a$ $7b$

38. $3w + 6 - 3w$ 6   **39.** $15c - c + 21$ $14c + 21$ **40.** $8j - 6 - 6j$ $2j - 6$

41. $16e + 2f - 16e - 2f$ 0   **42.** $12s + s - s$ $12s$ **43.** $8g + 8h - g + h$ $7g + 9h$

Write an expression for the phrase.

44. the product of some number n and 38 $(n)(38)$

45. x decreased by 16 $x - 16$

46. 14 greater than g $g + 14$

47. the sum of 54 and 16 added to w $54 + 16 + w$

48. c increased by n $c + n$

Solve.

49. A laboratory technician ordered 12 boxes of microscope slides.
 Let c = cost of each box.
 Then __?__ = the total cost. $12c$

50. Melba is taking a 7-day vacation.
 Let m = amount of spending money she has to spend.
 Then __?__ = average amount of money she can spend each day. $m \div 7$

2
Decimals

A picture is worth a thousand words. You can control the amount of light passing through the camera by adjusting the f-stop. Change it from 16 to 11 to increase the light, and from 5.6 to 8 to decrease the light.

2-1 Reading and Writing Decimals

Decimals represent a whole unit or part of a whole unit.

114.07
A

114.60
B

114.0 114.1 114.2 114.3 114.4 114.5 114.6 114.7 114.8 114.9 115.0

Point *A* shows the decimal one hundred fourteen and seven hundredths. Point *B* shows the decimals one hundred fourteen and six tenths, and one hundred fourteen and sixty hundredths. The decimals 114.6 and 114.60 are equal. **Equal decimals** name the same number.

Example 1   Read the decimal 13.0405.

Solution

millions	hundred-thousands	ten-thousands	thousands	hundreds	tens	ones	.	tenths	hundredths	thousandths	ten-thousandths	hundred-thousandths	millionths
					1	3	.	0	4	0	5		

Thirteen and four hundred five ten-thousandths

Example 2   Write the decimal sixty and four hundred thirteen thousandths.

Solution

millions	hundred-thousands	ten-thousands	thousands	hundreds	tens	ones	.	tenths	hundredths	thousandths	ten-thousandths	hundred-thousandths	millionths
					6	0	.	4	1	3			

Answer: 60.413

Your Turn
- Read the decimal 574.405. five hundred seventy-four and four hundred five-thousandths
- Write the decimal seven thousand five and two thousand two ten-thousandths. 7005.2002

Class Exercises

Complete.

1. 6.8 = __?__ and __?__ tenths $\overset{6;\ 8}{}$

2. 46.09 = __?__ and __?__ hundredths $\overset{46;\ 9}{}$

3. 9.031 = __?__ and __?__ thousandths $\overset{9;\ 31}{}$

4. 17.707 = __?__ and __?__ thousandths $\overset{17;\ 707}{}$

5. 0.88051 = __?__ hundred-thousandths $\overset{88051}{}$

6. 0.0004 = __?__ ten-thousandths $\overset{4}{}$

7. 5.500613 = __?__ and __?__ millionths $\overset{5;\ 500613}{}$

8. 0.234006 = __?__ millionths $\overset{234,006}{}$

Exercises

The number line below is divided into tenths and hundredths. Write the decimal for the given point.

24.0 G   D   C   L   Q   25.0

A 1. Point *C* 24.45   2. Point *Q* 24.88   3. Point *D* 24.22   4. Point *G* 24.08   5. Point *L* 24.61

The number line below is divided into hundredths and thousandths. Write two equal decimals for the given point.

86.70 M   B E   C   A 86.80

86.73; 86.730   86.79; 86.790   86.74; 86.740   86.77; 86.770   86.71; 86.710

6. Point *B*   7. Point *A*   8. Point *E*   9. Point *C*   10. Point *M*

Write *a*, *b*, or *c* to show how to read the decimal.

B 11. 0.12 c
   a. twelve thousandths
   b. twelve tenths
   c. twelve hundredths

12. 17.6 a
   a. seventeen and six tenths
   b. seventeen and six hundredths
   c. six and seventeen hundredths

13. 0.655 b
  a. six hundred fifty-five hundreds
  b. six hundred fifty-five thousandths
  c. six hundred five thousandths

14. 0.6505 b
  a. six hundred fifty-five ten-thousandths
  b. six thousand five hundred five ten-thousandths
  c. six thousand five hundred five thousandths

15. 4.00255 b
  a. two hundred fifty-five thousandths
  b. four and two hundred fifty-five hundred-thousandths
  c. four and two hundred fifty-five millionths

16. 10.005001 a
  a. ten and five thousand one millionths
  b. ten and five thousand one hundred-thousandths
  c. ten and five thousand one ten-thousandths

Write the decimal.

17. 7 tenths   0.7

18. 12 hundredths   0.12

19. 2401 ten-thousandths   0.2401

20. 98 millionths   0.000098

21. 17 and 6 thousandths   17.006

22. 500 and 5472 hundred-thousandths   500.05472

23. 4001 and 23 ten-thousandths   4001.0023

24. 80 and 7 millionths   80.000007

25. nine thousandths   0.009

26. twenty-two hundredths   0.22

27. four and six ten-thousandths   4.0006

28. thirty and two hundred twenty-five thousandths   30.225

29. six hundred forty and fifty thousand two hundred one millionths   640.050201

30. seven thousand thirteen and eight thousand eleven hundred-thousandths   7013.08011

Write a decimal for the given information.

C **31.** the part of a dollar represented by a dime   0.1

32. the part of a dollar represented by a nickel   0.05

33. the part of a decade represented by a year   0.1

34. the part of a century represented by a decade   0.1

35. the part of a centimeter represented by a millimeter   0.1

36. the part of a liter represented by a milliliter   0.001

37. the part of a meter represented by a centimeter   0.01

2-2 *Ordering Decimals*

The decimal coding system shown below is used to store merchandise at a store. Notice how the number of decimal places in the code increases as more information is given in the other charts.

RST Warehouse	3 Hair product	3.2 Shampoos	3.23 Natural
1 Stationery	3.1 Conditioners	3.21 Imperial	3.231 for normal hair
2 Cosmetics	3.2 Shampoos	3.22 Luster	3.232 for dry hair
3 Hair Products	3.3 Dyes/Tints	3.23 Natural	3.233 for oily hair
4 Soap Products	3.4 Perm Kits	3.24 Universal	3.234 for tinted hair
5 Miscellaneous	3.5 Combs/Brushes	3.25 Golden	3.235 for damaged hair

When an order needs to be filled, the code numbers from the order form are arranged in numerical order. To arrange decimals in numerical order, first recall how to compare decimals.

Example 1   Compare 5.46 and 5.41.

Solution   Start from the left and compare the digits in corresponding places.

5.46 __?__ 5.41

6 > 1   ⟵—— *The symbol* > *means*

so 5.46 > 5.41   *"is greater than."*

Example 2   Compare 27.4 and 27.456.

Solution   It may be helpful to write zeros after 27.4 so that both decimals have the same number of decimal places.

27.400 __?__ 27.456.

0 < 5   ⟵—— *The symbol* < *means*

so 27.4 < 27.456   *"is less than".*

30.72 > 30.62

Your Turn   • Compare 4.1 and 4.16. 4.1 < 4.16   • Compare 30.72 and 30.62.

Now use what you know about comparing decimals to arrange decimals in numerical order.

Example 3   Write the code numbers in
Form 6712 in order from
least to greatest.

Solution   3.246, 3.247, 3.31, 3.4

ORDER FORM 6712	
Code Number	Quantity
3.246	24
3.31	12
3.247	24
3.4	18

Class Exercises

Write > or < to compare the decimals.

1. 4.6 _?_ 5.2   <

2. 6.22 _?_ 6.32   <

3. 74.1 _?_ 74.4   <

4. 18.9 _?_ 19.4   <

5. 31.47 _?_ 31.48   <

6. 2.234 _?_ 2.214   >

7. 7.6 _?_ 7.63   <

8. 81.51 _?_ 81.5   >

9. 3.12 _?_ 31.2   <

10. 31.18 _?_ 31.187 <

11. 94.65 _?_ 946.5   <

12. 7.652 _?_ 7.65   >

13. 904.55 _?_ 904.5 >

14. 821.34 _?_ 821.3 >

15. 746.23 _?_ 74.623 >

Exercises

Write the decimals in order from least to greatest.

A

1. 3.7, 6.8, 5.2
3.7, 5.2, 6.8

2. 9.6, 9.4, 9.1
9.1, 9.4, 9.6

3. 3.2, 4.2, 3.3
3.2, 3.3, 4.2

4. 4.16, 3.16, 4.26
3.16, 4.16, 4.26

5. 52.3, 53.3, 52.2
52.2, 52.3, 53.3

6. 86.15, 96.15, 86.17
86.15, 86.17, 96.15

7. 87.78, 87.77, 87.87
87.77, 87.78, 87.87

8. 641.3, 641.4, 642.3
641.3, 641.4, 642.3

9. 9.103, 9.301, 9.013
9.013, 9.103, 9.301

10. 57.62, 37.72, 57.63, 57.61
37.72, 57.61, 57.62, 57.63

11. 413.32, 431.32, 413.23, 413.12
413.12, 413.23, 413.32, 431.32

12. 5.6642, 566.42, 56.642, 5664.2
5.6642, 56.642, 566.42, 5664.2

13. 2134.9, 21.349, 213.49, 2.1349
2.1349, 21.349, 213.49, 2134.9

Write the decimals in order from greatest to least.

B 14. 4.36, 4.3, 4.365
4.365, 4.36, 4.3

15. 0.008, 0.08, 0.8
0.8, 0.08, 0.008

16. 1.52, 1.522, 1.5
1.522, 1.52, 1.5

17. 39.954, 29.9, 29.95
39.954, 29.95, 29.9

18. 16.2, 16.23, 16.22
16.23, 16.22, 16.2

19. 71.45, 71.4, 71.455
71.455, 71.45, 71.4

20. 5.6432, 5.643, 5.64, 5.642
5.6432, 5.643, 5.642, 5.64

21. 7.2913, 7.291, 7.29, 7.28
7.2913, 7.291, 7.29, 7.28

22. 81.18, 81.187, 81.188, 81.178
81.188, 81.187, 81.18, 81.178

23. 190.9, 190.09, 190.099, 19.009
190.9, 190.099, 190.09, 19.009

24. 7.752, 7.7521, 7.75, 7.725
7.7521, 7.752, 7.75, 7.725

25. 61.008, 61.081, 610.8, 61.0813
610.8, 61.0813, 61.081, 61.008

Write < or > to compare the given numbers.

Example $b = 4.13;\ c = 4.1$ **Solution** $b > c$

C 26. $a = 2.7;\ b = 2.4$
$a \underline{\ ?\ } b \quad >$

27. $x = 30.4;\ y = 3.04$
$x \underline{\ ?\ } y \quad >$

28. $d = 5.16;\ c = 5.17$
$d \underline{\ ?\ } c \quad <$

29. $h = 304.1;\ q = 301.4$
$h \underline{\ ?\ } q \quad >$

30. $c = 0.09;\ t = 0.08$
$c \underline{\ ?\ } t \quad >$

31. $f = 61.16;\ z = 16.61$
$f \underline{\ ?\ } z \quad >$

32. $g = 7.13;\ s = 71.34$
$g \underline{\ ?\ } s \quad <$

33. $m = 8.64;\ w = 8.6$
$m \underline{\ ?\ } w \quad >$

34. $e = 32.7;\ y = 32.78$
$e \underline{\ ?\ } y \quad <$

35. $k = 50.05;\ r = 50.032$
$k \underline{\ ?\ } r \quad >$

36. $d = 16.62;\ y = 16.624$
$d \underline{\ ?\ } y \quad <$

37. $p = 7.5;\ b = 7.543$
$p \underline{\ ?\ } b \quad <$

Problems

Write an expression for the given sentence.

1. a is greater than 4.1. $a > 4.1$
3. s is equal to 5.21. $s = 5.21$
5. 7.45 is less than c. $7.45 < c$
7. h is greater than 7.04. $h > 7.04$
9. 7.6 is less than f. $7.6 < f$

2. p is less than 18.2. $p < 18.2$
4. 56.3 is greater than b. $56.3 > b$
6. 9.01 is equal to r. $9.01 = r$
8. w is equal to 32.6. $w = 32.6$
10. 9.211 is greater than q. $9.211 > q$

Challenge

You have six United States coins totaling $1.15 but no combination of the six coins totals $1.00. What are the six coins? 4 dimes, 1 quarter, 1 half dollar

2-3 The Rounding Process

Power and light companies sometimes add a fuel adjustment charge
to the monthly bills of their customers. This charge helps to cover any
increases in the cost of the fuel
needed to produce electricity.

One month a charge of $0.146 per
kilowatt hour was added to each
customer's bill. The number 0.146 is
shown on the number line below.

Example 1	Use the number line to round $0.146 to the nearest cent (hundredth of a dollar).
Solution	0.146 is closer to 0.15 than to 0.14, so $0.146 rounds to $0.15.

Example 2	Round 26.158 to the nearest whole number.
Solution	When the digit to the right of the place to which you are rounding is less than 5, always round down.

Given Decimal	Digit to the Right	Is it 5 or More?	Round the Number
26.158	1	no	down to 26

Example 3 Round 7.526 to the nearest hundredth.

Solution When the digit to the right of the place to which you are rounding is 5 or more, always round up.

Given Decimal	Digit to the Right	Is it 5 or More?	Round the Number
7.526	6	yes	up to 7.53

Your Turn • Round 7.03 to the nearest tenth. 7.0
• Round 18.7855 to the nearest thousandth. 18.786

Example 4 Round 46.96 to the nearest tenth.

Solution When the number in the place to which you are rounding is 9, and the digit to the right of that place is 5 or more, you'll need to round the number to its next greater place value.

Given Decimal	Digit to the Right	Is it 5 or More?	Round the Number
46.96	6	yes	up to 47.0

Your Turn • Round 0.596 to the nearest hundredth. 0.60

Class Exercises

Use the number line to round the given decimal to the nearest tenth.

9.5   9.51   9.52   9.53   9.54   9.55   9.56   9.57   9.58   9.59   9.6

1. 9.57 9.6   **2.** 9.54 9.5   **3.** 9.52 9.5   **4.** 9.55 9.6   **5.** 9.58 9.6

Complete the chart.

	Round to the Nearest	Given Decimal	Digit to the Right	Is it 5 or More?	Round the Number
6.	whole number	7.38625	? 3	? no	? 7
7.	tenth	7.38625	? 8	? yes	? 7.4
8.	hundredth	7.38625	? 6	? yes	? 7.39
9.	thousandth	7.38625	? 2	? no	? 7.386

Exercises

Measure the segment to the nearest centimeter.

Example **Solution** 3 cm

centimeters

A

1. _____ 5 cm

2. _____ 7 cm

3. _____ 10 cm

4. _____ 9 cm

5. _____ 12 cm

Round to the nearest whole number.

B

6. 0.6   1   **7.** 0.3   0   **8.** 1.5   2   **9.** 47.2   47   **10.** 45.5   46

11. 89.42 89   **12.** 538.81 539   **13.** 492.74 493   **14.** 389.554 390   **15.** 469.772   470

Round to the nearest tenth.

16. 0.45   0.5   **17.** 0.31   0.3   **18.** 4.76   4.8   **19.** 38.07   38.1   **20.** 42.03   42.0

21. 68.974 69.0   **22.** 72.213 72.2   **23.** 862.958 863.0   **24.** 497.0684   497.1   **25.** 766.3298   766.3

Round to the nearest hundredth.

26. 0.316   0.32   **27.** 0.567   0.57   **28.** 2.304   2.30   **29.** 31.209   31.21   **30.** 57.698   57.70

31. 38.4931   38.49   **32.** 757.6234   757.62   **33.** 840.3975   840.40   **34.** 624.8361   624.84   **35.** 590.0071   590.01

Round to the nearest thousandth.

36. 0.4567 ⟨0.457⟩   **37.** 0.1306 ⟨0.131⟩   **38.** 5.3496 ⟨5.350⟩   **39.** 18.5792 ⟨18.579⟩   **40.** 23.4575 ⟨23.458⟩

41. 86.0052 ⟨86.005⟩   **42.** 344.7214 ⟨344.721⟩   **43.** 877.0555 ⟨877.056⟩   **44.** 362.2397 ⟨362.240⟩   **45.** 440.3205 ⟨440.321⟩

Electrical energy is measured in kilowatt hours (kW · h). The chart at the right shows the amount of electrical energy used by some common electrical appliances in one year. Each amount has been rounded to the nearest whole number. What could the minimum and maximum amounts of electrical energy have been before they were rounded, if they had been measured to the nearest tenth?

		Electrical Appliance	Energy Used Per Year	
C	**46.**	toaster	38 kW · h	37.5; 38.4 kW · h
	47.	washer	100 kW · h	99.5; 100.4 kW · h
	48.	dryer	993 kW · h	992.5; 993.4 kW ·
	49.	stereo	109 kW · h	108.5; 109.4 kW ·
	50.	fan	43 kW · h	42.5; 43.4 kW · h
	51.	color TV	502 kW · h	501.5; 502.4 kW ·

Example   radio: 86 kW · h

Solution   minimum: 85.5 kW · h
              maximum: 86.4 kW · h

Self Test 1

Write the decimal.

1. 28 and 7 hundredths ⟨28.07⟩   **2.** 7013 and 62 ten-thousandths ⟨7013.0062⟩   **2-1**

3. six hundred and four thousandths ⟨600.004⟩   **4.** five and fourteen millionths ⟨5.000014⟩

Write the decimals in order from least to greatest.

5. 7.66, 8.66, 7.56, 7.67 ⟨7.56, 7.66, 7.67, 8.66⟩   **6.** 92.29, 82.29, 92.92, 92.28 ⟨82.29, 92.28, 92.29, 92.92⟩   **2-2**

7. 0.75, 0.7, 0.756, 0.76 ⟨0.7, 0.75, 0.756, 0.76⟩   **8.** 8.341, 8.3, 8.34, 8.44 ⟨8.3, 8.34, 8.341, 8.44⟩

Round to the nearest whole number.

9. 0.7 ⟨1⟩   **10.** 4.28 ⟨4⟩   **11.** 35.55 ⟨36⟩   **12.** 129.86 ⟨130⟩   **2-3**

Round to the nearest tenth.

13. 0.51 ⟨0.5⟩   **14.** 8.39 ⟨8.4⟩   **15.** 40.97 ⟨41.0⟩   **16.** 112.65 ⟨112.7⟩

2-4 Adding Decimals

The distance traveled each day on a biking trip was recorded as follows: Thursday 28.8 km, Friday 17.0 km, and Saturday 24.4 km.

You can find the total distance of the trip by adding the daily distances. Follow the same procedure for adding decimals as for adding whole numbers.

Let r = the total distance of the trip.
$$r = 28.8 + 17.0 + 24.4 \longleftarrow$$
$$r = 70.2$$
The total distance of the trip is 70.2 km.

Remember to line up the decimal points.

$$\begin{array}{r} 28.8 \\ 17.0 \\ +24.4 \\ \hline 70.2 \end{array}$$

To be sure that an answer is reasonable, estimate the sum.

Example 1   Estimate the total distance of the trip by rounding each addend to its greatest place value.

Solution
$$\begin{array}{rcr} 28.8 & \longrightarrow & 30 \\ 17.0 & \longrightarrow & 20 \\ +24.4 & \longrightarrow & +20 \\ \hline & & 70 \end{array}$$
The estimated distance of the trip is 70 km.
Since the estimated sum is close to the actual sum, 70.2 km is a reasonable answer.

Your Turn   • Estimate the sum of 13.17 and 25.56 by rounding each addend to the greatest place value. 40

Example 2 Solve the equation $g = 5.6 + 7.529$.

Solution $g = 5.6 + 7.529$ ←

5.600
+7.529
13.129

$g = 13.129$

Sometimes it's helpful to add zeros.

Your Turn • Solve the equation $y = 7.2 + 3.16 + 15.548$. 25.908

Class Exercises

Add.

1. 3.81
+2.7
6.51

2. 6
+47.2
53.2

3. 5.13
+0.652
5.782

4. 26.6
5
+117.8
149.4

5. 8.24
2.075
+0.6
10.915

Exercises

Add.

A **1.** $37.8 + 9.26$ 47.06

2. $41.4 + 13.2$ 54.6

3. $5.76 + 78.29$ 84.05

4. $4.658 + 24.1$ 28.758

5. $53.44 + 4$ 57.44

6. $378.62 + 2.1985$ 380.8185

7. $47 + 654.72$ 701.72

8. $85.111 + 26.81$ 111.921

9. $532.11 + 275.6$ 807.71

Round each addend to its greatest place value to estimate the sum.

10. $5.6 + 9.2$ 15

11. $13.42 + 27.8$ 40

12. $0.94 + 71.7$ 71

13. $652.1 + 71.5$ 770

14. $3.64 + 21.05$ 24

15. $61.5 + 20.4$ 80

16. $8.719 + 21.36$ 29

17. $86.2 + 9.4$ 99

18. $3.165 + 40.45$ 43

Evaluate the expression using the given value for the variable.

B **19.** $3.29 + n$; $n = 4.6$ 7.89

20. $7.31 + x$; $x = 26.5$ 33.81

21. $0.743 + y$; $y = 31.6$ 32.343

22. $0.81 + w$; $w = 31.7$ 32.51

23. $z + 36.257$; $z = 81$ *117.257*

24. $b + 2134$; $b = 7.65$ *2141.65*

25. $d + 31.66$; $d = 4.72$ *36.38*

26. $h + 3.007$; $h = 81.51$ *84.517*

27. $25.316 + m$; $m = 5.962$ *31.278*

28. $w + 18.934$; $w = 21.106$ *40.04*

29. $14 + t$; $t = 3.742$ *17.742*

30. $741.6 + r$; $r = 8.12$ *749.72*

Combine like terms.

C **31.** $8.4b + 3.6b$ *12b*

32. $0.7d + 4.6d$ *5.3d*

33. $32.4a + 1.44a$ *33.84a*

34. $1.75x + 12.1x$ *13.85x*

35. $21.14g + 4.657g$ *25.797g*

36. $0.321s + 52.1s$ *52.421s*

37. $31.24m + 5.0006m$ *36.2406m*

38. $17.012c + 3.04c$ *20.052c*

39. $162.34t + 31.17t$ *193.51t*

40. $4.7b + 0.81a + 31.4b$ *0.81a + 36.1b*

41. $0.91g + 21.4g + 3.77h$ *22.31g + 3.77h*

42. $8.8p + 3.07r + 24.1r$ *8.8p + 27.17r*

43. $8.3s + 57t + 16.61s$ *24.91s + 57t*

44. $4.8w + 3.1w + 0.07z$ *7.9w + 0.07z*

45. $0.24j + 3.9k + 7.7j$ *7.94j + 3.9k*

Problems

Write an expression for the given phrase.

1. 3.7 added to x *x + 3.7*

2. y plus 71.04   *y + 71.04*

3. b increased by 0.92   *b + 0.92*

4. 19.6 greater than p *p + 19.6*

5. a more than 5.61   *5.61 + a*

6. t added to 1.964   *1.964 + t*

Write an expression to complete.

7. The distance to the school is 2.3 km further than the distance to the park.

Let b = the distance to the park.

Then, __?__ = the distance to the school. *b + 2.3*

8. Science class enrollment is 47 more at Jefferson High School than at Washington High School.

Let w = science class enrollment at Washington High School.

Then, __?__ = science class enrollment at Jefferson High School. *w + 47*

Write an equation for the given sentence. Solve the equation.

9. The sum of 4.85 and 31.7 is equal to b.   *4.85 + 31.7 = b; 36.55*

10. 8.4 increased by 0.45 is equal to a.   *8.4 + 0.45 = a; 8.85*

11. 2.13 added to 71.6 is equal to g.   *71.6 + 2.13 = g; 73.73*

12. y is equal to the sum of 21.1 and 34.62.   *y = 21.1 + 34.62; 55.72*

13. n is equal to 12.62 more than 3.074.   *n = 3.074 + 12.62; 15.694*

14. 76.81 greater than 2.7 is equal to w.   *2.7 + 76.81 = w; 79.51*

2-5 Subtracting Decimals

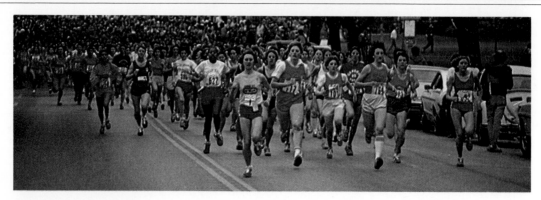

The qualifying time for entrants in a six-mile race is 51.6 min. One runner's time is 55.5 min.

Example 1 How much does the runner's time need to improve in order to qualify for the race?

Solution Let n = how much the runner's time needs to improve.

$n = 55.5 - 51.6$ ◀──────

$n = 3.9$

The runner's time needs to improve 3.9 min.

Remember to keep the decimal points in line.

$$\begin{array}{r} 55.5 \\ -51.6 \\ \hline 3.9 \end{array}$$

Sometimes all you need is an estimated answer.

Example 2 Estimate about how much the runner's time needs to improve in order to qualify for the race.

Solution

$$\begin{array}{r} 55.6 \longrightarrow 56 \\ -51.6 \longrightarrow -52 \\ \hline 4 \end{array}$$ ◀── *Round each number.*

The runner's time needs to improve about 4 min.

Your Turn • Estimate the difference between 44.6 and 7.2. 38

Example 3   Solve the equation $t = 17.1 - 5.62$.

Solution $t = 17.1 - 5.52$ ←

17.10	*If you wish, add zeros to help*
− 5.62	*keep the decimal points*
11.48	*aligned.*

$t = 11.48$

Your Turn   Solve the equation.
• $m = 12.6 - 4.71$ 7.89   • $d = 25 - 9.34$ 15.66

Class Exercises

Subtract.

1. 0.78	**2.** 0.758	**3.** 6.73	**4.** 6.306	**5.** 6.306
−0.32	−0.317	−0.26	−4.728	−0.72
0.46	0.441	6.47	1.578	5.586
6. 47.28	**7.** 0.7	**8.** 37.6	**9.** 9	**10.** 58
− 1.5	−0.36	− 7.746	−6.3	− 13.45
45.78	0.34	29.854	2.7	44.55

Exercises

Subtract.

A **1.** $0.963 - 0.721$ 0.242   **2.** $42.376 - 11.153$ 31.223   **3.** $14.76 - 10.59$ 4.17

4. $196.381 - 78.265$ 118.116   **5.** $321.15 - 76.28$ 244.87   **6.** $0.4765 - 0.24$ 0.2365

7. $78.1 - 59.35$ 18.75   **8.** $176 - 11.548$ 164.452   **9.** $476 - 0.2486$ 475.7514

Round each number to the nearest whole number to estimate the difference.

10. $8.1 - 3.97$ 4   **11.** $14.36 - 11.5$ 2   **12.** $38.514 - 19.01$ 20

13. $586.5 - 49.7$ 537   **14.** $32.058 - 19.67$ 12   **15.** $819.001 - 572.6$ 246

16. $31.64 - 2.247$ 30   **17.** $7.0892 - 0.99$ 6   **18.** $567.55 - 76.51$ 491

49

Solve the equation.

B 19. $4.97 - 3.06 = g$ 1.91

20. $567.8 - 324.5 = v$ 243.3

21. $0.963 - 0.302 = z$ 0.661

22. $1007.58 - 896.7 = d$ 110.88

23. $119.76 - 89.84 = p$ 29.92

24. $103.016 - 96.3 = h$ 6.716

25. $d = 0.83 - 0.543$ 0.287

26. $m = 96.13 - 3.257$ 92.873

27. $h = 7.138 - 2.4$ 4.738

28. $q = 42 - 36.245$ 5.755

29. $f = 781 - 560.31$ 220.69

30. $a = 13 - 9.1785$ 3.8215

Combine like terms.

31. $8.4a - 6.2a$ 2.2a

32. $13.7d - 9.4d$ 4.3d

33. $8.65x - 0.97x$ 7.68x

34. $16.43s - 8.4s$ 8.03s

35. $71.44b - 19.7b$ 51.74b

36. $364.2p - 1.0734p$ 363.1266p

37. $9v - 5.4v$ 3.6v

38. $48t - 17.93t$ 30.07t

39. $245z - 76.892z$ 168.108z

Evaluate the expression using the given value for the variable.

40. $a - 4.3;\ a = 7.02$ 2.72

41. $18.83 - d;\ d = 4.9$ 13.93

42. $47.4 - d;\ d = 41.82$ 5.58

43. $z - 21.3;\ z = 45.23$ 23.93

44. $g - 222.2;\ g = 232.41$ 10.21

45. $81.05 - k;\ k = 7.9$ 73.15

46. $21.3 - w;\ w = 3.91$ 17.39

47. $y - 77.7;\ y = 904.231$ 826.531

Add or subtract to write the missing digits.

C 48.
$$\begin{array}{r} 2.?317 \\ +8.6?2 \\ \hline 1?.28?7 \end{array}$$
6
5
1; 3

49.
$$\begin{array}{r} ?88.5?6 \\ -\ 68.?79 \\ \hline 32?.51? \end{array}$$
3; 9
0
0; 7

50.
$$\begin{array}{r} 2?1.3?02 \\ -17?.893? \\ \hline 114.?671 \end{array}$$
9; 6
6; 1
4

51.
$$\begin{array}{r} ?7.?03? \\ -\ 8.2?62 \\ \hline ?.75?4 \end{array}$$
1; 0; 6
4
8; 7

Problems

Write an addition or subtraction expression for the given phrase.

1. 8.3 minus t 8.3 − t

2. 4.08 subtracted from x x − 4.08

3. x decreased by 18.4   x − 18.4

4. 27.91 less than y y − 27.91

5. b increased by 7.41   b + 7.41

6. c more than 97.62   97.62 + c

Write an addition or subtraction equation for the given sentence. Solve the equation.

7. The difference between 21.073 and 4.68 is equal to r.   21.073 − 4.68 = r; 16.393

8. 67.9 decreased by 13.74 is equal to d.   67.9 − 13.74 = d; 54.16

9. The sum of 40.61 and 321.7 is equal to a.   40.61 + 321.7 = a; 362.31

10. 7.71 subtracted from 8.1 is equal to r.   8.1 − 7.71 = r; 0.39

2-6 *Problem Solving*

The answers to some problems must fall within a given set of limits. Quite often there will be key words such as *the greatest, the least, within,* and *at most,* to help determine if your answer is reasonable.

Example 1 A product planner spends from 2.75 to 4.9 hours per day making telephone calls. The planner estimates that about 23 h are spent on telephone calls during a 5-day week. Is that a reasonable estimate?

Solution Use the limits for the least and the greatest number of hours.

$$(2.75)(5) = 13.75 \qquad (4.9)(5) = 24.5$$
$$13.75 < 23 < 24.5 \longleftarrow \textit{The estimate falls within the limits.}$$

23 h is a reasonable estimate.

Example 2 At a certain bakery, a whole quiche sells for $7.95. A quiche cut into 8 slices is priced at $1.35 per slice. What is the greatest amount of money the bakery can get from selling 36 quiches?

Solution

$$(1.35)(8) = \$10.80 \longleftarrow \textit{price of one quiche when sold in slices}$$

$$\$10.80 > \$7.95$$
$$(\$10.80)(36) = \$388.80$$

Your Turn • A clerk in a credit department spends from 3.5 to 5.25 hours per day recording payments. The clerk estimates that about 26.5 h are spent recording payments during a 6-day week. Is the estimate reasonable? yes
• Suppose the bakery in Example 2 cuts each quiche into 6 slices and sells each slice for $1.40. What is the greatest amount of money it can get from selling 25 quiches? $210

51

Class Exercises

Appointment Schedule	
Morning	Afternoon
9:00 A.M. to 10:00 A.M.	3:00 P.M. to 4:00 P.M.

Listed below are the times when calls were made for appointments. Were the calls made according to the appointment schedule?

1. 9:10 A.M. yes   **2.** 9:15 A.M. yes   **3.** 8:45 A.M. no   **4.** 3:10 P.M. yes

5. 2:50 P.M. no   **6.** 11:00 A.M. no   **7.** 3:20 P.M. yes   **8.** 3:49 P.M. yes

Exercises

Use the table at the right to solve Exercises 1–5.

0.60	0.9	0.85	0.3
0.72	0.38	0.1	0.18
0.45	0.16	0.28	0.91
0.53	0.67	0.41	0.26

A

1. Find the greatest sum using three numbers. 2.66

2. Find the least sum using three numbers. 0.44

3. Which two numbers will produce the greatest product? 0.91, 0.9

4. Which two numbers will produce the least product? 0.1, 0.16

5. Two numbers are chosen so that the second number subtracted from the first produces a difference of 0.81. What are the two numbers? 0.91, 0.1

B

6. Alan has a roll of crepe paper 24 ft long. He is cutting the paper in strips measuring 9 in., 1.5 ft, or 2.4 ft each. What is the greatest and the least number of strips that Alan can cut from the roll? 32—9 in. strips; 10—2.4 ft strips

7. Three sets of tennis are scheduled for the championship play-off. It is estimated that each set will take 35 to 50 minutes. If the play-off begins at 2:30 P.M., what is the earliest and latest it can be expected to be completed? 4:15 P.M.; 5:00 P.M.

8. The label on an extension-type curtain rod states that the rod can be extended from 22 in. to 48 in. Will the rod be long enough for a window that measures 2 ft 6 in. across? Will it be too long? yes; no

2-7 *Multiplying Decimals*

A part-time job at a deli pays $4.85 per hour. How much would you earn in 4 hours?

Let d = the total amount
$d = 4 \times \$4.85$ ◄────────────
$d = \$19.40$

$\$ 4.85$ ◄──	*2 decimal places*
$\times 4$ ◄──	*+0 decimal places*
$\$19.40$ ◄──	*2 decimal places*

You would earn $19.40 in 4 hours.

Sometimes it may be necessary to write zeros in the product so you have the correct number of decimal places.

Example 1   Solve the equation $s = 0.03 \times 0.21$.

Solution $s = 0.03 \times 0.21$ ◄──────

0.21 ◄──	*2 decimal places*
$\times 0.03$ ◄──	*+2 decimal places*
0.0063 ◄──	*4 decimal places*

$s = 0.0063$

Your Turn   Solve the equation.
  • $y = 0.02 \times 0.42$ 0.0084 $x = 0.6 \times 0.031$ 0.0186

Example 2   Solve the equations $h = 10 \times 0.764$ and $p = 100 \times 4.3$.

Solution   Mentally move the decimal point one place to the right for each power of 10.

$h = 10 \times 0.764$ $p = 100 \times 4.3$
$h = 7.64$ $p = 430$

Your Turn   Solve the equation.
  • $100 \times 48.921 = a$ 4892.1   • $1000 \times 3.7006 = s$ 3700.6

53

Sometimes you may use a calculator to multiply decimals. Even with a calculator, mistakes can occur since you might press a wrong button.

Example 3 A calculator showed the product of 𝟕𝟓.𝟔 and 𝟑.𝟎𝟗 to be 𝟕𝟖.𝟔𝟗. To check that answer estimate the product.

Solution Round each factor.

$$75.6 \longrightarrow 80$$
$$\underline{\times 3.09} \longrightarrow \underline{\times 3}$$
$$240$$

Since 240 is nowhere near 78.69, we know we made a mistake. We pressed the ➕ button instead of the ✕ button. The correct product is 𝟐𝟑𝟑.𝟔𝟎𝟒.

Your Turn • Estimate the product of 26.731 and 481.2 by rounding each factor to the greatest place value. 15,000

Class Exercises

Multiply.

1. 0.3	**2.** 2.1	**3.** 0.7	**4.** 2.3	**5.** 4.5
$\underline{\times 6}$	$\underline{\times 3}$	$\underline{\times 0.5}$	$\underline{\times 0.4}$	$\underline{\times 0.2}$
1.8	6.3	0.35	0.92	0.9
6. 6.5	**7.** 1.47	**8.** 18.4	**9.** 0.4	**10.** 0.1
$\underline{\times 4.4}$	$\underline{\times 2.3}$	$\underline{\times 3.7}$	$\underline{\times 0.02}$	$\underline{\times 0.06}$
28.6	3.381	68.08	0.008	0.006

Multiply the given number by 10, 100, 1000, and 10,000.

	×	10	100	1000	10,000	
11.	7.8234	?	?	?	?	78.234; 782.34; 7823.4; 78,234
12.	47.236	?	?	?	?	472.36; 4723.6; 47,236; 472,360
13.	625.0035	?	?	?	?	6250.035; 62,500.35; 625,003.5; 6,250,035

Exercises

Multiply.

A 1. 4×5.2 20.8

2. 13×17.6 228.8

3. 7.4×11.4 84.36

4. 3.2×4.1 13.12

5. 7.6×0.9 6.84

6. 8.42×3.2 26.944

7. 0.07×0.1 0.007

8. 8.32×4.21 35.0272

9. 4.01×0.09 0.3609

Round each factor to its greatest place value to estimate the product.

10. 47×36.2 2000

11. 52×2.79 150

12. 345×41.4 12,000

13. 7.83×4.4 32

14. 3.19×21.6 60

15. 58.76×3.68 240

16. 8.99×876.1 8100

17. 76.5×4.321 320

18. 852.9×45.3 45,000

Solve the equation.

B 19. $7 \times 6.13 = x$ 42.91

20. $24 \times 0.15 = a$ 3.6

21. $27.9 \times 0.8 = c$ 22.32

22. $3.15 \times 2.6 = b$ 8.19

23. $621.4 \times 3.7 = m$ 2299.18

24. $0.003 \times 0.2 = g$ 0.0006

25. $z = 8 \times 73.9$ 591.2

26. $n = 41 \times 0.66$ 27.06

27. $p = 52.6 \times 0.7$ 36.82

28. $r = 0.473 \times 6.8$ 3.2164

29. $f = 0.06 \times 0.1$ 0.006

30. $t = 0.007 \times 0.4$ 0.0028

Find the value of the expression if $a = 10$.

31. $0.4a$ 4

32. $2.7a$ 27

33. $3.68a$ 36.8

34. $41.5a$ 415

35. $74.63a$ 746.3

36. $81.632a$ 816.32

Find the value of the expression if $y = 100$.

37. $0.63y$ 63

38. $7.85y$ 785

39. $9.634y$ 963.4

40. $24.31y$ 2431

41. $6.4y$ 640

42. $8.3y$ 830

Find the value of the expression if $z = 1000$.

43. $0.571z$ 571

44. $7.634z$ 7634

45. $9.8124z$ 9812.4

46. $27.6312z$ 27,631.2

47. $29.34z$ 29,340

48. $171.5z$ 171,500

Solve the equation.

C 49. $a = 2.1 + (0.4 \times 0.02)$ 2.108

50. $4.21 \times 3.2 - 6.41 = c$ 7.062

51. $z = 84.7 - (3.4 + 2.11)$ 79.19

52. $(8.7 \times 100) + 6.62 = g$ 876.62

53. $1.03 + 2.1 \times 10 = r$ 22.03

54. $s = 8.84 - 2.1 \times 0.03$ 8.777

Problems

Write an addition, subtraction, or multiplication expression for the given phrase.

$(d)(4.82)$

1. 3.7 times *b* 3.7*b*   **2.** 80.64 multiplied by *w* (80.64)*w* **3.** *d* multiplied by 4.82

4. *s* minus 4.6 *s* − 4.6   **5.** *m* added to 3.712 3.712 + *m*   **6.** *a* multiplied by 0.08

a(0.08)

Write an addition, subtraction, or multiplication expression to complete.

7. The length of the field is two times the width of the field. Let *h* = the width of the field. Then, __?__ = the length of the field. 2*h*

8. Rob's height is 2.4 cm less than Joe's height. Let *r* = Joe's height. Then, __?__ = Rob's height. *r* − 2.4

Add, subtract, or multiply to solve.

What is the cost of the given amount of Swiss cheese?

9. 0.89 lb $3.02 **10.** 0.45 lb $1.53 **11.** 1.12 lb $3.80

How much does the given amount of cole slaw cost?

12. 0.38 lb $.38 **13.** 0.66 lb $.65 **14.** 1.09 lb $1.08

What is the cost of the given amount of sliced roast beef?

15. 0.54 lb $2.69 **16.** 1.78 lb $8.86 **17.** 2.42 lb $12.05

Today's Special

Swiss cheese $3.39/lb

Cole slaw $.99/lb

Roast beef $4.98/lb

Using the Computer

This program will round a decimal to the nearest tenth.

```
 5  REM: ROUNDING DECIMALS
10  PRINT "WHAT IS YOUR DECIMAL";
20  INPUT D
30  PRINT D;" ROUNDED TO TENTHS IS";
40  PRINT INT(D*10+.5)/10
50  END
```

What is your decimal? 2.34
2.34 rounded to tenths is 2.3

This line prints a ?

What is your decimal? 2.36
2.36 rounded to tenths is 2.4

RUN this program for D = 2.34 and D = 2.36. Now try some other examples of your own.

2-8 *Dividing Decimals*

We follow the same procedure for dividing a decimal by a whole number as for dividing a whole number by a whole number.

Example 1   Solve the equation $y = 49.5 \div 9$.

Solution $y = 49.5 \div 9$ ←

$$y = 5.5$$

$$\begin{array}{r} 5.5 \\ 9\overline{)\ 49.5} \\ -45 \\ \hline 4\,5 \\ -4\,5 \\ \hline \end{array}$$

Notice that the decimal point in the quotient is placed to align with the decimal point in the dividend.

Example 2   Solve the equation $d = \dfrac{0.0048}{0.15}$.

Solution   Simplify the equation by multiplying the divisor and dividend by the power of 10 that makes the divisor a whole number.

$$\frac{0.0048 \times 100}{0.15 \times 100} = \frac{0.48}{15}$$

$d = \dfrac{0.48}{15}$ ←

$d = 0.032$

$$\begin{array}{r} 0.032 \\ 15\overline{)\ 0.480} \\ -45 \\ \hline 30 \\ -30 \\ \hline \end{array}$$

Write an extra zero after the 8 in the dividend so that you can complete the division.

Your Turn   • Solve the equation $t = \dfrac{3.71}{0.5}$.   7.42

57

To make sure that you put the decimal point in the correct place in a quotient, you can estimate the quotient.

Example 3   Estimate the quotient: $18.9 \div 35$.

Solution   Round the dividend and divisor to the nearest numbers that can be divided evenly.

$$35\overline{)18.9} \longrightarrow 40\overline{)20.0}^{\,0.5}$$

The estimated quotient is 0.5.

Your Turn   • Estimate the quotient of 3.71 divided by 0.5. 8

We can divide a decimal by a power of 10 mentally.

Example 4   Solve the equation $f = 4.1 \div 10$.

Solution   Move the decimal point one place to the left for each power of 10.

$$f = 4.1 \div 10$$
$$f = 0.41$$

Your Turn   • Solve the equation $d = 23.78 \div 100$. 0.2378

Class Exercises

Divide.

1. $8\overline{)4.24}$ 0.53

2. $6\overline{)0.45}$ 0.075

3. $51\overline{)9.18}$ 0.18

4. $23\overline{)89.7}^{\,3.9}$ 89.5

5. $2.9\overline{)185.6}$ 64

6. $0.38\overline{)24.32}$ 64

7. $0.4\overline{)632.16}$ 1580.4

8. $0.9\overline{)80.55}$

Divide the given number by 10, 100, 1000, or 10,000.

÷	10	100	1000	10,000
9. 13,276.48	?	?	?	?
10. 1.764	?	?	?	?

1327.648; 132.7648; 13.27648; 1.327648

0.1764; 0.01764; 0.001764; 0.0001764

Exercises

Divide.

A **1.** $22.5 \div 5$ 4.5   **2.** $5.32 \div 4$ 1.33   **3.** $14.4 \div 72$ 0.2   **4.** $1.35 \div 27$ 0.05

5. $72.8 \div 0.4$ 182   **6.** $46.72 \div 0.32$ 146   **7.** $8.16 \div 12$ 0.68   **8.** $19.3816 \div 3.46$ 5.6

9. $0.02 \div 0.5$ 0.04   **10.** $19.5 \div 0.6$ 32.5   **11.** $4.03 \div 0.325$ 12.4   **12.** $2.26 \div 0.452$ 5

Estimate the quotient.

B **13.** $23.8 \div 6.1$ 4   **14.** $30.2 \div 4.5$ 6   **15.** $41.6 \div .83$ 42   **16.** $64.29 \div 7.89$ 8

17. $177.6 \div 6.6$ 30   **18.** $235 \div 3.8$ 60   **19.** $419.1 \div 6.77$ 60   **20.** $387.2 \div 7.71$ 50

21. $36.2 \div 22.1$ 2   **22.** $77.1 \div 36.62$ 2   **23.** $119.8 \div 60.04$ 2   **24.** $897.65 \div 258.6$ 3

Find the value of the expression if $x = 100$.

25. $4523.6 \div x$ 45.236   **26.** $196.41 \div x$ 1.9641   **27.** $62.3 \div x$ 0.623   **28.** $0.16 \div x$ 0.0016

29. $5.5 \div x$ 0.055   **30.** $0.01 \div x$ 0.0001   **31.** $6.486 \div x$ 0.06486   **32.** $41.13 \div x$ 0.4113

Find the value of the expression if $y = 1000$.

33. $5886.1 \div y$ 5.8861   **34.** $7330.4 \div y$ 7.3304   **35.** $821.6 \div y$ 0.8216   **36.** $75.58 \div y$ 0.07558

37. $4.312 \div y$ 0.004312   **38.** $8.8 \div y$ 0.0088   **39.** $0.921 \div y$ 0.000921   **40.** $0.65 \div y$ 0.00065

Evaluate the expression using the given value for the variable.

41. $\dfrac{7.654}{s}$; $s = 5$ 1.5308   **42.** $\dfrac{41.16}{c}$; $c = 7$ 5.88   **43.** $\dfrac{46.72}{a}$; $a = 32$ 1.46

44. $\dfrac{4.24}{m}$; $m = 0.8$ 5.3   **45.** $\dfrac{1.962}{p}$; $p = 0.9$ 2.18   **46.** $\dfrac{0.08}{t}$; $t = 0.016$ 5

47. $\dfrac{62.3}{r}$; $r = 17.8$ 3.5   **48.** $\dfrac{4.7}{q}$; $q = 2.5$ 1.88   **49.** $\dfrac{142.48}{z}$; $z = 3.562$ 40

To find the miles per gallon (MPG) rating of an automobile, divide the distance traveled by the amount of gasoline used.

Example Find the MPG rating of an automobile which used 19.1 gal of gasoline when traveling 496.6 mi.

Solution $496.6 \div 19.1 = 26$
The MPG rating is 26.

Find the MPG rating of each car.

	Car	Distance Traveled	Gasoline Used	Miles per Gallon
C 50.	A	362.7 mi	15.5 gal	? 23.4
51.	B	462.5 mi	18.5 gal	? 25
52.	C	452.4 mi	17.4 gal	? 26
53.	D	537.6 mi	16.8 gal	? 32
54.	E	452.2 mi	13.3 gal	? 34
55.	F	519.1 mi	17.9 gal	? 29

Problems

Write an expression for the given phrase.

1. 7.3 times a $7.3a$
2. 84.2 divided by z $84.2 \div z$
3. 81.1 multiplied by b $(81.1)(b)$
4. h divided by 3.1 $h \div 3.1$
5. s multiplied by 3.8 $s(3.8)$
6. f times 3.7 $(f)(3.7)$
7. 47.2 decreased by d $47.2 - d$
8. r divided by 0.21 $r \div 0.21$
9. 5.18 divided by b $5.18 \div b$

Write an equation for the given sentence. Solve the equation.

10. The quotient of 157.6 divided by 2 is a. $157.6 \div 2 = a;\ 78.8$
11. The product of 2.13 and 1.5 is z. $(2.13)(1.5) = z;\ 3.195$
12. 4.116 divided by 2.1 is equal to s. $4.116 \div 2.1 = s;\ 1.96$
13. 80.08 decreased by 14.7 is equal to v. $80.08 - 14.7 = v;\ 65.38$
14. a is equal to the quotient of 82.0 divided by 4.1. $a = 82.0 \div 4.1;\ 20$

2-9 *Metric System*

The metric system of measurement has three basic units of measure. Length is measured in **meters** (m), mass in **grams** (g), and capacity in **liters** (L). The same prefixes are used for units of length, mass, and capacity. Each prefix represents a power of 10. To change a metric unit to a smaller metric unit, multiply by a power of 10. To change a metric unit to a larger metric unit, divide by a power of 10.

Example Change 0.48 m to centimeters and 7642 mg to grams.

Solution 0.48 m $\times$ 100 = 48 cm
7642 mg $\div$ 1000 = 7.642 g

larger	Metric Units of Length				smaller	
kilometer	hectometer	dekameter	meter	decimeter	centimeter	millimeter
(km)	(hm)	(dam)	(m)	(dm)	(cm)	(mm)

$\times 10 \qquad \times 10$

0.48 m $\times$ 100 = 48 cm

larger	Metric Units of Mass				smaller	
kilogram	hectogram	dekagram	gram	decigram	centigram	milligram
(kg)	(hg)	(dag)	(g)	(dg)	(cg)	(mg)

$\div 10 \qquad \div 10 \qquad \div 10$

7642 mg $\div$ 1000 = 7.642 g

Your Turn • Change 7 L to milliliters.   7000 mL
• Change 955 mL to hectoliters.   0.0095 hL

larger	Metric Units of Capacity				smaller	
kiloliter	hectoliter	dekaliter	liter	deciliter	centiliter	milliliter
(kL)	(hL)	(daL)	(L)	(dL)	(cL)	(mL)

Class Exercises

Would you multiply or divide to change metric units with the given prefixes? Write × or ÷.

1. centi to deka ÷   **2.** hecto to deci ×   **3.** centi to milli ×   **4.** deci to kilo ÷

Exercises

Complete.

A 1. 1 km = _?_ m   1000   **2.** 1 mm = _?_ cm   0.1   **3.** 1 m = _?_ dm   10

4. 1 g = _?_ mg   1000   **5.** 1 dag = _?_ kg   0.01   **6.** 1 cg = _?_ hg   0.0001

B 7. 6 m = _?_ cm   600   **8.** 0.456 km = _?_ m   456   **9.** 24 mm = _?_ cm   2.4

10. 7 hm = _?_ dm   7000   **11.** 8.6 cm = _?_ mm   86   **12.** 549 m = _?_ km   0.549

13. 0.85g = _?_ cg   85   **14.** 0.936 kg = _?_ g   936   **15.** 743 dg = _?_ kg   0.0743

16. 16.2 dag = _?_ dg   1620   **17.** 304 mg = _?_ g   0.304   **18.** 91 cg = _?_ mg   910

19. 8342 mL = _?_ L   8.342   **20.** 4.72 hL = _?_ L   472   **21.** 0.45 daL = _?_ dL   45

22. 3.4 cL = _?_ mL   34   **23.** 7.243 L = _?_ cL   724.3   **24.** 68 daL = _?_ kL   0.68

Self Test 2

Solve the equation.

1. $41.6 + 32.7 = f$ 74.3   **2.** $8.75 + 21.9 = d$ 30.65   **3.** $118.33 + 4.765 = c$ 123.095   **2-4**

4. $k = 8.96 - 4.38$ 4.58   **5.** $s = 17.86 - 9.9$ 7.96   **6.** $h = 325.8 - 27.65$ 298.15   **2-5**

Solve.

7. It usually takes a typist from 15 to 35 minutes to type a letter. He   **2-6**
finished 12 letters in 5 hours. Is that time within his usual range?   yes

Solve the equation.

8. $74 \times 2.36 = t$ 174.64   **9.** $0.02 \times 0.43 = a$ 0.0086   **10.** $1000 \times 8.65 = c$ 8650   **2-7**

11. $p = 220.8 \div 96$ 2.3   **12.** $w = 8.4 \div 3.5$ 2.4   **13.** $y = 36.2 \div 100$ 0.362   **2-8**

Complete.

14. 4562 mL = _?_ L   4.562   **15.** 0.841 kg = _?_ g   841   **16.** 724 m = _?_ km   0.724   **2-9**

Algebra Practice

Evaluate the expression using the given value for the variable.

1. $n(8 - n)$; $n = 2$ ₍12₎

2. $81 - (6x)$; $x = 6$ ₍45₎

3. $s \div 17$; $s = 51$ ₍3₎

Solve.

4. $15 = 15 + r$ ₍0₎

5. $22j = 22$ ₍1₎

6. $6 + 4 - 8 \div 2 = w$ ₍6₎

Simplify the expression.

7. $3.5r + 12.68r$ ₍16.18r₎

8. $4.3a + 9.7w + 8.12a$ ₍12.42a + 9.7w₎

9. $4.9c + 6.2f + 8.1c$ ₍13c + 6.2f₎

10. $15m - 12.78m$ ₍2.22m₎

11. $20.05b - 6.873b$ ₍13.177b₎

12. $31.05g - 0.982g$ ₍30.068g₎

13. $(6.6 - 3.97) + 4.806$ ₍7.436₎

14. $18.3 - 4.6 \times 0.9$ ₍14.16₎

15. $a(a + 4)$ ₍a² + 4a₎

Write an expression for the phrase.

16. the quotient of 263 and n ₍263 ÷ n₎

17. h used as a factor 4 times ₍h⁴₎

18. 14.2 greater than y ₍y + 14.2₎

19. g decreased by 2.6 ₍g − 2.6₎

20. c multiplied by 8.63 ₍8.63c₎

21. 7.5 divided by v ₍7.5 ÷ v₎

Write an equation for the sentence. Solve the equation.

22. 8090 minus 5989 is a. $8090 - 5989 = a$; 2101

23. 196 increased by 505 is n. $196 + 505 = n$; 701

24. The sum of 8.93 and 12.7 is equal to t. $8.93 + 12.7 = t$; 21.63

25. The difference between 36.409 and 19.7 is equal to h. $36.409 - 19.7 = h$; 16.709

26. 3.2 times 0.6 is equal to j. $3.2(0.6) = j$; 1.92

27. 18 divided by 3.6 is equal to b. $18 \div 3.6 = b$; 5

28. The product of 5.216 and 0.05 is f. $(5.216)(0.05) = f$; 0.2608

29. The numbers 11.097, 230.28, and 1.973 add to a sum of s. $11.097 + 230.28 + 1.973 = s$; 243.35

30. The quotient of 14.04 and 1.8 is z. $14.04 \div 1.8 = z$; 7.8

31. 21 increased by 804 is y. $21 + 804 = y$; 825

32. The number n is the quotient of 16 divided by 0.4. $n = 16 \div 0.4$; 40

33. 27.4 greater than 37 is q. $37 + 27.4 = q$; 64.4

34. The number t is the product of 0.16 and 0.042. $t = 0.16(0.042)$; 0.00672

35. The number j is 6 used as a factor twice. $j = 6^2$; 36

36. The factors 2.01 and 0.07 have a product m. $(2.01)(0.07) = m$; 0.1407

37. 86 decreased by 2.71 is h. $86 - 2.71 = h$; 83.29

38. The sum of 4 greater than 18 and 25 is x. $18 + 25 + 4 = x$; 47

39. The number n is the product of 2.01 and 0.009. $n = (2.01)(0.009)$; 0.01809

40. 4.01 decreased by itself is z. $4.01 - 4.01 = z$; 0

Problem Solving for the Consumer

Buying a Car

The amount of money a dealer pays a factory for a car is called the dealer cost. To make a profit a dealer must charge a customer more than the dealer cost. To give you an idea of a fair price for that charge, consumer magazines will estimate a cost factor. This cost factor is often expressed as a decimal. To determine dealer cost, just multiply the list price the dealer tells you by the cost factor.

Complete the chart to find the approximate dealer cost.

	Model	List Price	Cost Factor	Dealer Cost	
1.	Fire fly	$10,370	0.88	?	$9125.60
2.	Cruiser	$ 7095	0.86	?	$6101.70
3.	Wanderer	$ 6714	0.90	?	$6042.60
4.	Stallion	$ 8979	0.84	?	$7542.36

Options are not included in the basic price of a car, so you have to add those extra charges onto the cost. Here's a list of some options on one car model and the list prices. Answer the questions.

5. What's the total cost of these options? $1396.90 air conditioning and radio/tape

6. Which options total $881?

7. The cost factor on each of these options is 0.84. What is the dealer cost on the air conditioning? on the radio/tape? $575.82; $164.22

OPTIONS	LIST PRICE
POWER BRAKES	100.00
POWER STEERING	315.95
TINTED GLASS	99.95
AIR CONDITIONING	685.50
RADIO/TAPE	195.50

Often you can bargain with the car salesperson over the price you are willing to pay. The difference between dealer cost and the total list price is roughly the amount of bargaining room you have. Complete the chart on the next page.

	Basic Car			Options			(a) Total List Price	(b) Total Dealer Cost	Difference (a — b)
	List Price	Cost Factor	Dealer Cost	List Price	Cost Factor	Dealer Cost			
8.	$6278	0.88	? $5524.64	$1375	0.85	? $1168.75	? $7653	? $6693.39	? $959.61
9.	$7762	0.93	? $7218.66	$ 495	0.84	? $415.80	? $8257	? $7634.46	? $622.54
10.	$8449	0.87	? $7350.63	$1036	0.87	? $901.32	? $9485	? $8251.95	? $1233.05

It's smart to compare the gas mileage ratings of cars. The average driver might drive 12,000 mi per year. Suppose gas costs $1.08 a gallon. Complete the chart. Round the answers to the nearest hundredth.

	Model	Miles Per Gallon (Highway driving)	Number of Gallons Per Year	Cost of Gas Per Year
11.	Darter	42.6	281.69	? $304.23
12.	XM-Hawk	33.4	? 359.28	? $388.02
13.	Winslow	25.7	? 466.93	? $504.28

Solve.

14. A Cobra gets 39 mi per gallon. When air conditioning is running it gets 4.2 fewer miles per gallon. How many gallons of gas would be used for running the air conditioner constantly on a 420-mile trip? 1.3 gal

15. Suppose you have the following options, but you decide to buy only two of them. How many different combinations of two options do you have? 10 combinations
automatic transmission   air conditioning   power brakes
stereo with AM-FM system   fog lights

Enrichment

Binary Digits and the Computer

1. 100101 110100 100100 010010 010101 101001
2. 010001 010100 010100 011001 110011 011001 100110 10•
3. 010010 011001 100101 010001 101001 111000

You know that the number system we use is a decimal system. The digits 0–9 are used in this system. The only digits used in the binary system are 0 and 1. These binary digits are important to the operation of digital computers. If a circuit in a computer is open, the computer reads that as 1. If the circuit is closed, the computer reads that as 0. A listing of a code system called Binary Coded Decimal (BCD) is shown below.

4. 010011 100110 100100 100111 110100 110011 010101 101001
5. 100100 110100 100011 110011 011001 100111 100011 111000
6. 010100 011001 110101 011001 010100 010101

010001	010010	010011	010100	010101	010110	010111
A	B	C	D	E	F	G
011000	011001	100001	100010	100011	100100	100101
H	I	J	K	L	M	N
100110	100111	101000	101001	110010	110011	110100
O	P	Q	R	S	T	U
110101	110110	110111	111000	111001		
V	W	X	Y	Z		

7. 011000 100110 100100 010101 110110 100110 101001 100010
8. 010100 010101 010011 011001 100100 010001 100011

Notice that different combinations of the binary digits are used as codes for the letters of the alphabet.

The code for the word *math* is 100100 010001 110011 011000. The word 010001 010100 010100 is decoded as *add*.

Write the code for each word using the BCD system. See answers above.

1. number   2. addition   3. binary   4. computer

5. multiply   6. divide   7. homework   8. decimal

Use the BCD listing to decode the name of a famous mathematician who worked with binary digits. JOHN VON NEUMANN

9. 100001 J 100110 O 011000 H 100101 N   110101 V 100110 O 100101 N
   100101 N 010101 E 110100 U 100100 M 010001 A 100101 N 100101 N

Chapter Review

Match.

1. the standard form of 4 and 6 ten-thousandths C
2. 4000.551 rounded to the nearest tenth H
3. the product when you multiply 20.003 by 2 A
4. the sum when you add 1.453 and 2.54706 G
5. the standard form of four and six tenths F
6. 400.00618 rounded to the nearest thousandth E
7. the difference between 92.438 and 52.378 B
8. the quotient when you divide 1001.5 by 2.5 D

A. 40.006
B. 40.06
C. 4.0006
D. 400.6
E. 400.006
F. 4.6
G. 4.00006
H. 4000.6

Are the decimals in order? Write *Yes* or *No*.

9. 31.18, 31.1, 31.19, 32.19 no
10. 8.8, 8.89, 8.94, 8.9, 8.98 no
11. 34.14, 34.146, 34.15, 34.162 yes
12. 184.481, 18.4481, 18.48, 1848.1 no
13. 7.006, 7.007, 7.706, 7.707 yes
14. 21.01, 21.1, 21.12, 21.121, 21.122 yes

Choose the equivalent measure. Write *a*, *b*, or *c*.

15. 6.4 cm b   **a.** 64 m   **b.** 64 mm   **c.** 640 mm
16. 984 mg c   **a.** 9.84 g   **b.** 0.984 dg   **c.** 0.984 g
17. 7.4 km a   **a.** 7400 m   **b.** 740 m   **c.** 740 hm
18. 0.5 L b   **a.** 50 mL   **b.** 500 mL   **c.** 500 cL
19. 51.3 dag c   **a.** 5.13 g   **b.** 513 mg   **c.** 513 g

Solve the equation.

20. $4.002 + 31.6 = y$ 35.602
21. $48.9 - 21.75 = d$ 27.15
22. $1000 \times 6.75 = m$ 6750
23. $1.512 \div 3.6 = a$ 0.42
24. $0.84 \times 3.6 = z$ 3.024
25. $27.85 + 191.9 = b$ 219.75
26. $d = 93.2 \div 100$ 0.932
27. $s = 771.1 - 39.865$ 731.235
28. $m = 2.07 \div 4.6$ 0.45
29. $x = 4.7 \times 0.09$ 0.423
30. $n = 62 - 0.63$ 61.37
31. $10 \times 7.62 = n$ 76.2
32. $0.06(4.3 - 1.02) = m$ 0.1968
33. $(0.001)(5.8) = a$ 0.0058
34. $4.1(6.2 + 3.5) = c$ 39.77

Chapter Test

Write the decimal.

1. 36 and 4 thousandths 36.004
2. 424 and 307 ten-thousandths   424.0307   **2-1**
3. seventeen and four hundred five hundred-thousandths 17.00405
4. two and six thousand twelve millionths   2.006012

Write the decimals in order from least to greatest.

5. 6.12, 6.11, 6.22, 6.21   6.11, 6.12, 6.21, 6.22
6. 9.83, 9.8, 9.8347, 9.834   9.8, 9.83, 9.834, 9.8347   **2-2**
7. 766, 7.16, 7.1, 7.61   7.1, 7.16, 7.61, 766
8. 41.14, 41.1, 41.141, 41.41   41.1, 41.14, 41.141, 41.41

Round to the nearest tenth.

9. 0.2 0.2
10. 5.753 5.8
11. 16.545 16.5
12. 245.8364 245.8 **2-3**

Round to the nearest hundredth.

13. 2.476 2.48
14. 31.555 31.56
15. 0.8327 0.83
16. 7.5426 7.54

Solve the equation.

17. $8.62 + 4.09 = a$ 12.71
18. $74.5 + 2.13 = b$ 76.63
19. $684.2 + 39.754 = h$ 723.954   **2-4**

Solve the equation.

20. $24.36 - 9.75 = w$ 14.61
21. $45.2 - 3.16 = s$ 42.04
22. $745.3 - 74.536 = g$ 670.764   **2-5**

Solve.

23. A certain computer game ranges in price from \$29.95 to \$34.50, depending upon different store prices. What is the minimum you could pay for 4 of those games? The maximum? \$119.80; \$138.00   **2-6**

Solve the equation.

24. $87 \times 42.2 = y$ 3671.4
25. $0.04 \times 0.22 = v$ 0.0088
26. $100 \times 78.6 = m$ 7860   **2-7**

Solve the equation.

27. $15.51 \div 47 = n$ 0.33
28. $9.5 \div 0.25 = t$ 38
29. $8.45 \div 1000 = r$ 0.00845   **2-8**

Complete.

30. $45 \text{ cm} = \underline{}\text{ mm}$ 450
31. $0.64 \text{ daL} = \underline{}\text{ L}$ 6.4
32. $7.5 \text{ L} = \underline{}\text{ mL}$ 7500   **2-9**

Cumulative Review (Chapters 1–2)

Add, subtract, multiply, or divide.

1. $(1)(87,019)$ 87,019
2. $4.7 - 2.35$ 2.35
3. $(83.5)(0)$ 0
4. $16 \div 4 - 1.5$ 2.5
5. $3.5(2 + 8)$ 35
6. $14.08 - 2.4 \div 2$ 12.88
7. 10×7.4 74
8. $(10)(10)(16.83)$ 1683
9. $(100)(4.807)$ 480.7
10. $(10)(4.639)(0)$ 0
11. $(4.7)(0) + 84.213$ 84.213
12. $6.4 - (9.01)(0)$ 6.4
13. 0.004×1000 4
14. $2 \cdot 2 \cdot 2 \cdot 2$ 16
15. $3 \cdot 3 \cdot 3 \cdot 3$ 81

Round to the place of the underlined digit.

16. 4<u>3</u>81   4400
17. 52<u>9</u>4   5290
18. 0.7<u>1</u>1   0.71
19. 32<u>1</u>.6   322
20. <u>0</u>.9   1
21. <u>2</u>8,300   30,000
22. 0.4<u>6</u>6   0.47
23. 52<u>9</u>5   5300
24. 2<u>9</u>.9   30
25. 3.<u>9</u>8   4.0

Choose the best estimate.

26. $82 + 19$ b   **a.** 95   **b.** 100   **c.** 110   **d.** 115
27. $162 \div 43$ a   **a.** 4   **b.** 3   **c.** 40   **d.** 30
28. $78.8 \div 5.1$ c   **a.** 15   **b.** 25   **c.** 16   **d.** 18
29. $\$1.95 \times 9$ b   **a.** $20   **b.** $18   **c.** $9   **d.** $17

Simplify.

30. $a \cdot b$ ab
31. $a \cdot a$ a^2
32. $c \cdot c \cdot c \cdot c$ c^4
33. $5 \cdot a \cdot a \cdot a$ $5a^3$
34. $2 \cdot 2 \cdot n \cdot n$ $4n^2$
35. $5 \cdot x \cdot y \cdot z$ $5xyz$
36. $6 \cdot k^2$ $6k^2$
37. $4 \cdot t \cdot t \cdot w$ $4t^2w$
38. $x \cdot y \cdot z \cdot x$ x^2yz
39. $s \div s$ 1
40. $n(n + 1)$ $n^2 + n$
41. $j(7 + j)$ $7j + j^2$

Write an equation for the sentence. Solve the equation.

42. When 4.2 is increased by 18.9, the result is x. $4.2 + 18.9 = x$; 23.1
43. 83 is greater than 47.1 by g. $83 - 47.1 = g$; 35.9
44. 160 reduced by 45.5 is n. $160 - 45.5 = n$; 114.50
45. He traveled d by driving 55 mi per hour for 2 hours. $d = 55 \cdot 2$; 110 miles

Write an equation for the problem. Solve it.

46. The Norwalk High School band has twice as many members as the 45-member Drama Club. How many members does the band have? $x = 2 \cdot 45$; 90 members

3
Number Theory

Imagine knitting 20,160 squares! That's the number of 6-in. squares needed to make the largest blanket in the world. The length and width had to be multiples of 6 in., 68 ft by 100 ft to be exact.

3-1 Divisibility Tests

Some division problems have remainders. Others do not. On a calculator a remainder is indicated by decimal places in the quotient.

$650 \div 5 = 130$

650 is **divisible** by 5.

$650 \div 4 = 162.25$

650 is not divisible by 4.

A number a is divisible by another number b if the quotient $a \div b$ is a whole number.

Every number is divisible by 1. $a \div 1 = a$

No number is divisible by 0.   ~~$a \div 0 = ?$~~

To decide if a number is divisible by a number other than 1, you can divide the first number by the second number. At times you may wish to use a calculator to do the division. For certain divisors, however, it is often easier to use a few simple **divisibility tests.** In some cases you can determine divisibility just by looking at the number!

Divisor	Divisibility Tests
2	The last digit is 0, 2, 4, 6, or 8.
3	The sum of the digits is divisible by 3.
4	The number named by the last two digits is divisible by 4.
5	The last digit is 0 or 5.
6	The number is divisible by both 2 and 3.
8	The number named by the last three digits is divisible by 8.
9	The sum of the digits is divisible by 9.
10	The last digit is 0.

Notice that a number is divisible by 6 if it is divisible by its factors 2 and 3. In the same way a number is divisible by 12 if it is divisible by 3 and 4, a number is divisible by 15 if it is divisible by 3 and 5, and so on.

Example 1   Is 24,570 divisible by 3?

Solution   Sum of digits: $2 + 4 + 5 + 7 + 0 = 18$
Is 18 divisible by 3? ⟵———— $18 \div 3 = 6$
Then 24,570 is also divisible by 3.

Example 2   Is 1286 divisible by 4?

Solution   Look at last two digits: 1286
Is 86 divisible by 4? No. ⟵——— $86 \div 4 = 21.5$
Then 1286 is not divisible by 4.

Your Turn   • Is 92,424 divisible by the number?
• 2 yes   • 3 yes   • 4 yes   • 5 no   • 6 yes   • 10 no

The numbers 1, 2, 3, 4, 5, . . . are called **consecutive whole numbers.**
A number that is divisible by 2 is called an **even number.** A number
that is not divisible by 2 is called an **odd number.**

Consecutive even numbers: 2, 4, 6, 8, 10, . . .
Consecutive odd numbers: 1, 3, 5, 7, 9, . . .

Example 3   Is 117,594 an even number, or an odd number?

Solution   Look at the last digit: 117,594
The last digit is divisible by 2.
So 117,594 is divisible by 2 and 117,594 is an even
number.

Your Turn   • Is 20,371 an even number or an odd number? odd number
• What is the next consecutive whole number after 16? 17
• What is the next consecutive even number after 16? 18

Class Exercises

Look at the last digit of each number. Is the number divisible by 2? By 5? By 10?

yes; yes; yes

1. 528 yes; no; no **2.** 1730 yes; yes; yes **3.** 384 yes; no; no **4.** 3992 yes; no; no **5.** 2000
yes; yes; yes
6. 75 no; yes; no **7.** 5556 yes; no; no **8.** 328 yes; no; no **9.** 975 no; yes; no **10.** 850

11–20. Look at the last two digits of each number in Exercises 1–10. Tell whether the number is divisible by 4. **11.** yes **12.** no **13.** yes **14.** yes **15.** yes
16. no **17.** yes **18.** yes **19.** no **20.** no

21–30. Add the digits of each number in Exercises 1–10. Tell whether the number is divisible by 3. **21.** yes **22.** no **23.** yes **24.** no **25.** no
26. yes **27.** yes **28.** no **29.** yes **30.** no

Exercises

Is the first number divisible by the second number? Write *Yes* or *No*.

no
A **1.** 526 by 2 yes **2.** 1723 by 3 no **3.** 804 by 1 yes **4.** 157 by 0

yes
5. 630 by 5 yes **6.** 726 by 4 no **7.** 1938 by 6 yes **8.** 621 by 3

yes
9. 478 by 4 no **10.** 445 by 2 no **11.** 895 by 10 no **12.** 970 by 5

yes
13. 96 by 4 yes **14.** 490 by 0 no **15.** 836 by 6 no **16.** 802 by 2

Is the number divisible by 2? By 3? By 4? By 5? By 6? By 8? By 9?
By 10? **17.** yes; yes; yes; yes; yes; yes; no; yes **18.** no; no; no; no; no; no; no; no
19. yes; yes; yes; yes; yes; no; yes; yes **20.** yes; no; yes; yes; no; yes; no; yes
B **17.** 480 **18.** 373 **19.** 1980 **20.** 2000 **21.** 882
21. yes; yes; no; no; yes; no; yes; no **22.** yes; no; no; no; no; no; no; no
22. 98 **23.** 138 **24.** 575 **25.** 324 **26.** 2670
23. yes; yes; no; no; yes; no; no; no **24.** no; no; no; yes; no; no; no; no
27. 582 **28.** 777 **29.** 360 **30.** 517 **31.** 184
25. yes; yes; yes; no; yes; no; yes; no **26.** yes; yes; no; yes; yes; no; no; yes
32. 51,840 **33.** 68,672 **34.** 41,847 **35.** 502,164 **36.** 881,280
27. yes; yes; no; no; yes; no; no; no **28.** no; no; no; no; no; no; no; no

True or False? Write *T* or *F*. **29.** yes; yes; yes; yes; yes; yes; yes; yes
30. no; no; no; no; no; no; no; no
T
37. All even numbers are divisible by 2.
F **31.** yes; no; yes; no; no; yes; no; no
38. All odd numbers are divisible by 3. **32.** yes; yes; yes; yes; yes; yes; yes; yes
T **33.** yes; no; yes; no; no; yes; no; no
39. Some even numbers are divisible by 5. **34.** no; yes; no; no; no; no; no; no
F **35.** yes; yes; yes; no; yes; no; yes; no
40. The sum of two odd numbers is an odd number. **36.** yes; yes; yes; yes; yes; yes; yes; yes
T
41. The sum of two even numbers is an even number.

By which of the numbers is 17,844 divisible?

42. 3; 4; 12 — 3; 4; 12

43. 2; 5; 10 — 2

44. 2; 3; 6 — 2; 3; 6

45. 4; 6; 24 — 4; 6

Let n be a whole number. Write an expression for the next consecutive number.

46. n — $n + 1$

47. $2n$ — $2n + 1$

48. $n - 1$ — n

49. $n + 1$ — $n + 2$

50. $2n + 1$ — $2n + 2$

Let n be a whole number. Does the expression represent an even number?

C 51. $2n$ — yes

52. $2n + 1$ — no

53. $2n - 1$ — no

54. $2n + 2$ — yes

55. $4n + 2$ — yes

Problems

Solve.

1. For graduation, 96 students must be seated on stage. Each row must have the same number of seats. yes Is it possible to accomplish this with rows of 12 seats?

2. A teacher wishes to arrange 30 desks in a classroom. Each row is to have the same number of seats. List all the ways that this can be done. 5 rows of 6, 6 rows of 5; 1 row of 30, 2 rows of 15, 15 rows of 2, 3 rows of 10, 10 rows of 3

3. For a relay race 72 students are to be divided into teams of equal size. List all the possible ways that teams of more than 6 students may be formed. 8 teams of 9, 9 teams of 8, 2 teams of 36, 3 teams of 24, 4 teams of 18, 6 teams of 12

4. A "square" for a square dance is made up of 4 couples. If there are 156 people at a square dance, is it possible for all of them to dance in "squares" at the same time? no

Using the Calculator

An exclamation point is used in the following way to show multiplication of consecutive whole numbers.

$$2! = 1 \cdot 2, \quad 3! = 1 \cdot 2 \cdot 3, \quad 4! = 1 \cdot 2 \cdot 3 \cdot 4, \text{ and so on.}$$

The symbol 2! is read *2 factorial*.

Using a calculator find the value of the factorial expression.

1. 3! — 6

2. 6! — 720

3. 10! — 3,628,800

4. 5! · 3! — 720

5. 8! · 6! — 29,030,400

3-2 *Factors and Prime Numbers*

Alpha Games plans to ship a new electronic game to stores in cartons containing 12 games each. The shipping department recommends cartons with 3 stacks of 4 games in each.

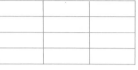

$3 \times 4 = 12$

The numbers 3 and 4 are called **factors** of 12. A number is divisible by each of its factors. Other factors of 12 are 1, 2, 6, and 12. The number 1 is a factor of every number.

Sometimes a number, like 7, has only two factors, itself and 1. Such a number is called a **prime number.** If a number has more than two factors, it is called a **composite number.** The number 1 is not considered to be a prime since we would have to show it as a factor in all examples such as Example 1 following. The number 0 is not considered to be a composite since, unlike any other composite number, it would have all numbers as its factors.

Factors of 7: 1 and 7   Factors of 6: 1, 2, 3, 6
7 is a prime number   6 is a composite number.

Composite numbers can be written as the product of prime factors, called the **prime factorization** of the number. The array of factors and connecting lines shown below is called a **factor tree.**

Example 1 Write the prime factorization of 42.

Solution First write 42 as a product of two factors. Replace composite factors with a product of two factors until all numbers are prime.

$42 = 2 \times 3 \times 7$

Sometimes there is more than one choice for a set of factors. However, the end result is always the same.

Example 2 Show two different ways of finding the prime factorization of 48.

Solution

$$48 = 2 \times 2 \times 2 \times 2 \times 3 \qquad 48 = 2 \times 3 \times 2 \times 2 \times 2$$

Because of the commutative property the order of the factors does not matter. The two solutions are equal.

Sometimes it's convenient to use exponents to write repeated factors.

Example 3 Write the prime factorization of 48 using exponents.

Solution Use the prime factorization of 48 in Example 2.

$$48 = \underbrace{2 \times 2 \times 2 \times 2}_{2^4} \times 3$$
$$= \qquad 2^4 \qquad \times 3$$

Your Turn Complete.

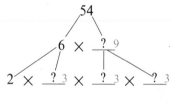

• $54 = 2 \times 3^{?\ 3}$

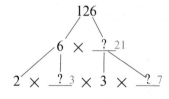

• $126 = 2 \times 3^{2} \times \underline{?\ 7}$

Divisibility tests can help you write the prime factorization of a number.

In Arithmetic	In Algebra
$12 \div 3 = 4$	$a \div b = c$
So both 3 and 4 are factors of 12.	So, b and c are factors of a.

Example 4   Write the prime factorization of 78.

Solution   The last digit of 78 is 8. So 78 is divisible by 2. Therefore 2 is a factor of 78 and $78 \div 2$, or 39, is also a factor.

$$
\begin{array}{c}
78 \\
\diagup\diagdown \\
2 \times 39 \qquad \longleftarrow \qquad \textit{39 is divisible by 3.} \\
\diagup \quad \diagup\diagdown \\
2 \times 3 \times 13 \qquad \longleftarrow \qquad \textit{3 and 39 ÷ 3, or 13, are} \\
\textit{factors of 39 and of 78.}
\end{array}
$$

$$78 = 2 \times 3 \times 13$$

Your Turn   Write the prime factorization of the number.
- 104   • 220   • 1350
  $2^3 \times 13$ $2^2 \times 5 \times 11$ $2 \times 3^3 \times 5^2$

Class Exercises

Complete the factor tree. State the prime factorization of the first number.

1.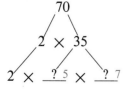

$70 = 2 \times \underline{?\ 5} \times \underline{?\ 7}$

2.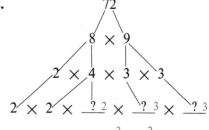

$72 = 2^{?\ 3} \times 3^{?\ 2}$

Exercises

Copy and complete the factor tree. Write the prime factorization of the first number.

A **1.**

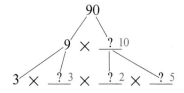

$$90 = 3 \times \underline{?\ 3} \times \underline{?\ 2} \times \underline{?\ 5}$$

2.

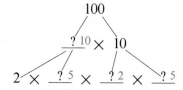

$$100 = 2 \times \underline{?\ 2} \times \underline{?\ 5} \times \underline{?\ 5}$$

Draw a factor tree. Write the prime factorization of the number.

B **3.** 24 $2^3 \times 3$ **4.** 50 2×5^2 **5.** 63 $3^2 \times 7$ **6.** 44 $2^2 \times 11$ **7.** 30 $2 \times 3 \times 5$

8. 140 $2^2 \times 5 \times 7$ **9.** 66 $2 \times 3 \times 11$ **10.** 112 $2^4 \times 7$ **11.** 128 2^7 **12.** 200 $2^3 \times 5^2$

13. 130 $2 \times 5 \times 13$ **14.** 900 $2^2 \times 3^2 \times 5^2$ **15.** 6300 $2^2 \times 3^2 \times 5^2 \times 7$ **16.** 512 2^9 **17.** 176 $2^4 \times 11$

Use exponents to write the prime factorization of the number.

18. 180 $2^2 \times 3^2 \times 5$ **19.** 378 $2 \times 3^3 \times 7$ **20.** 280 $2^3 \times 5 \times 7$ **21.** 660 $2^2 \times 3 \times 5 \times 11$ **22.** 550 $2 \times 5^2 \times 11$

23. 1600 $2^6 \times 5^2$ **24.** 1360 $2^4 \times 5 \times 17$ **25.** 784 $2^4 \times 7^2$ **26.** 1296 $3^4 \times 2^4$ **27.** 1225 $5^2 \times 7^2$

Solve.

C **28.** One of the largest known prime numbers is $2^{3217} - 1$. Is it an even number or an odd number? Give a reason for your answer. odd number; 2 raised to an odd power gives an even number and when 1 is subtracted, the result is odd.

29. How many prime numbers are there between 0 and 50? Between 50 and 75? 15; 6

Problems

Twin primes are two prime numbers whose difference is 2. Here are some examples of twin primes.

3 and 5   5 and 7   11 and 13

Solve.

1. How many pairs of twin primes are there less than 50? Name them. 6   3, 5; 5, 7; 11, 13; 17, 19; 29, 31; 41, 43

2. Janice claims that she can name a pair of even numbers that are twin primes. Evelyn says that she must have made a mistake. Who is right? Evelyn Why? Two is the only even-prime number.

3-3 *The Greatest Common Factor*

Sometimes two numbers have some of the same factors. These are called **common factors.**

Factors of 30: 1, 2, 3, 5, 6, 10, 15, 30
Factors of 54: 1, 2, 3, 6, 9, 18, 27, 54

Common factors of 30 and 54 are: 1, 2, 3, and 6. The **greatest common factor (GCF)** of 30 and 54 is 6.

Example 1 What is the GCF of 48 and 64?

Solution Factors of 48: 1, 2, 3, 4, 6, 8, 12, 16, 24, 48
Factors of 64: 1, 2, 4, 8, 16, 32, 64
Common factors: 1, 2, 4, 8, and 16
Greatest common factor: 16

Instead of listing all the factors as in Example 1, it is sometimes easier to use the prime factorization of each of the numbers.

Example 2 What is the GCF of 36 and 54?

Solution The GCF is the product of all common factors.
36 = 2 × 2 × 3 × 3
54 = 2 × 3 × 3 × 3
The GCF is 2 × 3 × 3, or 18.

15; 1, 3, 5, 15   12; 1, 2, 3, 4, 6, 12
50; 1, 2, 5, 10, 25, 50   32; 1, 2, 4, 8, 16, 32
GCF is 5.   GCF is 4.

Your Turn List the factors and write the GCF of the numbers.

8; 1, 2, 4, 8   • 8 and 12   • 15 and 50   • 12 and 32
12; 1, 2, 3, 4, 6, 12
GCF is 4.   Use the prime factorization to find the GCF of the
numbers.   12 = 2² × 3   9 = 3²   16 = 2⁴
            18 = 2 × 3²   30 = 2 × 3 × 5   24 = 2³ × 3
• 12 and 18 GCF is 6. • 9 and 30 GCF is 3. • 16 and 24 GCF is 8.

Class Exercises

Tell what numbers are missing.

1. Factors of 8: 1, 2, 4, 8
Factors of 12: 1, 2, 3, 4, 6, 12
Common factors: 1, 2, _?4_
GCF of 8 and 12: _?4_

2. Factors of 6: 1, 2, 3, 6
Factors of 15: 1, 3, 5, 15
Common factors: 1, _?3_
GCF of 6 and 15: _?3_

3. $14 = 2 \times 7$
$42 = 2 \times 3 \times$ _?7_
GCF of 14 and 42: $2 \times$ _?7_ $=$ _?14_

4. $16 = 2 \times 2 \times 2 \times 2$
$20 = 2 \times 2 \times$ _?5_
GCF of 16 and 20: $2 \times$ _?2_ $=$ _?4_

Exercises

List all the factors of each number.

A 1. 6 1, 2, 3, 6   **2.** 12 1, 2, 3, 4, 6, 12 **3.** 15 1, 3, 5, 15   **4.** 30 1, 2, 3, 5, 6, 10, 15, 30   **5.** 24 5. 1, 2, 3, 4, 6, 8, 12, 24

Use the answers to Exercises 1–5 to determine the GCF.

6. of 6 and 12 6   **7.** of 12 and 15 3   **8.** of 15 and 30 15   **9.** of 30 and 24 6

Copy and complete. Use the prime factorization of the numbers to find the GCF.

10. $4 = 2 \times$ _?2_
$6 = 2 \times$ _?3_
GCF: _?2_

11. $28 = 2 \times 2 \times$ _?7_
$70 = 2 \times 5 \times$ _?7_
GCF: $2 \times$ _?7_ $=$ _?14_

12. $30 = 2 \times 3 \times$ _?5_
$75 = 3 \times 5 \times$ _?5_
GCF: _?3_ $\times$ _?5_ $=$ _?15_

Write the GCF of the pair of numbers.

B 13. 4 and 8 4   **14.** 5 and 15 5   **15.** 6 and 18 6   **16.** 7 and 70 7

17. 12 and 16 4   **18.** 9 and 15 3   **19.** 6 and 15 3   **20.** 8 and 20 4

21. 36 and 54 18   **22.** 27 and 45 9   **23.** 12 and 18 6   **24.** 15 and 24 3

25. 48 and 112 16   **26.** 84 and 66 6   **27.** 99 and 108 9   **28.** 65 and 66 1

29. 180 and 168 12   **30.** 176 and 192 16   **31.** 216 and 180 36   **32.** 210 and 231 21

Two numbers are *relatively prime* if their GCF is 1. Tell if the pair of numbers is relatively prime.

C 33. 8 and 9 yes   **34.** 6 and 8 no   **35.** 9 and 15 no   **36.** 12 and 35 yes

3-4 *Factoring in Algebra*

To **factor** an expression means to write it as the product of factors.

$$6x^2 = 2 \cdot 3 \cdot x \cdot x \qquad 5a^2b = 5 \cdot a \cdot a \cdot b$$

We will call $2 \cdot 3 \cdot x \cdot x$ the **algebraic factorization** of $6x^2$.

In arithmetic, to find the greatest common factor (GCF), you first wrote the prime factorization of each number. Then the GCF was equal to the product of all the common prime factors.

In algebra, to find the GCF, you first write the algebraic factorization of each expression. The GCF is equal to the product of all the common factors of the algebraic factorizations.

Example 1   Write the GCF of $5a^2b$, $10a^3$, and $15a^2$.

Solution   Factor each expression.
$5a^2b = 5 \cdot a \cdot a \cdot b$
$10a^3 = 2 \cdot 5 \cdot a \cdot a \cdot a$
$15a^2 = 3 \cdot 5 \cdot a \cdot a$
GCF: $5 \cdot a \cdot a$, or $5a^2$

After a little practice you will be able to do this first step in your head.

Your Turn   Write the GCF of the set of expressions.
- $5m^2$ and $10m$ *5m*
- $6r^2$, $3rs$, and $9s^2$ *3*

When an expression has two or more terms you can often use the distributive property to factor the expression.

Distributive Property

In Arithmetic
$2 \cdot 6 + 2 \cdot 5 = 2(6 + 5)$
$2 \cdot 6 - 2 \cdot 5 = 2(6 - 5)$

In Algebra
$ab + ac = a(b + c)$
$ab - ac = a(b - c)$

81

Example 2   Use the distributive property to factor $9a + 6$.

Solution   What is the GCF of $9a$ and 6? The GCF is 3.
$9a + 6 = (3 \cdot 3a) + (3 \cdot 2)$ ⟵——— *Factor both 9a and 6.*
$\quad\quad = 3(3a + 2)$ ⟵——— *Use the distributive property.*
Check by multiplying.
$3(3a + 2) = 9a + 6$ ⟵——— *It checks.*

Example 3   Factor the expression $3p^2 - 6p$.

Solution   What is the GCF of $3p^2$ and $6p$? The GCF is $3p$.
$3p^2 - 6p = (3p \cdot p) - (3p \cdot 2)$ ⟵——— *Factor 3p² and 6p.*
$\quad\quad = 3p(p - 2)$ ⟵——— *Use the distributive property.*
Check by multiplying.
$3p(p - 2) = 3p^2 - 6p$ *It checks.*

Your Turn   Use the distributive property to factor the expression. $7(a + 2b - c)$
• $8x - 4$ $4(2x - 1)$ • $5y^2 + y$ $y(5y + 1)$ • $7a + 14b - 7c$

Class Exercises

Find the GCF.

1. **a.** 2 and 6   2
   b. a^2 and a a
   c. $2a^2$ and $6a$ $2a$

2. **a.** 5 and 7   1
   b. b^2 and b b
   c. $5b^2$ and $7b$ b

3. **a.** 10, 12, and 20   2
   b. c, c^2, and $c\,d$ c $2c$
   c. $10c$, $12c^2$, and $20cd$

Complete.

4. GCF of $6d^2$ and $3d$: __?__ $3d$
   $6d^2 + 3d = 3d\underline{?}\,(2d + \underline{?\,1})$

5. GCF of $30e$ and $20e^2$: __?__ $10e$
   $30e - 20e^2 = 10e\underline{?}\,(3 - 2e\underline{?})$

6. GCF of $5f^2$, $10f$, and 15: __?__ 5
   $5f^2 + 10f - 15 =$
   $\underline{?}\,5(\underline{?}\,f^2 + \underline{?}\,2f - 3)$

7. GCF of 8, $12g$, and $2g^2$: __?__ 2
   $8 + 12g - 2g^2$
   $\underline{?}\,2(4 + \underline{?}\,6g - \underline{?}\,g^2)$

Exercises

Write the GCF.

A
1. h^2 and $2h$ h **2.** $5j$ and 5 5 **3.** $2k^3$ and 6 2 **4.** $4m^2$ and $8m$ $4m$

5. n and $6n^2$ n **6.** $4p$ and $10p^2$ $2p$ **7.** q^2 and q q **8.** $6r^3$ and 18 6

Use the distributive property to complete.

9. $3s^2 - 3 = 3(\underline{?\,s^2} - \underline{?\,1})$ **10.** $4u + u^2 = u(\underline{?\,4} + \underline{?\,u})$

11. $5v^2 - 10 = \underline{?\,5}(v^2 - \underline{?\,2})$ **12.** $3w + w^2 = \underline{?\,w}(3 + \underline{?\,w})$

13. $12x^3 - 4 = \underline{?\,4}(3x^3 - \underline{?\,1})$ **14.** $10y + 15y^2 = \underline{5y\,?}(2 + \underline{3y\,?})$

Use the distributive property to factor the expression.

B
15. $a^2 + 2a$ $a(a + 2)$ **16.** $30 + 10b^2$ $10(3 + b^2)$ **17.** $c^2 - 2c$ $c(c - 2)$

18. $d + d^2$ $d(1 + d)$ **19.** $e - 2e^2$ $e(1 - 2e)$ **20.** $10f - 25$ $5(2f - 5)$

21. $6g^2 - 3g$ $3g(2g - 1)$ **22.** $12h - 4h^2$ $4h(3 - h)$ **23.** $15j + 20j^2$ $5j(3 + 4j)$

24. $18k - 12k^2$ $6k(3 - 2k)$ **25.** $30m + 25m^2$ $5m(6 + 5m)$ **26.** $24n - 20n^2$ $4n(6 - 5n)$

27. $6pq + p^2q^2$ $pq(6 + pq)$ **28.** $4rs + 8r^2$ $4r(s + 2r)$ **29.** $12u^2v - 8uv^2$ $4uv(3u - 2v)$

30. $3x^2 - 6x + 9$ $3(x^2 - 2x + 3)$ **31.** $ay^2 + ay + a$ $a(y^2 + y + 1)$ **32.** $12 + 4z - 8z^2$ $4(3 + z - 2z^2)$

33. $12 + 8a - 6a^2$ $2(6 + 4a - 3a^2)$ **34.** $10b - 5b^2 - 15$ $5(2b - b^2 - 3)$ **35.** $12c^2 - 8c - 4cd$ $4c(3c - 2 - d)$

Self Test 1

Is 12,550 divisible by the given number?

1. 2 yes   **2.** 4 no   **3.** 3 no   **4.** 5 yes   **3-1**

Write the prime factorization of each number.

5. 84 $2^2 \times 3 \times 7$ **6.** 920 $2^3 \times 5 \times 23$ **7.** 147 3×7^2 **8.** 1880 $2^3 \times 5 \times 47$ **3-2**

Write the GCF of each set of numbers.

9. 18 and 28 2 **10.** 20 and 45 5 **11.** 6, 10, and 15 1 **3-3**

Use the distributive property to factor the expression.

12. $3a - 12$ $3(a - 4)$ **13.** $5b^2 + 10b$ $5b(b + 2)$ **14.** $2 + 6c - 4c^2$ $2(1 + 3c - 2c^2)$ **3-4**

Self Test answers and Extra Practice are at the end of the book.

3-5 *Problem Solving*

Finding and using a pattern can be the key to solving certain kinds of problems.

Example 1   A city planner needs to know the number of street intersections before ordering new traffic lights. If there are 20 North-South streets intersecting with 20 East-West streets, how many intersections are there?

Solution   First we'll find how many intersections there are if there are fewer streets in each direction. We draw diagrams and count to determine the number of intersections if there are 1, 2, 3, or 4 streets in each direction.

Next, record the results and look for a pattern.

Number of streets in each direction	Number of intersections
1	1
2	4
3	9
4	16
⋮	⋮
20	400

Pattern:

$1^2 = 1$

$2^2 = 4$

$3^2 = 9$

$4^2 = 16$

The last step is to extend the pattern:

$20^2 = 400$

If 20 North-South streets intersect 20 East-West streets, there are 400 intersections in all.

In Example 1, the numbers 1, 4, 9, 16, . . . form a **sequence.** Each number, or **term** of a sequence, is obtained by applying a rule. You are probably already familiar with many sequences that you can use in problem solving.

Example 2   If January 1 is a Sunday, what is the date for the last Sunday of January? Write a sequence and state the rule.

Solution   You know that there are 7 days from one Sunday to the next. The Sundays of January are the following:

January 1,   8,   15,   22,   29   36

+7 +7   +7   +7   +7

Rule: The first term is 1. Each of the other terms is obtained by adding 7 to the term before it. No term is greater than 31, so the last Sunday of January is January 29.

Your Turn   • Beginning at 7:45 A.M. buses leave Lawrence for Macon every 45 minutes. What is the departure time that is closest to 12 Noon? Write a sequence and state the rule.

7:45 A.M., 8:30 A.M., 9:15 A.M., 10:00 A.M., 10:45 A.M., 11:30 A.M., 12:15 P.M. The first term is 7:45. Each successive term is obtained by adding 45 min to the term before it. The departure time closest to noon is 12:15 P.M.

Class Exercises

State the next three terms of the sequence.

1. 10, 20, 30, 40, . . .   50, 60, 70

2. 1, 3, 5, 7, . . .   9, 11, 13

3. 1980, 1984, 1988, 1992, . . .   1996, 2000, 2004

4. A, C, E, G, I, K, M, . . .   O, Q, S

5. A, V, B, Ǝ, C, Ɔ, . . .   D, ᗡ, E

6. Jan 31, Feb 28, Mar 31, . . .   Apr 30, May 31, June 30

7. 0, 1, 10, 11, 100, 101, . . .   1000, 1001, 10,000

8. 12:00, 12:20, 12:40, 1:00, . . .   1:20, 1:40, 2:00

9. 2, 4, 8, 16, . . .   32, 64, 128

10. Sun., Tues., Thurs., . . .   Sat., Mon., Wed.

11. ZYX, YXW, XWV, . . .   WVU, VUT, UTS

12. 3, 9, 27, 81, . . .   243, 729, 2187

85

Exercises

Solve.

A **1.** Four people can be seated at a single card table. If two tables are placed end to end, 6 people can be seated. How many tables must be placed end to end to seat 22 people? 10

2. January 1, 2000 will be a Saturday. On what day of the week will July 4 be that year? (The year 2000 will be a leap year.) Tuesday

3. A signature of a book resembles a small booklet of 32 pages. It is made by folding a large piece of paper several times and cutting the edges so that the pages will open. How many times must a piece of paper be folded to make a signature? 4

B **4.** Buses that go up Temple Avenue stop at every even-numbered street (Second Street, Fourth Street, Sixth Street, etc.). Houses on Temple Avenue that are numbered 10 to 19 are between First Street and Second Street. Houses numbered 20–29 are between Second Street and Third Street, and so on. What is the closest bus stop to 178 Temple Avenue? 18th St.

5. How many squares, of any size, are there on a standard, 8 × 8-square checkerboard? 204

Most comets travel around the sun in orbits that are oval shaped. The time it takes a comet to complete an orbit is called its period. We can calculate its approximate period from records of previous observations and then predict the approximate date of the comet's return. Solve.

C **6.** Halley's comet is one of the most famous and brilliant of comets. It was observed in 1531, 1607, 1682, 1759, 1835, and 1910.

    a. What is the average period (number of years from one observation to the next)? 75.8 years

    b. Use the average period to predict when Halley's comet will next be visible. 1985

3-6 *The Least Common Multiple*

Tennis balls are sold in cans containing 3 balls each. There are 3 balls in 1 can, 6 balls in 2 cans, 9 balls in 3 cans, and so on. The numbers 3, 6, 9, . . . are **multiples** of 3.

A multiple of a number is any product of that number and a natural number. Multiples of a number, *n*, are *n*, 2*n*, 3*n*, 4*n*, ...

A pair of numbers may have **common multiples.**

Multiples of 4: 4, 8, 12, 16, 20, 24, . . . , 36, . . . , 48, . . .
Multiples of 6: 6, 12, 18, 24, . . . , 36, . . . , 48, . . .

The numbers 12, 24, 36, 48, . . . are common multiples of 4 and 6.
The **least common multiple (LCM)** of 4 and 6 is 12.

Example 1 Write the LCM of 4, 6, and 10.

Solution Multiples of 4: 4, 8, 12, . . . , 60, . . . , 120, . . .
Multiples of 6: 6, 12, 18, . . . , 60, . . . , 120, . . .
Multiples of 10: 10, 20, 30, . . . , 60, . . . , 120, . . .
Common multiples: 60, 120, . . .
LCM: 60

Your Turn Write the LCM of the numbers.
• 3, 8, and 12 24
• 4, 9, and 15 180

87

The LCM of two or more numbers contains as factors all the factors of each number. You can use the prime factorization of a set of numbers to write the LCM. The highest power of each factor is used in the LCM.

Example 2 Use the prime factorizations of 100, 80, and 54 to write the LCM.

Solution Write the prime factorizations.

$100 = 2 \cdot 2 \cdot 5 \cdot 5$ $80 = 2 \cdot 2 \cdot 2 \cdot 2 \cdot 5$ $54 = 2 \cdot 3 \cdot 3 \cdot 3$
$ = 2^2 \cdot 5^2$ $ = 2^4 \cdot 5$ $ = 2 \cdot 3^3$

The highest power of 2 in any factor is 2^4.
The highest power of 3 in any factor is 3^3.
The highest power of 5 in any factor is 5^2.
The LCM is $2^4 \cdot 3^3 \cdot 5^2$, or 10,800

Example 3 Write the LCM of $10a^2$, $5a$, and 40.

Solution Factor each expression.

$10a^2 = 2 \cdot 5 \cdot a^2$ $5a = 5 \cdot a$ $40 = 2^3 \cdot 5$

Use the highest power of each factor to form the LCM.
The LCM is $2^3 \cdot 5 \cdot a^2$, or $40a^2$

Your Turn Use prime factorization to write the LCM.
- 6 and 8 24
- 9, 15, and 75 225
- $2x^2$, $4x$, and 16 $16x^2$

Class Exercises

State the first five multiples of each number.

1. 3 3, 6, 9, 12, 15
2. 10 10, 20, 30, 40, 50
3. 5 5, 10, 15, 20, 25
4. 9 9, 18, 27, 36, 45
5. m $m, 2m, 3m, 4m, 5m$
6. $2p$ $2p, 4p, 6p, 8p, 10p$

State the common multiples less than 30. What is the LCM?

7. 2 and 3 6, 12, 18, 24; 6
8. 2 and 5 10, 20; 10
9. 3 and 4 12, 24; 12
10. 3 and 5 15; 15

Exercises

Write the numbers.

A **1.** Multiples of 8 less than 40   8, 16, 24, 32   **2.** Multiples of 12 less than 50   12, 24, 36, 48

3. Multiples of 4 between 10 and 20   12, 16   **4.** Multiples of 5 between 20 and 40   25, 30, 35

Write the common multiples less than 100. Ring the LCM.

5. 5 and 6   ㉚, 60, 90   **6.** 6 and 9   ⑱, 36, 54, 72, 90   **7.** 2 and 7   ⑭, 28, 42, 56, 70, 84, 98   **8.** 8 and 12   ㉔, 48, 72, 96

9. 6 and 15   ㉚, 60, 90   **10.** 5 and 7   ㉟, 70   **11.** 10 and 12   ⑥⓪   **12.** 8 and 10   ㊵, 80

Write the LCM of the numbers.

B **13.** 2 and 4   4   **14.** 3 and 7   21   **15.** 3 and 9   9   **16.** 4 and 10   20

17. 4 and 9   36   **18.** 5 and 9   45   **19.** 4 and 10   20   **20.** 3 and 12   12

21. 6 and 10   30   **22.** 8 and 20   40   **23.** 10 and 15   30   **24.** 7 and 8   56

25. 18 and 30   90   **26.** 42 and 56   168   **27.** 48 and 60   240   **28.** 64 and 72   576

29. a^2 and $2a$ $2a^2$ **30.** $3b$ and $6b^3$ $6b^3$ **31.** $4c$ and $8c^2$ $8c^2$ **32.** $5d^2$ and $6d$ $30d^2$

33. $10e^3$ and $15e^2$ $30e^3$ **34.** $4f$ and $2f^2$ $4f^2$ **35.** h and j hj **36.** $2k$ and $3m$ $6km$

Use prime factorizations to write the LCM.

37. 10, 20, and 25   100   **38.** 20, 60, and 45   180   **39.** 24, 30, and 36   360

40. 12, 18, and 20   180   **41.** 15, 20, 25, and 30   300   **42.** 6, 9, 15, 18, and 24   360

43. $25d$, $15d^2$, and $5d^3$ $75d^3$ **44.** $3n^2$, $6n^3$, and $4n$ $12n^3$ **45.** $12x^2$, $6xy$, and $8y^2$ $24x^2y^2$

Using the Computer

This program will find pairs of factors of a whole number. RUN this program for 500, 600, and 700. Then try some examples of your own.

```
 5  REM: FACTORING A WHOLE NUMBER
10  PRINT "WHAT IS YOUR WHOLE NUMBER";
20  INPUT N
30  FOR F=1 TO N
40  LET Q=N/F
50  IF Q <> INT(Q) THEN 70
60  PRINT F;Q,
70  NEXT F
80  END
```

Output for 500:
What is your whole number? 500

1	500	2	250	4	125	5	100	10	50
20	25	25	20	50	10	100	5	125	4
250	2	500	1						

3-7 Scientific Notation

Over 2.1×10^5 cubic feet of water flow over Niagara Falls each second. The number 2.1×10^5 is written in **scientific notation.**

Scientific notation is especially useful when you are working with very large or very small numbers. Many calculators and computers use scientific notation for these numbers to save space. In a future course you will learn how to write numbers less than 1 using scientific notation.

A number written in scientific notation is the product of two factors.

The first factor is a $\qquad$ 2.1×10^5 $\qquad$ *The second factor is a*
number between 1 and 10. $\qquad$ *power of 10.*

Example 1 Are these numbers written in scientific notation?
36×10^5; $\qquad$ 7.2×10^3; $\qquad$ 4.0×5^2

Solution 36×10^5 ———— No, 36 is not between 1 and 10.
7.2×10^3 ———— Yes.
4.0×5^2 ———— No, 5^2 is not a power of 10.

Any number in scientific notation can be written in standard notation. To do this you multiply. You can think of moving the decimal point as many places as the power of 10.

Example 2 Write 8.6×10^9 in standard form.

Solution $8.6 \times 10^9 = 8,600,000,000$
9 places

Your Turn Is the number written in scientific notation?
- 8.7×10^3 yes $\qquad$ • 19×10^7 no $\qquad$ • 1.2×100^2 no

Write the number in standard form.
- 1.2×10^5 120,000 $\qquad$ • 6.1×10^{10} 61,000,000,000 $\qquad$ • 7.5×10^8 750,000,000

If a number is given in standard form, you can write it in scientific notation.

Example 3   Write the number 361,000,000,000 in scientific notation.

Solution   First, move the decimal point to the left to obtain a number between 1 and 10. The number of places the decimal moves is the exponent of 10.

$$361,000,000,000. = 3.61 \times 10^{11}$$

11 places

Your Turn   Write the number in scientific notation.
- 54,000 5.4×10^4 • 2,038,000,000 2.038×10^9• 3,100,000 3.1×10^6

See p. T18

Class Exercises

Is the number in scientific notation? Answer *Yes* or *No*.

1. 2.0×10^7 yes   **2.** 1.2×5^5 no   **3.** 86×10^9 no   **4.** 7.0×10^{32} yes

What is the standard form of the number?

5. 3.1×10^1 31   **6.** 8.6×10^3 8600   **7.** 5.4×10^2 540   **8.** 1.2×10^3 1200

Tell what number completes the equation.

9. $679,000 = 6.79 \times 10^?$ 5   **10.** $5,800,000,000 = 5.8 \times 10^?$ 9

11. $20,000 = \underline{\ ?\ } \times 10^4$ 2.0   **12.** $15,000,000,000 = \underline{\ ?\ } \times 10^{10}$ 1.5

Exercises

Write the number in standard form.   4. 100,000,000; 900,000,000; 930,000,000

A   **1. a.** 10^3 1000   **2. a.** 10^6 1,000,000   **3. a.** 10^5 100,000   **4. a.** 10^8
   b. 3×10^3 3000   **b.** 4×10^6 4,000,000   **b.** 2×10^5 200,000   **b.** 9×10^8
   c. 3.1×10^3 3100   **c.** 4.9×10^6 4,900,000   **c.** 2.1×10^5 210,000   **c.** 9.3×10^8

91

Write the number in scientific notation.

5. a. 10,000 1.0×10^4 **6. a.** 1000 1.0×10^3 **7. a.** 1,000,000 $^{1.0 \times 10^6}$ **8. a.** 100,000 1.0×10^5
   b. 50,000 5.0×10^4 **b.** 6000 6.0×10^3 **b.** 7,000,000 $^{7.0 \times 10^6}$ **b.** 400,000 4.0×10^5
   c. 51,000 5.1×10^4 **c.** 6100 6.1×10^3 **c.** 7,200,000 $^{7.2 \times 10^6}$ **c.** 432,000 4.32×10^5

Write the number in standard form.

B

  9300
9. 9.3×10^3

  810,000
10. 8.1×10^5

  17,000
11. 1.7×10^4

  3,000,000
12. 3.0×10^6

  180
13. 1.8×10^2

  76
14. 7.6×10^1

  380,000
15. 3.8×10^5

  690,000,000
16. 6.9×10^8

  3,900,000,000,000
17. 3.9×10^{12}

  92,000,000,000
18. 9.2×10^{10}

  7,100,000,000
19. 7.1×10^9

  8,500,000,000,000,000
20. 8.5×10^{15}

Write the underlined number in standard form.

21. An ocean sunfish may lay as many as $\underline{3.0 \times 10^8}$ eggs at one time. 300,000,000
22. There are about $\underline{3.9 \times 10^5}$ known types of plants in existence.   390,000
23. There are over $\underline{1.23 \times 10^6}$ known types of animals in existence.   1,230,000

Write the underlined number in scientific notation.

24. The deepest mine on Earth is the Western Deep Levels Mine in
the Transvaal, South Africa. It is $\underline{12,600}$ ft deep. 1.26×10^4
25. The temperature of Earth at its core is about $\underline{76000}$°F. 7.6×10^4
26. The maximum take-off weight of a "Jumbo Jet" is $\underline{775,000}$ lb. 7.75×10^5

Self Test 2

Solve by using a pattern.

1. January 1, 2000 will be a Saturday. On what day of the week will   **3-5**
July 3 be that year? (The year 2000 will be a leap year.)   Monday

Write the LCM of each set of expressions.

2. 60 and 72 $_{360}$ **3.** $3a$ and $2a$ $_{6a}$ **4.** $2b$, $6b^2$, and 8 $_{24b^2}$ **3-6**

Write the number in standard form.

5. 8.0×10^3 $_{8000}$ **6.** 1.7×10^5 $_{170,000}$ **7.** 9.4×10^8 $_{940,000,000}$ **3-7**

Write the number in scientific notation.

8. 2,800,000 $_{2.8 \times 10^6}$ **9.** 96,000 $_{9.6 \times 10^4}$ **10.** 54,000,000 $_{5.4 \times 10^7}$

Algebra Practice

Write an equation for the sentence. Solve the equation.

1. 2398 increased by 9746 is *r*. $2398 + 9746 = r$; 12,144

2. The difference between 5000 and 2509 is *a*. $5000 - 2509 = a$; 2491

3. The product of 780 and 67 is *m*. $780 \cdot 67 = m$; 52,260

4. 2 used as a factor 3 times is *w*. $2 \cdot 2 \cdot 2 = w$; 8

5. 2784 divided by 87 is equal to *f*. $2784 \div 87 = f$; 32

6. 1000 minus 19.65 is equal to *t*. $1000 - 19.65 = t$; 980.35

7. The numbers 1986.21, 8.005, and 497.6 add to a sum of *d*. $1986.21 + 8.005 + 497.6 = d$; 2491.815

8. The quotient of 1.424 and 1.6 is *n*. $\frac{1.424}{1.6} = n$; 0.89

9. 0.41 times 0.25 is equal to *y*. $(0.41)(0.25) = y$; 0.1025

Simplify the expression.

10. $6.8h + 2.5h$ 9.3h

11. $7.5a + 5.2b + 3.6a$ 11.1a + 5.2b

12. $12k - 8.53k$ 3.47k

13. $9.2p - 4.8q - 2.3p$ 6.9p − 4.8q

14. $8.63 - (2.08 + 3.5)$ 3.05

15. $14.2 - (0.33 \times 26.8)$ 5.356

Write the GCF of each set of expressions.

16. $3c^2$ and 6   3

17. $2r^3$ and $10r^2$ 2r²

18. $3h^2$, $12h$, and $9h^2$ 3h

19. $12m$ and $4m^2$ 4m

20. 14 and $2b^2$ 2

21. $4y^2$, $8y$, and $2xy$ 2y

Use the distributive property to factor each expression.

22. $30k^3 + 24k^2$ 6k²(5k + 4)

23. $2s^3 - 6s^2t + 10s$ 2s(s² − 3st + 5)

24. $3m^2 + 6n$ 3(m² + 2n)

25. $5b^3 - 15b$ 5b(b² − 3)

26. $4j^2k - (jk)^2 + jk^3$ jk(4j − jk + k²)

27. $(fg)^2 + f^2g - fg^2$ fg(fg + f − g)

28. $6mn^2 - 18m^2$ 6m(n² − 3m)

29. $8x^2y - (2x)^2 + 4xy^2$ 4x(2xy − x + y²)

30. $9a^2t^2 + 12at^2 - 15a^2t$ 3at(3at + 4t − 5a)

Write the LCM of each set of expressions.

31. w^2 and $3w$ 3w²

32. $2d$ and $8d^3$ 8d³

33. $3q$ and $5q^2$ 15q²

34. 15 and *a*   15a

35. $3k^2$ and *n*   3k²n

36. $5h^2$ and $7h$ 35h²

37. 12, $5d^2$, and $3d$ 60d²

38. $8y$, $6x$, and $3y$ 24xy

39. $10s$, r^2, and $4r$ 20r²s

40. $3m^2$, $6mn$, and m^2n^2 6m²n²

41. $4a^2b$, $12b^2$, and $16a^2$ 48a²b²

42. $5d$, $20h$, $4d^2h$ 20d²h

Problem Solving On The Job

Administrative Assistant

Judy Alison is administrative assistant to Mrs. Eastland, a senior vice-president at Hampton Associates.

```
ADMINISTRATIVE ASSISTANT

DESCRIPTION: Coordinate secretarial
services and handle details so that
the head person in an office can
attend to other matters.

QUALIFICATION: High school; college
or business school desirable; on-
the-job training

JOB OUTLOOK: Excellent opportuni-
ties for individuals who want to
work their way up
```

One of Judy's duties is to keep attendance records for all the staff in the office. Use the table below to do Exercises 1–9.

	Years of Service Completed	Days Absent This Year	
		Sickness	Vacation
Mike	2	0	5
Judy	4	3	6
Frank	5	1	3
Kim	1	5	1

Up to 10 days a year are allowed each person for sickness. How many more days are allowed each person for sickness this year?

1. Mike 10 days   **2.** Judy 7 days   **3.** Frank 9 days   **4.** Kim 5 days

5. If a person is absent from work for 2–4 hours, one-half day is deducted from the 10 days allowed for sickness. Because of a doctor's appointment. Mike was out of the office for 3 hours. How many more days is Mike allowed for sickness this year? $9\frac{1}{2}$ days

During the first two years of service, each person has 10 vacation days. After two years, 15 days are allowed. How many more days are allowed each person for vacation this year?

6. Mike 10 days   **7.** Judy 9 days   **8.** Frank 12 days   **9.** Kim 9 days

Mrs. Eastland has asked Judy to have copies of these documents made.

Document A: 2 pages, 100 copies   Document B: 32 pages, 15 copies
Document C: 10 pages, 125 copies   Document D: 60 pages, 10 copies

Sometimes Judy sends material to a copy center to be copied. For each page of a document, the copy center charges $.05 per page for the first 100 copies and $.03 per page for additional copies. The copy center will also assemble and staple the documents for $.03 per staple.

How much will it cost the company to have the documents copied, assembled and stapled at the copy center?

10. Document A $13   **11.** Document B $24.45   **12.** Document C $61.25   **13.** Document D $30.30

Judy calls The Temporary Agency for assistance when there is a work overload. The agency charges $7.10 an hour for a general typist and $11.50 an hour for a word processor operator (WP operator). How much does The Temporary Agency charge Hampton Associates each week?

14. Week 1:   **15.** Week 2:   **16.** Week 3:
     Typist: 18 hours $403.80   Typist: 30 hours $443.00   Typist: 8 hours $194.80
     WP operator: 24 hours   WP operator: 20 hours   WP operator: 12 hours

Mrs. Eastland is planning a conference for 50 people. It becomes Judy's job to make reservations for a meeting room and a catered lunch. Solve the problem.

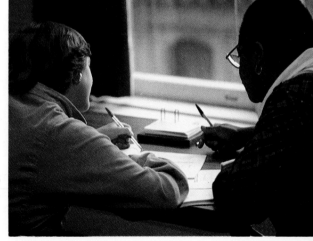

17. The Bay View Hotel charges $8.95 per person for lunch. There is no additional charge for the meeting room if lunch is served. If the conference is held at the Bay View Hotel, how much will it cost? $447.50

18. Renting a hall for one day costs $225. A caterer will serve lunch for $5.50 per person. If Judy $500.00 rents the hall for the conference and has the lunch catered, how much will it cost the company?

95

Enrichment

Arithmetic Sequences

In the sequence 3, 7, 11, 15, 19, . . . each term is obtained by adding 4 to the previous term. The difference between any two consecutive terms is 4.

$$3 \quad , \quad 7 \quad , \quad 11 \quad , \quad 15 \quad , \quad 19$$
$$+4 \qquad +4 \qquad +4 \qquad +4$$

Such a sequence is called an **arithmetic sequence** and 4 is called the **common difference.**

An arithmetic sequence is a sequence in which the difference obtained when any term is subtracted from the next is always the same number.

We can use a pattern to find the nth term of an arithmetic sequence. Suppose a is the first term of an arithmetic sequence. Then $a + d$ is the second term, and $a + d + d$ or $a + 2d$ is the third term, and so on. The coefficient of d is always 1 less than the number of the term. The sequence looks like this.

Term 1	Term 2	Term 3	Term 4	. . .	Term n
a	$a + 1d$	$a + 2d$	$a + 3d$	. . .	$a + (n - 1)d$

$$+d \qquad +d \qquad +d$$

We can find the 100th term of the sequence 3, 7, 11, 15, 19, ... The first term, a, is 3. The common difference, d, is 4.

nth term $= a + (n - 1)d$

100th term $= 3 + (100 - 1)\,4$ ← *Since we are looking for the*
$\qquad\qquad = 3 + (99)\,4$ *100th term, n is 100.*
$\qquad\qquad = 3 + 396$, or 399

Find the specified term of the sequence 5, 10, 15, 20, ...

1. 10th term 50 **2.** 50th term 250 **3.** 80th term 400 **4.** 200th term 1000

Find the 100th term of each sequence.

5. 1, 3, 5, 7, 9, . . . 199 **6.** $1.50, $3.00, $4.50, $6.00, . . . $150

96

Chapter Review

Match. An answer may be used more than once.

1. A number that is divisible by 6 and 10   c

2. A number that is divisible by 2 but not by 4   d

3. A number that is divisible by 3 and 5   c

4. An odd number that is not divisible by 3   b

5. An even number that is divisible by 5   c

a. 132
b. 91
c. 780
d. 98

Match. An answer may be used more than once.

6. The prime factorization of 60   c

7. The prime factorization of 108   d

8. The LCM of 12 and 15   c

9. The LCM of 36 and 27   d

10. The GCF of 54 and 162   a

11. The GCF of 48 and 144   e

12. Scientific notation for 2000   b

a. $2 \cdot 3^3$
b. $2 \cdot 10^3$
c. $2^2 \cdot 3 \cdot 5$
d. $2^2 \cdot 3^3$
e. $2^4 \cdot 3$

Use the distributive property to factor each expression.

13. $6a + 2$ $2(3a + 1)$ **14.** $5b^2 - b$ $b(5b - 1)$ **15.** $2c - 4c^2 + 6$ $2(c - 2c^2 + 3)$

True or False? Write *T* or *F*.

16. The LCM of $4x^2$ and $6x$ is $12x^2$. T

17. Standard notation for 2.8×10^5 is 2,800,000. F

18. Scientific notation for 57,000 is 57×10^3. F

19. The GCF of $32a^2$ and $18a$ is $2a$. T

20. An odd number is always 1 more than an even number. T

Solve by using a pattern.

21. A movie which lasts for 1 h 45 min starts at 1:15 P.M. and runs for 5 shows. There are 20 min between showings. At what time does the last show start? 9:35 P.M.

Chapter Test

Is the first number divisible by the second number? Answer *Yes* or *No*.

1. 528 by 4 yes **2.** 729 by 3 yes **3.** 1001 by 2 no **3-1**

4. 940 by 5 yes **5.** 765 by 10 no **6.** 94 by 6 no

Use exponents to write the prime factorization of each number.

7. 840 $2^3 \cdot 3 \cdot 5 \cdot 7$ **8.** 98 $2 \cdot 7^2$ **9.** 416 $2^5 \cdot 13$ **3-2**

Write the GCF of each set of expressions.

10. 12 and 20 4 **11.** 16 and 36 4 **12.** 15, 30, and 40 5 **3-3**

13. $2n$ and 8 2 **14.** a^2 and $2a$ a **15.** $3b^3$, $6b^2$, and 96 3 **3-4**

Use the distributive property to factor each expression.

16. $5x - 10$ $5(x - 2)$ **17.** $y^2 + 2y$ $y(y + 2)$ **18.** $4s^2 + 2s + 10$ $2(2s^2 + s + 5)$

19. $3m - 12m^2$ $3m(1 - 4m)$ **20.** $5h + 25h^2$ $5h(1 + 5h)$ **21.** $6d^2 - 18$ $6(d^2 - 3)$

Solve by using a pattern.

22. Subway trains leave Central Station for Uptown Station every **3-5**
4 min during rush hour. The trip takes 22 min. How many trips
are completed during a two-hour period? 25 trips

Write the LCM of each set of expressions.

23. 15 and 20 60 **24.** $2n$ and n^2 $2n^2$ **25.** 6, $2a$, and $4a^2$ $12a^2$ **3-6**

26. $3m$, $12m^2$, 4 $12m^2$ **27.** d^2, $5d$, 20 $20d^2$ **28.** 7, $14h^2$, $2h$ $14h^2$

Write the number in scientific notation.

29. 8,000,000 8.0×10^6 **30.** 1200 1.2×10^3 **31.** 93,000,000 9.3×10^7 **3-7**

32. 51,200 5.12×10^4 **33.** 806,000 8.06×10^5 **34.** 4,570,000 4.57×10^6

Write the number in standard form.

35. 2.0×10^3 2000 **36.** 4.9×10^5 490,000 **37.** 1.8×10^6 1,800,000

38. 6.2×10^4 62,000 **39.** 8.4×10^6 8,400,000 **40.** 1.1×10^7 11,000,000

Cumulative Review (Chapters 1–3)

Add, subtract, multiply, or divide.

1. 100×6.7 670

2. $356 \div 10$ 35.6

3. $2 \cdot 2 \cdot 2$ 8

4. $10 \cdot 10 \cdot 10 \cdot 10$ 10,000

5. $10 \cdot 10 \cdot 10 \cdot 10 \cdot 10$ 100,000

6. $(4.1 + 5)(2.01 - 1)$ 9.191

7. 5^3 125

8. $2^3 + 7$ 15

9. $10^2 + 7^2 - 6$ 143

10. $3 \times 12 \div 9$ 4

11. $4^2 \div 8 + 8$ 10

12. $21 - 3^2 \cdot 2$ 3

Simplify.

13. $4(a + 1) + a(7 - 3)$ $8a + 4$

14. $r(12 - 3) + 5(5 - r)$ $4r + 25$

15. $2p + 8y - p + 6y - 2$ $p + 14y - 2$

16. $(15 - 14)x + (8 + 9)x$ $18x$

17. $a \cdot 1 + 4a - b$ $5a - b$

18. $23s - (5)(s) + s(6 + 1)$ $25s$

Factor.

19. $3x + 3$ $3(x + 1)$

20. $9a - 9$ $9(a - 1)$

21. $8 - 2c$ $2(4 - c)$

22. $n^2 + n$ $n(n + 1)$

23. $5y^2 + 10$ $5(y^2 + 2)$

24. $6j^2 + 3j$ $3j(2j + 1)$

25. $6s^2 - 3s + 15$ $3(2s^2 - s + 5)$

26. $8p^2 - 8$ $8(p^2 - 1)$

27. $10f^2 + 5f - 25$ $5(2f^2 + f - 5)$

Write an expression for the phrase.

28. $2x$ increased by 9 $2x + 9$

29. 35 decreased by n $35 - n$

30. m greater than the sum of n and 17 $(n + 17) + m$

31. the sum of 12 and the product of 5 and y $12 + 5y$

Solve.

32. Chris is 5 years older than her sister Martha.
Let $y =$ Chris' age.
Then ___?___ = Martha's age. $y - 5$

33. It took a carpenter 3 weeks to complete a job.
Let $d =$ the number of days worked per week.
Then ___?___ = the number of days spent on the job. $3d$

34. For each hour of classroom time in a college course, students are expected to spend from 2 to $2\frac{1}{2}$ hours on homework. Libby spent 15 hours on homework for 8 hours of classroom time. Was her homework time within the expected range? no

4
Fractions

You can vary the length of a column of air inside a flute by opening and closing holes at different locations. One-half of the column will give a sound with pitch higher than the whole column.

4-1 Fraction Concept

On the number line below, the distance from 0 to 1 is divided into 8 equal parts. The distance from 0 to point P is five of those eight parts, or $\frac{5}{8}$ of the distance from 0 to 1.

Every fraction has a **numerator** and a **denominator**.

$$\frac{5}{8} \longleftarrow \begin{array}{l} numerator \\ denominator \end{array} \qquad \frac{x}{y} \longleftarrow \begin{array}{l} numerator \\ denominator \end{array}$$

The numerator of a fraction can be any whole number, while the denominator can be any whole number except zero. For the fraction $\frac{x}{y}$, y cannot be 0. We write $y \neq 0$ to mean y is not equal to zero.

You can see from the number line that $\frac{5}{8}$ is less than 1. Not all fractions are less than 1. Study the number line and notice that the fraction $\frac{8}{8}$ could replace the whole number 1. The fraction $\frac{8}{8}$ is an example of a fraction that is equal to 1.

The fact that $a \div b = \frac{a}{b}$ enables us to write other whole numbers as fractions.

$$\text{Since } 18 \div 6 = \frac{18}{6}, \frac{18}{6} = 3$$

$$\text{Since } 10 \div 1 = \frac{10}{1}, \frac{10}{1} = 10$$

$$\text{Since } 6 \div 6 = \frac{6}{6}, \frac{6}{6} = 1$$

In Arithmetic	In Algebra
$8 \div 8 = \frac{8}{8} = 1$	$x \div x = \frac{x}{x} = 1 \qquad (x \neq 0)$
$10 \div 1 = \frac{10}{1} = 10$	$y \div 1 = \frac{y}{1} = y$

The number line below is divided into sixths. We know that $\frac{6}{6}$ is 1. The fraction $\frac{7}{6}$, therefore, can be written as the mixed number $1\frac{1}{6}$.

The examples below show how to write a fraction as a mixed number and a mixed number as a fraction.

Example 1   Write $\dfrac{28}{9}$ as a mixed number.

Solution $\dfrac{28}{9}$ ▷ $9\overline{)\begin{array}{r} 3 \\ 28 \\ -27 \\ \hline 1 \end{array}}$ ▷ $3\dfrac{1}{9}$ ◀——— *Write the remainder as a fractional part of the divisor 9.*

Your Turn   • Write $\dfrac{35}{8}$ and $\dfrac{26}{9}$ as mixed numbers. $4\frac{3}{8}$; $2\frac{8}{9}$

Example 2   Write $3\dfrac{4}{5}$ as a fraction.   See p. T18

Solution $5 \times 3 = 15$ ◀——— *Multiply the denominator and the whole number.*

$15 + 4 = 19$ ◀——— *Add the numerator to the product.*

$\dfrac{19}{5}$ ◀——— *Write the sum over the denominator.*

Shortcut: $\dfrac{(5 \times 3) + 4}{5} = \dfrac{19}{5}$

Your Turn   • Write $6\dfrac{2}{7}$ and $8\dfrac{1}{6}$ as fractions. $\frac{44}{7}$; $\frac{49}{6}$

Class Exercises

Name the fraction at point *A*.

1.

$\frac{3}{8}$ 0 $\frac{1}{8}$ 1

2.

$\frac{7}{8}$ 0 $\frac{1}{8}$ 1

3.

$\frac{5}{9}$ 0 $\frac{1}{9}$ $\frac{8}{9}$

4.

$\frac{4}{7}$ 0 $\frac{1}{7}$

5.

$\frac{3}{2}$ 0 $\frac{1}{2}$ 1   2   3

6.

$\frac{11}{6}$ 0   1   2

Exercises

Write the whole number as a fraction. Use 1 as the denominator.

A **1.** 6 $\frac{6}{1}$ **2.** 7 $\frac{7}{1}$ **3.** 8 $\frac{8}{1}$ **4.** 9 $\frac{9}{1}$ **5.** 10 $\frac{10}{1}$ **6.** 11 $\frac{11}{1}$

7. 12 $\frac{12}{1}$ **8.** 13 $\frac{13}{1}$ **9.** 14 $\frac{14}{1}$ **10.** 15 $\frac{15}{1}$ **11.** 16 $\frac{16}{1}$ **12.** 17 $\frac{17}{1}$

Write as a fraction.

13. $4 \div 1$ $\frac{4}{1}$ **14.** $5 \div 3$ $\frac{5}{3}$ **15.** $7 \div 2$ $\frac{7}{2}$ **16.** $8 \div 5$ $\frac{8}{5}$ **17.** $9 \div 4$ $\frac{9}{4}$

18. $6 \div 7$ $\frac{6}{7}$ **19.** $8 \div 11$ $\frac{8}{11}$ **20.** $12 \div 11$ $\frac{12}{11}$ **21.** $5 \div 13$ $\frac{5}{13}$ **22.** $14 \div 6$ $\frac{14}{6}$

Write the mixed number as a fraction.

B **23.** $1\frac{1}{2}$ $\frac{3}{2}$ **24.** $1\frac{1}{3}$ $\frac{4}{3}$ **25.** $2\frac{1}{2}$ $\frac{5}{2}$ **26.** $2\frac{1}{3}$ $\frac{7}{3}$ **27.** $1\frac{1}{4}$ $\frac{5}{4}$

28. $2\frac{1}{4}$ $\frac{9}{4}$ **29.** $1\frac{3}{4}$ $\frac{7}{4}$ **30.** $2\frac{2}{3}$ $\frac{8}{3}$ **31.** $3\frac{1}{2}$ $\frac{7}{2}$ **32.** $2\frac{2}{5}$ $\frac{12}{5}$

Write a mixed number or a whole number for the variable.

33. $\frac{3}{2} = a$ $1\frac{1}{2}$ **34.** $\frac{4}{3} = b$ $1\frac{1}{3}$ **35.** $\frac{6}{5} = c$ $1\frac{1}{5}$ **36.** $\frac{7}{3} = d$ $2\frac{1}{3}$ **37.** $\frac{8}{4} = e$ 2

38. $\frac{9}{4} = f$ $2\frac{1}{4}$ **39.** $\frac{7}{1} = g$ 7 **40.** $\frac{9}{2} = h$ $4\frac{1}{2}$ **41.** $\frac{8}{1} = j$ 8 **42.** $\frac{10}{7} = k$ $1\frac{3}{7}$

103

Write a fraction for the variable.

43. $5\frac{1}{4} = l$ $\frac{21}{4}$ **44.** $3\frac{2}{5} = m$ $\frac{17}{5}$ **45.** $8\frac{1}{6} = n$ $\frac{49}{6}$ **46.** $7\frac{3}{5} = p$ $\frac{38}{5}$ **47.** $6\frac{2}{7} = q$ $\frac{44}{7}$

48. $9\frac{6}{7} = r$ $\frac{69}{7}$ **49.** $10\frac{3}{5} = s$ $\frac{53}{5}$ **50.** $11\frac{5}{8} = t$ $\frac{93}{8}$ **51.** $12\frac{9}{10} = v$ $\frac{129}{10}$ **52.** $13\frac{5}{9} = w$ $\frac{122}{9}$

Substitute. Write the fraction as a whole number or as a mixed number.

53. $\frac{a}{b}$ when $a = 5$ and $b = 4$ $\quad 1\frac{1}{4}$

54. $\frac{c}{d}$ when $c = 11$ and $d = 8$ $\quad 1\frac{3}{8}$

55. $\frac{e}{f}$ when $e = 12$ and $f = 5$ $\quad 2\frac{2}{5}$

56. $\frac{c}{h}$ when $c = 18$ and $h = 6$ $\quad 3$

57. $\frac{a}{p}$ when $a = 24$ and $p = 7$ $\quad 3\frac{3}{7}$

58. $\frac{e}{s}$ when $e = 36$ and $s = 1$ $\quad 36$

59. $\frac{t}{u}$ when $t = 32$ and $u = 16$ $\quad 2$

60. $\frac{l}{m}$ when $l = 14$ and $m = 13$ $\quad 1\frac{1}{13}$

61. $\frac{e}{d}$ when $e = 31$ and $d = 20$ $\quad 1\frac{11}{20}$

62. $\frac{c}{g}$ when $c = 35$ and $g = 35$ $\quad 1$

Problems

Three groups of people were asked if they would use Brite-White toothpaste. Write a fraction for the given response.

1. In a group of 21 people, n people answered yes. $\quad \frac{n}{21}$

2. In a group of x people, 15 people answered no. $\quad \frac{15}{x}$

3. In a group of 30 people, m people were undecided. $\quad \frac{m}{30}$

The first year class at the Taft School voted for a class president. The results were posted on the bulletin board as shown at the right.

4. What part of the class voted for Peter? $\quad \frac{20}{81}$

5. What part of the class voted for Helen? $\quad \frac{28}{81}$

6. What part of the class did not vote for Joel? $\quad \frac{64}{81}$

7. What part of the class did not vote for Marie? $\quad \frac{65}{81}$

8. Who got the larger fraction of the votes, Helen or Joel? Helen

9. Suppose every one voted for Helen. What fraction of the votes did she get? $\quad \frac{81}{81}$

Election Results	
Candidate	Votes
Helen Ling	28
Peter Allard	20
Joel Lopes	17
Marie Stevens	16

4-2 *Renaming Fractions*

When you rename a fraction you can either multiply or divide the numerator and the denominator by the same nonzero number. By doing so you do not actually change the value of the fraction. You simply find a fraction that is equal to the given fraction.

Example 1   Write a fraction that is equal to $\dfrac{7}{10}$.   See p. T18

Solution

$$\frac{7}{10} = \frac{7 \times 3}{10 \times 3} \longleftarrow \quad \textit{Multiply the numerator and the denominator by 3.}$$

$$= \frac{21}{30}$$

Here are other examples of fractions that are equal to $\frac{7}{10}$: $\frac{14}{20}$, $\frac{28}{40}$, and $\frac{35}{50}$.

When you divide to find an equal fraction, you rename the original fraction with a different numerator and denominator. If you divide by the greatest common factor (GCF), you rename the fraction in **lowest terms.**

Example 2   Write $\dfrac{16}{20}$ in the lowest terms.

Solution

$$\frac{16}{20} = \frac{16 \div 4}{20 \div 4} \longleftarrow \quad \textit{4 is the GCF of 16 and 20.}$$

$$= \frac{4}{5}$$

Here is a shortcut you may have learned before.

$$\frac{\overset{4}{\cancel{16}}}{\underset{5}{\cancel{20}}} = \frac{4}{5} \longleftarrow \quad \textit{If you cannot think of the GCF right away, you can do the division in several steps.}$$

105

You can also use the factors of the numerator and denominator to help you find a fraction in lowest terms.

Example 3   Write $\dfrac{18}{24}$ in lowest terms.

Solution $\dfrac{18}{24} = \dfrac{3 \cdot 2 \cdot 3}{2 \cdot 2 \cdot 2 \cdot 3}$ ⟵ *Notice that the GCF is 2 · 3.*

$$= \dfrac{3 \cdot \overset{1}{\cancel{2}} \cdot \overset{1}{\cancel{3}}}{2 \cdot 2 \cdot \underset{1}{\cancel{2}} \cdot \underset{1}{\cancel{3}}} = \dfrac{3}{4}$$

Example 4   Write $\dfrac{6x^2}{9x}$ in lowest terms.

Solution $\dfrac{6x^2}{9x} = \dfrac{\overset{2}{\cancel{6}} \cdot \overset{1}{\cancel{x}} \cdot x}{\underset{3}{\cancel{9}} \cdot \underset{1}{\cancel{x}}}$

$$= \dfrac{2x}{3}$$

Your Turn   Write the fraction in lowest terms.

- $\dfrac{2xy}{2x}$ y
- $\dfrac{4a}{8ab}$ $\dfrac{1}{2b}$
- $\dfrac{5ac^2}{10ac}$ $\dfrac{c}{2}$

Class Exercises

Complete.

1. $\dfrac{3 \times 2}{4 \times 2} = \dfrac{?}{8}$ 6

2. $\dfrac{1 \times ?}{3 \times 3} = \dfrac{3}{9}$ 3

3. $\dfrac{4 \times ?}{5 \times ?} = \dfrac{16}{20}$ $\dfrac{4}{4}$

4. $\dfrac{8 \div 2}{10 \div 2} = \dfrac{4}{?}$ 5

5. $\dfrac{7 \div ?}{14 \div ?} = \dfrac{1}{2}$ $\dfrac{7}{7}$

6. $\dfrac{16 \div ?}{20 \div ?} = \dfrac{4}{5}$ $\dfrac{4}{4}$

Exercises

Complete to find an equal fraction.

A **1.** $\dfrac{3}{7} = \dfrac{?}{14}$ 6   **2.** $\dfrac{4}{5} = \dfrac{?}{35}$ 28   **3.** $\dfrac{7}{9} = \dfrac{?}{63}$ 49   **4.** $\dfrac{5}{8} = \dfrac{?}{24}$ 15

5. $\dfrac{1}{14} = \dfrac{3}{?}$ 42   **6.** $\dfrac{7}{19} = \dfrac{14}{?}$ 38   **7.** $\dfrac{24}{36} = \dfrac{2}{?}$ 3   **8.** $\dfrac{56}{64} = \dfrac{?}{8}$ 7

Write in lowest terms.

9. $\dfrac{6}{9}$ $\dfrac{2}{3}$ **10.** $\dfrac{10}{12}$ $\dfrac{5}{6}$ **11.** $\dfrac{15}{30}$ $\dfrac{1}{2}$ **12.** $\dfrac{8}{20}$ $\dfrac{2}{5}$

13. $\dfrac{8}{32}$ $\dfrac{1}{4}$ **14.** $\dfrac{9}{24}$ $\dfrac{3}{8}$ **15.** $\dfrac{18}{12}$ $\dfrac{3}{2}$ **16.** $\dfrac{35}{21}$ $\dfrac{5}{3}$

B **17.** $\dfrac{x}{x}$ 1   **18.** $\dfrac{3y}{y}$ 3   **19.** $\dfrac{2b}{2}$ b **20.** $\dfrac{2a}{a}$ 2

21. $\dfrac{3}{6c}$ $\dfrac{1}{2c}$ **22.** $\dfrac{4}{4m}$ $\dfrac{1}{m}$ **23.** $\dfrac{2e}{4e}$ $\dfrac{1}{2}$ **24.** $\dfrac{10n}{5n}$ 2

25. $\dfrac{3xy}{3x}$ y **26.** $\dfrac{4st}{4s}$ t **27.** $\dfrac{2ab}{6b}$ $\dfrac{a}{3}$ **28.** $\dfrac{9cd}{3d}$ $3c$

29. $\dfrac{6mc}{9mc}$ $\dfrac{2}{3}$ **30.** $\dfrac{4nb}{12b}$ $\dfrac{n}{3}$ **31.** $\dfrac{10cv}{15v}$ $\dfrac{2c}{3}$ **32.** $\dfrac{7xu}{21x}$ $\dfrac{u}{3}$

33. $\dfrac{21t}{28t^2}$ $\dfrac{3}{4t}$ **34.** $\dfrac{8ax}{4a^2x}$ $\dfrac{2}{a}$ **35.** $\dfrac{9m^2b}{6m}$ $\dfrac{3mb}{2}$ **36.** $\dfrac{15cd^2}{10cd}$ $\dfrac{3d}{2}$

Simplify.

Example $\dfrac{6a + 12}{6} = \dfrac{6(a + 2)}{6} = a + 2$

C **37.** $\dfrac{3x + 3}{3}$ $x + 1$ **38.** $\dfrac{5n + n}{2n}$ 3   **39.** $\dfrac{7b + b}{b}$ 8   **40.** $\dfrac{2x + x}{x}$ 3

41. $\dfrac{8c + 4c}{4c}$ 3   **42.** $\dfrac{6a + 3a}{3a}$ 3   **43.** $\dfrac{2x}{4x + 2x}$ $\dfrac{1}{3}$ **44.** $\dfrac{10b}{5b + 5b}$ 1

45. $\dfrac{6r}{10r + 4}$ $\dfrac{3r}{5r + 2}$ **46.** $\dfrac{5d + 10}{15d}$ $\dfrac{d + 2}{3d}$ **47.** $\dfrac{12e + 4}{8}$ $\dfrac{3e + 1}{2}$ **48.** $\dfrac{16a}{4a + 8}$ $\dfrac{4a}{a + 2}$

4-3 Adding Fractions

Students at Eastdale High School are sponsoring concerts to buy band uniforms. Profits from the first concert paid for $\frac{1}{8}$ of the cost of the uniforms. Profits from the second concert paid for another $\frac{3}{8}$. What part of the cost of the uniforms is paid for by the two concerts?

To find the answer, you can add $\frac{1}{8}$ and $\frac{3}{8}$. We add fractions with like denominators by writing the sum of the numerators over the denominator.

In Arithmetic	In Algebra
$\dfrac{2}{5} + \dfrac{1}{5} = \dfrac{2+1}{5} = \dfrac{3}{5}$	$\dfrac{a}{c} + \dfrac{b}{c} = \dfrac{a+b}{c} \qquad (c \neq 0)$

Example 1 Solve $n = \dfrac{1}{8} + \dfrac{3}{8}$. Write the sum in lowest terms.

Solution $n = \dfrac{1+3}{8}$ ⟵ *Add the numerators.* See p. T18

$= \dfrac{4}{8} = \dfrac{1}{2}$

Example 2 Find the sum. $\dfrac{5}{a} + \dfrac{4}{a}$

Solution $\dfrac{5}{a} + \dfrac{4}{a} = \dfrac{5+4}{a} = \dfrac{9}{a}$ ⟵ *Add the numerators.*

To add fractions with different denominators we must first rewrite the fractions with a common denominator and then add. Try to choose the least common multiple (LCM) as the common denominator. We call that number the **least common denominator** (LCD).

Example 3 Write the sum of $\dfrac{5}{12}$ and $\dfrac{3}{8}$ in lowest terms.

Solution The LCM for 12 and 8 is 24, so the LCD is 24.

$$\frac{5}{12} = \frac{10}{24} \text{ and } \frac{3}{8} = \frac{9}{24}$$

$$\frac{10}{24} + \frac{9}{24} = \frac{19}{24} \longleftarrow \textit{Add the numerators.}$$

Example 4 Write the sum: $5\dfrac{3}{10} + 3\dfrac{2}{5}$.

Solution

$$
\begin{array}{r}
5\dfrac{3}{10} = 5\dfrac{3}{10} \\[2ex]
+3\dfrac{2}{5} = +3\dfrac{4}{10} \\[2ex]
\hline
8\dfrac{7}{10}
\end{array}
$$

Your Turn Find the sum.

- $2\dfrac{3}{4} + 3\dfrac{2}{3}$ $6\dfrac{5}{12}$
- $\dfrac{5}{d} + \dfrac{7}{d}$ $\dfrac{12}{d}$
- $\dfrac{e}{6} + \dfrac{e}{6}$ $\dfrac{e}{3}$

Class Exercises

Write the sum in lowest terms.

1. $\dfrac{2}{3} + \dfrac{4}{5}$ $1\dfrac{7}{15}$

2. $\dfrac{2}{3} + \dfrac{5}{8}$ $1\dfrac{7}{24}$

3. $\dfrac{3}{4} + \dfrac{7}{9}$ $1\dfrac{19}{36}$

4. $9 + \dfrac{4}{7}$ $9\dfrac{4}{7}$

5. $\dfrac{3}{4} + \dfrac{3}{5}$ $1\dfrac{7}{20}$

6. $\dfrac{7}{10} + 10$ $10\dfrac{7}{10}$

7. $\dfrac{11}{20} + \dfrac{3}{8}$ $\dfrac{37}{40}$

8. $\dfrac{4}{5} + 13$ $13\dfrac{4}{5}$

109

Exercises

Simplify the expression using the given value for the variable.

A 1. $5\frac{2}{9} + e;\ e = 4\frac{3}{8}$ $\quad 9\frac{43}{72}$

2. $6\frac{1}{7} + p;\ p = 3\frac{5}{8}$ $\quad 9\frac{43}{56}$

3. $2\frac{1}{12} + r;\ r = 4\frac{5}{8}$ $\quad 6\frac{17}{24}$

4. $3\frac{4}{11} + l;\ l = 5\frac{1}{4}$ $\quad 8\frac{27}{44}$

5. $4\frac{5}{11} + w;\ w = 6\frac{3}{8}$ $\quad 10\frac{73}{88}$

6. $8\frac{5}{6} + v;\ v = 4\frac{4}{9}$ $\quad 13\frac{5}{18}$

7. $b + 9\frac{4}{7};\ b = 3\frac{6}{7}$ $\quad 13\frac{3}{7}$

8. $a + 2\frac{7}{8};\ a = 7\frac{1}{12}$ $\quad 9\frac{23}{24}$

9. $c + 6\frac{1}{11};\ c = 4\frac{2}{3}$ $\quad 10\frac{25}{33}$

Is the first expression greater than the second expression? Guess first, then check your guess. Assume the variable is greater than zero.

B 10. $\dfrac{1}{x} + \dfrac{5}{x}$ $\qquad \dfrac{2}{x} + \dfrac{3}{x}$ $\quad$ yes

11. $\dfrac{3}{a} + \dfrac{5}{a}$ $\qquad \dfrac{1}{a} + \dfrac{3}{a} + \dfrac{2}{a}$ $\quad$ yes

12. $\dfrac{5y}{7} + \dfrac{2y}{7}$ $\qquad \dfrac{3y}{7} + \dfrac{y}{7}$ $\quad$ yes

13. $\dfrac{4e}{5} + \dfrac{e}{5}$ $\qquad \dfrac{2e}{5} + \dfrac{e}{5} + \dfrac{3e}{5}$ $\quad$ no

Find the sum.

14. $\dfrac{6}{a} + \dfrac{7}{b}$ $\quad \dfrac{6b + 7a}{ab}$

15. $\dfrac{8}{c} + \dfrac{2}{w}$ $\quad \dfrac{8w + 2c}{cw}$

16. $\dfrac{5}{m} + \dfrac{5}{r}$ $\quad \dfrac{5r + 5m}{mr}$

17. $\dfrac{3}{b} + \dfrac{2}{c}$ $\quad \dfrac{3c + 2b}{bc}$

18. $\dfrac{x}{2} + \dfrac{x}{3}$ $\quad \dfrac{5x}{6}$

19. $\dfrac{b}{4} + \dfrac{b}{8}$ $\quad \dfrac{3b}{8}$

20. $\dfrac{x}{2} + \dfrac{y}{3}$ $\quad \dfrac{3x + 2y}{6}$

21. $\dfrac{m}{10} + \dfrac{f}{5}$ $\quad \dfrac{m + 2f}{10}$

Problems

Write an equation. Solve.

1. The sum of $4\frac{1}{2}$ and $\frac{3}{5}$ is some number. What is it? $\quad 4\frac{1}{2} + \frac{3}{5} = n;\ 5\frac{1}{10}$

2. Some number is the total of 15 and $6\frac{5}{8}$. What is it? $\quad n = 15 + 6\frac{5}{8};\ 21\frac{5}{8}$

3. Brian bought $\frac{3}{4}$ lb of grapes and $\frac{1}{2}$ lb of plums. How many pounds of fruit did he buy? $\quad \frac{3}{4} + \frac{1}{2} = p;\ 1\frac{1}{4}$ lb

4. A board $\frac{3}{4}$ in. thick is placed on top of a board $\frac{5}{8}$ in. thick. What is the total thickness of the two boards? $\quad \frac{3}{4} + \frac{5}{8} = n;\ 1\frac{3}{8}$ in.

5. Beth cycled $\frac{5}{8}$ mi from home to school, $\frac{5}{6}$ mi from school to the library, $\frac{2}{3}$ mi from the library to work, and $\frac{1}{4}$ mi from work to her home. How many miles did Beth travel? $\quad \frac{5}{8} + \frac{5}{6} + \frac{2}{3} + \frac{1}{4} = m;\ 2\frac{3}{8}$ mi

4-4 Subtracting Fractions

The rules for subtracting fractions are similar to the rules for adding fractions. We subtract fractions with like denominators by writing the difference of the numerators over the denominator.

In Arithmetic	In Algebra
$\dfrac{5}{7} - \dfrac{3}{7} = \dfrac{5-3}{7} = \dfrac{2}{7}$	$\dfrac{a}{c} - \dfrac{b}{c} = \dfrac{a-b}{c} \qquad (c \neq 0)$

Example 1 Find the difference. $\dfrac{25}{a} - \dfrac{16}{a}$

Solution $\dfrac{25}{a} - \dfrac{16}{a} = \dfrac{25-16}{a}$ ⟵ *Subtract the numerators.*

$$= \dfrac{9}{a}$$

To subtract fractions with unlike denominators, we first rewrite the fractions with a common denominator, then subtract.

Example 2 Find the difference: $\dfrac{a}{4} - \dfrac{a}{6}$.

Solution The LCD is 12.

$\dfrac{a}{4} = \dfrac{?}{12}$ ⟵ *4 must be multiplied by 3 to get 12.*

$= \dfrac{3a}{12}$ ⟵ *So multiply a by 3 to get 3a.*

$\dfrac{a}{6} = \dfrac{2a}{12}$

$\dfrac{3a}{12} - \dfrac{2a}{12} = \dfrac{a}{12}$

Your Turn   Find the difference.

- $\dfrac{12}{x} - \dfrac{3}{x}$ $\dfrac{9}{x}$
- $\dfrac{5}{xy} - \dfrac{2}{xy}$ $\dfrac{3}{xy}$
- $\dfrac{2a}{4} - \dfrac{a}{5}$ $\dfrac{3a}{10}$

When you subtract mixed numbers you may have to regroup. A mixed number is said to be in simplest form if the fraction part is in lowest terms.

Example 3   Write the difference in simplest form.

$$8\dfrac{1}{3} - 6\dfrac{5}{7}$$

Solution $8\dfrac{1}{3} - 6\dfrac{5}{7}$ $\Rightarrow$ $8\dfrac{7}{21} - 6\dfrac{15}{21}$ $\longleftarrow$ *Rewrite $\dfrac{1}{3}$ and $\dfrac{5}{7}$ with the LCD.*

Write $8\dfrac{7}{21}$ as $7\dfrac{28}{21}$ so that you can subtract $\dfrac{15}{21}$ from $\dfrac{28}{21}$.

$$7\dfrac{28}{21} - 6\dfrac{15}{21} = 1\dfrac{13}{21}$$

Your Turn   Write the difference in simplest form.

- $\dfrac{b}{3} - \dfrac{b}{6}$ $\dfrac{b}{6}$
- $4\dfrac{2}{5} - 3\dfrac{4}{5}$ $\dfrac{3}{5}$
- $6\dfrac{1}{2} - 4\dfrac{3}{5}$ $1\dfrac{9}{10}$

$$\dfrac{2b - b}{6} = \dfrac{b}{6}$$

Class Exercises

Rewrite the fraction with the given denominator.

1. $\dfrac{a}{5} = \dfrac{?}{10}$ $2a$

2. $\dfrac{b}{6} = \dfrac{?}{12}$ $2b$

3. $\dfrac{c}{4} = \dfrac{?}{12}$ $3c$

4. $\dfrac{d}{3} = \dfrac{?}{18}$ $6d$

5. $2\dfrac{1}{4} = 1 + \dfrac{?}{4} + \dfrac{1}{4}$ 4

6. $3\dfrac{5}{6} = 2 + \dfrac{?}{6} + \dfrac{5}{6}$ 6

7. $4\dfrac{3}{8} = 3 + \dfrac{?}{8} + \dfrac{?}{8}$ $8; \dfrac{3}{8}$

8. $5\dfrac{1}{12} = \dfrac{?}{12} + \dfrac{12}{12} + \dfrac{1}{12}$ 4

9. $\dfrac{?}{11} = 6 + \dfrac{11}{11} + \dfrac{3}{11}$ $7\dfrac{3}{11}$

10. $\dfrac{?}{12} = 7 + \dfrac{12}{12} + \dfrac{7}{12}$ $8\dfrac{7}{12}$

Exercises

Write the difference in lowest terms.

A

1. $\dfrac{7}{6} - \dfrac{5}{6}$ $\quad \dfrac{1}{3}$
2. $\dfrac{5}{8} - \dfrac{2}{8}$ $\quad \dfrac{3}{8}$
3. $\dfrac{17}{10} - \dfrac{16}{10}$ $\quad \dfrac{1}{10}$
4. $\dfrac{11}{12} - \dfrac{4}{12}$ $\quad \dfrac{7}{12}$

5. $\dfrac{7}{10} - \dfrac{3}{10}$ $\quad \dfrac{2}{5}$
6. $\dfrac{11}{18} - \dfrac{5}{18}$ $\quad \dfrac{1}{3}$
7. $\dfrac{17}{15} - \dfrac{7}{15}$ $\quad \dfrac{2}{3}$
8. $\dfrac{23}{24} - \dfrac{5}{24}$ $\quad \dfrac{3}{4}$

9. $\dfrac{1}{2} - \dfrac{1}{20}$ $\quad \dfrac{9}{20}$
10. $\dfrac{6}{10} - \dfrac{1}{3}$ $\quad \dfrac{4}{15}$
11. $\dfrac{4}{7} - \dfrac{3}{14}$ $\quad \dfrac{5}{14}$
12. $\dfrac{5}{8} - \dfrac{11}{32}$ $\quad \dfrac{9}{32}$

B

13. $\dfrac{15}{y} - \dfrac{10}{y}$ $\quad \dfrac{5}{y}$
14. $\dfrac{31}{g} - \dfrac{29}{g}$ $\quad \dfrac{2}{g}$
15. $\dfrac{21}{s} - \dfrac{11}{s}$ $\quad \dfrac{10}{s}$
16. $\dfrac{32}{f} - \dfrac{29}{f}$ $\quad \dfrac{3}{f}$

17. $\dfrac{3a}{n} - \dfrac{2a}{n}$ $\quad \dfrac{a}{n}$
18. $\dfrac{4e}{q} - \dfrac{3e}{q}$ $\quad \dfrac{e}{q}$
19. $\dfrac{10m}{3} - \dfrac{10m}{3}$ $\quad 0$
20. $\dfrac{16r}{8} - \dfrac{9r}{8}$ $\quad \dfrac{7r}{8}$

21. $\dfrac{b}{3} - \dfrac{b}{9}$ $\quad \dfrac{2b}{9}$
22. $\dfrac{2r}{3} - \dfrac{r}{6}$ $\quad \dfrac{r}{2}$
23. $\dfrac{m}{6} - \dfrac{m}{8}$ $\quad \dfrac{m}{24}$
24. $\dfrac{3d}{4} - \dfrac{d}{12}$ $\quad \dfrac{2d}{3}$

Solve the equation. Write the difference in lowest terms.

25. $\dfrac{7}{8} - \dfrac{3}{24} = a$ $\quad \dfrac{3}{4}$
26. $\dfrac{5}{6} - \dfrac{2}{30} = b$ $\quad \dfrac{23}{30}$
27. $\dfrac{7}{10} - \dfrac{1}{4} = c$ $\quad \dfrac{9}{20}$
28. $\dfrac{11}{12} - \dfrac{3}{8} = d$ $\quad \dfrac{13}{24}$

29. $3\dfrac{1}{9} - 2\dfrac{2}{3} = j$ $\quad \dfrac{4}{9}$
30. $4\dfrac{1}{2} - 2\dfrac{3}{5} = k$ $\quad 1\dfrac{9}{10}$
31. $6\dfrac{3}{4} - 5\dfrac{1}{6} = l$ $\quad 1\dfrac{7}{12}$
32. $7\dfrac{1}{4} - 5\dfrac{5}{8} = m$ $\quad 1\dfrac{5}{8}$

33. $4\dfrac{7}{9} - 2\dfrac{3}{4} = n$ $\quad 2\dfrac{1}{36}$
34. $5\dfrac{3}{7} - 3\dfrac{2}{3} = p$ $\quad 1\dfrac{16}{21}$
35. $6\dfrac{2}{3} - 2\dfrac{2}{15} = q$ $\quad 4\dfrac{8}{15}$
36. $4\dfrac{1}{10} - 2\dfrac{3}{4} = r$ $\quad 1\dfrac{7}{20}$

Subtract.

Example $\dfrac{5n + 8}{6} - \dfrac{1}{6} = \dfrac{5n + 8 - 1}{6}$

$$= \dfrac{5n - 7}{6}$$

C

37. $\dfrac{7a + 5}{8} - \dfrac{1}{8}$ $\quad \dfrac{7a + 4}{8}$
38. $\dfrac{4b + 7}{9} - \dfrac{2}{9}$ $\quad \dfrac{4b + 5}{9}$
39. $\dfrac{8c + 5}{12} - \dfrac{c}{12}$ $\quad \dfrac{7c + 5}{12}$

40. $\dfrac{6a - 3}{3}$ $\quad 2a - 1$
41. $\dfrac{4a - 4b}{2}$ $\quad 2a - 2b$
42. $\dfrac{10x - 5m}{5}$ $\quad 2x - m$

Problems

Write an equation. Solve.

1. $4\frac{2}{3}$ decreased by $1\frac{1}{3}$ is what number? $\quad 4\frac{2}{3} - 1\frac{1}{3} = n;\ 3\frac{1}{3}$

2. $6\frac{4}{5}$ increased by $\frac{1}{2}$ is some number. What is it? $\quad 6\frac{4}{5} + \frac{1}{2} = n;\ 7\frac{3}{10}$

3. How much greater is $\frac{5}{8}$ than $\frac{1}{3}$? $\quad \frac{5}{8} - \frac{1}{3} = n;\ \frac{7}{24}$

4. The librarian shelved the books in $\frac{5}{6}$ h yesterday and in $\frac{3}{5}$ h today. Find the decrease in time, expressed as a fraction. $\quad \frac{5}{6} - \frac{3}{5} = n;\ \frac{7}{30}$ h

5. Joan jogged $\frac{7}{8}$ of a mile, and Sarah jogged $\frac{7}{10}$ of a mile. How much farther did Joan jog than Sarah? $\quad \frac{7}{8} - \frac{7}{10} = n;\ \frac{7}{40}$ mi

6. A nut has a center hole $\frac{21}{64}$ in. across. The hole must be enlarged to $\frac{3}{8}$ in. How much wider will the new hole be? $\quad \frac{3}{8} - \frac{21}{64} = n;\ \frac{3}{64}$ in.

Self Test 1

Write a fraction for the variable.

1. $7\frac{2}{3} = t \quad \frac{23}{3}$ 2. $4\frac{5}{6} = m \quad \frac{29}{6}$ 3. $5\frac{4}{9} = x \quad \frac{49}{9}$ 4. $10\frac{1}{7} = b \quad \frac{71}{7}$ **4-1**

Substitute. Write the fraction or whole number as a mixed number.

5. $\frac{x}{y}$ when $x = 21$ and $y = 10$ $\quad 2\frac{1}{10}$ 6. $\frac{c}{p}$ when $c = 24$ and $p = 8$ $\quad 3$

Write the fraction in lowest terms.

7. $\frac{12ab}{6ab}$ $\quad 2$ 8. $\frac{9dx^2}{3d}$ $\quad 3x^2$ 9. $\frac{7c^2m}{14cm}$ $\quad \frac{c}{2}$ 10. $\frac{10a}{16b}$ $\quad \frac{5a}{8b}$ **4-2**

Find the sum.

11. $\frac{5x}{8} + \frac{x}{8}$ $\quad \frac{3x}{4}$ 12. $\frac{6}{b} + \frac{7}{b}$ $\quad \frac{13}{b}$ 13. $\frac{10}{c} + \frac{1}{c}$ $\quad \frac{11}{c}$ **4-3**

Simplify the expression using the given value for the variable.

14. $y + 7\frac{3}{5};\ y = 2\frac{7}{15}$ $\quad 10\frac{1}{15}$ 15. $8\frac{3}{7} + p;\ p = \frac{5}{28}$ $\quad 8\frac{17}{28}$

Write the difference in lowest terms.

16. $\frac{12n}{r} - \frac{9n}{r}$ $\quad \frac{3n}{r}$ 17. $\frac{5s}{3} - \frac{3s}{8}$ $\quad \frac{31s}{24}$ 18. $10\frac{3}{16} - 8\frac{7}{12}$ $\quad 1\frac{29}{48}$ **4-4**

4-5 *Multiplying Fractions*

The average weight of a pilot whale is $\frac{3}{4}$ t.
You can find the weight of five pilot whales
by multiplying $\frac{3}{4}$ by 5. To multiply a fraction
and a whole number, you multiply the whole
number and the numerator and write the
product over the denominator.

Example 1 Solve $w = \frac{3}{4} \times 5$. Write the product in lowest terms.

See p. T19

Solution $w = \dfrac{3 \times 5}{4}$ ⟵——— *Multiply the numerator and the whole number.*

$= \dfrac{15}{4}$

$= 3\dfrac{3}{4}$ ⟵——— *Write $\dfrac{15}{4}$ in simplest form.*

You know that the whole number 5 can be written as a fraction. So, in Example 1 above, you could rewrite the equation as $w = \dfrac{3}{4} \times \dfrac{5}{1}$.

Example 2 Solve the equation. Write the product in lowest terms.
$$t = \frac{2}{3} \times \frac{7}{8}$$

See p. T19

Solution $t = \dfrac{2 \times 7}{3 \times 8}$ ⟵——— *Multiply the numerators. Multiply the denominators.*

$= \dfrac{14}{24} = \dfrac{7}{12}$

115

Notice that in Example 2 we could have divided by common factors before multiplying. When you divide first, the multiplication is usually made easier since you will be multiplying smaller numbers.

$$\frac{\overset{1}{\cancel{2}}}{3} \times \frac{7}{\underset{4}{\cancel{8}}} = \frac{1 \times 7}{3 \times 4} = \frac{7}{12} \longleftarrow$$

> Divide the numerator 2 and the denominator 8 by 2.

Example 3 Write the product in lowest terms.

$$2\frac{1}{2} \cdot \frac{x}{5}$$

Solution $$2\frac{1}{2} \cdot \frac{x}{5} = \frac{5}{2} \cdot \frac{x}{5} \longleftarrow \text{ Write } 2\frac{1}{2} \text{ as the fraction } \frac{5}{2}.$$

$$= \frac{\overset{1}{\cancel{5}}}{2} \cdot \frac{x}{\underset{1}{\cancel{5}}} = \frac{x}{2}$$

Your Turn Find the product in lowest terms.

- $\frac{4}{5} \times \frac{1}{2}$ $\frac{2}{5}$
- $3\frac{1}{2} \times \frac{a}{10}$ $\frac{7a}{20}$

In Arithmetic	In Algebra
$\frac{1}{2} \times \frac{3}{5} = \frac{1 \times 3}{2 \times 5} = \frac{3}{10}$	$\left(\frac{a}{b}\right) \cdot \left(\frac{c}{d}\right) = \frac{ac}{bd} \qquad (b \neq 0, d \neq 0)$

Class Exercises

Write the mixed number or whole number as a fraction.

1. $1\frac{1}{2}$ $\frac{3}{2}$

2. $2\frac{2}{3}$ $\frac{8}{3}$

3. $2\frac{3}{4}$ $\frac{11}{4}$

4. 3 $\frac{3}{1}$

5. $1\frac{4}{5}$ $\frac{9}{5}$

6. $2\frac{1}{4}$ $\frac{9}{4}$

7. 9 $\frac{9}{1}$

8. $3\frac{5}{6}$ $\frac{23}{6}$

9. $4\frac{2}{7}$ $\frac{30}{7}$

10. $4\frac{3}{8}$ $\frac{35}{8}$

Exercises

Write the product in lowest terms.

A **1.** $\dfrac{1}{2} \cdot 5$ $2\dfrac{1}{2}$

2. $\dfrac{1}{3} \cdot 8$ $2\dfrac{2}{3}$

3. $\dfrac{7}{12} \cdot 6$ $3\dfrac{1}{2}$

4. $3 \cdot \dfrac{2}{3}$ 2

5. $\dfrac{4}{7} \cdot 7$ 4

6. $\dfrac{3}{5} \cdot 15$ 9

7. $16 \cdot \dfrac{1}{16}$ 1

8. $6 \cdot \dfrac{7}{12}$ $3\dfrac{1}{2}$

9. $\dfrac{1}{2} \cdot \dfrac{2}{3}$ $\dfrac{1}{3}$

10. $\dfrac{1}{2} \cdot \dfrac{1}{4}$ $\dfrac{1}{8}$

11. $\dfrac{1}{2} \cdot \dfrac{1}{2}$ $\dfrac{1}{4}$

12. $\dfrac{1}{3} \cdot 3$ 1

Write the product in lowest terms.

B **13.** $\dfrac{1}{b} \cdot 8$ $\dfrac{8}{b}$

14. $\dfrac{9}{11} \cdot g$ $\dfrac{9g}{11}$

15. $\dfrac{7}{13} \cdot f$ $\dfrac{7f}{13}$

16. $\dfrac{x}{6} \cdot \dfrac{3}{x}$ $\dfrac{1}{2}$

17. $\dfrac{1}{b} \cdot \dfrac{b}{3}$ $\dfrac{1}{3}$

18. $\dfrac{2}{a} \cdot \dfrac{a}{8}$ $\dfrac{1}{4}$

19. $\dfrac{2c}{c} \cdot \dfrac{4e}{e}$ 8

20. $\dfrac{5}{d} \cdot \dfrac{2d}{15}$ $\dfrac{2}{3}$

21. $3\dfrac{1}{7} \cdot \dfrac{m}{3}$ $\dfrac{22m}{21}$

22. $2\dfrac{2}{3} \cdot \dfrac{3}{x}$ $\dfrac{8}{x}$

23. $3\dfrac{1}{3} \cdot \dfrac{b}{5}$ $\dfrac{2b}{3}$

24. $4\dfrac{1}{2} \cdot \dfrac{2}{y}$ $\dfrac{9}{y}$

Write the given expression as shown below.

Example $\dfrac{1}{2} \cdot x = \dfrac{1 \cdot x}{2} = \dfrac{x}{2}$

25. $\dfrac{1}{3} \cdot b$ $\dfrac{b}{3}$

26. $\dfrac{1}{5} \cdot c$ $\dfrac{c}{5}$

27. $\dfrac{1}{6} \cdot g$ $\dfrac{g}{6}$

28. $\dfrac{1}{7} \cdot p$ $\dfrac{p}{7}$

29. $\dfrac{1}{8} \cdot q$ $\dfrac{q}{8}$

Problems

Write an equation. Solve.

1. Twice $\frac{3}{4}$ is some number. What is the number? $2 \cdot \dfrac{3}{4} = n;\ 1\dfrac{1}{2}$
2. The product of $\frac{2}{3}$ and 20 is some number. What is the number? $\dfrac{2}{3} \cdot 20 = n;\ 13\dfrac{1}{3}$
3. 25 times $\frac{4}{5}$ is some number. What is the number? $25 \cdot \dfrac{4}{5} = n;\ 20$
4. A gas tank holds 18 gal of gasoline. When the tank is $\frac{3}{4}$ full, how many gallons does it contain? $\dfrac{3}{4} \cdot 18 = n;\ 13\dfrac{1}{2}$ gal
5. Twenty-five students in an art class were each given $\frac{2}{3}$ lb of clay. What was the total weight of the clay distributed to the 25 students?

$25 \cdot \dfrac{2}{3} = n;\ 16\dfrac{2}{3}$ lb   **117**

4-6 *Dividing Fractions*

Before you divide fractions and mixed numbers, it is useful to know about **reciprocals.** Two numbers are reciprocals if their product is 1. The numbers 4 and $\frac{1}{4}$ are reciprocals because $4 \times \frac{1}{4} = 1$. Since the product of 0 and another number is always 0 and never 1, the number 0 has no reciprocal.

Suppose you have to share $\frac{2}{3}$ of a lasagna equally among four people. You would write the problem as $\frac{2}{3} \div 4$.

Instead of dividing by 4, you could multiply by $\frac{1}{4}$, since dividing by a number is the same as multiplying by its reciprocal.

$$\frac{2}{3} \div 4 = \frac{2}{3} \times \frac{1}{4} = \frac{\overset{1}{2} \times 1}{3 \times \underset{2}{4}} = \frac{1}{6}$$

In Arithmetic

$$\frac{2}{3} \div \frac{4}{1} = \frac{2}{3} \times \frac{1}{4} = \frac{1}{6}$$

In Algebra

$$\frac{a}{b} \div \frac{d}{c} = \frac{a}{b} \times \frac{c}{d} \qquad (b \neq 0,\ c \neq 0,\ d \neq 0)$$

Example 1 Solve the equation. Write the quotient in lowest terms.

$$x = \frac{5}{16} \div 10$$

Solution $x = \dfrac{5}{16} \times \dfrac{1}{10}$ ⟵ *Dividing by 10 is the same as multiplying by $\frac{1}{10}$.*

$$= \frac{\overset{1}{5}}{16} \times \frac{1}{\underset{2}{10}}$$

$$x = \frac{1}{32}$$

Example 2 Write the quotient in lowest terms: $\dfrac{x}{5} \div x$.

Solution $\dfrac{x}{5} \div x = \dfrac{x}{5} \times \dfrac{1}{x}$ ⟵ *Dividing by x is the same as multiplying by $\dfrac{1}{x}$.*

$$\dfrac{\overset{1}{\cancel{x}}}{5} \times \dfrac{1}{\underset{1}{\cancel{x}}} = \dfrac{1}{5}$$

Your Turn Write the quotient in lowest terms.

- $\dfrac{4}{7} \div 4 \quad \dfrac{1}{7}$
- $\dfrac{d}{6} \div d \quad \dfrac{1}{6}$
- $\dfrac{5}{m} \div 10 \quad \dfrac{1}{2m}$

Class Exercises

Write the reciprocal.

1. $3 \quad \dfrac{1}{3}$ **2.** $5 \quad \dfrac{1}{5}$ **3.** $6 \quad \dfrac{1}{6}$ **4.** $7 \quad \dfrac{1}{7}$ **5.** $8 \quad \dfrac{1}{8}$ **6.** $10 \quad \dfrac{1}{10}$

7. $\dfrac{1}{2} \quad 2$ **8.** $\dfrac{3}{2} \quad \dfrac{2}{3}$ **9.** $\dfrac{4}{5} \quad \dfrac{5}{4}$ **10.** $\dfrac{4}{9} \quad \dfrac{9}{4}$ **11.** $\dfrac{7}{2} \quad \dfrac{2}{7}$ **12.** $\dfrac{14}{1} \quad \dfrac{1}{14}$

Exercises

Write the quotient in lowest terms.

A **1.** $\dfrac{1}{2} \div 3 \quad \dfrac{1}{6}$ **2.** $\dfrac{1}{3} \div 3 \quad \dfrac{1}{9}$ **3.** $\dfrac{1}{4} \div 5 \quad \dfrac{1}{20}$ **4.** $\dfrac{3}{4} \div 2 \quad \dfrac{3}{8}$

5. $\dfrac{2}{3} \div \dfrac{1}{5} \quad 3\dfrac{1}{3}$ **6.** $\dfrac{1}{4} \div \dfrac{3}{8} \quad \dfrac{2}{3}$ **7.** $\dfrac{7}{2} \div \dfrac{2}{3} \quad 5\dfrac{1}{4}$ **8.** $\dfrac{3}{5} \div \dfrac{1}{5} \quad 3$

9. $\dfrac{3}{8} \div \dfrac{3}{8} \quad 1$ **10.** $\dfrac{2}{5} \div \dfrac{4}{3} \quad \dfrac{3}{10}$ **11.** $\dfrac{3}{5} \div \dfrac{6}{15} \quad 1\dfrac{1}{2}$ **12.** $\dfrac{4}{7} \div \dfrac{1}{14} \quad 8$

B **13.** $4\dfrac{1}{2} \div \dfrac{9}{x} \quad \dfrac{x}{2}$ **14.** $3\dfrac{1}{4} \div \dfrac{4}{b} \quad \dfrac{13b}{16}$ **15.** $2\dfrac{1}{8} \div \dfrac{8}{c} \quad \dfrac{17c}{64}$ **16.** $4\dfrac{1}{6} \div \dfrac{m}{5} \quad \dfrac{125}{6m}$

17. $2\frac{1}{2} \div \frac{3}{2e}$ $\frac{5e}{3}$

18. $3\frac{1}{3} \div \frac{7f}{3}$ $\frac{10}{7f}$

19. $4\frac{1}{4} \div \frac{13}{4g}$ $\frac{17g}{13}$

20. $2\frac{1}{5} \div \frac{5}{6h}$ $\frac{66}{25h}$

21. $\frac{11}{10} \div \frac{7r}{2}$ $\frac{11}{35r}$

22. $2\frac{2}{5} \div \frac{3}{4n}$ $\frac{16n}{5}$

23. $2\frac{1}{16} \div \frac{9e}{4}$ $\frac{11}{12e}$

24. $1\frac{5}{6} \div \frac{11}{3b}$ $\frac{b}{2}$

Write the given expression with a fraction as the coefficient of the variable. Write the coefficient in lowest terms if possible.

Example $\quad 2a \div 3 = \frac{2a}{3} = \frac{2 \cdot a}{3} = \frac{2}{3}a$

25. $4b \div 5$ $\frac{4}{5}b$

26. $6x \div 7$ $\frac{6}{7}x$

27. $3m \div 8$ $\frac{3}{8}m$

28. $2b \div 6$ $\frac{1}{3}b$

29. $3m \div 9$ $\frac{1}{3}m$

30. $7e \div 14$ $\frac{1}{2}e$

31. $8r \div 14$ $\frac{4}{7}r$

32. $10p \div 30$ $\frac{1}{3}p$

Problems

Write an expression for the phrase.

1. The quotient of 24 divided by x. $\frac{24}{x}$

2. The quotient of some number divided by 16. $\frac{n}{16}$

Solve.

3. At the science fair, four students plan to display their exhibits on a table $18\frac{1}{2}$ ft long. How long will each section be if the students divide the space equally among themselves? $18\frac{1}{2} \div 4 = n;\ 4\frac{5}{8}$ ft

4. Joan plans to stake 5 tomato plants in her garden. How tall will each stake be if she cuts a pole $21\frac{1}{4}$ ft long into 5 stakes of equal length? $21\frac{1}{4} \div 5 = n;\ 4\frac{1}{4}$ ft

5. How many small pillows can be made from a piece of fabric that measures $3\frac{1}{3}$ yd? 4

6. How many large pillows can be made from $6\frac{2}{3}$ yd of fabric? 4

7. How many yards of fabric do you need for three large pillows and four small ones? $8\frac{1}{3}$ yd

Decorative Pillows
Material needed

$\frac{5}{6}$ yd (small pillow)

$1\frac{2}{3}$ yd (large pillow)

4-7 *Problem Solving*

Suppose that you are in charge of ordering ingredients for the "Potato Pancake Fest" your class is sponsoring. You know that 230 tickets have been sold. You also know that the recipe for 20 pancakes includes the ingredients listed below.

> **Potato Pancakes (makes 20)**
>
> 6 large potatoes   salt & pepper to taste
> 1 onion   2 T flour
> 2 eggs   2½ T vegetable oil

Using the information you know, you can work backward to determine the amount of each ingredient to buy. First, decide how many pancakes 230 people might eat. Let's say each person might eat 5.

$$230 \times 5 = 1150$$

Next, how many recipes of pancakes are needed to make 1150.

$$\begin{array}{c}\textit{pancakes needed} \longrightarrow \\ \textit{pancakes in 1 recipe} \longrightarrow\end{array} \frac{1150}{20} = 57\frac{1}{2}$$

You can now multiply the amount of ingredient in one recipe by the number of recipes to find the amount of each ingredient to buy.

Example 1 How many pounds of potatoes should you order if 6 large potatoes weigh about 2 lb?

Solution Use the information you know:
6 potatoes are needed for 1 recipe.
6 potatoes weigh about 2 lb.
$57\frac{1}{2}$ recipes are needed.

$$2 \times 57\frac{1}{2} = 115$$

So, you should order 115 lb of potatoes.

When you work backward to solve a problem, you often have to reverse the operation.

Example 2   Each year an automobile is worth about $\frac{4}{5}$ of what its value was the previous year. If an automobile is now worth $6000, what was its value last year?

Solution   You know that last year's value was multiplied by $\frac{4}{5}$ to get $6000.
Reverse the operation to find the value you want.

$$\$6000 \div \frac{4}{5} = \overset{1500}{\cancel{6000}} \times \frac{5}{\underset{1}{\cancel{4}}} = \$7500$$

Your Turn   • This year a machine is worth $\frac{3}{5}$ of what it was worth last year. If the machine is worth $1600 this year, what was it worth last year? $2666.67

Class Exercises

Write a new exercise by reversing the operation, then solve the new exercise.

$4\frac{1}{8} \times \frac{3}{5}; \; 2\frac{19}{40}$

1. $\$200 \times \dfrac{5}{3}$ $\$200 \div \frac{5}{3}; \$120$

2. 48×16 $48 \div 16; \; 3$

3. $4\dfrac{1}{8} \div \dfrac{3}{5}$

4. $24p \times 20p$ $24p \div 20p; \; 1\frac{1}{5}$

5. $15y \times 1\dfrac{1}{4}$ $15y \div 1\frac{1}{4}; \; 12y$

6. $\dfrac{9}{11} \div 3\dfrac{2}{3}$

$\dfrac{9}{11} \times 3\frac{2}{3}; \; 3$

Exercises

Solve. Use the recipe for potato pancakes to answer questions 1–2.

A   **1.** How many cups of vegetable oil do you need for 10 recipes, if 1 c contains 16 T? $1\frac{9}{16}$ c

2. If one carton contains 12 eggs, how many cartons of eggs do you need for 60 recipes? 10 cartons

B **3.** Each year a bicycle is worth about $\frac{3}{4}$ of its value the previous year. If a bicycle is now worth \$45, what was its value one year ago? Two years ago? $60; $80

4. A highway construction crew can build $\frac{3}{8}$ mi of highway per day. How many working days should be allowed to meet the time deadline for constructing 12 mi of highway? 32 days

5. Suppose that you have a minibike that can travel $24\frac{1}{2}$ mi on 1 qt of gas. You have $2\frac{1}{4}$ qt of gas and want to make a 52-mi trip without buying more gas. Can you make the trip? yes

6. The price of a Super Sedan is now $\frac{9}{5}$ times what the price was last year. If the sedan now sells for \$6700, what was last year's price? $3722.22

7. The price tag on a car stereo is now $\frac{5}{8}$ of last week's price. If the price is now \$230, what was last week's price? $368

8. A magazine club has 3125 subscribers this month. This is $\frac{1}{4}$ more than the number of subscribers last month. How many subscribers were there last month? 2500 subscribers

9. City Cab charges a flat fee of \$2.05 plus \$.15 for every $\frac{1}{6}$ mile. A City Cab driver charged Jane Norton a total of \$4.75 for a trip from her home to the airport. How many miles is Jane's home to the airport? 3 mi

10. An architect estimates that the average person in a dense crowd requires a fraction of a square yard of space. Based on this estimate she decided that a 4000 yd² shopping mall will hold 10,000 people. Find the fraction. $\frac{2}{5}$

4-8 Fractions and Decimals

The label on the package of ground beef that Jason bought reads 0.75 lb. Did he buy the amount of ground beef that is shown on the list?

To find out, we can change $\frac{3}{4}$ to a decimal and then compare.

$$\frac{3}{4} = 3 \div 4$$

$\frac{3}{4}$ lb is equal to 0.75 lb.

Jason's Shopping List

$\frac{3}{4}$ lb ground beef

$\frac{1}{2}$ gal milk

1 lb carrots

We say that $\frac{3}{4}$ is equal to the **terminating decimal** 0.75. Sometimes when we divide, the division process does not end.

Example 1   Write $\frac{3}{11}$ as a decimal.

Solution $\frac{3}{11} = 3 \div 11 = 0.2727\ldots$

You can see that $\frac{3}{11}$ is equal to the **repeating decimal** 0.2727 . . . We may write this decimal as $0.\overline{27}$. The bar indicates that 27 repeats.

A terminating decimal can be written as a fraction or mixed number. Such a fraction will have a power of 10 as its denominator.

Example 2   Write 0.352 as a fraction in lowest terms.

Solution $0.352 = \dfrac{352}{1000}$ ⟵———— *Remember that 0.352 is $\dfrac{352}{1000}$.*

$\qquad\qquad = \dfrac{352 \div 8}{1000 \div 8}$ ⟵———— *The GCF of 352 and 1000 is 8.*

$\qquad\qquad = \dfrac{44}{125}$

Your Turn Write as a fraction or as a decimal.

- $0.25 \; \frac{1}{4}$ - $\frac{2}{3} \; 0.\overline{6}$ - $\frac{5}{6} \; 0.8\overline{3}$

Class Exercises

Is the decimal repeating or terminating? Write R for repeating and T for terminating.

1. 0.4   T   **2.** 0.7   T   **3.** 0.10   T   **4.** 0.1$\overline{2}$ R   **5.** 018$\overline{6}$ R

6. 2.18   T   **7.** 4.27$\overline{33}$ R   **8.** 0.005   T   **9.** 7.19$\overline{93}$ R   **10.** 6.$\overline{6}$ R

Exercises

Write the fraction as a terminating or repeating decimal.

A   **1.** $\frac{5}{2}$ 2.5   **2.** $\frac{3}{20}$ 0.15   **3.** $\frac{6}{25}$ 0.24   **4.** $\frac{7}{11}$ 0.$\overline{63}$ **5.** $\frac{5}{8}$ 0.625

6. $\frac{4}{3}$ 1.$\overline{3}$ **7.** $\frac{5}{9}$ 0.$\overline{5}$ **8.** $\frac{7}{2}$ 3.5   **9.** $\frac{5}{4}$ 1.25   **10.** $\frac{3}{8}$ 0.375

11. $\frac{7}{8}$ 0.875   **12.** $\frac{5}{16}$ 0.3125   **13.** $\frac{4}{20}$ 0.2   **14.** $\frac{5}{12}$ 0.41$\overline{6}$ **15.** $\frac{7}{15}$ 0.4$\overline{6}$

Write the decimal as a fraction or mixed number in lowest terms.

16. 0.34 $\frac{17}{50}$ **17.** 0.96 $\frac{24}{25}$ **18.** 0.100 $\frac{1}{10}$ **19.** 0.220 $\frac{11}{50}$ **20.** 0.165 $\frac{33}{200}$

21. 0.37 $\frac{37}{100}$ **22.** 0.009 $\frac{9}{1000}$ **23.** 2.7 $2\frac{7}{10}$ **24.** 6.12 $6\frac{3}{25}$ **25.** 1.125 $1\frac{1}{8}$

26. 1.025 $1\frac{1}{40}$ **27.** 1.625 $1\frac{5}{8}$ **28.** 2.215 $2\frac{43}{200}$ **29.** 7.024 $7\frac{3}{125}$ **30.** 4.666 $4\frac{333}{500}$

Write a terminating or repeating decimal for the variable.

B   **31.** $\frac{32}{10} = a$ 3.2   **32.** $\frac{21}{16} = b$ 1.3125   **33.** $\frac{19}{11} = c$ 1.$\overline{72}$ **34.** $\frac{53}{30} = d$ 1.7$\overline{6}$ **35.** $\frac{41}{12} = e$ 3.41$\overline{6}$

36. $\frac{49}{25} = f$ 1.96   **37.** $\frac{87}{20} = g$ 4.35   **38.** $\frac{65}{40} = h$ 1.625   **39.** $\frac{77}{50} = j$ 1.54   **40.** $\frac{95}{45} = k$ 2.$\overline{1}$

If $x = 10$, write the fraction as a decimal.

41. $\frac{x}{15}$ 0.$\overline{6}$ **42.** $\frac{x}{25}$ 0.4   **43.** $\frac{x}{30}$ 0.$\overline{3}$ **44.** $\frac{x}{45}$ 0.$\overline{2}$ **45.** $\frac{x}{50}$ 0.2

Using the Computer

This program will change a fraction to a decimal. You will need to input the numerator and denominator separately. RUN it for 11/16 and 11/15 and then try some examples of your own.

```
 5  REM: CHANGING A FRACTION TO A DECIMAL
10  PRINT "WHAT IS THE NUMERATOR";
20  INPUT N
30  PRINT "WHAT IS THE DENOMINATOR";
40  INPUT D
50  PRINT N;" /";D;" =";N/D
60  END
```

What is the numerator? 11
What is the denominator? 16
11/16 = .6875
What is the numerator? 11
What is the denominator? 15
11/15 = .733333

Self Test 2

Write the product in lowest terms.

1. $\dfrac{7}{13} \cdot p$ $\dfrac{7p}{13}$

2. $10 \cdot \dfrac{x}{5}$ $2x$

3. $4\dfrac{4}{5} \cdot \dfrac{d}{12}$ $\dfrac{2d}{5}$ **4-5**

Write the quotient in lowest terms.

4. $\dfrac{5n}{6} \div \dfrac{18}{n}$ $\dfrac{5n^2}{108}$

5. $\dfrac{12b}{11} \div 7\dfrac{1}{3}$ $\dfrac{18b}{121}$

6. $\dfrac{8}{9}p \div 8p$ $\dfrac{1}{9}$ **4-6**

Work backward to find the answer.

7. A carton contains enough cereal mix to make $8\dfrac{1}{3}$ c of cooked cereal. The $8\dfrac{1}{3}$ c is enough for $12\dfrac{1}{2}$ servings. How many cups of cereal is one serving? $\dfrac{2}{3}$ c   **4-7**

Write a terminating or repeating decimal for the variable.

8. $\dfrac{2}{33} = w$ $0.\overline{06}$

9. $\dfrac{7}{40} = y$ 0.175

10. $\dfrac{9}{16} = h$ 0.5625 **4-8**

Write a fraction or mixed number for the variable.

11. $b = 0.59$ $\dfrac{59}{100}$

12. $d = 0.010$ $\dfrac{1}{100}$

13. $f = 5.65$ $5\dfrac{13}{20}$

126 *Self Test answers and Extra Practice are at the back of the book.*

Algebra Practice

Solve.

1. $12 = 12r$ 1   **2.** $63 = 63 + q$ 0   **3.** $3 + 5 \times 2$ 13

4. $4 + 4 \times 4 \div 4$ 8   **5.** $4 + 4 \div 4 - 4$ 1   **6.** $4 \times 4 + 4 \div 4$ 17

Use the distributive property to factor each expression.

           $3b(b^2 + 2c + 5)$ $rs(rs + 2s + 5r^2)$ $jk(3k + jk + 2j)$

7. $3b^3 + 6bc + 15b$ **8.** $(rs)^2 + 2rs^2 + 5r^3s$ **9.** $3jk^2 + (jk)^2 + 2j^2k$

Write the LCM of each set of expressions.

                                                                      $10m^2n$

10. 12 and $9x$ $36x$ **11.** $3a$, $4b$, and $6a^2$ $12a^2b$ **12.** m^2n, $5m$, and $2n$

Substitute. Write the fraction as a whole number or as a mixed number.

13. $\dfrac{c}{r}$ when $c = 28$ and $r = 14$ 2   **14.** $\dfrac{y}{m}$ when $y = 13$ and $m = 4$ $3\frac{1}{4}$

Write the fraction in lowest terms.

15. $\dfrac{18}{3b}$ $\dfrac{6}{b}$ **16.** $\dfrac{17h}{2h}$ $8\frac{1}{2}$ **17.** $\dfrac{d^2e}{de^2}$ $\dfrac{d}{e}$ **18.** $\dfrac{15c^3}{10cf}$ $\dfrac{3c^2}{2f}$

Write an equation. Solve.

19. The difference between 4073 and 2981 is a. $4073 - 2981 = a$; 1092

20. 7680 increased by 1979 is equal to g. $7680 + 1979 = g$; 9659

21. The quotient of 9632 and 112 is u. $9632 \div 112 = u$; 86

22. 7.18 times 6.82 is equal to n. $(7.18)(6.82) = n$; 48.9676

23. The sum of 86.28, 100.5, and 1.097 is t. $86.28 + 100.5 + 1.097 = t$; 187.877

24. 2.3018 divided by 0.17 is equal to r. $2.3018 \div 0.17 = r$; 13.54

25. Some number is the sum of $2\frac{1}{3}$ and $1\frac{1}{4}$. $n = 2\frac{1}{3} + 1\frac{1}{4}$; $3\frac{7}{12}$

26. How much greater is $\dfrac{11}{16}$ than $\dfrac{17}{32}$? $\dfrac{11}{16} - \dfrac{17}{32} = n$; $\dfrac{5}{32}$

27. The product of $\dfrac{3}{4}$ and 18 is some number. $\dfrac{3}{4} \cdot 18 = n$; $13\frac{1}{2}$

28. The quotient of $4\frac{3}{8}$ divided by $1\frac{3}{4}$ is some number. $4\frac{3}{8} \div 1\frac{3}{4} = n$; $2\frac{1}{2}$

29. $2\frac{2}{5}$ multiplied by $1\frac{7}{8}$ is some number. $2\frac{2}{5} \cdot 1\frac{7}{8} = n$; $4\frac{1}{2}$

30. $4\frac{1}{5}$ divided by $1\frac{1}{3}$ is some number. $4\frac{1}{5} \div 1\frac{1}{3} = n$; $3\frac{3}{20}$

Problem Solving for the Consumer

Investing in Stocks

A shareholder, or stockholder, is a person who buys one or more shares of stock in a corporation. A share of stock represents part ownership in a corporation. Stock prices are published each day in the business sections of daily newspapers. Prices are usually quoted in eighths of a dollar. Below is a listing of stocks.

Stock	Open	High	Low	Close	Chg	
Balloongram	$64\frac{5}{8}$	$65\frac{1}{2}$	$64\frac{3}{8}$	$64\frac{1}{2}$	$-\frac{1}{8}$	⟵ *The price of stock went down.*
NJK	$98\frac{1}{2}$	$100\frac{1}{8}$	98	$98\frac{1}{8}$	$-\frac{3}{8}$	
ECO	$25\frac{1}{8}$	$26\frac{3}{8}$	25	$25\frac{3}{4}$	$+\frac{5}{8}$	⟵ *The price of stock went up.*
Winter Ice	$30\frac{3}{8}$	$31\frac{1}{8}$	$30\frac{3}{8}$	$30\frac{3}{4}$	$+\frac{3}{8}$	
Fructose	$36\frac{3}{4}$	$36\frac{3}{4}$	$35\frac{1}{2}$	$35\frac{1}{2}$	$-1\frac{1}{4}$	
Tots	49	$50\frac{1}{2}$	$48\frac{3}{4}$	49	0	
Techtron	$36\frac{7}{8}$	39	$36\frac{7}{8}$	$38\frac{1}{8}$	$+1\frac{1}{4}$	
Reliable Motors	$64\frac{1}{2}$	$65\frac{1}{2}$	$64\frac{3}{8}$	$64\frac{1}{2}$	0	
Windpower Electric	$42\frac{3}{4}$	$44\frac{7}{8}$	$42\frac{3}{4}$	$43\frac{3}{4}$	$+1$	
Top Notch Equipment	$96\frac{3}{8}$	$101\frac{1}{4}$	$95\frac{5}{8}$	99	$+2\frac{5}{8}$	

Notice that Winter Ice's highest and lowest prices for the day were $31\frac{1}{8}$ and $30\frac{3}{8}$. The stock opened at $30\frac{3}{8}$ and closed at $30\frac{3}{4}$. The closing price was $\frac{3}{8}$ higher than the closing price on the previous day. If you owned 100 shares of Winter Ice's stock, the value of your investment would have increased $\frac{3}{8}$ per share that day.

$$\$\frac{3}{8} \cdot 100 = \frac{300}{8} = \$37.50$$

Use the stock price listing to give the answer.

1. Write the closing price of NJK. $\$98\frac{1}{8}$
2. Write the high price of Tots. $\$50\frac{1}{2}$
3. Write the low price of Reliable Motors. $\$64\frac{3}{8}$
4. Write the opening price of Top Notch Equipment. $\$96\frac{3}{8}$

5. Find the difference between the high and low prices of Reliable Motors. $1\frac{1}{8}$
6. If you owned 30 shares of Techtron, how much would your investment have increased between closing times? $52.50
7. If you owned 40 shares of ECO, what was the highest value of your investment during the day? $1055
8. What would it have cost you to purchase 10 shares of Tots at its low price? $487.50
9. If you had $500 to buy stock, how many shares of Windpower Electric could you have purchased at its opening price? 11 shares
10. Fructose stock opened at $36\frac{3}{4}$ and closed at $35\frac{1}{2}$. Did the value increase or decrease during that day? By how much did it increase or decrease? decrease; $1\frac{1}{4}$

When a stock splits "*n* for 1", the number of shares are multiplied by *n*, and the price is divided by *n*, so that the stockholders investment keeps its value.

Use the low price from the listing to find the value for the stock split.

Example   Suppose a stockholder owns 10 shares of a stock at $60 per share. The value is $60 · 10, or $600. If the stock splits 3 for 1, the stockholder now owns 10 · 3, or 30 shares. The value is $\frac{\$60}{3}$ · 30, or $600.

11. ECO: 4 for 1
10 shares $250

12. Tots: 2 for 1
10 shares $487.50

13. NJK: $1\frac{1}{2}$ for 1
10 shares $980

Enrichment

Repeating Decimals as Fractions

You have seen that every terminating decimal can be written as a fraction. Repeating decimals can also be written as fractions. One method for finding a fraction for a repeating decimal is shown below. Study each step carefully.

Write $7.\overline{82}$ as a fraction in lowest terms.

Step 1: Write an equation using n to represent the fraction you want to find.
$n = 7.\overline{82}$ or $n = 7.82\overline{82}$ ⟵ *82 is called the repetend because it repeats.*

Step 2: Since there are two digits in the repetend, we multiply both sides of the equation by 10^2 or 100.
$n \cdot 100 = 7.82\overline{82} \cdot 100$
$100n = 782.\overline{82}$ ⟵ *The decimal point moves two places to the right.*

Step 3: Subtract the original equation from the new equation.
$100n = 782.\overline{82}$
$\underline{-n = \quad 7.\overline{82}}$
$99n = 775$

Step 4: Solve $99n = 775$ ⟵ *Divide by 99 to solve for* n.
$n = \dfrac{775}{99}$ ⟵ $\dfrac{775}{99}$ *is already in lowest terms.*

Check: Divide 775 by 99. ⟹
$$
\begin{array}{r}
7.82 \\
99{\overline{\smash{\big)}\,775.00}} \\
\underline{693} \\
82\,0 \\
\underline{79\,2} \\
2\,80 \\
\underline{1\,98} \\
82
\end{array}
$$

Write each repeating decimal as a fraction in lowest terms.

1. $0.\overline{3}$ $\frac{1}{3}$
2. $0.\overline{9}$ $\frac{9}{9}$ or $\frac{1}{1}$
3. $1.\overline{2}$ $\frac{11}{9}$
4. $3.\overline{4}$ $\frac{31}{9}$
5. $2.\overline{35}$ $\frac{233}{99}$

6. $7.\overline{19}$ $\frac{712}{99}$
7. $0.\overline{62}$ $\frac{62}{99}$
8. $8.\overline{07}$ $\frac{799}{99}$
9. $2.\overline{135}$ $\frac{711}{333}$
10. $4.\overline{731}$ $\frac{4727}{999}$

Chapter Review

Match.

1. a fraction that equals 1   f   **a.** $\dfrac{21}{11}$

2. $2\dfrac{1}{9}$ expressed as a fraction   h

    b. $\dfrac{7}{8}$

3. $\dfrac{21}{10}$ expressed as a mixed number   e

    c. $3\dfrac{1}{8}$

4. $\dfrac{7}{25}$ expressed as a terminating decimal   g

    d. $0.8\overline{3}$

5. 3.125 expressed as a mixed number   c   **e.** $2\dfrac{1}{10}$

6. 0.875 expressed as a fraction   b

    f. $\dfrac{871}{871}$

7. $\dfrac{5}{6}$ expressed as a repeating decimal   d

    g. 0.28

8. the reciprocal of $\dfrac{11}{21}$ a   **h.** $\dfrac{19}{9}$

Choose the answer that renames the expression. Write a, b, or c.

9. $\dfrac{12}{4x}$ b   **a.** $\dfrac{1}{3x}$ **b.** $\dfrac{3}{x}$ **c.** $\dfrac{3}{4}$

10. $\dfrac{17df}{d^2f}$ a   **a.** $\dfrac{17}{d}$ **b.** $\dfrac{17}{f}$ **c.** $\dfrac{17}{df}$

11. $\dfrac{18em^2}{24em}$ c   **a.** $\dfrac{18}{24}$ **b.** $\dfrac{2m}{3}$ **c.** $\dfrac{3m}{4}$

Solve.

12. $\dfrac{3}{x} + \dfrac{8}{x}$ $\dfrac{11}{x}$ 13. $\dfrac{c}{8} + \dfrac{3c}{8}$ $\dfrac{c}{2}$ 14. $\dfrac{9x}{n} - \dfrac{5x}{n}$ $\dfrac{4x}{n}$ 15. $\dfrac{7r}{8} - \dfrac{5r}{12}$ $\dfrac{11r}{24}$

16. $5\dfrac{1}{2} \cdot \dfrac{2}{y}$ $\dfrac{11}{y}$ 17. $\dfrac{4b}{b} \cdot \dfrac{4c}{c}$ 16   18. $\dfrac{3n}{8} \div \dfrac{n}{16}$ 6   19. $\dfrac{m^2r}{r} \div mr$ $\dfrac{m}{r}$

Simplify the expression using the given value for the variable.

20. $g + 4\dfrac{5}{9}$; $g = 2\dfrac{3}{4}$ $7\dfrac{11}{36}$ 21. $m + \dfrac{14}{15}$; $m = 1\dfrac{2}{5}$ $2\dfrac{1}{3}$ 22. $k + 4\dfrac{1}{6}$; $k = \dfrac{6}{7}$ $5\dfrac{1}{42}$

23. $8\dfrac{3}{7} - p$; $p = 7\dfrac{1}{14}$ $1\dfrac{5}{14}$ 24. $4\dfrac{5}{12} - y$; $y = 1\dfrac{2}{9}$ $3\dfrac{7}{36}$ 25. $10\dfrac{1}{4} - t$; $t = \dfrac{9}{10}$ $9\dfrac{7}{20}$

Chapter Test

Write a fraction for the variable.

1. $8\dfrac{2}{3} = m$ $\;\;\frac{26}{3}$ **2.** $9\dfrac{1}{5} = t$ $\;\;\frac{46}{5}$ **3.** $7\dfrac{3}{4} = a$ $\;\;\frac{31}{4}$ **4.** $6\dfrac{10}{11} = b$ $\;\;\frac{76}{11}$ **4-1**

Write a mixed number or a whole number for the variable.

5. $c = \dfrac{7}{3}$ $\;\;2\frac{1}{3}$ **6.** $d = \dfrac{8}{5}$ $\;\;1\frac{3}{5}$ **7.** $f = \dfrac{10}{2}$ $\;\;5$ **8.** $g = \dfrac{16}{1}$ $\;\;16$

Write the fraction in lowest terms.

9. $\dfrac{10x}{12xy}$ $\;\;\frac{5}{6y}$ **10.** $\dfrac{7ab}{14b}$ $\;\;\frac{a}{2}$ **11.** $\dfrac{18cd^2}{16cd}$ $\;\;\frac{9d}{8}$ **12.** $\dfrac{9f^2}{27f}$ $\;\;\frac{f}{3}$ **4-2**

Find the sum.

13. $\dfrac{4}{c} + \dfrac{6}{c} + \dfrac{1}{c}$ $\;\;\frac{11}{c}$ **14.** $\dfrac{2f}{5} + \dfrac{3f}{5} + \dfrac{f}{5}$ $\;\;\frac{6f}{5}$ **15.** $\dfrac{0}{a} + \dfrac{1}{a} + \dfrac{7}{a}$ $\;\;\frac{8}{a}$ **4-3**

Simplify the expression using the given value for the variable.

16. $4\dfrac{5}{7} + y; y = 1\dfrac{3}{14}$ $\;\;5\frac{13}{14}$ **17.** $p + 3\dfrac{4}{9}; p = 2\dfrac{1}{6}$ $\;\;5\frac{11}{18}$

Write the difference in lowest terms.

18. $\dfrac{9m}{x} - \dfrac{7m}{x}$ $\;\;\frac{2m}{x}$ **19.** $\dfrac{3b}{4} - \dfrac{2b}{8}$ $\;\;\frac{b}{2}$ **20.** $9\dfrac{5}{6} - 7\dfrac{4}{5}$ $\;\;2\frac{1}{30}$ **4-4**

Write the product in lowest terms.

21. $15 \cdot \dfrac{b}{3}$ $\;\;5b$ **22.** $\dfrac{x}{14} \cdot \dfrac{7}{2x}$ $\;\;\frac{1}{4}$ **23.** $\dfrac{t}{20} \cdot 2\dfrac{2}{9}$ $\;\;\frac{t}{9}$ **4-5**

Write the quotient in lowest terms.

24. $\dfrac{3r}{8} \div 2\dfrac{1}{2}$ $\;\;\frac{3r}{20}$ **25.** $4\dfrac{1}{6} \div \dfrac{5}{2x}$ $\;\;\frac{5x}{3}$ **26.** $\dfrac{4}{7}p \div 4p$ $\;\;\frac{1}{7}$ **4-6**

Work backward to find the answer.

27. Susan Chu can drive 304 mi on a full tank of gasoline. On the average, she can drive 22 mi on a gallon of gasoline. How many gallons of gasoline does the gas tank of Susan's car hold? $13\frac{9}{11}$ gallons **4-7**

Write a terminating or repeating decimal for the variable.

28. $\dfrac{12}{25} = y$ $\;\;0.48$ **29.** $\dfrac{3}{16} = p$ $\;\;0.1875$ **30.** $\dfrac{5}{11} = j$ $\;\;0.\overline{45}$ **4-8**

Cumulative Review (Chapters 1–4)

Solve the equation.

1. $17.4 \div 10 = y$ 1.74
2. $x = (4.82)(4)$ 19.28
3. $12 + 18 - 12 = m$ 18

4. $17.1 \div 3.8 = s$ 4.5
5. $5^2 - 2^2 = r$ 21
6. $(3.2 + 4)(1.8 - 1) = y$ 5.76

7. $\dfrac{1}{3} + \dfrac{2}{3} = n$ 1
8. $w = \dfrac{3}{8} \times \dfrac{2}{3}$ $\dfrac{1}{4}$
9. $\dfrac{1}{2} \times \dfrac{2}{5} = k$ $\dfrac{1}{5}$

10. $j = \dfrac{3}{4} \div \dfrac{3}{5}$ $1\dfrac{1}{4}$
11. $1\dfrac{1}{2} + 6\dfrac{3}{4} = m$ $8\dfrac{1}{4}$
12. $x = 12 \div \dfrac{6}{7}$ 14

13. $15 \cdot \dfrac{1}{15} + \dfrac{2}{5} = n$ $1\dfrac{2}{5}$
14. $\dfrac{4}{5} \cdot \dfrac{10}{13} = c$ $\dfrac{8}{13}$
15. $y = 1\dfrac{2}{3} \div 3$ $\dfrac{5}{9}$

16. $\dfrac{3}{8} \times \dfrac{8}{3} = s$ 1
17. $16.3 + \dfrac{1}{3} - 16.3 = p$ $\dfrac{1}{3}$
18. $25 \cdot \dfrac{1}{25} + 50 = a$ 51

Simplify.

19. $8y - 2x - 6y + 13x$ $2y + 11x$
20. $9m - 6 + 7m - 7m$ $9m - 6$
21. $12 - 6p + 6p$ 12

22. $x \div x$ 1
23. $5 + 6n - 5$ $6n$
24. $2x + 3y + z - x$ $x + 3y + z$

25. $4x(x + 1)$ $4x^2 + 4x$
26. $12r - 8 + 8$ $12r$
27. $9(x - 2)$ $9x - 18$

28. $4 \cdot \dfrac{1}{r}$ $\dfrac{4}{r}$
29. $\dfrac{1}{8} \cdot d$ $\dfrac{d}{8}$
30. $s \cdot \dfrac{1}{4}$ $\dfrac{s}{4}$

31. $\dfrac{24x^2}{x}$ $24x$
32. $\dfrac{12n^2}{3n}$ $4n$
33. $\dfrac{5ab}{20a^2b}$ $\dfrac{1}{4a}$

Solve.

34. The temperature at 9:00 A.M. was 68°.
    The temperature at 2:00 P.M. went up to t degrees.
    Then __?__ = the number of degrees the temperature went up. $t - 68$
35. The average family throws out 17 lb of trash per day.
    Let t = time in days.
    Then __?__ = amount of trash it throws out in t days. $17t$
36. A dime is about 1 mm thick. If a stack of dimes is 3 cm high, about how many dimes are in the stack?   30 dimes
37. Every two years Jo has to pay to register her car in her state. Last year the charge was $14. The cost has been increasing $2 every year. At this rate, how much will Jo be charged the next time she registers? the time after that? $18; $22

5
Solving Equations

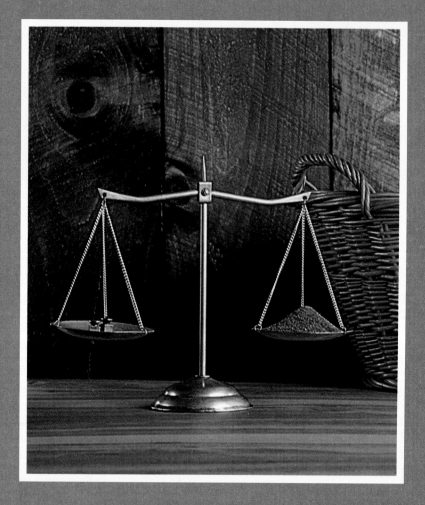

Most American cookbooks use volume measure for the ingredients of recipes. Did you know, however, that European cooks and professional chefs often use balance scales to measure their ingredients?

5-1 Equations

A statement that two expressions are equal is called an **equation.** A set of scales in balance can be used to picture an equation.

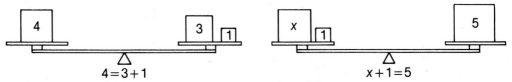

$$4 = 3 + 1 \qquad\qquad x + 1 = 5$$

Some equations, like $x + 1 = 5$, contain a **variable.** If you substitute 4 for x in the equation $x + 1 = 5$, the scales are in balance and the equation is true. The number 4 is called the **solution** of $x + 1 = 5$. We write $x = 4$.

Example 1 Is 3 a solution of $5 + y = 7$?

Solution Substitute 3 for y in the equation.

$$5 + y = 7$$

$$
\begin{array}{c|c}
5 + 3 & 7 \\
\hline
8 & 7
\end{array}
$$

$8 \neq 7 \longleftarrow \neq$ *means is not equal to*

So 3 is not a solution and $y \neq 3$.

Example 2 Is 2 a solution of $5 + y = 7$?

Solution Substitute 2 for y in the equation.

$$5 + y = 7$$

$$
\begin{array}{c|c}
5 + 2 & 7 \\
\hline
7 & 7
\end{array}
$$

$7 = 7 \;\; \checkmark$

So 2 is a solution and $y = 2$.

Your Turn
- Is 2 a solution of $x + 8 = 10$? yes
- Is 10 a solution of $n - 5 = 7$? no
- Is 3 a solution of $5x = 15$? yes

Example 3 Solve $c - 5 = 13$.

Solution What number minus 5 equals 13?
$18 - 5 = 13$
So, $c = 18$.

Example 4 Solve $12 = 2x$.

Solution 12 equals 2 times what number?
$12 = 2 \cdot 6$
So, $x = 6$.

Your Turn
- Solve $3h = 15$. 5
- Solve $10 = y - 4$. 14
- Solve $\frac{1}{2}z = 20$. 40

Class Exercises

Is 5 a solution of the equation?

1. $x + 1 = 6$ yes
2. $y - 4 = 10$ no
3. $20 = 5z$ no
4. $5 - n = 3$ no

5. $2 + a = 3$ no
6. $3b = 15$ yes
7. $\frac{1}{4}c = 20$ no
8. $p + 7 = 8$ no

Solve the equation.

9. $p - 2 = 8$ 10
10. $4q = 20$ 5
11. $3 + r = 9$ 6
12. $q - 4 = 5$ 9

13. $10u = 30$ 3
14. $32 = 8v$ 4
15. $\frac{w}{2} = 7$ 14
16. $7s = 14$ 2

Exercises

Is the given number a solution of the equation? Write *Yes* or *No*.

A **1.** $2a = 16$; 8 yes   **2.** $b + 9 = 10$; 9 no   **3.** $g - 6 = 37$; 31 no

4. $81 = 3x$; 6 no   **5.** $39 = d - 12$; 27 no   **6.** $4h = 56$; 14 yes

7. $4 + e = 28$; 32 no   **8.** $2f = 46$; 23 yes   **9.** $3x = 21$; 24 no

Solve the equation.

10. $k + 9 = 15$ 6   **11.** $m - 4 = 12$ 16   **12.** $3n = 36$ 12   **13.** $\frac{1}{2}p = 6$ 12

14. $4 + q = 6$ 2   **15.** $15 = r - 5$ 20   **16.** $16 = 8s$ 2   **17.** $u - 7 = 3$ 10

Tell which of the numbers is a solution.

B **18.** $48 = x + 9$ 39 or 57? 39   **19.** $a - 7 = 75$ 82 or 68? 82

20. $124 = 4b$ 31 or 120? 31   **21.** $\frac{1}{2}c = 80$ 40 or 160? 160

22. $2f + 1 = 5$ 2 or 3? 2   **23.** $7 = 3g - 2$ 3 or 5? 3

24. $5(h + 2) = 30$ 4 or 8? 4   **25.** $2k + 8 = 12$ 1 or 2? 2

26. $5(q - 3) = 0$ 3 or 12? 3   **27.** $2r + 9 = 19$ 3 or 5? 5

Solve the equation.

28. $24 + a = 32$ 8   **29.** $46 = 2b$ 23   **30.** $c + 17 = 100$ 83   **31.** $d - 30 = 66$ 96

32. $e + 13 = 51$ 38   **33.** $5f = 65$ 13   **34.** $130 = 13g$ 10   **35.** $\frac{h}{3} = 10$ 30

36. $j + 25 = 52$ 27   **37.** $16 - k = 9$ 7   **38.** $64 = m - 14$ 78   **39.** $r + 7 = 92$ 85

These equations have fractions or decimals. Solve.

40. $\frac{1}{5}x = 20$ 100   **41.** $y - 0.1 = 2.1$ 2.2 **42.** $v + \frac{1}{2} = 39\frac{1}{2}$ 39   **43.** $s + 1.3 = 2.9$ 1.6

44. $4\frac{1}{4} = q - \frac{1}{2}$ $4\frac{3}{4}$ **45.** $1 = 2p$ $\frac{1}{2}$ **46.** $2r = 1.6$ 0.8   **47.** $\frac{2}{3}w = 2$ 3

Answers may vary. One possible
Write another equation that has the same solution. equation is given for each exercise.

C **48.** $a + 8 = 10$ **49.** $12 = \frac{1}{2}e$ **50.** $7c = 35$ $\frac{1}{5}c = 1$ **51.** $8 - d = 7$
       $a + 10 = 12$ $2e + 36 = 60$ $d + 7 = 8$

137

5-2 *Using Subtraction*

Julie wants to weigh her puppy. When she holds the puppy and steps on the scale, the scale shows 54 lb. Julie knows that she weighs 48 lb. How much does the puppy weigh?

$$\text{Puppy's weight} + \text{Julie's weight} = 54 \text{ lb}$$
$$p \quad + \quad 48 \quad = 54$$

To solve an equation like $p + 48 = 54$, you can picture a two-pan balance scale.

If you remove 48 lb from each side, the scales remain in balance. Likewise, if you subtract 48 from each side of the equation, the equation remains true.

$$p + 48 - 48 = 54 - 48$$
$$p + 0 = 6$$
$$p = 6$$

Julie's puppy weighs 6 lb.

Example 1 Solve $a + 4 = 27$.

Solution
$$a + 4 = 27$$
$$a + 4 - 4 = 27 - 4 \longleftarrow \text{ To "undo" addition of 4,}$$
$$a + 0 = 23 \qquad\qquad \text{you subtract 4.}$$
$$a = 23$$

Example 2 Solve $7 + b = 37$. Check the solution.

Solution
$$7 + b = 37$$
$$7 + b - 7 = 37 - 7$$
$$b = 30$$

Check:

$7 + b = 37$	
$7 + 30$	37
37	37
$37 = 37$	$\checkmark$

So $b = 30$.

Your Turn
- Solve $c + 9 = 49$. Check the solution. 40; $40 + 9 = 49$
- Solve $6 + d = 58$. Check the solution. 52; $6 + 52 = 58$
- Solve $18 = 9 + e$. Check the solution. 9; $18 = 9 + 9$

Class Exercises

Tell what number must be subtracted from each side of the equation to solve for x.

1. $x + 3 = 5$ 3
2. $x + 7 = 19$ 7
3. $x + 6 = 21$ 6
4. $9 + x = 25$ 9

5. $6 + x = 37$ 6
6. $54 = x + 13$ 13
7. $8 + x = 10$ 8
8. $30 = 29 + x$ 29

Exercises

Solve the equation. Check the solution.

A **1.** $a + 2 = 11$ 9 **2.** $b + 5 = 9$ 4 **3.** $7 + c = 12$ 5 **4.** $d + 8 = 15$ 7

5. $13 = 9 + e$ 4 **6.** $f + 6 = 20$ 14 **7.** $9 + g = 15$ 6 **8.** $21 = h + 10$ 11

9. $4 + j = 6$ 2 **10.** $k + 3 = 9$ 6 **11.** $6 + m = 7$ 1 **12.** $4 + p = 10$ 6

13. $5 = 1 + q$ 4 **14.** $10 + r = 23$ 13 **15.** $9 + s = 20$ 11 **16.** $17 = 9 + v$ 8

B **17.** $96 + a = 99$ 3 **18.** $63 = 17 + b$ 46 **19.** $c + 12 = 51$ 39 **20.** $d + 7 = 104$ 97

21. $e + 17 = 33$ 16 **22.** $29 + f = 72$ 43 **23.** $37 = 19 + g$ 18 **24.** $8 + h = 126$ 118

25. $j + 9 = 206$ 197 **26.** $113 = 29 + k$ 84 **27.** $852 = 9 + m$ 843 **28.** $37 + n = 94$ 57

29. $p + 17 = 36$ 19 **30.** $12 + q = 41$ 29 **31.** $104 + r = 117$ 13 **32.** $300 = 52 + s$ 248

These equations have fractions and decimals. Solve and check.

33. $8.8 = b + 3.3$ 5.5
34. $3.1 + u = 9.3$ 6.2
35. $9.9 + v = 10.0$ 0.1

36. $7\frac{2}{3} = w + 3\frac{1}{3}$ $4\frac{1}{3}$
37. $x + 4\frac{1}{2} = 9\frac{3}{4}$ $5\frac{1}{4}$
38. $0.81 = 0.06 + y$ 0.75

39. $c + \frac{1}{2} = 3\frac{1}{2}$ 3
40. $a + 8.8 = 16.16$ 7.36
41. $9.75 + a = 12.99$ 3.24

C **42.** In the equation $x + a = b$, b is greater than a. State a rule you can use to solve the equation for x. $x = b - a$; subtract a from b

5-3 *Using Division*

A pair of running shoes weighs 800 g. How much does each shoe weigh?

Of course you can solve this problem by dividing 800 by 2. We can also show how to solve it by writing an equation with a variable.

Let *s* represent the weight of one shoe. Then 2*s* represents the weight of the pair. So 2*s* equals 800.

To solve the equation $2s = 800$, you can divide each side of the equation by 2. Then *s* equals 400. Each shoe weighs 400 g.

$$2s = 800$$
$$\frac{2s}{2} = \frac{800}{2}$$
$$s = 400$$

Some equations can be solved by dividing each side by the same non-zero number. Division by a non-zero number "undoes" multiplication by that number.

Example 1 Solve $24 = 4y$.

Solution
$$24 = 4y$$
$$\frac{24}{4} = \frac{4y}{4} \longleftarrow \quad \textit{To "undo" multiplication by 4, divide by 4.}$$
$$6 = 1y$$
$$6 = y$$

Example 2   Solve $2a = 9$. Check the solution.

Solution $2a = 9$

$$\frac{2a}{2} = \frac{9}{2}$$

$$a = 4\frac{1}{2}$$

Check: $2a = 9$

$$2 \cdot 4\frac{1}{2} \quad \bigg| \quad 9$$

$$9 \quad \bigg| \quad 9$$

$$9 = 9 \quad \checkmark$$

Your Turn   • Solve $5b = 30$. Check the solution. $6; 5(6) = 30$
   • Solve $27 = 3c$. Check the solution. $9; 27 = 3(9)$
   • Solve $9d = 152$. Check the solution. $16\frac{8}{9}; 9\left(\frac{152}{9}\right) = 152$

How can you tell which operation to use to solve an equation?
Remember to use the opposite operation.

Example 3   Solve $8d = 40$ and $e + 3 = 12$.

Solution   You must "undo" the operation performed on the variable.

$$8d = 40 \qquad\qquad\qquad e + 3 = 12$$

To "undo" multiplication
by 8, divide by 8.

$$\frac{8d}{8} = \frac{40}{8}$$

$$d = 5$$

To "undo" addition of 3,
subtract 3.

$$e + 3 - 3 = 12 - 3$$

$$e = 9$$

Your Turn   • To solve $5p = 20$, would you subtract 5 from each
     side, or would you divide each side by 5? Solve the
     equation.   divide by 5; 4
   • To solve $s + 10 = 16$ would you subtract 10 from
     each side, or would you divide each side by 10? Solve
     the equation.   subtract 10; 6

141

Class Exercises

You are to solve for *x*. By what number would you divide each side of the equation?

1. $5x = 35$ 5   **2.** $24 = 3x$ 3   **3.** $7x = 14$ 7   **4.** $4x = 48$ 4

5. $27 = 9x$ 9   **6.** $80 = 8x$ 8   **7.** $13x = 13$ 13   **8.** $30 = 2x$ 2

Exercises

Use division to solve. Check the solution.

A

1. $2b = 6$ 3   **2.** $18 = 9c$ 2   **3.** $8d = 48$ 6   **4.** $5e = 15$ 3

5. $72 = 8f$ 9   **6.** $3g = 12$ 4   **7.** $2h = 8$ 4   **8.** $5j = 35$ 7

9. $3k = 21$ 7   **10.** $20 = 4m$ 5   **11.** $10n = 65$ 6.5   **12.** $8p = 12$ $1\frac{1}{2}$

Solve. Check the solution.

B

13. $9a = 270$ 30   **14.** $186 = 6b$ 31   **15.** $15c = 75$ 5   **16.** $11d = 913$ 83

17. $244 = 4e$ 61   **18.** $93 = 31f$ 3   **19.** $14g = 420$ 30   **20.** $9h = 972$ 108

21. $25j = 175$ 7   **22.** $640 = 16k$ 40   **23.** $960 = 30m$ 32   **24.** $40n = 1600$ 40

25. $65p = 130$ 2   **26.** $75q = 600$ 8   **27.** $360 = 18r$ 20   **28.** $19s = 76$ 4

These equations have fractions or decimals. Solve and check.

29. $6a = 7.2$ 1.2   **30.** $4.5 = 15w$ 0.3   **31.** $0.6m = 120$ 200   **32.** $1.2q = 36$ 30

33. $1.8 = 0.2x$ 9   **34.** $0.01y = 2$ 200   **35.** $1.4d = 28$ 20   **36.** $15 = 0.5r$ 30

37. $\frac{1}{2}n = 8$ 16   **38.** $\frac{4}{5} = 2e$ $\frac{2}{5}$ **39.** $\frac{1}{3}q = 4$ 12   **40.** $18 = \frac{1}{4}s$ 72

Decide which operation to use. Solve and check.

41. $10u = 400$ 40   **42.** $v + 16 = 25$ 9   **43.** $16 + s = 29$ 13   **44.** $1100 = 20t$ 55

45. $20x = 160$ 8   **46.** $12 + y = 48$ 36   **47.** $19 = j + 19$ 0   **48.** $12k = 84$ 7

Solve and check.

C

49. $\frac{2}{3}p = 165$ $247\frac{1}{2}$ **50.** $\frac{3}{4}q = 180$ 240   **51.** $\frac{1}{2}x = 4\frac{1}{2}$ 9

52. $3p + p = 16$ 4   **53.** $4d - 3 + 2d = 5$ $1\frac{1}{3}$ **54.** $9d - 3d = 30 + d$ 6

5-4 *Using Addition*

To solve an equation like $x + 3 = 8$, we subtracted 3 from each side of the equation. Subtracting 3 is the opposite of adding 3.

$$\frac{x+3-3 \qquad\qquad 8-3}{\triangle}$$

$$x + 3 = 8$$
$$x + 3 - 3 = 8 - 3$$
$$x + 0 = 5$$
$$x = 5$$

In the equation $y - 7 = 9$, the number 7 is subtracted from y. To "undo" the subtraction of 7, we add 7 to each side of the equation.

$$\frac{y-7+7 \qquad\qquad 9+7}{\triangle}$$

$$y - 7 = 9$$
$$y - 7 + 7 = 9 + 7$$
$$y + 0 = 16$$
$$y = 16$$

Example Solve $a - 8 = 37$. Check the solution.

Solution

$$a - 8 = 37$$
$$a - 8 + 8 = 37 + 8$$
$$a = 45$$

Check: $a - 8 = 37$

$45 - 8$	37
37	37
$37 = 37$ ✓	

Your Turn
- Solve $a - 4 = 22$. Check the solution. 26; $26 - 4 = 22$
- Solve $29 = c - 7$. Check the solution. 36; $29 = 36 - 7$

Class Exercises

You are to solve for x. Tell what number you would add to each side of the equation.

1. $x - 4 = 6$ 4   **2.** $12 = x - 10$ 10   **3.** $2 = x - 9$ 9   **4.** $x - 8 = 72$ 8

5. $14 = x - 19$ 19   **6.** $100 = x - 32$ 32   **7.** $x - 3 = 5$ 3   **8.** $x - 1 = 8$ 1

143

Exercises

You are to solve the equation for *n*. What number must you add to each side of the equation?

A **1.** $n - 6 = 7$ 6   **2.** $n - 3 = 7$ 3   **3.** $12 = n - 5$ 5   **4.** $n - 10 = 7$ 10

    5. $6 = n - 14$ 14   **6.** $n - 6 = 14$ 6   **7.** $n - 18 = 2$ 18   **8.** $3 = n - 5$ 5

B **9–16.** Solve the equations in Exercises 1–8.   **9.** 13   **10.** 10   **11.** 17   **12.** 17
                                            13. 20   **14.** 20   **15.** 20   **16.** 8

Solve and check.

17. $a - 7 = 39$ 46   **18.** $84 = b - 19$ 103   **19.** $c - 201 = 10$ 211   **20.** $d - 13 = 156$ 169

21. $13 = e - 47$ 60   **22.** $117 = f - 39$ 156   **23.** $g - 32 = 68$ 100   **24.** $79 = h - 57$ 136

25. $112 = j - 14$ 126   **26.** $k - 76 = 52$ 128   **27.** $m - 61 = 80$ 141   **28.** $p - 17 = 118$ 135

These equations have fractions or decimals. Solve and check.

29. $\dfrac{2}{3} = a - \dfrac{1}{3}$ 1   **30.** $b - \dfrac{1}{2} = 1\dfrac{1}{2}$ 2   **31.** $5 = c - \dfrac{1}{4}$ $5\dfrac{1}{4}$ **32.** $d - \dfrac{1}{10} = \dfrac{3}{10}$ $\dfrac{2}{5}$

33. $e - 1.2 = 3.8$ 5   **34.** $f - 1 = 3.6$ 4.6   **35.** $4.5 = g - 0.5$ 5   **36.** $0.01 = h - 1.10$ 1.11

Solve and check.

37. $4p = 64$ 16   **38.** $5 + q = 82$ 77   **39.** $71 = r - 3$ 74   **40.** $17h = 51$ 3

41. $8 + v = 102$ 94   **42.** $91 = w - 16$ 107   **43.** $x - 21 = 52$ 73   **44.** $a - 9 = 73$ 82

45. $b - 3.9 = 7.1$ 11   **46.** $c + 8.5 = 10$ 1.5   **47.** $1.2d = 0.84$ 0.7   **48.** $84 = 0.7h$ 120

Problems

Write an expression for the number described.

1. 5 times a number *n* $5n$ **2.** 3 less than the number *p* $p - 3$

3. 5 more than the number *x* $x + 5$ **4.** a third of the number *q* $\dfrac{1}{3}q$

Solve.

5. Pat delivered 16 papers more than Mike.
Pat delivered 71 papers. In the equation $m + 16 = 71$, *m* represents the number of papers that Mike delivered. Solve the equation for *m*. 55 papers

5-5 *Using Multiplication*

Nurses must record the pulse rate of patients often. Instead of counting the number of heartbeats in a minute, often they count the number of beats in 15 seconds, which is $\frac{1}{4}$ of a minute. Suppose a patient's heart beats 18 times in $\frac{1}{4}$ of a minute. How many times does it beat in 1 minute?

Let h = number of heartbeats in 1 minute.

Then $\frac{h}{4}$ = number of heartbeats in $\frac{1}{4}$ minute.

To solve an equation like $\frac{h}{4} = 18$, we can multiply each side of the equation by 4.

$$\frac{h}{4} \cdot 4 = 18 \cdot 4$$

$$h = 72$$

The patient's heart beats 72 times per minute.

Example 1 Solve $\frac{y}{3} = 9$.

Solution $\frac{y}{3} = 9$

$3 \cdot \frac{y}{3} = 9 \cdot 3$ ⟵———— *To "undo" division by 3, multiply by 3.*

$y = 27$

To "undo" multiplication by a fraction, you can multiply by the reciprocal of the fraction.

Example 2   Solve $\frac{2}{3}x = 16$. Check the solution.

Solution $\frac{2}{3}x = 16$

$\frac{3}{2} \cdot \frac{2}{3}x = 16 \cdot \frac{3}{2}$ ⟵ _To "undo" multiplication by_ $\frac{2}{3}$, _multiply by its reciprocal,_ $\frac{3}{2}$.

$x = 24$

Check: $\frac{2}{3}x = 16$

$\frac{2}{3} \cdot 24 \quad \big| \quad 16$

$16 \quad \big| \quad 16$

$16 = 16 \quad \checkmark$

Your Turn   • Solve $\frac{w}{5} = 7$. Check the solution. $35;\ \frac{35}{5} = 7$

• Solve $\frac{3}{4}v = 15$. Check the solution. $20;\ \frac{3}{4} \cdot 20 = 15$

• Solve $10 = \frac{2}{3}n$. Check the solution. $15;\ 10 = \frac{2}{3} \cdot 15$

Class Exercises

You are to solve each equation for y. Tell by what number you should multiply each side of the equation.

1. $\frac{y}{4} = 9$ 4

2. $\frac{y}{8} = 6$ 8

3. $3 = \frac{y}{5}$ 5

4. $\frac{y}{10} = 4$ 10

5. $\frac{1}{2}y = 7$ 2

6. $10 = \frac{1}{3}y$ 3

7. $\frac{2}{3}y = 8$ $\frac{3}{2}$

8. $\frac{3}{4}y = 12$ $\frac{4}{3}$

Exercises

You are to solve for *n*. By what number should you multiply each side of the equation?

A　**1.** $\dfrac{n}{2} = 4$　2　　　**2.** $\dfrac{n}{3} = 5$　3　　　**3.** $6 = \dfrac{n}{4}$　4　　　**4.** $\dfrac{n}{5} = 7$　5

5. $\dfrac{1}{2}n = 5$　2　　　**6.** $6 = \dfrac{1}{3}n$　3　　　**7.** $\dfrac{1}{4}n = 7$　4　　　**8.** $\dfrac{1}{5}n = 8$　5

B　**9–16. Solve the equations in Exercises 1–8.**　**9.** 8　　**10.** 15　**11.** 24　**12.** 35
　　　　　　　　　　　　　　　　　　　　　　　　13. 10　**14.** 18　**15.** 28　**16.** 40

Solve each equation. Check the solution.

17. $\dfrac{x}{4} = 6$　24　　　**18.** $\dfrac{2}{5}y = 20$　50　　　**19.** $60 = \dfrac{a}{5}$　300　　**20.** $7 = \dfrac{b}{4}$　28

21. $\dfrac{5}{8}c = 10$　16　　**22.** $\dfrac{3}{5}d = 6$　10　　**23.** $80 = \dfrac{2}{3}e$　120　**24.** $16 = \dfrac{f}{5}$　80

25. $\dfrac{2}{3}g = 24$　36　　**26.** $48 = \dfrac{h}{5}$　240　　**27.** $\dfrac{k}{4} = 19$　76　　**28.** $\dfrac{1}{5}m = 32$　160

These equations have fractions or decimals. Solve and check.

29. $\dfrac{3}{5}d = 10.5$　17.5　　**30.** $\dfrac{e}{4} = 1.2$　4.8　　**31.** $3.7 = \dfrac{p}{2}$　7.4　　**32.** $0.02 = \dfrac{2}{3}q$　0.03

33. $\dfrac{5}{6}g = 2.5$　3　　**34.** $\dfrac{1}{2}h = \dfrac{5}{8}$　$1\dfrac{1}{4}$　　**35.** $1.7 = \dfrac{1}{3}r$　5.1　**36.** $\dfrac{5}{9} = \dfrac{1}{3}s$　$1\dfrac{2}{3}$

Decide which operation to use. Solve and check.

37. $\dfrac{z}{5} = 12$　60　　　**38.** $y - 3 = 61$　64　　**39.** $19 = \dfrac{1}{2}x$　38　　**40.** $105 = 21d$　5

41. $w + 19 = 81$　62　　**42.** $82 = v + 21$　61　　**43.** $\dfrac{2}{3}u = 120$　180　**44.** $76 = e - 15$　91

45. $100 = a - 59$　159　**46.** $36 + b = 172$　136　**47.** $15c = 180$　12　　**48.** $19q = 76$　4

Solve and check.

Example　$\dfrac{250}{n} = 5$　▷　$\dfrac{250}{n} \cdot n = 5 \cdot n$　▷　$\dfrac{250}{5} = \dfrac{5 \cdot n}{5}$　▷　$50 = n$

C　**49.** $\dfrac{18}{a} = 6$　3　　　**50.** $\dfrac{32}{b} = 8$　4　　　**51.** $\dfrac{75}{c} = 25$　3　　**52.** $\dfrac{96}{d} = 2$　48

Using the Computer

This program will solve equations of the form $Ax + B = C$ and $Ax - B = C$. RUN it to solve $3x + 5 = 17$ and $5x - 3 = 27$. Now try some examples of your own.

```
10   REM: SOLVING SIMPLE EQUATIONS
20   PRINT "TO SOLVE AN EQUATION"
30   PRINT "   AX @ B = C"
40   PRINT "WHERE @ CAN BE + OR -:"
50   PRINT "WHAT SIGN DO YOU WISH FOR @"
60   PRINT "(TYPE + OR -)";
70   INPUT S$
80   IF S$="+" THEN 110
90   IF S$="-" THEN 110
100  GOTO 60
110  PRINT "WHAT IS A";
120  INPUT A
130  PRINT "WHAT IS B";
140  INPUT B
150  PRINT "WHAT IS C";
160  INPUT C
170  IF S$="-" THEN 200
180  PRINT "X =";(C-B)/A
190  GOTO 210
200  PRINT "X =";(C+B)/A
210  END
```

To solve an equation
  AX @ B = C
Where @ can be + or −:
What sign do you wish for @ (type + or −)? +
What is A? 3
What is B? 5
What is C? 17
X = 4

To solve an equation
  AX @ B = C
Where @ can be + or −:
What sign do you wish for @ (type + or −)? −
What is A? 5
What is B? 3
What is C? 27
X = 6

Self Test 1

Answer *Yes* or *No*.

1. Is 26 a solution of $x + 27 = 53$? yes   **5-1**

2. Is 36 a solution of $73 = 2y + 1$? yes

Solve the equation.

3. $a + 13 = 71$ 58	**4.** $32 = b + 7$ 25	**5.** $51 + c = 69$ 18 **5-2**
6. $7d = 91$ 13	**7.** $400 = 8e$ 50	**8.** $3f = 693$ 231 **5-3**
9. $g - 17 = 74$ 91	**10.** $102 = h - 21$ 123	**11.** $j - 43 = 12$ 55 **5-4**
12. $\dfrac{k}{5} = 105$ 525	**13.** $\dfrac{1}{3}m = 13$ 39	**14.** $\dfrac{2}{5}p = 16$ 40 **5-5**

5-6 *Using Two Steps*

Solving some equations may require more than one operation.

Example 1 Solve $2a + 6 = 14$. Check the solution.

Solution First, subtract 6 from each side of the equation. That leaves only one term with the variable on the left of the "=" sign.

$$2a + 6 - 6 = 14 - 6$$
$$2a + 0 = 8$$
$$2a = 8$$

Then solve $2a = 8$ by dividing each side of the equation by 2.

$$2a = 8$$
$$\frac{2a}{2} = \frac{8}{2}$$
$$a = 4$$

Check:

$$
\begin{array}{c|c}
2a + 6 & = 14 \\
\hline
2 \cdot 4 + 6 & 14 \\
8 + 6 & 14 \\
14 & 14 \\
14 = 14 & \checkmark
\end{array}
$$

Example 2 Solve $3b - 8 = 13$.

Solution
$$3b - 8 = 13$$
$$3b - 8 + 8 = 13 + 8 \quad \longleftarrow \text{ } Add \text{ } 8 \text{ } to \text{ } each \text{ } side.$$
$$3b = 21$$
$$\frac{3b}{3} = \frac{21}{3} \quad \longleftarrow \text{ } Divide \text{ } each \text{ } side \text{ } by \text{ } 3.$$
$$b = 7$$

149

Example 3 Solve $\frac{1}{2}c - 7 = 2$.

Solution
$$\frac{1}{2}c - 7 = 2$$

$$\frac{1}{2}c - 7 + 7 = 2 + 7 \quad \longleftarrow \quad \textit{Add 7 to each side.}$$

$$\frac{1}{2}c = 9$$

$$2 \cdot \frac{1}{2}c = 2 \cdot 9 \quad \longleftarrow \quad \textit{Multiply each side by 2.}$$

$$c = 18$$

Your Turn • Solve $6 + 4d = 30$. Check the solution. 6; $6 + 4(6) = 30$
• Solve $3x - 2 = 13$. Check the solution. 5; $3(5) - 2 = 13$
• Solve $\frac{1}{3}e - 4 = 9$. Check the solution. 39; $\frac{1}{3}(39) - 4 = 9$

Some equations require you to use the distributive property to solve. Recall that the property states the following: $a(b + c) = ab + ac$.

Example 4 Solve $2(x + 3) = 18$.

Solution
$$2(x + 3) = 18 \quad \longleftarrow \quad \textit{Recall the distributive property.}$$
$$2x + 6 = 18$$
$$2x + 6 - 6 = 18 - 6 \quad \longleftarrow \quad \textit{Subtract 6 from each side.}$$
$$2x = 12$$
$$\frac{2x}{2} = \frac{12}{2} \quad \longleftarrow \quad \textit{Divide each side by 2.}$$
$$x = 6$$

Your Turn • Solve $3(x - 1) = 21$. Check the solution. 8; $3(8 - 1) = 21$
• Solve $30 = 5(x + 2)$. Check the solution. 4; $30 = 5(4 + 2)$

Class Exercises

Tell what steps you would take to solve the equation.

Example $5f + 9 = 54$

Solution Subtract 9 from each side. Then divide each side by 5.

subtract 3, divide by 2   add 3, divide by 4   add 3, multiply by 2   add 7, divide by 2

1. $3 + 2g = 11$ **2.** $4h - 3 = 21$ **3.** $\frac{1}{2}j - 3 = 4$ **4.** $2k - 7 = 19$

add 4, multiply by 3   add 13, divide by 7   subtract 9, divide by 8   subtract 3, multiply by 4

5. $\frac{1}{3}m - 4 = 9$ **6.** $7n - 13 = 22$ **7.** $8p + 9 = 65$ **8.** $3 + \frac{1}{4}q = 9$

add 6, divide by 3   add 1, divide by 5   subtract 4, multiply by 3   add 3, multiply by 4

9. $3q - 6 = 12$ **10.** $5r - 1 = 29$ **11.** $\frac{1}{3}s + 4 = 13$ **12.** $\frac{1}{4}t - 3 = 2$

Exercises

Follow the steps to solve the equation. Remember, the same operation must be performed on each side of the equation.

A   **1.** $2a + 4 = 16$ **2.** $3b - 5 = 28$ **3.** $\frac{x}{2} + 10 = 13$ **4.** $6c - 2 = 22$

Subtract 4.   Add 5.   Subtract 10.   Add 2.
Divide by 2. $\quad a = 6$ Divide by 3. $\quad b = 11$ Multiply by 2. $\quad x = 6$ Divide by 6. $\quad c = 4$

5. $5 + \frac{3}{4}d = 20$ **6.** $\frac{4}{5}e - 2 = 30$ **7.** $8f - 9 = 31$ **8.** $\frac{2}{3}g + 8 = 22$

Subtract 5.   Add 2.   Add 9.   Subtract 8.

Multiply by $\frac{4}{3}$. $\quad d = 20$ Multiply by $\frac{5}{4}$. $\quad e = 40$ Divide by 8. $\quad f = 5$ Multiply by $\frac{3}{2}$. $\quad g = 21$

Solve. Check the solution.

B   **9.** $\frac{1}{2}u - 9 = 9$ 36   **10.** $4v + 3 = 15$ 3   **11.** $7w - 9 = 19$ 4   **12.** $9 + \frac{1}{2}x = 19$ 20

13. $\frac{1}{6}y - 2 = 1$ 18   **14.** $9 + 4n = 25$ 4   **15.** $2a + 5 = 15$ 5   **16.** $3b - 8 = 19$ 9

17. $5 + 4c = 25$ 5   **18.** $\frac{1}{4}d + 9 = 25$ 64   **19.** $1 + 3e = 10$ 3   **20.** $5f - 9 = 51$ 12

21. $\frac{1}{4}g - 3 = 1$ ₁₆ **22.** $3h - 2 = 1$ ₁ **23.** $4j - 8 = 0$ ₂ **24.** $\frac{1}{3}k - 2 = 0$ ₆

25. $6 + 5m = 51$ ₉ **26.** $6n + 3 = 27$ ₄ **27.** $9p - 9 = 0$ ₁ **28.** $7q - 7 = 7$ ₂

29. $\frac{1}{2}r - 1 = 1$ ₄ **30.** $6s + 8 = 26$ ₃ **31.** $9 + 2n = 57$ ₂₄ **32.** $9 + 9u = 99$ ₁₀

33. $4 = \frac{1}{4}v - 4$ ₃₂ **34.** $1 = 3w + 1$ ₀ **35.** $2 = 5x + 2$ ₀ **36.** $24 = 2y + 22$ ₁

Solve the equation. Check the solution. Remember to use the distributive property.

37. $2(a - 2) = 6$ ₅ **38.** $5(b + 1) = 45$ ₈ **39.** $12 = 6(c - 7)$ ₉

40. $30 = 3(d + 8)$ ₂ **41.** $4(e + 3) = 32$ ₅ **42.** $10 = 2(f - 4)$ ₉

43. $42 = 7(g - 1)$ ₇ **44.** $9(h + 5) = 72$ ₃ **45.** $8(k + 5) = 96$ ₇

46. $3(x - 1) + 4 = 13$ ₄ **47.** $2(y + 1) - 3 = 9$ ₅ **48.** $5(z - 5) + 2 = 7$ ₆

49. $12 + 2(3p - 4) = 14$ $1\frac{2}{3}$ **50.** $52 = 4(2q + 5) + 8$ ₃ **51.** $3(2r - 6) + 6 = 11$ $3\frac{5}{6}$

Is the given number a solution? Write *Yes* or *No*.

Example $5x + 6 > 21$; 2   Check:
$$\begin{array}{c|c} 5x + 6 & > 21 \\ \hline 5(2) + 6 & 21 \\ 10 + 5 & 21 \\ 16 & 21 \end{array}$$

No. 16 is not greater than 21, so 2 is not a solution.

52. $2a - 5 > 7$; 4 ₙₒ **53.** $3 + 5n > 24$; 5 yₑₛ **54.** $3x - 10 < 35$; 5 ʸᵉˢ

55. $2y + 3y < 18$; 4 ₙₒ **56.** $6(x + 2) < 20$; 5 ₙₒ **57.** $3(d + 25) < 100$; 2 ʸᵉˢ

Challenge

Alice has accepted a special 15-day assignment with ABC Corporation. She may choose to be paid according to one of two plans.

If Alice chooses Plan A, she will be paid $25,000 when the assignment is completed. If Alice chooses Plan B, she will be paid $1 on the first day. Each day thereafter she will be paid an amount equal to 2 times the amount she received the day before. Which plan should Alice choose? Plan B

5-7 *Equations with More Steps*

Some equations have the variable on both sides. To solve, you need to get the variable alone on one side of the equation.

Example 1 Solve $3a + 6 = 2a + 14$.

Solution First, let's subtract $2a$ from each side of the equation. That will result in an equation having the variable on one side only.

$$3a - 2a + 6 = 2a - 2a + 14$$
$$a + 6 = 14$$

The variable is now on one side. Now, subtract 6 from each side.

$$a + 6 - 6 = 14 - 6$$
$$a = 8$$

In the example above, we first subtracted $2a$ from each side. Then we subtracted 6. You could solve the same equation by subtracting 6 from each side first and then subtracting $2a$ from each side. You would get the same answer.

Example 2 Solve $9b + 4 = 6b + 22$.

Solution

$$9b + 4 = 6b + 22$$
$$9b - 6b + 4 = 6b - 6b + 22 \longleftarrow \text{\textit{Subtract 6b from each side.}}$$
$$3b + 4 = 22 \longleftarrow \text{\textit{The variable is on one side.}}$$
$$3b + 4 - 4 = 22 - 4 \longleftarrow \text{\textit{Subtract 4 from each side.}}$$
$$3b = 18$$
$$\frac{3b}{3} = \frac{18}{3} \longleftarrow \text{\textit{Divide each side by 3.}}$$
$$b = 6$$

Your Turn
- Solve $2d = d + 3$. Check the solution. $\quad$ 3; $2(3) = 3 + 3$
- Solve $5f - 3 = 2f + 15$. Check the solution. 6; $5(6) - 3 = 2(6) + 15$

Class Exercises

Tell what steps you would take to solve the equation.

add h, divide by 6 $\qquad$ subtract $2k$, divide by 2 $\quad$ subtract $3m$, divide by 2 $\quad$ add $3x$, divide by 8
1. $5h = 12 - h$ $\qquad$ **2.** $4k = 2k + 4$ $\qquad$ **3.** $5m = 3m + 6$ $\qquad$ **4.** $5x = 8 - 3x$
subtract $2n$, divide by 6 $\quad$ subtract $4p$ $\qquad\qquad$ add $3r$, divide by 5 $\qquad\quad$ subtract $3y$, divide by 4
5. $8n = 2n + 6$ $\qquad$ **6.** $5p = 4p + 4$ $\qquad$ **7.** $2r = 5 - 3r$ $\qquad$ **8.** $7y = 3y + 12$

Exercises

Follow the steps to solve the equation. Remember to perform the same operation on each side of the equation.

A $\quad$ **1.** $5e = 3e + 8$ $\qquad$ **2.** $4f = 10 - f$ $\qquad$ **3.** $3g = 12 - 3g$ $\qquad$ **4.** $h = 9 - 2h$
$\qquad\quad$ Subtract $3e$. $_{e\,=\,4}$ $\qquad$ Add f. $\quad_{f\,=\,2}$ $\qquad\quad$ Add $3g$. $\quad_{g\,=\,2}$ $\qquad$ Add $2h$. $_{h\,=\,3}$
$\qquad\quad$ Divide by 2. $\qquad\qquad$ Divide by 5. $\qquad\qquad$ Divide by 6. $\qquad\qquad$ Divide by 3.

Solve each equation. Check the solution.

B $\quad$ **5.** $2a = a + 11$ $\;$ 11 $\quad$ **6.** $3b = 10 - b$ $\;$ $2\frac{1}{2}$ $\;$ **7.** $4c = 2c + 8$ $\;$ 4 $\quad$ **8.** $8n = 6n + 4$ $\,^{2}$

$\qquad$ **9.** $3d = 2d + 9$ $\;$ 9 $\quad$ **10.** $5e = 2e + 12$ $\;$ 4 $\quad$ **11.** $7f = 18 - 3f$ $1\frac{4}{5}$ $\,$ **12.** $9g = 5g + 4$ $\,_{1}$

$\qquad$ **13.** $7h = 5h + 8$ $\;$ 4 $\quad$ **14.** $4j = 18 - 2j$ $\;$ 3 $\quad$ **15.** $6k = 9 - 3k$ $\;$ 1 $\quad$ **16.** $7m = 5m + 6$ $\,_{3}$

$\qquad$ **17.** $3t - 12 = 2t + 4$ $\quad$ 16 $\quad$ **18.** $8u + 1 = 7u + 1$ $\quad$ 0 $\qquad$ **19.** $12v + 5 = 11v + 7$ $\,_{7}^{2}$

$\qquad$ **20.** $4w - 7 = 3w + 1$ $\quad$ 8 $\quad$ **21.** $6x + 4 = 5x + 10$ $\quad$ 6 $\qquad$ **22.** $2y - 2 = y + 8$ $\,_{10}$

$\qquad$ **23.** $5z + 4 = 4z + 11$ $\quad$ 7 $\quad$ **24.** $7s - 3 = 6s + 2$ $\quad$ 5 $\qquad$ **25.** $32t - 8 = 31t + 17$ $\,_{5}^{25}$

$\qquad$ **26.** $7g + 2 = 2g + 12$ $\quad$ 2 $\quad$ **27.** $9h + 1 = 4h + 11$ $\quad$ 2 $\qquad$ **28.** $5k - 1 = 2k + 14$ $\,_{4}$

$\qquad$ **29.** $12m - 9 = 5m + 5$ $\;$ 2 $\quad$ **30.** $14n - 8 = 2n + 16$ 2 $\qquad$ **31.** $5p + 9 = p + 25$ $\,_{8}$

$\qquad$ **32.** $14q - 4 = 10q + 20$6 $\quad$ **33.** $8r + 5 = 6r + 7$ $\quad$ 1 $\qquad$ **34.** $8s - 1 = 6s + 15$ $\,_{1}$

$\qquad$ **35.** $4t + 4 = 2t + 6$ $\quad$ 1 $\quad$ **36.** $7u - 3 = 3u + 5$ $\quad$ 2 $\qquad$ **37.** $10v + 8 = 3v + 15$ $\,_{1}$

$\qquad$ **38.** $5w + 8 = 3w + 26$ 9 $\quad$ **39.** $18 + 3x = x + 40$ $\quad$ 11 $\qquad$ **40.** $7 + 4y = 16 - 5y$ $\,_{6}$

C $\quad$ **41.** $5(a + 2) = 30 + a$ $\;$ 5 $\quad$ **42.** $b + 2(b + 1) = 7 - 2b$ 1 $\;$ **43.** $3(d - 4) + d = 2d$

5-8 *Writing Algebraic Expressions*

Algebra is a powerful tool. To develop skill in using algebra you will need more practice in writing expressions. The first step in writing an expression is to decide what the variable will represent.

Example 1   The Panthers won 7 more games than the Cougars. Write an algebraic expression to show the number of games won by the Panthers.

Solution   Let c = number of games won by Cougars.
Panthers won 7 games more than Cougars.

$$7 \qquad + \qquad c$$

So, $7 + c$ = number of games won by Panthers.

Example 2   Susan is twice as tall as her brother John.
Paul is 5 in. taller than Susan.
Write an expression for the height of each person.

Solution   First, decide what the variable will represent.
Let b = John's height in inches.
Then $2b$ = Susan's height in inches. ⟵ *2 times John's height*
And $2b + 5$ = Paul's height in inches. ⟵ *5 in. taller*
                                                        than Susan

Your Turn   Complete.
● Barney ran three times as far as Sal.
Ann ran 1 km farther than Barney.
Let s = number of kilometers that Sal ran.
Then __?__ = number of kilometers that Barney ran. $3s$
And __?__ = number of kilometers that Ann ran. $3s + 1$

155

Using a pattern may help you write some expressions.

Example 3 Write expressions for three consecutive whole numbers.

Solution Think of examples of three consecutive whole numbers.
Then look for a pattern.

First	Second	Third
3	4	5
17	18	19
216	217	218

Pattern: *Add 1.*   *Add 1 again.*

Let x = first of three whole numbers. Use the pattern.

First	Second	Third
x	$x + 1$	$(x + 1) + 1$ or $x + 2$

Add 1.   *Add 1 again.*

Your Turn
- Let $2x$ = an even number.
  Write an expression for the next even number. $2x + 2$
- Let n be a number.
  Write an expression for twice the number. $2n$
  Write an expression for 1 more than twice the number. $2n + 1$

Class Exercises

Lou is 5 years older than Sam. Complete the chart.

	If Sam's age is . . . ,	then Lou's age is . . .	
1.	2	2 + 5, or __?__	7
2.	13	13 + __?__ or __?__	5; 18
3.	a	__?__ + 5	a
4.	$2b$	__?__ + __?__	$2b$; 5

Complete the expression.

5. a. 1 less than 3 is $3 - \underline{\ ?\ }$, or $\underline{\ ?\ }$ 1; 2

b. 1 less than r is $r - \underline{\ ?\ }$ 1

c. 1 less than $2r$ is $\underline{\ ?\ } - 1$ 2r

d. 1 less than 3 times n is $\underline{\ ?\ } - \underline{\ ?\ }$ 3n; 1

6. Let $2x$ be an even number.

a. the next odd number is $\underline{\ ?\ }$ 2x + 1

b. the next even number is $\underline{\ ?\ }$ 2x + 2

c. 3 more than $2x$ is $2x + \underline{\ ?\ }$ 3

d. 6 less than $2x$ is $\underline{\ ?\ } - \underline{\ ?\ }$ 2x; 6

Exercises

Choose the expression at the right that represents the number described.

A

1. 5 less than a number x d
2. a number x decreased by 3   h
3. 5 times the number x k
4. 3 more than x a
5. the number x increased by 2   c
6. the number x doubled   e
7. the number x divided by 3   g
8. one-half of x j
9. 3 more than 2 times x b
10. 3 less than 4 times x f

a. $x + 3$
b. $2x + 3$
c. $x + 2$
d. $x - 5$
e. $2x$
f. $4x - 3$
g. $\dfrac{x}{3}$
h. $x - 3$
j. $\dfrac{1}{2}x$
k. $5x$

Complete by writing an algebraic expression for each phrase.

B 11. a. 1 more than a number n is $\underline{\ ?\ }$ $n + 1$

b. 1 more than a number $2x$ is $\underline{\ ?\ }$ $2x + 1$

c. 1 more than 3 times the number p is $\underline{\ ?\ }$ $3p + 1$

d. 1 more than twice a number r is $\underline{\ ?\ }$ $2r + 1$

12. a. the sum of 2 and n is $\underline{\ ?\ }$ $2 + n$

b. the sum of 2 and $3y$ is $\underline{\ ?\ }$ $2 + 3y$

c. the sum of x and $3a$ is $\underline{\ ?\ }$ $x + 3a$

d. the sum of x and 4 times h is $\underline{\ ?\ }$ $x + 4h$

13. **a.** 10 less than 50 is __?__ $50 - 10$
    b. 10 less than m is __?__ $m - 10$
    c. 10 less than $2x$ is __?__ $2x - 10$
14. Let $2x$ be an even number.
    a. The next consecutive number is __?__ $2x + 1$
    b. The next consecutive even number is __?__ $2x + 2$
15. Paula is 3 in. taller than Sue.
    Let $s = $ Sue's height in inches.
    a. Paula's height $= $ __?__ in. $s + 3$
    b. Jim is 1 in. shorter than Paula. Jim's height $= $ __?__ in. $s + 2$
16. Carl is 6 years older than Jerry.
    Let $j = $ Jerry's age.
    a. Carl's age $= $ __?__ $j + 6$
    b. Betty is 2 years older than Carl. Betty's age $= $ __?__ $j + 8$
17. Sara ran half as far as Al.
    Let $a = $ number of km that Al ran.
    a. Sara ran __?__ km. $\frac{1}{2}a$
    b. Leo ran 3 km farther than Sara. Leo ran __?__ km. $\frac{1}{2}a + 3$
18. Ned had twice as many strikes as Jo.
    Let $j = $ number of strikes by Jo.
    a. Number of strikes by Ned $= $ __?__ $2j$
    b. Kim had 2 more strikes than Ned. Number of strikes by
    Kim $= $ __?__ $2j + 2$
19. Ken has twice as much money as Cora.
    Let $c = $ amount of money that Cora has.
    a. Amount of money that Ken has $= $ __?__. $2c$
    b. Max has \$5 more than Ken. Amount of money that Max
    has $= $ __?__. $2c + 5$

**To write an expression for these problems you will have to supply some
information. For example, 1 week has 7 days. Complete.**

C 20. Let $c = $ number of weeks Paul will be at camp.
    Then __?__ $= $ number of days Paul will be at camp. $7c$
21. Let $d = $ number of dimes in a parking meter.
    Then __?__ $= $ the value of the dimes in dollars. $0.1d$
22. Let $w = $ number of words you can type in 1 hour.
    Then __?__ $= $ number of words you can type in 1 min. $\frac{w}{60}$
23. Let $h = $ height of a rectangle in millimeters.
    Then __?__ $= $ height of the rectangle in centimeters. $\frac{h}{10}$

5-9 *Writing Equations*

To write an equation you need to write two equal expressions. One of the expressions may be just a number.

Example 1 The Rams won 1 game more than the Trojans. If the Rams won 6 games, how many games did the Trojans win?

Solution Let t = games won by Trojans.
Then $t + 1$ = games won by Rams.

Games won by Rams = Games won by Rams
$$t + 1 = 6 \longleftarrow \text{\textit{Write two equal expressions.}}$$
$$t + 1 - 1 = 6 - 1 \longleftarrow \text{\textit{Solve the equation.}}$$
$$t = 5$$

The Trojans won 5 games.

Example 2 An apple has about 70 calories. That is 2 times the number of calories in a peach. How many calories are in a peach?

Solution Let p = calories in a peach.
Then $2p$ = calories in an apple.

Calories in an apple = Calories in an apple
$$2p = 70 \longleftarrow \text{\textit{Write two equal expressions.}}$$
$$\frac{2p}{2} = \frac{70}{2} \longleftarrow \text{\textit{Solve the equation.}}$$
$$p = 35$$

A peach has 35 calories.

Your Turn • Josie is 2 in. shorter than Ken.
Josie is 58 in. tall.
How tall is Ken? 60 in.

159

Class Exercises

Complete the steps to solve the problem.

Problem: Linda's bowling score is 50 points more than Al's.
Linda's score is 83.
What is Al's score?

1. Let a = Al's score. Then, Linda's score = $a +$ __?__. 50
2. The problem says that Linda's score = __?__. 83
3. State two equal expressions for Linda's bowling score. $a + 50$; 83
4. An equation for the problem is $a +$ __?__ = __?__. 50; 83

Problem: Sal has half as much money as Karen.
Sal has $16.
How much money does Karen have?

5. Let k = number of dollars that Karen has. Then, Sal has __?__ $\cdot k$ $\frac{1}{2}$
dollars.
6. The problem states that Sal has __?__ dollars. 16
7. State two equal expressions for the number of dollars that Sal has. $\frac{1}{2}k$; 16
8. An equation for the problem is __?__ $\cdot k =$ __?__. $\frac{1}{2}$; 16

Exercises

**Choose the equation that matches the problem. Write a, b, c, or d.
Then solve the problem.**

a. $m + 8 = 24$ **b.** $m - 8 = 24$ **c.** $8m = 24$ **d.** $\dfrac{m}{8} = 24$

A **1.** Vera is 8 years older than Marco.
Vera is 24 years old.
How old is Marco? a; 16 years
(Let m = Marco's age.)
2. Kim has $8 less than Maria.
Kim has $24.
How much money does Maria have? b; $32
(Let m = money Maria has.)
3. Mrs. Molloy divided a roll of twine evenly among 8 students in
Home Ec class. Each student received a piece of twine 24 in. long.
How many inches of twine did Mrs. Molloy have originally? (Let
m = inches of twine that Mrs. Molloy had.) d; 192 in.

4. The annual rainfall in Warwick last year was 24 in. That was 8 times the amount that fell in March. How many inches of rain fell in Warwick during March? (Let m = inches of rainfall in March.) c; 3 in.

Write an equation and solve the problem. Some equations may vary. One possible equation is given for each problem.

B

5. One number is 13 more than another. The greater number is 35. What is the lesser number? $s + 13 = 35$; 22 (Let s = lesser number.)

6. Mario's age is $\frac{1}{2}$ of his sister's. Mario is 8 years old. How old is his sister? $\frac{1}{2}s = 8$; 16 years (Let s = Mario's sister's age.)

7. Susan is 3 in. shorter than Tom. Susan's height is 62 in. How tall is Tom? $t - 3 = 62$; 65 in. (Let t = Tom's height in inches.)

8. One number is twice another. Their sum is 24. $n + 2n = 24$; 8 and 16 What are the two numbers? (Let n = the first number.)

9. A baseball team played 27 games. They won 5 games more than they lost. How many games did they win? $x + x + 5 = 27$; 16 games

10. There are 28 students in Home Room 107. There were 3 students absent on Tuesday. How many students were present? $28 - 3 = p$; 25 students

11. Suso sold three times as many tickets to the school play as Len. Suso sold 18 tickets to the school play. How many tickets did Len sell? $3s = 18$; 6 tickets

12. Ana swam 10 yd farther than Ivan. Ana swam 42 yd. How far did Ivan swim? $x + 10 = 42$; 32 yards

13. There are 952 students in Valley Central School. There are 38 more girls than boys. $x + x + 38 = 952$; How many boys are there? 457 boys How many girls are there? 495 girls

5-10 *Problem Solving*

Architects and engineers solve many equations to make certain that designs for bridges and buildings will be safe. In this chapter we use simple equations to solve problems. These equations are much easier than many used by engineers. However, the methods you learn in this chapter are the bases of methods used to solve more difficult equations.

When you use an equation to solve a problem it is often helpful to let the variable represent the number you want to know. Using the variable, write two equal expressions. Then write an equation and solve it. Let's start with a simple example.

Example 1   Suppose so far this year you have saved $648. Your savings goal is $700. How much more must you save to meet your goal?

Solution   Let x = amount of money you still need to save.

Write two equal expressions. Then write an equation and solve it.

Savings goal = $700
Savings goal = $648 + x ⟵—— *amount already saved + amount you must save*

$$\text{Savings goal} = \text{Savings goal}$$
$$\$648 + x = \$700$$
$$x + 648 = 700 \quad \longleftarrow \text{\textit{Commutative Property:}}$$
$$x + 648 - 648 = 700 - 648 \qquad \textit{648 + x = x + 648}$$
$$x = 52$$

You must still save $52 to meet your goal.

Your Turn   Use an equation to solve the problem.
- Marjorie's business is growing. She now employs 29 people. In two months she plans to employ 57 people. How many more people does she need to hire?

$x + 29 = 57$; 28 people

Class Exercises

Complete the steps to write an equation for the problem.

1. There are 4 times as many carpenters as electricians at a construction site. If there are 52 carpenters, how many electricians are there? Let e = number of electricians. Then __?__ = number of carpenters. $4e$; $4e = 52$

2. Craig and Jane Conroy together earned $1200 last week. If Jane earned $110 more than Craig earned, how much did each earn last week? Let c = amount Craig earned. Then __?__ = amount Jane earned. $c + 110$; $c + c + 110 = 1200$

Exercises

Write an equation, solve it, then answer the question.

A 1. In Sue Crogen's office 14 people go to lunch at 12 noon. This leaves 29 people in the office. How many people work in the office? $x - 14 = 29$; 43 people

2. The sum of two numbers is 456. One of the numbers is 286. What is the other number? $x + 286 = 456$; 170

3. Omega Manufacturers recently doubled the number of computers produced each day. They now make 54 computers each day. How many computers did Omega Manufacturers make each day before they increased production? $2n = 54$; 27 computers

4. Herb traveled 279 miles on the first day of a 548-mile trip. How many more miles must he travel on the second day to reach his destination? $279 + m = 548$; 269 mi

5. The product of two numbers is 486. One of the factors is 6. What is the other factor? $6x = 486$; 81

6. Madeline wants to delete 10 programs from a computer memory. This will leave 437 programs in memory. How many programs are in memory now? $x - 10 = 437$; 447 programs

163

B   7. The sum of two numbers is 687. One number is 2 times the other. What are the two numbers? $2t + t = 687$; 229, 458

8. An auto dealer has 468 cars. He has 3 times as many four-door cars as two-door cars. How many 2-door cars does he have? How many 4-door cars does he have? $x + 3x = 468$; 117 2-door, 351 4-door

9. Jonas has a paper route. He has 20 customers more than Janice. Together they have 78 customers. How many customers does Jonas have? How many does Janice have? $c + c + 20 = 78$; 49 customers, 29 customers

10. Milton and Molton are neighboring towns. Molton has 18,112 more residents than Milton. Their combined populations is 478,658. What is the population of each town? $x + x + 18,112 = 478,658$; 230,273 people; 248,385 people

11. A pet store sold half as many pets in December as it sold during January through November. If 1272 pets were sold in all that year, how many pets were sold in December? What was the average number of pets sold in one month that year? $\frac{1}{2}x + x = 1272$; 424 pets; 106 pets

12. When you double a number and add 16, you get 86. What is the number?
$2x + 16 = 86$; 35

Self Test 2

Solve the equation.

1. $2a - 3 = 27$ 15   2. $31 = 5b + 6$ 5   3. $97 = 9c + 16$ 9   **5-6**

4. $3d - 4 = 2d + 7$ 11   5. $e + 4 = 8 - e$ 2   6. $5f - 1 = 2f + 8$ 3 **5-7**

Fran is 5 years older than Jim. Let j = Jim's age. Complete by writing an algebraic expression.

7. Fran's age = __?__ $j + 5$ **5-8**
8. Dean is 3 years younger than Fran. Dean's age = __?__ $j + 2$

Write an equation. Solve the problem.

9. Marlene has twice as much money as Nick.   **5-9**
   Marlene has $16.
   How much money does Nick have? $2n = 16$; $8
   (Let n = amount Nick has.)   **5-10**
10. Choose a number. Add seven. Multiply the sum by 3. If the total is 54, what is the original number? $(x + 7)3 = 54$; 11

Algebra Practice

Write an equation. Solve.

1. The product of 308 and 280 is k. $308 \cdot 280 = k$; 86,240

2. The quotient of 156,204 and 36 is d. $156{,}204 \div 36 = d$; 4339

3. 56.07 minus 9.806 is equal to w. $56.07 - 9.806 = w$; 46.264

4. The numbers 12.83, 1.509, and 304.89 add to a sum of m.
$12.83 + 1.509 + 304.89 = m$; 319.229

5. 52.635 divided by 8.7 is equal to f. $52.635 \div 8.7 = f$; 6.05

6. 0.52 times 0.16 is equal to s. $(0.52)(0.16) = s$; 0.0832

7. The difference between $7\frac{1}{2}$ and $3\frac{5}{6}$ is some number. $7\frac{1}{2} - 3\frac{5}{6} = k$; $3\frac{2}{3}$

8. How much is $2\frac{6}{7}$ times $2\frac{4}{5}$? $2\frac{6}{7}\left(2\frac{4}{5}\right) = p$; 8

9. What is the sum of $3\frac{1}{2}$, $1\frac{1}{8}$, and $4\frac{3}{4}$? $3\frac{1}{2} + 1\frac{1}{8} + 4\frac{3}{4} = h$; $9\frac{3}{8}$

10. $2\frac{4}{7}$ divided by $\frac{5}{3}$ is some number. $2\frac{4}{7} \div \frac{5}{3} = m$; $1\frac{19}{35}$

Use the distributive property to factor each expression.

11. $8uv^2 + 2(uv)^2 + u^3v$
    $uv(8v + 2uv + u^2)$

12. $6c^3 + 3c^2d^2 + 15c$
    $3c(2c^2 + cd^2 + 5)$

13. $7qr + (qr)^2 + qr^2$
    $qr(7 + qr + r)$

Write the LCM of each set of expressions.

14. m^3 and $5m$ $\quad 5m^3$

15. $3g$, $2h^2$, and 4 $\quad 12gh^2$

16. $6a^2$, $9ab$, and $2b^2$
    $18a^2b^2$

Solve the equation. Check the solution.

17. $m + 5 = 12$ $\quad$ 7

18. $14 = r + 3\frac{1}{2}$ $\quad 10\frac{1}{2}$

19. $16.3 + w = 40$ $\quad$ 23.7

20. $7l = 56$ $\quad$ 8

21. $4.3k = 7.74$ $\quad$ 1.8

22. $7\frac{1}{2} = 3\frac{1}{8}s$ $\quad 2\frac{2}{5}$

23. $4.1 = g - 2.6$ $\quad$ 6.7

24. $a - 13 = 20$ $\quad$ 33

25. $t - \frac{1}{3} = \frac{1}{2}$ $\quad \frac{5}{6}$

26. $\frac{e}{3} = 2.5$ $\quad$ 7.5

27. $4 = \frac{1}{6}v$ $\quad$ 24

28. $\frac{3}{8}l = \frac{15}{16}$ $\quad 2\frac{1}{2}$

29. $4b - 5 = 23$ $\quad$ 7

30. $\frac{2}{3}d + 5 = 11$ $\quad$ 9

31. $54 = 6(j - 2)$ $\quad$ 11

165

Problem Solving on the Job

Office Cashier

The duties of a cashier may vary somewhat from one company to another. In general, cashiers are responsible for handling money and for keeping accurate records of receipts and expenditures. Although computers are used to help with the recordkeeping, a cashier is still needed to handle the money and to deal with customers.

Mason Jones is a cashier at Franck Enterprises. He maintains a petty cash fund of $100, a fund used to pay for small, unforeseen expenses. The items in Exercises 1–3 were paid out of the petty cash fund one week.

```
OFFICE CASHIER

DESCRIPTION: Maintain petty-cash
fund; take money for goods and
services; keep records

QUALIFICATIONS: High school; good
recordkeeping skills; maturity and
good judgment

JOB OUTLOOK: Good, especially if
individual also has typing and
bookkeeping skills
```

What is the total of each kind of expense for the week?

1. Delivery Expenses: $12.83, $20.00, $4.60 $37.43

2. Office Expenses: $1.50, $2.98, $4.98, $1.50 $10.96

3. Miscellaneous Expenses: $7.50, $8.50, $21.80 $37.80

4. When the petty cash fund has $25 or less, Mason must get more money to bring the fund up to $100. After paying for the items in Exercises 1–3, how much more money is needed to bring the fund up to $100? $86.19

A cashier in a store may accept payments from customers on charge accounts and layaway items. When merchandise is returned, it is often the cashier who refunds the money or credits the customer's account. The amount that a customer owes on an account is the balance due.

How much will the customer owe after the payment or credit shown?

5. Balance due: $68.37
   Payment: $25.00
   $43.37

6. Balance due: $107.82
   Credit: $58.63
   $49.19

7. Balance due: $306.34
   Credit: $19.98
   Payment: $45.00
   $241.36

8. A customer makes a down payment of $20 on a coat that costs $150 and puts the coat on layaway. There is a sales tax of $7.50 on the purchase. After the customer makes 3 payments of $15, what is the balance due? $92.50

Cashiers also count and wrap money and prepare bank deposit slips. The First Bank provides Costello Industries with the following types of wrappers.

BILLS

Bill	$1	$5	$10	$20
Number in Wrapper	50	50	50	50

COINS

Coin	Penny	Nickel	Dime	Quarter
Number in Roll	50	40	50	40

Sue Schwartz is the cashier at A-Z, Inc. At the end of each day she counts and wraps the money and sees to it that the money is deposited in the bank. The following cash and checks are to be deposited.

Bill	Wrapped	Unwrapped
$1	7 pkg	32
$5	2 pkg	16
$10	3 pkg	43
$20	1 pkg	3

Coin	Wrapped	Unwrapped
Pennies	4 rolls	37
Nickels	3 rolls	19
Dimes	5 rolls	8
Quarters	3 rolls	29

Checks
250.00
36.83
179.47
230.94

9. What is the total value of the bills to be deposited? $3952
10. What is the total value of the coins to be deposited? $72.37
11. What is the total value of the checks to be deposited? $697.24
12. What is the total value of the money to be deposited? $4721.61

Enrichment

Venn Diagrams

Sometimes it is useful to illustrate certain statements with diagrams like the ones shown below. Such diagrams are called **Venn Diagrams.**

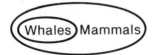

Lions Birds

Some cats are wild. All whales are mammals. No lion is a bird.

A single diagram can be used to picture several statements.

Some humans are vegetarians.
All giraffes are vegetarians.
No human is a giraffe.

Draw Venn Diagrams to illustrate the statements. Check students' drawings.

1. All kangaroos are marsupials.
2. No hares are carnivores.
3. Some tortoises weigh over 400 lb.
4. Penguins are found only in the southern hemisphere.
5. Frogs lay eggs. Birds lay eggs. Turtles lay eggs.
6. Some birds sing. Some whales sing.
7. Snakes and lizards have scales. Some fish have scales.
8. Some cats, like the lion, are social animals. Some cats, like the leopard, are solitary animals.
9. Mammals and birds are warm-blooded animals. No reptile is warm-blooded.
10. Some mammals are nocturnal animals (active at night). Leopards are nocturnal mammals. No bat is not a nocturnal mammal.

168

Chapter Review

Which number is a solution of the equation? Answer *a*, *b*, or *c*.

1. $171 + a = 376$ *a*
   a. 205   **b.** 547   **c.** 195

2. $247 = 19b$ *b*
   a. 228   **b.** 13   **c.** 4693

Solve the equation.

3. $c + 7 = 26$ 19   **4.** $16 + d = 70$ 54   **5.** $43 = e + 39$ 4

6. $4f = 64$ 16   **7.** $78 = 3g$ 26   **8.** $15h = 225$ 15

9. $j - 12 = 82$ 94   **10.** $95 = k - 25$ 120   **11.** $m - 48 = 102$ 150

12. $\dfrac{n}{3} = 14$ 42   **13.** $\dfrac{1}{2}p = 21$ 42   **14.** $\dfrac{2}{5}q = 98$ 245

15. $2r - 3 = 21$ 12   **16.** $3s + 7 = 34$ 9   **17.** $5u - 9 = 71$ 16

18. $9v - 4 = 8v + 7$ 11   **19.** $6w + 1 = 3w + 10$ 3   **20.** $7x - 5 = 5x + 17$ 11

Match the expression at the right with the number described.

21. a number divided by 3   c

22. a number increased by 3   a

23. 3 less than a number   e

24. 5 times a number   b

25. twice a number   d

26. 3 more than 5 times a number   g

27. twice a number decreased by 3   f

a. $n + 3$
b. $5n$
c. $\dfrac{n}{3}$
d. $2n$
e. $n - 3$
f. $2n - 3$
g. $3 + 5n$

Write an equation. Solve the problem.

28. Paulo is buying a calculator at half price.
He pays $6 for the calculator.
What is the regular price of the calculator? $\dfrac{1}{2}n = 6$; $12
(Let n = regular price.)

29. Suppose you choose a number and multiply it by 6. Then
you add 9 to the product. If the total is 345, what is
the number? $6n + 9 = 345$; 56

Chapter Test

Which number is a solution of the equation?

1. $7a = 364$ 52 or 92? 52   **2.** $16 + b = 93$ 77 or 109? 77   **5-1**

Solve the equation.

3. $c + 8 = 17$ 9   **4.** $6 + h = 21$ 15   **5.** $57 = 19 + r$ 38   **5-2**

6. $5e = 45$ 9   **7.** $132 = 6p$ 22   **8.** $9s = 540$ 60   **5-3**

9. $d - 4 = 11$ 15   **10.** $49 = n - 3$ 52   **11.** $x - 12 = 39$ 51   **5-4**

12. $\dfrac{1}{2}f = 7$ 14   **13.** $\dfrac{g}{3} = 4$ 12   **14.** $\dfrac{3}{5}y = 42$ 70   **5-5**

15. $8a + 4 = 28$ 3   **16.** $6x - 1 = 17$ 3   **17.** $4v + 5 = 53$ 12   **5-6**

18. $9w - 1 = 8w + 7$ 8 **19.** $2b - 1 = 13 - b$ $\dfrac{14}{3}$ **20.** $5c + 5 = 2c + 23$ 6   **5-7**

Complete by writing an algebraic expression.

21. a. 5 less than $12 = \underline{\ ?\ }$ $12 - 5$ **5-8**
   b. 5 less than $n = \underline{\ ?\ }$ $n - 5$
   c. 5 less than $3x = \underline{\ ?\ }$ $3x - 5$
   d. 5 less than twice the number $p = \underline{\ ?\ }$ $2p - 5$
22. Carl worked 3 hours more than Janet last week.
   Let j = number of hours Janet worked.
   a. Number of hours Carl worked $= \underline{\ ?\ }$ $j + 3$
   b. Max worked 2 hours less than Carl worked last week.
   Number of hours Max worked $= \underline{\ ?\ }$ $j + 1$

Write an equation. Solve the problem.

23. Bart earned $15 more than Norma.   **5-9**
   Bart earned $44.
   How much did Norma earn? $n + 15 = 44$; $29
   (Let n = amount that Norma earned.)
24. Carol sold 6 more tickets to the school play than Bob.
   Carol sold 13 tickets. $x + 6 = 13$; 7 tickets
   How many tickets did Bob sell?
25. A number is doubled, then the result is increased by 17. The final   **5-10**
   result is 41. What is the original number? $2n + 17 = 41$; 12

Cumulative Review (Chapters 1–5)

Add, subtract, multiply, or divide.

1. $361 + 8.2 + 19$ 388.2

2. $7491 \times 0 \times 84$ 0

3. $17 + 35 \cdot 4$ 157

4. $(4.2 + 5) \div 4$ 2.3

5. $8002 - 36.21$ 7965.79

6. 100×483.21 48,321

7. $3 \cdot 3 \cdot 3 \cdot 3$ 81

8. $10 \cdot 10 \cdot 10 \cdot 10 \cdot 10$ 100,000

9. $36 \div 4 + 7$ 16

10. $\dfrac{1}{2} \cdot \dfrac{1}{8} \cdot \dfrac{2}{3}$ $\dfrac{1}{24}$

11. $\dfrac{3}{4} \cdot \dfrac{2}{5} \cdot \dfrac{5}{6}$ $\dfrac{1}{4}$

12. $\dfrac{2}{3} + \dfrac{1}{4} - \dfrac{1}{4}$ $\dfrac{2}{3}$

13. $32 + 4 \cdot 9$ 68

14. $(3645)(0)(1)$ 0

15. $(6.2)(8) - 49.6$ 0

16. $\dfrac{1}{8} \times 8$ 1

17. $2004 \div 1.2$ 1670

18. $\left(1\dfrac{1}{2}\right) \div \left(1\dfrac{1}{2}\right) + 1^2$

Factor.

$\dfrac{1}{2}(a + b + c)$ $2(a + 2n - 3x)$ $5y(y - 2)$

19. $\dfrac{1}{2}a + \dfrac{1}{2}b + \dfrac{1}{2}c$

20. $2a + 4n - 6x$

21. $5y^2 - 10y$

22. $2j^2 - 3j$ $j(2j - 3)$

23. $5n^2 - 25$ $5(n^2 - 5)$

24. $12p^2 - 6p - 2$ $2(6p^2 - 3p - 1)$

Solve.

25. A first number is 47 greater than a second number. Let $n =$ the first number. Then __?__ = the second number. $n - 47$

26. A florist told Rocky that his plant would grow from 10 to 12 cm during the summer if conditions were right. The plant grew from 14.7 cm to 15.9 cm. Was the growth within the limits the florist gave?   no

Write an equation. Solve the problem.

27. Sue worked 8 hours at $9.50 per hour, then at time and one half for 4 hours. How much did she earn in all? $(9.50)(8) + (9.50)(1.5)(4) = x$; $133.00

28. I'm thinking of a number. If I multiply it by 6 and then add 7, the result is 31. What is my number? $6x + 7 = 31$; 4

29. There are 56 members of a volunteer group. Twenty-four are women. How many are men? $56 - 24 = x$; 32

30. Mike's little sister has half as much money as Mike. Together they have $63. How much does each have? $x + \dfrac{1}{2}x = 63$; $42, $21

6
Formulas

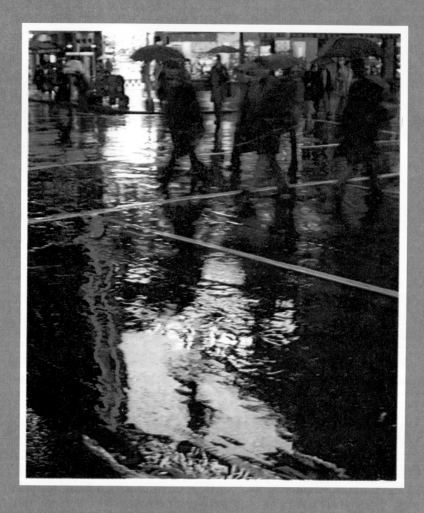

You often see skid marks on the road when a motorist brakes to come to a quick stop. Based on the condition of the road surface, you can use a formula to estimate the rate of speed before braking.

6-1 Perimeter

Some airports are enclosed by cyclone fencing. The diagram below is a drawing of one such airport. To find the total length of fencing around the airport, you add the lengths of the sides. If your addition is correct, you get 9487 ft.

The distance around a figure is called its **perimeter.** Some figures have special formulas for their perimeters. To use any of these formulas, simply replace the variables in the formula with the numbers you know.

<table>
<tr><td>Square
$P = 4s$</td><td>Rectangle
$P = 2l + 2w$</td><td>Triangle
$P = a + b + c$</td></tr>
</table>

Example 1   A rectangle is 25 ft long and 15 ft wide. What is its perimeter?

Solution $P = 2l + 2w$ ⟵ *Use the formula for rectangle.*
$ = 2 \times 25 + 2 \times 15$ ⟵ *Replace the variables with the numbers.*

So, the perimeter is 80 ft.

Your Turn   • A rectangle is 24 ft long and 18 ft wide. What is its perimeter? 84 ft

173

For some figures there are no general perimeter formulas. To find the perimeter of such figures, you simply add the lengths of the sides as we did when we found the distance around the airport. In some cases you might even need to find the lengths of one or more sides before you do the addition.

Example 2 Find the perimeter of the figure shown below.

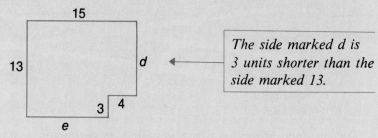

The side marked d is 3 units shorter than the side marked 13.

Solution The distance marked d must be $13 - 3$, or 10.
The distance marked e must be $15 - 4$, or 11.
$P = 13 + 15 + 10 + 4 + 3 + 11 = 56$

Your Turn • Find the perimeter of the figure at the right. 65

Class Exercises

Complete the formula for the perimeter of the figure.

1. rectangle
$P = 2l +$ __?__ 2w

2. square
$P =$ __?__ s 4

3. triangle   b, c
$P = a +$ __?__ $+$ __?__

Complete.

4. side a is 15 in. long
side b is 4 in. shorter than side a
side b is __?__ in. long 11

5. side x is 20 in. long
side y is 7 in. shorter than side x
side y is __?__ in. long 13

Exercises

Use a formula to find the perimeter of the figure.

A **1.**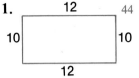

12   44
10   10
12

2.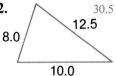

30.5
12.5
8.0
10.0

3.

7.1   28.4
7.1   7.1
7.1

$$P = 2l + 2w \qquad P = a + b + c \qquad P = 4s$$

Use a formula to find the perimeter of the figure.

B **4.**

136 m
46 m
22 m

5.

4.2 mi   16.8 mi
4.2 mi

6.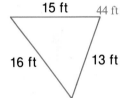

15 ft   44 ft
16 ft   13 ft

7.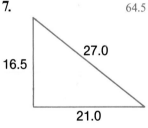

64.5
27.0
16.5
21.0

8.

$12l + 8w$
$4w$
$6l$

9.

28s
7s
7s

Find the perimeter of the figure.

10.

3 ft   26 ft
1 ft →
4 ft
5 ft   5 ft
5 ft
← 1 ft
2 ft

11.

13.2 m   78.9 m
9.5 m
7.0 m
12.4 m   11.6 m
25.2 m

12.

12 km   82 km
7 km
18 km   x
y
23 km

13. In the triangle shown, $a = 15$,
$b = 18$, and $P = 49$. What is the
length of c? 16

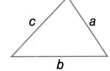

c   a
b

6-2 Circumference

The curved section in the drawing of the window is one half of a circle or a semicircle. The segment that passes through the center of the circle at point O and divides the circle in half is a **diameter** (d). The distance around the circle, called the **circumference** (C), has a special relationship to the diameter. A formula that relates the diameter to the circumference is $C \div d = \pi$. Complete each division in the table below to find an approximation for the Greek letter π (pi).

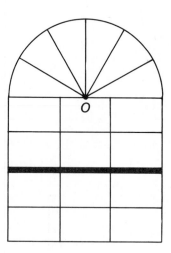

Round the quotient to the nearest hundredth			
Item	C	d	Quotient
bicycle tire	88 in.	28 in.	$88 \div 28 = 3.14$
flower bed	22 yd	7 yd	$22 \div 7 = ?$
manhole cover	125.6 in.	40 in.	$125.6 \div 40 = ?$

Since $C \div d$ results in the same number for all circles, you can use the formula $C \div d = \pi$ to find the circumference of any circle. We usually write $\pi \approx 3.14$. The symbol $\approx$ means *is approximately equal to.*

Example 1   A circular swimming pool has a diameter of 76 m. What is its circumference?

Solution
$$C \div d = \pi$$
$$C \div d \times d = \pi \times d \longleftarrow \quad \textit{Rewrite the formula to get}$$
$$C = \pi d \qquad\qquad\qquad \textit{C on the left of the = sign.}$$
$$\approx 3.14 \times 76$$
$$\approx 238.64$$

Remember from the drawing of the window that the diameter touches the circle twice. A **radius** (*r*) is drawn from the center and touches the circle once. The diameter of a circle is twice as long as the radius. The formula that relates the radius to the circumference is $C = 2\pi r$.

Example 2   The radius of a circle is 32.5 cm. What is its circumference?

Solution $C = 2\pi r$

$\approx 2 \times 3.14 \times 32.5$ ⟵ *Replace π with 3.14.*
Replace r with 32.5.

$\approx 3.14 \times 65$
≈ 204.1

Sometimes the fraction $\frac{22}{7}$ is used as an approximation for π. Change $\frac{22}{7}$ to a decimal to see that $\frac{22}{7} \approx 3.14$. Here is an example of when it is more convenient to use $\pi \approx \frac{22}{7}$.

Example 3   The diameter of a circle is $3\frac{1}{2}$ in. What is its circumference?

Solution $C = \pi d$

$= \pi \times 3\frac{1}{2}$ ⟵ *Replace d with $3\frac{1}{2}$*

$\approx \frac{22}{7} \times \frac{7}{2}$ ⟵ *Replace π with $\frac{22}{7}$.*
Write $3\frac{1}{2}$ as the fraction $\frac{7}{2}$.

$\approx \frac{\overset{11}{\cancel{22}}}{\underset{1}{\cancel{7}}} \times \frac{\overset{1}{\cancel{7}}}{\underset{1}{\cancel{2}}}$

≈ 11

Your Turn   What is the circumference of the circle? Use $\pi \approx \frac{22}{7}$, or $\pi \approx 3.14$.

28.26 yd or $28\frac{2}{7}$ yd
• $d = 9$ yd   • $r = 5.5$ in.   34.54 in.   • $d = 21$ m   66 m

Class Exercises

Complete.

1. $r = 8$
$C = 2 \times \pi \times \underline{\ ?\ }\ 8$

2. $r = 12$
$C = \underline{\ ?\ } \times \pi \times 12\ \ 2$

3. $r = 7.4$
$C = \underline{\ ?\ } \times \pi \times \underline{\ ?\ }$ $2;\ 7.4$

4. $d = 20$
$C = \pi \times \underline{\ ?\ }\ 20$

5. $d = 16.70$
$\underline{\ ?\ } = \pi \times \underline{\ ?\ }\ C;\ 16.70$

6. $d = 0.98$
$C = \underline{\ ?\ } \times \underline{\ ?\ }\pi;\ 0.98$

Exercises

Use $\pi \approx 3.14$ to find the circumference.

A **1.** 31.4

2. 43.96

3. 15.7

Find the circumference of the circle described. Use $\pi \approx 3.14$ for 4–9.

Use $\pi \approx \dfrac{22}{7}$ for 10–15.

B **4.** diameter = 20 in. 62.8 in.

5. diameter = 76 m 238.64 m

6. diameter = 40 in. 125.6 in.

7. radius = 15 m 94.2 m

8. radius = 1.6 mi 10.048 mi

9. radius = 3.12 km 19.5936 km

10. diameter = 28 88

11. diameter = 42 132

12. diameter = 49 154

13. radius = $\dfrac{14}{33}$ $2\dfrac{2}{3}$

14. radius = $\dfrac{21}{22}$ 6

15. radius = $\dfrac{21}{44}$ 3

Problems

1. The curved section of the figure is a semicircle. Which figure has the greater perimeter: the shaded figure or the unshaded one?
neither, the perimeters are equal

4 cm

←—8 cm—→|←—8 cm—→

2. The front wheel of a certain tricycle has a radius of 14 in. Each back wheel has a radius of 6 in. How much larger is the circumference of the front wheel than the circumference of a back wheel? 50.24 in.

6-3 Angle Measurement

You are probably very familiar with the type of angle marked (⌐) in the square, the rectangle, and the right triangle shown below. The measure of this angle is 90°, and it is referred to as a **right angle.**

Right angle

Square
4 right angles

Rectangle
4 right angles

Right triangle
1 right angle

There are four right angles, or 360°, in one complete revolution around any given point. Therefore, every circle contains 360°.

One complete revolution

There are two right angles, or 180° in one half of a revolution. An angle that measures 180° is usually referred to as a **straight angle.**

Half of one revolution

Angles are classified by their measures. Study the table below to see how some angles are classified.

Angle	Name	Measure
	Acute	Less than 90°
	Right	90°
	Obtuse	More than 90° but less than 180°
	Straight	180°

179

We generally use three letters to name an angle, but an angle is sometimes named using only the letter at the **vertex.** The symbol for angle is ∠.

∠ *NOP,* or ∠ *PON,* or ∠ *O*

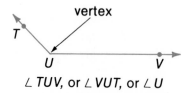

∠ *TUV,* or ∠ *VUT,* or ∠ *U*

Example 1 Use the diagram below to name an angle as indicated.
- right angle
- straight angle
- acute angle
- obtuse angle

Solution

right angle: ∠ *CED*
straight angle: ∠ *AED*
acute angle: ∠ *AEB*
obtuse angle: ∠ *BED*
Notice that ∠ *CEA* is also a right angle and ∠ *BEC* is also an acute angle.

The diagram on the right shows two lines that intersect to form right angles. Two lines that form right angles are said to be **perpendicular.** The symbol for perpendicular is ⊥. We write $\overleftrightarrow{LM}$ to mean line *LM*.

Now look at these two lines. They are the same distance apart and will never intersect. Two lines in a plane that do not intersect are **parallel.** We write $\overleftrightarrow{AB}\|\overleftrightarrow{CD}$ to mean $\overleftrightarrow{AB}$ is parallel to $\overleftrightarrow{CD}$.

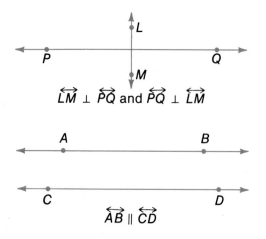

$\overleftrightarrow{LM} \perp \overleftrightarrow{PQ}$ and $\overleftrightarrow{PQ} \perp \overleftrightarrow{LM}$

$\overleftrightarrow{AB} \| \overleftrightarrow{CD}$

Example 2   In the diagram shown below, name two parallel lines and two perpendicular lines.

Solution   parallel lines: $\overleftrightarrow{HJ} \| \overleftrightarrow{FG}$
perpendicular lines: $\overleftrightarrow{AB} \perp \overleftrightarrow{FG}$

Your Turn   Use the diagram in Example 2 to complete the statement.

- $GF \| \underline{\quad?\quad}$ *JH*   • $GF \perp \underline{\quad?\quad}$ *AB*

Class Exercises

Match the statement with the correct letter.

1. The angle measure is less than 90°. C   **A.** right angle
2. The angle measure is 90°.   A   **B.** straight angle
3. The angle measure is 180°.   B   **C.** acute angle
4. *B* is at the vertex of the angle. E   **D.** ∠CAB
5. *C* is at the vertex of the angle. F   **E.** ∠CBA
6. *A* is at the vertex of the angle. D   **F.** ∠ACB

Exercises

Write *yes* or *no* to answer the question.
Use the diagram shown at right.

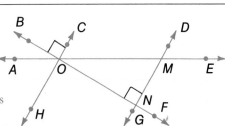

A 1. Is $\overleftrightarrow{BF} \perp \overleftrightarrow{CH}$? yes   2. Is $\overleftrightarrow{HC} \| \overleftrightarrow{GD}$? yes
3. Is $\overleftrightarrow{AE} \| \overleftrightarrow{DG}$? no   4. Is $\overleftrightarrow{GD} \perp \overleftrightarrow{BF}$? yes
5. Is $\overleftrightarrow{AE} \perp \overleftrightarrow{HC}$? no   6. Is $\overleftrightarrow{CH} \| \overleftrightarrow{EA}$? no

181

The measure of an angle is given below. Tell whether it is an acute, obtuse, right, or straight angle.

B **7.** 60° acute **8.** 25° acute **9.** 180° straight **10.** 92° obtuse **11.** 100° obtuse

12. 90° right **13.** 105° obtuse **14.** 37° acute **15.** 172° obtuse **16.** 87° acute

Use the figures above for Exercises 17–22.

17. Name two sides in the triangle that are perpendicular. *ST, TV*

18. Name two pairs of parallel sides in the rectangle. *AD, BC; AB, DC*

Find the sum of the angle measures.

19. $\angle STV + \angle TVS + \angle VST$ 180°

20. $\angle EFG + \angle FGH + \angle GHE$ 250°

21. $\angle ABC + \angle CDA + \angle DAB$ 270°

22. $\angle HEF + \angle TSV + \angle ADC$ 255°

In the diagram shown at right $\angle MPN = 50°$.

C **23.** What is the measure of $\angle MPR + \angle RPQ$? 180°

24. Are $\overleftrightarrow{MQ}$ and $\overleftrightarrow{NR}$ parallel? Explain. no, they intersect

25. Are $\overleftrightarrow{MQ}$ and $\overleftrightarrow{NR}$ perpendicular? Explain.
no, they do not form right angles

Self Test 1

Find the perimeter of the figure described.

1. square 44 ft
$s = 11$ ft

2. rectangle 68 in.
$l = 18$ in.
$w = 16$ in.

3. triangle 53.8 cm
sides $= 16.7$ cm, 18.0 cm, 19.1 cm

6-1

Find the circumference of the circle described. Use $\pi \approx 3.14$.

4. diameter $= 21$ yd 65.94 yd

5. radius $= 3.2$ m 20.096 m

6. radius $= 1.1$ mi 6.908 mi **6-2**

Write whether the angle is acute, obtuse, right, or straight.

7. 90° right **8.** 101° obtuse **9.** 180° straight **10.** 13° acute **11.** 3° acute **6-3**

6-4 Area of Polygons

When you measure the surface inside a closed figure, you are really finding the area (A) of the figure. Area is measured in square units. Some familiar square units used for measuring small areas are square inch (in.^{2}) and square centimeter (cm^2). Square miles (mi^2) and square kilometers (km^2) are generally used to measure large areas.

$A = bh$ $A = bh$ $A = \frac{1}{2}bh$ $A = s^2$

The area formulas for some common polygons are given above. We use b to represent the length of the base and h to represent the height. Any side of a parallelogram can be its base. Its height is the perpendicular distance between the base and the opposite side.

You can use the area formula $A = bh$ to find the area of a square, but the formula that is most often used is $A = s^2$. The variable s is used to represent the length of any side.

Example 1   A parallelogram is $4\frac{1}{2}$ in. high and its base is $3\frac{1}{2}$ in. What is its area?

Solution

$A = bh$ ←——— *Use the area formula for a parallelogram.*

$ = 3\frac{1}{2} \times 4\frac{1}{2}$ ←——— *Replace the variables with the numbers.*

$ = \frac{7}{2} \times \frac{9}{2}$ ←——— *Write the mixed numbers as fractions.*

$ = \frac{63}{4} = 15\frac{3}{4}$ ←——— *Multiply the fractions, then simplify the answer.*

The area is $15\frac{3}{4}$ in.^{2}

Your Turn • A rectangle is $2\frac{1}{2}$ in. high and its base is 4 in. What is its area? 10 in.²

Sometimes you may want to find the area of only a part of a figure. Example 2 below shows one way to find a partial area.

Example 2 Find the area of the shaded portion of the figure.

Solution Find the area of the square.

$$A = s^2$$
$$= 8^2$$
$$= 64 \quad \longleftarrow \quad \textit{Remember that } 8^2 \textit{ means } 8 \times 8.$$

Find the area of the rectangle.

$$A = bh = 5 \times 6$$
$$= 30$$

Find the difference in area.

$$(64 - 30) \text{ cm}^2 \quad \longleftarrow \quad \textit{The area of the square is 64 cm}^2.$$
$$= 34 \text{ cm}^2 \qquad\qquad \textit{The area of the rectangle is 30 cm}^2.$$

Your Turn • Find the area of the shaded portion of the figure. 26 cm²

Class Exercises

Use a formula to find the area of the figure.

1. 24.5 m²   2.   40 ft²   3.   8 in.²

3.5 m   5 ft   4 in.

7.0 m   8 ft   4 in.

Exercises

Find the area of the figure described below.

A **1.** triangle 17.5 ft²
$b = 7$ ft
$h = 5$ ft

2. parallelogram 154 cm²
$b = 14$ cm
$h = 11$ cm

3. square 110.25 m²
$s = 10.5$ m

B **4.** rectangle $35\frac{3}{4}$ ft²
$b = 6\frac{1}{2}$ ft
$h = 5\frac{1}{2}$ ft

5. triangle $43\frac{1}{20}$ in.²
$h = 8\frac{2}{5}$ in.
$b = 10\frac{1}{4}$ in.

6. parallelogram 208.98 cm²
$h = 12.9$ cm
$b = 16.2$ cm

Find the area of the shaded section.

7.

12 cm

12 cm 72 cm²

8.

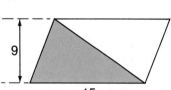

9

15 67.5 sq units

9.

12   18
12

24 288 sq units

Problems

Solve.

1. 7 yd times some length is 63 yd². 9 yd
2. $\frac{1}{2}b$ times 14 is 112. 16
3. 400 yd² divided by h is 20 yd. 20 yd
4. A tennis court is 26 yd long and has an area of 312 yd². What is its width? 12 yd
5. Table tennis is played on a table that has an area of 5 yd² and is 5 ft wide. What is the length of the table? 9 ft
6. The area of the tennis court is how many times larger than the area of the table tennis table?
$62\frac{2}{5}$ times larger

185

6-5 Area of Circles

You know that the area for many polygons is related to the height and base of the individual figure. The area formula of a circle is not usually described in terms of height and base, but the diagrams below suggest that we can use a parallelogram to show how a formula for finding the area of a circle is developed.

 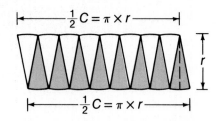

Notice that the base of the parallelogram is really the same as one half the circumference of the circle. The height of the parallelogram is just about the same as the radius of the circle. So, the area formula for the circle can be stated as $A = \frac{1}{2}C \cdot r$. You know that $C = 2\pi r$. So you can replace C with $2\pi r$ and rewrite the area formula.

$$A = \frac{1}{2} \cdot 2\pi r \cdot r$$
$$= \pi r^2 \longleftarrow \quad \frac{1}{\cancel{2}} \cdot \cancel{2}\pi r \cdot r = \pi r^2$$

Example 1   The radius of a circle is 8 cm. What is its area? Use $\pi \approx 3.14$.

Solution $A = \pi r^2 \longleftarrow$ *Use the area formula for a circle.*
          $\approx 3.14 \times 8^2$
          ≈ 200.96
The area is 200.96 cm².

Your Turn • The radius of a circle is 6 cm. What is its area? Use $\pi \approx 3.14$. 113.04 cm²

Sometimes you may have to find the area of two different figures, then subtract the smaller area from the larger area.

Example 2 Find the area of the shaded portion of the figure shown. Use $\pi \approx 3.14$.
Larger radius = 15 ft.
Smaller radius = 6 ft.

Solution Find the area of the large circle.
$A \approx 3.14 \times 15^2$ ←——— *The radius of the large circle is 15 ft.*
$\approx 3.14 \times 225$
≈ 706.5
Find the area of the small circle.
$A \approx 3.14 \times 6^2$ ←——— *The radius of the small circle is 6 ft.*
$\approx 3.14 \times 36$
≈ 113.04
Find the difference.
$(706.5 - 113.04) = 593.46 \text{ ft}^2$
The area of the shaded portion is 593.46 ft^2.

Your Turn Find the area of the shaded portion of the figure shown above. Use $\pi \approx 3.14$.
- larger radius = 6 34.54   • larger radius = 11 226.08
  smaller radius = 5   smaller radius = 7

Class Exercises

Write the correct number to complete. Use $\pi \approx 3.14$.

1. $r = 6$
   $A \approx \underline{\ ?\ } \times 6^2$ 3.14

2. $r = 8$
   $A \approx 3.14 \times \underline{\ ?\ }$ 8^2

3. $r = 10.2$ 10.2^2
   $A \approx 3.14 \times \underline{\ ?\ }$

4. $r = 7.5$
   $A \approx \underline{\ ?\ } \times \underline{\ ?\ }$ 3.14; 7.5^2

5. $d = 14$
   $A \approx \underline{\ ?\ } \times 7^2$ 3.14

6. $d = 18$ 3.14; 9^2
   $A \approx \underline{\ ?\ } \times \underline{\ ?\ }$

187

Exercises

Find the area of the circle. Use $\pi \approx 3.14$.

A **1.** 200.96 in.²

8 in.

2. 176.625 m²

7.5 m

3. 5538.96 yd²

84 yd

4. 1519.76 ft²

44 ft

Find the area of the circle described. Use $\pi \approx 3.14$.

B **5.** $r = 3.5$ in. 38.465 in.²

6. $r = 6.1$ ft 116.8394 ft²

7. $r = 9$ yd 254.34 yd²

8. $d = 17$ m 226.865 m²

9. $d = 20$ mi 314 mi²

10. $d = 24$ cm 452.16 cm²

Which figure has the greater area? What is the difference in area?

11. circle; 481.5 in.²

15 in.

15 in.

15 in.

15 in.

12. triangle; 52.815 m²

38 m

21 m

21 m

13. circle; 15.94 ft²

14 ft

26 ft

22 ft

14. circle; 115.44 km²

20 km

25 km

28 km

Find the area of the shaded part. Use $\pi \approx 3.14$.

15. 18.84

2.5 3.5

16. 17.415

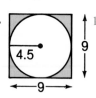

4.5

9

9

17. 100.48

16

18. 14.52

7

12

Find the area of the figure. Each curve is a semicircle. Use $\pi \approx 3.14$.

C **19.** 1316.16 yd²

24 yd

36 yd

20. 4719.465 ft²

43 ft

76 ft

6-6 *Problem Solving*

The formulas you have studied so far are useful for solving problems that are related to perimeter and area. There are other useful formulas that you can use to solve a variety of problems.

When you use formulas, it is important that you know which number or quantity each variable represents. For example, a weight applied at one end of a lever can move a much heavier weight at the other end. To use the lever formula correctly you must be able to tell which variable represents the heavier weight and which represents the lighter weight.

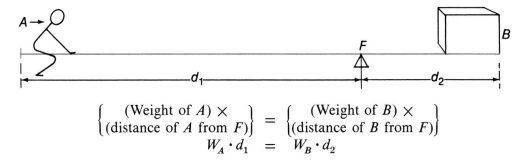

$$\left\{\begin{array}{c}\text{(Weight of } A) \times \\ \text{(distance of } A \text{ from } F)\end{array}\right\} = \left\{\begin{array}{c}\text{(Weight of } B) \times \\ \text{(distance of } B \text{ from } F)\end{array}\right\}$$
$$W_A \cdot d_1 = W_B \cdot d_2$$

Example In the drawing shown above, B represents a 160-lb box and is 4 ft from F. The person, A, is 10 ft from F. Find the weight of the person that will move the box.

Solution Use the lever formula.
$$W_A \cdot d_1 = W_B \cdot d_2$$
$$W_A \cdot 10 = 160 \cdot 4 \quad \longleftarrow \quad \textit{Divide both sides of the equation by 10.}$$
$$10\,W_A = 640$$
$$W_A = 64$$
The weight of the person to move the box is 64 lb.

Your Turn • In the drawing above, the box weighs 120 lb. F is 3 ft from the box and 8 ft from the person. Find the weight of the person that will move the box. 45 lb

189

Class Exercises

Copy the table and use the formula to
complete. Round to the nearest thousandth.

$$\text{batting average} = \frac{\text{number of hits}}{\text{times at bat}}$$

$$A = \frac{h}{t}$$

	h	t	$h \div t$	
1.	40	85	?	0.471
2.	60	210	?	0.286
3.	24	85	?	0.282
4.	32	94	?	0.340

Exercises

Use the formula $W = \dfrac{11(h - 40)}{2}$ to solve.

A **1.** $h = 64$ in.
  $W = \underline{\ ?\ }$ 132

2. $h = 67$ in.
  $W = \underline{\ ?\ }$ 148.5

3. $h = 59$ in.
  $W = \underline{\ ?\ }$ 104.5

4. $h = 72$ in.
  $W = \underline{\ ?\ }$ 176

5. $h = 49\frac{1}{2}$ in.
  $W = \underline{\ ?\ }$ 52.25

6. $h = 60\frac{1}{3}$ in.
  $W = \underline{\ ?\ }$ $111\frac{5}{6}$

More Formulas

Skid marks: $L = s^2 \div 18.6 \longleftarrow$ L = length of skid marks (ft)
  s = speed (mi/h)

Air speed: $a - h = g \longleftarrow$ a = airspeed (mi/h)
  h = head wind speed
  g = ground speed

Electricity: $I = W \div V \longleftarrow$ I = current (amps)
  W = power (W)
  V = force (volts)

Choose the correct formula and use it to solve problems 7–10.

B **7.** Two children are balanced on
the seesaw (lever) as shown.
How far is the heavier child
from point F? 6.6 ft

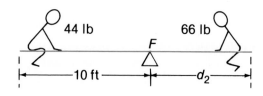
44 lb   66 lb F 10 ft d_2

8. Marsha was driving at a speed of 40 mi/h when a football rolled into the street. She applied her brakes immediately. How long were the skid marks made by the tires? 86.02 ft

9. A pilot reports an air speed of 625 mi/h. If the plane is flying into a head wind of 30 mi/h, what is the ground speed? 595 mi/h

10. A 20-amp fuse will burn out if more than 20 amps of current try to flow through the fuse. Suppose a hair styler using 1000 W of current, a humidifier using 177 W, and an electric iron using 1008 W are all connected to the same 110-volt line. If all these appliances are turned on at the same time, will the 20-amp fuse burn out? no

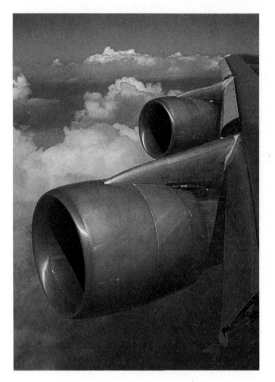

Self Test 2

Find the area of the figure described.

1. triangle 16 ft²
$b = 8$ ft
$h = 4$ ft

2. rectangle 150.96 in.²
$b = 13.6$ in.
$h = 11.1$ in.

3. parallelogram 120.36 yd²
$b = 11.8$ yd
$h = 10.2$ yd
6-4

Find the area of the circle described. Use $\pi \approx 3.14$.

4. $r = 2.5$ ft 19.625 ft²

5. $d = 22$ yd 379.94 yd²

6. $r = 8.8$ cm 243.1616 cm²
6-5

Use the formula $a - h = g$ to solve. (a = airspeed, h = head wind speed, and g = ground speed)

7. An airplane is flying into a 25 mi/h wind. Its air speed is 650 mi/h. What is the ground speed? 625 mi/h
6-6

Self Test answers and Extra Practice are at the back of the book.

6-7 Volume of Prisms and Pyramids

A **prism** is a solid figure with two identical bases. The volume (V) of a prism is the amount of space it contains. Some standard units of volume are cubic centimeter (cm^3), cubic foot (ft^3), and cubic yard (yd^3). Study the prisms shown below.

Rectangular Prism

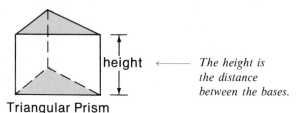

Triangular Prism

height ← *The height is the distance between the bases.*

The shaded portions of each prism are the bases. Notice that the shape of the base determines the name of the prism. The base area of a prism is the area of one base. The formula for the volume of a prism is $V = Bh$. ← *B means base area; h means height.*

Example 1 Find the volume of the prism shown at the right.

Solution
$B = 9 \times 4 = 36 \text{ m}^2$
$V = Bh$
$\quad = 36 \cdot 5$
$\quad = 180 \text{ m}^3$ ← *Notice that we express the answer in cubic meters.*

5 m

4 m   9 m

The figures below are pyramids. Like the prisms you studied above, the base of a pyramid determines its name. The formula for the volume of a pyramid is $V = \frac{1}{3}Bh$. ← *B means base area; h means height.*

Triangular Pyramid

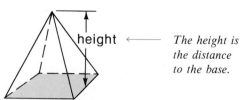

Square Pyramid

height ← *The height is the distance to the base.*

Example 2 The base area of the pyramid shown is 24 ft² and the height is 17 ft. What is its volume?

Solution
$$V = \frac{1}{3}Bh$$

$$= \frac{1}{\underset{1}{3}} \cdot \overset{8}{24} \cdot 17$$

$$= 8 \cdot 17 = 136$$
The volume is 136 ft³.

Your Turn • The base area of a pyramid is 18 cm² and the height is 10 cm. What is its volume? 60 cm³

Class Exercises

Complete.

8 m

8 m

8 m

10.5 cm

25.0 cm²

9 cm

11 cm

4 cm

1. $V = (\underset{64}{\underline{\ ?\ }} \cdot 8)$ m³

2. $V = (\overset{25.0;\ 10.5}{\underline{\ ?\ } \cdot \underline{\ ?\ }})$ cm³

3. $V = \left(\frac{1}{3} \cdot \overset{44;\ 9}{\underline{\ ?\ } \cdot \underline{\ ?\ }}\right)$ cm³

Exercises

Find the volume of the prism.

A **1.** $h = 7$ in.
$B = 22$ in.² 154 in.³

2. $h = 12$ cm
$B = 19$ cm² 228 cm³

3. $h = 11$ yd
$B = 30$ yd² 330 yd³

4. $h = 18$ cm
$B = 49$ cm² 882 cm³

5. $h = 8$ ft
$B = 25$ ft² 200 ft³

6. $h = 10$ yd
$B = 26.75$ yd² 267.5 yd³

193

Find the volume of the figure.

B **7.** square prism (cube) 6331.625 yd³

$B = 18.5$ yd by 18.5 yd

$h = 18.5$ yd

8. triangular prism 1785 cm³

$B = \left(\frac{1}{2} \cdot 17 \cdot 15\right) \text{cm}^2$

$h = 14 \, \text{cm}$

9. triangular pyramid 29.75 m³

$B = \left(\frac{1}{2} \cdot 21\right) \text{m}^2$

$h = 8.5 \, \text{m}$

10. rectangular pyramid $139\frac{1}{3}$ ft³

$B = 19 \, \text{ft} \times 13.2 \, \text{ft}$

$h = 20 \, \text{in.}$

11. 7644 in.³

39 in.
7 in.
28 in.

12. 20 yd³

10 yd
3 yd   4 yd

13. 1521 ft³

26 ft
9 ft   13 ft

Problems

Solve.

1. B times 8 yd is 128 yd³.   16 yd²
2. B times 12 m is 216 m³.   18 m²
3. 49 m² times h is 294 m³.   6 m
4. $\frac{1}{3}B$ times 9 ft is 54 ft³.   18 ft²
5. 27 times $\frac{1}{3}$ times h is 99.   11
6. The original plan for the Great Pyramid of Cheops, near Cairo, Egypt, includes these measurements: $B = 765$ ft², $h = 320$ ft. Use the measurements to find the volume.   81,600 ft³
7. A plan for the Pyramid at Meydum includes these measurements: $B = 476$ ft², $h = 298$ ft. Find the volume. $47,282\frac{2}{3}$ ft³

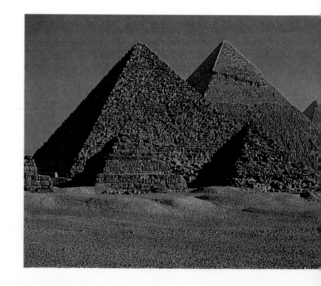

6-8 *Volume of Cylinders and Cones*

Formulas for the volume of a cylinder and a cone are similar to the formulas for the volume of a prism and a pyramid.

The height is the distance between the bases.

Cylinder
$V = Bh$

$B = \pi r^2$

Cone
$V = \frac{1}{3} Bh$

The height is the distance to the base.

Notice that the base of both a cylinder and a cone are circular. You will use what you know about the area of a circle to find the base area (*B*) of these two figures.

Example 1   The radius of a cylinder is 10 in. and the height is 12 in. What is the volume? Use $\pi \approx 3.14$.

Solution   Step 1: Solve for *B*.
$$B = \pi r^2$$
$$\approx 3.14 \cdot 10^2$$
$$\approx 314 \text{ in.}^2$$

Step 2: Solve for *V*.
$$V = Bh$$
$$\approx 314 \cdot 12$$
$$\approx 3768 \text{ in.}^3$$

Example 2   The base area and the height of a cone are the same as the base area and height of the cylinder in Example 1. What is the volume of the cone?

Solution   Step 1: $B = \pi r^2$
$$\approx 3.14 \cdot 10^2$$
$$\approx 314 \text{ in.}^2$$

Step 2: $V = \frac{1}{3} \cdot 314 \cdot 12$
$$= 1256 \text{ in.}^3$$

Your Turn   A cylinder and a cone have the same base area and the same height. The radius is 8 in. and the height is 20 in.
  • Find the volume of the cylinder. 4019.2 in.³
  • Find the volume of the cone.   1339.7̄3 in.³

195

Class Exercises

Complete the formula by writing the correct number from the diagram on the right.

$B = \pi r^2$

$V = Bh \qquad V = \frac{1}{3} Bh$

8 in.

20 in.

1. $B = \underline{\;?\;} \cdot 8^2$ ³·¹⁴

2. $V = 3.14 \cdot 8^2 \cdot \underline{\;?\;}$ ²⁰

3.14; 14

3. $B = 3.14 \cdot \underline{\;?\;}$ ⁹²

4. $V = \frac{1}{3} \cdot \underline{\;?\;} \cdot 9^2 \cdot \underline{\;?\;}$

14 cm

5. $\underline{\;?\;} = (3.14 \cdot 81)$ cm² ᴮ

6. $V = \frac{1}{3} \cdot 3.14 \cdot 81 \cdot \underline{\;?\;}$ ¹⁴

9 cm

Exercises

Find the volume of the figure. Use $\pi \approx 3.14$

A 1. 2769.48 in.³

7 in.

|←——18 in.——→|

2. 1058.70$\overline{3}$ cm³

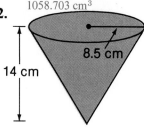

8.5 cm

14 cm

3. 2207.8125 m³

7.5 m

12.5 m

B 4. 904.32 cm³

3 cm

32 cm

5. 4521.6 in.³

12 in.

|←———30 in.———→|

6. 1004.8 yd³

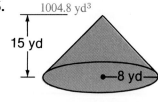

15 yd

8 yd

7. 1959.36 cm³

6 cm

10 cm

|←14 cm→|

8. 6028.8 in.³

12 in.

12 in.

20 in. ┊ 20 in.

9. 221.37 ft³ |←—4 ft—→|←——6.5 ft——→|

3 ft

10. The cylinder and the cone have equal radii and equal heights. The volume of the cylinder is 90 ft³. What is the volume of the cone?

30 ft³

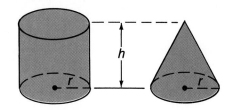

C 11. Assume that the top part of the bottle is a cone and the bottom part is a cylinder. What is the volume? 602.88 cm³

9 cm

9 cm

8 cm

12. Find the total volume of the cup and the funnel. 15,147.36 cm³

16 cm

18 cm

22 cm

12 cm

10 cm

Using the Computer

Computer programs can be written to evaluate formulas. This program will find the volume of a cylinder when the height and the radius of the base are given. RUN this program for R = 3 and H = 6. Now try some examples of your own.

```
 5  REM: VOLUME OF A CYLINDER
10  PRINT "WHAT IS THE RADIUS OF THE BASE";
20  INPUT R
30  PRINT "WHAT IS THE HEIGHT";
40  INPUT H
50  LET P=3.14159
60  PRINT "VOLUME =";P*R*R*H
70  END
```

What is the radius of the base? 3
What is the height? 6
Volume = 169.646

6-9 Surface Area

If you have to paint the entire outside surface of the birdhouse shown at right, you will probably paint one section at a time until all nine sections are painted. The entire outside surface of a figure is referred to as the **surface area** (S).

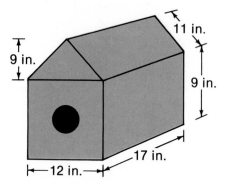

Like the birdhouse shown at right, many of the objects you see every day are made up of flat surfaces called **faces.**

Example 1 Find the surface area of the birdhouse shown above.

Solution

Face	Area	How many?	Total
roof side (rectangle)	$11 \times 17 = 187$ in.²	2	374 in.²
roof end (triangle)	$\frac{1}{2} \times 12 \times 9 = 54$ in.²	2	108 in.²
front (rectangle)	$12 \times 9 = 108$ in.²	1	108 in.²
back (rectangle)	$12 \times 9 = 108$ in.²	1	108 in.²
side (rectangle)	$17 \times 9 = 153$ in.²	2	306 in.²
bottom (rectangle)	$17 \times 12 = 204$ in.²	1	204 in.²
		Surface area =	1208 in.²

The surface area is a little less than 1208 in.² since the area of the entrance must be subtracted.

Your Turn • Find the surface area of the figure at right.
552 in.²

The surface area for the soup can at right includes the area of the circular bases plus the area of the curved surface. Study the diagram to see that the curved surface can be flattened out to form a rectangle. Can you see that the base of the rectangle will have the same measure as the circumference of a circular base?

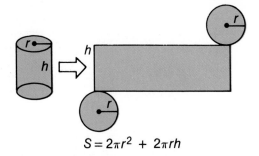

$$S = 2\pi r^2 + 2\pi rh$$

Example 2 Find the surface area of the object shown. Use $\pi \approx \dfrac{22}{7}$.

7 cm

30 cm

Solution $S = 2\pi r^2 + 2\pi rh$

$$\approx \left(2 \cdot \frac{22}{7} \cdot 7^2\right) + \left(2 \cdot \frac{22}{7} \cdot 7 \cdot 30\right)$$

$$\approx \left(\frac{2}{1} \cdot \frac{22}{7} \cdot \frac{\overset{7}{49}}{1}\right) + \left(\frac{2}{1} \cdot \frac{22}{7} \cdot \frac{\overset{1}{7}}{1} \cdot \frac{30}{1}\right) \approx 1628 \text{ cm}^2$$

Your Turn • Find the surface area of a cylinder with a radius of $3\dfrac{1}{2}$ in. and a height of 8 in. Use $\pi \approx \dfrac{22}{7}$.   253 in.²

Class Exercises

Determine the number of faces in the figure.

1. __? 6__ rectangular faces
    __? 0__ triangular faces

2. __? 2__ triangular faces
    __? 3__ rectangular faces

3. __? 2__ circular faces
    __? 1__ rectangular faces

199

Exercises

Find the surface area. Use $\pi \approx 3.14$.

A 1. 384

8
8
8

2. 574

9
7
14

3. 533.8

5
12

The height of each triangular face is 8 ft. Find the surface area.

B 4. 336 ft²

12 ft
12 ft

5. 465 ft²

15 ft
15 ft

6. 176 ft²

12 ft
8 ft
10 ft   10 ft

What is the least amount of paper needed to wrap the object? Use $\pi \approx 3.14$.

7. 468 cm²

15 cm
10 cm
Cheese
9 cm   12 cm

8. 722.2 cm²

|←——18 cm——→|
5 cm→
GOLDEN   CORN MEAL

9. 1628 cm²

|←28 cm→|
19 cm
CRISPY Cereal
6 cm

Self Test 3

Find the volume of the figure described. Use $\pi \approx 3.14$.

1. triangular prism 1200 cm³
   $B = 80$ cm², $h = 15$ cm

2. rectangular prism 360 mm³   **6-7**
   $B = 45$ mm², $h = 8$ mm

3. cylinder 2260.8 in.³
   $r = 6$ in., $h = 20$ in.

4. cone 615.44 cm³   **6-8**
   $r = 7$ cm, $h = 12$ cm

Find the surface area of the figure. Use $\pi \approx 3.14$.

5. 72 m²

3 m
2 m
6 m

6. 18,463.2 mm² **6-9**

42 mm
28 mm

Algebra Practice

Write an equation. Solve.

1. The product of 355 and 982 is r. $355 \cdot 982 = r$; $348,610$

2. The sum of 16.74, 39.1, and 26.492 is m. $16.74 + 39.1 + 26.492 = m$; 82.332

3. 0.0861 divided by 0.07 is equal to x. $0.0861 \div 0.07 = x$; 1.23

4. The difference between $5\frac{1}{2}$ and $2\frac{4}{9}$ is d. $5\frac{1}{2} - 2\frac{4}{9} = d$; $3\frac{1}{18}$

5. $\frac{1}{8}$ of $4\frac{4}{5}$ is equal to q. $\frac{1}{8} \cdot 4\frac{4}{5} = q$; $\frac{3}{5}$

Use the distributive property to factor each expression.

6. $s^3t + (st)^2 + 5st^2$
$st(s^2 + st + 5t)$

7. $6bc + 2b^2 + 4b^2c$
$2b(3c + b + 2bc)$

8. $3gh^2 + g^2h + gh^3$
$gh(3h + g + h^2)$

Solve the equation. Check the solution.

9. $a + 2\frac{3}{4} = 3\frac{1}{8}$ $\frac{3}{8}$

10. $42 = 12t$ $3\frac{1}{2}$

11. $k - \frac{1}{8} = \frac{3}{4}$ $\frac{7}{8}$

12. $\frac{2}{5} = \frac{5}{6}d$ $\frac{12}{25}$

13. $3(r - 2) = 12$ 6

14. $6z - 14 = z + 1$ 3

Write an equation. Solve.

$2(4.8) + 2(3.6) = P$; 16.8 m

15. The perimeter of a rectangle 4.8 m long and 3.6 m wide is P.

$5.3 + 7.5 + 4.4 = P$; 17.2 ft

16. The perimeter of a triangle with sides 5.3 ft, 4.4 ft, and 7.5 ft is P.

$2(3.14)14 = C$; 87.92 yd

17. The circumference of a circle with a radius of 14 yd is C.

18. The area of a triangle with a base of 6.2 km and a height of 2.6 km is A. $\frac{(6.2)(2.6)}{2} = A$; 8.06 km²

19. The area of a circle with a radius of 5 m is A. $(3.14)5^2 = A$; 78.5 m²

20. The area of a circle with a diameter of 28 ft is A. $(3.14)14^2 = A$; 615.44 ft²

21. The volume of a pyramid with a base area of 10 m² and a height of 6 m is V. $\frac{(10)6}{3} = V$; 20 m³

22. The volume of a cylinder with a radius of 4 yd and a height of 5 yd is V. $(3.14)(4^2)(5) = V$; 251.2 yd³

23. The surface area of a box 5 cm wide, 3 cm high, and 10 cm long is S. $(2 \cdot 5 \cdot 10) + (2 \cdot 10 \cdot 3) + (2 \cdot 5 \cdot 3) = S$; 190 cm²

24. The surface area of a cylinder with a radius of 5 ft and a height of 20 ft is S. $2(3.14)5^2 + 2(3.14)(5)(20) = S$; 785 ft²

Problem Solving for the Consumer

The Do-It-Yourselfer

Have you ever wondered how much money people can save by doing at-home repairs themselves rather than hiring someone to do them? Doing the job yourself does cost money, though. Let's take a look at some of the hidden costs in do-it-yourself work.

Project: Renovate Dining Room
Dimensions—13 ft long, 10 ft wide, 8 ft high

Problem: Peeling paint, cracking plaster in spots
Solution: Scrape existing paint, patch plaster, sand down rough spots, and paint

First you need to figure how much paint is needed and how much it will cost.

1. How many square feet of ceiling space is there? 130 ft²
2. How many square feet of wall space is there? (Don't worry about doors and windows. Just pretend there are none.) 368 ft²
3. One quart of paint covers about 100 ft² on the first coat. How many quarts of ceiling paint will be needed for the first coat? How many quarts of wall paint will be needed? 2 quarts; 4 quart
4. Ceiling paint costs $14 per gallon and $3.75 per quart. What is the least amount of money the paint will cost? $7.50
5. Wall paint costs $15.50 per gallon and $4.50 per quart. What is the least amount of money the wall paint will cost? $15.50

6. Copy and complete the chart. Find the total costs of other materials to do the job.

	Price per Unit	Number of Units	Total	
scraper	$2.98	1	?	$2.98
plaster	$4.50	1	?	$4.50
sandpaper	$1.05 (pkg.)	2	?	$2.10
paint brush	$5.89	1	?	$5.89
paint roller covers	$1.69	2	?	$3.38
roller, roller pan	$6 (set)	1	?	$6.00
goggles	$2.95	1	?	$2.95
protective masks	$1.99	1	?	$1.99
			?	$29.79

A unit is one package, one can, etc. →

Needed at the → *sanding stage* { goggles, protective masks }

7. A professional painter will do the job for about $100 (including all materials). What is the difference in price when the job is done by the do-it-yourselfer instead of the professional? $47.21 Does the do-it-yourselfer save money? yes

8. Suppose the do-it-yourselfer buys all the materials and pays an apprentice $5.50 an hour to do the work. If the apprentice completes the work in $6\frac{1}{2}$ h, what is the total cost of renovating the room? $88.54

9. If a second room needs to be done at another time, the do-it-yourselfer can use the following materials again: scraper, paint brush, roller and pan, goggles, protective masks. How much of a savings is this off the cost of supplies for the second room? $19.81

Enrichment

Functions

A function is sometimes referred to as a rule that takes a given value as an input and produces an output. For example, the rate of a certain long distance telephone call is 50¢ for the first minute and 34¢ for each additional minute. You can make up a rule or function for computing the costs of telephone calls. If you use n to represent the length of the phone call in minutes, then you can write a function as follows.

$$n \rightarrow 0.50 + (0.34)(n - 1)$$

Use the function to check the outputs in the table at right. For each input (n) there is one output (cost).

Input (n)	Output (cost)
5	$1.86
10	$3.56
15	$5.26

Use the given function to complete the table of outputs.

1. $n \rightarrow 4n + 1$
- $1 \rightarrow$ 5
- $2 \rightarrow$? 9
- $3 \rightarrow$? 13
- $4 \rightarrow$? 17
- $5 \rightarrow$? 21
- $6 \rightarrow$? 25
- $7 \rightarrow$? 29
- $8 \rightarrow$? 33

2. $n \rightarrow 5n - 3$
- $1 \rightarrow$ 2
- $2 \rightarrow$? 7
- $3 \rightarrow$? 12
- $4 \rightarrow$? 17
- $5 \rightarrow$? 22
- $6 \rightarrow$? 27
- $7 \rightarrow$? 32
- $8 \rightarrow$? 37

3. $n \rightarrow n^2 + 3$
- $1 \rightarrow$ 4
- $2 \rightarrow$? 7
- $3 \rightarrow$? 12
- $4 \rightarrow$? 19
- $5 \rightarrow$? 28
- $6 \rightarrow$? 39
- $7 \rightarrow$? 52
- $8 \rightarrow$? 67

4. $n \rightarrow 3n^2$
- $1 \rightarrow$ 3
- $2 \rightarrow$? 12
- $3 \rightarrow$? 27
- $4 \rightarrow$? 48
- $5 \rightarrow$? 75
- $6 \rightarrow$? 108
- $7 \rightarrow$? 147
- $8 \rightarrow$? 192

Complete the table of outputs, then write a function.

5.

Input	1	2	3	4	5	6	7	8
Output	3	8	15	?	?	?	?	?

Function: $n \rightarrow n^2 + 2n$ 24   35   48   63   80

6.

Input	1	2	3	4	5	6	7	8
Output	1	7	17	31	?	?	?	?

Function: $n \rightarrow 2n^2 - 1$ 49   71   97   127

Chapter Review

Match.

1. perimeter of a rectangle d
2. $A = \pi r^2$ a
3. perimeter of a square h
4. $P = a + b + c$ k
5. perpendicular l
6. $C = 2r \times \pi$ e
7. area of a parallelogram j
8. $A = s^2$ b
9. an angle measuring less than 90° o
10. obtuse angle g
11. an angle that measures 90° n
12. $V = \frac{1}{3}Bh$ i
13. parallel c
14. volume of a prism f
15. surface area of a prism m

a. area of a circle
b. area of a square
c. lines that are the same distance apart
d. $P = 2l + 2w$
e. circumference of a circle
f. $V = Bh$
g. more than 90° but less than 180°
h. $P = 4s$
i. volume of a pyramid
j. $A = bh$
k. perimeter of a triangle
l. lines that form right angles
m. sum of the areas of all the faces
n. right angle
o. acute angle

Choose the correct answer. Write *a*, *b*, or *c*.

16. perimeter of a triangle with sides 4.5 ft, 4.4 ft, and 4.1 ft c
    a. 11 ft   b. 12 ft   c. 13 ft

17. circumference of a circle with diameter = 9 mm. Use $\pi \approx 3.14$. c
    a. 26.28 mm   b. 22.86 mm   c. 28.26 mm

18. an angle that measures 180° b
    a. acute angle   b. straight angle   c. obtuse angle

19. the letter at the vertex of $\angle ABC$ a
    a. B   b. C   c. A

20. One circle has a radius of 25 in. Another circle has a radius of 12 in. Find the difference in the areas of the two circles. 1510.34 in.²

Chapter Test

Find the perimeter of the figure described.

1. rectangle 52.4 ft
$l = 14.2$ ft, $w = 12.0$ ft

2. triangle 36.05 m
sides = 15.0 m, 9.75 m, 11.3 m

6-1

What is the circumference of the circle? Use $\pi \approx 3.14$.

3. $d = 18$ in. 56.52 in.

4. $r = 4$ yd 25.12 yd

5. $d = 35$ ft 109.9 ft

6-2

True or False? Write *T* or *F*.

6. An angle that measures 180° is a right angle.   F

7. An angle that measures 65° is an acute angle.   T

8. An angle that measures 108° is an obtuse angle. T

What is the area of the polygon described?

9. rectangle 368 ft²
$b = 23$ ft, $h = 16$ ft

10. triangle 99 cm²
$b = 18$ cm, $h = 11$ cm

6-4

What is the area of the circle? Use $\pi \approx 3.14$.

11. $r = 15$ ft 706.5 ft²

12. $d = 118$ mi 10,930.34 mi²

13. $r = 8.3$ in. 216.3146 in.²

6-5

Use the formula to solve: Power (kW) · Time (h) = Energy (kW · h).

14. In a certain experiment, 14 kW of power were used in 4 h. How much energy was used? 56 kW · h

6-6

Find the volume of the figure described. Use $\pi \approx 3.14$.

15. rectangular prism 60 ft³

$B = 15$ ft², $h = 4$ ft

16. triangular pyramid 60 in.³

$B = 24$ in.², $h = 7\frac{1}{2}$ in.

6-7

17. cylinder 1130.4 m³
$r = 6$ m, $h = 10$ m

18. cone 122.46 yd³
$r = 3$ yd, $h = 13$ yd

6-8

What is the surface area of the figure shown? Use $\pi \approx 3.14$.

19. 3086 cm²

20. 697.08 in.²

6-9

19 cm
15 cm
37 cm

6.0 in.
12.5 in.

Cumulative Review (Chapters 1–6)

Solve the equation.

1. $y = 2704 - 96$ 2608
2. $0.4 \times 36 = x$ 14.4
3. $6.2 \times 10 = n$ 62

4. $\frac{1}{2} \times 84.2 = t$ 42.1
5. $\frac{3}{4} \cdot 284 = s$ 213
6. $\frac{4}{5} = \frac{x}{10}$ 8

7. $(12)(4.2) - 6 = y$ 44.4
8. $10 \cdot 10 \cdot 10 = z$ 1000
9. $A = (6.2)(5)$ 31

10. $i = \$100 \cdot \frac{1}{8} \cdot 2$ $25
11. $a = 4 + 7 \cdot 9$ 67
12. $j = \frac{1}{3} \cdot 426$ 142

13. $100 \times 0.46 = f$ 46
14. $3.7 + 8 - 3.7 = w$ 8
15. $1000 \times 8.92 = g$ 8920

16. $\frac{2}{5} = \frac{c}{100}$ 40
17. $A = \frac{1}{2}(16)(7)$ 56
18. $n = 5(2 + 5.6)$ 38

19. $m = \frac{5}{8} \cdot 264$ 165
20. $24 = 0.2n$ 120
21. $0.25d = 1000$ 4000

Evaluate the expression.

22. ab; $a = 2$, $b = 7$ 14
23. $x + y$; $x = 7$, $y = 9$ 16
24. $4n - 1$; $n = 2.7$ 9.8

25. n^2; $n = 4$ 16
26. r^2; $r = 7$ 49
27. $6p^2$; $p = 9$ 486

28. $y^2 - 8$; $y = 8$ 56
29. $2(x + 1)$; $x = 2.3$ 6.6
30. $2xy$; $x = 5$, $y = 8$ 80

Write an equation. Solve.

31. What number times 10 equals 4.6? $n \cdot 10 = 4.6$; 0.46

32. Some number is $\frac{3}{4}$ of 60. What is it? $n = \frac{3}{4} \cdot 60$; 45

33. $\frac{2}{3}$ of 63 is what number? $\frac{2}{3} \cdot 63 = n$; 42

34. What number times 150 is 50? $n \cdot 150 = 50$; $\frac{1}{3}$

35. $\frac{1}{4}$ of what number is 35? $\frac{1}{4}n = 35$; 140

Solve.

36. What is the sixth term of this sequence: 2, 5, 9, 14, 20, . . . ? 27

37. Tom's first computer had 16K memory. His next one had twice the memory. His third has twice the memory of the second. How much memory does the third one have? (One K equals 1000 units of memory.) 64K

7
Ratio, Proportion, Percent

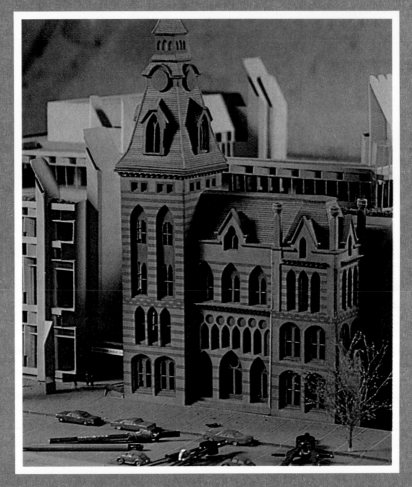

Scale models are used by architects to test their designs. The models make it possible to simulate various scenarios and test the overall appropriateness of the design.

7-1 *Ratio*

A theater owners group hired Pulse Polls, Inc. to conduct a survey in five cities. In each city 100 people were asked, "Would you attend the play *It's a Short Time from September to April?*" The results of the survey are shown in the table.

City	Brunswick	Eastway	Arbor Haven	Cuttiwell	Donnett
Favorable Responses	32	42	61	75	53

A **ratio** uses division to compare two numbers. The ratio of *a* to *b* can be written in three ways:

$$a \text{ to } b, \frac{a}{b}, \text{ or } a{:}b$$

You can write a ratio in lowest terms by dividing both terms by their GCF.

Example 1 Write a ratio in lowest terms to compare the number of favorable responses in Cuttiwell to all responses in that city.

Solution $\dfrac{75}{100} = \dfrac{75 \div 25}{100 \div 25}$ ⟵ *The GCF of 75 and 100 is 25.*

$= \dfrac{3}{4}$

Example 2 Write a ratio to compare the number of favorable responses in Brunswick to the favorable responses in Eastway.

Solution $\dfrac{\text{Brunswick}}{\text{Eastway}}$ ⟹ $\dfrac{32}{42} = \dfrac{32 \div 2}{42 \div 2} = \dfrac{16}{21}$

For every 16 favorable responses in Brunswick, there were 21 favorable responses in Eastway.

Your Turn
- Write a ratio as a fraction in lowest terms to compare 12 chickens to 4 eggs. $\frac{3}{1}$
- Write a ratio as a fraction in lowest terms to compare 400 musicians to 250 instruments. $\frac{8}{5}$
- A news report stated that 27 out of 30 people voted for Tom Mathews. Write this ratio in lowest terms. $\frac{9}{10}$

Class Exercises

Write the ratio as a fraction in lowest terms.

1. 5 to 100 $\frac{1}{20}$ **2.** a to b $\frac{a}{b}$ **3.** 25 to 50 $\frac{1}{2}$

4. 35 to 80 $\frac{7}{16}$ **5.** 31 to 40 $\frac{31}{40}$ **6.** c to d $\frac{c}{d}$

7. 65 to 15 $\frac{13}{3}$ **8.** 36 to 8 $\frac{9}{2}$ **9.** 40 to 120 $\frac{1}{3}$

10. 12d to 18b $\frac{2d}{3b}$ **11.** 7x to 56y $\frac{x}{8y}$ **12.** 39t to 13n $\frac{3t}{n}$

Exercises

Write the ratio as a fraction in lowest terms.

A
1. 35 patients to 10 children $\frac{7}{2}$ **2.** 35 apartments to 5 vacant $\frac{7}{1}$

3. 12 trucks to 3 pickups $\frac{4}{1}$ **4.** 36 roads to 4 unpaved $\frac{9}{1}$

5. 45 players to 5 injured $\frac{9}{1}$ **6.** 16 puppets to 4 on strings $\frac{4}{1}$

7. 27 departments to 9 sold out $\frac{3}{1}$ **8.** 48 parking spaces to 8 empty $\frac{6}{1}$

Write as a ratio in lowest terms using the ":" notation.

9. $\frac{2}{3}$ 2:3   **10.** $\frac{4}{7}$ 4:7   **11.** $\frac{19}{20}$ 19:20   **12.** $\frac{m}{n}$ $m:n$ **13.** $\frac{47}{92}$ 47:92

14. $\frac{95}{100}$ 19:20   **15.** $\frac{x}{y}$ $x:y$ **16.** $\frac{95}{108}$ 95:108   **17.** $\frac{46}{80}$ 23:40   **18.** $\frac{p}{q}$ $p:q$

B 19. Use the table to write a ratio in lowest terms to compare the responses in each category to the total responses. $\frac{7}{15}; \frac{2}{5}; \frac{2}{15}$

Viewer Survey of Janet Effmar Show

Liked	Disliked	No Opinion
35	30	10

Use the table to complete the exercise.

20. Write a ratio in lowest terms to compare each response to the total responses for each candidate.

Voter Survey on Mayoral Candidates

Candidate	Like	Dislike	No Opinion
Carp	25	40	15
Nolan	34	34	12
Dorado	60	16	4
Owens	14	12	54
Thompson	15	45	20

$\frac{5}{16}; \frac{1}{2}; \frac{3}{16}$

$\frac{17}{40}; \frac{17}{40}; \frac{3}{2C}$

$\frac{3}{4}; \frac{1}{5}; \frac{1}{20}$

$\frac{7}{40}; \frac{3}{20}; \frac{2?}{4C}$

$\frac{3}{16}; \frac{9}{16}; \frac{1}{4}$

Problems

Solve.

1. Of 120 people polled, 48 said they would not vote for Fenner for Congress. All others said they would.
  a. Write the following ratios:
   No Votes for Fenner:Total votes 48:120
   Yes Votes for Fenner:No Votes for Fenner. 72:48
  b. For each ratio in **a** write a fractional ratio in lowest terms. Express the ratio using the ":" notation. $\frac{2}{5}$, 2:5; $\frac{3}{2}$, 3:2

2. In order to receive research funds, John Eston had to show that people favored his product by a ratio of at least 5:4 over the competition. (His product:competition = 5:4)
  In a survey of 4000 people, 2400 favored Eston's product while 1600 favored that of the competitor. Will Mr. Eston receive the research funds? yes

SALE OF TENNIS RACKETS

Sales of tennis rackets were studied by Delor Management Group. Since the totals were not available, they assigned letters to stand for the numbers, and constructed this table.

Tennis Racket	Super Serve	Smooth Hit	Volley
Number Sold	N	P	Q

3. a. Write a ratio comparing these sales, using the letters given.

Example $\dfrac{\text{Super Serve}}{\text{Smooth Hit}} = \dfrac{N}{P}$ $\frac{N}{Q}; \frac{P}{Q}$

  b. If $N = 4650$, $P = 8962$, and $Q = 2384$, write a ratio in lowest terms for each pair of tennis rackets. $\frac{2325}{4481}; \frac{4481}{1192}; \frac{2325}{1192}$

211

7-2 *Proportions*

A national health agency asked 60 parents in a random sample if their children had had chickenpox. Of those asked, 50 said, "Yes." If 600 parents had been asked, about how many would you expect to say "Yes"? You can write equal ratios to solve the problem. An equation that shows equal ratios is called a **proportion.**

$$\frac{\text{Yes responses}}{\text{total responses}} = \frac{50}{60} \quad \diamond \quad \frac{50}{60} = \frac{n}{600} \quad \diamond \quad \frac{50 \times 10}{60 \times 10} \quad \diamond \quad \frac{500}{600}$$

$$n = 500$$

You would expect 500 parents to say "Yes."

Example 1 A car model is being built with a scale of 3 cm to 20 cm. The length of the car is 400 cm. What is the length of the model?

Solution Let n = length of the model in centimeters.
$$\frac{3}{20} = \frac{n}{400} \quad \diamond \quad \frac{3}{20} = \frac{3 \times 20}{20 \times 20} = \frac{60}{400} \quad \diamond \quad n = 60$$
The model is 60 cm long.

Example 2 The length of the model car's hood is 18 cm. How long is the hood of the actual car?

Solution Let n = the length of the hood in centimeters.
$$\frac{3}{20} = \frac{18}{n} \quad \diamond \quad \frac{3}{20} = \frac{3 \times 6}{20 \times 6} = \frac{18}{120} \quad \diamond \quad n = 120$$
The hood is 120 cm long.

Your Turn • A tire company sells 2 tires for $87. How much will 4 tires cost? $174.00

You can **cross multiply** to solve proportions that aren't easily solved by using equal ratios.

In Arithmetic	In Algebra
If $\dfrac{2}{5} = \dfrac{6}{15}$	If $\dfrac{a}{b} = \dfrac{c}{d}$ $(b \neq 0,\ d \neq 0)$
Then $2 \times 15 = 5 \times 6$	Then $ad = bc$

Example 3   Mr. Jones paid $9 for 4 kg of grass seed. How much would 10 kg cost?

Solution   Let $n =$ the cost of 10 kg of seed.

$$\dfrac{9}{4} = \dfrac{n}{10}$$

$9 \times 10 = 4n$ ⟵——— *Cross multiply.*

$90 = 4n$

$$\dfrac{90}{4} = \dfrac{4n}{4}$$ ⟵——— *Divide both sides by 4.*

$\$22.50 = n$

The cost of 10 kg of grass seed is $22.50.

Your Turn
- It took an equipment truck 3 hours to travel 200 km. How long will it take to travel 500 km? $7\frac{1}{2}$ hours
- A car maintains a speed of 80 km per hour. How far will it travel in 3.5 hours? 280 km

Class Exercises

Solve the proportion.

1. $\dfrac{3}{4} = \dfrac{n}{12}$ 9

2. $\dfrac{2}{3} = \dfrac{6}{n}$ 9

3. $\dfrac{n}{6} = \dfrac{21}{18}$ 7

4. $\dfrac{5}{7} = \dfrac{n}{35}$ 25

5. $\dfrac{1}{2} = \dfrac{n}{8}$ 4

6. $\dfrac{5}{3} = \dfrac{20}{n}$ 12

7. $\dfrac{3}{1} = \dfrac{n}{400}$ 1200

8. $\dfrac{n}{40} = \dfrac{3}{5}$ 24

213

Exercises

Solve the proportion.

A **1.** $\dfrac{2}{14} = \dfrac{n}{21}$ $\quad$ 3

2. $\dfrac{3}{15} = \dfrac{x}{35}$ $\quad$ 7

3. $\dfrac{a}{6} = \dfrac{9}{54}$ $\quad$ 1

4. $\dfrac{7}{y} = \dfrac{4}{9}$ $\quad$ $15\frac{3}{4}$

5. $\dfrac{4}{18} = \dfrac{6}{n}$ $\quad$ 27

6. $\dfrac{6}{n} = \dfrac{15}{35}$ $\quad$ 14

7. $\dfrac{12}{27} = \dfrac{8}{y}$ $\quad$ 18

8. $\dfrac{18}{21} = \dfrac{b}{28}$ $\quad$ 24

Cars and trucks of various lengths are to have models made. The ratio will be $\dfrac{\text{model length}}{\text{vehicle length}} = \dfrac{1}{8}$. Complete the table for the length of each model.

		Vehicle Name	Vehicle Length	Model Length
B	**9.**	Cat bird	360 cm	*n* 45 cm
	10.	Forma	400 cm	*n* 50 cm
	11.	Invit	560 cm	*n* 70 cm
	12.	Torp	*m* 480 cm	60 cm
	13.	Granda	*m* 720 cm	90 cm
	14.	Macin	*m* 656 cm	82 cm
	15.	Fash	433 cm	*n* 54.125 cm
	16.	Sparka	528 cm	*n* 66 cm
	17.	Dan Man	984 cm	*n* 123 cm
	18.	Welton	288 cm	*n* 36 cm

Solve.

C **19.** A square with sides of 5 cm has each side doubled. What effect does this have on the perimeter? The perimeter is doubled.

20. In a large room, the ratio of length to width is 3:1.
   a. If the length is 18 m, how wide is the room? 6 m
   b. Find the perimeter and area of the room. 48 m; 108 m²
   c. The dimensions of the room are doubled. Does this affect the ratio of length to width? no
   d. Find the perimeter of the room using the new dimensions. How does the "doubling" affect the perimeter? 96 m; It is doubled.
   e. How does the "doubling" affect the area? The area is quadrupled.

Problems

Solve. If necessary, round to the nearest tenth.

1. A truck driver can travel 200 miles in 3 days. How far will he travel in 12 days? 800 mi

2. On a map of Fairview County, 12 km are represented by 1 cm. How many kilometers would be shown by 7 cm? 84 km

3. At Green's Department Store, shirts are on sale at 3 for $50. How much will 8 shirts cost? $133.33

4. In a sample of 75 light bulbs, a store owner found 9 that were broken. How many broken bulbs can she expect to find in a case of 200? 24 light bulbs

5. A baseball pitcher allowed 2 runs in 9 innings. About how many runs would he allow in 54 innings at the same rate? 12 runs

6. A Metro car travels 450 km on 40 L of gas. How far will it travel on 110 L of gas? 1237.5 km

7. A TV station broadcasts 5 out of 6 playoff games every year. This year there will be about 58 playoff games. About how many games will the station broadcast? 48 games

8. In Medfield, 3 out of 10 people attended the circus. The town has 900 residents. How many attended the circus? Estimate how many would have attended if the town had 1800 residents. 270 people; 540 people

Using the Calculator

The diagram is drawn to a scale of $\dfrac{1 \text{ cm diagram length}}{48 \text{ cm tent length}}$. Measure the length on the diagram and calculate the corresponding length of the tent.

1. a   **2.** b   **3.** c   **4.** d
120 cm   230.4 cm   153.6 cm   105.6 cm

If the scale were $\dfrac{1 \text{ cm diagram length}}{56 \text{ cm tent length}}$ what would the tent measurements be?

140 cm   268.8 cm   179.2 cm   123.2 cm

5. a   **6.** b   **7.** c   **8.** d

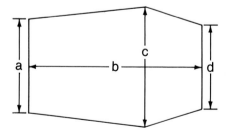

Floor plan of a
2-person tent

7-3 *Percents*

Two surveys were conducted to test voter opinion about a candidate for the state assembly. The candidate received 96 out of 400 votes in the first survey and 84 out of 300 votes in the second survey. In which survey did the candidate do better?

You can compare the ratios by writing a proportion with a denominator of 100.

First Survey

$$\frac{96}{400} = \frac{n}{100}$$

$400n = 96 \times 100$
$400n = 9600$
$n = 24$

In the first survey, the candidate received 24 out of 100 votes.

Second Survey

$$\frac{84}{300} = \frac{m}{100}$$

$300m = 84 \times 100$
$300m = 8400$
$m = 28$

In the second survey, the candidate received 28 out of 100 votes.

The candidate did slightly better in the second survey.

When you compare groups to 100 or find out how many out of 100, you're finding a **percent.** Percent means "per 100." The symbol % means percent.

Example 1 A candidate received 57 out of 300 votes. What percent is this?

Solution Let $a =$ the number of votes out of 100.

$$\frac{57}{300} = \frac{a}{100}$$

$300a = 57 \times 100$ ⟵ *Cross multiply to solve for* a.
$300a = 5700$
$a = 19$

The candidate received 19 out of every 100 votes.
The candidate received 19% of the vote by receiving 57 out of 300 votes.

Your Turn   Write the ratio as a percent.
- 7 out of 100   7%
- 45 out of 300   15%
- 56 votes out of 400   14%

You can write percents as decimals as well as fractions.

Example 2   Write 44% as a fraction and as a decimal.

Solution $44\% = \dfrac{44}{100} = 0.44$

Your Turn   Write the percent as a fraction and as a decimal.
- 37% $\dfrac{37}{100}$; 0.37
- 9% $\dfrac{9}{100}$; 0.09
- 83% $\dfrac{83}{100}$; 0.83

Some fractions cannot easily be written with a denominator of 100. When this happens, use division to write the fraction as a decimal, then write the decimal as a percent.

Example 3   Write $\dfrac{9}{37}$ as a percent.

Solution $\dfrac{9}{37}$ $\Rightarrow$ $37\overline{)9.000}$ $\dfrac{0.243\ldots}{} \approx 0.24$ ← *Since the answer is a repeating decimal, it is convenient to round to the nearest hundredth.*

$0.24 = \dfrac{24}{100} = 24\%$ ← *Move the decimal point two places to the right.*

Class Exercises

Write as a percent. Round to the nearest hundredth.

1. 7 out of 100   7%

2. 9 out of 100   9%

3. 23 out of 100   23%

4. 99 out of 100   99%

5. 90 out of 225   40%

6. 30 out of 75   40%

7. 16 out of 85   19%

8. 720 out of 1250   58%

217

Exercises

Write as a percent.

A **1.** 0.07 7%   **2.** 0.56 56%   **3.** 0.99 99%   **4.** 0.63 63%   **5.** 0.12 12%   **6.** 0.81 81%

7. 0.03 3%   **8.** 0.05 5%   **9.** 0.15 15%   **10.** 0.25 25%   **11.** 0.90 90%   **12.** 0.33 33%

Write the percent as a fraction and a decimal.

13. 5% $\frac{1}{20}$; 0.05   **14.** 18% $\frac{9}{50}$; 0.18   **15.** 45% $\frac{9}{20}$; 0.45   **16.** 28% $\frac{7}{25}$; 0.28   **17.** 8% $\frac{2}{25}$; 0.08

18. 10% $\frac{1}{10}$; 0.10   **19.** 91% $\frac{91}{100}$; 0.91   **20.** 77% $\frac{77}{100}$; 0.77   **21.** 50% $\frac{1}{2}$; 0.50   **22.** 1% $\frac{1}{100}$; 0.01

Write as a percent. Round to the nearest hundredth if necessary.

B **23.** $\frac{1}{5}$ 20%   **24.** $\frac{5}{8}$ 63%   **25.** $\frac{9}{10}$ 90%   **26.** $\frac{3}{4}$ 75%   **27.** $\frac{3}{8}$ 38%

28. $\frac{5}{12}$ 42%   **29.** $\frac{3}{25}$ 12%   **30.** $\frac{39}{50}$ 78%   **31.** $\frac{1}{3}$ 33%   **32.** $\frac{5}{6}$ 83%

33. $\frac{1}{7}$ 14%   **34.** $\frac{4}{9}$ 44%   **35.** $\frac{15}{62}$ 24%   **36.** $\frac{18}{75}$ 24%   **37.** $\frac{68}{135}$ 50%

Write the percent.

38. What percent of 100 is 22? 22%   **39.** What percent of 200 is 150? 75%

40. What percent of 50 is 6? 12%   **41.** What percent of 58 is 25? 43%

42. What percent of 75 is 25? 33%   **43.** What percent of 550 is 250? 45%

Using the Computer

This program will find one number as a percent of another. RUN it using P = 27, B = 135, and R = 20. Now try some other examples.

```
10  PRINT "TO FIND WHAT PERCENT P IS OF B:"
20  PRINT "WHAT IS P";
30  INPUT P
40  PRINT "WHAT IS B";
50  INPUT B
60  PRINT P;" IS";(P/B)*100;"% OF";B;"."
70  END
```

To find what percent P is of B:
What is P? 27
What is B? 135
27 is 20% of 135.

7-4 *Percent of a Number*

To approve of a new camera at least 40% of the people in a survey must respond favorably. If there are 300 people in the survey, how many favorable responses are needed?

You can write and solve an equation to answer the question "What number is 40% of 300?"

Let n = the number of favorable responses needed

Then n is 40% of 300 ⟵—— *In percent problems, "of" means multiply.*

$n = 0.40 \times 300$ ⟵—— *Write the percent as a decimal and solve.*

$n = 120$

At least 120 people must give favorable responses.

When you compute sales tax and interest you're finding a percent of a number.

Example 1   The Wilcox family bought camping gear that cost $439.98. If the sales tax rate is 5%, how much was the sales tax? What was the price including tax?

Solution   Let n = the amount of the sales tax

Then n = 5% of $439.98

$n = 0.05 \times 439.98$

$n = \$21.999$ ⟵—— *Round to the nearest cent.*

$\$439.98 + \$22 = \$461.98$ ⟵—— *Add the tax to the total cost.*

The sales tax was $22 and the price including tax was $461.98.

Your Turn   • Riverdale High chartered a bus for a class trip. The cost of the charter was $178.45 plus 4% sales tax. What was the amount of the tax? $7.14

219

You can use the following formula to find the amount of interest paid on a loan or deposit.

interest (i) = principal (p) × rate (r) × time (t)

The principal is the amount on which the interest is being computed, the rate is the rate of interest being paid, and the time is the length of time, in years, over which interest is being earned.

Example 2 Jeremy borrowed $400 for 6 months to buy a computer. The rate of interest is 15%. How much interest does he pay?

Solution $i = p \times r \times t$
$i = 400 \times 0.15 \times 0.5$ ⟵ *Use* t = 0.5 *since 6 months is 0.5 year.*
$i = 30$
Jeremy pays $30 interest.

Your Turn Compute the interest
• Max has $375 in a savings account. How much interest will he earn in one year if the annual rate is 5%? $18.75
• Maria borrowed $950 to take a course in TV production. The annual interest rate is 14%. How much interest will she pay if she borrows the money for two years? $266.00

Class Exercises

Find the number. Round to the nearest whole number.

1. 10% of 200 is n 20
2. 32% of 25 is y 8
3. 9% of 800 is c 72
4. 42% of 50 is z 21
5. 63% of 1500 is p 945
6. 5% of 20 is d 1
7. 99% of 2500 is t 2475
8. 1% of 2500 is w 25
9. 14% of 25 is m 4

Exercises

Write an equation. Solve. Round to the nearest whole number.

A
1. 32% of 900 is r 288
2. 14% of 800 is s 112
3. 90% of 20 is z 18

4. 12% of 25 is q 3
5. 3% of 4682 is d 140
6. 18% of 775 is c 140

7. 3% of 35,482 is n 1064
8. 9% of 1186 is y 107
9. 20% of 689 is b 138

10. 89% of 1752 is m 1559
11. 43% of 27 is t 12
12. 55% of 3002 is z 1651

Allied Appliance is having a 20% off sale. What is the sale price for the item?

B
13. Toaster   —$39.98 $31.98
14. Microwave oven   —$578 $462.40

15. Refrigerator   —$637.50 $510.00
16. Hair dryer   —$42.50 $34.00

17. Food processor —$138.98 $111.18
18. Stove   —$588.88 $471.10

Find the total price for each item after a 20% price reduction and a 7% sales tax.

19. Electric wok   —$45.50 $38.95
20. Foot massager   —$33.75 $28.89

21. Electric shaver —$29.98 $25.66
22. Electric pencil sharpener—$15.88 $13.59

23. Vacuum cleaner—$158.59 $135.75
24. Blender   —$95.89 $82.08

Problems

Solve.

1. A team of 8 people was paid $4000 for work completed on a project. The payment was divided as follows: Malloy—30%; Hodge— $1200 25%; Hemmer—18%; Sullivan—13%; Miller—10%; Belini—8%; $720 $520 $400 $320 Cowens—6%; and Ling—3%. How much did each person receive? $1000 $240 $120 What is wrong with the total amount? The amount is more than $4000 because the sum of the percents > 100%.

2. An author received $8000 in advances for the sale of a book. She paid 25% of the advance to an assistant. The assistant paid 50% of his share to a researcher. The researcher paid 50% of her share to a fact finding company. The company paid 50% of its share to a systems analyst who set up their system. How much did each person receive? How much did each person have left after paying out part of his or her share? author: $8000, $6000; assistant: $2000, $1000; researcher: $1000, $500; fact finder: $500, $250; analyst: $250

7-5 Problem Solving

Suppose you want to open a NOW account at a bank. In order to compare the features of each bank, it's helpful to make a chart to **organize the information.**

NOW ACCOUNT - SNOW BANK

The checking account that pays you 5.25% annual interest compounded daily from day of deposit to day of withdrawal.

- NO CHARGE for this service as long as you keep a balance of $500.

- If your balance falls below $500 at any time, there will be a $2.00 account maintenance fee plus a 15¢ charge per check for all checks written during that month's statement period.

River Bank **NOW Accounts.**

There will be no monthly service charge if the minimum balance in your NOW Account is $500 or more during the statement period. Otherwise, the service charge will be $1.75 and an additional $.25 for each check.

Earn 5¼% compounded daily.

Example 1 Which bank offers the more economical plan if you write about 15 checks per month?

Solution Make a chart to organize the information.

Bank	Interest Rate	Service Charge	Minimum Balance	Check Charge
Snow	5.25%	$2.00	$500	$.15/check
River	5.25%	$1.75	$500	$.25/check

The interest rates and minimum balances are the same, so look at the other two columns. You need to compare the service charges and check charges.

Snow Bank			River Bank		
Checks	*Check Charge*	*Fee*	*Checks*	*Check Charge*	*Fee*
15	× $.15	= $2.25	15	× $.25	= $3.75
	Service Charge	+2.00		Service Charge	+1.75
		$4.25			$5.50

Snow Bank is slightly more economical.

Your Turn • At the Diamond Bank, the service charge is $3.00 per month. The check charge is $.15 per check. If you write 20 checks per month, will you pay less at River Bank or Diamond Bank? Diamond Bank

Class Exercises

Use the chart for Exercises 1 and 2.

Bank	Interest Rate	Service Charge	Min. Bal.	Check Charge
Wilde	6.09	$1.75	$300	$.20/check
Data	6.09	$2.15	$300	$.15/check
Roman	6.09	$1.60	$300	$.25/check
Justice	6.09	$2.10	$300	$.12/check

1. If you write about 30 checks per month, which bank's plan is more economical, Wilde's or Data's? Data's
2. If you write about 45 checks per month, which bank's plan is more economical, Roman's or Justice's? Justice's

Exercises

Solve. Check students' charts for Exercises 1 through 5.

A   1. At a sporting goods store golf balls are sold in packages of 3. Each package costs $3.75. Make a chart to show the cost of from 1 to 10 packages.
2. Bus tokens cost 55¢ apiece. Make a chart to show the cost of from 1 to 10 tokens.
3. A math teacher gave a quiz containing 15 questions. She figured each student's grade by multiplying the number of correct answers by 6 and adding 10. Make a chart to show the possible grades.

B   4. At a photo shop reprints cost 65¢ each plus 3% sales tax. Make a chart to show the cost of from 1 to 10 reprints. How much will 18 reprints cost? $12.05

5. A billing clerk must calculate interest charges for charge customers before preparing their bills. The charges are as follows: $1\frac{1}{2}\%$ for the first $500, 1% for the amounts over $500. Make a chart to show the interest charge and total amount of bills for customers owing the following amounts: Mr. Wang—$186.50, Mrs. Toon—$468.25, Miss Saunders—$86.75, Ms. Kopek—$675.82, Mr. Laffer—$572.39, Miss Golden—$888.69.

Self Test 1

1. Use the table to write a ratio in lowest terms to compare the responses in each category to the total responses for each brand.   **7-1**

Customer Survey of Toothpaste Preference

Brand	Like	Dislike	No Opinion	
Glisten	55	22	8	$\frac{11}{17}$; $\frac{22}{85}$; $\frac{8}{85}$
PearlyWhite	63	18	7	$\frac{63}{88}$; $\frac{9}{44}$; $\frac{7}{88}$
Shine'n'Smile	19	75	2	$\frac{19}{96}$; $\frac{25}{32}$; $\frac{1}{48}$

Solve the proportion.

2. $\frac{1}{7} = \frac{n}{28}$ 4
3. $\frac{6}{y} = \frac{3}{9}$ 18
4. $\frac{b}{22} = \frac{5}{10}$ 11
5. $\frac{5}{15} = \frac{7}{q}$ 21   **7-2**

Write as a percent.

6. $\frac{4}{25}$ 16%
7. $\frac{6}{24}$ 25%
8. $\frac{15}{75}$ 20%
9. $\frac{5}{20}$ 25%   **7-3**

A-1 Auto parts offers a 15% discount on all purchases. Find the discounted price for the item.

10. case of oil—$9.00 $7.65
11. windshield wipers—$4.85 $4.12 **7-4**

12. antenna—$12.50 $10.63

13. At the Town Rink, it costs $.75 to rent ice skates and $1.85 for an afternoon's skating pass. Make a chart to show the cost of skating for from 1 to 10 days. If you can get a 12% discount for buying a 5-day pass that includes skate rental, how much will you save?   **7-5**

Check students' chart; $1.56

7-6 *More Percents*

The Alair Rug Company installed 200 m² of carpeting. In the process of trimming the rug, 1 m² was wasted. What percent of the rug was wasted?

Let w = the percent of the rug wasted

Then $w = \dfrac{1}{200}$

$= 0.005$ ⟵ *Move the*
$= 0.5\%$ *decimal point two places to the right.*

We say that 0.5% or $\dfrac{1}{2}\%$ of the rug was wasted. This means that

5 tenths of 1% or $\dfrac{1}{2}$ of 1% was wasted. Decimal or fractional percents

mean an amount less than $\dfrac{1}{100}$ or 1%.

Example 1 What is $\dfrac{3}{4}\%$ of 582?

Solution Let $n = \dfrac{3}{4}\%$ of 582

$\dfrac{3}{4}\% = 0.75\% = 0.0075$ ⟵
Write the fraction as a decimal. Move the decimal point two places to the left. Add zeros as needed.

$n = 0.0075 \times 582$
$n = 4.365$

Your Turn • What is $\dfrac{1}{5}\%$ of 750? 1.5 • What is $4\dfrac{1}{2}\%$ of 88? 3.96

Be careful not to confuse fractions and decimals with fractional and decimal percents.

Example 2 Are $\frac{1}{3}\%$ of 600 and $\frac{1}{3}$ of 600 the same?

Solution Let $n = \frac{1}{3}\%$ of 600   Let $m = \frac{1}{3}$ of 600.

$\frac{1}{3}\% \approx 0.33\% = 0.0033$ $\frac{1}{3} = 0.333$

$n = 0.0033 \times 600$ $m = 0.333 \times 600$
$n = 1.98 \approx 2$ $m = 199.8 \approx 200$

Since 2 is less than 200, $\frac{1}{3}\%$ of 600 is not the same as $\frac{1}{3}$ of 600.

Your Turn • Sturn Corporation earned $8000 one week. Of the week's earnings, $\frac{3}{4}\%$ was spent on office supplies and $\frac{3}{4}$ was spent on salaries. How much was spent in each area?

$60; $6000

Last week's sales at Walder Company totalled $6000. The sales manager would like to see this week's sales be 150% of last week's. This means that the sales manager would like to see sales increase by 50% or be $\frac{1}{2}$ again as large as last week's. Percents greater than 100 are equal to numbers greater than 1. Here's how to find the actual amount of this week's sales goal.

$$150\% = \frac{150}{100} = 1.50 \longleftarrow \textit{Move the decimal point two places to the left.}$$
$$n = 1.5 \times 6000$$
$$n = 9000 \qquad \text{This week's sales goal is \$9000.}$$

Your Turn • What is 135% of 86?   • What is 200% of 75?

116.1   150

Class Exercises

Write as a decimal.

1. $\frac{1}{4}\%$ 0.0025 **2.** 0.4% 0.004 **3.** $\frac{1}{10}\%$ 0.001 **4.** 0.7% 0.007 **5.** $\frac{1}{3}\%$ $0.00\overline{3}$

6. $4\frac{1}{2}\%$ 0.045 **7.** $12\frac{3}{5}\%$ 0.126 **8.** 9.5% 0.095 **9.** $15\frac{7}{8}\%$ 0.15875 **10.** 75.75% 0.7575

Exercises

Write as a percent.

A **1.** $\frac{4}{50}$ 8% **2.** $\frac{6}{500}$ 1.2% **3.** $7\frac{1}{2}$ 750% **4.** $\frac{3}{750}$ 0.4% **5.** $5\frac{1}{8}$ 512.5%

6. 0.56 56% **7.** 0.003 0.3% **8.** 0.469 46.9% **9.** 3.62 362% **10.** 4.615 461.5%

11. $\frac{15}{1200}$ 1.25% **12.** 0.0909 9.09% **13.** $\frac{12}{1500}$ 0.8% **14.** 15.2 1520% **15.** $\frac{15}{3000}$ 0.5%

Find the number. Round to the nearest hundredth.

B **16.** $\frac{1}{3}\%$ of 450 is y 1.49 **17.** $\frac{2}{5}\%$ of 500 is n 2 **18.** $\frac{9}{10}\%$ of 368 is r 3.31

19. 125% of 993 is b 1241.25 **20.** 250% of 2166 is t 5415 **21.** $3\frac{2}{3}\%$ of 1230 is z 45.10

Problems

Solve.

1. Compedium, Inc. sold 3598 electric mixers last year. This year they hope to have sales 133% of last years sales. What is the company's goal in units? 4786 mixers

2. A six-month bank certificate pays $11\frac{1}{2}\%$ interest. How much interest will be earned on a $10,000 investment? $575

3. The population of Aldersville is increasing at the rate of $3\frac{1}{2}\%$ per year. If last year's population was 7816, what should this year's be? 8090

227

7-7 Finding the Base

In a recent shipment, a local supermarket received 75 cases of soup. The soup represented only 25% of the cases in the shipment. How many cases were in the shipment?

To solve this problem you need to find the **base** or total number of cases that were to be in the shipment.

Let s = the base
Then 25% of $s = 75$
$0.25 s = 75$ ⟵———— *Write the percent as a decimal and solve.*

$$s = \frac{75}{0.25}$$

$$s = 300$$

The base number of cases was 300.

Example   An agent for a musical group earns a 12% commission based on the group's earnings. How much must the group earn for the agent to earn $36,000?

Solution   Let g = group's earnings
Then $12\% \, g = 36{,}000$
$0.12 \, g = 36{,}000$

$$g = \frac{36{,}000}{0.12}$$

$$g = \$300{,}000$$

The group must earn $300,000 for the agent's commission to be $36,000.

Your Turn   • Season's attendance at Larchmont's football games was 2876. This is a 130% of last years attendance. What was last year's attendance? 2212
• There are 386 books on loan from the East High library. This represents 9% of the books owned by the library. How many books does the library own? 4288 books

Class Exercises

Solve. Round to the nearest whole number.

1. $60 = 0.10\,n$ 600

2. $90 = 0.30\,b$ 300

3. $45 = 0.05x$ 900

4. $66 = 0.66\,a$ 100

5. $44 = 0.15\,z$ 293

6. $37 = 0.99\,y$ 37

7. $570 = 0.25\,n$ 2280

8. $56 = 0.75\,b$ 75

9. $999 = 0.12\,x$ 8325

Exercises

Write and solve an equation to find the base. Round to the nearest whole number.

A

1. 120 is 8% of what number?   1500
2. 1200 is 10% of what number? 12,000
3. 1586 is 2% of what number?   79,300
4. 2100 is 7% of what number?   30,000
5. 108 is 9% of what number?   1200
6. 725 is 8% of what number?   9063

B

7. 6 is 0.5% of what number?   1200
8. 14 is $\frac{3}{4}$% of what number?   1867
9. 25 is 0.25% of what number? 10,000
10. 82 is $\frac{1}{2}$% of what number?   16,400
11. 65 is 125% of what number?   52
12. 130 is 200% of what number?   65
13. 88 is 33.5% of what number? 263
14. 235 is 5.5% of what number?   4273

Problems

Solve.

1. On the average, families should expect to pay about 25% of income for housing costs. If the rent on an apartment is $575 per month, how much must a family earn to afford the rent? $2300

2. Union Utilities requested a 17% increase in electricity rates. This will raise the Cooper Company's monthly bill to $380. How much are they now paying? $324.79

3. "With an 8% increase in production we can produce 400 more transmissions per month," said the production manager at Central Transmission Co. How many are they currently producing? 5000 transmissions

229

7-8 *Percent of Increase or Decrease*

Sue and Mary work for a law firm. Sue earns $400 per week and Mary earns $650 per week. Sue recently received a raise to $436 while Mary received a raise to $700. Mary received the higher dollar amount but you should compare the percent of increase to see who received a higher percent of salary.

To find the percent of increase, first subtract to find the amount of increase.

Sue: $436 - 400 = 36$ Mary: $700 - 650 = 50$

Next write an equation and solve for the percent of increase.

Sue: Let t = the % of increase   Mary: Let m = the % of increase

$400\,t = 36$ $650\,m = 50$

$$t = \frac{36}{400} = 0.09 = 9\%$$ $$m = \frac{50}{650} = 0.077 = 7.7\%$$

Sue's raise was 9%.   Mary's raise was 7.7%.

Sue's percent of increase was greater than Mary's.

Example 1   Jerry bought a table for $480 that originally cost $600. What was the percent of discount?

Solution $600 - 480 = 120$ ⟵ *Subtract to find the amount of discount.*
Let n = % of discount
$600\,n = 120$

$$n = \frac{120}{600} = 0.20 = 20\%$$

Jerry received a 20% decrease or discount.

Your Turn
- A news staff director must reduce his staff from 40 to 25. What is the percent of decrease? 37.5%
- Joan scored 80 on her first test and 96 on her second test. What was the percent of increase? 20%

Class Exercises

Complete to find the percent of change. Round to the nearest whole percent.

	Original Price	New Price	Amount of Change	Percent of Change
1.	$485	$425	? $60	? 12%
2.	$ 65	$ 75	? $10	? 15%
3.	$188	$206	? $18	? 10%
4.	$238	$200	? $38	? 16%
5.	$344	$328	? $16	? 5%

Exercises

Find the percent of decrease. Round to the nearest whole percent.

A **1.** old price: $170
decrease: $45 26%

2. old price: $45
decrease: $6 13%

3. old price: $3591
decrease: $659 18%

4. old price: $15.98
decrease: $2.75 17%

5. old price $239.50
decrease: $23.95 10%

6. old price: $87.99
decrease: $22.00 25%

Find the percent of increase. Round to the nearest whole percent.

7. old price: $65
increase: $10 15%

8. old price: $359
increase: $36 10%

9. old price: $1500
increase: $300 20%

10. old price: $69.85
increase: $3.50 5%

11. old price: $78.35
increase: $11.75 15%

12. old price: $1.29
increase: $1.94 150%

Find the percent of change. Round to the nearest whole percent.

13. old price: $18.25
new price: $15.79 13%

14. old price: $33.12
new price: $42.26 28%

15. old price: $56.89
new price: $47.59 16%

Find the percent of increase or decrease to the nearest tenth of a percent.

B **16.** from 675 to 580 14.1%   **17.** from 33 to 77   133.3%   **18.** from 186 to 200 7.5%

19. from 300 to 178 40.7%   **20.** from 5 to 65   1200%   **21.** from 78 to 56 28.2%

22. from 87 to 35   59.8%   **23.** from 4786 to 3955 17.4%   **24.** from 1350 to 866 35.9%

25. from 98 to 125   27.6%   **26.** from 116 to 88 24.1%   **27.** from 760 to 670 11.8%

C **28.** A company employs 100 people. If the staff is decreased to 90, what is the percent of decrease? If the staff is increased from 90 to 100 what is the percent of increase? Explain. 10%; 11.1%; the bases are different

Problems

Solve.

1. The value of a mining stock rose from $36 to $40 per share. What is the percent of increase? 11.$\overline{1}$%
2. The price of a stereo set was raised from $300 to $315. What is the percent of increase? 5%
3. A salesperson drove 450 miles in October. In November she drove 360 miles. What is the percent of decrease? 20%

Self Test 2

Find the number. Round to the nearest hundredth.

1. $\frac{1}{2}$% of 300 is x 1.5   **2.** 150% of 450 is y 675   **3.** $4\frac{3}{4}$% of 80 is b 3.8   **7-6**

Write and solve an equation to find the base. Round to the nearest whole number.

4. 15 is 10% of what number? 150   **5.** 7 is 2% of what number? 350   **7-7**

Find the percent of change to the nearest tenth of a percent.

6. from 48 to 84 75%   **7.** from 100 to 35 65%   **8.** from 650 to 605 6.9% **7-8**

Algebra Practice

Write an equation. Solve.

1. 487 times 503 is equal to s. $487 \cdot 503 = s$; 244,961

2. 229,392 divided by 72 is equal to n. $229{,}392 \div 72 = n$; 3186

3. The difference between 20 and 5.683 is d. $20 - 5.683 = d$; 14.317

4. The quotient of 0.0567 and 0.09 is g. $0.0567 \div 0.09 = g$; 0.63

5. The sum of $\dfrac{2}{15}$ and $\dfrac{29}{30}$ is w. $\dfrac{2}{15} + \dfrac{29}{30} = w$; $1\dfrac{1}{10}$

6. $11\dfrac{3}{4}$ times $8\dfrac{1}{3}$ is equal to b. $\left(11\dfrac{3}{4}\right)\left(8\dfrac{1}{3}\right) = b$; $97\dfrac{11}{12}$

7. The perimeter of a rectangle $2\dfrac{5}{8}$ in. long and $1\dfrac{2}{8}$ in. wide is p. $2\left(2\dfrac{5}{8}\right) + 2\left(1\dfrac{2}{8}\right) = p$; 7.75 in.

8. The circumference of a circle with a diameter of 2.5 cm is c. $(3.14)(2.5) = c$; 7.85 cm

9. The area of a triangle with a base of $4\dfrac{1}{2}$ in. and a height of $2\dfrac{1}{4}$ in. is a. $\left(4\dfrac{1}{2}\right)\left(2\dfrac{1}{4}\right)\left(\dfrac{1}{2}\right) = a$; $5\dfrac{21}{16}$ in.²

10. The volume of a pyramid with base area of 12 m² and a height of 3 m is v. $(12)(3)\left(\dfrac{1}{3}\right) = v$; 12 m³

11. The surface area of a cylinder with a radius of 2 ft and a height of 4 ft is s. $(2)(2^2)(3.14) + (4)(4)(3.14) = s$; 75.36 ft²

Write the LCM of each set of expressions.

12. a^2 and $3ab$ $3a^2b$

13. $2r$, 3, and s^2 $6rs^2$

14. $9h^3$, $6gh$, and g^2 $18g^2h^3$

Solve the equation. Check the solution.

15. $3\dfrac{1}{2}m = \dfrac{3}{4}$ $\dfrac{3}{14}$

16. $12 = 9a - 15$ 3

17. $2s + 5 = 6s - 9$ 3.5

Solve. Round to the nearest hundredth.

18. $\dfrac{3}{8} = \dfrac{b}{32}$ 12

19. $\dfrac{4}{1} = \dfrac{y}{144}$ 576

20. $\dfrac{12}{4} = \dfrac{m}{10}$ 30

23. 10% of 40 is c. 4

24. 20% of 60 is w. 12

25. 4% of 40 is s. 1.6

26. $\dfrac{3}{4}$% of 1200 is n. 9

27. $33\dfrac{1}{3}$% of 600 is h. 200

28. 125% of 64 is e. 80

29. 9 is 12.5% of d. 72

30. 6 is $\dfrac{3}{5}$% of f. 1000

31. 2.9 is 116% of x. 2.5

233

Problem Solving on the Job

Landscape Architect

> **LANDSCAPE ARCHITECT**
>
> **DESCRIPTION:** Plan the type and location of plants and shrubs for homes and buildings.
> **QUALIFICATIONS:** 4–5 years of college
> **JOB OUTLOOK:** Openings are expected to grow faster than average throughout the next decade.

A landscaper submitted the following estimate for planting and lawn care services to the National Boat Company.

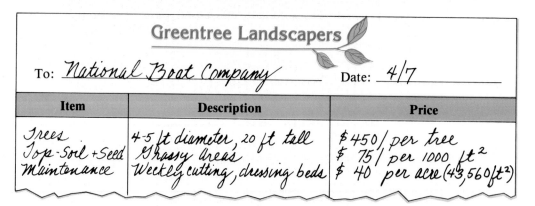

Greentree Landscapers

To: *National Boat Company*   Date: _4/7_

Item	Description	Price
Trees	4-5 ft diameter, 20 ft tall	$450/ per tree
Top-Soil + Seed	Grassy Areas	$ 75/ per 1000 ft^2
Maintenance	Weekly cutting, dressing beds	$ 40 per acre (43,560/ft^2)

Use the estimate to figure out some costs for National Boat Company.

1. The company expects to plant 30 large trees. How much will this cost? $13,500

2. The area to be seeded will cover 200,000 ft². How much will this cost? $15,000

3. The grassy area covers about 5 acres. How much will grass cutting cost per week? for a 26 week season? $200; $5200

4. What is the total cost of planting, seeding, and maintenance for one season? $33,700

5. The landscape company receives a 12% commission on the total bill for their design work. How much is the commission? $4044

6. The National Boat Company is planning on planting an additional 23 trees and seeding an additional 18 acres of lawn at another site. What would the cost be, including maintenance, for one season? $87,876

Solve.

7. Each spring and fall the landscaper's crew fertilizes the grassy areas. They use 10 lb of fertilizer for every 1000 ft^2 of grass. If fertilizer costs $.20 per pound how much will it cost to fertilize 200,000 ft^2? $400

8. Greentree Landscapers employs 20 workers to do their planting and maintenance work. Each worker is paid $7.58 per hour. Compute the total payroll if each worker works a 40 hour week. $6064

9. Greentree Landscapers recently purchased two trucks for $6982 each. They traded in an old truck and received a trade-in allowance of $735. What was the final cost of the new trucks? $13,229

Greentree Landscapers does planting, seeding, and maintenance work for private homes as well as businesses. Complete the monthly bills below.

10.

Greentree Landscapers

Mr. Thomas Hawkins
48 Leland Road
Hackensack, MA 02167

Bill for June	
Monthly maintenance	$75.00
Fertilizer	18.00
Tree Trimming	65.00
Total	? $158.00

11.

Greentree Landscapers

Ms. Leona Chan
19 Waverly Rd.
Myopia, MA 02212

Bill for June	
Monthly maintenance	$60.00
Mulch	55.00
2 Azaleas @ $27.50 each	$55.00 ?
Total	? $170.00

Enrichment

Direct and Inverse Variation

The area of the rectangle shown is
$3 \times 8 = 24$ sq. ft. What happens to
the area if one of the dimensions is
doubled while the other remains the
same? What if the one dimension is
tripled?

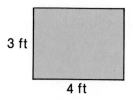

3 ft

4 ft

$A = l \times w$
$\quad = 3 \times 8$
$\quad = 24$

$A = l \times w$
$\quad = (2 \times 3) \times 8$
$\quad = 48$

$A = l \times w$
$\quad = (3 \times 3) \times 8$
$\quad = 72$

As one dimension varies by a factor of 2, the area varies by a factor
of 2. As one dimension varies by a factor of 3, the area varies by a
factor of 3. This is an example of **direct variation.**

Direct Variation

One factor remains unchanged as a second factor and the product
change by the same factor.

Inverse Variation

The product remains constant as one factor increases and the other
factor decreases by the same factor.

Complete.

1.

Length	× Width	= Area
1	3	? 3
5	3 ·	? 15
25	3	? 75
125	3	? 375

Length	× Width	= Area
1	36	36
2	18	? 36
3	12	? 36
4	9	? 36

3. Is Exercise 1 an example of direct or inverse variation? direct Exercise 2? inverse

Chapter Review

True or false? Write *T* or *F*.

1. A ratio compares two numbers using division. T

2. Percent means per one thousand. F

3. An equation that shows equal ratios is called a percent. F

4. In the proportion $\frac{3}{4} = \frac{9}{x}$, x is equal to 12. T

5. When computing 150% of y, the product will be greater than y. T

Match.

6. $\frac{150}{300} = y\%$ c

7. 0.3% of 3000 is y a

8. 15 is 75% of y d

9. $0.009 = y\%$ e

10. $\frac{6}{5} = y$ b

a. $y = 9$
b. $y = 120\%$
c. $y = 50$
d. $y = 20$
e. $y = 0.9$

Choose the best answer. Write *a*, *b*, or *c*.

11. Two tires cost $87, so 8 tires will cost ___?___. c
    a. $174   **b.** $870   **c.** $348

12. In a shipment of TVs, 4 out of 80 had defects. This is $x\%$. b
    a. $x = 50$ **b.** $x = 5$ **c.** $x = 20$

13. In a recent fund raising campaign, 35% of the 820 people contacted made contributions. Which equation could be solved to find the number of contributors? b
    a. $0.35x = 820$ **b.** $(0.35)(820) = x$ **c.** $0.35 = 820 + x$

14. Max's rent went from $585 per month to $731.25 per month. This is a ___?___% increase. c
    a. 20   **b.** 125   **c.** 25

Chapter Test

1. Use the table to write a ratio in lowest terms to compare the attendance each day to the total for the week. **7-1**

Symphony Attendance

Day	Mon.	Tues.	Wed.	Thurs.
Attendance	725	430	520	320

$\frac{145}{399}$; $\frac{86}{399}$; $\frac{104}{399}$; $\frac{64}{399}$

2. Four out of 5 people attending a concert were adults. Use the table to find how many adults attended a concert each night. **7-2**

580; 344; 416; 256

Write as a percent.

3. $\frac{2}{5}$ 40%   4. $\frac{8}{200}$ 4%   5. $\frac{35}{75}$ $46\frac{2}{3}\%$ 6. $\frac{100}{300}$ $33\frac{1}{3}\%$ 7. $\frac{14}{28}$ 50% **7-3**

Dudley saves 7% of his pay each month. How much does he have left from each check after deducting his savings?

8. March—$1588 $1476.84   9. April—$1176 $1093.68   10. May—$1701 $1581.93 **7-4**

11. At Pippin's Garage it costs $.75 to park for the first half-hour and $1.35 for each additional hour or fraction of an hour up to a maximum of $7.00. Make a chart to show the cost of parking for from 1 to 4 hours. How much would it cost to park for 1 hour 20 min? **7-5**

Check students' chart; $2.10

Find the number. Round to the nearest hundredth.

12. $\frac{4}{5}\%$ of 75 is y 0.6   13. 135% of 68 is b 91.8   14. $2\frac{1}{2}\%$ of 55 is z 1.38 **7-6**

Write and solve an equation to find the base. Round to the nearest whole number.

15. 26 is 50% of what number? 52   16. 150 is 8% of what number? 1875 **7-7**

Find the percent of increase or decrease to the nearest tenth of a percent.

17. from 155 to 100 35.5%   18. from 17 to 25 47.1%   19. from 12 to 5 58.3% **7-8**

Cumulative Review (Chapters 1–7)

Add, subtract, multiply, or divide.

$7\frac{11}{24}$

1. $9\frac{2}{3} - 6$ $3\frac{2}{3}$

2. $8 - 3\frac{3}{5}$ $4\frac{2}{5}$

3. $14\frac{1}{8} - 6\frac{2}{3}$

4. $5.6 - 4 \div 2$ 3.6

5. $(8.1)(9.6)(100)(0)$ 0

6. 1000×0.83 830

7. $(100)(0.2)$ 20

8. $62 - 4.837$ 57.163

9. $1.06 \div 0.2$ 5.3

10. $2.04 \div 2.4$ 0.85

11. $\frac{1}{4} \cdot 36 \cdot \frac{5}{8}$ $5\frac{5}{8}$

12. $\left(\frac{25}{4.7}\right)(4.7)$ 25

13. $3 - 1 - 1 - 1$ 0

14. $(10)(3.52)(10)$ 352

15. $(10^3)(8.34)$ 8340

Find the area. 16. $64\,\text{cm}^2$ 17. $33\,\text{ft}^2$ 18. $2.52\,\text{cm}^2$ 19. $28.08\,\text{m}^2$ 20. $42\,\text{cm}^2$ 21. $28.26\,\text{m}^2$

16.
8 cm   8 cm

17.
6 ft   11 ft

18.
1.2 cm   2.1 cm

19.
5.2 m   5.4 m

20.
8 cm   4 cm   13 cm

21.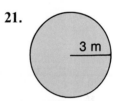
3 m

The formula $D = 16t^2$ relates the distance in feet (D) an object will fall with the time (t) in seconds it will fall. Solve the problem.

22. A broken tree branch fell directly from a tree to the ground. The branch took 1.1 seconds to hit the ground. How far did it fall? 19.36 ft

23. How long will it take an object to fall 256 ft from the roof of a building? 4 seconds

Write an equation. Solve.

24. An empty truck weighs 8200 lb. Its load weighs 4100 lb less than the truck. How much do both the truck and the load weigh in all? 12,300 lb

25. A tire for Charlie's van cost $42 two years ago. This year the price is $5 less than $1\frac{1}{2}$ times the old price. What's this year's price? $58.00

26. The regular price of a camera is $259. It's now on sale for 20% off the regular price. What's the savings? $51.80

8
Integers and Rational Numbers

Negative charges of electricity at the bottom of a thunderhead are attracted by positive charges in the ground causing the powerful burst of energy that is a lightning bolt.

8-1 Integers on the Number Line

The highest spot on Earth is the top of Mt. Everest, about 29,000 ft above sea level. The lowest spot is the bottom of the Mariana Trench in the Pacific Ocean, about 36,000 ft below sea level.

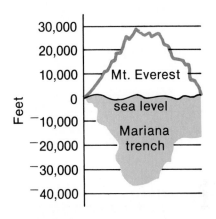

We can think of sea level as being 0 on a vertical number line. Numbers above 0 are called positive numbers. Numbers below 0 are called negative numbers.

Positive 29,000 is written as 29,000 or $^+$29,000. Negative 36,000 is written as $^-$36,000.

On a horizontal number line, we show negative numbers to the left of 0, and positive numbers to the right of 0.

Numbers such as $^-$2 and 2 that are the same distance from 0 but on opposite sides of it are called **opposite** numbers, or **additive inverses.** The numbers 1, 2, 3, 4, . . . , together with their opposites $^-$1, $^-$2, $^-$3, $^-$4, . . . , and 0 are called the **integers.**

On the number line below, points A, B, and C are the **graphs** of $^-$5, $^-$2, and 3. The numbers $^-$5, $^-$2, and 3 are the **coordinates** of their graphs.

Of any two numbers on the number line, the one at the right is the greater. Thus, for example:

$$^-2 > ^-5 \qquad 3 > ^-2 \qquad 0 > ^-4$$

This also means that the number at the left is the lesser:

$$^-3 < ^-1 \qquad ^-2 < 1 \qquad 0 < 3$$

Example 1 Complete. Compare the numbers, 4 __?__ 0.

Solution 4 > 0

Your Turn Complete. Compare the numbers, $^-12$ __?__ $^-2$. $<$

Class Exercises

What is the opposite?

1. Up Down   **2.** East West   **3.** Hot Cold   **4.** Win Lose   **5.** North South

Exercises

What is the opposite?

A **1.** 8 $^-8$ **2.** $^-9$ 9   **3.** $^-23$ 23   **4.** 17 $^-17$ **5.** $^-17$ 17

On the number line, what is the co-ordinate of the graph?

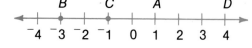

B **6.** Point A 1   **7.** Point B $^-3$

8. Point C $^-1$ **9.** Point D 4

Draw a number line and on it graph the number. Check students' number lines.

10. Point A at 4   **11.** Point B at $^-2$ **12.** Point C at 0   **13.** Point D at 1

Write a number sentence using $>$ to show which number is greater. $67 > ^-57$

14. 8 or $^-9$ $8 > ^-9$ **15.** 12 or 0 $12 > 0$ **16.** $^-18$ or 18 $18 > ^-18$ **17.** $^-57$ or 67

How many units do you travel, and in which direction do you go, to make the move on the number line? 7 units to right

C **18.** From 3 to 10 7 units to right   **19.** From 10 to 3 7 units to left   **20.** From $^-5$ to 2

21. From 2 to $^-7$ 9 units to left   **22.** From 0 to $^-4$ 4 units to left   **23.** From $^-3$ to $^-12$

9 units to left

Let n be negative and t be positive. Is the statement true or false? false

24. $n > t$ false   **25.** $t > n$ true   **26.** $t < 0$ false   **27.** $0 < n$

242

8-2 Adding Negative Integers

Pete carried the ball twice during the first quarter of the game. He lost 4 yd the first time and 2 yd the second time. He lost 6 yd in all. We add two negative integers to find the total lost yardage.

$$^-4 + {}^-2 = {}^-6$$

By using a number line you can see that the sum of two negative integers is always negative.

Example 1   Use a number line to find the sum $^-3 + {}^-5$.

Solution   You start at $^-3$ on the number line and move 5 units to the left, stopping at $^-8$.

$$^-3 + {}^-5 = {}^-8$$

Your Turn   • Use a number line to find the sum $^-2 + {}^-7$. $^-9$

You already know from past experience that the sum of two positive numbers is positive. When you add two negative numbers on a number line you always start to the left of 0 and then move farther to the left. Thus the sum of two negative numbers is always negative.

> The sum of two positive numbers is positive.
> The sum of two negative numbers is negative.

243

Class Exercises

What sum is shown on the number line?

1.

$0 + ^-6 = ^-6$

2.

$^-3 + ^-2 = ^-5$

3.

$^-8 + ^-5 = ^-13$

4.

$^-4 + ^-6 = ^-10$

Exercises

Use a number line to find the sum.

A 1. $^-4 + ^-3$ $^-7$ 2. $^-1 + ^-7$ $^-8$ 3. $^-6 + ^-6$ $^-12$ 4. $^-8 + ^-5$ $^-13$

5. $^-2 + ^-10$ $^-12$ 6. $^-8 + ^-1$ $^-9$ 7. $^-11 + ^-3$ $^-14$ 8. $^-4 + ^-9$ $^-13$

Find the sum.

B 9. $^-6 + ^-7$ $^-13$ 10. $^-8 + ^-2$ $^-10$ 11. $^-5 + ^-9$ $^-14$ 12. $^-10 + ^-6$ $^-16$

13. $^-2 + ^-18$ $^-20$ 14. $^-26 + ^-5$ $^-31$ 15. $^-4 + ^-30$ $^-34$ 16. $^-11 + ^-7$ $^-18$

Solve the equation.

17. $m = ^-12 + ^-8$ $^-20$ 18. $b = ^-4 + ^-15$ $^-19$ 19. $^-18 + ^-17 = d$ $^-35$

20. $h = ^-8 + ^-25$ $^-33$ 21. $f = ^-13 + ^-31$ $^-44$ 22. $^-26 + ^-15 = t$ $^-41$

23. $^-9 + ^-42 = x$ $^-51$ 24. $w = ^-27 + ^-32$ $^-59$ 25. $n = ^-43 + ^-38$ $^-81$

26. $c = ^-56 + ^-17$ $^-73$ 27. $^-31 + ^-42 = t$ $^-73$ 28. $^-65 + ^-19 = m$ $^-84$

Combine like terms.

29. $^-5x + ^-2x$ ^-7x 30. $^-h + ^-8h$ ^-9h 31. $^-8t + ^-12t$ ^-20t 32. $^-7d + ^-16d$ ^-23d

33. $^-13g + ^-12g$ ^-25g 34. $^-26m + ^-7m$ ^-33m 35. $^-19y + ^-y$ ^-20y 36. $^-14p + ^-17p$ ^-31p

C 37. $^-6n + ^-7p + ^-5p + ^-3n$ $^-9n + ^-12p$ 38. $^-8k + ^-t + ^-9k + ^-14t$ $^-17k + ^-15t$

39. $^-12a + ^-14x + ^-4x + ^-8a$ $^-20a + ^-18x$ 40. $^-3f + ^-12g + ^-21f + ^-18g$ $^-24f + ^-30g$

8-3 *Adding Integers of Opposite Sign*

During the first week of August, Jim and Jean's Yard Care Service took in $75 for work done and paid out $84 for gasoline, fertilizer and repair of equipment. Since they paid out more than they took in they had a loss of $9. We can show this as ⁻$9.

Number lines are helpful when learning to add positive and negative numbers.

Example 1 Find the sum 5 + ⁻7.

Solution Start at 5 on the number line. To add ⁻7, move 7 units to the left. You stop at ⁻2.

$$5 + {}^-7 = {}^-2$$

Example 2 Find the sum ⁻5 + 9.

Solution Start at ⁻5. To add 9, move 9 units to the right. You stop at 4.

$$^-5 + 9 = 4$$

Example 3   Find the sum $6 + {}^-6$.

Solution   Start at 6. To add $^-6$, move 6 units to the left. You stop at 0.

$$6 + {}^-6 = 0$$

The last example above displays the following property.

The sum of two opposite numbers is 0.
$$a + {}^-a = 0 \qquad {}^-a + a = 0$$

You can use the following rules to add a positive and negative integer without drawing a number line.

1. Think of both numbers as positive and subtract the smaller from the larger.
2. Notice the sign of the addend that is farther from 0. This will be the sign of the sum.
3. Write the number found in Step 1 with the sign found in Step 2. This is the sum.

Example 4   Solve the equation $n = 5 + {}^-8$.

Solution   Step 1. If both numbers were positive they would be 5 and 8. Subtracting, $8 - 5 = 3$.
Step 2. $^-8$ is farther from 0 than 5. The sign of the sum is negative.
Step 3. The sum is $^-3$. So, $n = {}^-3$.

Your Turn   • Solve the equation $y = {}^-6 + 2$. $^-4$

Class Exercises

What sum is shown on the number line?

1.

$5 + {}^-3 = 2$

2.

${}^-6 + 2 = {}^-4$

Exercises

Use a number line to find the sum. Check students' number lines.

A 1. $8 + {}^-2$ 6
2. ${}^-5 + 4$ ${}^-1$
3. ${}^-8 + 6$ ${}^-2$
4. ${}^-4 + 5$ 1

5. $9 + {}^-9$ 0
6. $12 + {}^-8$ 4
7. $4 + {}^-7$ ${}^-3$
8. ${}^-6 + 9$ 3

Find the sum.

B 9. ${}^-2 + 3$ 1
10. ${}^-6 + 1$ ${}^-5$
11. $2 + {}^-7$ ${}^-5$
12. $8 + {}^-10$ ${}^-2$ 9

13. ${}^-12 + 12$ 0
14. $13 + {}^-4$ 9
15. $12 + {}^-10$ 2
16. ${}^-9 + 18$ 9

17. ${}^-11 + 7$ ${}^-4$
18. $3 + {}^-20$ ${}^-17$
19. ${}^-14 + 16$ 2
20. $9 + {}^-21$ ${}^-12$

Solve the equation.

21. $x = 15 + {}^-4$ 11
22. $b = {}^-6 + 13$ 7
23. $14 + {}^-19 = t$ ${}^-5$

24. $d = {}^-2 + 18$ 16
25. $g = 23 + {}^-8$ 15
26. ${}^-28 + 16 = m$ ${}^-12$

27. $c = {}^-5 + 32$ 27
28. $56 + {}^-18 = y$ 38
29. $x = 84 + {}^-92$ ${}^-8$

30. $g = {}^-37 + 67$ 30
31. $n = 41 + {}^-37$ 4
32. $33 + {}^-53 = p$ ${}^-20$

Combine like terms.

33. $3a + {}^-2a$ a
34. ${}^-d + 5d$ $4d$
35. $7y + {}^-8y$ ${}^-y$
36. ${}^-4n + 4n$ 0

37. ${}^-8x + 12x$ $4x$
38. $10g + {}^-16g$ ${}^-6g$
39. $14m + {}^-8m$ $6m$
40. ${}^-k + {}^-16k$ ${}^-17k$

41. ${}^-13p + 12p$ ${}^-p$
42. ${}^-16y + {}^-4y$ ${}^-20y$
43. $18n + 12n$ $30n$
44. $7a + {}^-a$ $6a$

C 45. ${}^-3x + 2y + 4x + 5y + 6$ $x + 7y + 6$

46. $5d + {}^-2h + {}^-6d + 5h + 7$ ${}^-d + 3h + 7$

47. $9t + 12p + 10 + {}^-6p + {}^-11t$ ${}^-2t + 6p + 10$

48. ${}^-12 + {}^-8k + 7m + {}^-2k + {}^-9m$ ${}^-10k + {}^-2m + {}^-12$

49. $4g + {}^-15n + {}^-g + {}^-8 + 12n$ $3g + {}^-3n + {}^-8$

50. ${}^-6x + 13y + {}^-5x + {}^-13y + 4$ ${}^-11x + 4$

247

8-4 Subtracting Integers

The number line below can be read as either $4 - 6 = {}^-2$ or $4 + {}^-6 = {}^-2$.

For any subtraction equation we can always write a related addition equation.

$$12 - 9 = 3 \qquad\qquad 12 + {}^-9 = 3$$
$$24 - 11 = 13 \qquad\qquad 24 + {}^-11 = 13$$
$$18 - 12 = 6 \qquad\qquad 18 + {}^-12 = 6$$

We use this fact to subtract integers.

To subtract a number, we add its opposite.
$$a - b = a + {}^-b$$

Example 1 Subtract $3 - {}^-5$.

Solution $3 - {}^-5 = 3 + 5 = 8$

Example 2 Subtract ${}^-5 - 2$.

Solution ${}^-5 - 2 = {}^-5 + {}^-2 = {}^-7$

Your Turn Subtract

- $2 - 5$ ${}^-3$ - $6 - {}^-8$ 14   - ${}^-3 - 4$ ${}^-7$ - $9 - {}^-2$ 11

Class Exercises

Write the opposite.

1. 5 ₋5   **2.** ⁻12 12   **3.** 56 ₋56   **4.** ⁻75 75   **5.** 101 ₋101   **6.** ⁻92 92

Complete the equation.

7. $7 - 5 = 7 +$ _?_ ₋5   **8.** $8 - ⁻1 = 8 +$ _?_ 1   **9.** $⁻5 - 3 = ⁻5 +$ _?_ ₋3

10. $⁻12 - 14 = ⁻12 +$ _?_ ₋14   **11.** $⁻7 - ⁻4 = ⁻7 +$ _?_ 4   **12.** $13 - 23 = 13 +$ _?_ ₋23

Exercises

Write a related addition equation.

A **1.** $12 - 3 = 9$ $12 + ⁻3 = 9$ **2.** $⁻5 - 6 = ⁻11$ $⁻5 + ⁻6 = ⁻11$ **3.** $4 - ⁻10 = 14$ $4 + 10 = 14$

4. $⁻18 - 20 = ⁻38$ $⁻18 + ⁻20 = ⁻38$ **5.** $⁻9 - 6 = ⁻15$ $⁻9 + ⁻6 = ⁻15$ **6.** $14 - 23 = ⁻9$ $14 + ⁻23 = ⁻9$

7. $17 - ⁻8 = 25$ $17 + 8 = 25$ **8.** $⁻13 - ⁻8 = ⁻5$ $⁻13 + 8 = ⁻5$ **9.** $⁻8 - ⁻19 = 11$ $⁻8 + 19 = 11$

10. $22 - 34 = ⁻12$ $22 + ⁻34 = ⁻12$ **11.** $16 - ⁻23 = 39$ $16 + 23 = 39$ **12.** $⁻15 - 8 = ⁻23$ $⁻15 + ⁻8 = ⁻23$

Subtract.

B **13.** $8 - ⁻2$ 10   **14.** $⁻3 - ⁻2$ ₋1   **15.** $12 - 22$ ₋10   **16.** $7 - ⁻16$ 23

17. $⁻9 - 18$ ₋27   **18.** $4 - 21$ ₋17   **19.** $⁻13 - 5$ ₋18   **20.** $⁻25 - ⁻16$ ₋9

21. $38 - 38$ 0   **22.** $⁻15 - 12$ ₋27   **23.** $21 - ⁻21$ 42   **24.** $⁻17 - 34$ ₋51

Solve the equation.

25. $t = ⁻4 - 8$ ₋12   **26.** $n = 12 - 9$ 3   **27.** $13 - ⁻9 = p$ 22

28. $x = ⁻18 - 12$ ₋30   **29.** $b = ⁻21 - ⁻21$ 0   **30.** $g = 27 - 32$ ₋5

31. $19 - ⁻28 = m$ 47   **32.** $33 - ⁻16 = y$ 49   **33.** $n = ⁻42 - 5$ ₋47

Combine like terms.

34. $8n - 2n$ 6n   **35.** $⁻6d - 3d$ ₋9d   **36.** $4t - ⁻5t$ 9t   **37.** $12x - ⁻6x$ 18x

38. $⁻7k - ⁻4k$ ₋3k   **39.** $⁻8h - 3h$ ₋11h   **40.** $10y - ⁻y$ 11y   **41.** $⁻9p - ⁻11p$ 2p

C **42.** $7t - 5n + ⁻3t - 4n$ $4t + ⁻9n$ **43.** $12x - ⁻3y - 2x + 4y$ $10x + 7y$

44. $⁻9p + 12d - ⁻6d - 3p$ $⁻12p + 18d$ **45.** $15g + ⁻8n - ⁻4g + 5n$ $19g + ⁻3n$

249

8-5 Multiplying Integers

Monica lost 3 points on each of 5 rounds in a card game. Dale lost 3 yd on each of 5 running plays in a football game. In each case we could use addition to find the total loss.

$$^-3 + {}^-3 + {}^-3 + {}^-3 + {}^-3 = {}^-15$$

Since $^-3$ is used as an addend 5 times, we could also use multiplication.

$$5 \times {}^-3 = {}^-15$$

On the number line it looks like this.

Example 1   Solve the equation $y = 6(^-2)$.

Solution $y = {}^-12$

Example 2   Solve the equation $12(^-4) = n$.

Solution $^-48 = n$

Your Turn   Solve the equation.
- $y = 8(^-7)$ $^-56$ • $15(^-2) = p$ $^-30$

To multiply a negative number times a positive number we use the commutative property.

We know that $\longrightarrow$ $^-6 \times 2 = 2 \times {}^-6$ $\longleftarrow$ *the commutative property*

and that $\longrightarrow$ $2 \times {}^-6 = {}^-12$

so $\longrightarrow$ $^-6 \times 2 = {}^-12$

Example 3   Solve the equation $d = {}^-4(5)$.

Solution $d = {}^-20$

When you multiply a positive and a negative number, the product is negative.

In the pattern at the right, as the multiplier of $^-2$ decreases from 4 to 0, the product increases. This pattern does not stop when the multiplier becomes a negative number. You can see that the product becomes positive.

$$4 \times {}^-2 = {}^-8$$
$$3 \times {}^-2 = {}^-6 \ \searrow +2$$
$$2 \times {}^-2 = {}^-4 \ \searrow +2$$
$$1 \times {}^-2 = {}^-2 \ \searrow +2$$
$$0 \times {}^-2 = 0 \ \searrow +2$$
$${}^-1 \times {}^-2 = 2 \ \searrow +2$$
$$-2 \times {}^-2 = 4 \ \searrow +2$$

When you multiply two negative numbers the product is positive.

Example 4   Solve the equation.
    a. $x = {}^-7({}^-10)$ **b.** $n = {}^-6({}^-8)$

Solution   **a.** $x = 70$ **b.** $n = 48$

Your Turn   Solve the equation.
    • $p = {}^-9(3)$ $^-27$ • ${}^-8({}^-7) = g$ 56

The following table summarizes the rules for signs when multiplying integers.

Factors	Product
Both positive	Positive
Both negative	Positive
One positive, one negative	Negative

251

Class Exercises

Is the product positive or negative?

1. $^-5(2)$ negative   **2.** $6 \cdot 10$ positive   **3.** $^-8(^-12)$ positive   **4.** $9(^-4)$ negative

5. $^-15 \cdot ^-21$ positive   **6.** $30(^-7)$ negative   **7.** $28 \cdot 43$ positive   **8.** $^-32(3)$ negative

Exercises

Multiply.

A   **1.** $8(^-11)$ $^-88$ **2.** $^-9 \cdot 3$ $^-27$ **3.** $^-12(4)$ $^-48$ **4.** $^-5(^-3)$ 15

   5. $7 \cdot 6$ 42   **6.** $^-3 \cdot 4$ $^-12$ **7.** $^-5(^-6)$ 30   **8.** $2(^-7)$ $^-14$

   9. $8(^-4)$ $^-32$ **10.** $^-6(^-2)$ 12   **11.** $3 \cdot 5$ 15   **12.** $6(^-3)$ $^-18$

   13. $12(^-10x)$ ^-120x **14.** $^-2 \cdot 9d$ ^-18d **15.** $7 \cdot ^-4h$ ^-28h **16.** $2 \cdot 13p$ $26p$

Solve the equation.

B   **17.** $h = ^-8(^-11)$ 88   **18.** $x = 3(^-6)$ $^-18$ **19.** $t = 4(^-30)$ $^-120$

   20. $^-2(8) = m$ $^-16$ **21.** $p = ^-8 \cdot 6$ $^-48$ **22.** $^-4(^-5) = d$ 20

   23. $f = ^-6(2)$ $^-12$ **24.** $y = 6 \cdot 4$ 24   **25.** $2(^-15) = n$ $^-30$

   26. $^-3(8) = g$ $^-24$ **27.** $^-7(^-5) = m$ 35   **28.** $h = ^-8(5)$ $^-40$

Evaluate the expression using the given value for the variable.

   29. $^-7y;\ y = 4$ $^-28$ **30.** $8x;\ x = ^-3$ $^-24$ **31.** $^-4d;\ d = ^-2$ 8

   32. $5m;\ m = ^-5$ $^-25$ **33.** $9t;\ t = ^-2$ $^-18$ **34.** $^-6g;\ g = 9$ $^-54$

   35. $^-10p;\ p = ^-3$ 30   **36.** $8y;\ y = ^-6$ $^-48$ **37.** $^-2k;\ k = 20$ $^-40$

Solve the equation.

   38. $x = ^-1(3)(^-2)(4)$ 24   **39.** $h = 2(^-3)(2)(^-1)$ 12   **40.** $p = ^-3(7)(2)(^-2)(^-1)$ $^-84$

   41. $n = 2(^-5)(3)(4)$ $^-120$ **42.** $^-3(2)(^-1)(^-5) = m$ $^-30$ **43.** $k = 4(^-2)(3)(^-5)$ 120

Multiply.

C   **44.** $^-2(^-a + ^-3)$ $2a + 6$ **45.** $(^-4x + 7)4$ $^-16x + 28$ **46.** $^-4(2y - 6)$ $^-8y + 24$

   47. $(5d - ^-4)3$ $15d + 12$ **48.** $^-7(^-h + 6)$ $7h + ^-42$ **49.** $8(^-3k + ^-4)$ $^-24k + ^-32$

   50. $^-6(g + ^-8)$ $^-6g + 48$ **51.** $4(^-9t - ^-7)$ $^-36t + 28$ **52.** $(^-7n + 10)(^-5)$ $35n + ^-50$

8-6 *Dividing Integers*

We can use what we know about multiplying integers to help us learn how to divide integers.

Using whole numbers you can write a related division equation for any multiplication equation.

$$4 \times 3 = 12 \qquad 12 \div 3 = 4$$
$$7 \times 2 = 14 \qquad 14 \div 2 = 7$$
$$a \times b = c \qquad c \div b = a$$

The same pattern holds true for integers.

$$a \times b = c \qquad\qquad c \div b = a$$

$^-5 \times 6 = ^-30$	$^-30 \div 6 = ^-5 \longleftarrow$ *negative* $\div$ *positive* = *negative*
$^-8 \times ^-4 = 32$	$32 \div ^-4 = ^-8 \longleftarrow$ *positive* $\div$ *negative* = *negative*
$3 \times ^-2 = ^-6$	$^-6 \div ^-2 = 3 \longleftarrow$ *negative* $\div$ *negative* = *positive*

From the above we can write the following rules for the sign of the quotient when dividing integers.

Numbers being divided	Quotient
Both positive	Positive
Both negative	Positive
One positive and one negative	Negative

Example 1 Solve the equation $x = \dfrac{^-15}{5}$.

Solution $\dfrac{^-15}{5} = {^-15} \div 5$. We are dividing a negative integer by a positive integer, therefore the quotient is negative.

$$x = \frac{^-15}{5} = {^-15} \div 5 = {^-3}$$

Your Turn • Solve the equation $y = \dfrac{24}{^-4}$. $^-6$

253

Class Exercises

Tell whether the quotient will be positive or negative.

1. $8 \div {}^-2$ neg.
2. ${}^-10 \div 5$ neg.
3. $12 \div 6$ pos.
4. ${}^-18 \div 9$ neg.

5. $\dfrac{-24}{-6}$ pos.
6. $\dfrac{22}{-11}$ neg.
7. $\dfrac{-32}{8}$ neg.
8. $\dfrac{42}{21}$ pos.

Exercises

Divide.

A **1.** $63 \div {}^-9$ $^-7$
2. $35 \div {}^-7$ $^-5$
3. ${}^-77 \div {}^-7$ 11
4. ${}^-32 \div {}^-8$ 4

5. $\dfrac{-42}{6}$ $^-7$
6. ${}^-90 \div 10$ $^-9$
7. $\dfrac{49}{-7}$ $^-7$
8. ${}^-36 \div {}^-4$ 9

9. ${}^-39 \div 13$ $^-3$
10. $\dfrac{-84}{4}$ $^-21$
11. $121 \div {}^-11$ $^-11$
12. ${}^-75 \div {}^-5$ 15

B **13.** $6x \div 3$ $2x$
14. ${}^-12m \div 4$ ^-3m
15. $10d \div {}^-5$ ^-2d
16. ${}^-8t \div {}^-8$ t

17. $\dfrac{18m}{-9}$ ^-2m
18. $\dfrac{-21h}{3}$ ^-7h
19. $\dfrac{26k}{-2}$ ^-13k
20. $\dfrac{-72a}{9}$ ^-8a

21. ${}^-50x \div 25$ ^-2x
22. $84n \div {}^-4$ ^-21n
23. ${}^-180y \div 9$ ^-20y
24. ${}^-69g \div 3$ ^-23g

25. $\dfrac{45h}{5}$ $9h$
26. $\dfrac{-120t}{-60}$ $2t$
27. $\dfrac{-200n}{25}$ ^-8n
28. $\dfrac{124b}{-4}$ ^-31b

Solve the equation.

29. $y = {}^-64 \div 8$ $^-8$
30. ${}^-45 \div {}^-3 = n$ 15
31. $a = 108 \div {}^-9$ $^-12$

32. $\dfrac{-144}{-12} = x$ 12
33. $d = \dfrac{150}{-15}$ $^-10$
34. $\dfrac{-36}{-18} = g$ 2

35. $88 \div {}^-11 = n$ $^-8$
36. $x = {}^-180 \div 9$ $^-20$
37. $p = 175 \div {}^-5$ $^-35$

38. $n = \dfrac{-84}{-4}$ 21
39. $d = \dfrac{-210}{-70}$ 3
40. $\dfrac{-160}{20} = y$ $^-8$

41. $110 \div 10 = m$ 11
42. ${}^-140 \div 7 = y$ $^-20$
43. $a = {}^-96 \div {}^-3$ 32

44. $x = \dfrac{320}{-8}$ $^-40$
45. $t = \dfrac{-360}{-18}$ 20
46. $\dfrac{-284}{4} = b$ $^-71$

Solve the equation. Remember to perform the operations in the parentheses first.

C **47.** $d = (^-65 \div {}^-5) \times (^-3)$ $\quad$ $^-39$

48. $(95 \div 5) - (117 \div {}^-3) = x$ $\quad$ 58

49. $n = \dfrac{48}{^-4} - \dfrac{^-60}{^-5}$ $\qquad$ $^-24$

50. $y = \dfrac{36}{^-2} + (^-15 \div {}^-3)$ $\qquad$ $^-13$

51. $\dfrac{^-60}{5} - (^-48 \div 4) = t$ $\quad$ 0

52. $(^-72 \div 9) + \dfrac{^-35}{7} = b$ $\qquad$ $^-13$

Problems

Decide which operation to use, then solve.

1. At noon the temperature was $3°C$. Between noon and 10 P.M. it fell $6°$, rose $8°$, and then fell $12°$. What was the temperature at 10 P.M.? $^-7°C$

2. Jane had $126 in a checking account on March 1. For each of the next 8 weeks she withdrew $16. How did her account stand then? $-$2.00

3. Sue and Sam borrowed $4000 to open a sports equipment shop. Over the next 6 months they had fixed expenses of $1535 per month. During those months they took in the following amounts: $1289, $1562, $2874, $3925, and $5201. How much could Sue and Sam pay off on the $4000? What profit, if any, did they make? all; $1641 profit

Self Test 1

Write a number sentence using $>$ to show which number is greater.

1. 5 or $^-6$ $\;5 > {}^-6$ **2.** $^-8$ or 3 $\;3 > {}^-8$ **3.** $^-12$ or 20 $\;20 > {}^-12$ **4.** 18 or $^-4$ $\qquad$ **8-1**

$\qquad\qquad\qquad\qquad\qquad\qquad\qquad\qquad\qquad\qquad\qquad\qquad$ $18 > {}^-4$

Solve the equation.

5. $x = {}^-3 + {}^-8$ $\;{}^-11$ $\qquad$ **6.** $n = {}^-12 + {}^-10$ $\;{}^-22$ $\qquad$ **7.** $t = {}^-22 + {}^-7$ $\;{}^-29$ **8-2**

8. $d = 7 + {}^-4$ $\;3$ $\qquad$ **9.** $k = {}^-15 + 9$ $\quad {}^-6$ $\qquad$ **10.** $y = 12 + {}^-20$ $\;{}^-8$ **8-3**

11. $m = 4 - 12$ $\;{}^-8$ $\qquad$ **12.** $a = {}^-6 - 12$ $\quad {}^-18$ $\qquad$ **13.** $h = {}^-8 - {}^-5$ $\quad {}^-3$ **8-4**

14. $p = 7(^-8)$ $\quad {}^-56$ $\qquad$ **15.** $t = {}^-10(4)$ $\qquad {}^-40$ $\qquad$ **16.** $x = {}^-6(^-11)$ $\quad 66$ **8-5**

17. $n = 24 \div {}^-3$ $\;{}^-8$ $\qquad$ **18.** $d = {}^-15 \div 3$ $\quad {}^-5$ $\qquad$ **19.** $x = {}^-36 \div {}^-9$ $\;4$ **8-6**

Self Test answers and Extra Practice are at the back of the book. $\qquad$ **255**

8-7 Adding/Subtracting Rationals

A share of Satellite Communications Company stock was selling for $60. Over the next 2 days it went up $2.50 and then down $3.38. We can show changes as positive and negative decimals and operate with them as we did with integers.

Example 1 By how much did the price of a share of the stock change? What was the final price?

Solution Let c = the amount by which the price changed.

$c = 2.50 + {}^-3.38$

$c = {}^-0.88$ ◄─────── *To add, follow the rules for adding integers.*

The price dropped $0.88.

$$\begin{array}{r} {}^-3.38 \\ +\ 2.50 \\ \hline {}^-0.88 \end{array}$$

Let f = the final price

$f = 60 + {}^-0.88$

$\ \ = 59.12$

The final price was $59.12.

A number represented by a fraction whose numerator is an integer and whose denominator is any integer other than 0 is called a **rational number**.

Example 2 Solve the equation $n = \dfrac{{}^-1}{2} + \dfrac{{}^-3}{4}$.

Solution $n = \dfrac{{}^-1}{2} + \dfrac{{}^-3}{4} = \dfrac{{}^-2}{4} + \dfrac{{}^-3}{4}$

$\qquad\ = \dfrac{{}^-5}{4} = {}^-1\dfrac{1}{4}$

Your Turn   Solve the equation.

• $t = {}^-6.17 + {}^-2.52$ ${}^-8.69$ • $\dfrac{{}^-3}{8} + \dfrac{{}^-1}{4} = n$ ${}^-\dfrac{5}{8}$

You can also subtract positive and negative decimals and fractions just as you do integers.

Example 3   Solve the equation $y = 8.62 - {}^-4.31$.

Solution
$$y = 8.62 - {}^-4.31$$
$$= 8.62 + 4.31 \longleftarrow$$
$$= 12.93$$

| *To subtract, you* |
| *add the opposite.* |

Example 4   Solve the equation ${}^-6\dfrac{2}{3} - 4\dfrac{1}{6} = k$.

Solution
$$ {}^-6\dfrac{2}{3} + {}^-4\dfrac{1}{6} = k $$

$$ {}^-6\dfrac{4}{6} + {}^-4\dfrac{1}{6} = k $$

$$ {}^-10\dfrac{5}{6} = k $$

Your Turn   • Solve the equation ${}^-5\dfrac{3}{8} - 4\dfrac{1}{4} = h$. ${}^-9\dfrac{5}{8}$

Class Exercises

The graph of which number is farther from 0 on the number line?

1. 8.3 or 10.2   *10.2*
2. 5.6 or ${}^-6.3$ *${}^-6.3$*
3. ${}^-4.5$ or ${}^-5.4$ *${}^-5.4$*
4. 12.7 or ${}^-14.5$ *${}^-14.5$*

5. 9.61 or ${}^-9.62$ *${}^-9.62$*
6. 0.05 or ${}^-0.50$ *${}^-0.50$*
7. ${}^-18.59$ or ${}^-18.63$ *${}^-18.63$*
8. ${}^-23.92$ or 29.63   *29.63*

9. $8\dfrac{2}{3}$ or $8\dfrac{1}{3}$ *$8\dfrac{2}{3}$*
10. ${}^-5\dfrac{3}{8}$ or $5\dfrac{5}{8}$ *$5\dfrac{5}{8}$*
11. ${}^-6\dfrac{2}{5}$ or ${}^-6\dfrac{4}{5}$ *${}^-6\dfrac{4}{5}$*
12. $12\dfrac{5}{6}$ or ${}^-12\dfrac{1}{6}$ *$12\dfrac{5}{6}$*

13. $3\dfrac{1}{4}$ or ${}^-3\dfrac{1}{3}$ *${}^-3\dfrac{1}{3}$*
14. ${}^-8\dfrac{2}{5}$ or ${}^-8\dfrac{3}{10}$ *${}^-8\dfrac{2}{5}$*
15. $14\dfrac{5}{6}$ or ${}^-14\dfrac{7}{12}$ *$14\dfrac{5}{6}$*
16. ${}^-11\dfrac{3}{8}$ or $11\dfrac{5}{16}$ *${}^-11\dfrac{3}{8}$*

Exercises

Is the sum positive or negative?

A **1.** $5.4 + {}^-6.2$ negative **2.** $8.7 + 0.3$ positive **3.** ${}^-6.1 + 7.4$ positive **4.** ${}^-5.9 + {}^-2.1$ negative

5. ${}^-8\frac{1}{3} + 6\frac{2}{3}$ negative **6.** $12\frac{1}{2} + {}^-8\frac{3}{4}$ positive **7.** $13\frac{1}{8} + 5\frac{11}{16}$ positive **8.** ${}^-7\frac{1}{5} + {}^-1\frac{7}{10}$

Solve the equation.

B **9.** $t = 9.8 + {}^-9.2$ 0.6 **10.** $y = {}^-4.7 + 8.5$ 3.8 **11.** $7.5 + 0.8 = m$ 8.3

12. $x = {}^-8.8 - {}^-9.7$ 0.9 **13.** $6.2 - {}^-6.1 = h$ 12.3 **14.** $b = {}^-8.3 - 5.2$ ${}^-13.5$

15. ${}^-5.01 + 6.52 = n$ 1.51 **16.** $t = {}^-7.85 + {}^-12.31$ ${}^-20.16$ **17.** $y = 12.41 + {}^-12.41$ 0

18. $9.55 - {}^-10.71 = b$ 20.26 **19.** $t = {}^-12.76 - {}^-19.18$ 6.42 **20.** $h = {}^-13.44 - 23.44$ ${}^-36.88$

21. $d = {}^-4\frac{1}{3} + 5\frac{2}{3}$ $1\frac{1}{3}$ **22.** ${}^-7\frac{2}{5} + {}^-3\frac{3}{5} = f$ ${}^-11$ **23.** $x = 6\frac{3}{8} + {}^-7\frac{5}{8}$ ${}^-1\frac{1}{4}$

24. $n = 8\frac{3}{8} - {}^-9\frac{1}{8}$ $17\frac{1}{2}$ **25.** $y = {}^-5\frac{1}{3} - 8\frac{2}{3}$ ${}^-14$ **26.** ${}^-7\frac{5}{6} - {}^-10\frac{1}{6} = n$ $2\frac{1}{3}$

27. $m = 6\frac{2}{3} + {}^-5\frac{1}{6}$ $1\frac{1}{2}$ **28.** $x = {}^-12\frac{2}{5} + {}^-6\frac{7}{10}$ ${}^-19\frac{1}{10}$ **29.** $t = {}^-15\frac{3}{8} + 5\frac{3}{4}$ ${}^-9\frac{5}{8}$

30. $12\frac{1}{2} - {}^-9\frac{3}{4} = t$ $22\frac{1}{4}$ **31.** $h = {}^-15\frac{2}{3} - 10\frac{4}{9}$ ${}^-26\frac{1}{9}$ **32.** $b = {}^-8\frac{1}{2} - {}^-16\frac{5}{8}$ $8\frac{1}{8}$

C **33.** $n = 0.8 - (3.6 - {}^-8.4)$ ${}^-11.2$ **34.** $t = {}^-12.3 + ({}^-7.4 + {}^-5.6)$ ${}^-25.3$

Using the Calculator

Here is one week's record of the checking account for the Music Club.

Use a calculator to find the final balance. Has the club lost or gained money during the week? lost money

Date	Deposits (Add)	Checks (Subtract)	Balance Forward
			$396.17
3/7		$95.16	$301.01
3/10	$23.71		$324.72
3/11		$189.05	$135.67
3/12		$74.19	$61.48
	Final Balance		$61.48

8-8 *Multiplying/Dividing Rationals*

A chemist was preparing 5 samples for an experiment. For each sample he used 2.7 mL of a starch solution that he took from a bottle containing 94.5 mL of the solution. How much less starch solution was in the bottle when he finished?

We can show the amount he took for each sample as a negative decimal and multiply.

$$5(^-2.7) = {}^-13.5$$

The amount of starch solution in the bottle had changed by $^-13.5$ mL.

We use the same rules of signs when multiplying or dividing decimals and fractions as we do for integers.

Example 1 Solve the equation $d = {}^-3.6 \div 0.4$.

Solution Since a negative number is divided by a positive number, the quotient is negative.

$$d = {}^-3.6 \div 0.4 = {}^-9 \qquad 0.4\overline{){}^-3.6}^{\,\,{}^-9}$$

Example 2 Solve the equation $n = \dfrac{^-3}{5}\left(\dfrac{^-1}{2}\right)$.

Solution Since both factors are negative, the product is positive.

$$n = \frac{^-3}{5}\left(\frac{^-1}{2}\right) = \frac{3}{10}$$

259

Example 3   Solve the equation $g = \dfrac{3}{8} \div \dfrac{^-2}{3}$.

Solution   Since a positive number is being divided by a negative number, the quotient is negative.

$$g = \frac{3}{8} \div \frac{^-2}{3} = \frac{3}{8} \times \frac{^-3}{2} = \frac{^-9}{16}$$

Class Exercises

Is the product or quotient positive or negative?

1. $7.5(^-8.2)$ negative
2. $^-12.3(^-6.4)$ positive
3. $^-16.48(3.02)$ negative
4. $12.59(10.61)$ positive

5. $\dfrac{^-5}{8}\left(\dfrac{3}{4}\right)$ negative
6. $\dfrac{1}{3}\left(\dfrac{3}{16}\right)$ positive
7. $\dfrac{^-2}{5}\left(\dfrac{^-1}{2}\right)$ positive
8. $\dfrac{4}{9}\left(\dfrac{^-2}{3}\right)$ negative

9. $^-9.2 \div {^-6.3}$ positive
10. $^-6.7 \div 9.4$ negative
11. $12.3 \div 3.1$ positive
12. $15.6 \div {^-0.03}$ negative

13. $\dfrac{4}{5} \div \dfrac{^-1}{3}$ negative
14. $\dfrac{^-2}{5} \div \dfrac{3}{8}$ negative
15. $\dfrac{^-5}{6} \div \dfrac{^-3}{4}$ positive
16. $\dfrac{5}{8} \div \dfrac{1}{2}$

Exercises

Multiply.

A
1. $2.3(^-4)$ $^-9.2$
2. $^-1.7(3)$ $^-5.1$
3. $^-5.6(^-3.1)$ 17.36
4. $^-4.2(^-5.1)$ 21.42

5. $\dfrac{^-2}{3}\left(\dfrac{3}{8}\right)$ $\dfrac{^-1}{4}$
6. $\dfrac{^-5}{6}\left(\dfrac{^-3}{4}\right)$ $\dfrac{5}{8}$
7. $\dfrac{^-1}{2}\left(\dfrac{4}{5}\right)$ $\dfrac{^-2}{5}$
8. $\dfrac{4}{9}\left(\dfrac{^-3}{10}\right)$ $\dfrac{^-2}{15}$

Divide.

9. $^-5.7 \div 3$ $^-1.9$
10. $8.4 \div {^-2.1}$ $^-4$
11. $^-6.9 \div 1.5$ $^-4.6$
12. $^-9.1 \div {^-1.3}$ 7

13. $\dfrac{1}{2} \div \dfrac{^-5}{8}$ $\dfrac{^-4}{5}$
14. $\dfrac{^-4}{5} \div \dfrac{^-3}{10}$ $2\dfrac{2}{3}$
15. $\dfrac{7}{8} \div \dfrac{3}{4}$ $1\dfrac{1}{6}$
16. $\dfrac{^-2}{9} \div \dfrac{4}{3}$ $\dfrac{^-1}{6}$

Solve the equation.

B
17. $d = 16.2(3.1)$ 50.22
18. $t = 5.8(^-7.6)$ $^-44.08$
19. $^-4.6(^-9.3) = g$ 42.78

20. $n = 12.5(^-6.3)$ $^-78.75$
21. $p = {^-22.3}(^-0.7)$ 15.61
22. $m = {^-14.4}(8.5)$ $^-122.4$

23. $g = \dfrac{3}{5}\left(\dfrac{^-5}{6}\right)$ $\quad \dfrac{^-1}{2}$

24. $\dfrac{^-2}{9}\left(\dfrac{^-3}{8}\right) = d$ $\quad \dfrac{1}{12}$

25. $\dfrac{3}{4}\left(\dfrac{^-1}{6}\right) = n$ $\quad \dfrac{^-1}{8}$

26. $k = \dfrac{^-3}{16}\left(\dfrac{^-8}{9}\right)$ $\quad \dfrac{1}{6}$

27. $h = \dfrac{^-7}{8}\left(\dfrac{3}{14}\right)$ $\quad \dfrac{^-3}{16}$

28. $\dfrac{^-5}{16}\left(\dfrac{4}{5}\right) = p$ $\quad \dfrac{^-1}{4}$

29. $t = 12.8 \div {}^-3.2$ $\quad ^-4$

30. $8.4 \div {}^-1.4 = n$ $\quad ^-6$

31. $g = {}^-11.2 \div 2.8$ $\quad ^-4$

32. $\dfrac{3}{8} \div \dfrac{^-1}{4} = p$ $\quad ^-1\dfrac{1}{2}$

33. $n = \dfrac{^-5}{6} \div \dfrac{^-2}{3}$ $\quad 1\dfrac{1}{4}$

34. $t = \dfrac{1}{2} \div \dfrac{^-7}{8}$ $\quad \dfrac{^-4}{7}$

Simplify.

C 35. $\dfrac{^-2a(^-3 + {}^-1.5)}{3}$ $\quad 3a$

36. $\dfrac{(2.4d - 0.8d)1.2}{^-4}$ $\quad ^-0.48d$

37. $\dfrac{0.5n(4.2 - {}^-1.8)}{^-0.2}$ $\quad ^-15n$

Using the Computer

This program demonstrates multiplication and division of rational numbers. RUN it for $\dfrac{^-3}{4} \times \dfrac{4}{5}$ and then try some other exercises from this chapter. Check students' printouts.

```
  5  REM: TO MULTIPLY OR DIVIDE RATIONAL NUMBERS
 10  PRINT "FOR MULTIPLICATION, TYPE 1."
 20  PRINT "FOR DIVISION, TYPE 2."
 30  PRINT "WHICH";
 40  INPUT C
 50  PRINT "WHAT ARE NUMERATOR AND"
 60  PRINT "DENOMINATOR OF FIRST FRACTION";
 70  INPUT N1,D1
 80  PRINT "WHAT ARE NUMERATOR AND"
 90  PRINT "DENOMINATOR OF SECOND FRACTION";
100  INPUT N2,D2
110  IF C=1 THEN 160
120  PRINT N1;" /";D1;" /";N2;" /";D2;
130  PRINT " =";N1*D2;" /";D1*N2;
140  PRINT " OR";N1*D2/(D1*N2)
150  GOTO 190
160  PRINT N1;" /";D1;" X ";N2;" /";D2;
170  PRINT " =";N1*N2;" /";D1*D2;
180  PRINT " OR";N1*N2/(D1*D2)
190  END
```

8-9 *Problem Solving*

An elevator started at the 29th floor, went up 2 floors, down 3 floors, down 1 more floor, up 5 floors, and down 6 floors. At what floor did the elevator stop last?

A diagram is useful in solving a problem like this. It helps you to picture the situation more clearly.

$$2 + {}^-3 + {}^-1 + 5 + {}^-6 = {}^-3$$
$$29 + {}^-3 = 26$$

The last stop was on the 26th floor.

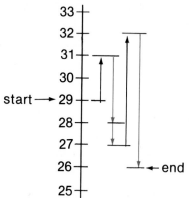

Following are other situations in which a diagram is helpful.

Example 1   You have invited 3 friends to dinner. In how many different ways can the four of you be seated at a round table if you occupy a particular position.

Solution   Let's number your friends 1, 2, and 3. First draw diagrams showing friend 1 on your left. Next show friend 2 on your left. Finally show friend 3 on your left. There are 6 arrangements in all.

Example 2 The Computer Club entered a game contest. To determine the best 3 players to represent the club, all 8 members were to play each other. How many games would be played?

Solution We can represent the members of the club by 8 dots, labeled *A* through *H*, placed in a circle. We show a game between two members by a line segment. Now our problem is to count the number of line segments connecting two dots.

There are 7 segments connecting *A* and the other dots, shown in black in the diagram. For *B* there are only 6 segments, the red ones, because *B* has already been connected to *A*. For *C* there will be only 5 segments because *C* is already connected to *A* and *B*. Now we can make a table to continue the count and find the total.

Dot	*A*	*B*	*C*	*D*	*E*	*F*	*G*	*H*
Number of segments	$7 + 6 + 5 + 4 + 3 + 2 + 1 + 0 = 28$							

A total of 28 games would be played.

Class Exercises

Draw a diagram for the problem.

1. A dolphin started at the surface of the ocean, dove 20 ft down, rose 12 ft, dove 16 ft down, rose 18 ft, and dove 33 ft down. How far below the surface was the dolphin then? 39 ft below

2. In how many ways can you, Al, Mimi, and Pat be seated at a round table if you always occupy the same seat and Mimi sits opposite you? 2 ways

Problems

Draw a diagram to help you solve the problem.

1. There are 5 people at a meeting. If each person shakes the hand of everyone else, how many handshakes will there be? 10 handshakes

2. A group of 6 friends play tennis together. They plan to have each person play all the others. How many games will be played? 15 games

3. In how many ways can 3 people be seated at a round table if each person is free to occupy any seat? 6 ways

4. In how many ways can Elsie, John, Lucia, and Manuel be seated at a round table so that boys and girls alternate? 8 ways

5. In how many ways can Jill, Lisa, Chris, and Pedro be seated at a round table if Jill and Chris want to sit next to each other? 16 ways

6. Each Saturday a pair of members of the Nature Club leads a field trip. There are 8 members in the club. If all the different possible pairs are made, how many field trips can be lead? 28 field trips

7. A ball is dropped from a height of 16 ft. Each time it bounces it reaches half its previous height. How high is the 5th bounce? How far has the ball traveled at the top of that bounce? $\frac{1}{2}$ ft; $46\frac{1}{2}$ ft

8. In a 100-m race, Marie is given a headstart of 20 m over Rena. If Rena runs 30 m in the same time that Marie runs 20 m, who wins the race? If Marie can run 10 m in 2 s, how long does it take her to finish the race? How long does it take Rena? Rena; 16 s; $13\frac{1}{3}$ s

9. A 50-ft rope is cut into 3 sections. The longest section is 5 times as long as the shortest section, and the remaining section is 3 times as long as the shortest section. How long is each section? $5\frac{5}{9}$ ft, $16\frac{2}{3}$ ft, $27\frac{7}{9}$ ft

Copy and label the diagram at the right to help solve the problem.

10. Scott knows the following distances:

home to Steve's house	0.5 mi
home to the library	0.6 mi
home to the store	0.7 mi
library to the store	0.2 mi
library to Steve's house	0.4 mi
store to Steve's house	0.3 mi

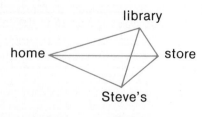

What is the shortest round trip that Scott can make to go from home to the store, to the library, and to Steve's, not necessarily in that order, and then back home? home to library, library to store store to Steve's, Steve's to home; 1.6 mi

8-10 *Equations with Rationals*

Thirty shares of Vidword stock dropped $150 in value. How much did each share drop?

You can use an equation to solve this problem.

Let s = amount each share dropped.

$$\text{Then } 30s = {}^-150$$

$$\frac{30s}{30} = \frac{{}^-150}{30} \quad \longleftarrow \text{ Divide each side by 30.}$$

$$s = {}^-5$$

Each share dropped $5 in value.

We use the same rules for solving equations involving both negative and positive numbers as we do for equations involving just positive numbers.

Example 1   Solve the equation $y + {}^-6 = 8$

Solution
$$y + {}^-6 = 8$$
$$y + {}^-6 - {}^-6 = 8 - {}^-6 \quad \longleftarrow \text{ Subtract } {}^-6 \text{ from each side.}$$
$$y + 0 = 8 + 6$$
$$y = 14$$

Example 2   Solve the equation $\frac{{}^-2}{3}t = 18$

Solution
$$\frac{{}^-2}{3}t = 18$$

$$\left(\frac{{}^-3}{2}\right)\left(\frac{{}^-2}{3}\right)t = \frac{{}^-3}{2}(18) \quad \longleftarrow \text{ Multiply each side by } \frac{{}^-3}{2}.$$

$$t = {}^-27$$

Your Turn   Solve the equation.

• $3n = {}^-21$ • $k + {}^-6 = {}^-4$ • $\frac{1}{4}m = {}^-6.2$ • $\frac{a}{{}^-7} = 3.1$

$^{-7}$ ^{2} $^{-24.8}$ $^{-21.7}$

Class Exercises

Answers may vary for Exercises 1–16. One possible solution is given for each exercise.

What number would you add or subtract to solve the equation?

1. $t - 6 = {}^-2$ add 6   *subtract 3*   2. $p - {}^-3 = 8$ 3. $x - 4 = {}^-7$ add 4   *subtract 10*   4. $y - {}^-10 = 9$

5. $n + 12 = 13$ *subtract 12*   6. $k + {}^-4 = 15$ add 4   7. $m + {}^-9 = {}^-3$ add 9   *subtract 11*   8. $d + 11 = {}^-7$

What number would you multiply or divide by to solve the equation?

multiply by 5   *multiply by $^-6$*   *multiply by $^-4$*   *multiply by $^-3$*

9. $\dfrac{h}{5} = {}^-20$ 10. $\dfrac{{}^-n}{6} = 3$ 11. $\dfrac{{}^-d}{4} = {}^-5$ 12. $\dfrac{x}{{}^-3} = 8$

divide by $^-6$ *divide by 8*   *multiply by $^-1$*   *divide by $^-5$*

13. $^-6t = 4$ 14. $8m = {}^-2$ 15. $^-y = 7$ 16. $^-5n = {}^-9$

Exercises

Solve the equation.

A 1. $x - 5 = {}^-6$ $^-1$ 2. $m - {}^-3 = 9$ 6   3. $t - {}^-7 = {}^-5$ $^-12$ 4. $k - 12 = 13$ 25

5. $d + 8 = {}^-4$ $^-12$ 6. $y + {}^-5 = 7$ 12   7. $a + {}^-9 = {}^-2$ 7   8. $n + 11 = {}^-7$ $^-18$

9. $\dfrac{n}{{}^-2} = 6$ $^-12$ 10. $\dfrac{t}{7} = {}^-4$ $^-28$ 11. $\dfrac{h}{{}^-5} = {}^-3$ 15   12. $\dfrac{b}{{}^-8} = 6$ $^-48$

13. $^-10p = 3$ $\dfrac{{}^-3}{10}$ 14. $^-6d = {}^-5$ $\dfrac{5}{6}$ 15. $^-k = {}^-7$ 7   16. $^-t = {}^-12$ 12

B 17. $p - 3.2 = 4.7$ 7.9   18. $h - {}^-4.3 = 2.5$ $^-1.8$

19. $x - 7.1 = {}^-8.2$ $^-1.1$ 20. $y - {}^-6.5 = {}^-1.4$ $^-7.9$

21. $h + {}^-5.4 = 7.2$ 12.6   22. $y + 6.9 = {}^-3.8$ $^-10.7$

23. $m + {}^-7.4 = 2.6$ 10   24. $n + {}^-6.3 = {}^-5.1$ 1.2

25. $\dfrac{x}{4} = {}^-1.2$ $^-4.8$ 26. $\dfrac{k}{{}^-5} = 1.3$ $^-6.5$ 27. $\dfrac{d}{{}^-3} = {}^-2.2$ 6.6   28. $\dfrac{h}{6} = {}^-4.2$ $^-25.2$

29. $^-5m = 12.5$ $^-2.5$ 30. $7t = {}^-14.7$ $^-2.1$ 31. $^-8g = {}^-7.2$ 0.9   32. $^-6n = 8.4$ $^-1.4$

33. $h - \dfrac{3}{4} = \dfrac{{}^-1}{4}$ $\dfrac{1}{2}$ 34. $y - \dfrac{{}^-1}{8} = \dfrac{3}{8}$ $\dfrac{1}{4}$ 35. $t + \dfrac{2}{3} = \dfrac{{}^-1}{6}$ $\dfrac{{}^-5}{6}$ 36. $x + \dfrac{{}^-5}{8} = \dfrac{1}{4}$ $\dfrac{7}{8}$

37. $\dfrac{1}{3}p = \dfrac{{}^-1}{2}$ $^-1\dfrac{1}{2}$ 38. $\dfrac{{}^-3}{4}m = \dfrac{1}{8}$ $\dfrac{{}^-1}{6}$ 39. $\dfrac{{}^-2}{5}h = \dfrac{{}^-3}{5}$ $1\dfrac{1}{2}$ 40. $\dfrac{3}{8}t = \dfrac{{}^-5}{8}$ $^-1\dfrac{2}{3}$

C 41. $2.4k + {}^-1.2 = {}^-3.6$ $^-1$ 42. $^-1.5t - 7.4 = 1.6$ $^-6$ 43. $6.2n - {}^-10.4 = {}^-8.2$ $^-3$

8-11 *Inequalities*

There is a greater number of tape cassettes in stock than stereos.

65 is greater than 32.

Stock Inventory

Tape Cassettes	Stereos
65	32

This is an inequality. An **inequality** is a statement that two quantities are unequal.

Inequalities	
In words	In symbols
65 is greater than 32.	$65 > 32$
n is less than $^-5$.	$n < ^-5$
y is equal to or greater than $^-17$.	$y \geq ^-17$
t is equal to or less than $5\frac{1}{2}$.	$t \leq 5\frac{1}{2}$

We use the same rules to solve inequalities as we do to solve equations *except* when we multiply or divide the inequality by a negative number.

Rules for Solving Inequalities

Add or subtract the same number.	$n - 3 > 10$ $n - 3 + 3 > 10 + 3$ $n > 13$	$d + ^-5 > 7$ $d + ^-5 - ^-5 > 7 - ^-5$ $d > 12$
Multiply or divide by the same positive number.	$\dfrac{x}{5} \geq ^-7$ $5\left(\dfrac{x}{5}\right) \geq 5(^-7)$ $x \geq ^-35$	$6t \leq 18$ $\dfrac{6t}{6} \leq \dfrac{18}{6}$ $t \leq 3$
Multiply or divide by the same *negative* number and *reverse* the inequality symbol.	$\dfrac{a}{^-3} > 6$ $^-3\left(\dfrac{a}{^-3}\right) < ^-3(6)$ $a < ^-18$	$^-4m < 8$ $\dfrac{^-4m}{^-4} > \dfrac{8}{^-4}$ $m > ^-2$

The last rule tells you to reverse the inequality symbol when you multiply or divide by a negative number. You can see why this is so by looking at the following.

$$8 > 6$$
$$^-2(8) \underline{\quad ? \quad} {}^-2(6)$$
$$^-16 \underline{\quad ? \quad} {}^-12$$
$$^-16 < {}^-12$$

Example 1   Solve the inequality $y - 7 > {}^-5$.

Solution
$$y - 7 > {}^-5$$
$$y - 7 + 7 > {}^-5 + 7$$
$$y > 2$$

Example 2   Solve the inequality $^-8d < 16$.

Solution
$$^-8d < 16$$
$$\frac{^-8d}{^-8} > \frac{16}{^-8}$$
$$d > {}^-2$$

Your Turn   Solve the inequality.

- $t + 6 < 10$ - $x - 5 > 2$

$t < 4$ $x > 7$

We can graph inequalities on the number line.

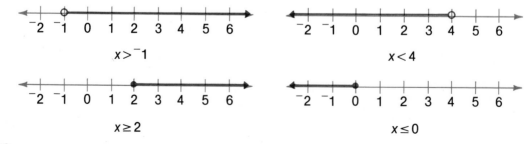

$x > {}^-1$ $x < 4$

$x \geq 2$ $x \leq 0$

Notice that an open dot shows that a number *is not* included in a graph and a filled-in dot shows that a number *is* included in a graph.

Example 3   Write an inequality for the graph.

Solution $x < 2$

Your Turn   • Write an inequality for the graph.

$x \geq {}^{-}1$

Class Exercises

Write the inequality in symbols.

1. 8 is greater than 3. $8 > 3$ **2.** 6 is less than 9. $6 < 9$ **3.** $^{-}7$ is less than $^{-}1$. $^{-}7 < {}^{-}1$

4. 2 is greater than $^{-}5$. $2 > {}^{-}5$ **5.** $^{-}3$ is greater than $^{-}6$. $^{-}3 > {}^{-}6$ **6.** $^{-}3$ is less than 6. $^{-}3 < 6$

Is the given number a solution of the inequality? Write Yes or No.

7. $x > 6$; 12 yes   **8.** $n > {}^{-}3$; 2 yes   **9.** $m < 4$; 8 no   **10.** $d < 5$; 0 yes

11. $t > {}^{-}5$; $^{-}6$ no   **12.** $p < 9$; $^{-}9$ yes   **13.** $h > 0$; $^{-}7$ no   **14.** $p < 6$; 1 yes

Exercises

Answers may vary for Exercises 1-4. One possible solution is given for each exercise.

What step would you take to solve the inequality?

A   **1.** $t - 7 > 4$ add 7   **2.** $x + {}^{-}5 < 10$ add 5   **3.** $6d > {}^{-}12$ divide by 6   **4.** $\dfrac{a}{{}^{-}6} > 2$ multiply by $^{-}6$

Would you reverse the inequality symbol when solving the inequality? Write Yes or No.

5. $x + 7 > 4$ no   **6.** $^{-}3y < 6$ yes   **7.** $\dfrac{n}{2} \geq {}^{-}5$ no   **8.** $m + 3 \leq {}^{-}4$ no

9. $\dfrac{t}{{}^{-}8} > 3$ yes   **10.** $h + 2 \leq 3$ no   **11.** $^{-}9d > {}^{-}3$ yes   **12.** $b - 2 \geq 6$ no

Solve the inequality.

B **13.** $a + 5 < 2$ $a < {}^-3$ **14.** $d - 6 \geq 3$ $d \geq 9$ **15.** $p + {}^-4 > 2$ $p > 6$ **16.** $5t \leq 10$ $t \leq 2$

17. ${}^-2b > 8$ $b < {}^-4$ **18.** $h - {}^-7 < 8$ $h < 1$ **19.** $\dfrac{n}{9} < 3$ $n < 27$ **20.** $\dfrac{x}{{}^-4} > 5$ $x < {}^-20$

21. $n + 8 > {}^-2$ $n > {}^-10$ **22.** $p - 4 < {}^-5$ $p < {}^-1$ **23.** ${}^-5y < {}^-3$ $y > \dfrac{3}{5}$ **24.** $6n \leq {}^-18$ $n \leq {}^-3$

25. $\dfrac{a}{4} \geq {}^-5$ $a \geq {}^-20$ **26.** $t + {}^-3 > {}^-7$ $t > {}^-4$ **27.** $x - 6 \leq {}^-1$ $x \leq 5$ **28.** $8n \geq 0$ $n \geq 0$

29. $\dfrac{d}{{}^-5} > 6$ $d < {}^-30$ **30.** ${}^-x < {}^-9$ $x > 9$ **31.** $h - {}^-3 \leq 7$ $h \leq 4$ **32.** ${}^-4n < {}^-2$ $n > \dfrac{1}{2}$

Write an inequality for the graph.

33. $x > {}^-2$ **34.** $x \leq 7$

35. $x \geq 3$ **36.** $x < 5$

Solve the inequality.

C **37.** $2x - 5 > 3$ $x > 4$ **38.** $7n + {}^-4 \geq 6$ $n \geq \dfrac{10}{7}$ **39.** ${}^-3m + 4 > {}^-9$ $m < \dfrac{13}{3}$

Self Test 2

Solve the equation.

1. $b = 7.5 + {}^-7.1$ 0.4   **2.** $x = {}^-8.3 + 4.6$ -3.7   **3.** $n = {}^-2.4 - {}^-8.3$ 5.9   **8-7**

4. $t = {}^-3(2.1)$ ${}^-6.3$ **5.** $y = 1.2({}^-1.2)$ ${}^-1.44$ **6.** $h = {}^-3.9 \div {}^-3$ 1.3   **8-8**

Draw a diagram to help you solve the problem.

7. In how many ways can Lee, Mike, Nan, and Oliver be seated at a   **8-9**
round table if Mike and Nan do not sit next to each other? 8 ways

Solve the equation.

8. $m - 1.5 = 6.2$ 7.7   **9.** $d + {}^-3.4 = 4.2$ 7.6   **10.** ${}^-6t = 12.6$ ${}^-2.1$ **8-10**

Solve the inequality.

11. $y + 3 > 5$ $y > 2$ **12.** $x - {}^-9 < 12$ $x < 3$ **13.** ${}^-4b > 12$ $b < {}^-3$ **8-11**

Algebra Practice

Write an equation. Solve.

1. The product of 761 and 1002 is equal to r. $761(1002) = r;$ 762,522
2. 156,204 divided by 36 is equal to p. $156,204 \div 36 = p;$ 4339
3. The sum of 364.8, 1.065, and 98.37 is d. $364.8 + 1.065 + 98.37 = d;$ 464.235
4. 9.6 times 0.875 is equal to b. $9.6(0.875) = b;$ 8.4
5. The difference between $17\frac{8}{9}$ and $5\frac{3}{8}$ is m. $17\frac{8}{9} - 5\frac{3}{8} = m;$ $12\frac{37}{72}$
6. $2\frac{11}{14}$ divided by $\frac{3}{7}$ is equal to y. $2\frac{11}{14} \div \frac{3}{7} = y;$ $6\frac{1}{2}$
7. The perimeter of a triangle with sides $2\frac{1}{2}$, $3\frac{5}{8}$, and $5\frac{3}{4}$ is P. $2\frac{1}{2} + 3\frac{5}{8} + 5\frac{3}{4} = p;$ $11\frac{7}{8}$
8. The area of a parallelogram with a base of 12.8 cm and a height of 7.2 cm is A. $(12.8)(7.2) = A;$ 92.16 cm²
9. The volume of a cylinder with a radius of 2 m and a height of 4 m is V. $(3.14)(2^2)(4) = V;$ 50.24 m³

Use the distributive property to factor each expression.

10. $c^3d + cd^2 + 3c^2d$ $cd(c^2 + d + 3c)$
11. $5r^2q + 5rq^2 + 10q^2$ $5q(r^2 + rq + 2q)$
12. $2b^2h + (bh)^2 + bh^2$ $bh(2b + bh + h)$

Solve.

13. $\frac{3}{8}j = \frac{1}{6}$ $\frac{4}{9}$
14. $7 = 6w + 3$ $\frac{2}{3}$
15. $2t + 2 = 5t - 1.6$ 1.2

16. 52% of 70 is h. 36.4
17. $4\frac{3}{8}$% of 200 is y. 8.75
18. 6.12 is 7.2% of a. 85

19. $r = {}^-4 + {}^-5$ ⁻9
20. $d = {}^-29 + {}^-18$ ⁻47
21. $g = {}^-7 + {}^-4$ ⁻11
22. $j = {}^-6 - 3$ ⁻9
23. $m = 7 - {}^-5$ 12
24. $c = {}^-10 - {}^-8$ ⁻2
25. $t = {}^-9({}^-3)$ 27
26. $k = {}^-2 \cdot 5$ ⁻10
27. $u = 7({}^-9)$ ⁻63
28. $f = 6 + ({}^-3 \times 3)$ ⁻3
29. $j = ({}^-9 \times 2) + 4$ ⁻14
30. $p = 8 - (6 \div 2) + {}^-2$ 3
31. $v = {}^-8.63 - 4.68$ ⁻13.31
32. $q = \frac{{}^-1}{8} + \frac{{}^-3}{4}$ $\frac{{}^-7}{8}$
33. $z = 3\frac{1}{6} - {}^-2\frac{1}{2}$ $5\frac{2}{3}$
34. $e = 88.56 \div {}^-2.7$ ⁻32.8
35. $g = {}^-1\frac{1}{6} \times {}^-1\frac{1}{3}$ $1\frac{5}{9}$
36. $r = {}^-3\frac{1}{3} \div 2\frac{1}{3}$ $^-1\frac{3}{7}$
37. $2x + {}^-3 > 5$ $x > 4$
38. ${}^-4 - 2b < 6$ $b > {}^-5$
39. $\frac{m}{{}^-4} + 2 > {}^-3$ $m < 20$

Problem Solving for the Consumer

Travel Rates

If air travel is ever in your plans, it pays to think smart and to compare prices on different airlines and special deals. Listed below are sample air fares from City A to City B. All the prices are for coach class. Notice that you can save quite a bit of money if you can take advantage of a special deal.

Airline	Regular Fare	Night Fare
XYZ	$269 one way	$236 one way
ABC	$295 one way	$236 one way
FUN	$280 one way	—

Airline	Special Fare
XYZ	$99 one way
FUN	$99 one way

←—— Limited seats. Fares only good through a specified date.

Airline	Advance Purchase Fare
XYZ	$189 one way
ABC	$189 one way
FUN	$189 one way

←—— Must be purchased at least 7 days before flight.

Children fly free on XYZ Airline.

Solve.

1. What's the least expensive rate available for a round-trip ticket? $198
2. Suppose the special fares on airlines XYZ and FUN are good through April 1, and you wish to fly on April 10. What is the least expensive fare? When must you purchase your ticket? $189 one way; on or before Apr. 3
3. To travel first class costs 20% more than to travel in coach at the regular fare. What is the first class fare on ABC Airline? $354, one way
4. A parent with two children wants to make a round trip and leave in two days. If there are no special fare seats left, what is the least expensive way to make the trip? How much will it cost? Night Fare XYZ; $472

272

Hotels, resorts, and airlines all want the consumer's business, and sometimes they offer good deals to get it. Rates can vary quite a bit, so it pays to examine these deals carefully. Here's an example of a tour package that includes all transportation and hotel space.

Hotel	8 Days, 7 Nights*	
	Feb–April	May–June
Economy	$419	$399
Superior	$519	$499
Deluxe	$569	$489

* All rates per person, double occupancy. All rates plus 15% tax.

5. How much would the package deal cost per person, for an economy hotel in April, including the tax? $481.85
6. Suppose meals will average $35 per day, and the traveler wants to bring $200 extra for spending money. How much will the trip at a superior hotel in April cost? $1076.85

Package rates are usually based upon the fact that people will arrive and leave on a Saturday or Sunday. If they don't, usually they'll have to pay individual rates. Here are some typical ones for the same trip described above.

Individual Rates, April*	
Round-trip air fare	$359
Superior hotel per night	$ 50
Limousine to hotel**	$ 6

* Prices include taxes.   **One way

7. How much would the trip cost if you paid the individual rates? Include $35 per day for meals and $200 for spending money. $1201.00
8. By taking the package deal in April and staying at the superior hotel, how much money do you save? $124.15

273

Enrichment

Absolute Value

On a number line, $^-3$ and 3 are each 3 units in distance from 0. The distance of a number from 0 is called its **absolute value.** It is always a positive number or zero. The absolute value of both $^-3$ and 3 is 3.

The absolute value of a number x is written $|x|$. We write $|^-3| = 3$ and $|3| = 3$.

Here is a complete definition of absolute value.

$$|x| = x \text{ if } x \geq 0 \text{ and } |x| = {}^-x \text{ if } x < 0$$

Thus
$$|19| = 19 \text{ because } 19 \geq 0$$
$$|^-23| = 23 \text{ because } {}^-23 < 0$$

What is the value of the expression?

1. $^-|7|$ $^-7$ **2.** $|^-50|$ 50 **3.** $^-|^-12|$ $^-12$ **4.** $|18.3|$ 18.3 **5.** $-\left|\dfrac{7}{10}\right|$ $\dfrac{^-7}{10}$

Which is greater?

6. $|^-7|$ or $|5|$ $\quad|^-7|$ **7.** $^-|8|$ or $|^-8|$ $\quad|^-8|$ **8.** $|12|$ or $^-|22|$ $\quad|12|$ **9.** $|^-9|$ or $|^-15|$ $\quad|^-15|$

10. $^-|^-2|$ or $|^-2|$ $\quad|^-2|$ **11.** $|25|$ or $|^-50|$ $\quad|^-50|$ **12.** $|^-18|$ or $^-|16|$ $\quad|^-18|$ **13.** $^-|^-23|$ or $|^-24|$ $\quad|^-24|$

Arrange in order from smallest to largest.

14. $|^-9|, \; ^-|8|, \; ^-|^-7|, \; |6|, \; |^-10|$ $\quad ^-|8|, \; ^-|^-7|, \; |6|, \; |^-9|, \; |^-10|$ **15.** $|5|, \; ^-|4|, \; |^-3|, \; |^-4|, \; |0|$ $\quad ^-|4|, \; |0|, \; |^-3|, \; |^-4|, \; |5|$

16. $\left|\dfrac{1}{2}\right|, \; \left|\dfrac{^-3}{4}\right|, \; ^-\left|\dfrac{3}{8}\right|, \; \left|\dfrac{1}{4}\right|, \; \left|\dfrac{^-1}{8}\right|$ $\quad ^-\left|\dfrac{3}{8}\right|, \; \left|\dfrac{^-1}{8}\right|, \; \left|\dfrac{1}{4}\right|, \; \left|\dfrac{1}{2}\right|, \; \left|\dfrac{^-3}{4}\right|$ **17.** $|^-4.3|, \; |5.6|, \; ^-|3.8|, \; |7.1|, \; |^-6.2|$ $\quad ^-|3.8|, \; |^-4.3|, \; |5.6|, \; |^-6.2|, \; |7.1|$

Let $a = {}^-5$ and $b = 3$. Evaluate the expression.

18. $|3a|$ $\quad 15$ **19.** $|3a + 4b|$ $\quad 3$ **20.** $|^-3a + b| - |2b|$ $\quad 12$

21. $|^-5b|$ $\quad 15$ **22.** $|5a + 2b|$ $\quad 19$ **23.** $|^-9a + 3b| - |3a|$ $\quad 39$

24. $|a - b|$ $\quad 8$ **25.** $|^-4b + a|$ $\quad 17$ **26.** $|3b + {}^-2a| - |6b|$ $\quad 1$

When will these be true statements?

$a = \pm b$

27. $|a| = |b|$ **28.** $|a + b| = |a| + |b|$ $\quad a \text{ and } b \geq 0 \text{ or } a \text{ and } b \leq 0$ **29.** $|a + b| = |a| - |b|$

29. $|a| > |b|, \; a \geq 0 \text{ and } b \leq 0 \text{ or } |a| > |b|, \; a \leq 0 \text{ and } b \geq 0$

Chapter Review

Complete, using < or >, to make a true statement.

1. $^-12$ _?_ $3 <$
2. $^-5$ _?_ $8 <$
3. 14 _?_ $^-3 >$
4. 2 _?_ $^-20$ $>$

Choose the correct answer. Write a, b, or c.

5. $x = {^-7} + 5$
   a. $x = 2$ c
   b. $x = 12$
   c. $x = {^-2}$

6. $n = 8 - {^-4}$
   a. $n = 12$ a
   b. $n = 4$
   c. $n = {^-4}$

7. $d = {^-6}(^-3)$
   a. $d = {^-18}$ b
   b. $d = 18$
   c. $d = 9$

8. $t = 16 \div {^-2}$
   a. $t = {^-32}$ b
   b. $t = {^-8}$
   c. $t = 8$

Is the given number a solution of the equation? Write Yes or No.

9. $m + 8 = {^-6}$; 2 no
10. $g - 5 = {^-7}$; $^-12$ no
11. $k + {^-3} = 9$; 12 yes
12. $t - {^-4} = 5$; 9 no
13. $h + {^-10} = {^-12}$; 2 no
14. $b - 7 = 0$; 7 yes
15. $\dfrac{n}{6} = {^-3}$; $^-2$ no
16. $\dfrac{b}{^-4} = 2$; $^-8$ yes
17. $\dfrac{a}{^-3} = {^-5}$; $^-15$ no
18. $7x = {^-21}$; 3 no
19. $^-4g = 20$; $^-5$ yes
20. $^-3d = {^-33}$; $^-11$ no

Solve the equation.

21. $n + 7 = {^-3}$ $^-10$
22. $t - {^-12} = {^-8}$ $^-20$
23. $m + {^-9} = 1$ 10
24. $^-3h = 24$ $^-8$
25. $\dfrac{a}{7} = {^-5}$ $^-35$
26. $5t = {^-40}$ $^-8$
27. $d + {^-3.3} = 7.4$ 10.7
28. $k - 7.1 = 5.5$ 12.6
29. $b + 9.6 = {^-0.4}$ $^-10$
30. $\dfrac{n}{11} = {^-1.21}$ $^-13.31$
31. $^-4x = {^-4.8}$ 1.2
32. $\dfrac{m}{^-4.3} = 5$ $^-21.5$

Solve the inequality.

33. $y - 6 < {^-3}$ $y < 3$
34. $x + {^-12} > 6$ $x > 18$
35. $g + {^-4} > {^-18}$ $g > {^-14}$
36. $^-8t > {^-4}$ $t < \dfrac{1}{2}$
37. $\dfrac{a}{6} < {^-9}$ $a < {^-54}$
38. $7h < {^-12}$ $h < \dfrac{^-12}{7}$
39. $\dfrac{x}{^-5} < 4$ $x > {^-20}$
40. $^-6d < {^-36}$ $d > 6$
41. $13y > {^-39}$ $y > {^-3}$

275

Chapter Test

Write a number sentence using $>$ to show which number is greater.

1. $^-3$ or 2 $2 > {}^-3$ **2.** 10 or $^-12$ $10 > {}^-12$ **3.** $^-4$ or $^-14$ $^-4 > {}^-14$ **4.** $^-30$ or 20 $20 > {}^-30$ **8-1**

Solve the equation.

5. $t = {}^-8 + {}^-4$ $^-12$ **6.** $b = {}^-2 + {}^-13$ $^-15$ **7.** $h = {}^-20 + {}^-9$ $^-29$ **8-2**

8. $x = {}^-7 + {}^-12$ $^-19$ **9.** $n = {}^-9 + {}^-21$ $^-30$ **10.** $d = {}^-23 + {}^-14$ $^-37$

11. $x = {}^-3 + 8$ 5 **12.** $n = 12 + {}^-1$ 11 **13.** $y = 4 + {}^-16$ $^-12$ **8-3**

14. $d = 15 + {}^-18$ $^-3$ **15.** $k = {}^-32 + 4$ $^-28$ **16.** $t = 35 + {}^-16$ 19

17. $m = 8 - {}^-3$ 11 **18.** $g = {}^-7 - 10$ $^-17$ **19.** $d = {}^-2 - {}^-9$ 7 **8-4**

20. $a = 2 - 13$ $^-11$ **21.** $t = 15 - {}^-8$ 23 **22.** $b = {}^-4 - 2$ $^-6$

23. $b = 5({}^-6)$ $^-30$ **24.** $k = {}^-8({}^-3)$ 24 **25.** $g = {}^-12(5)$ $^-60$ **8-5**

26. $x = {}^-9(3)$ $^-27$ **27.** $m = 12({}^-6)$ $^-72$ **28.** $y = {}^-14({}^-3)$ 42

29. $h = {}^-18 \div 2$ $^-9$ **30.** $m = 24 \div {}^-6$ $^-4$ **31.** $t = {}^-20 \div 5$ $^-4$ **8-6**

32. $y = 16 \div {}^-8$ $^-2$ **33.** $d = {}^-32 \div 4$ $^-8$ **34.** $b = {}^-38 \div {}^-2$ 19

35. $d = 4.5 + {}^-3.2$ 1.3 **36.** $p = {}^-3.8 + {}^-2.1$ $^-5.9$ **37.** $n = {}^-9.6 - 5.4$ $^-15$ **8-7**

38. $x = {}^-6.3 - 7.4$ $^-13.7$ **39.** $y = 8.2 - {}^-4.3$ 12.5 **40.** $t = {}^-5.1 + {}^-3.4$ $^-8.5$

41. $x = 5({}^-4.1)$ $^-20.5$ **42.** $b = {}^-7({}^-3.4)$ 23.8 **43.** $y = {}^-3.5 \div 7$ $^-0.5$ **8-8**

44. $n = {}^-6.3 \div {}^-9$ 0.7 **45.** $p = 2.4({}^-4)$ $^-9.6$ **46.** $a = 12.6 \div {}^-3$ $^-4.2$

Draw a diagram to help you solve the problem.

47. A board 12 ft long is cut into 2 pieces, one piece 3 times longer than the other. How long is each piece? 3 ft, 9 ft   **8-9**

Solve the equation.

48. $t + {}^-5.6 = 3.3$ 8.9 **49.** $x - 4.5 = {}^-2.5$ 2 **50.** $^-3n = 36$ $^-12$ **8-10**

51. $\dfrac{a}{4} = {}^-1.2$ $^-4.8$ **52.** $5n = {}^-2.5$ $^-0.5$ **53.** $\dfrac{m}{^-6} = 2.3$ $^-13.8$

Solve the inequality.

54. $n + {}^-6 < 4$ $n < 10$ **55.** $t - 5 > {}^-9$ $t > {}^-4$ **56.** $^-6d < 30$ $d > {}^-5$ **8-11**

57. $\dfrac{x}{^-5} > 7$ $x < {}^-35$ **58.** $b - {}^-7 > 10$ $b > 3$ **59.** $3a < {}^-12$ $a < {}^-4$

Cumulative Review (Chapters 1–8)

Add, subtract, multiply, or divide.

1. $6.2 - 0.465$ 5.735
2. $4.25 \div 0.17$ 25
3. 6.3×2.09 13.167
4. $16 - 5 \times 3.1$ 0.5
5. $6(12 + 8)$ 120
6. 0.25×100 25
7. $1\frac{1}{3} - \frac{4}{5}$ $\frac{8}{15}$
8. $\frac{5}{9} \times \frac{3}{8} \times 1\frac{1}{2}$ $\frac{5}{16}$
9. $(10^2)\left(1\frac{3}{5}\right)$ 160
10. $(12)(10)(0.6)$ 72
11. $26 + 3 \div 2$ $27\frac{1}{2}$
12. $(10)(17.1)(10)$ 1710
13. $\frac{1}{5} \div \frac{1}{8}$ $1\frac{3}{5}$
14. $\frac{1}{8} \cdot \frac{2}{3} \cdot 15$ $1\frac{1}{4}$
15. $\left(2\frac{1}{2}\right)\left(\frac{1}{2}\right)$ $1\frac{1}{4}$
16. $(4.6)^2$ 21.16
17. $42 + 8.5$ 50.5
18. $12 \div 4 + 4 \cdot 8$ 35

Solve.

19. 76% of 50 is what number?   38
20. 50 out of 80 is what percent? $62\frac{1}{2}\%$
21. 24% of what number is 5.76?   24
22. 36% of 180 is what number?   64.8
23. What is 18% of 45?   8.1
24. 16 out of 56 is what percent? $28\frac{4}{7}\%$
25. 150% of what number is 375?   250
26. What is 4% of 300?   12
27. What is 8% of 600?   48
28. $33\frac{1}{3}\%$ of 282 is what number?   94

Find the volume.

29.   120 in.³
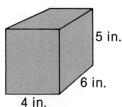
5 in.
6 in.
4 in.

30.   100 m³

4 m
2 m
2 m
6 m
5 m

31.   50.24 cm³

2 cm
4 cm

Write an equation. Solve.

32. The area of a rectangle is 225 m² and one side is 15 m. What are the lengths of the other sides?   15 m, 15 m, 15 m
33. In a figure skating competition a skater scored twice as many points in the freestyle event as in the school figures. The total of the two events was 14.7 points. How many points did he score in each event?   4.9 points, 9.8 points

9
Graphing in the Coordinate Plane

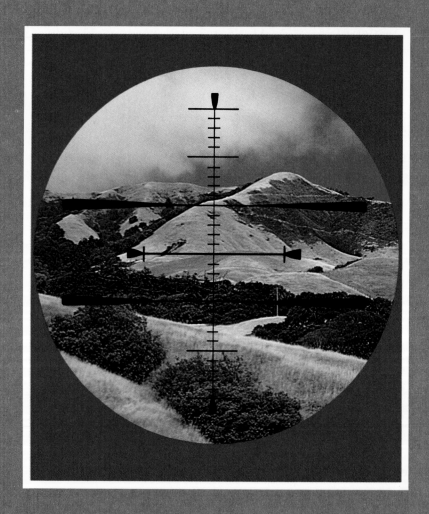

A surveyor looking through a transit, a form of telescope, uses horizontal and vertical lines to map positions. In this chapter we use grids of horizontal and vertical lines to graph points.

9-1 Collecting Data

Draw a square and mark a point in it. How many regions are formed if you draw one line through the point? 2 lines? 3 lines? 4 lines?

 1 line
2 regions

 2 lines
4 regions

 3 lines
6 regions

 4 lines
8 regions

The data are shown in the diagrams. We can also show the data in a table.

No. of lines	1	2	3	4
No. of regions	2	4	6	8

Constant change = 2

+2 +2 +2

We see that each time we draw a line, 2 regions are added. We call 2 the *constant change* of the sequence of terms, 2, 4, 6, 8. We also see that the number of regions in each case is twice the number of lines. We can predict the table will continue as follows:

No. of lines	1	2	3	4	5	6	7	8	. . .	n
No. of regions	2	4	6	8	10	12	14	16	. . .	$2n$

Example 1 How many regions are formed by 25 lines?

Solution If $n = 25$, then $2n = 2(25) = 50$. Therefore, 50 regions are formed.

Your Turn How many regions are formed by the following number of lines?

- 16 32 regions
- 150 300 regions
- 1492 2984 regions
- 2001 4002 regions

Here is another experiment. Arrange different numbers of blocks using the following rules:

Rule 1. Blocks must always touch   This , not this
face-to-face.

Rule 2. Blocks must be placed in   This , not this
a straight line.

Our object is to count the number of visible faces in each arrangement and to look for a pattern. Shown below are data collected for the first five arrangements.

No. of blocks	1	2	3	4	5
No. of visible faces	5	8	11	14	17

Each time we add a block, we add 3 visible faces. We have produced the sequence of five terms, 5, 8, 11, 14, 17, with a constant change of 3. We might expect that for n blocks there should be $3n$ visible faces. However, the first block has 5, or 2 *more* than 3, visible faces. So we write the expression $3n + 2$ for the number of visible faces when n blocks are in a row.

No. of blocks	1	2	3	4	5	6	7	...	n
No. of visible faces	5	8	11	14	17	20	23	...	$3n + 2$

Constant change = 3

+3 +3 +3 +3 +3 +3

Example 2   What is the 18th term in the sequence shown above?

Solution   When $n = 18$, $3n + 2 = 3(18) + 2$
$$= 54 + 2 = 56.$$
The 18th term is 56. So 56 faces are visible when 18 blocks are in a row.

Your Turn   How many faces are visible when the following numbers of blocks are in a row?
- 8   26 faces   • 10   32 faces   • 50   152 faces   • 100   302 faces

Class Exercises

Find the constant change for each sequence of numbers. Then give the next 5 terms.

	Term							Term				
	1st	2nd	3rd	4th	5th			1st	2nd	3rd	4th	5th
1.	1	3	5	7	9	2; 11 13 15 17 19	**2.**	5	6	7	8	9

1; 10 11 12 13 14 (for 2.)

	1st	2nd	3rd	4th	5th			1st	2nd	3rd	4th	5th
3.	4	7	10	13	16	3; 19 22 25 28 31	**4.**	6	9	12	15	18

3; 21 24 27 30 33 (for 4.)

	1st	2nd	3rd	4th	5th			1st	2nd	3rd	4th	5th
5.	8	12	16	20	24	4; 28 32 36 40 44	**6.**	6	11	16	21	26

5; 31 36 41 46 51 (for 6.)

Exercises

Find the constant change for each sequence of numbers. Then find the next 5 terms.

A

		1st	2nd	3rd	4th	5th			1st	2nd	3rd	4th	5th
		24; 132 156 180 204 228							35; 198 233 268 303 338				
1.		12	36	60	84	108		**2.**	23	58	93	128	163
		127; 638 765 892 1019 1146							28; 282 310 338 366 394				
3.		3	130	257	384	511		**4.**	142	170	198	226	254
		$^-$24; 444 420 396 372 348							$^-$52; 438 386 334 282 230				
5.		564	540	516	492	468		**6.**	698	646	594	542	490

Find the first five terms of the sequence of numbers produced by the given expression.

Example $6x + 3$

Solution When $x = 1$, $6x + 3 = 6(1) + 3 = 6 + 3 = 9$, the 1st term
When $x = 2$, $6x + 3 = 6(2) + 3 = 12 + 3 = 15$, the 2nd term
When $x = 3$, $6x + 3 = 6(3) + 3 = 18 + 3 = 21$, the 3rd term
When $x = 4$, $6x + 3 = 6(4) + 3 = 24 + 3 = 27$, the 4th term
When $x = 5$, $6x + 3 = 6(5) + 3 = 30 + 3 = 33$, the 5th term

B

9, 10, 11, 12, 13
7. $n + 8$

6, 8, 10, 12, 14
8. $2x + 4$

0, 5, 10, 15, 20
9. $5s - 5$

28, 31, 34, 37, 40
10. $3n + 25$

10, 8, 6, 4, 2
11. $^-2n + 12$

4, 1, $^-$2, $^-$5, $^-$8
12. $^-3n + 7$

$^-$7, $^-$20, $^-$33, $^-$46, $^-$59
13. $^-13z + 6$

14. $^-16a - 13$
14. $^-$29, $^-$45, $^-$61, $^-$77, $^-$93

Find the required terms of the given expression.

258; 758
15. $5n + 8$, 50th and 150th terms

857; 1097
16. $12z - 7$, 72nd and 92nd terms

1215; 825
17. $15x - 45$, 84th and 58th terms

1322; 2429
18. $27a + 80$, 46th and 87th terms

281

9-2 *Finding Expressions for Data*

In the preceding section we found expressions for any term for two sequences of numbers with constant changes.

$$2, 4, 6, 8, 10, \ldots, 2n \qquad 5, 8, 11, 14, 17, \ldots, 3n + 2$$

We can find an expression for any term of *any* sequence of numbers with a constant change.

Example   Find an expression for any term of the sequence 9, 14, 19, 24, ...

Solution   1. Find the constant change by subtracting the first term from the second, the second term from the third, and so on: $14 - 9 = 5$, $19 - 14 = 5$, and so on. The constant change is 5, so $5n$ is one part of the expression.
2. Subtract the constant change from the first term. $9 - 5 = 4$.
3. Write an expression to show that 4 is added to a multiple of 5: $5n + 4$.

Check: Use $5n + 4$ to find the 3rd term.
If $n = 3$, then $5n + 4 = 5(3) + 4 = 19$
The 3rd term is 19, as shown above.

Your Turn   • Find an expression for any term of 5, 7, 9, 11, 13, ... $2n + 3$

Class Exercises

For the sequence 7, 11, 15, 19, 23, ..., do the following:

1. Find the constant change. 4

2. Subtract the constant change from the first term. 3

3. Write an expression for any term: $\underset{4}{\underline{}}n + \underset{3}{\underline{}}$

4. Use the expression to find the 5th term. Does it check with the 5th term given above? yes

5. Find the 10th and 20th terms. 43; 83

Exercises

Write an expression for any term of the given sequence. Then find the 10th and 15th terms.

A **1.** 4, 8, 12, 16, 20, . . . $4n$; 40; 60

2. 5, 9, 13, 17, 21, . . . $4n + 1$; 41; 61

3. 7, 10, 13, 16, 19, . . . $3n + 4$; 34; 49

4. 14, 20, 26, 32, 38, . . . $6n + 8$; 68; 98

5. 10, 17, 24, 31, 38, . . . $7n + 3$; 73; 108

6. 12, 21, 30, 39, 48, . . . $9n + 3$; 93; 138

Find the constant change for each sequence of numbers. Then find the next five terms.

B **7.** 7, 6, 5, 4, 3, . . . $^-1$; 2, 1, 0, $^-1$, $^-2$

8. 4, 2, 0, $^-2$, $^-4$, . . . $^-2$; $^-6$, $^-8$, $^-10$, $^-12$, $^-14$

9. $^-25$, $^-20$, $^-15$, $^-10$, $^-5$, . . . 5; 0, 5, 10, 15, 20

10. $^-5$, $^-10$, $^-15$, $^-20$, $^-25$, . . . $^-5$; $^-30$, $^-35$, $^-40$, $^-45$, $^-50$

11. $^-9$, $^-6$, $^-3$, 0, 3, . . . 3; 6, 9, 12, 15, 18

12. 9, 6, 3, 0, $^-3$, . . . $^-3$; $^-6$, $^-9$, $^-12$, $^-15$, $^-18$

Write an expression for any term of the sequence. Then find the 10th and 50th terms.

12, 10, 8, 6, 4

Find the constant change: $10 - 12 = ^-2$
Subtract constant change from 1st term: $12 - ^-2 = 14$
Write an expression for any term: $^-2n + 14$
10th term: $^-2(10) + 14 = ^-6$ 50th term: $^-2(50) + 14 = ^-86$

13. 10, 9, 8, 7, 6, . . . $^-n + 11$; 1; $^-39$

14. 8, 4, 0, $^-4$, $^-8$, . . . $^-4n + 12$; $^-28$; $^-188$

15. $^-5$, $^-1$, 3, 7, 11, . . . $4n, - 9$; 31; 191

16. 11, 8, 5, 2, $^-1$, . . . $^-3n + 14$; $^-16$; $^-136$

17. 3, 8, 13, 18, 23, . . . $5n - 2$; 48; 248

18. 2, 10, 18, 26, 34, . . . $8n - 6$; 74; 394

C **19.** 8, $10\frac{1}{2}$, 13, $15\frac{1}{2}$, 18, . . . $\frac{5}{2}n + \frac{11}{2}$; $30\frac{1}{2}$; $130\frac{1}{2}$

20. 5, $8\frac{3}{4}$, $12\frac{1}{2}$, $16\frac{1}{4}$, 20, . . . $\frac{15}{4}n + \frac{5}{4}$; $38\frac{3}{4}$; $188\frac{3}{4}$

21. 16, $14\frac{2}{5}$, $12\frac{4}{5}$, $11\frac{1}{5}$, $9\frac{3}{5}$, . . . $\frac{^-8}{5}n + \frac{88}{5}$; $1\frac{3}{5}$; $^-62\frac{2}{5}$

22. $6\frac{2}{3}$, 4, $1\frac{1}{3}$, $^-1\frac{1}{3}$, $^-4$, . . . $\frac{^-8}{3}n + \frac{28}{3}$; $^-17\frac{1}{3}$; $^-124$

Problems

Solve.

1. On the first week in January, Edna put 75¢ in her piggy bank. On each following week she added 25¢.
   a. How much money was in her piggy bank after 5 weeks? 10 weeks? 50 weeks? $1.75; $3.00; $13.00
   b. How long did it take Edna to save $20. 78 weeks

The tables in the Seven Seas Restaurant are square-shaped and can seat one person on each side. They can be arranged in rows, as shown at the right, for parties who want to sit together. How many can be seated in a row with the given number of tables?

2. 1 4   **3.** 2 6   **4.** 3 8   **5.** 4 10   **6.** 5 12   **7.** 10 22   **8.** 15 32

9. A party of 15 persons has made reservations at the Seven Seas for lunch. If the tables are arranged in a row, how many of them are needed? 7 tables

10. a. Thirty members of the Ecology Club arrived for dinner at the Seven Seas. Only 12 tables were available for them. What is the least number of rows of tables which can seat them exactly if there are the same numbers of tables in each row. How are the tables arranged? 3 rows of 4 tables
    b. Just as the 30 members of the Ecology Club were about to sit down, 2 more members joined them. How could the tables be rearranged to seat all 32 members exactly? The least number of rows of tables should be used.   4 rows of 3 tables

9-3 *The Coordinate Plane*

We can display data like those in the two preceding sections by graphing them on a *coordinate plane.* First we write the data as *ordered pairs* of numbers. The numbers in an ordered pair are called **coordinates.**

The ordered pairs below display the data for the first experiment in Section 9-1.

No. of lines	No. of regions	Ordered pairs
1	2	(1, 2)
2	4	(2, 4)
3	6	(3, 6)
4	8	(4, 8)

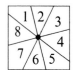

In the ordered pair (3, 6), the first coordinate, 3, tells the number of lines drawn through a point in a square. The second coordinate, 6, tells the number of regions formed.

To graph (3, 6) on the coordinate plane, start at 0, move 3 units to the right, then move 6 units up.

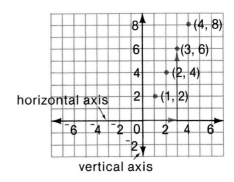

In general, to graph an ordered pair (*a, b*):
- Start at 0.
- Move along the horizontal axis the number named by the first coordinate, *a* units.
- Move along the vertical axis the number named by the second coordinate, *b* units.

Example 1 Graph the ordered pairs on a coordinate plane.
 a. (6, 3) Is (6, 3) the same as (3, 6)?
 b. (3, −2)   **c.** (⁻4, 1)   **d.** (⁻2, ⁻3)   **e.** (0, 4)   **f.** (⁻3, 0)

Solution In each case, start at 0.
 a. Move 6 right and 3 up.
    No.
 b. Move 3 right and 2 down.
 c. Move 4 left and 1 up.
 d. Move 2 left and 3 down.
 e. Do not move on the hori-
    zontal axis. Move 4 up.
 f. Move 3 left and stop.

   In the example above, we see that the ordered pair (6, 3) is not the same as the ordered pair (3, 6). In general, the ordered pair (a, b) is not the same as (b, a), unless a = b.

Example 2 Write the ordered pair for the point on the coordinate plane.
 a. A   **b.** B
 c. C   **d.** D

Solution **a.** (2, 3) **b.** (5, ⁻3)
 c. (⁻5, ⁻3) **d.** (⁻4, 5)

Your Turn Graph the ordered pairs on a
 coordinate plane. Check students' graphs.
 • (3, 5)   • (⁻4, 4)
 • (0, 2)   • (1, ⁻4)

 Write the ordered pair for the
 point on the coordinate plane.
 • E   • F   • G   • H
 (⁻5, ⁻3) (1, 2) (⁻4, 2) (1, ⁻5)

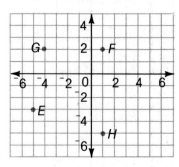

286

Class Exercises

How far would you move and in what direction for the given coordinate?

1. 2 in (2, 3) ² ʳⁱᵍʰᵗ **2.** ⁻3 in (1, ⁻3) ³ ᵈᵒʷⁿ **3.** ⁻5 in (⁻5, 4) ⁵ ˡᵉᶠᵗ **4.** 0 in (2, 0) ⁰

5. ⁻4 in (0, ⁻4) ⁴ ᵈᵒʷⁿ **6.** 20 in (20, 32) ²⁰ ʳⁱᵍʰᵗ **7.** 8 in (⁻8, 8) ⁸ ᵘᵖ **8.** 0 in (0, 7) ⁰

Exercises

Graph the ordered pairs on a coordinate plane. Check students' graphs.

A

1. (7, ⁻2)	**2.** (5, 0)	**3.** (⁻6, 1)	**4.** (⁻3, ⁻3)
5. (0, 8)	**6.** (⁻4, 0)	**7.** (0, 0)	**8.** (0, ⁻10)
9. (⁻4, ⁻1)	**10.** (6, ⁻2)	**11.** (5, 7)	**12.** (⁻2, 4)

Write the ordered pair for the point on the coordinate plane.

13. *M* (⁻6, 3) **14.** *N* (4, 5)

15. *P* (5, ⁻3) **16.** *Q* (⁻5, ⁻5)

17. *R* (0, ⁻3) **18.** *S* (0, 3)

19. *T* (⁻4, 0) **20.** *U* (5, 0)

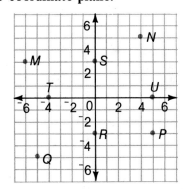

For each exercise, graph the ordered pairs on a coordinate plane, then join the graphs in order, connecting the last graph with the first graph. What geometric figure have you drawn? Check students' graphs.

B **21.** (3, 3), (⁻3, 3), (⁻3, ⁻3), (3, ⁻3) square **22.** (4, 0), (0, 6), (⁻4, 0) triangle

23. (2, ⁻3), (6, ⁻3), (6, ⁻7) triangle **24.** (⁻4, 3), (6, 3), (3, ⁻2), (⁻7, ⁻2) parallelogram

25. (0, 5), (5, 0) (0, ⁻5), (⁻5, 0) square **26.** (2, 6), (5, 3), (⁻3, ⁻5), (⁻6, ⁻2) rectangle

27. (⁻1, 3), (5, 3), (3, ⁻1), (⁻3, ⁻1) parallelogram **28.** (⁻4, 1), (⁻2, ⁻2), (2, ⁻2), (4, 1) trapezoid

287

9-4 Graphing Data

In the preceding lesson, we graphed ordered pairs of numbers which showed the number of regions formed by drawing lines through a point. The graph is repeated at the right. Notice that the points graphed lie on a straight line. By extending the line we can predict that 6 lines form 12 regions, 7 lines form 14 regions, and so on.

We can also graph the data we collected in section 9-1 involving the number of visible faces of blocks arranged in a row:

No. of blocks	No. of visible faces	Ordered pairs
1	5	(1, 5)
2	8	(2, 8)
3	11	(3, 11)
4	14	(4, 14)
5	17	(5, 17)

Notice that, like the preceding graph, the plotted points lie on a straight line. By extending the line we can predict that 6 blocks have 20 visible faces, 7 blocks have 23 visible faces, and so on.

In each case above we have graphed a sequence of numbers with a constant change and have found that the graphs lie on a straight line. This is true of any sequence of numbers with a constant change.

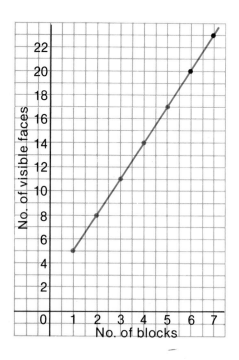

Example   What is the constant change for the sequence of numbers shown at the right? Graph the sequence and use the graph to predict the 6th term.

No. of term	Sequence
1	4
2	8
3	12

Solution $4 + 4 = 8$, $8 + 4 = 12$. The constant change is 4. Write the data as ordered pairs and then graph them on a coordinate plane.

Ordered pairs
—————————
(1, 4)
(2, 8)
(3, 12)

From the graph, the 6th term is 24.

Class Exercises

1. (1, 5), (2, 7), (3, 9), (4, 11), (5, 13)   **2.** (1, 4), (2, 7), (3, 10), (4, 13), (5, 16)

Use the graph to write the first 5 terms of each sequence.

1.

2.

289

Exercises

Graph the following data. Use your graph to find the 8th term. Check students' graphs.

A

1. (11)

No. of term	Sequence
1	4
2	5
3	6
4	7
5	8

2. (24)

No. of term	Sequence
1	3
2	6
3	9
4	12
5	15

3. (15)

No. of term	Sequence
1	1
2	3
3	5
4	7
5	9

4. (30)

No. of term	Sequence
1	2
2	6
3	10
4	14
5	18

5. (14)

No. of term	Sequence
1	0
2	2
3	4
4	6
5	8

6. (1)

No. of term	Sequence
1	8
2	7
3	6
4	5
5	4

7. (23)

No. of term	Sequence
1	2
2	5
3	8
4	11
5	14

8. (1)

No. of term	Sequence
1	15
2	13
3	11
4	9
5	7

B

9. ($^-1$)

No. of term	Sequence
1	6
2	5
3	4
4	3
5	2

10. ($^-10$)

No. of term	Sequence
1	4
2	2
3	0
4	$^-2$
5	$^-4$

11. (16)

No. of term	Sequence
1	$^-5$
2	$^-2$
3	1
4	4
5	7

12. ($^-6$)

No. of term	Sequence
1	15
2	12
3	9
4	6
5	3

C

13. ($15\frac{1}{2}$)

No. of term	Sequence
1	$1\frac{1}{2}$
2	$3\frac{1}{2}$
3	$5\frac{1}{2}$
4	$7\frac{1}{2}$
5	$9\frac{1}{2}$

14. (14)

No. of term	Sequence
1	$3\frac{1}{2}$
2	5
3	$6\frac{1}{2}$
4	8
5	$9\frac{1}{2}$

15. ($^-5\frac{3}{4}$)

No. of term	Sequence
1	$8\frac{1}{4}$
2	$6\frac{1}{4}$
3	$4\frac{1}{4}$
4	$2\frac{1}{4}$
5	$0\frac{1}{4}$

16. ($3\frac{1}{2}$)

No. of term	Sequence
1	$12\frac{1}{4}$
2	11
3	$9\frac{3}{4}$
4	$8\frac{1}{2}$
5	$7\frac{1}{4}$

Problems

Solve. Check students' graphs.

1. A partially full swimming pool contains 6000 gal of water. It is being filled at the rate of 300 gal per h. When full it holds 27,000 gal. Draw a graph to show how much water is in the pool after 10 h, 20 h, and 30 h. Use your graph to predict how long it will take to fill the pool. 70 h

2. Comchip Company produced 15,000 computer chips in January. The production manager has set a goal of increasing production by 2000 chips each month for the rest of the year. Draw a graph to show the production figures for January through March. Then use your graph to predict the production figures for each of the remaining months. April, 21,000; May, 23,000; June, 25,000; July, 27,000; August, 29,000; September, 31,000; October, 33,000; November, 35,000; December, 37,000

Self Test 1

Find the first five terms of the sequence of numbers produced by the given expression.

1. $x - 2$ $^{-1, 0, 1, 2, 3}$ 2. $3y + 5$ $^{8, 11, 14, 17, 20}$ 3. $-2n - 4$ $^{-6, -8, -10, -12, -14}$ 4. $-t + 5$ $^{4, 3, 2, 1, 0}$ **9-1**

Write an expression for any term of the sequence. Then find the 10th and 50th terms.

5. 1, 4, 7, 10, 13 $3n - 2$; 28; 148   6. $^-3$, 0, 3, 6, 9 $3n - 6$; 24; 144   **9-2**

7. 9, 5, 1, $^-3$, $^-7$ $-4n + 13$; $^-27$; $^-187$ 8. 11, 16, 21, 26, 31 $5n + 6$; 56; 256

Graph the ordered pairs on a coordinate plane. Check students' graphs.

9. (3, 5)   10. ($^-4$, 0)   11. (6, $^-2$)   12. ($^-5$, $^-1$)   **9-3**

Check students' graphs.

Graph the following data. Use your graph to find the 8th term.

13.
No. of term	1	2	3	4	5
Sequence	3	7	11	15	19

31   **9-4**

14.
No. of term	1	2	3	4	5
Sequence	8	5	2	$^-1$	$^-4$

$^-13$

Self Test answers and Extra Practice are at the back of the book.

9-5 Equation of a Line

In Section 9-2 you learned that you can write an expression for any sequence of numbers with a constant change. For example, the expression $3x + 2$ produces the sequence of numbers 5, 8, 11, 14, . . . , which has a constant change of 3.

In algebra, we often write an expression like $3x + 2$ in an equation with two variables, as $y = 3x + 2$. Then we graph the equation on the coordinate plane. The horizontal axis is called the x-axis and the vertical axis is called the y-axis. We substitute values for x in $y = 3x + 2$ to find values for y. Then we form ordered pairs and graph them.

x	$y = 3x + 2$	(x, y)
$^-2$	$y = 3(^-2) + 2 = {}^-4$	$(^-2, {}^-4)$
0	$y = 3(0) + 2 = 2$	$(0, 2)$
2	$y = 3(2) + 2 = 8$	$(2, 8)$

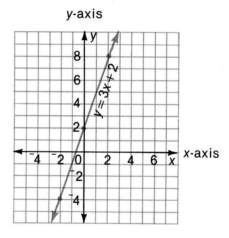

The points all lie on a straight line. The ordered pairs $(-2, -4)$, $(0, 2)$, and $(2, 8)$ are called **solutions** of the equation $y = 3x + 2$. Every point on the line we have graphed has an ordered pair that is a solution of $y = 3x + 2$.

Example Is the ordered pair a solution of the equation $y = 3x + 2$?
a. $(1, 4)$ **b.** $(^-5, {}^-13)$

Solution

a. $4 \stackrel{?}{=} 3(1) + 2$

4	$3 + 2$
4	5

$4 \neq 5$, so $(1, 4)$ is not a solution.

b. $^-13 \stackrel{?}{=} 3(^-5) + 2$

$^-13$	$^-15 + 2$
$^-13$	$^-13$

$^-13 = {}^-13$, so $(^-5, {}^-13)$ is a solution.

Your Turn Is $(10, 32)$ a solution of $y = 3x + 2$? yes

Class Exercises

Complete the ordered pair so that it is a solution of the given equation. Use the graph.

$y = 2x - 3$
(x, y)

1. $(^-4, ?)$ $^-11$
2. $(^-2, ?)$ $^-7$
3. $(0, ?)$ $^-3$
4. $(?, 1)$ 2
5. $(?, 5)$ 4

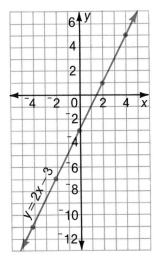

$y = 3x + 1$
(x, y)

6. $(^-3, ?)$ $^-8$
7. $(^-1, ?)$ $^-2$
8. $(0, ?)$ 1
9. $(?, 4)$ 1
10. $(?, 10)$ 3

Exercises

Complete the ordered pair so that it is a solution of the given equation.

	x	$y = 2x - 1$	(x, y)
A 1.	$^-2$	$y = 2(^-2) - 1 = ^-5$	$(^-2, ?)$ $^-5$
2.	0	$y = 2(0) - 1 = ^-1$	$(?, ^-1)$ 0
3.	3	$y = 2(3) - 1 = ?$ 5	$(3, ?)$ 5
4.	5	$y = 2(5) - 1 = ?$ 9	$(?, ?)$ $5; 9$

	x	$y = 4x + 2$	(x, y)
5.	$^-5$	$y = 4(^-5) + 2 \overset{-18}{=} ?$	$(?, ?)$ $^-5; ^-18$
6.	$^-1$	$y = 4(^-1) + 2 \overset{-2}{=} ?$	$(?, ?)$ $^-1; ^-2$
7.	0	$y = 4(0) + 2 = ?$ 2	$(?, ?)$ $0; 2$
8.	5	$y = 4(5) + 2 = ?$ 22	$(?, ?)$ $5; 22$

Find three ordered pairs that are solutions of the given equation, then graph them and draw the line for the equation. Check students' graphs.

B 9. $y = x - 6$ 　　10. $y = x + 5$ 　　11. $y = 2x + 1$

12. $y = 2x - 2$ 　　13. $y = ^-x + 3$ 　　14. $y = ^-x - 3$

15. $y = 3x - 1$ 　　16. $y = ^-2x + 2$ 　　17. $y = ^-3x - 1$

18. $y = 4x + 5$ 　　19. $y = ^-3x + 1$ 　　20. $y = 4x - 8$

C 21. $y = \frac{1}{2}x + 3$ 　　22. $y = 2x + \frac{1}{3}$ 　　23. $y = \frac{1}{3}x + \frac{2}{3}$

293

9-6 Slope and Intercept

Integers that differ by 1 are called **consecutive integers.** For example, 1, 2, 3, and 4 are consecutive integers, as are $^-15$, $^-14$, and $^-13$.

As shown in the table below, if we substitute the consecutive integers 1, 2, 3, and 4 for x in the equation $y = 2x + 5$, we obtain the values 7, 9, 11, and 13 for y. Thus we produce a sequence of numbers with the constant change of 2, which is the coefficient of x in $y = 2x + 5$.

x	$y = 2x + 5$	(x, y)
1	$y = 2(1) + 5 = 7$	$(1, 7)$
2	$y = 2(2) + 5 = 9$	$(2, 9)$
3	$y = 2(3) + 5 = 11$	$(3, 11)$
4	$y = 2(4) + 5 = 13$	$(4, 13)$

The constant change, or coefficient of x, can also be found by looking at the graph of $y = 2x + 5$. On the graph at the right we can find the constant change by moving from point A to point B horizontally 3 units (the **run**), then vertically 6 units (the **rise**). The ratio of rise to run equals the coefficient of x in the equation $y = 2x + 5$.

$$\frac{\text{rise}}{\text{run}} = \frac{6}{3} = 2, \text{ the coefficient of } x$$

$$\frac{rise}{run} = slope$$

vertical distance

horizontal distance

This ratio of rise to run is the same when moving from any point on the line to any other point on the line and is called the **slope** of the line. The slope is a measure of the steepness of a line.

Notice that the line crosses the y-axis 5 units up. This 5 corresponds to the 5 in the equation $y = 2x + 5$ and is called the **y-intercept.**

An equation of the form $y = mx + b$ is called a **linear** equation. Its graph is a straight line whose slope is m and whose y-intercept is b.

Example 1   Find the slope and y-intercept for the line at the right. Then use them to write an equation for the line.

Solution   From point A to point B the run is 3 and the rise is 2.

$$\text{slope} = \frac{\text{rise}}{\text{run}} = \frac{2}{3}$$

The line crosses the y-axis 2 units up, so the y-intercept is 2.

The equation for the line is $y = \frac{2}{3}x + 2$.

Your Turn   • Find the slope and y-intercept for the line at the right. Then use them to write an equation for the line. 4, ⁻2; $y = 4x - 2$

Example 2   What is the slope and y-intercept of the graph of the equation?
a. $y = 3x + 4$ **b.** $y = 5x - 7$ **c.** $y = ⁻12x + 8$

Solution   **a.** slope = 3   **b.** slope = 5   **c.** slope = ⁻12
    y-intercept = 4 y-intercept = ⁻7 y-intercept = 8

Your Turn   What is the slope and y-intercept of the graph of the equation?
• $y = 6x + 9$ 6; 9   • $y = 4x - 3$ 4; ⁻3   • $y = ⁻7x - 2$ ⁻7; ⁻2

295

So far we have shown lines with positive slope. Notice that these lines slant upward from left to right.
Lines that have negative slope slant downward from left
to right. Look at the graph of the equation $y = -3x + 1$.

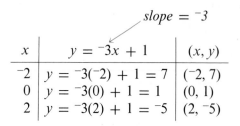

x	$y = ^-3x + 1$	(x, y)
$^-2$	$y = ^-3(^-2) + 1 = 7$	$(^-2, 7)$
0	$y = ^-3(0) + 1 = 1$	$(0, 1)$
2	$y = ^-3(2) + 1 = ^-5$	$(2, ^-5)$

slope $= ^-3$

Class Exercises

1–3. Answers may vary for the rise and the
run, but the ratio should remain the same.

1. $3, 6, \dfrac{1}{2}$ **2.** $5, 3, \dfrac{5}{3}$ **3.** $2, 6, \dfrac{1}{3}$

Find the rise, the run, and the slope, for each line.

1.

2.

3.
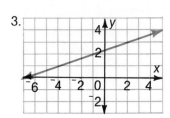

What is the slope and y-intercept of the graph of the equation?

4. $y = 2x + 7$ 2; 7   **5.** $y = ^-3x + 8$ $^-3$; 8   **6.** $y = \dfrac{3}{5}x - 4$ $\dfrac{3}{5}$; $^-4$

Exercises

1. $1, 3; y = x + 3$ **2.** $3, ^-15; y = 3x - 15$ **3.** $^-4, 20; y = ^-4x + 20$

Find the slope and y-intercept for the line. Then use them to write an equation for the line.

A 1.

2.

3.

What is the slope and *y*-intercept of the graph of the equation? Does the graph slant upward from left to right, or downward?

$^{-}12; \frac{1}{2};$ downward

4. $y = 6x + 5$ 6; 5; upward   **5.** $y = \frac{3}{5}x - 4$ $\frac{3}{5};$ $^{-}4;$ upward   **6.** $y = ^{-}12x + \frac{1}{2}$

1.5; 7.2; upward $^{-}0.42;$ $^{-}3.6;$ downward   7.3; $^{-}12.6;$ upward
7. $y = 1.5x + 7.2$ **8.** $y = ^{-}0.42x - 3.6$ **9.** $y = 7.3x - 12.6$

For each exercise, what do you notice about the slopes of the graphs of the equations? Graph the equations. What do you notice about the lines?

Check students' graphs.

B **10.** $y = 2x + 5,$ $y = 2x - 3,$ $y = 2x + 7$ same; parallel

11. $y = 5x - 2,$ $y = 5x,$ $y = 5x + 1$ same; parallel

12. $y = ^{-}3x + 1,$ $y = ^{-}3x - 3,$ $y = ^{-}3x + 2$ same; parallel

13. $y = 4x + 1,$ $y = \frac{^{-}1}{4}x + 3$ product is $^{-}1;$ perpendicular

14. $y = \frac{2}{3}x + 2,$ $y = \frac{^{-}3}{2}x + 4$ product is $^{-}1;$ perpendicular

Check students' graphs.

Graph each equation. Is the line slanted, vertical, or horizontal?

vertical
C **15.** $y = 3$ horizontal   **16.** $y = ^{-}5$ horizontal   **17.** $x = 2$ vertical   **18.** $x = ^{-}3$

Problems

Solve.

1. The foot of a ramp is 8 ft from the base of a house. The ramp reaches a doorway that is 18 in. above the ground. What is the slope of the ramp? $\frac{3}{16}$

2. The foot of a ladder is 3 ft. from the base of a house. Its top rests against a window sill 28 ft from the ground. What is the slope of the ladder? $\frac{28}{3}$

9-7 *Linear Inequalities*

Inequalities in two variables, such as $y > \frac{1}{2}x + 3$, are called **linear inequalities.** The graph of a linear inequality is not a line but a region.

In the diagram at the right, the following graphs are shown:

- graph of $y = \frac{1}{2}x + 3$: the line

- graph of $y > \frac{1}{2}x + 3$: the region above the line

- graph of $y < \frac{1}{2}x + 3$: the region below the line

In graphing linear inequalities we use dashed and solid lines in a special way as shown in these two graphs. The graph of $y < 4x - 3$ is shown at the left. In it, the graph of $y = 4x - 3$ is a dashed line, indicating that it is not included in the graph of $y < 4x - 3$. The graph of $y \le 4x - 3$ is shown at the right. In it, the graph of $y = 4x - 3$ is a solid line, indicating that it is included in the graph of $y \le 4x - 3$.

$y < 4x - 3$ $y \le 4x - 3$

We can use a graph to determine whether an ordered pair is a solution of a linear inequality.

Example 1   Use the graph of $y < 4x - 3$ above to determine whether or not $(0, {}^-3)$ is a solution of $y < 4x - 3$.

Solution   Plotting $(0, {}^-3)$ we find its graph is the point P on the dashed line. Therefore, $(0, {}^-3)$ is not a solution of $y < 4x - 3$.

In Example 2 we determine whether an ordered pair is a solution of a linear inequality by substituting its values in the inequality.

Example 2 Use substitution to determine whether (4, 2) is a solution of $y \leq 4x - 3$.

Solution $y \leq 4x - 3$
Is $2 \leq 4(4) - 3$ true?
$2 \leq 13$ is true. Therefore, (4, 2) is a solution.

You can draw the graph of the inequality in Example 2 by first drawing the graph of $y = 4x - 3$; then, of the two possible regions, shade the region containing the known solution (4, 2).

Your Turn
- Use the graph of $y < 4x - 3$ above to determine whether ($^-$2, 2) is a solution of the inequality. not a solution
- Use substitution to determine whether (3, 4) is a solution of $y \geq 5x - 3$. not a solution   See p. T28

Class Exercises

Is the point a graph of a solution of $y \geq 2x + 1$?

1. *A* yes   2. *B* yes   3. *C* no

4. *D* no   5. *E* no   6. *F* yes

$y \geq 2x + 1$

Exercises

Use the graph at the right to determine whether the ordered pair is a solution of $y < 5x - 4$.

A   1. (0, 1) no   2. (1, 0) yes   3. (3, 2) yes   4. (3, $^-$2) yes

5. ($^-$2, 3) no   6. (0, $^-$4) no   7. (4, $^-$6) yes   8. (1, 1) no

In each exercise, is the ordered pair a solution of the linear inequality?

B 9. $(2, 1)$, $y > x - 3$ yes 10. $(8, ^-8)$, $y > 5x - 48$ no 11. $(^-3, ^-33)$, $y \leq 12x + 3$ yes

12. $(6, 5)$, $y \leq \frac{1}{2}x + \frac{1}{4}$ no 13. $(7, 8)$, $y \geq \frac{2}{3}x - \frac{2}{3}$ yes 14. $(^-16, 0)$, $y > \frac{5}{8}x + 4$ yes

Draw the graph of the linear inequality. Check students' graphs.

15. $y > x + 2$ 16. $y < 3x - 7$ 17. $y \geq -2x + 4$ 18. $y \leq 6x - 9$

Using the Computer

This program will find the slope of the line through two points. RUN it for these pairs of points:

$(2, 3)$ and $(4, 7)$; $(^-3, 2)$ and $(1, 8)$; $(^-3, 1)$ and $(0, ^-4)$

```
 5  REM: SLOPE OF LINE THROUGH TWO POINTS
10  PRINT "WHAT ARE THE COORDINATES--"
20  PRINT "OF THE FIRST POINT";
30  INPUT X1,Y1
40  PRINT "OF THE SECOND POINT";
50  INPUT X2,Y2
60  PRINT "SLOPE =";Y2-Y1;" /";X2-X1;
70  PRINT " =";(Y2-Y1)/(X2-X1)
80  END
```

What are the coordinates --
of the first point? 2, 3
of the second point? 4, 7
Slope = 4/2 = 2
$(^-3, 2)$ and $(1, 8)$: $\frac{6}{4} = 1.5$
$(^-3, 1)$ and $(0, ^-4)$: $\frac{^-5}{3} = 1.\overline{6}$

Self Test 2

Find three ordered pairs that are solutions of the given equation. Then graph them and draw the line for the equation. Check students' graphs.

1. $y = x + 1$ 2. $y = 3x - 5$ 3. $y = ^-2x + 4$ **9-5**

What is the slope and y-intercept of the graph of the equation? Graph the equation. Check students' graphs.

4. $y = 4x - 1$ 4; $^-1$ 5. $y = ^-x + 2$ $^-1$; 2   6. $y = 3x + 4$ 3; 4   **9-6**

Is the ordered pair a solution of the linear inequality?

7. $(3, 2)$, $y < x + 4$ yes 8. $(^-1, 1)$, $y \geq x - 3$ yes 9. $(2, 0)$, $y > 2x + 1$ no   **9-7**

Algebra Practice

Write an equation. Solve.

1. 49,452 divided by 78 is equal to c. $\quad$ 49,452 ÷ 78 = c; 634

2. 216 times 980 is equal to f. $\quad$ (216)(980) = f; 211,680

3. The sum of 103 and 99.44 is v. $\quad$ 103 + 99.44 = v; 202.44

4. The quotient of 0.2313 and 0.09 is m. $\quad$ 0.2313 ÷ 0.09 = m; 2.57

5. The sum of $4\frac{2}{3}$ and $4\frac{7}{16}$ is t. $\quad$ $4\frac{2}{3} + 4\frac{7}{16} = t;\ 9\frac{53}{48}$

6. $\frac{5}{6}$ of $3\frac{3}{10}$ is equal to b. $\quad$ $\frac{5}{6} \cdot 3\frac{3}{10} = b;\ 2\frac{3}{4}$

7. The perimeter of a square with side $6\frac{7}{8}$ in. is P. $\quad$ $4\left(6\frac{7}{8}\right) = P;\ 27\frac{1}{2}$ in.

8. The area of a circle with a radius of 2.5 m is A. $\quad$ $(3.14)(2.5)^2 = A;\ 19.625m^2$

9. The volume of a prism with a base area of 20 ft² and a height of 6 ft is V. $\quad$ (20)(6) = V; 120 ft³

Use the distributive property to factor each expression.

10. $2g^2h + g^2h^2 + 5g^2$ $\quad$ $g^2(2h + h^2 + 5)$

11. $3st^2 + s^2t^2 + 2s^2t$ $\quad$ $st(3t + st + 2s)$

12. $4ab + 8a^2 + 6ab^2$ $\quad$ $2a(2b + 4a + 3b^2)$

Solve.

13. $2f + 8 = 4$ $\quad$ -2

14. $5j - 6 = ^{-}21$ $\quad$ -3

15. $9s - 4 = ^{-}40$ $\quad$ -4

16. $7 > ^{-}2w + 3$ $\quad$ -2

17. $6 + ^{-}3m < 12$ $\quad$ -2

18. $\frac{a}{2} - 5 > ^{-}1$ $\quad$ 8

Find the first five terms of the sequence produced by the given expression.

19. $n + 5$ $\quad$ 6, 7, 8, 9, 10

20. $25a - 12$ $\quad$ 13, 38, 63, 88, 113

21. $^{-}4x + 5$ $\quad$ 1, ⁻3, ⁻7, ⁻11, ⁻15

Write an expression for any term of the sequence. Then find the 12th and 20th terms.

22. $^{-}4, ^{-}1, 2, 5, 8, \ldots$ $\quad$ 3n − 7; 29; 53

23. $12\frac{5}{7}, 10\frac{3}{7}, 8\frac{1}{7}, 5\frac{6}{7}, 3\frac{4}{7}, \ldots$ $\quad$ $\frac{^{-}16}{7}n + 15;\ ^{-}12\frac{3}{7};\ ^{-}30\frac{5}{7}$

Find three ordered pairs that are solutions of the given equation. Answers may vary.

24. $y = x + 4$

25. $y = 4x - 3$

26. $y = ^{-}2x + 3$

What is the slope and y-intercept of the equation?

27. $y = 5x + 3$ $\quad$ 5; 3

28. $y = 2x - 1$ $\quad$ 2; ⁻1

29. $y = ^{-}3x + 6$ $\quad$ ⁻3; 6

Is the ordered pair a solution of the linear inequality?

30. $(3, ^{-}5), y > x + 2$ $\quad$ no

31. $(4, 4), y < 3x - 5$ $\quad$ yes

32. $(2, 0), y \geq ^{-}2x + 4$ $\quad$ yes

Problem Solving on the Job

Engineering Technician

Are you interested in radio, television, electronics, computers, or scientific research and development? Technicians work in every field of science and engineering. Design technicians must be able to sketch objects and must be creative. Other technicians work closely with production or sales departments.

```
ENGINEERING TECHNICIAN

DESCRIPTION: Analyze and solve en-
gineering and science problems.
Prepare formal reports on experi-
ments, tests, and other projects.
QUALIFICATIONS: 1-4 years training
at a technical school, or on-the-
job training, or a combination.
JOB OUTLOOK: Increase in high tech-
nology jobs and the trend toward
automation in industry will require
more technicians.
```

The government employs engineering technicians in many fields. For example, as an aircraft is built a technician checks it for conformance to specifications. If you applied for a job as an engineering technician working for the government, you would have to take a civil service exam. The following problems are similar to those appearing on such an exam. Why don't you see how you would do?

Write a, b, c, or d to show the correct answer.

1. *PQ* is 42 in. long. The ratio of *PR* to *RQ* is 5 to 2. How long is *PR*? d

   a. 14 in.   b. 20 in.
   c. 28 in.   d. 30 in.

2. There are *b* boys and *g* girls in a class. What is the ratio of the number of boys to the total number of students? b

   a. $\dfrac{b}{g}$ b. $\dfrac{b}{b+g}$ c. $\dfrac{b+g}{b}$ d. $\dfrac{g}{b+g}$

3. If 60 ft of wire weighs 80 lb, what is the weight of 141 ft of the wire? d
   a. 160 lb   b. 162 lb   c. 165 lb   d. 188 lb

4. If *t* tons of snow falls in *h* hours, how many tons fall at this rate in *m* minutes? b

   a. $\dfrac{mt}{h}$ b. $\dfrac{mt}{60h}$ c. $\dfrac{60mt}{h}$ d. $\dfrac{60t}{mh}$

5. 0.6927 ft is most nearly how many inches? c

   a. $8\dfrac{1}{4}$ in.   b. $8\dfrac{9}{32}$ in.   c. $8\dfrac{5}{16}$ in.   d. $8\dfrac{11}{32}$ in.

6. The distance between two points on the ground is measured with a 100-ft steel tape and found to be 1012.60 ft. If the tape is 0.04 ft too long which measurement is closest to the true distance? d
   a. 1012.15 ft   b. 1012 ft   c. 1012.75 ft   d. 1013.00 ft

7. A gallon of paint covers 350 ft². About how many gallons are required to paint the inner walls of the hall with 1 coat of paint? d

   a. 6 gal   b. 7 gal
   c. 4 gal   d. 5 gal

8. About how many 9" × 9" pieces of tile are needed for the hall floor? c

   a. 2600   b. 2840
   c. 2400   d. 2260

   4′ × 7′ Door (1)
   Wall 12′ high
   30′   Plan of hall
   45′
   3′ × 7′ Windows (5)

9. The scale of a drawing is 1/8 in. = 1 ft. A rectangle on the drawing measures 7 1/8 in. by 6 1/4 in. About how many square feet are there in the area of the actual rectangle? d
   a. 2725 ft²   b. 2580 ft²   c. 2675 ft²   d. 2850 ft²

Enrichment

Systems of Equations

When we graph two linear equations on the same set of axes, sometimes the graphs intersect. The ordered pair of the point of intersection
is a common solution of the two equations. We call this ordered pair a
solution of the given **system of equations.**

System of equations
$$x + 2y = 3$$
$$2x - y = {}^-4$$

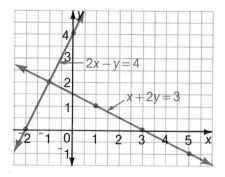

The graphs of the two equations
intersect at the point whose coordinates are $(^-1, 2)$. We check to see
that $(^-1, 2)$ is a solution of the system of equations by substituting in
each of the equations.

$x + 2y = 3$	
$^-1 + 2(2)$	3
$^-1 + 4$	3
3	3

$2x - y = {}^-4$	
$2(^-1) - 2$	$^-4$
$^-2 - 2$	$^-4$
$^-4$	$^-4$

$(^-1, 2)$ is a solution of the system of equations.

Sometimes the graphs of two equations in a system are parallel and
do not intersect. In this case the system has no solution. Sometimes the
graphs coincide, in which case there are an infinite number of solutions.

Is the given ordered pair a solution of the system of equations.

1. $2x - y = 3$; $(3, 3)$ yes
$\quad x + y = 6$

2. $x + 2y = 5$; $(2, 3)$ no
$\quad x - y = 1$

3. $x + 3y = {}^-4$; $(2, {}^-2)$ yes
$\quad 2x - y = 6$

Graph the system of equations. Find and check its solution. Check students' graphs.

4. $3x - y = 4$ $(3, 5)$
$\quad x + y = 8$

5. $x + 2y = 4$ $(10, {}^-3)$
$\quad x + 3y = 1$

6. $x - 4y = 6$ $(2, {}^-1)$
$\quad 2x + y = 3$

7. $2x - y = 1$ $(1, 1)$
$\quad x + 3y = 4$

8. $3x + y = 6$ $(2, 0)$
$\quad x - 2y = 2$

9. $4x - y = 2$ $(^-1, {}^-6)$
$\quad 2x - y = 4$

304

Chapter Review

Match the expression with the sequence.

1. 3, 7, 11, 15, 19 d

2. 9, 7, 5, 3, 1 e

3. 5, 1, ⁻3, ⁻7, ⁻11 c

4. 1, 6, 11, 16, 21 b

5. 6, 3, 0, ⁻3, ⁻6 a

a. $^-3x + 9$

b. $5n - 4$

c. $^-4t + 9$

d. $4d - 1$

e. $^-2y + 11$

Write an expression for any term of the sequence, then find the 15th and 20th terms.

6. 2, 6, 10, 14, 18 $4n - 2$; 58; 78

7. 1, 6, 11, 16, 21 $5n - 4$; 71; 96

8. 4, 1, ⁻2, ⁻5, ⁻8 $^-3n + 7$; ⁻38; ⁻53

9. ⁻5, ⁻2, 1, 4, 7 $3n - 8$; 37; 52

Graph the ordered pair on a coordinate plane. Check students' graphs.

10. $(4, 6)$ **11.** $(4, ^-3)$ **12.** $(2, 0)$ **13.** $(^-7, 1)$ **14.** $(^-2, ^-4)$

Is the ordered pair a solution of the given equation?

15. $y = 2x + 1$; $(2, 5)$ yes

16. $y = 4x - 1$; $(0, ^-1)$ yes

17. $y = ^-3x - 2$; $(1, 5)$ no

18. $y = 4x + 6$; $(^-2, ^-4)$ no

19. $y = ^-x + 7$; $(3, 10)$ no

20. $y = ^-4x - 2$; $(3, ^-14)$ yes

Find three ordered pairs that are solutions of the given equation, then graph them and draw the line for the equation. Check students' graphs.

21. $y = 3x + 1$ **22.** $y = 2x - 3$ **23.** $y = 4x - 3$

What is the slope and y-intercept of the graph of the equation? Graph the equation. Check students' graphs.

24. $y = 2x + 6$ 2; 6 **25.** $y = 4x - 5$ 4; ⁻5 **26.** $y = 3x - 3$ 3; ⁻3

Is the ordered pair a solution of the linear inequality?

27. $y < 2x + 3$; $(1, 6)$ no **28.** $y > 3x - 6$; $(2, 5)$ yes **29.** $y > x + 8$; $(1, 3)$ no

30. $y < 2x - 6$; $(1, 4)$ no **31.** $y < 4x + 2$; $(2, 10)$ no **32.** $y > 5x - 3$; $(3, 13)$ yes

305

Chapter Test

Find the first five terms of the sequence of numbers produced by the given expression.

1. $m + 3$ 4, 5, 6, 7, 8

2. $3y - 1$ 2, 5, 8, 11, 14

3. $-2x + 5$ 3, 1, -1, -3, -5

4. $-n - 6$ -7, -8, -9, -10, -11

9-1

Write an expression for any term of the sequence, then find the 12th and 30th terms.

5. 5, 9, 13, 17, 21 $4n + 1$; 49; 121

6. 12, 9, 6, 3, 0 $-3n + 15$; -21; -75

9-2

7. -4, -1, 2, 5, 8 $3n - 7$; 29; 83

8. 6, 1, -4, -9, -14 $-5n + 11$; -49; -139

Graph the ordered pairs on a coordinate plane. Check students' graphs.

9. $(7, 5)$ 10. $(4, -6)$ 11. $(-8, 3)$ 12. $(2, 0)$ 9-3

Check students' graphs.

Graph the following data. Use your graph to find the 8th term.

13.

28

No. of term	1	2	3	4	5
Sequence	7	10	13	16	19

9-4

14.

-8

No. of term	1	2	3	4	5
Sequence	20	16	12	8	4

Find three ordered pairs that are solutions of the given equation, then graph them and draw the line for the equation. Check students' graphs.

15. $y = 2x + 5$ 16. $y = 3x - 2$ 17. $y = 4x + 2$ 9-5

What is the slope and y-intercept of the graph of the equation. Graph the equation. Check students' graphs.

18. $y = 3x - 4$ 3; -4   19. $y = 2x + 7$ 2; 7   20. $y = \dfrac{1}{2}x + 3$ $\dfrac{1}{2}$; 3   9-6

Is the ordered pair a solution of the linear inequality?

21. $(0, 3)$, $y < 2x - 4$ no   22. $(2, 3)$, $y \geq 4x - 5$ yes   9-7

23. $(-1, 2)$, $y > x - 2$ yes

306

Cumulative Review (Chapters 1–9)

Add, subtract, multiply, or divide.

1. $3\frac{1}{2} \times 1\frac{1}{8}$ $\ 3\frac{15}{16}$

2. $2\frac{1}{3} - 1\frac{5}{8}$ $\ \frac{17}{24}$

3. $\frac{7}{8} \cdot \frac{1}{3} \cdot \frac{12}{21}$ $\ \frac{1}{6}$

4. $4.02 - 9.6$ $\ ^-5.58$

5. $8 - 6.04$ $\ 1.96$

6. $218.7 \div 8.1$ $\ 27$

7. $23 - 7 \cdot 2 \div 7$ $\ 21$

8. $46 + 28 \div 4$ $\ 53$

9. 10×19 $\ 190$

10. $(100)(2.6)$ $\ 260$

11. $(^-2)(5)$ $\ ^-10$

12. $8 + {}^-5$ $\ 3$

13. $^-20 - 7$ $\ ^-27$

14. $14 + {}^-9$ $\ 5$

15. $^-8 - {}^-10$ $\ 2$

16. $(12)(6)$ $\ 72$

17. $(^-8)(^-3)$ $\ 24$

18. $^-3 \div {}^-1$ $\ 3$

19. $56 \div {}^-7$ $\ ^-8$

20. $(^-9)(^-2) \div (^-3)$ $\ ^-6$

21. $45 \div {}^-9 - 7$ $\ ^-12$

Solve the equation.

22. $a - 6 = 4$ $\ 10$

23. $14 + n = 25$ $\ 11$

24. $6y = 42$ $\ 7$

25. $9f = 81$ $\ 9$

26. $\frac{a}{7} = 30$ $\ 210$

27. $\frac{1}{3}c = 12$ $\ 36$

28. $a + 2a = 60$ $\ 20$

29. $3x - 1 = 29$ $\ 10$

30. $4n + 17 = 31$ $\ 3\frac{1}{2}$

31. $5p - 1 = 3p + 7$ $\ 4$

32. $12 + 8s = 20$ $\ 1$

33. $6d + 7 = 31 - 2d$ $\ 3$

Solve.

34. In a computer game, if a player can score between 450 and 500 points (no more, no less) within 10 minutes, he or she wins. Lois scored the following points in 10 minutes: 80, $^-60$, 90, $^-50$, 110, 70, 40, $^-10$. Did she win? no

35. In riding his bike around town Adam went north 2 blocks, then west 5 blocks, then south 10 blocks, then east 6 blocks, then north 8 blocks. How many blocks from his starting point was he then? 1

36. Eight years ago the monthly rent on the Coopers' apartment was $210. That was $\frac{1}{3}$ of what it is today. What is it today? $630

37. Here's a formula to relate the surface area (A) of a cube with the length of a side (s).

$$A = 6s^2$$

A cube has sides 12 cm by 12 cm. What's the surface area? 864 cm²

38. On Sunday the temperature at noon in Minneapolis was $^-7°C$. On Monday the noon temperature was 4 degrees warmer. What was the temperature at noon on Monday? $^-3°C$

10
Statistics

Statistics helps us know when a new world record for an event is established. In 1980, Juoko Tormanen of Finland achieved the longest ski jump in Olympic history at Lake Placid, NY by jumping 117 m!

10-1 Introduction to Statistics

The traffic safety division of a large city received a request to install a traffic light at the intersection of Thompson and Maynard Streets. The city policy is to install lights at intersections where the average number of vehicles passing through the intersection per day is 1200 or more. Therefore a 7-day electronic vehicle count was conducted at the Thompson and Maynard intersection. The results are shown below.

VEHICLE COUNT—THOMPSON AND MAYNARD INTERSECTION							
Day	1	2	3	4	5	6	7
Number of Vehicles	1254	1189	1261	1304	1295	1083	1285

Numerical facts such as those shown in the chart above are called **data.** The study of the collection, organization, and interpretation of data is called **statistics.**

The traffic safety division used the data to compute the **mean** number of vehicles using the intersection per day. To find the mean of data, divide the sum of the numbers by the total number of addends.

Example 1   Find the mean number of vehicles using the intersection per day.

Solution   Let b = the mean.

$$b = \frac{1254 + 1189 + 1261 + 1304 + 1295 + 1083 + 1285}{7}$$

$$b = \frac{8671}{7}, \text{ or about } 1238.7$$

Since the mean number of vehicles using the intersection per day is more than 1200, the traffic light will be installed.

Other terms often used in statistics are **range, mode,** and **median.** The range is the difference between the greatest and least numbers in a set of data. The range of the data above is $1304 - 1083$, or 221.

The mode is the number that occurs most frequently in a set of data. Sometimes a set of data has no mode. The median is the middle number when data are arranged in numerical order. If there is an even number of data, the median is the mean of the two middle numbers.

Example 2   Find the mode of 44 kg, 36 kg, 43 kg, 44 kg, 36 kg, and 44 kg.

Solution   44 kg occurs most frequently so the mode is 44 kg.

Example 3   Find the median of 6.2 m, 0 m, 7 m, 5.7 m, 4.7 m, and 5.9 m.

Solution   Arrange the data in order:
0 m, 4.7 m, 5.7 m, 5.9 m, 6.2 m, 7 m
Find the mean of the two middle numbers:
$$\frac{5.7 + 5.9}{2} = \frac{11.6}{2} = 5.8$$
The median is 5.8 m.

Your Turn   • Find the mean, range, mode and median of 17 L, 12 L, 14 L, 12 L, 17 L, and 12 L. $^{14 L;\ 5 L;\ 12 L;\ 13 L}$

Class Exercises

Write mean, mode, median, or range to complete the sentence.

1. 18 + 25 + 24 + 25 = 92
    92 ÷ 4 = 23
    The _?_ is $23. mean

SAVINGS			
Month	Jan.	Feb.	Mar.	Apr.
Amount	$18	$25	$24	$25

2. 18, 24, 25, 25
    (24 + 25) ÷ 2 = 24.5
    The _?_ is $24.50. median

3. 18, 25, 24, 25
    The _?_ is $25. mode

4. 25 − 18 = 7 ^{range}
    The _?_ is $7.

Exercises

Find the mean and mode of the given data.

A **1.** 18, 21, 20, 18
19.25; 18

2. 0.7, 0.6, 0.6, 0.4
0.575; 0.6

3. $\dfrac{5}{6}, \dfrac{1}{8}, \dfrac{1}{8}, \dfrac{7}{12}$
$\dfrac{5}{12}; \dfrac{1}{8}$

Find the median and range of the given data.

4. 8, 4, 9, 5, 2
5; 7

5. 4.2, 3.6, 3.1, 4.4
3.9; 1.3

6. $\dfrac{5}{8}, \dfrac{1}{4}, \dfrac{7}{16}, \dfrac{3}{8}$
$\dfrac{13}{32}; \dfrac{3}{8}$

Find the mean, mode, median, and range of the given data.

B **7.**
71°; 72°; 72°; 5°

AVERAGE TEMPERATURE							
Day	S	M	T	W	Th	F	S
Degrees Fahrenheit	70°	73°	72°	68°	72°	70°	72°

8.
88%; 92%; 86%; 11%

TEST SCORES							
Week	1	2	3	4	5	6	7
Percent	83%	84%	86%	85%	94%	92%	92%

9.
$57.45; $49.95; $49.95; $100

CALCULATOR PRICES							
Type	A	B	C	D	E	F	G	H
Price	$19.95	$49.95	$69.95	$49.95	$119.95	$49.95	$29.95	$69.95

Problems

Solve.

1. The attendance figures at the first four games of a season were 64,532; 58,711; 62,871; and 64,334. What was the mean attendance? 62,612

2. One team's scores for the first five games of a season were 4, 3, 5, 2, and 1. What was the range of the scores? 4

3. Ticket prices for a home game are as follows: $3.50, $4.50, $5.00, and $3.25. What is the median price of a ticket? $4.00

4. The ages of the six youngest players on a team are 24, 26, 25, 24, 23, and 27. What is the mode of the ages of these players? 24

10-2 Circle Graphs

A **circle graph** presents data as a circular region divided into sections. The size of each section corresponds to the part of the data represented.

This circle graph shows the voting status of 72,000 people eligible for voter registration in one city for a recent election.

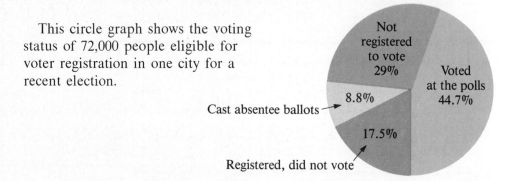

VOTING STATUS

Not registered to vote 29%

Voted at the polls 44.7%

Cast absentee ballots — 8.8%

17.5%

Registered, did not vote

Example About how many people were not registered to vote?

Solution 29% of 72,000 = __?__
0.29 × 72,000 = 20,880

Your Turn • How many people cast absentee ballots? 6336 people

Class Exercises

The circle graph at the right shows the types of computers sold by a company in one year.

1. What percent of the computer sales were personal computers? 28%
2. What type of computer accounted for the smallest percent of computer sales? educational

COMPUTER SALES

54%
Business/
Professional

Educational — 8%

28%

10%

Scientific

Personal

3. Were more scientific or educational computers sold? scientific

4. What type of computer accounted for 54% of the computer sales? business/professional

Exercises

The circle graph at the right shows one family's proposed budget. Use the graph to answer the following questions. Write your answers in dollar amounts.

ANNUAL BUDGET ($20,000)

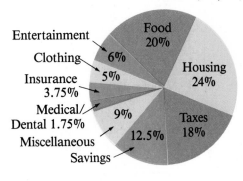

A **1.** About how much do they plan to spend for food? $4000

2. What are their anticipated housing costs for the year? $4800

3. Clothing costs will account for how much of their budget? $1000

B **4.** About how much more do they plan to put in savings than to spend on entertainment? $1300

5. What are they expecting to pay for insurance and taxes altogether? $4350

6. By how much do they expect miscellaneous costs to exceed medical and dental costs? $1450

7. How much money is budgeted monthly for entertainment? $100

8. How much more is budgeted monthly for clothing than insurance? $20.83

A survey of 620 students was conducted to determine the popularity of four radio stations. The chart below shows the results of the survey. Compute the percent of students favoring each station then copy and complete the circle graph, labeling each wedge with the corresponding station and percent. Check students' graphs.

C **9.**

SURVEY RESULTS

Station	Student Votes	
WROQ	279	45%
WCLS	31	5%
WCAW	124	20%
WANY	186	30%

SURVEY RESULTS

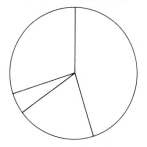

313

10-3 Pictographs

A **pictograph** uses a symbol to represent a number. In the graph below, each token represents $40,000. The data in the graph are rounded to the nearest $10,000.

MASON BUS LINES

Quarter	Earnings
1 (Jan – Mar)	⑤ ⑤
2 (April – June)	⑤ ⑤ ⑤
3 (July – Sept)	⑤ ⑤
4 (Oct – Dec)	⑤ ⑤

⑤ = $40,000

The first quarter earnings were approximately equal to $40,000 + $40,000, or $80,000.

Amounts less than $40,000 are represented by a fraction of a token.

⑤	⑤	⌣
$40,000	$20,000	$10,000

Example 1   What were the fourth quarter earnings?

Solution $2\frac{1}{4} \times \$40,000 = \frac{9}{4} \times \$40,000 = \$90,000$

The fourth quarter earnings were about $90,000.

Example 2   It is estimated that Mason Bus Lines will earn $112,000 during the first quarter of next year. Draw symbols that represent this amount.

Solution   Round to the nearest $10,000: $112,000 \approx \$110,000$

$\$110,000 \div \$40,000 = 2\frac{3}{4}$ ▷ ⑤ ⑤ ⑤

314

Your Turn Let $\boxed{\$\,\$\,\$\,\$}$ represent $20,000. How much money do these symbols represent? $30,000 $15,000 $55,000

$\cdot\boxed{\$\,\$\,\$\,\$}$ $\boxed{\$\,\$}$ $\cdot\boxed{\$\,\$\,\$}$ $\cdot\boxed{\$\,\$\,\$\,\$}$ $\boxed{\$\,\$\,\$\,\$}$ $\boxed{\$\,\$\,\$}$

Draw symbols to represent these amounts. $\boxed{\$\$\$\$}\boxed{\$\$\$\$}\boxed{\$\$\$\$}\boxed{\$\$\$\$}\boxed{\$\$\$\$}\boxed{\$}$

- $50,000   - $75,000   - $102,413.72

$\boxed{\$\$\$\$}\boxed{\$\$\$\$}\boxed{\$\$}$ $\boxed{\$\$\$\$}\boxed{\$\$\$\$}\boxed{\$\$\$\$}\boxed{\$\$\$}$

Class Exercises

Use the pictograph to tell about how many working women there were in the United States in the given year.

30 million   45 million   25 million
1. 1970   **2.** 1980   **3.** 1960

WORKING WOMEN IN THE U.S.

1960	♀ ♀ ♀
1970	♀ ♀ ♀
1980	♀ ♀ ♀ ♀ ♀

♀ represents 10 million women

Estimates have been made of the number of working women there will be in the United States in the future. How many ♀ symbols are needed to represent the estimates given?

about $6\frac{1}{2}$ symbols

about $5\frac{1}{2}$ symbols
4. 1990: 56 million women   **5.** 2000: 63,900,000 women

Exercises

**The pictograph shows the monthly budget for the Pendleton Family.
About how much is budgeted for each item? Complete.**

A 1. Housing: $4 \times \$100 =$ _?_ $\$400$

2. Food: $3 \times$ _?_ $=$ _?_ $\$100; \$300$

3. Insurance: $\dfrac{1}{2} \times$ _?_ $=$ _?_ $\$100; \$50$

4. Telephone: $\dfrac{1}{4} \times$ _?_ $=$ _?_ $\$100; \$25$

5. Clothing: _?_ $\times \$100 =$ _?_ $2\dfrac{1}{2}; \$250$

6. Entertainment: $1 \times$ _?_ $=$ _?_ $\$100; \$100$

7. Savings: _?_ $\times \$100 =$ _?_ $2\dfrac{1}{4}; \$225$

8. Miscellaneous: _?_ $\times$ _?_ $=$ _?_ $1\dfrac{1}{2}; \$100; \$150$

**PENDLETON FAMILY
MONTHLY BUDGET**

Housing	$ $ $ $
Food	$ $ $
Insurance	$
Telephone	▯
Clothing	$ $ $
Entertainment	$
Savings	$ $ ▯
Miscellaneous	$ $

$ represents $100

B 9. About how much more is budgeted for clothing than for entertainment? $\$150$

10. What is the total amount budgeted for one month? $\$1500$

The data in the table show the number of students enrolled in institutions of higher education in the United States for selected years.

Round the numbers in the table to the nearest 1 million. Let 🚶 represent 2 million students. Draw symbols to represent the data.

Example   1960: $3{,}789{,}000 \approx 4{,}000{,}000$
$4{,}000{,}000 \div 2{,}000{,}000 = 2$
🚶🚶

11. 1965: $5{,}921{,}000 \approx 6{,}000{,}000$
$6{,}000{,}000 \div 2{,}000{,}000 =$ _?_ 3
Check students' drawings.

12. 1970 $4\dfrac{1}{2}$ 13. 1975 $5\dfrac{1}{2}$ 14. 1980 6

Enrollment in Institutions of Higher Education (U.S.)	
Year	Enrollment
1960	3,789,000
1965	5,921,000
1970	8,581,000
1975	11,185,000
1980	12,070,000

Check students' graphs.

15. Draw a pictograph to show enrollment in institutions of higher education in the United States for the five years given in the table.

C 16. Make a pictograph from the data in the table. Let ☐ represent 10 million households and Γ, 5 million households. Check students' graphs.

U.S. Households with TV Sets (in millions)

1960	Black/White	46.2
	Color	xxxx
1965	Black/White	55.9
	Color	5.5
1970	Black/White	63.2
	Color	27.2
1975	Black/White	72.6
	Color	54.1
1980	Black/White	79.3
	Color	63.4

Self Test 1

Find the mean, mode, median, and range of the given data.

30.5 mi; 36 mi; 31 mi; 12 mi

1. 24 mi, 36 mi, 26 mi, 36 mi

9.525 km; 9.4 km; 9.4 km; 0.9 km

2. 9.4 km, 10.1 km, 9.4 km, 9.2 km

10-1

Use the circle graph to answer the following questions. Write your answers in dollar amounts.

CLASS PROJECTS

Bake Sale 7%
Car Wash 33%
Craft Sale 60%

Total Earnings: $240

3. About how much was earned at the car wash? $79

4. About how much was earned at the craft sale? $144

10-2

Use the pictograph to answer the following questions.

200 people

5. About how many people attended the 7:00 show on Friday?

6. About how many people attended the 9:20 Saturday show?

160 people

THEATER ATTENDANCE

Fri. 7:00	▲ ▲ ▲ ▲ ▲ ▲ ▲ ▲ ▲ ▲
Fri. 9:20	▲ ▲ ▲ ▲ ▲ ▲
Sat. 7:00	▲ ▲ ▲ ▲ ▲
Sat. 9:20	▲ ▲ ▲ ▲ ▲ ▲ ▲

▲ = 20 people

10-3

Self Test answers and Extra Practice are at the back of the book.

10-4 Bar Graphs

A **bar graph** is used to compare data. The bar graph below shows the approximate mean weekly salaries of four different job categories in one city.

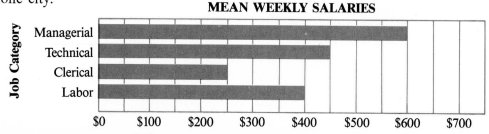

MEAN WEEKLY SALARIES

Example 1   What is the approximate mean weekly salary of the clerical and labor job categories?

Solution $250 + $400 = $650
$650 ÷ 2 = $325

Your Turn   • What is the approximate mean weekly salary of all four job categories? $425

Multiple bar graphs are used to compare more complex data. The triple bar graph below shows the post-graduation plans of the sophomores, juniors, and seniors at one high school.

POST GRADUATION PLANS

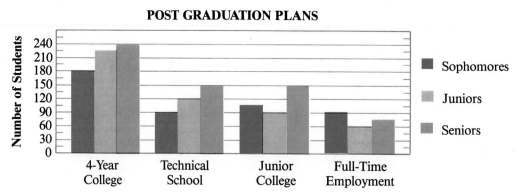

Example 2 How many more seniors than sophomores plan to attend a four-year college?

Solution 60 more seniors

Your Turn • What is the total number of students who plan to attend junior college? 345 students

Class Exercises

Use the weekly salaries graph to answer the following questions.

1. What is the approximate mean weekly salary of technical employees? $450
2. Which job category has the lowest weekly salary? clerical
3. What is the approximate difference between the weekly salary of a clerical worker and that of a laborer? $150

Exercises

Use the post-graduation plans graph to answer the following questions.

A
1. How many juniors plan to attend junior college? 90
2. Which class has the greatest number of students planning to attend a four-year college? seniors

B
3. How many seniors participated in the survey? 615
4. How many students plan to attend a technical school? 360
5. How many more students plan to attend a four-year college than a junior college? 300
6. What is the mean number of students who plan to work full time? 75
7. What is the range in the number of students who plan to attend a four-year college? 60
8. What is the median number of students who plan to attend a junior college or a four-year college? 165
9. What percent of the students planning to attend a technical school are sophomores? 25%

319

A **shaded bar graph** is used to compare individual sets of data as well as combined sets of data. The shaded bar graph below shows the sources of funds for three candidates in a recent election. For example, Thomas received about $10,000 from party funds.

CAMPAIGN FUND SOURCES

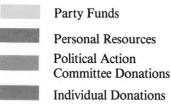

Party Funds

Personal Resources

Political Action Committee Donations

Individual Donations

Use the graph to answer the following questions.

C 10. Which candidate received the greatest amount of individual donations? Thomas

11. Did Mingle receive more campaign contributions from political action committees or from individuals? political action

12. About how much did Caldwell receive in all? $50,000

13. Personal resources accounted for how much of Thomas' campaign funds? $15,000

14. What is the range of the amount of funds donated by individuals? $32,000

15. What is the approximate median amount of donations from political action committees? $13,000

Problems

Construct the graph. Check students' graphs.

1. Construct a bar graph comparing the swimming speeds given in the table.

SWIMMING SPEEDS

Sailfish	60 mph
Flying fish	40 mph
Dolphin	37 mph
Trout	15 mph
Human	5.19 mph

2. Construct a double bar graph comparing the number of general admission tickets and reserved seat tickets sold for each game.

TICKETS SOLD				
Game	1	2	3	4
General Admission	525	473	681	725
Reserved Seats	54	73	58	104

Challenge

A group of fitness experts rated the benefits of certain activities. Each activity was rated from 0 to 100 relative to physical fitness and general health. Construct a shaded bar graph comparing the benefits of the activities. Check students' graphs.

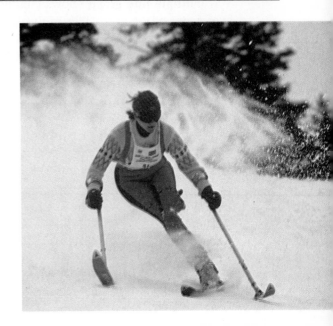

←Fitness→←Health→							
Total	Jogging	Bicycling	Swimming	Basketball	Tennis	Skiing	Walking
Physical Fitness	80	76	78	76	72	70	50
General Health	61	60	55	51	50	50	47
Total	141	136	133	127	122	120	97

10-5 Line Graphs

A **line graph** is used to show
changes in data over a period of
time. The line graph at the right
shows the temperature changes in a
city in twelve hours. It shows that
the greatest temperature increase
occurred between the hours of
10 A.M. and 12 noon.

TEMPERATURE READINGS

A **multiple line graph** shows changes in more than one set of data
over a period of time. The multiple line graph below shows the
changes in the percent of the population that received national political campaign information from various media from 1952 to 1980.

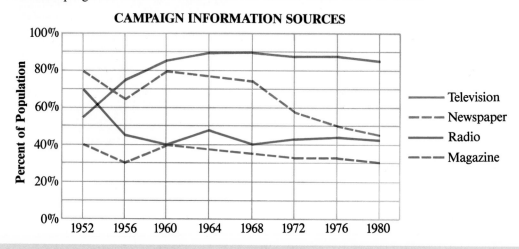

CAMPAIGN INFORMATION SOURCES

Example   Which medium declined the most as a source of campaign information from 1968 through 1980?

Solution   newspaper

Your Turn   • Which medium increased the most as a source of
campaign information from 1952 to 1960?   television

Class Exercises

Use the temperature readings line graph to answer the questions.

1. Did the temperature increase or decrease from 10 A.M. to 12 noon? *increase*
2. During what two-hour interval did the temperature decrease 10°? *6 P.M. and 8 P.M.*
3. How much did the temperature increase from 8 A.M. to 10 A.M.? *5°*
4. How much did the temperature decrease from 2 P.M. to 8 P.M.? *about 17° to 18°*
5. During what four-hour interval did the temperature increase 15°? *8 A.M. to 12 Noon*

Exercises

Use the campaign information sources multiple line graph to answer the following questions.

A

1. Did the use of the radio as a source of campaign information increase or decrease from 1952 to 1956? *decrease*
2. During what four-year interval did the use of magazines as a source of campaign information decrease the most? *1952 to 1956*
3. During what twenty-year interval did the use of television as a source of campaign information stay about the same? *1960 to 1980*
4. Which medium gained the most popularity as a source of campaign information from 1952 to 1968? *television*
5. Which medium experienced the least change as a source of campaign information from 1952 to 1980? *magazine*

B

6. About how much did the percent of the population using TV as a source of campaign information increase from 1952 to 1960? *30%*
7. About how much did the percent of the population using the newspaper as a source of campaign information decrease from 1960 to 1980? *35%*
8. What is the approximate difference between the percent of the population using television as a source of campaign information when television was at its highest peak and the percent of the population using radio as a source of campaign information when radio was at its highest peak? *20%*
9. What is the approximate difference between the decrease in the percent of the population using the radio as a source of campaign information from 1952 to 1956 and the decrease in the percent of the population using the magazine as a source of campaign information from 1952 to 1956? *15%*

A **shaded multiple line graph** shows changes in individual sets of data as well as combined sets of data over a period of time. The shaded multiple line graph below shows the population growth of each region in the continental United States as well as the combined regional population growth.

REGIONAL POPULATIONS

Use the regional populations graph to answer the following questions.

Example About 20 million people lived in the north central region in 1895.

C 10. Which region had the greatest population in 1900? Northeast
11. Which region has consistently had the lowest population? West
12. When did the population of the west begin to increase? 1850
13. Did the population of the Northeast increase more before or after 1870? After
14. About what was the total population in 1900? 73 million
15. About what was the total population in 1870? 41 million

Problems

Use the data from the chart to construct a double line graph. Check students' graphs.

1.

CLASS ENROLLMENT								
Year	1956	1960	1964	1968	1972	1976	1980	1984
Science	70%	79%	68%	60%	75%	81%	79%	81%
Math	74%	69%	61%	58%	62%	68%	74%	85%

Using the Computer

The following program will draw a bar graph horizontally. (If you have a microcomputer with graphics capabilities, you will be able to draw vertical lines according to the given instructions.) RUN the program for ten items with values 3, 5, 7, 9, 15, 12, 8, 6, 2, 1. Check students' printouts.

```
  5  REM: TO DRAW A BAR GRAPH        80  FOR I=1 TO T
 10  PRINT "HOW MANY ITEMS";         90  PRINT "!";
 20  INPUT T                        100  FOR J=1 TO F(I)
 30  PRINT "WHAT IS THE VALUE"      110  PRINT "*";
 40  FOR I=1 TO T                   120  NEXT J
 50  PRINT "FOR ITEM";I;            130  PRINT
 60  INPUT F(I)                     135  PRINT "!"
 70  NEXT I                         140  NEXT I
 75  PRINT                          150  END
```

Self Test 2

Use the multiple bar graph to answer the following questions.

1. About how many more turntable sales than amplifier sales were reported from Store A? 10

2. About how many recorder sales were reported in all? 70

SALES REPORT (June)

10-4

Use the multiple line graph to answer the following questions.

3. Who increased their savings the most from May to June? Kim

4. During which period of time did both Kim and Dave decrease their savings? June to July

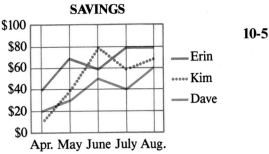

SAVINGS

10-5

Self Test answers and Extra Practice are at the back of the book.

10-6 Problem Solving

A problem usually includes a set of facts and asks a question. Problems in real life are usually decisions you must make or tasks you must do. You usually have to research your own facts and ask your own questions. In this lesson you will write the questions that could help you make a good decision or do the task well.

Example 1 Decision: Whether to rent a telephone or buy a telephone
Facts: You can rent a telephone for $1.50 per month.
You can buy a similar telephone for $60.
Write a question that will help you decide whether to buy the telephone or not. Then solve the problem and answer the question.

Solution "If I rent a telephone at $1.50 per month, how long will it be before rental charges equal the cost of buying the phone?"

$$\$60 \div \$1.50 = 40$$

"At the present rate, I can rent my telephone for 40 months for $60."

Your Turn Write a question that will help you make the decision and that can be answered with the facts given. Then solve the problem. Answers may vary. One possible solution is given.
- Decision: When to leave home to go to the concert
Facts: The concert starts at 7:30 P.M. It takes 5 min to walk to the bus stop from your house. Buses leave the corner near your home every 20 min after 6:15 P.M. The bus ride takes 15 min. After you get off the bus, it takes 10 min to walk to the concert hall.

What is the latest I can leave home to get to the concert before 7:30 P.M.? Must leave home at 6:50 P.M.

Class Exercises

Ask two questions that can help you make a good decision or do the task. Answers may vary.

Example   You want to open a savings account and need to choose a bank.

Solution   • What rate of interest is offered by each bank?
   • How often is interest added to savings accounts?

1. Your class must decide how much to spend on the Spring Dance.
2. You must choose between two job offers for the summer.
3. Choose the most valuable player on the baseball team.
4. You want to change the wallpaper in your bedroom.

Exercises

Suppose you must do the task specified or make the decision. Write a question that can be answered from the facts given. Solve the problem and answer the question. Answers may vary. One possible solution is given.

A 1. Decision: Whether to buy or rent a TV
      Facts: You can rent a TV for $25 a month.
         You can buy a similar TV for $300.

   How long will it be before rental charges equal the cost of buying the TV? 12 months

2. Task: Tell a friend how your grade average compares with the rest of the class.
   Facts: The mean grade average for the class is 82.6.
      Your grades this term are 78, 85, 86, 80, 77, 85.

   How does my grade average compare with the rest of the class? It is about one less than the average.

B 3. Task: Buy milk and laundry detergent.
      Facts: Milk costs $1.13 for a half gallon or $.59 a quart
         Detergent costs $1.95 for 32 oz or $2.99 for 64 oz.
         You have $4.00.

   What is the greatest amount of milk and detergent you can buy for $4.00? $\frac{3}{4}$ gal milk, 32 oz detergent

4. Task: Plan your time after school.

   At what times will you study if you go to work right after school? 6:30 to 8:00; 9:00 to 10:30

      Facts: School dismissal is at 2:30 P.M. Your job requires $2\frac{1}{2}$ hours.
         Transportation from school to your job and then home takes about 45 minutes in all. Dinner is served at 6:00 P.M. You must study for 3 hours. Your favorite TV show is from 8:00–9:00 P.M. and bedtime is at 10:30 P.M.

327

5. Task: Prepare dinner and serve at 6:30 P.M.

Facts: Each dish requires the preparation time and cooking time given. When should you start preparing dinner so that it is ready for 6:30? Start preparing f at 4:20. Put meat in at 4:30 and insert other items as their cooking time requires.

Dish	Preparation Time	Cooking Time
Meat	10 minutes	2 hours
Potatoes	5 minutes	1 hour
Vegetable	10 minutes	15 minutes
Salad	15 minutes	none
Dessert	30 minutes	45 minutes

6. Task: Eat foods that satisfy the recommended daily allowance (RDA) for iron. How many more milligrams of iron are needed to satisfy the RDA? 5.8 mg

Facts: The RDA for iron is 10 mg. Foods eaten so far today with their iron content are the following:

Orange....0.6 mg   Egg ....0.7 mg
Toast .....0.3 mg   Tuna sandwich ...1.9 mg
Milk.......Trace   Carrot sticks .....0.7 mg

7. Decision: Whether or not to buy a battery charger

Facts: A battery charger costs about $30. You usually spend about $5 a month on batteries for your calculator, flashlights, etc. Rechargeable batteries will cost about $35 and can be re-charged many times. How long will it be before the cost of buying batteries equal the cost of buying a charger and rechargeable batteries? 13 r

C 8. Decision: Decide which carpet to buy for your bedroom. Can you afford Royal Plush? No

Facts: Your bedroom is 10 ft by 12 ft. Royal Plush carpet costs $22.79 per sq yd. Soft Step carpet costs $18.79 per sq yd. Your state has a 5% sales tax. You have $300 to spend.

10-7 Histograms

The fuel efficiency rating of an automobile is important to consider when buying a car. The data in the chart below show the fuel efficiency ratings of several different cars.

FUEL EFFICIENCY RATINGS														
Cars	A	B	C	D	E	F	G	H	I	J	K	L	M	N
Rating (mi/gal)	27	33	24	33	30	23	36	26	31	32	28	38	37	36

   To analyze the data, you can **tally** the number of times each rating occurs. If the list of data is quite long or if the data covers a wide range of numbers it may be more convenient to group the data into intervals. We can tally the data above using intervals of 5 miles per gallon.

TALLY

Rating (mi/gal)	20–24	25–29	30–34	35–39
Frequency (number of cars)	||	|||	⊬⊬	||||

   A summary of the number of items in each interval is called a **frequency distribution.**

Example 1 Use the tally above to show the frequency distribution of the fuel efficiency ratings.

Solution

FREQUENCY DISTRIBUTION CHART			
Rating (mi/gal)	20–24	25–29	30–34	35–39
Frequency (number of cars)	2	3	5	4

Frequency distribution may be shown on a **histogram.** A histogram is similar to a bar graph; however, there are no spaces between the bars.

FUEL EFFICIENCY RATING

Rating (mi/gal)

Example 2   Which fuel efficiency rating interval occurs most frequently?

Solution   the 30–34 mi/gal interval

Frequency distribution may also be shown as a **frequency polygon.** A frequency polygon is the broken line connecting the midpoints of the top of each bar of a histogram.

FUEL EFFICIENCY RATING

Rating (mi/gal)

Example 3   Did the frequency increase or decrease from the 20–24 mi/gal interval to the 25–29 mi/gal interval?

Solution   increase

Your Turn   • How much did the frequency decline from the 30–34 mi/gal interval to the 35–39 mi/gal interval?

Class Exercises

The data in the chart below show ten students' absences during the first semester of the school year. Check students' charts.

STUDENT ABSENCES—FIRST SEMESTER										
Student	A	B	C	D	E	F	G	H	I	J
Number of absences	2	0	1	2	5	2	4	3	5	3

1. Tally the data from the chart.
2. Make a frequency distribution chart.

Exercises

Tally the data in the chart below in 4-percent intervals. Then use the tally to make a frequency distribution chart. Check students' chart.

A **1.**

CLASS TEST SCORES											
Student	A	B	C	D	E	F	G	H	I	J	K	L
Score	77%	86%	78%	93%	76%	92%	96%	88%	81%	98%	87%	99%

Copy and complete the histogram using the data from the frequency distribution chart. Use the completed histogram to answer the following questions.

STUDENT WEEKLY INCOME					
Amount in Dollars	0–4	5–9	10–14	15–19	20–24
Frequency (number of students)	13	15	28	21	16

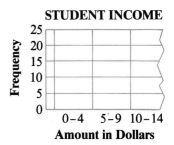

B **2.** Which income interval occurs most frequently? $10–$14
3. How much greater is the frequency of the $10–$14 income interval than the frequency of the $20–$24 income interval? $1\frac{3}{4}$ times greater
4. What is the mean frequency of all of the income intervals? 18.6
5. What is the frequency range of all of the income intervals? 15

331

The histogram shows the weekly television viewing times of one hundred seventy people. Copy the histogram and make a frequency polygon. Use the frequency polygon to answer the following questions.

Check students' graphs.

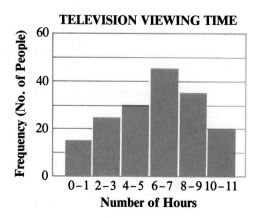

TELEVISION VIEWING TIME

6. Did the frequency increase or decrease from the 0–1 hour interval to the 2–3 hour interval? increase
7. The greatest decrease in frequency occurred between what two consecutive intervals? between 8–9 and 10–11
8. How much did the frequency increase from the 0–1 hour interval to the 2–3 hour interval? 10

A **cumulative histogram** shows the data for each interval added to the data in all preceding intervals. From a cumulative histogram we can more easily answer questions which refer to cumulative data. The cumulative histogram below shows the mean number of miles jogged each week by eighteen joggers.

Use the histogram to answer the following questions.

Example How many people run 7–9 mi each week?

Solution 2 people

C 9. How many people run 1–3 mi each week? 2 people
10. How many people run 6 or fewer miles each week? 5 people
11. How many people run fewer than 10 mi each week? 7 people
12. How many people run 13–15 mi each week? 5 people
13. How many people run more than 15 mi each week? 3 people

JOGGING RECORD

10-8 Scattergrams

A **scattergram** shows the relationship among given data. The scattergram at the right shows the results of a survey about the relationship between the heights of 20 parents and their adult children.

PARENT/CHILD HEIGHTS

Point P represents a parent's height of 68 in. whose child's height is 66 in. Point M represents a parent's height of 70 in. whose child's height is 71 in. Notice that the points slope upward to the right. There is a **positive association** between the heights of the parents and children; the taller parents have taller children. The line to which the scattered points are closest is the **regression** or **trend line.** The trend line best represents the relationship between the parents' and children's heights.

A scattergram may be used to predict future trends. The Parent/Child Height scattergram shows that knowing the height of a parent may help in guessing the height of the child; however, the wide scattering of points shows that there is still room for error.

Example 1 Using the trend line, about what would you expect a child's height to be if the parent's height is 72 in?

Solution about 70 in.

Your Turn • Using the trend line, about what would you expect a child's height to be if the parent's height is 66 in.? about 67 in.

333

The scattergram below shows the relationship between the distance a player was from the target in a baseball toss game and the score.

Point A represents a 6-ft distance from the target and a score of 45. Point B represents a 9-ft distance from the target and a score of 30. Notice that the points slope downward to the right. There is a **negative association** between the distance from the target and the score; the further the distance from the target, the lower the score.

BASEBALL TOSS GAME

Score

Distance from Target (ft)

Example 2   Using the trend line, what would you expect the score to be if the distance from the target is 15 ft?

Solution   15

Your Turn   • Using the trend line, what would you expect the score to be if the distance from the target is 18 ft? about 5

Class Exercises

Use the Parent/Child scattergram to answer the following questions.

1. Which point represents a parent's height of 74 inches whose child height is 72 inches? point D
2. Which point represents a parent's height of 65 inches whose child height is 64 inches? point B

Use the Baseball Toss Game scattergram to answer the following questions.

3. Which point represents a 3-ft distance from the target and a score of 50? point D
4. Which point represents a 6-ft distance from the target and a score of 40? point C

Exercises

The scattergram below shows the relationship between the height and weight of several students. Use it to answer the following questions.

A 1. Which points represent students who weigh 140 lb? points L, R, P

2. Which points represent students who are 72 in. tall? points A, B

3. Which point represents a student 64 in. tall who weighs 140 lb? point R

4. Which point represents a student 68 in. tall who weighs 130 lb? point S

B 5. Does the scattergram show a positive or a negative association? negative

6. Does the trend line indicate that a tall person will usually weigh more or less than a short person? less

7. Using the trend line, how much would you expect a person who is 70 in. tall to weigh? 150 lb

8. Using the trend line, how much would you expect a person who is 72 in. tall to weigh? 145 lb

The scattergram below shows the relationship between the world records for the one-mile run and the years elapsed from 1860 to 1980. Use the One-Mile Run scattergram to answer the following questions.

C 9. Does this scattergram show a positive or a negative association between the year and the time? negative

10. Does the trend line indicate that the time will increase or decrease as the years progress? decrease

11. Using the trend line, what would you expect the time for the one-mile run to be in the year 2000? What does that conclusion indicate to you about predicting future trends from the data on a scattergram? Under 3:40; the time will decrease as the years progress

335

Problems

The data in the chart below shows the number of students enrolled in industrial arts class at one high school for ten years.

INDUSTRIAL ARTS CLASS ENROLLMENT										
Year	1	2	3	4	5	6	7	8	9	10
Number of students	36	65	51	42	32	68	55	49	64	59

1. Use the data to construct a scattergram. Check students' scattergrams.

2. What did you discover about the association between the number of students enrolled in industrial arts class and the progression of years? positive

Self Test 3

Use the histogram and frequency polygon to answer the following questions.

1. Which age group attended outdoor concerts most frequently? 18–21
2. How much did the frequency increase from the 12–15 year old age group to the 15–18 year old age group? 2

OUTDOOR CONCERT ATTENDANCE

10-6

10-7

Use the scattergram to answer the following questions.

3. Using the trend line, what would you expect the average salary to be for a person with eight years of experience? $30,000
4. Using the trend line, about how many years of experience would you expect a person with an average salary of $35,000 to have? 10 years

TECHNICAL SALARIES
(In thousands of $)

10-8

Algebra Practice

Write an equation. Solve.

1. The product of 385 and 124 is *y*. $385 \cdot 124 = y$; 47,740

2. 613,718 divided by 826 is *a*. $613,718 \div 826 = a$; 743

3. The sum of 70.54, 8.346, and 21.43 is *n*. $70.54 + 8.346 + 21.43 = n$; 100.316

4. 0.39 times 0.27 is equal to *g*. $(0.39)(0.27) = g$; 0.1053

5. The difference between $5\frac{1}{2}$ and $3\frac{4}{5}$ is *s*. $5\frac{1}{2} - 3\frac{4}{5} = s$; $1\frac{7}{10}$

6. $\frac{4}{9}$ divided by $\frac{5}{18}$ is equal to *d*. $\frac{4}{9} \div \frac{5}{18} = d$; $1\frac{3}{5}$

7. The circumference of a circle with a radius of 6.2 cm is *C*. $C = 2(3.14)(6.2)$ 38.936 cm

8. The volume of a cone with a radius of 4 in. and a height of 6 in. is *V*.
$$V = \frac{1}{3}(3.14)(4)^2(6)\ 100.48\text{ in.}^3$$

Write the LCM of each set of expressions.

9. $2rs$ and r^3 $2r^3s$

10. c^2, 5, and $2d$ $10c^2d$

11. $6jk$, $4j^3$, and k^2 $12j^3k^2$

Solve.

12. $\frac{j}{4} = ^-1$ $^-4$

13. $7s - 7 = 7$ 2

14. $5y = 2 + 4y$ 2

15. 80% of 160 is *c*. 128

16. $16\frac{2}{3}\%$ of 90 is *m*. 15

17. 60 is 80% of *r*. 75

18. $6y + 6 = 0$ $^-1$

19. $11n + 7 < ^-70$ $n < ^-7$

20. $4f - 1 > ^-21$ $f > ^-5$

Find the first five terms of the sequence produced by the given expression.

21. $c + 5$ 6, 7, 8, 9, 10

22. $5t - 3.8$ 1.2, 6.2, 11.2, 16.2, 21.2

23. $6 + 3w$ 9, 12, 15, 18, 21

Write an equation and solve the problem.

24. In Ward Two there are 1614 registered voters.
There are 44 more women registered than men.
How many men are registered voters? $m + m + 44 = 1614$; 785 voters
How many women are registered voters? 829 voters

Problem Solving for the Consumer

Consumer Awareness

Consumer publications provide consumers with information which may be helpful when buying a product.

Suppose you are planning to buy a new 10-speed bicycle. The chart below shows data for six 10-speed bicycles.

BICYCLE						
	A	**B**	**C**	**D**	**E**	**F**
Price ($)	169	198	220	220	190	155
Weight (lb)	$33\frac{1}{2}$	$30\frac{1}{4}$	33	$28\frac{1}{4}$	$34\frac{1}{2}$	$31\frac{3}{4}$

Use the chart to answer the following questions.

1. What is the price range for the six bicycles? $65
2. If you are interested in purchasing a bicycle that is closest in weight to the average weight of all six bicycles, which bicycle will you choose? F
3. What is the average price of bicycles weighing over 31 lb? $183.50
4. What is the difference in weight between the two bicycles that are the same price? $4\frac{3}{4}$ lb
5. If you are interested in buying a bicycle that is closest in price to the average price of all six bicycles, which bicycle will you choose? E

It is important to compare many different features when purchasing a product. The chart below shows the ratings of four different features for each of the six bicycles.

BICYCLE RATINGS						
Features	**A**	**B**	**C**	**D**	**E**	**F**
Ease of Pedaling	3	4	4	4	3	3
Precision of Handling	4	4	4	2	4	5
Ease of Shifting	5	2	5	2	5	4
Braking Control	4	3	4	3	2	4
Overall Rating (Av.)	? _4_	? _3_	? _4_	? _3_	? _4_	? _4_

RATING CODE	
5	Excellent
4	Very Good
3	Good
2	Fair
1	Poor

6. Complete the chart to show the average overall rating for each bicycle.

Use the data from the chart above and the chart on the facing page to answer the following questions.

7. Which bicycles with an overall rating of 3 or more could you purchase for less than $200. A, B, E, F

8. Do any of the bicycles weighing less than 31 lb have an average overall rating of 4 or more? no

9. What is the average overall rating for all of the bicycles together? 4

Several students identified the features which were most important to them when purchasing a bicycle. Which bicycle is best suited to each person's needs?

10. Student 1 F
- priced less than $200
- very good or excellent braking control
- excellent precision of handling

11. Student 2 C
- weight 33 lb or less
- very good or excellent ease of shifting
- very good ease of pedaling

Enrichment

Percentiles

Standardized test results often indicate scores within a **percentile.** A percentile shows each student's score in comparison to other students' scores in a particular group. The chart below shows forty students' test scores in order from least to greatest. The 90th percentile is the score at which 90% of the scores are at or below and 10% are at or above.

$$90\% \text{ of } 40 = 36 \qquad\qquad 10\% \text{ of } 40 = 4$$

36 scores are at or below the score in the 90th percentile and 4 scores are at or above that score. You can now use the chart.to locate the score in the 90th percentile. It is the score of Student 36.

Student Number	1	2	3	4	5	6	7	8	9	10	11	12	13	14	15	16
Score	45	46	47	52	53	56	56	58	60	61	65	67	68	70	73	73

Student Number	17	18	19	20	21	22	23	24	25	26	27	28	29	30	31	32
Score	75	76	78	79	80	82	82	84	85	86	87	91	91	91	92	93

Student Number	33	34	35	36	37	38	39	40
Score	93	93	94	95	96	96	97	98

Student 36 had a score of 95. The score in the 90th percentile is 95.

How many scores are at or above the given percentile?

1. 95th 2   **2.** 20th 32   **3.** 65th 14   **4.** 30th 28   **5.** 70th 12   **6.** 55th 18

Find the score for the given data.

7. 22 scores at or below; 18 at or above 82   **8.** 8 scores at or below; 32 at or above 58

Find the score for the given percentile.

9. 25th 61   **10.** 50th 79   **11.** 75th 91   **12.** 40th 73   **13.** 60th 84   **14.** 80th 93

Chapter Review

Write the letter for the graph that presents the data needed to answer the question. Use the data to answer the question.

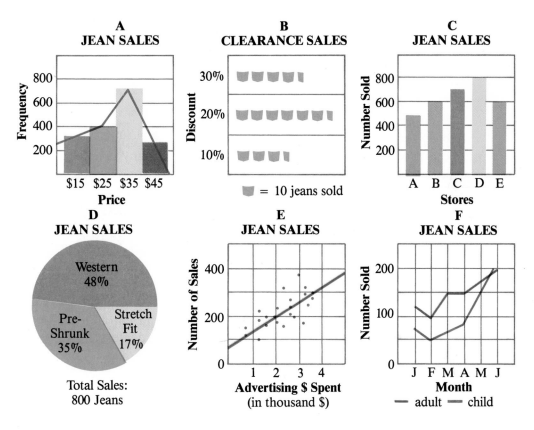

A
JEAN SALES

Frequency / Price
$15 $25 $35 $45

B
CLEARANCE SALES

Discount
30% 20% 10%

= 10 jeans sold

C
JEAN SALES

Number Sold / Stores
A B C D E

D
JEAN SALES

Western 48%
Pre-Shrunk 35%
Stretch Fit 17%

Total Sales:
800 Jeans

E
JEAN SALES

Number of Sales
Advertising $ Spent
(in thousand $)
1 2 3 4

F
JEAN SALES

Number Sold / Month
J F M A M J
— adult — child

1. About how many more jeans were sold at a 20% discount than a 10% discount? *B*; 30 jeans
2. Did the sales of adults' jeans or children's jeans increase more from January to June? *F*; children's
3. What was the price range of jeans? *A*; $30
4. About how many western-look jeans were sold? *D*; 384 jeans
5. About how many stretch-to-fit jeans were sold? *D*; 136 jeans
6. Does the scattergram show a positive or a negative association? *E*; positive
7. What was the median number of jeans sold at all of the stores? *C*; 600 jeans
8. Using the trend line, how many sales would you expect if $4000 was spent on advertising? *E*; 300 jeans
9. Use the data in Graphs C and D to write and solve a problem. Answers may vary.

341

Chapter Test

Find the mean of the given data.

1. 87, 92, 88, 96, 87 90

2. 42.3, 40.6, 42.1, 42.1 41.775

10-1

Use the corresponding graph to answer the following questions.

MUSIC FESTIVALS

Total Attendance. 4,500

COMMUTING

● = 100 people

3. About how many people attended the folk music festival? 1845 people

4. About how many people commute to work by bus? 550 people

10-2, 3

5. About how many more T.E. games than Star games were sold at Store B? 100 games

6. How much did enrollment in exercise class decrease from May to July? 20 people

10-4, 5

Write a question and solve the problem.

10-6

7. Sandi typed a page 40 lines long in 10 minutes. The mean number of words on each line was 15. How many words did Sandi type in 10 min? 600 words

Use the graph to answer the question.

USED CAR SALES

DETERGENT PRICES

8. Did the frequency increase or decrease from the $2000–$3000 price range to the $4000–$5000 price range? decrease

9. Using the trend line, about how much would you expect the unit price of a 32-oz box of detergent to be? 12¢

10-7, 8

Cumulative Review (Chapters 1–10)

Add, subtract, multiply, or divide.

1. $28 - 6 \div 2$ 25

2. $1.183 \div 2.6$ 0.455

3. 5.6×10 56

4. 4.3×10^2 430

5. $27.263 \div 100$ 0.27263

6. $185 + 16 \div 4 \times 0$ 185

7. $\dfrac{1}{5} \times 6\dfrac{3}{4}$ $1\dfrac{7}{20}$

8. $2\dfrac{1}{8} \times 20$ $42\dfrac{1}{2}$

9. $4\dfrac{1}{3} + \dfrac{5}{6}$ $5\dfrac{1}{6}$

10. $17 - 3\dfrac{3}{5}$ $13\dfrac{2}{5}$

11. $24\dfrac{1}{9} - 5\dfrac{3}{4}$ $18\dfrac{13}{36}$

12. $21 \div 1\dfrac{3}{4}$ 12

Solve the equation.

13. $2x + 3 = 9$ 3

14. $25 = 9y - 20$ 5

15. $7(p + 4) = 28$ 0

16. $24 = 6(g - 2)$ 6

17. $56 = 8(2 + w)$ 5

18. $5n = 2n + 9$ 3

19. $4h - 12 = h$ 4

20. $2p - 1 = 4p - 15$ 7

21. $3 + 8r = r + 17$ 2

Solve.

22. What is 20% of 48? 9.6

23. 65% of 99 is what? 64.35

24. 2% of 74 is what number? 1.48

25. What is 5.5% of $840? 46.2

26. 150% of 350 is what number? 525

27. 65 out of 80 is what percent? 81.25%

Add, subtract, multiply, or divide.

28. $^-2 + 7$ 5

29. $^-7 - 5$ $^-12$

30. $^-21 \div ^-3$ 7

31. $6 \times ^-35$ $^-210$

32. $^-15 - ^-6$ $^-9$

33. $^-26 - ^-4$ $^-22$

34. $^-8 \times ^-12$ 96

35. $45 \div ^-9$ $^-5$

What is the slope and y-intercept of the equation?

36. $y = 2x - 3$ 2; $^-3$

37. $y = ^-5x$ $^-5$; 0

38. $y = ^-x + 9$ $^-1$; 9

39. $y = \dfrac{1}{2}x + 8$ $\dfrac{1}{2}$; 8

40. $y = \dfrac{^-1}{3}x - 1$ $\dfrac{^-1}{3}$; $^-1$

41. $y = ^-16x + 4$ $^-16$; 4

Solve.

42. The rent on Jerry's apartment increased 5%. The rent used to be $250 per month. What is the rent now? $262.50

43. Jacob Eberhart's father and his father's father both married at 20. Each had their only child when they were 21. If Jacob continues the pattern, how old will Jacob's grandfather be when Jacob's son or daughter is born? 63

11
Special Triangles

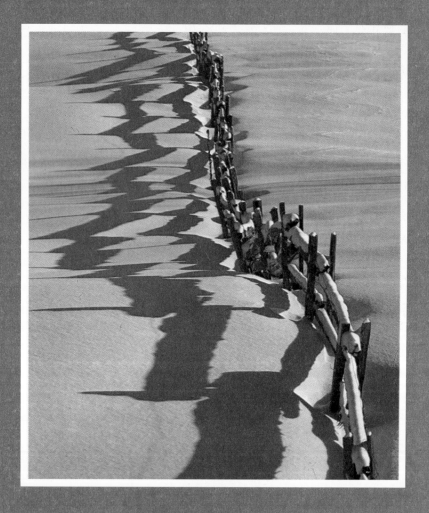

When the sun is at a given angle, the shadows of nearby objects are in proportion to the heights of the objects themselves. You can use this fact to solve a variety of practical problems.

11-1 Similar Triangles

Two triangles are said to be similar if the **corresponding angles** have
equal measure and the **corresponding sides** are in proportion. Similar
triangles have the same shape but not always the same size.

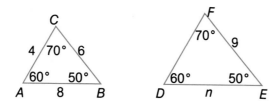

Triangles *ABC* and *DEF* are similar, with vertex *A* corresponding to
vertex *D*, vertex *B* corresponding to vertex *E*, and vertex *C* corresponding to vertex *F*. This statement can be written as $\triangle ABC \sim \triangle DEF$.
You can identify the corresponding angles by looking for pairs of
angles with equal measure. To identify a pair of corresponding sides,
notice that both $\overline{AC}$ and $\overline{DF}$ are opposite 50° angles. We say that
$\overline{AC}$ corresponds to $\overline{DF}$. The corresponding angles and sides of triangles
ABC and *DEF* are listed below.

Corresponding Angles

∠ *A* and ∠ *D*
∠ *B* and ∠ *E*
∠ *C* and ∠ *F*

Corresponding Sides

$\overline{AC}$ and $\overline{DF}$ ←— *The notation* $\overline{AC}$ *is often*
$\overline{AB}$ and $\overline{DE}$ *used to mean side* AC
$\overline{BC}$ and $\overline{EF}$ *or segment* AC.

You can find an unknown length by writing a proportion using corresponding sides.

Example 1   Find the length of $\overline{DE}$. Use the similar triangles shown above.

Solution $\dfrac{DE}{AB} = \dfrac{EF}{BC}$ ←— *The notation EF is used to*
           represent the length of $\overline{EF}$.

    $\dfrac{n}{8} = \dfrac{9}{6}$ ⇨ $6n = 72$ ←— *An easy way to solve this equation*
           $n = 12$ *is to use cross multiplication.*

  The length of $\overline{DE}$ is 12 units.

Sometimes similar triangles are drawn so that one angle is common to both triangles. In the diagram shown at right, notice that $\angle F$ is common to $\triangle FHL$ and $\triangle FGM$. Study the diagram to see that $\overline{HL}$ corresponds to $\overline{GM}$ and $\overline{FL}$ corresponds to $\overline{FM}$.

Example 2   Use the similar triangles *FHL* and *FGM* above to find *a*.   Use the following facts:
$$HL = 8, \ GM = 4, \text{ and } FM = 10.$$

Solution $\dfrac{FL}{FM} = \dfrac{HL}{GM}$ ➩ $\dfrac{a}{10} = \dfrac{8}{4}$

$$4a = 80$$
$$a = 20$$

Your Turn   • In the similar triangles *FHL* and *FGM* above, $FL = 12$, $HL = 6$ and $GM = 3$. Find the length of $\overline{FM}$. 6

Class Exercises

In the similar triangles *GHK* and *LMN* the corresponding angles are marked alike. Write the corresponding side or angle.

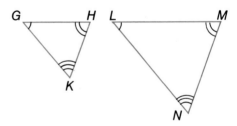

1. $\overline{GH}$ *LM*   2. $\overline{HK}$ *MN*   3. $\overline{LN}$ *GK*

4. $\angle M$ *∠H*   5. $\angle N$ *∠K*   6. $\angle G$ *∠L*

Complete the proportion.

7. $\dfrac{GH}{LM} = \dfrac{GK}{?}$ *LN*

8. $\dfrac{MN}{HK} = \dfrac{LN}{?}$ *GK*

9. $\dfrac{ML}{HG} = \dfrac{?}{KG}$ *NL*

Exercises

For each pair of similar triangles, find *n*.

A

1. 4.5

2. 2

3. 3

4. 12

B

5. 14

6. 6.75

7. 6

8. 12

9. 12

10. 12.5
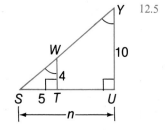

347

11-2 *Similar Right Triangles*

You can use similar right triangles to solve a variety of problems. For example, you can find the height of a tree without actually measuring it. The diagram shows a particular tree that casts a 9-ft shadow while a 5-ft pole casts a 3-ft shadow. The triangle formed by the tree and its shadow is similar to the triangle formed by the pole and its shadow.

Example   Use the similar triangles in the diagram to find the height of the tree.

Solution $\dfrac{\text{height of the tree}}{\text{height of the pole}} = \dfrac{\text{shadow of the tree}}{\text{shadow of the pole}}$

$$\frac{h}{5} = \frac{9}{3} \quad \diamond \quad 3h = 45 \quad \diamond \quad h = 15$$

The height of the tree is 15 ft.

Your Turn   • A student 5 ft 4 in. tall casts a shadow that is 5 ft 4 in. long. At the same time, a flag pole casts a shadow that is 45 ft long. What is the height of the flag pole? 45 ft

Class Exercises

The two triangles are similar. Complete the proportion.

1. $\dfrac{h}{16} = \dfrac{?}{8}$ 12

2. $\dfrac{h}{4} = \dfrac{?}{6}$ 9

Exercises

Use the similar right triangles to find *h* to the nearest tenth.

A **1.** 7.5 ft

2. 18 m

B **3.** 69 ft

4. 22.7 m

5. 21.8 ft

6. 37.1 ft

Problems

1. To find the length of Sun Lake, Nancy made the measurements shown in the diagram. Triangles *ABC* and *AFG* are similar. How long is Sun Lake? 200 m

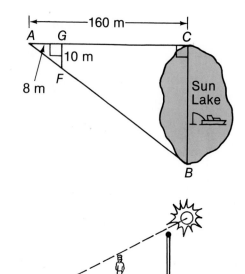

2. A forest tower is 20 m high and casts a shadow of 4 m. At the same time, a ranger standing nearby casts a shadow of 0.5 m. How tall is the ranger? 2.5 m

3. To find the height of the pole, Alan made use of shadows as suggested by the diagram shown. By measuring, he found that *AB* = 11 ft and *AC* = 20 ft 8 in. If Alan is 5 ft 6 in. tall, how tall is the pole? 10 ft 4 in.

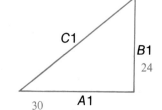

4. A utility pole casts a shadow of 7 m. At the same time, a pedestrian standing next to the pole casts a shadow of 0.6 m. If the pedestrian is 1.8 m tall, how tall is the utility pole? 21 m

Using the Computer

This program will calculate the lengths of two sides of a triangle when the length of one side is known, and the lengths of the corresponding sides of a similar triangle are known. RUN it for A = 10, B = 8, C = 12, C1 = 36, then try it for some examples of your own.

```
10  PRINT "TO FIND THE SECOND AND THIRD "
20  PRINT "SIDES OF A SIMILAR TRIANGLE:"
30  PRINT "WHAT ARE A, B, C, C1";
40  INPUT A,B,C,C1
50  PRINT "THE SIDES ARE:"
60  PRINT "A =";A,"A1 =";A*C1/C
70  PRINT "B =";B,"B1 =";B*C1/C
80  PRINT "C =";C,"C1 =";C1
90  END
```

11-3 Pythagorean Theorem

Surely you have seen a ladder set up against a building. The ladder and the building form a right triangle. One side of the triangle is at ground level, from the foot of the ladder to the building. The building forms another side, and the ladder forms the third side. It is interesting to note that the ladder always forms the longest side. In any right triangle, the side opposite the right angle is called the **hypotenuse.** The other two sides are called **legs.**

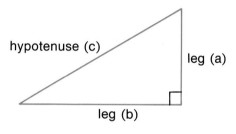

An important property of right triangles is known as the Pythagorean Theorem.

Pythagorean Theorem

For any right triangle, the square of the length of the hypotenuse is equal to the sum of the squares of the lengths of the other two sides.

You can write the Pythagorean Theorem as an equation.

$$c^2 = a^2 + b^2 \qquad \text{or} \qquad a^2 + b^2 = c^2$$

It is also true that if a triangle has the property in which c^2 is equal to $a^2 + b^2$, it is a right triangle.

Example 1   Is the triangle shown a right triangle?

Solution

$$c^2 = a^2 + b^2$$

5^2	$4^2 + 3^2$
25	$16 + 9$
25	25

$25 = 25$, so the triangle is a right triangle.

You know that $5^2 = 25$. You also know that $(^-5)^2 = 25$. Since $5^2 = 25$ and $(^-5)^2 = 25$, both 5 and $^-5$ are **square roots** of 25. The positive square root of a number n is shown by the symbol $\sqrt{n}$, and the negative square root is shown by the symbol $^-\sqrt{n}$.

Example 2   Write the positive square root of 18.

Solution   18 is between 16 and 25, so $\sqrt{18}$ is between $\sqrt{16}$ and $\sqrt{25}$. $\sqrt{18}$ is between 4 and 5. From the table of square roots on page 470, $\sqrt{18}$ is approximately 4.243.

   If you know the lengths of two sides of a right triangle, you can use the Pythagorean Theorem and the positive square root to calculate the length of the third side.

Example 3   Calculate the length of the hypotenuse.

Solution

$$c^2 = a^2 + b^2$$
$$c^2 = 5^2 + 12^2$$
$$c^2 = 25 + 144 = 169$$
$$c = \sqrt{169} = 13$$

Your Turn   • If $a = 1$ and $b = 2$, what is the length of the hypotenuse? 2.236

Class Exercises

Complete.

1. $2^2 + 3^2 = \underline{\;?\;}$ 13
2. $5^2 + 6^2 = \underline{\;?\;}$ 61
3. $4^2 + 1^2 = \underline{\;?\;}$ 17

4. $10^2 - 6^2 = \underline{\;?\;}$ 64
5. $12^2 - 8^2 = \underline{\;?\;}$ 80
6. $13^2 - 12^2 = \underline{\;?\;}$ 25

Exercises

Write the positive square root. Use the table of square roots on page 470, if necessary.

A **1.** $\sqrt{36}$ 6
2. $\sqrt{49}$ 7
3. $\sqrt{81}$ 9
4. $\sqrt{100}$ 10
5. $\sqrt{1}$ 1 3.742

6. $\sqrt{12}$ 3.464
7. $\sqrt{6}$ 2.449
8. $\sqrt{10}$ 3.162
9. $\sqrt{13}$ 3.606
10. $\sqrt{14}$

The lengths of the sides of a triangle are given. Is the triangle a right triangle?

B **11.** $a = 9, b = 12, c = 15$ yes
12. $a = 4, b = 5, c = 6$ no

13. $a = 10, b = 15, c = 20$ no
14. $a = 10, b = 24, c = 26$ yes

15. $a = 5, b = 12, c = 13$ yes
16. $a = 20, b = 21, c = 29$ yes

The lengths of two sides of a right triangle are given. Find the length of the hypotenuse.

17. 2 km, 3 km 3.606 km
18. 3 m, 5 m 5.831 m
19. 6 cm, 8 cm 10 cm

20. 4 mm, 2 mm 4.472 mm
21. 7 m, 5 m 8.602 m
22. 5 mm, 5 mm 7.071 mm

A right triangle has sides of lengths a, b, and c, with c the length of the hypotenuse. Find the length of the missing side of the triangle to the nearest thousandth.

Example $a = 7, c = 9$

Solution $a^2 + b^2 = c^2$
$49 + b^2 = 81$
$b^2 = 81 - 49 = 32$

You must find $\sqrt{32}$ to find b. $\longrightarrow$ $b = 5.657$

23. $a = 3, c = 7$ 6.325
24. $a = 4, c = 6$ 4.472
25. $a = 5, c = 9$ 7.483

26. $b = 1, c = 4$ 3.873
27. $b = 4, c = 9$ 8.062
28. $a = 5, b = 7$ 8.602

Problems

Solve. Write the answer to the nearest tenth.

1. A rectangle is 5 ft long and 2 ft wide. How long is a diagonal of the rectangle? 5.4 ft
2. A square measures 6 yd on one side. What is the length of a diagonal of the square? 8.5 yd
3. Marie and Kevin hiked 3 mi east and then 6 mi north. How far were they from their starting point? 6.7 mi
4. A pole is 8 ft high. A wire is attached to the top of the pole and fastened to an anchor in the ground. The anchor is 5 ft from the foot of the pole. What is the length of the wire? 9.4 ft

5. A ladder 25 ft long is placed so that its top reaches 24 ft up the side of a house. How far from the house is the foot of the ladder? 7 ft

Self Test 1

Triangles *SRT* and *WYZ* are similar. Find the length of $\overline{SR}$.

1.   2.   11-1

Use the similar triangles to find the height marked *h.*

3.   4.   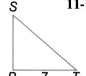   11-2

The lengths of the two legs of a right triangle are given. Find the length of the hypotenuse to the nearest tenth.

5. 6 in., 5 in. 7.8 in.   6. 4 cm, 6 cm 7.2 cm   7. 7 in., 7 in. 9.9 in. 11-3

11-4 *Tangent of an Angle*

Triangle *ABC* is a right triangle. In relation to ∠ *B*, $\overline{BC}$ is called the adjacent leg and $\overline{AC}$ is called the opposite leg.

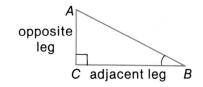

In a right triangle, the ratio of the length of the leg opposite an angle to the length of the leg adjacent to the angle is called the tangent of the angle. We write the tangent of angle *B* as "tan *B*."

$$\tan B = \frac{\text{length of the opposite leg}}{\text{length of the adjacent leg}} = \frac{AC}{BC}$$

Triangles *PQR* and *PTS* shown at the right are similar triangles. Notice that ∠ *P* is common to both triangles. You can find the tangent of ∠ *P* as shown below.

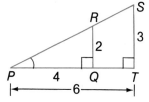

Triangle *PQR*

$$\tan P = \frac{RQ}{PQ} \quad \Rightarrow \quad \frac{2}{4} = \frac{1}{2}$$

Triangle *PTS*

$$\tan P = \frac{ST}{PT} \quad \Rightarrow \quad \frac{3}{6} = \frac{1}{2}$$

For both similar right triangles, tan *P* = $\frac{1}{2}$. You can see that the tangent of ∠ *P* depends on the measure of the angle itself, not on the size of the triangle.

Example 1   For the given right triangle, find the value of tan *G*.

Solution   Use the Pythagorean Theorem to find *x*.

$$3^2 + x^2 = 5^2$$
$$x^2 = 25 - 9 = 16$$
$$x = \sqrt{16} = 4$$

$$\tan G = \frac{\text{opposite leg}}{\text{adjacent leg}} = \frac{3}{4}$$

Example 2 For the given triangle, find the value of tan C.

Solution Find the value of y.
$$5^2 + y^2 = 6^2$$
$$y^2 = 36 - 25 = 11$$
$$y = \sqrt{11}$$

$$\tan C = \frac{\text{opposite leg}}{\text{adjacent leg}} = \frac{5}{\sqrt{11}}$$

$$\approx \frac{5}{3.317} \approx 1.507$$

Your Turn • Find the value of tan B, in the triangle above. 0.6634

Class Exercises

Use triangle NBC to complete.

1. $\overline{NB}$ is opposite ∠ _?_. C

2. $\overline{BC}$ is opposite ∠ _?_. N

3. $\overline{BC}$ is _?_ to ∠C. adjacent

4. $\overline{BN}$ is _?_ to ∠N. adjacent

5. $\tan C = \dfrac{NB}{?}$ BC

6. $\tan N = \dfrac{?}{BN}$ CB

Exercises

Write the value of tan A and tan B in lowest terms.

A **1.** $\frac{1}{2}$; 2 **2.** $\frac{4}{5}$; $\frac{5}{4}$ **3.** $\frac{3}{2}$; $\frac{2}{3}$

4. $\frac{7}{4}$; $\frac{4}{7}$ **5.** 4; $\frac{1}{4}$ **6.** $\frac{2}{3}$; $\frac{3}{2}$

For the given triangle, find the value of tan A to the nearest tenth.

B 7. 0.8

8. 0.6

9. 0.9

10. 2.5

11. 1.9

12. 0.3

13. 1.8

14. 0.7

15. 4.4

Use the diagram at the right to find the tangent of the angle to the nearest tenth.

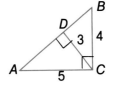

16. ∠A 0.8

17. ∠B 1.3

18. ∠ACD 1.3

19. ∠DCB 0.9

20. For any right triangle *ABC* with the right angle at *C*, is it true that tan A · tan B = 1? Show how you discovered this. yes

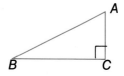

Using the Calculator

Find the value of the symbol in the table on page 470, use a calculator to evaluate the expression, and round to the nearest whole number.

1. $\sqrt{3} \cdot \sqrt{3}$ 3 **2.** $\sqrt{7} \cdot \sqrt{7}$ 7 **3.** $\sqrt{15} \cdot \sqrt{15}$ 15 **4.** $\sqrt{23} \cdot \sqrt{23}$ 23 **5.** $\sqrt{49} \cdot \sqrt{49}$ 49

6. Is the following statement true? $\sqrt{n} \cdot \sqrt{n} = n$ yes

11-5 Sine and Cosine of an Angle

In addition to the tangent ratio, you can write two other important ratios, the **sine** ratio and the **cosine** ratio. Notice that $\triangle MLS$ is a right triangle. We write the sine of $\angle M$ as sin M and the cosine of $\angle M$ as cos M.

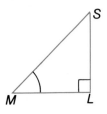

$$\sin M = \frac{\text{length of opposite leg}}{\text{length of hypotenuse}} = \frac{SL}{MS}$$

$$\cos M = \frac{\text{length of adjacent leg}}{\text{length of hypotenuse}} = \frac{ML}{MS}$$

In the diagram at the right, triangles ADE and AFG are similar right triangles. You can compute sin A and cos A for both triangles.

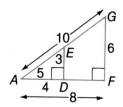

Triangle ADE

$$\sin A = \frac{ED}{AE} = \frac{3}{5}$$

$$\cos A = \frac{AD}{AE} = \frac{4}{5}$$

Triangle AFG

$$\sin A = \frac{GF}{AG} = \frac{6}{10} = \frac{3}{5}$$

$$\cos A = \frac{AF}{AG} = \frac{8}{10} = \frac{4}{5}$$

You can see that sin A and cos A depend on the size of $\angle A$, not on the size of the triangle.

Example   Find sin T and cos T in the given triangle.

Solution   Find the value of x.

$$12^2 + x^2 = 13^2$$
$$x^2 = 169 - 144 = 25$$
$$x = \sqrt{25} = 5$$

$$\sin T = \frac{PE}{PT} = \frac{5}{13} \qquad \cos T = \frac{ET}{PT} = \frac{12}{13}$$

Your Turn • Find sin P and cos P. $\frac{3}{5}; \frac{4}{5}$ • Find sin M and cos M. $\frac{3}{5}; \frac{4}{5}$

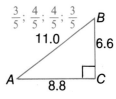

Class Exercises

Use the triangles shown to complete.

1. $\sin A = \dfrac{BC}{?}$ *AC*

2. $\sin C = \dfrac{?}{AC}$ *AB*

3. $\cos A = \dfrac{AB}{?}$ *AC*

4. $\cos C = \dfrac{?}{AC}$ *BC*

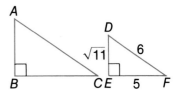

5. $\sin F = \dfrac{?}{6}$ $\sqrt{11}$

6. $\cos D = \dfrac{\sqrt{11}}{?}$ 6

7. $\sin \underline{\ ?\ } = \dfrac{5}{6}$ *D*

8. $\underline{\ ?\ }\, F = \dfrac{5}{6}$ cos

Exercises

For each triangle, find the value of sin A, cos A, sin B, and cos B. Write the ratio in lowest terms.

A 1. $\frac{5}{13}; \frac{12}{13}; \frac{12}{13}; \frac{5}{13}$

2. $\frac{5}{7}; \frac{5}{7}; \frac{5}{7}; \frac{5}{7}$

3. $\frac{3}{5}; \frac{4}{5}; \frac{4}{5}; \frac{3}{5}$

4. $\frac{20}{21}; \frac{20}{63}; \frac{20}{63}; \frac{20}{21}$

5. $\frac{70}{99}; \frac{70}{99}; \frac{70}{99}; \frac{70}{99}$

6. $\frac{3}{5}; \frac{4}{5}; \frac{4}{5}; \frac{3}{5}$

359

Find the value of *x*, then find sin *A*. 8.602; 0.8138

B **7.** 40; $\frac{40}{41}$

8.

9. 8; $\frac{8}{17}$
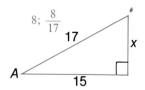

Find the value of *x*, then find cos *A*. 8.602; 0.8138

10. 5.385; 0.9285

11.

12. 7; $\frac{7}{25}$

For the triangles shown at the right, find the value of the ratio.

13. sin ∠ *BCD* $\frac{4}{5}$

14. cos ∠ *BCD* $\frac{3}{5}$

15. sin ∠ *ACD* 0.7071

16. cos ∠ *ACD* 0.7071

17. sin *A* 0.7071

18. cos *A* 0.7071

19. cos *B* $\frac{4}{5}$

20. sin *B* $\frac{3}{5}$

Refer to rectangle *ABCD* to find the value of the ratio.

C **21.** tan ∠2 $\frac{3}{4}$

22. sin ∠1 $\frac{4}{5}$

23. cos ∠1 $\frac{3}{5}$

24. tan ∠3 $\frac{4}{3}$

25. sin ∠4 $\frac{3}{5}$

26. cos ∠4 $\frac{4}{5}$

27. Find the values of sin *M* and cos *N* in △ MNP.
What do you notice? Is this result always true
for every right triangle? $\frac{3}{5}$; $\frac{3}{5}$; sin *M* = cos *N*; yes

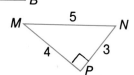

To express $\frac{5}{\sqrt{2}}$ without the symbol in the denominator, you can multiply the numerator and the denominator by $\sqrt{2}$. Write the following
expressions without the symbol in the denominator.

1. $\frac{1}{\sqrt{6}}$ $\frac{\sqrt{6}}{6}$

2. $\frac{1}{\sqrt{3}}$ $\frac{\sqrt{3}}{3}$

3. $\frac{2}{\sqrt{5}}$ $\frac{2\sqrt{5}}{5}$

4. $\frac{3}{\sqrt{8}}$ $\frac{3\sqrt{8}}{8}$

5. $\frac{7}{\sqrt{3}}$ $\frac{7\sqrt{3}}{3}$

11-6 *Using Trigonometry Tables*

In order to solve some practical problems involving right triangles, you must have access to the values of certain sine, cosine, and tangent ratios. A few of these can be easily computed using the properties of special triangles and the Pythagorean Theorem. Study triangle ABC shown below to see how the statement sin 30° = 0.5000 is derived.

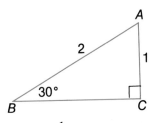

Angle	Sine	Cosine	Tangent
26°	.4384	.8988	.4877
27°	.4540	.8910	.5095
28°	.4695	.8829	.5317
29°	.4848	.8746	.5543
30°	.5000	.8660	.5774

$$\sin 30° = \frac{1}{2} = 0.5$$

$\sin 30° = 0.5000$ ⟵ *Remember that 0.5000 has the same value as 0.5.*

Most values of trigonometric ratios have to be computed by advanced methods. The table on page 471 gives approximate values of the sine, cosine, and tangent of angles with measures 1° to 90°. A portion of the table is shown above. You can use the table to find the lengths of sides of right triangles.

Example Use the tangent ratio to find the length of $\overline{XE}$ in the given triangle.

Solution $\tan 30° = \dfrac{XE}{AE}$

Substitute the value of tan 30° from the table.

$0.5774 = \dfrac{XE}{5}$ ⟵ *Use multiplication to solve the equation.*

$5 \times 0.5775 = XE$

$2.8875 = XE$

361

Your Turn
- If $AE = 4$, use the tangent ratio to find the length of $\overline{XE}$ in the triangle above. 2.3096
- If $XE = 3$, use the sin ratio to find the length of $\overline{AX}$. 6

Class Exercises

Use the table on page 471 to write the measure of the angle.

1. sin ___?___ = .1736 10° **2.** sin ___?___ = .2588 15° **3.** cos ___?___ = .9703 14°

4. cos ___?___ = .9962 5° **5.** tan ___?___ = 11.4301 85° **6.** tan ___?___ = 6.3138 81°

Exercises

Use the tangent values from the table on page 471 to find the length of a to the nearest tenth.

A **1.**

B 6

2.

a   B 11.9

3.

4.6
5.5

Use the table on page 471 to find the length of x to the nearest tenth.

B **4.**

4.2

5.

13.0

6.

x 12.1 A

7.

x 5.7

8.

18.8

9.
18.1

Problems

Use the table on page 471 to solve.

1. What is the distance across the lake to the nearest meter? 477 m

2. What is the height of the tree to the nearest foot? 41 ft

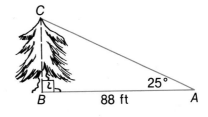

3. A trail bike is driven along a straight path from point *D* to point *C*. At point *C* the driver makes a 90° turn and travels to point *A*. The bike is then driven along a straight path from point *A* back to point *D*. Find the total distance the bike is driven to the nearest mile. 55 mi

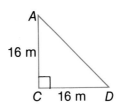

4. Lisa and her brother Eric are flying their kite. Eric is standing at point *E*. The kite is directly over his head at point *K*. The kite string makes an angle of 54° with the ground. To the nearest meter, how high is the kite above Eric's head? 179 m

11-7 Finding Angle Measures

You can use trigonometry tables to find the approximate measure of an angle in a right triangle if you know the lengths of two sides.

Example   Find the measure of $\angle A$ to the nearest degree, then find the measure of $\angle B$.

Solution $\sin A = \dfrac{BC}{BA} = \dfrac{5}{8}$

$\dfrac{5}{8} = 0.625$ ⟵ *Write $\frac{5}{8}$ as a decimal since the entries in the table are decimals.*

Use the table on page 471 to estimate the measure of the angle with a sine of 0.6250.

Sin 38° = 0.6157 and sin 39° = 0.6293.

Since 0.6250 is closer to 0.6293 than it is to 0.6157, $\angle A = 39°$ to the nearest degree.

$\angle B = (180° - 90°) - 39° = 51°$ ⟵ *The sum of the measures of the angles of a triangle is 180°.*

Your Turn   • Find the measure of $\angle A$ to the nearest degree, then find the measure of $\angle B$. 37°; 53°

Class Exercises

In triangle ABC, $\angle C = 90°$. The measure of one other angle is given below. Find the measure of the angle that is not given.

1. $\angle A = 53°$ 37°   **2.** $\angle B = 88°$ 2°   **3.** $\angle A = 71°$ 19°   **4.** $\angle B = 63°$ 27°

5. $\angle B = 47°$ 43°   **6.** $\angle A = 39°$ 51°   **7.** $\angle B = 29°$ 61°   **8.** $\angle A = 55°$ 35°

Exercises

Use the table on page 471 to find the measure of the angle to the nearest degree.

A **1.** $\sin A = 0.5625$ _34°_

2. $\cos B = 0.7049$ _45°_

3. $\cos A = 0.44$ _64°_

4. $\sin B = 0.3846$ _23°_

5. $\sin A = 0.875$ _61°_

6. $\tan B = 1.0758$ _47°_

Find the measures of $\angle A$ and $\angle B$ to the nearest degree.

7. _63°; 27°_

8. _24°; 66°_

9. _48°; 42°_

B **10.** _53°; 37°_

11. _34°; 56°_

12. _45°; 45°_

In triangle ABC, $\angle C = 90°$. Find the measures of $\angle A$ and $\angle B$ to the nearest degree.

13. $AB = 5$ and $AC = 2$ _66°; 24°_

14. $AB = 6$ and $AC = 4$ _48°; 42°_

15. $BC = 3$ and $AB = 6$ _30°; 60°_

16. $AC = 7$ and $AB = 9$ _39°; 51°_

Triangles ABC and ADE are similar. Find the measure of the angle to the nearest degree.

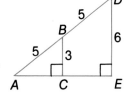

17. $\angle A$ _37°_

18. $\angle ABC$ _53°_

19. $\angle D$ _53°_

Find the measures of the angles and sides that are not given. Round each measure to the nearest unit.

C **20.**

21.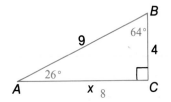

365

Problems

1. The picture at the right shows a section of the roof of a house. What is the approximate measure of the angle that the rafters form with the attic floor? (Hint: The rafters and the attic floor form the angle with vertex at *R*.) 23°

2. Engineers at point *P* would like to get to point *T*, 15 m below ground level. They can get to point *T* by tunnelling at an angle of 40°. How long will the tunnel be to the nearest meter? 23 m

Self Test 2

For the given triangle, find the value of tan *A*.

1.

2. A $\frac{3}{4}$

3.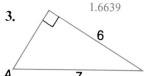

11-4

Find the value of the ratio for the triangle shown.

4. sin *B* 0.4472

5. cos *B* 0.8945

6. cos *A* 0.4472

7. sin *A* 0.8945

11-5

Use the table on page 471 to find *x*. Round to the nearest tenth.

8.

9.

10.

11-6

In △*ABC*, ∠*C* = 90°. Find the measures of ∠*A* and ∠*B* to the nearest degree.

11. AB = 7.5 and AC = 4.5 53°; 37°

12. BC = 2 and AC = 1.5 53°; 37°

11-7

Algebra Practice

Write an equation. Solve.

1. The quotient of 293,675 and 425 is *m*. $293{,}675 \div 425 = m$; 691

2. 768 times 392 is equal to *k*. $768 \cdot 392 = k$; 301,056

3. 700 minus 469.89 is equal to *c*. $700 - 469.89 = c$; 230.11

4. 510.2 divided by 46.8 is equal to *y*. $510.2 \div 46.8 = y$; 10.901709

5. The sum of $12\frac{3}{5}$ and $5\frac{9}{10}$ is *g*. $12\frac{3}{5} + 5\frac{9}{10} = g$; $18\frac{1}{2}$

6. The product of $11\frac{1}{5}$ and $1\frac{3}{7}$ is *n*. $11\frac{1}{5} \cdot 1\frac{3}{7} = n$; 16

7. The area of a circle with a diameter of 8.4 in. is *A*. $(3.14)(4.2)^2 = A$; 55.3896 in.²

8. The surface area of a box 8 cm wide, 9 cm high, and 14 cm long is *S*. $2(8 \cdot 9) + 2(9 \cdot 14) + 2(8 \cdot 14) = S$; 620 cm²

Use the distributive property to factor each expression.

9. $2g^2 - 2g + 6g^2$ $2g(g - 1 + 3g)$

10. $6ab - 2a^2b + ab^2$ $ab(6 - 2a + b)$

11. $12c^2d + 3c^2d^2 - 3cd^3$ $3cd(4c + cd - d^2)$

Solve.

12. $\frac{1}{2}d = 5\frac{1}{2}$ 11

13. $3 - 2c = 15$ ⁻6

14. $8r = 7r - 3$ ⁻3

15. 15% of 60 is *m*.   9

16. $\frac{3}{4}$% of 800 is *y*.   6

17. 39 is 12.5% of *h*.   312

18. $10 = 20 + {}^-5x$ 2

19. $10v - 12 > {}^-42$ $v > {}^-3$

20. ${}^-14 - 3q > 7$ $q < {}^-7$

Write an expression for any term of the sequence. Then find the 15th and 30th terms.

21. ⁻7, ⁻2, 3, 8, 13 $5n - 12$; 63; 138

22. ⁻10.7, ⁻9.4, ⁻8.1, ⁻6.8, ⁻5.5 $1.3n - 12$; 7.5; 27

Write an equation and solve the problem.

23. The base of a triangle is 2.8 cm more than its height. The height of the triangle is 5.3 cm. What is the base of the triangle? $5.3 + 2.8 = b$; 8.1 cm

24. In triangle *ABC*, the measure of $\angle A$ is 92°. The measure of $\angle A$ is twice the measure of $\angle B$. What is the measure of $\angle B$? $2x = 92$; 46°

Problem Solving on the Job

Medical Records Administrator

Many hospitals, health insurance companies and health equipment manufacturers require the service of medical record administrators.

```
MEDICAL RECORD ADMINISTRATOR

Description: Develop systems for
recording, storing and retrieving
patients' medical information--com-
pile medical statistics--supervise
the medical record staff

Qualifications: Bachelor's degree
in medical record administration

Job Outlook: Openings are expected
to grow faster than average for all
occupations
```

The medical record department at a large hospital compiled the following statistics on 470 male and 530 female surgery patients over a three-year period. Statistics such as these are useful when plans are being made for patient turn-over and room assignments.

Recovery Time			
Age Group	Male	Female	Days
0–15	35	45	12
16–30	90	85	11
31–45	105	110	13
46–60	135	155	15
61+	105	135	18

1. 43.75%; 51.43%; 48.84%; 46.55%; 43.75%
2. 56.25%; 48.57%; 51.16%; 53.45%; 56.25%

1. What percent of the patients in each age group were male? See answers above.
2. What percent in each age group were female? See answers above.
3. What percent of the patients were over 60 years old? 24%
4. What percent were under 16 years old? 8%
5. Of the patients under 46 years old, what percent was female? 51.06%
6. Of the patients under 31 years old, what percent was male? 49.02%

7. How much greater was the average recovery time for the 61+ age group than for the 31–45 age group? 5*d*

8. Copy and complete the chart to find the average recovery time for each male patient. 14*d*

Age Group	Number of Male Patients	Number of Days	Total Recovery Time
0–15	35	12	420
16–30	90	11	? 990
31–45	105	13	? 1365
46–60	135	15	? 2025
61+	105	18	? 1890
Total	? 470		? 6690

$$\text{Average Recovery Time} = \frac{\text{total recovery time}}{\text{total number of male patients}}$$

9. What was the average recovery time for each female patient? 14*d*

10. A full-time medical record administrator usually works 40 hours per week. One part-time medical record administrator works 21 hours per week. What percent of the week does she work? $52\frac{1}{2}\%$

11. Salaries are often based on training and experience. Six medical records administrators received these salaries in a recent year: $14,500, $15,200, $19,500, $18,000, $23,600, $30,000. What was the range in salary? What was the mean salary? $15,500; $20,133.33

12. In a recent year 15,000 medical record administrators were employed in hospitals. Of these about 6500 were RRA's (Registered Record Administrators). What fraction was RRA's? $\frac{13}{30}$

13. During the summer Bill McLean worked 12 hours per week as a medical record administrator intern at City Hospital. The table shows the number of hours he worked at each task in one week.

How many hours credit will Bill have in each section after 15 weeks?

Task	Hours
Verify information	2 30 h
Code forms	$4\frac{1}{2}$ 67.5 h
Transcribe information to patients charts	4 60 h
Maintain files	$1\frac{1}{2}$ 22.5 h

369

Enrichment

Special Right Triangles

Right triangles are so important in construction and in many other areas of work that it is worthwhile to study them in detail. One special right triangle has two 45° angles. Also, the two legs are equal in length. In the right triangle shown below, each leg is 1 unit long. Through the Pythagorean Theorem, we know that the hypotenuse is $\sqrt{2}$.

$$c^2 = 1^2 + 1^2$$
$$c^2 = 2$$
$$c = \sqrt{2}$$

45°-45° Right Triangle Property:
If each leg of a 45°-45° right triangle has length x, then the hypotenuse has length $x\sqrt{2}$.

Triangle SPQ is drawn so that each side is 2 units long. The 30°-60° right triangle, $\triangle PRQ$, can be thought of as half of $\triangle SPQ$. Since $\overline{RQ}$ is half of $\overline{SQ}$, then $\overline{RQ}$ is 1 unit long.

$$(RQ)^2 + (RP)^2 = (PQ)^2 \longleftarrow \text{Pythagorean Theorem}$$
$$1^2 + (RP)^2 = 2^2 \longleftarrow \text{Subtract } 1^2 \text{ to solve for } (RP)^2.$$
$$(RP)^2 = 3$$
$$RP = \sqrt{3}$$

30°-60° Right Triangle Property:
If the shorter leg of a 30°-60° right triangle has length x, then the other leg has length $x\sqrt{3}$, and the hypotenuse has length $2x$.

Find the length of each side labeled with a variable.

1.

2.

3.

4.

5.

6.

Chapter Review

How high is the tree? Write a, b, or c.

1. An 8-ft pole casts a shadow 5.5 ft long. At the same time a tree casts a shadow 16.5 ft long. b **a.** 16 ft **b.** 24 ft **c.** 10.5 ft

The lengths of the two legs of a triangle are given. Find the length of the hypotenuse to the nearest tenth.

2. 6 ft, 8 ft 10 ft

3. 4 m, 6 m 7.2 m

8.6 in.
4. 7 in., 5 in.

Find the tangent of the angle. Write a, b, or c.

5. ∠A a
   a. 1.6 **b.** 16 **c.** 0.6

6. ∠B c
   a. 10 **b.** 1.6 **c.** 0.625

7. Triangles *ABC* and *DEF* are similar. Choose the correct measure for *n*.
   a. 28 **b.** 50 **c.** 7 a

Use the table on page 471 to find the length of *n* to the nearest tenth.

8.

9.

10.

In triangle *RNP*, ∠*N* = 90°. Find the measures of ∠*R* and ∠*P* to the nearest degree.

37°; 53°
11. *RP* = 15, *RN* = 12

53°; 37°
12. *NP* = 10, *RP* = 12.5

41°; 49°
13. *RN* = 12, *RP* = 16

Find the value of *x*, then find the value of the ratio.

14. sin *M* $\frac{3}{5}$

15. cos *M* $\frac{4}{5}$

16. sin *N* $\frac{4}{5}$

17. cos *N* $\frac{3}{5}$

Chapter Test

For each pair of similar triangles, find *n*.

1. 13.5

2. 8

11-1

Use the similar right triangles to find the missing height.

3. 21 ft

4. 12.8 ft

11-2

A right triangle has sides of lengths *a*, *b*, and *c*, with *c* the length of the hypotenuse. Find the length of the missing side to the nearest tenth.

5. $a = 6$, $c = 10$ 8   **6.** $c = 12$, $b = 10$ 6.6   **7.** $b = 11$, $c = 13$ 6.9 **11-3**

Find the value of tan *B*.

8. $\frac{3}{4}$

9. $\frac{4}{3}$

10. $\frac{3}{4}$ **11-4**

In $\triangle MRP$ $\angle R = 90°$, $MR = 6$, $RP = 8$, and $MP = 10$. Find the value of the ratio.

11. $\sin M$ $\frac{5}{6}$ **12.** $\sin P$ $\frac{1}{2}$ **11-5**

13. $\cos P$ $\frac{5}{6}$ **14.** $\cos M$ $\frac{1}{2}$

Use the table on page 471 to find the length of *x* to the nearest tenth.

15. 31.5

16. 27° 26.4

17. 5.9 **11-6**

Find the measure of $\angle A$ and $\angle B$ to the nearest degree.
32°; 58°   34°; 56°   73°; 17°

18. 8

19. 9

20. 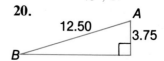 **11-7**

372

Cumulative Review (Chapters 1–11)

Write the fraction in lowest terms.

1. $\dfrac{4}{18}$ $\quad \frac{2}{9}$

2. $\dfrac{7}{49}$ $\quad \frac{1}{7}$

3. $\dfrac{12}{48}$ $\quad \frac{1}{4}$

4. $\dfrac{35}{70}$ $\quad \frac{1}{2}$

5. $\dfrac{18}{32}$ $\quad \frac{9}{16}$

6. $\dfrac{9}{27}$ $\quad \frac{1}{3}$

7. $\dfrac{14}{27}$ $\quad \frac{14}{27}$

8. $\dfrac{16}{40}$ $\quad \frac{2}{5}$

9. $\dfrac{18}{45}$ $\quad \frac{2}{5}$

10. $\dfrac{15}{35}$ $\quad \frac{3}{7}$

11. $\dfrac{56}{72}$ $\quad \frac{7}{9}$

12. $\dfrac{24}{56}$ $\quad \frac{3}{7}$

13. $\dfrac{42}{48}$ $\quad \frac{7}{8}$

14. $\dfrac{20}{32}$ $\quad \frac{5}{8}$

15. $\dfrac{27}{81}$ $\quad \frac{1}{3}$

16. $\dfrac{32}{72}$ $\quad \frac{4}{9}$

Solve.

17. What percent is 9 out of 15? 60%

18. 12 out of 50 is what percent? 24%

19. 64 percent of 86 is what number? 55.04

20. What is 93% of 82? 76.26

21. 24% of what number is 8.4? 35

22. $\dfrac{1}{2}$% of 44 is what number? 0.22

23. How much simple interest will $1000 make at $7\dfrac{1}{2}$% for 2 years? $150

24. If you invest $500 and the money increases by $4\dfrac{1}{2}$%, how much money do you gain? $22.50

Add, subtract, multiply, or divide.

25. $^-2 + 0$ $^-2$

26. $^-5 + {}^-7$ $^-12$

27. $6 + {}^-13$ $^-7$

28. $^-4 + 25$ 21

29. $^-9 - 2$ $^-11$

30. $6 - {}^-4$ 10

31. $0 - {}^-8$ 8

32. $^-2 \cdot {}^-7$ 14

33. $4 \cdot {}^-12$ $^-48$

34. $^-5 \div {}^-1$ 5

35. $^-35 \div 7$ $^-5$

36. $^-80 \div {}^-10$ 8

Draw the graph of the equation. Check students' graphs.

37. $y = x + 7$

38. $y = x + 3$

39. $y = 4x - 6$

40. $y = 2x + 1$

41. $y = 3x - 2$

42. $y = \dfrac{1}{2}x - 3$

43. Record albums range from $4.95 to $10.95 at Dave's Record City. What is the minimum and maximum you could spend for 5 albums? $24.75; $54.75

12
Probability

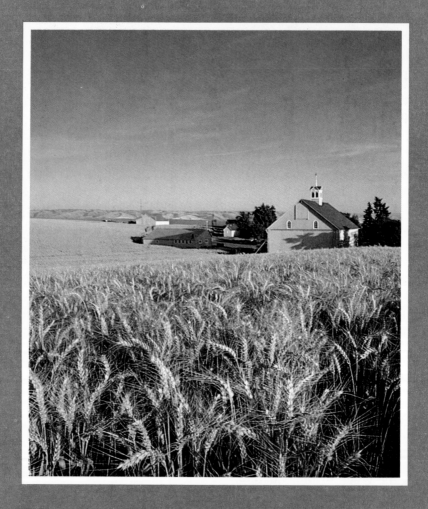

A package of certified wheat seed must be 96% "pure live seed." That is, the probability that a seed in the package will be a wheat seed, and that it will sprout under proper conditions must be 96%.

12-1 Probability

One student from Granville High School will be interviewed on a TV program called "Students Speak Out." To select the student, names are written on cards and placed in a box. One card will be drawn at **random.** That is, the outcome of the drawing is strictly a matter of chance.

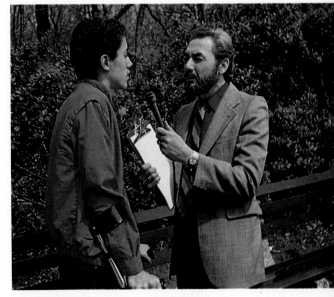

There are 520 students at Granville High School. We say that there are 520 **outcomes.** A set of one or more outcomes is called an **event.** The outcomes are **equally likely** if each card is as likely to be chosen as any other card. Stephen hopes that the card with his name will be drawn. As far as he is concerned, there is only 1 **favorable outcome.** The **probability** that Stephen's name will be drawn is 1 out of 520, or $\frac{1}{520}$. We write $P(Stephen) = \frac{1}{520}$.

If all outcomes are equally likely, the probability of an event is the ratio of the number of favorable outcomes to the total number of outcomes.

$$P(\text{event}) = \frac{\text{number of favorable outcomes}}{\text{total number of outcomes}}$$

Since a ratio may be written as an equivalent decimal or as a percent, the probability of an event may also be written as a decimal or a percent.

Example 1 What is *P*(even number)
on the spinner? Write the
probability as a ratio, as a
decimal, and as a percent.

Solution There are 2 favorable outcomes: 10 and 20.
There are 5 outcomes in all: 5, 10, 15, 20, and 25.

$$P(\text{even number}) = \frac{2}{5} = 0.4 = 40\% \longleftarrow \quad \begin{array}{l} 2 \div 5 = 0.4 \\ 0.4 = 0.40 = 40\% \end{array}$$

Example 2 What is *P*(6)? What is *P*(whole number)?

Solution There is no 6 on the spinner. We say that 6 is an **impossible event.** Every number on the spinner is a whole number. Getting a whole number is a **certain event.**

$$P(6) = \frac{0}{5} = 0 \qquad P(\text{whole number}) = \frac{5}{5} = 1, \text{ or } 100\%$$

Your Turn There are 100 beads in a bag. Of these, 50 are red, 30
are blue, and 20 are yellow. You draw one bead without
looking. State the probability as a ratio, as a decimal,
and as a percent.

- *P*(red)   • *P*(blue or yellow)   • *P*(colored bead)   • *P*(green)
  $\frac{1}{2}$, 0.5, 50% $\frac{1}{2}$, 0.5, 50%   1, 1, 100%   0, 0, 0%

Examples 1 and 2 show some useful properties of probabilities.

- The probability of an impossible event is 0.
- The probability of a certain event is 1, or 100%.
- The probability of an event that is neither certain nor impossible is
  a number between 0 and 1.

Class Exercises

A game cube has six faces numbered 0, 3, 6, 9, 12, and 15. The cube is tossed once. State the probability as a ratio.

1. $P(9)$ $\frac{1}{6}$ **2.** $P(0$ or $15)$ $\frac{1}{3}$ **3.** $P(\text{odd number})$ $\frac{1}{2}$

4. $P(\text{not } 6)$ $\frac{5}{6}$ **5.** $P(1)$ 0 **6.** $P(\text{number} < 16)$ 1

State the probability as a percent.

7. $P(A) = \frac{1}{2} = \underline{\ ?\ }\%$ 50 **8.** $P(B) = \frac{3}{5} = \underline{\ ?\ }\%$ 60 **9.** $P(C) = \frac{7}{10} = \underline{\ ?\ }\%$ 70

Exercises

A record store is giving away a randomly selected album free with each purchase of a new album. The free albums are selected from a group of 500 albums. They include 250 rock albums, 150 country albums, and 100 classical albums. Complete to determine the probability of the album selected for the first customer.

A **1.** $P(\text{rock album}) = \frac{250}{500} = \frac{?}{2}$ 1 **2.** $P(\text{not a rock album}) = \frac{250}{?} = \frac{?}{?}$ 1; 500; 2

3. $P(\text{classical album}) = \frac{?}{500} = \frac{?}{?}$ 100; 1; 5 **4.** $P(\text{country album}) = \frac{?}{?} = \frac{?}{?}$ 150; 3; 500; 10

5. 50% 6. 50% 7. 20% 8. 30%

5–8. State the probabilities in Exercises 1–4 as percents.

At a school carnival students can buy chances to spin the wheel for the prizes shown. State the probability as a ratio.

Outcome	Prize
Red	Free lunches for 1 week
White	Free spin

B **9.** $P(\text{yellow})$ $\frac{1}{4}$ **10.** $P(\text{blue})$ $\frac{1}{4}$ **11.** $P(\text{yellow or blue})$ $\frac{1}{2}$

12. $P(\text{free lunches})$ $\frac{1}{4}$ **13.** $P(\text{free spin})$ $\frac{1}{4}$ **14.** $P(\text{prize})$ $\frac{1}{2}$

15. $P(\text{no prize})$ $\frac{1}{2}$ **16.** $P(\text{white})$ $\frac{1}{4}$ **17.** $P(\text{not white})$ $\frac{3}{4}$

18. $P(\text{red})$ $\frac{1}{4}$ **19.** $P(\text{not red})$ $\frac{3}{4}$ **20.** $P(\text{purple})$ 0

The table shows the percent of students at Rockbury School whose ages are 15, 16, 17, or 18. No student is older than 18, but some are younger than 15. If a student is selected at random, write the probability as a percent.

Age at Last Birthday	Percent
15	20%
16	30%
17	25%
18	18%

21. P(age 16) 30% **22.** P(age at least 15) 93%

23. P(age 19) 0% **24.** P(age less than 15) 7%

25. P(not 15) 80% **26.** P(age greater than 15) 73%

On the spinner, $P(A)$ equals $\frac{1}{3}$, and $P(\text{not } A)$ equals $1 - \frac{1}{3}$, or $\frac{2}{3}$. Event A and Event (not A) are called **complementary events.**

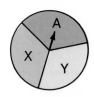

$$P(\text{not } A) = 1 - P(A)$$

Let $P(R) = \frac{1}{3}$, $P(S) = \frac{3}{4}$, and $P(T) = 0.4$. Determine the probability.

C **27.** P(not S) $\frac{1}{4}$ **28.** P(not T) $\frac{3}{5}$ **29.** P(not R) $\frac{2}{3}$

Problems

Solve. To the nearest whole percent, what is the probability?

1. Nathan randomly answered a true-false question on a quiz. What is the probability that he answered correctly? 50%
2. Lisa randomly selected 1 of 5 choices on a multiple choice question. What is the probability that she selected the one correct answer? 20%
3. One student from Valleyview Central School will be chosen at random to be "Principal For a Day." If 52% of the students are girls, what is the probability that a boy will be chosen? 48%
4. At Dee's Bike Shop 50% of the customers pay for their purchases with cash and 30% use a credit card. The rest pay with a check. What is the probability that a customer will pay with a check? 20%

12-2 *Sample Spaces*

Ace Tours offers passengers a choice of three routes from Los Angeles to St. Louis and two routes from St. Louis to New York. The sketch shows the possible routes from Los Angeles to New York through St. Louis.

The Northern, Scenic Route is outlined in red.

The first prize in a contest is a trip from Los Angeles to New York. We write *P*(*Northern, Scenic*) to represent the probability that the Northern Route *and* the Scenic Route will be chosen.

To determine the probability of an event, you first need to know the number of possible outcomes. The set of all outcomes is called the **sample space.** One way to find the number of outcomes in a sample space is to list them. A **tree diagram** can help you do this.

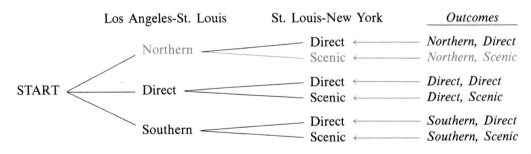

Example 1   What is *P*(Northern, Scenic)?

Solution   There are 6 outcomes in all; only 1 is favorable.

$$P(\text{Northern, Scenic}) = \frac{1}{6}$$

Your Turn   In addition to the cities on the preceding page, Ace Tours offers a choice of two routes from New York to Boston, a direct route and an historical route. Check students' diagrams.
- Draw a tree diagram to list all the routes from Los Angeles to Boston through St. Louis and New York.
- If you select one route from Los Angeles to Boston at random, what is the probability that part of the trip will be via a direct route? $\frac{5}{6}$

Class Exercises

Suppose you spin the spinner and then toss a coin. The outcomes of the two-stage activity are shown in the tree diagram.

1. Complete the list of outcomes.

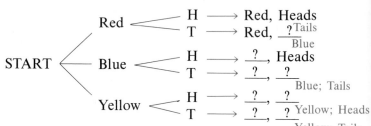

Outcomes

Red — H ⟶ Red, Heads
     T ⟶ Red, ? Tails
Blue
Blue — H ⟶ ?, Heads
      T ⟶ ?, ?
                Blue; Tails
Yellow — H ⟶ ?, ?
        T ⟶ ?, ? Yellow; Heads
                Yellow; Tails

What is the probability?

2. P(Red, Heads) $\frac{1}{6}$ 3. P(Red or Heads) $\frac{2}{3}$ 4. P(Green, Tails) 0

Exercises

For his birthday, Jason's parents will buy tickets to a movie or a game for him and a friend. Jason will choose one of four friends: Jack, Bill, Tim, or Chris. Copy and complete the tree diagram. Use the tree diagram to determine the probability.

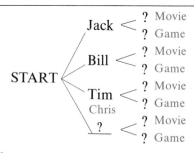

START
Jack < ? Movie / ? Game
Bill < ? Movie / ? Game
Tim < ? Movie / ? Game
Chris
? < ? Movie / ? Game

A 1. P(Jack, movie) $\frac{1}{8}$ 2. P(Bill, game) $\frac{1}{8}$ 3. P(Tim or Chris, game) $\frac{1}{4}$

4. P(not Harry, movie) $\frac{1}{2}$ 5. P(Bill, not movie) $\frac{1}{8}$ 6. P(not Bill or Chris, game) $\frac{1}{4}$

Jason decides to go with Jack, Tim, or Chris to either a football game or a baseball game. Use a tree diagram to determine the probability.

B **7.** P(Jack, football) $\frac{1}{6}$ **8.** P(Tim, game) $\frac{1}{3}$

9. P(Chris, soccer) 0 **10.** P(Jack or Chris, baseball) $\frac{1}{3}$

11. P(not Tim, football) $\frac{1}{3}$ **12.** P(not Jack, not football) $\frac{1}{3}$

A coin is tossed. Then a game cube is rolled. The game cube has faces numbered 1 to 6. Use a tree diagram to determine the probability.

13. P(H, 4) $\frac{1}{12}$ **14.** $P(T, 6)$ $\frac{1}{12}$ **15.** $P(T, 8)$ 0 $\frac{5}{12}$

16. P(H, even number) $\frac{1}{4}$ **17.** P(H or T, 6) $\frac{1}{6}$ **18.** P(not H, not 5)

19. P(T, prime number) $\frac{1}{4}$ **20.** P(H or T, odd number) $\frac{1}{2}$ **21.** P(H, $n > 4$) $\frac{1}{6}$

A chart is sometimes used to give additional information about a two-stage activity. For example, the Tourist-Day flight costs $110. Use the chart to determine the probability. Let r represent the rate.

Jetaway Airline
Carlton to Oxbow Rate Chart

	Day	Night
1st Class	$125	$100
Tourist	$110	$90
Standby	$80	$70

C **22.** P(least expensive) $\frac{1}{6}$ **23.** $P(r < \$100)$ $\frac{1}{2}$

24. $P(r > \$100)$ $\frac{1}{3}$ **25.** P(Tourist or Night) $\frac{2}{3}$

Problems

Draw a tree diagram and solve. Check students' diagrams.

1. Susette plans a trip from Chicago to an island off the coast of Maine. She can go to the coast by plane, by car, by train, or by bus. She then has a choice of going by plane or by boat from the coast to the island. What is the probability that she will fly on both parts of the trip if she chooses at random? $\frac{1}{8}$

2. Daily specials at a restaurant offer customers these choices:

Meat: roast beef, chicken, turkey, ham
Potato: baked, mashed
Vegetable: salad, squash, peas

If a customer selects a meal at random, what is the probability that the customer will not select either ham or peas? $\frac{1}{2}$

381

12-3 Counting Principle

It is not always necessary to list all the outcomes in a sample space to determine the number of possible outcomes. You can use the **counting principle** to find the number of outcomes for an activity with two or more stages.

The number of outcomes for an activity with two or more stages equals the product of the number of outcomes for each stage.

Suso is buying a telephone. He has a choice of these colors, styles, and dials.

Colors	Styles	Dials
black	antique	dial
white	modern	push-button
yellow	futura	
red	standard	
tan		
blue		
green		

Example 1 From how many different telephones must Suso choose?

Solution This is a three-stage activity.

Stage 1	Stage 2	Stage 3
Color	Style	Dial
7 choices	4 choices	2 choices

There are $7 \times 4 \times 2$, or 56 different outcomes possible.

Example 2   If Suso chooses a telephone at random, what is the probability that he will select a yellow or red, futura, push-button phone?

Solution   There are 2 favorable outcomes:

yellow, futura, push-button
red, futura, push-button

There are 56 possible outcomes.

P(yellow or red, futura, push-button) $= \dfrac{2}{56}$, or $\dfrac{1}{28}$.

Your Turn   • Jan has won a vacation trip for two to Bermuda, Hawaii, Jamaica, or Puerto Rico. She will go with either Sue, Pamela, or Fran. She can go by plane all the way or she can take a boat cruise. If she chooses at random, what is P(Hawaii, Fran, boat cruise)? $\dfrac{1}{24}$

Class Exercises

How many different paths are there?

1. from A to B 3   **2.** from B to C 5

3. from A to C 15   **4.** from C to D 3

5. from B to D 15   **6.** from A to D 45

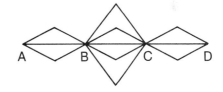

During the Fall, John will participate in one sport and one club.

> **Sports:**   soccer, football, swimming
> **Clubs:**   drama, photography, French, computer

If John selects at random from the lists above, what is the probability? $\dfrac{1}{12}$

7. P(football, drama) $\dfrac{1}{12}$ **8.** P(baseball, drama) 0   **9.** P(swimming, computer)

10. How many 2-digit numerals are there if there are 9 digits to choose from for the tens' place, and 10 digits for the ones' place? How many 3-digit numerals are there? 90; 900

Exercises

Four activities are used for Exercises 1–20. They are tossing a coin, rolling a game cube, spinning the spinner shown, and drawing one of three cards marked *A, B, C*. The faces of the game cube are numbered 1 through 6.

Complete to determine the number of outcomes for each set of activities.

A **1.** Toss the coin; then spin the spinner. $2 \times 5 = \underline{?}$ 10

2. Roll the game cube; then draw a card. $6 \times \underline{?} = \underline{?}$ 3; 18

3. Toss the coin twice; then spin the spinner. $2 \times \underline{?} \times \underline{?} = \underline{?}$ 2; 5; 20

4. Roll the game cube twice; then toss the coin. $6 \times \underline{?} \times \underline{?} = \underline{?}$ 6; 2; 72

Determine the number of outcomes for each set of activities.

B **5.** Spin the spinner 3 times.   125

6. Spin the spinner twice; then draw a card.   75

7. Draw card; spin the spinner; then roll the game cube.   90

8. Toss the coin 3 times; roll the game cube; then draw a card.   144

Suppose you spin the spinner and draw a card. What is the probability?

9. $P(\text{red}, B)$ $\frac{1}{15}$ **10.** $P(\text{yellow}, D)$ 0   **11.** $P(\text{white}, A \text{ or } C)$ $\frac{2}{15}$

Suppose you toss the coin, roll the game cube, and draw a card. What is the probability? $\frac{1}{12}$

12. $P(H, 5, B)$ $\frac{1}{36}$ **13.** $P(T, 4, A \text{ or } C)$ $\frac{1}{18}$ **14.** $P(H, \text{even number}, A)$

Suppose you roll the game cube, spin the spinner, and draw a card. What is the probability? $\frac{1}{30}$ $\frac{1}{30}$

15. $P(1, \text{blue}, B)$ $\frac{1}{90}$ **16.** $P(\text{prime number}, \text{red}, C)$ **17.** $P(\text{even number}, \text{red}, B)$

Suppose you toss the coin, roll the game cube, spin the spinner, and draw a card. What is the probability?

18. $P(\text{H, 1, red, } A)$ $\frac{1}{180}$ **19.** $P(\text{H or T, 3, red, } A)$ $\frac{1}{90}$ **20.** $P(\text{H, 1 or 2, red, } B)$ $\frac{1}{90}$

Two bowling teams, the Strikers and the All-Stars, are tied for the league championship. The four bowlers on each team are ranked 1, 2, 3, and 4. For the playoff, one person, selected at random, from each team will bowl. Answer the question.

C **21.** How many possible combinations of players are there for the playoff? 16

22. What is the probability that Player 1 of the Strikers will bowl against Player 3 of the All-Stars? $\frac{1}{16}$

23. What is the probability that both players will have even numbers? $\frac{1}{4}$

Problems

Solve.

1. A club has 5 seniors, 3 juniors, and 4 sophomores. How many senior-junior-sophomore combinations are possible for a three-person committee? 60

2. A baseball team has 5 pitchers and 2 catchers. How many pitcher-catcher combinations are possible? 10

3. A car dealer offers 15 body colors and 10 interior colors. How many color combinations are possible? 150

4. Barbara has 8 mystery books. 6 science fiction books, and 5 animal books. She wants to take one of each on a camping trip. From how many combinations can Barbara choose? 240

5. A clothing manufacturer makes dresses in 10 styles. Each style is made in 4 different colors and 6 sizes. A different code number is used for each style-color-size combination. How many code numbers are there? 240

6. A department store sells TVs from 5 different manufacturers. Each manufacturer offers a choice of screen in 8 different sizes. All TVs are available in either color or black and white. If one TV is chosen at random as a prize in a contest, what is the probability that it will be a Brand *X* color TV in the largest size available? $\frac{1}{80}$

12-4 Independent Events

Suppose you spin the spinner then toss the coin. The outcome on the spinner in no way affects the outcome on the coin. A *4* on the spinner and *heads* on the coin are **independent events.** If two events are independent, you can use the following rule to determine the probability of both events occurring.

If Event *A* and Event *B* are independent, then $P(A$ and $B)$ equals $P(A)$ times $P(B)$.

$$P(A, B) = P(A) \cdot P(B)$$

In general, the probability of two or more independent events occurring is the product of the probabilities of the individual events.

Example 1   If you spin the spinner then toss a coin, what is P(odd number, H)?

Solution   First, determine the probability of each event separately.

$$P(\text{odd number}) = \frac{3}{5} \qquad P(\text{H}) = \frac{1}{2}$$

Then multiply: $P(\text{odd number, H}) = \frac{3}{5} \cdot \frac{1}{2}$

$$= \frac{3}{10}$$

Your Turn   If you spin the spinner above two times, what is the probability?
- P(even number, odd number) $\frac{6}{25}$ • P(not 4, 4) $\frac{4}{25}$

Example 2 If a coin is tossed three times, what is $P(\text{H, H, T})$?

Solution $P(\text{H, H, T}) = P(\text{H}) \cdot P(\text{H}) \cdot P(\text{T})$

$$= \frac{1}{2} \cdot \frac{1}{2} \cdot \frac{1}{2}$$

$$= \frac{1}{8}$$

Your Turn A game cube has faces numbered 1 through 6. If the cube is rolled three times, what is the probability?
- $P(1, 1, 6)$ $\frac{1}{216}$
- $P(\text{even number, odd number, 6})$ $\frac{1}{24}$

Class Exercises

Suppose you spin the spinner shown twice. Complete to determine the probability.

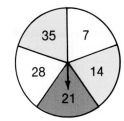

1. $P(7, 7) = \frac{1}{5} \cdot \underline{\ ?\ } = \underline{\ ?\ }$ $\frac{1}{5}; \frac{1}{25}$

2. $P(\text{even number, 7}) = \frac{2}{?} \cdot \frac{1}{5} = \underline{\ ?\ }$ $5; \frac{2}{25}$

3. $P(\text{prime number, composite number}) = \frac{?}{5} \cdot \frac{?}{5} = \underline{\ ?\ }$ $1; 4; \frac{4}{25}$

4. $P(\text{multiple of 3, odd number}) = \frac{?}{5} \cdot \frac{?}{5} = \underline{\ ?\ }$ $1; 3; \frac{3}{25}$

Exercises

Two game cubes each have faces numbered 1 through 6. Determine the probability.

A
1. $P(2, 5)$ $\frac{1}{36}$ **2.** $P(6, 6)$ $\frac{1}{36}$ **3.** $P(\text{even number, 3})$ $\frac{1}{12}$

4. $P(\text{odd number, 1})$ $\frac{1}{12}$ **5.** $P(n < 6, 6)$ $\frac{5}{36}$ **6.** $P(4, n > 4)$ $\frac{1}{18}$

387

One boy and one girl from each class at Taylor High School will be chosen at random for an exchange program. The table shows the number of boys and the number of girls in each class as well as the number of girls named Mary and the number of boys name Bill in each class. Use the table for Exercises 7-21.

What is *P*(Bill, Mary) in each class?

Taylor High School Enrollment

Class	Boys	Girls	Bill	Mary
Freshman	28	32	7	4
Sophomore	30	35	6	7
Junior	25	27	5	9
Senior	24	30	6	5

B 7. Freshman $\frac{1}{32}$ 8. Sophomore $\frac{1}{25}$
9. Junior $\frac{1}{15}$ 10. Senior $\frac{1}{24}$

What is *P*(neither Bill nor Mary) in each class?

11. Freshman $\frac{21}{32}$ 12. Sophomore $\frac{16}{25}$
13. Junior $\frac{8}{15}$ 14. Senior $\frac{5}{8}$

Determine the probability.

15. *P*(Mary in all 4 classes) $\frac{1}{720}$ 16. *P*(Bill in all 4 classes) $\frac{1}{400}$

17. *P*(no girl named Mary is chosen) $\frac{7}{18}$ 18. *P*(no boy named Bill is chosen) $\frac{9}{25}$

19. *P*(Mary in all 4 classes, Bill in all 4 classes) $\frac{1}{288,000}$

Solve.

C 20. In which of the classes is it most likely that a boy named Bill and a girl named Mary will be chosen? (Hint: Before comparing the probabilities, write them as decimals.) Junior
21. In which class is it least likely that a boy named Bill and a girl named Mary will be chosen? Freshman

Problems

Solve.

1. The probability that a healthy child will contract a particular disease after exposure is 0.8. What is the probability of two children who have been exposed to it getting the disease? 0.64
2. The probability that a person is allergic to a new drug is 0.004. What is the probability that the first three persons for whom a doctor prescribes this drug will all be allergic? 0.000000064

Using the Calculator

Statistics about past events can sometimes be used to estimate the probability of future events if conditions remain unchanged. Recent statistics about child births in the United States show that for every 100 girls that are born 105 boys are born. Let $P(G, B)$ represent the probability that the first child is a girl and the second child is a boy.

What is the probability, rounded to the nearest thousandth?

1. $P(B)$ $^{0.512}$ **2.** $P(G)$ $^{0.488}$ **3.** $P(B, G)$ $^{0.250}$ **4.** $P(B, B, B)$ $^{0.134}$ **5.** $P(G, G, B, B)$ $^{0.062}$

Self Test 1

The letters of the word "CALCULATOR" are each printed on a separate card. A game cube has faces numbered 1 through 6. Use these cards and this game cube for Exercises 1–11.

C A L C U L A T O R

One card is selected at random. Write the probability as a ratio.

1. $P(C)$ $\frac{1}{5}$ **2.** $P(\text{vowel})$ $\frac{2}{5}$ **3.** $P(\text{not A})$ $\frac{4}{5}$ **4.** $P(\text{L or A})$ $\frac{2}{5}$ **12-1**

Draw a tree diagram to list the outcomes. Check students' diagrams.

5. Toss a coin; then roll the game cube. **12-2**
6. Choose a card; then toss a coin.

How many outcomes are there for each set of activities?

7. Choose a card; then roll the game cube. $_{60}$ **12-3**

8. Toss a coin twice; then roll the game cube. $_{24}$

Suppose you choose a card, and then toss a coin. What is the probability?

9. $P(\text{A, Heads})$ $\frac{1}{10}$ **10.** $P(\text{vowel, Tails})$ $\frac{1}{5}$ **11.** $P(\text{L or A, Tails})$ $\frac{1}{5}$ **12-4**

Self Test answers and Extra Practice are at the back of the book.   **389**

12-5 Dependent Events

Mary and Marty are twins. The 25 members of their class have decided to draw names for a gift swap at a party. If Mary draws first and Marty second, what is the probability that each will draw the other's name?

Mary draws 1 name out of 25 and does not replace the name she has drawn. Then Marty draws 1 name out of 24. This is called *drawing without replacement*. The occurrence of the first event affects the occurrence of the second. Such events are called **dependent events.**

To calculate the probability of two dependent events occurring you first determine the probability of each event separately in the order in which it occurs. Then multiply the probabilities.

Example 1 What is P(Marty, then Mary)? ◄——— *This means Marty on the first draw, and Mary on the second.*

Solution On the first draw $P(\text{Marty}) = \dfrac{1}{25}$.

On the second draw $P(\text{Mary}) = \dfrac{1}{24}$.

$P(\text{Marty, then Mary}) = \dfrac{1}{25} \cdot \dfrac{1}{24} = \dfrac{1}{600}$

Your Turn Two of the seven cubes shown are drawn at random, one after the other, without replacement. What is the probability?
- P(R, then R) $\dfrac{2}{7}$ • P(B, then R) $\dfrac{2}{7}$

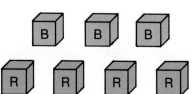

Class Exercises

A box contains 4 green, 5 red and 6 yellow marbles. If a green marble is drawn first and not replaced, what is the probability for the second draw?

1. $P(\text{green})$ $\frac{3}{14}$ **2.** $P(\text{red})$ $\frac{5}{14}$ **3.** $P(\text{yellow})$ $\frac{3}{7}$

If a red marble is drawn first and not replaced, what is the probability for the second draw?

4. $P(\text{green})$ $\frac{2}{7}$ **5.** $P(\text{red})$ $\frac{2}{7}$ **6.** $P(\text{yellow})$ $\frac{3}{7}$

If a yellow marble is drawn first and a green marble is drawn second without replacement, what is the probability for the third draw?

7. $P(\text{green})$ $\frac{3}{13}$ **8.** $P(\text{red})$ $\frac{5}{13}$ **9.** $P(\text{yellow})$ $\frac{5}{13}$

Exercises

Events A and B are dependent events. The probability of A is given, as well as the probability of B after the occurrence of A. Complete the steps to determine $P(A, \text{then } B)$.

A **1.** $P(A)$: $\frac{1}{4}$ **2.** $P(A)$: $\frac{1}{3}$ **3.** $P(A)$: 0.2
$P(B)$ after A: 0.1

$P(B)$ after A: $\frac{2}{3}$ $P(B)$ after A: $\frac{6}{7}$ $P(A, \text{then } B) = \underline{\ ?\ }$ 0.02

$P(A, \text{then } B) = \frac{1}{4} \cdot \underline{\ ?\ }$ $\frac{2}{3}$ $P(A, \text{then } B) = \frac{1}{3} \cdot \underline{\ ?\ }$ $\frac{6}{7}$

A drawer contains 6 black socks, 4 blue socks, and 2 white socks. Two socks are drawn at random without replacement. If a black sock is drawn first, determine the probability for the second draw.

4. $P(\text{black})$ $\frac{5}{11}$ **5.** $P(\text{blue})$ $\frac{4}{11}$ **6.** $P(\text{white})$ $\frac{2}{11}$

What is the probability of the given sequence of events?

B **7.** $P(\text{black, then black})$ $\frac{5}{22}$ **8.** $P(\text{black, then white})$ $\frac{1}{11}$

9. $P(\text{white, then white})$ $\frac{1}{66}$ **10.** $P(\text{blue, then blue})$ $\frac{1}{11}$

11. $P(\text{blue, then black})$ $\frac{2}{11}$ **12.** $P(\text{white, then blue})$ $\frac{2}{33}$

Two students from the class executive committee are to be president and vice president. The committee includes 5 girls (Kim, Jennifer, Lisa, Maria, and Alice) and 3 boys (John, Charles, and Nathaniel). The names are placed in a container and two are drawn at random without replacement. The first person whose name is drawn is president and the second is vice president. Find the probability.

13. P(boy, then boy) $\frac{3}{28}$ **14.** P(girl, then girl) $\frac{5}{14}$

15. P(boy, then girl) $\frac{15}{56}$ **16.** P(girl, then boy) $\frac{15}{56}$

17. P(Kim, then Charles) $\frac{1}{56}$ **18.** P(Lisa, then Nathaniel) $\frac{1}{56}$

19. P(John, then Charles) $\frac{1}{56}$ **20.** P(Maria, then Alice) $\frac{1}{56}$

Twelve cards are numbered 1 to 12 and placed in a container. Two cards are drawn at random, one after the other, without replacement. What is the probability of each sequence of draws? Let m and n represent whole numbers from 1 to 12.

21. P(10, then 3) $\frac{1}{132}$ **22.** $P(n$, then $2n)$ $\frac{1}{22}$ **23.** $P(n$, then $n+1)$ $\frac{1}{12}$

C   **24.** $P(2n$, then $2m)$ $\frac{5}{22}$ **25.** $P(n < 6$, then $m > 6)$ $\frac{5}{22}$ **26.** $P(2n$, then $2n+1)$ $\frac{5}{132}$

Problems

Encourage students to use exponential notation.

Six-digit numbers are used for license plate numbers in some states. Suppose zero is never the first digit, and that license numbers are chosen at random. Solve the problem.

1. What is the probability that no two digits will be the same? $\frac{9 \cdot 8 \cdot 7 \cdot 6 \cdot 5}{10^5}$

2. What is the probability that each digit is 1 more than the preceding digit? $\frac{4}{9 \cdot 10^5}$

3. What is the probability that all digits will be the same? $\frac{1}{10^5}$

4. What is the probability that all digits will be even? $\frac{4}{9} \cdot \left(\frac{5}{10}\right)^5$

5. What is the probability that no two digits will be the same and that all digits will be even?   0

6. Some states use a combination of letters and numbers for license plates. Suppose license plates are to have a three-digit number followed by three letters and that plates are assigned at random. What is the probability that an individual will be assigned *100-WOW*? $\frac{1}{9 \cdot 10^2 \cdot 26^3}$

12-6 Odds

A civic association is sponsoring a raffle to raise money for a children's summer sports camp. They plan to sell 2000 tickets to a local concert and will award door prizes by drawing names at random.

Summer Camp Raffle

1 First Prize: Bicycle
5 Second Prizes: Radio
10 Third Prizes: Calculator

If you buy 1 ticket, there is only 1 chance that you will win first prize and 1999 chances that you will not win first prize. We say that the **odds in favor** of your winning first prize are 1 to 1999, or $\dfrac{1}{1999}$. The **odds against** your winning first prize are 1999 to 1, or $\dfrac{1999}{1}$.

If for an event there are a favorable outcomes and b unfavorable outcomes, then the following is true.

$$\text{Odds in favor: } \dfrac{a}{b} \qquad \text{Odds against: } \dfrac{b}{a}$$

Example 1   A total of 16 prizes will be awarded in all. If you buy only 1 ticket, what are the odds of winning a prize?

Solution   Number of favorable outcomes: 16
Number of unfavorable outcomes: $2000 - 16 = 1984$

Odds in favor of winning: $\dfrac{16}{1984}$, or $\dfrac{1}{124}$

Example 2 If you do not win the first prize, what are the odds against your winning another prize?

Solution Number of favorable outcomes: 15 ◄──── *5 second prizes + 10 third prizes*

Number of unfavorable outcomes: 1984

Odds against winning second or third prize: $\dfrac{1984}{15}$

Your Turn • After the first and second prizes have been awarded, what are the odds in favor of winning a third prize? $\dfrac{5}{992}$
What are the odds against winning a third prize? $\dfrac{992}{5}$
State the answers in lowest terms.

Class Exercises

There are 10 beads in a bag. Of these, 5 are blue, 3 are red, and 2 are green. You draw one bead at random. What are the odds in favor of each draw? What are the odds against each draw?

1. red bead $\dfrac{3}{7}; \dfrac{7}{3}$ **2.** green bead $\dfrac{1}{4}; \dfrac{4}{1}$ **3.** blue bead $\dfrac{1}{1}; \dfrac{1}{1}$ **4.** red or green bead $\dfrac{1}{1}; \dfrac{1}{1}$

The odds in favor of an event are given. What are the odds against this event occurring?

5. 4 to 1 $\dfrac{1}{4}$ **6.** 3 to 10 $\dfrac{10}{3}$ **7.** 2 to 7 $\dfrac{7}{2}$ **8.** 4 to 3 $\dfrac{3}{4}$

Exercises

If you spin the spinner shown once, what are the odds in favor of each event? State the answers in lowest terms.

 A **1.** blue $\dfrac{1}{1}$ **2.** red $\dfrac{1}{2}$ **3.** yellow $\dfrac{1}{5}$
4. 3 $\dfrac{1}{5}$ **5.** 1 or 4 $\dfrac{1}{2}$ **6.** even number $\dfrac{1}{1}$

7. blue or even number $\frac{2}{1}$ **8.** blue and even number $\frac{1}{2}$

9. yellow or odd number $\frac{2}{1}$ **10.** yellow and odd number $\frac{0}{6}$

What are the odds against the event?

11. blue $\frac{1}{1}$ **12.** odd number $\frac{1}{1}$ **13.** 1 or red $\frac{2}{1}$ **14.** 1 and red $\frac{5}{1}$

The odds in favor of an event are given. Write the odds against the event.

B   **15.** $\frac{2}{3}$ $\frac{3}{2}$ **16.** $\frac{2}{1}$ $\frac{1}{2}$ **17.** $\frac{4}{5}$ $\frac{5}{4}$ **18.** $\frac{7}{10}$ $\frac{10}{7}$ **19.** $\frac{1}{n}$ $\frac{n}{1}$ **20.** $\frac{p}{q}$ $\frac{q}{p}$

The number given is the number of favorable outcomes. If there are 100 possible outcomes in all, what are the odds in favor of each event?

21. 30 $\frac{3}{7}$ **22.** 5 $\frac{1}{19}$ **23.** 80 $\frac{4}{1}$ **24.** 50 1 **25.** n $\frac{n}{100-n}$ **26.** $2a$ $\frac{a}{50-a}$

The odds against four events are given in the table.

27. Which event is least likely to occur (has the worst odds)?   A

28. Which event is most likely to occur (has the best odds)?   C

Event	Odds Against
A	10 to 1
B	7 to 3
C	5 to 4
D	9 to 2

The number given is the probability that an event will occur. If the total number of possible outcomes is 120, what are the odds in favor of each event?

C   **29.** $\frac{4}{5}$ $\frac{4}{1}$ **30.** $\frac{2}{3}$ $\frac{2}{1}$ **31.** $\frac{1}{3}$ $\frac{1}{2}$ **32.** $\frac{1}{5}$ $\frac{1}{4}$ **33.** $\frac{1}{n}$ $\frac{1}{n-1}$ **34.** $\frac{a}{b}$ $\frac{a}{b-a}$

Solve.

35. The odds in favor of an event are 3 to 5. The total number of outcomes is 10 more than the number of favorable outcomes. How many outcomes are there? What is the probability that the event will occur?   16 outcomes; $\frac{3}{8}$

36. The odds against an event are 2 to 3. The total number of outcomes is 1 less than 3 times the number of unfavorable outcomes. How many outcomes are there? What is the probability that the event will occur?   5; $\frac{3}{5}$

12-7 *Experimental Probability*

The results of an experiment repeated many times can be used to get a good idea of the probability of an event. We call the result the **experimental probability** of the event.

Experimental Probability $= \dfrac{\text{Number of favorable outcomes}}{\text{Number of experiments}}$

Experimental Probability $\approx P(\text{event})$

You can approximate the probability of an event by finding the experimental probability. A greater number of experiments usually gives a closer approximation than a lesser number of experiments.

Example 1   Pedro and his 24 classmates each tossed a coin 20 times. Pedro got 8 Heads out of 20 tosses. Altogether, the entire class counted 251 Heads out of 500 tosses. Determine $P(\text{H})$ experimentally for Pedro and for the entire class.

Solution $P(\text{event}) \approx \dfrac{\text{Number of favorable outcomes}}{\text{Number of experiments}}$

Pedro: $P(\text{H}) \approx \dfrac{8}{20} = \dfrac{2}{5}$, or 0.4

Class: $P(\text{H}) \approx \dfrac{251}{500}$, or 0.502

Your Turn   Suppose you spin a spinner 300 times. The spinner stops on red 200 times, on blue 40 times, and on yellow 60 times. What is the approximate probability?
  • $P(\text{red})$ $0.\overline{6}$ • $P(\text{blue})$ $0.1\overline{3}$ • $P(\text{yellow})$ 0.2

Example 1 illustrates an important property of experimental probability. You know that if a coin is "fair", then $P(H) = \dfrac{1}{2}$, or 0.5. In Example 1 the greater number of experiments (tosses) gave the closer approximation to 0.5. Try tossing a coin yourself 10 times, then 100 times to approximate $P(H)$. Which set of experiments gives you the better approximation?

Statistics about past events are often considered as experiments to approximate the probability of a future event. A baseball player's batting average is based on statistics of past performances. It is often used to approximate the probability of a hit the next time at bat.

Example 2   A baseball player hit the ball 48 times out of the last 150 times at bat. What is the probability that that player will hit the ball next time at bat?

Solution $P(\text{hit}) \approx \dfrac{\text{Number of hits}}{\text{Number of times at bat}}$ ⟵   *This ratio is called the "batting average."*

$P(\text{hit}) \approx \dfrac{48}{150}$, or 0.320

Your Turn   • A baseball player hit the ball 72 times out of 320 times at bat. What is the approximate probability that that player will hit the ball next time at bat?   0.225

Class Exercises

If a bottle cap is tossed in the air, it will land either "up" or "down." Use the results of these experiments to determine $P(\text{up})$ and $P(\text{down})$.

1. 50 tosses
Up: 33   0.66
Down: 17   0.34

2. 100 tosses
Up: 67   0.67
Down: _?_   33; 0.33

3. 200 tosses   0.65
Up: 130
Down: _?_ 70; 0.35

397

Exercises

A game cube is weighted so that not all outcomes are equally likely. The faces of the cube are each painted a different color. The cube is rolled 200 times and the results recorded in the table. About what is the probability of each event?

Red	Blue	White	Green	Yellow	Orange
21	30	43	76	15	15

A **1.** P(red) 0.105 **2.** P(blue) 0.15 **3.** P(white) 0.215 **4.** P(green) 0.38 **5.** P(orange) 0.075

When tossed, a paper cup can land up, down, or on its side. Four friends experimented to determine the probability of each event. Use their results for Exercises 6–20.

What is the approximate probability based on each person's experiments?

	Up	Down	Side
Pam	3	5	8
Max	4	6	14
Sue	2	3	7
Lee	6	9	15

B **6.** Pam, P(up) 0.1875 **7.** Max, P(up) $0.1\overline{6}$ **8.** Sue, P(up) $0.1\overline{6}$ **9.** Lee, P(up) 0.2
10. Pam, P(down) 0.3125 **11.** Max, P(down) 0.25 **12.** Sue, P(down) 0.25 **13.** Lee, P(down) 0.3
14. Pam, P(side) 0.5 **15.** Max, P(side) $0.58\overline{3}$ **16.** Sue, P(side) $0.58\overline{3}$ **17.** Lee, P(side) 0.5

What is the approximate probability of each event based on the total of all the experiments?

18. P(up) $\frac{15}{82}$ **19.** P(down) $\frac{23}{82}$ **20.** P(side) $\frac{22}{41}$

Problems

During the first two baseball games of the season, a player hit the ball 4 times out of 10 times at bat. During the entire season, that same player hit the ball 157 times out of 600 times at bat. Solve.

1. What is the batting average for that player for the first two games? 0.400
2. What is the batting average for that player for the season? 0.262
3. Which average is a better approximation of P(hit) for that player? Why? season
Greater number of times at bat gives a better approximation

12-8 *Using Samples*

You can approximate the probability of an event by examining a **random sample.** A sample is a relatively small set of outcomes which we analyze and from which we draw conclusions.

Characteristics of a random sample:
- Each element of the sample space is as likely to be examined as any other element of the sample space.
- The sample is large enough to reflect the variety of the sample space.

Example 1 Heidi closed her eyes and opened her Math book at random 10 times. She found photos on 5 of the 20 pages. About what is the probability of finding a photo on a given page?

Solution $P(\text{photo}) \approx \dfrac{5}{20}$, or 0.25

Your Turn
- Suppose that out of 20 pages of this book, chosen at random, you find photos on 7 pages. Based on your sample, about what is the probability of finding a photo on any given page? $\dfrac{7}{20}$
- John used his computer to obtain a random set of 50 page numbers of his textbook. He found photos on 10 of the 50 pages. Based on John's sample, about what is the probability of finding a photo on a particular page? $\dfrac{1}{5}$

The way you choose a sample is very important. Suppose you looked only at the first page of each chapter of this book. You would find a photo on each page. You might then falsely conclude that $P(\text{photo})$ is $\frac{14}{14}$, or 100%. The first page of each chapter is not a random sample.

399

We often use a random sample to draw conclusions about the entire sample space. Surveys and opinion polls are frequently conducted for this purpose.

Example 2 A new school district conducted a survey to determine the needs of its students for bike racks, bus service, and parking. The question "How do you plan to get to and from school?" was asked of 200 students. Here are the results.

Walk	55	Ride a bus	85
Ride in a car	40	Ride a bike	15
Drive a car	5		

The school district has 10,000 students. Approximately how many students plan to drive a car?

Solution Based on the survey, the probability that a student will drive is about $\dfrac{5}{200}$, or 0.025.

$$0.025 \times 10,000 = 250$$

About 250 students will probably drive.

Your Turn Approximately how many students plan to use each method of transportation to and from school?
- Walk 2750   • Bus 4250   • Bike 750

Class Exercises

A box contains 1000 marbles. A random sample of 20 marbles contains 10 red, 2 blue, 5 yellow, and 3 green marbles. Complete to approximate the number of each color marble.

1. Number of red marbles
   $P(\text{red}) \cdot 1000 = \underline{\ ?\ } \cdot 1000$ 0.5
   $= \underline{\ ?\ }$ 500

2. Number of blue marbles
   $P(\text{blue}) \cdot 1000 = \underline{\ ?\ } \cdot 1000$ 0.1
   $= \underline{\ ?\ }$ 100

Exercises

Opinions on 4 brands of toothpaste were obtained from a random sample of toothpaste users. The results are shown in the table. Based on the poll, what is the probability that an individual will prefer the brand specified?

Brand	Number Favoring
A	240
B	320
Y	160
Z	80
Total	800

A **1.** Brand A 0.3 **2.** Brand Z 0.1 **3.** Brand B or Y 0.6

The Midvale High School Student Council asked 50 randomly chosen students to vote on the name of the school mascot. The results are shown in the table. Based on the poll, what is the probability that a student will favor the name specified?

Tigers	15
Cougars	21
Bears	6
Muskrats	8

B **4.** Tigers 0.3 **5.** Cougars 0.42 **6.** Bears or Muskrats 0.28

Use the results of the Midvale Student Council survey to estimate how many of the 1200 Midvale students favor the given mascot name.

7. Tigers 360 **8.** Cougars 504 **9.** Bears or Muskrats 336

The Committee to Re-elect the Mayor randomly surveyed 60 of the 4000 Hardyville eligible voters. Of the 60, 28 favored re-electing the mayor, 20 favored Opponent A, and 12 favored Opponent B. About how many eligible voters favor each candidate?

10. Mayor 1867 **11.** Opponent A 1333 **12.** Opponent B 800

Solve. Assume that each sample is random.

13. When 50 ninth graders were questioned, 18 said they participate in a sport. About how many of the 450 ninth graders participate in a sport? 162

14. A survey indicated that 75% of Midville High School students plan to attend college. How many of the 120 students interviewed said they planned to attend college? 90

15. A grower chose 30 trees in an orchard of 1450 trees and found that fruit on 24 trees was ripe enough to pick. About how many trees in the orchard are ripe enough to pick? 1160

401

Using the Computer

You can use something called the random number function to simulate a coin tossing experiment on a computer. The following program may need to be adjusted for use on your computer to provide different results on every RUN. RUN the program several times for N = 20.

Answers will vary.
Check students' printouts.

```
  5  REM: SIMULATING TOSSING A COIN
 10  PRINT "HOW MANY TOSSES";
 20  INPUT N
 30  FOR I=1 TO N
 40  LET A=RND(1)
 50  IF A<.5 THEN 90
 60  LET T=T+1
 70  PRINT "  T"
 80  GOTO 110
 90  LET H=H+1
100  PRINT "H"
110  NEXT I
120  PRINT "H =";H,"T =";T,"H/N =";H/N
130  END
```

40 LET A=RND(1) ⟵ *To get different tosses on every RUN, you may need to alter line 40. Check the manual for your computer.*

Self Test 2

A seed package contains seeds for 6 red flowers, 6 blue flowers, 8 white flowers, and 4 yellow flowers. What is the probability for the first two seeds planted?

1. P(red, then red) $\frac{5}{92}$ **2.** P(red, then blue) $\frac{3}{46}$ **3.** P(red, then white) $\frac{2}{23}$ **12-5**

What are the odds in favor of the event for the first flower planted?

4. red $\frac{1}{3}$ **5.** red or white $\frac{7}{5}$ **6.** red, white, or blue $\frac{5}{1}$ **12-6**

A survey of 200 people showed that 60 read the paper only on Sunday and 40 read the paper every day. Approximate the probability.

7. P(read paper only on Sunday) 0.3 **8.** P(read paper every day) 0.2 **12-7**

The newspaper survey above was conducted in an area with about 12,000 people. About how many people in the area read the paper?

9. only on Sunday 3600 **10.** every day 2400 **12-8**

Algebra Practice

Write an equation. Solve.

1. The product of 304 and 465 is *b*. $(304)(465) = b$; 141,360

2. 327,012 divided by 916 is *v*. $327,012 \div 916 = v$; 357

3. The sum of 5.84, 9.473, and 6.958 is *j*. $5.84 + 9.473 + 6.958 = j$; 22.271

4. 0.208 times 0.41 is equal to *q*. $(0.208)(0.41) = q$; 0.08528

5. The difference between $20\frac{3}{8}$ and $12\frac{5}{6}$ is *h*. $20\frac{3}{8} - 12\frac{5}{6} = h$; $7\frac{13}{24}$

6. $8\frac{1}{3}$ divided by $\frac{5}{9}$ is equal to *c*. $8\frac{1}{3} \div \frac{5}{9} = c$; 15

7. The perimeter of a rectangle 6.2 m long and 5.9 m wide is *P*. $2(6.2) + 2(5.9) = P$; 24.2 m

8. The volume of a cylinder with a radius of 6 ft and a height of 20 ft is *V*. $(3.14)(6^2)(20) = V$; 2260.8 ft³

Use the distributive property to factor each expression.

9. $48x^3 - 42x^2$ $6x^2(8x - 7)$

10. $5fg + f^2g - f^2g^2$ $fg(5 + f - fg)$

11. $2r^3 - 6r^2s + 4rs^3$ $2r(r^2 - 3rs + 2s^3)$

Solve.

12. $0 = \frac{m}{3}$ 0

13. $4 - 8r = 20$ ⁻2

14. $b = 12 - 2b$ 4

15. 4% of 96 is *j* 3.84

16. 300% of 21 is *w* 63

17. 13 is $16\frac{2}{3}\%$ of *t* 78

18. $^-3h + 5 = {}^-4$ 3

19. $4 - \frac{3}{2}k > {}^-5$ $k < 6$

20. $7d + 3 < {}^-6$ $d < \frac{^-9}{7}$

Find three ordered pairs that are solutions of the given equation.

Answers may vary for Exercises 21-23. One possible answer is given for each exercise.

21. $y = x - 6$ (⁻1, ⁻7), (0, ⁻6), (1, ⁻5)

22. $y = 3x + 2$ (⁻1, ⁻1), (0, 2), (1, 5)

23. $y = 8 - 5x$ (⁻1, 13), (0, 8), (1, 3)

Write an equation and solve the problem.

24. The probability of snow today is 30%.

    The probability of snow is $\frac{2}{3}$ the probability of rain.

    What is the probability of rain today? $30\% = \frac{2}{3}x$; 45%

25. Last month the Lees spent $58.42 on clothing.
    They spent $18.79 less on clothing than on gasoline.
    How much did they spend on gasoline? $g - 18.79 = 58.42$; $77.21

Problem Solving for the Consumer

Polls and Surveys

Many ads claim that surveys have been made and that people prefer a particular product. All surveys are not necessarily good ones. Consumers should be aware of what makes a survey good and what makes a survey poor or even worthless. Here's a typical ad.

"Four out of five doctors recommend Clean Gel for deep cleaning oily skin."

There are two ways the survey could have been conducted.

One Survey	**Another Survey**
Doctors surveyed: 10	Doctors surveyed: 200
Doctors recommending Clean Gel: 8	Doctors recommending Clean Gel: 160

Study the two possible surveys.

1. In each survey, what is the ratio of doctors recommending Clean Gel to those not recommending it? $\frac{4}{1}$
2. Which survey stands the greater chance of representing the opinion of doctors in general? second survey
3. If 1000 doctors had been surveyed and the results of the survey had been the same, how many doctors would have recommended Clean Gel? 800

Let's consider an opinion poll.

> Issue: Whether or not members of the senior class at Stamford High School should be given any special privileges in buying school play or school concert tickets.

Here are results of five different polls.

	Description of Group Polled	No. of Persons Polled	"Yes" Votes	"No" Votes	"Maybe" Votes
Poll 1	members, senior class	90	82	3	5
Poll 2	members, freshman class	85	0	80	5
Poll 3	members, sophomore class	82	0	78	4
Poll 4	members, junior class	86	6	78	2
Poll 5	randomly selected students	95	24	66	5

4. If you want a poll to represent the general opinion of the school body, which poll does that best? Poll 5
5. Suppose all five polls are conducted. Which will be more reliable to use, the result of Poll 5, or the sum of the results from Polls 1–4? sum of the results from Polls 1–4
6. If 50 more seniors are asked their opinion, about how many of them will most likely vote "yes"? 46

Barnes, a candidate for mayor, comes from the south part of town. His campaign workers conducted two independent surveys. In the first survey, 120 people from the south part of town were polled. A second survey selected 150 people at random from the telephone book.

7. If you were Barnes, which survey would you trust more? telephone book survey

The results of the poll of 150 people selected at random from the telephone book are given in the table. Twelve people are undecided.

8. Set up another table to show the results of this political poll. In the last column of your table show the percent of people polled who said they were going to vote for the candidate.
9. Make a circle graph to represent the results of the poll.

Candidate	Number Favoring	
Barnes	45	30%
Lipinsky	48	32%
Nathan	33	22%
Stowe	12	8%

Check students' graphs.

Enrichment

Logical Thinking

Let's look at three key statements from a sports broadcast.

> 1: "That's right, folks, if Jones steals only one more base, then he will hold the new world record for stolen bases."
> 2: "He's done it! Al Jones has just stolen another base."
> 3: "Al Jones holds the new world record for stolen bases."

A statement in the form "If . . ., then . . ." is called a **conditional statement.** Sometimes the word "then" is understood. A conditional statement has two parts.

"If Jones steals one more base, (then) he will break the record."

| Condition | Conclusion |

The three statements above are in a special form called a **syllogism.** Syllogisms are often used in logical thinking.

Syllogism
1: If A, then B. ⟵—— *A conditional statement*
2: A ⟵—— *States that the condition is true*
3: Therefore, B. ⟵—— *Draws the conclusion*

Complete the syllogism.

1. If it is snowing, then it is cold.
It is snowing.
Therefore, __?__. it is cold

2. If $a + 6 < b + 6$, then $a < b$.
$a + 6 < b + 6$
Therefore, __?__. $a < b$

3. If a number has only two factors, itself and 1, then it is a prime number. The number 13 has only two factors, 13 and 1. Therefore, __?__. 13 is a prime number

4. If riddles are fun, then we'll talk in riddles. Riddles are fun. Therefore, __?__. we'll talk in riddles

5. If a number is a multiple of 12, it is also a multiple of 4. 48 is a multiple of 12. Therefore, __?__. 48 is a multiple of 4

6. If two triangles are similar, corresponding sides are proportional. $\triangle ABC \sim \triangle XYZ$. Therefore, __?__. corresponding sides are proportional

7. If you win the race, you will receive $1000. If you win the race, you will be on TV. If you have money and you are on TV, you will be a celebrity. You win the race. Therefore, __?__.
you will receive $1000; you will be on TV; you will be a celebrity.

Chapter Review

A bus has 30 orange seats and 20 green seats. If passengers choose seats at random, what is the probability for the first passenger?

1. P(orange) $\frac{3}{5}$ **2.** P(green) $\frac{2}{5}$ **3.** P(red) 0

4. What are the odds that the first passenger will choose a green seat? $\frac{2}{3}$

Suppose the first passenger gets off before the second passenger gets on. What is the probability that the first two passengers will select the seat colors in the order specified?

5. P(orange, orange) $\frac{9}{25}$ **6.** P(green, orange) $\frac{6}{25}$

7. P(green, green) $\frac{4}{25}$ **8.** P(orange, green) $\frac{6}{25}$

If the second passenger gets on before the first passenger gets off, what is the probability?

9. P(orange, then green) $\frac{12}{49}$ **10.** P(green, then green) $\frac{38}{245}$

11. P(orange, then orange) $\frac{87}{245}$ **12.** P(green, then orange) $\frac{12}{49}$

Jim, Joan and Jane are the first three passengers on the bus.

13. Draw a tree diagram to show all the possible combinations of passenger and seat color. Check students' diagrams.

14. How many outcomes are there in the sample space? 8

A random sample of 500 passengers shows that 300 use tokens and 200 pay with exact change. For any given passenger, what is the probability?

15. P(token) $\frac{3}{5}$ **16.** P(exact change) $\frac{2}{5}$

17. If a bus driver counts 1200 passengers a day, about how many pay with a token? 720

18. What are the odds that a passenger will use exact change? $\frac{2}{3}$

One-half of the green seats and one-half of the orange seats are next to a window. The other seats are on the aisle.

19. What is the probability that the first passenger will choose an orange seat next to a window? $\frac{3}{10}$

20. What is the probability that the first two passengers will each choose a green seat on the aisle? $\frac{9}{245}$

Chapter Test

A game cube has faces numbered 10, 20, 30, 40, 50, 60. Each letter of MATH is printed on one of four cards. Use this game cube, these cards, and the spinner shown to do the exercises on this page.

The game cube is rolled once. What is the probability, written as a ratio?

1. $P(10)$ $\frac{1}{6}$
2. P(even number) 1
3. P(odd number) 0
12-1

Draw a tree diagram to list the outcomes. Check students' diagrams.

4. Choose a card; then spin the spinner.
5. Spin the spinner; then toss a coin.
12-2

How many outcomes are there for each set of activities?

6. Roll the game cube; 18 then spin the spinner.
7. Spin the spinner twice; 36 then choose a card.
12-3

If you roll the game cube; then choose a card, what is the probability?

8. $P(10, M)$ $\frac{1}{24}$
9. $P(10$ or $20, A)$ $\frac{1}{12}$
10. $P(60,$ consonant$)$ $\frac{1}{8}$
12-4

Suppose you choose two cards, one after the other, without replacement. What is the probability?

11. $P(M,$ then A$)$ $\frac{1}{12}$
12. $P(A,$ then T or H$)$ $\frac{1}{6}$
12-5

What are the odds for each event?

13. Odds in favor of choosing the card marked A $\frac{1}{3}$
12-6
14. Odds against a multiple of 3 on the game cube $\frac{2}{1}$

You spin the spinner 12 times and it stops on red 6 times, on blue 4 times, and on yellow 2 times. What is the experimental probability?

15. P(red) $\frac{1}{2}$
16. P(blue) $\frac{1}{3}$
17. P(yellow) $\frac{1}{6}$
12-7

A survey of 120 voters shows that 60 afe in favor of a new mall, 40 oppose it, and 20 have no opinion. What is the probability?

18. P(favor) $\frac{1}{2}$
19. P(oppose) $\frac{1}{3}$
20. P(no opinion) $\frac{1}{6}$
12-8

21. If there are 10,000 voters, about how many can be expected to vote in favor of the new mall? 5000
12-9

Cumulative Review (Chapters 1–12)

Add, subtract, multiply, or divide.

1. $4\frac{3}{4} - 1\frac{1}{3}$ $\;4\frac{5}{12}$

2. $6\frac{7}{8} - 1\frac{3}{5}$ $\;5\frac{11}{40}$

3. $2\frac{1}{9} - \frac{3}{5}$ $\;1\frac{23}{45}$

4. $14.06 - 0.32$ $\;13.74$

5. $24.9 \div 0.3$ $\;83$

6. 6.7×10^3 $\;6700$

7. $63.92 \div 0.02$ $\;3196$

8. $^-6 \cdot \,^-27$ $\;162$

9. $^-1 - \,^-18$ $\;17$

10. $^-12 \div 4$ $\;^-3$

11. $^-35 \div \,^-5$ $\;7$

12. $28 - \,^-9$ $\;37$

Find the measure of the missing angle in triangle ABC.

13. $\angle A = 27°$, $\angle B = 41°$ $\;112°$

14. $\angle C = 18°$, $\angle B = 45°$ $\;117°$

15. $\angle C = 90°$, $\angle A = 40°$ $\;50°$

16. $\angle A = 104°$, $\angle C = 12°$ $\;64°$

17. $\angle C = 25°$, $\angle A = 56°$ $\;99°$

18. $\angle B = 80°$, $\angle C = 38°$ $\;62°$

Find the area.

19. rectangle $\;32.4 \text{ cm}^2$
$b = 12.0$ cm
$h = 2.7$ cm

20. triangle $\;21 \text{ in.}^2$
$b = 14$ in.
$h = 3$ in.

21. square $\;17.64 \text{ m}^2$
$s = 4.2$ m

Solve.

22. An $80 pair of ice skates is on sale at 30% off. How much will the skates cost on sale? $56

23. A child's plastic swimming pool is a cylinder in shape. It is 6 ft in diameter and 1 ft deep. What is its volume? 28.26 ft^3

24. A certain subway car used to be able to carry 80 passengers. When the seats were rearranged, there was a 15% increase in the number of passengers the car could carry. How many passengers could the subway car then carry? 92 passengers

Write an equation. Solve the problem.

$420 + m = 725$; 305 mi

25. Emily plans to drive 725 mi to visit a relative. If she drives 420 mi the first day, how far will she have to drive the second day?

26. The sum of two numbers is 693. One number is twice as great as the other. What are the two numbers? $2x + x = 693$; 231, 462

27. The Keep Our City Green Club raised money to plant trees and shrubs. Team A raised $160 more than Team B. Team C raised $70 less than Team B. Together the teams raised $1860. How much money did each team raise? $x + x + 160 + x - 70 = 1860$;
Team A, $750; Team B, $590; Team C, $520

409

13
Geometry

The art of quiltmaking often relies on the use of geometric shapes. Look carefully and you'll see squares, triangles, and windmills of various sizes hiding in the myriad shapes.

13-1 Points, Lines, and Planes

Did you know that the photos you see reproduced in books, magazines, and newspapers are made up of thousands of closely packed dots? The dots are so small and so close together that they can only be seen when the photo is enlarged.

In geometry, dots and capital letters are used to represent **points.** **Lines** are made up of an infinite number of **collinear points** (points in a line) and have no starting or ending point. We often work with parts of lines that do have endpoints; these parts are called line **segments.**

Point *A*

• *A*

A

Line *AB*

$\overset{\longleftrightarrow}{A \quad B}$

$\overleftrightarrow{AB}$

Segment *AB*

$\overline{A \quad B}$

$\overline{AB}$

Example 1   Name the points, lines, and segments in the figure.

$\overset{\longleftrightarrow}{B \quad O \quad G}$

Solution   Points: *B*, *O*, *G* ← *Points are identified by letters.*

Lines: $\overleftrightarrow{BG}$, $\overleftrightarrow{GB}$, $\overleftrightarrow{BO}$, $\overleftrightarrow{OB}$, $\overleftrightarrow{GO}$, $\overleftrightarrow{OG}$ ← *Any two points in any order can be used to name the line.*

Segments: $\overline{BG}$, $\overline{GB}$ ← *A segment is named by its endpoints. There are three different segments each with two possible names.*
$\overline{BO}$, $\overline{OB}$
$\overline{OG}$, $\overline{GO}$

A **plane** is a set of points that extends forever in all directions. We usually deal with parts of a plane as suggested by a sheet of paper or pane of glass. An actual plane does not have sides, but is often represented by a four-sided figure.

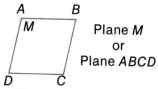

Plane *M*
or
Plane *ABCD*

When two planes intersect, their intersection is a line. If two planes do not intersect they are parallel.

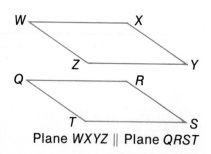

Plane *WXYZ* ∥ Plane *QRST*

Planes *ABCD* and *LMNO*
intersect in $\overleftrightarrow{PS}$

Example 2 Name the parallel planes in the figure.

Solution   Plane *MNOP* ∥ Plane *ABCD*
Plane *MPDA* ∥ Plane *NOCB*
Plane *MNBA* ∥ Plane *POCD*

Your Turn Use the figure in Example 2 to complete.
● Plane *MNBA* intersects plane *NOCB* in line ___?___ . $\overleftrightarrow{NB}$

For lines to be parallel, they must be in the same plane. Look at lines $\overleftrightarrow{AB}$ and $\overleftrightarrow{CD}$. They will never intersect but they are not parallel because they are not in the same plane. $\overleftrightarrow{AB}$ and $\overleftrightarrow{CD}$ are called **skew** lines.

Example 3 Write skew or parallel to describe the lines.
$\overleftrightarrow{TY}$ and $\overleftrightarrow{QN}$ $\overleftrightarrow{LT}$ and $\overleftrightarrow{QN}$

Solution $\overleftrightarrow{TY}$ and $\overleftrightarrow{QN}$ are skew.
$\overleftrightarrow{LT}$ and $\overleftrightarrow{QN}$ are parallel.

Your Turn   Use the figure in Example 3. Write skew or parallel to describe the lines.

• $\overleftrightarrow{BR}$ and $\overleftrightarrow{QN}$ _parallel_   • $\overleftrightarrow{MB}$ and $\overleftrightarrow{LT}$ _skew_

A **transversal** is a line that intersects two lines in two different points. If the two lines are parallel, then the transversal forms several pairs of equal angles. Angles 3 and 5, called **alternate interior** angles, are equal as are angles 4 and 6. Angles 2 and 6, called **corresponding angles,** are equal. Other pairs of equal corresponding angles are angles 1 and 5, 4 and 8, and 3 and 7.

Example 4   In the figure, $\overleftrightarrow{LM} \parallel \overleftrightarrow{NO}$, and $\angle 4 = 140°$. What are the measures of angles 8, 2, and 6?

Solution $\angle 8 = 140°$ ⟵ _Angles 4 and 8 are equal since they are corresponding angles._

$\angle 2 = 140°$ ⟵ _Angles 8 and 2 are equal since they are alternate interior angles._

$\angle 6 = 140°$ ⟵ _Angles 6 and 2 are equal since they are corresponding angles._

Your Turn   • Use the figure in Example 4. Suppose $\angle 1 = 50°$. What are the measures of angles 3, 7, and 5? _50°; 50°; 50°_

Class Exercises

1. Give three examples of models that could represent each of the following: point, line, segment, plane. _Answers may vary._

Answers may vary. One possible answer is given for each exercise.

Use the figure on the right. $\overline{RS}, \overline{ST}, \overline{UY}, \overline{YX}, \overline{ZY}$

2. Name five different segments in the figure.
3. Name three different planes. _RSTU, RSWZ, RUYZ, UTXY_
4. Name a pair of parallel lines. $\overleftrightarrow{RU}, \overleftrightarrow{ZY}$
5. Name a pair of skew lines. $\overleftrightarrow{RZ}, \overleftrightarrow{UT}$

413

Exercises

True or false? Write *T* or *F*.
For Exercises 1–5 use the figure on the right. Assume that $\overleftrightarrow{AB} \parallel \overleftrightarrow{CD}$.

A 1. Angles 1 and 5 are alternate interior angles. F
2. Angles 6 and 13 are corresponding angles. F
3. $\overleftrightarrow{AB}$ is a transversal. T
4. Angles 10 and 14 are equal. T
5. $\angle 5$ measures 110° so $\angle 1$ measures 110°. T

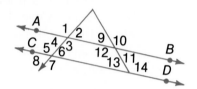

For Exercises 6–10 use the figure on the right.

6. Plane *ABCD*‖Plane *EFGH*. T
7. Planes *ABCD* and *ADHE* intersect in $\overleftrightarrow{EH}$. F
8. Lines $\overleftrightarrow{AD}$ and $\overleftrightarrow{BC}$ are skew. F
9. Planes *BCGF* and *ABFE* intersect in $\overleftrightarrow{BF}$. T
10. $\angle ADC = \angle EHG$. T

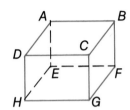

For Exercises 11–18 use the figure on the right. $\overleftrightarrow{WX} \parallel \overleftrightarrow{YZ}$.
Give the special names for the following pairs of angles.

B 11. $\angle 3$ and $\angle 9$ alternate interior 12. $\angle 6$ and $\angle 16$ alternate interior
13. $\angle 5$ and $\angle 13$ corresponding 14. $\angle 7$ and $\angle 15$ corresponding
15. Name four pairs of alternate interior angles.
16. Name eight pairs of corresponding angles.
17. $\angle 8 = 125°$ so $\angle 16 = \underline{\ ?\ }$. 125°
18. $\angle 2 = 70°$ so $\angle 12 = \underline{\ ?\ }$. 70°

15. $\angle 7, \angle 13; \ \angle 6, \angle 16; \ \angle 3, \angle 9; \ \angle 2, \angle 12$
16. $\angle 8, \angle 16; \ \angle 7, \angle 15; \ \angle 5, \angle 13; \ \angle 6, \angle 14; \ \angle 4, \angle 12; \ \angle 3, \angle 11; \ \angle 1, \angle 9; \ \angle 2, \angle 10$

Use the figure at the right for Exercises 19–24. If two lines are cut by a transversal and the resulting corresponding angles are equal, then the lines are parallel. If two lines are cut by a transversal and the resulting alternate interior angles are equal, then the lines are parallel.

Write *Yes* or *No* to tell if the information given is enough to prove that $\overleftrightarrow{AB} \parallel \overleftrightarrow{CD}$.

C 19. $\angle 14 = \angle 7$ yes
22. $\angle 12 = \angle 14$ no
20. $\angle 1 = \angle 5$ yes
23. $\angle 10 = \angle 7$ no
21. $\angle 5 = \angle 8$ yes
24. $\angle 11 = \angle 5 + \angle 6$ no

13-2 *Polygons*

A **polygon** is a closed, plane figure formed when three or more line segments are connected at their endpoints. Polygons can be concave or convex. To decide if a polygon is convex you can think of stretching an elastic band around its perimeter. If the band fits snugly, the polygon is convex. Our discussion will focus on convex polygons.

Convex Polygon   Concave Polygon

A polygon is classified by the number of its sides. The table shows some of the polygons with which you are familiar.

Name	Number of sides
Triangle	3
Quadrilateral	4
Pentagon	5
Hexagon	6
Octagon	8

A polygon in which all the sides are the same length and all the angles are equal is called a **regular polygon.**

Regular Polygons

A **vertex** is a point where two adjacent sides of a polygon intersect. When referring to a polygon, we name the vertices (plural of vertex) in order. The polygon shown could be called *LMNO* but not *OMLN*. A **diagonal** is a segment that joins two non-consecutive vertices.

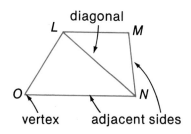

415

Example 1 Write *Yes* or *No* to tell whether the segment is a diagonal of polygon *ABCD*.

1. $\overline{AC}$
2. $\overline{AB}$
3. $\overline{CD}$
4. $\overline{DB}$

Solution　　　　　1. Yes　2. No　3. No　4. Yes

If you could arrange the angles of a triangle so they were side-by-side, you would see they form a straight angle which measures 180°. This is true of any triangle, no matter what its size. You can draw a diagonal in a quadrilateral to form two triangles. Since the sum of the angles in a triangle is 180°, you can see that the sum of the angles in a quadrilateral is twice as large or 360°. A pentagon can be divided into three triangles. So the sum of the angles of a pentagon is 3 × 180° = 540°.

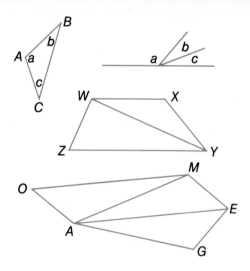

In general, the sum of the angles of a polygon with *n* sides is 180°(*n* − 2).

Example 2 What is the sum of the angles of the polygon?

Solution　　　Let *s* = the sum of the angles

Then *s* = 180°(*n* − 2) ⟵——— *Since the polygon has*
　　　　= 180°(6 − 2)　　　　 *6 sides, n = 6.*
　　　　= 180°(4)
　　　　= 720°

The sum of the angles is 720°.

Class Exercises

Is the figure a polygon? Write *Yes* or *No*. If *Yes* is it a regular polygon?

1. yes; no

2. no

3. yes; no

Exercises

True or false? Write *T* or *F*.

A **1.** A polygon has six sides. F
  2. A diagonal connects consecutive vertices in a convex polygon. F
  3. A triangle has two possible diagonals. F
  4. In a regular polygon all the sides are of equal length. T
  5. The sum of the angles of a triangle is 180°. T

Use the figure on the right for Exercises 6–9.

B **6.** Is figure *LAUNCH* a hexagon? yes
  7. Do the letters *CHLNUA* describe the figure? no
  8. How many diagonals can be drawn from vertex *C*? 3 from vertex *U*? 3
  9. Are *C* and *N* consecutive vertices? *A* and *N*? no
    yes

For Exercises 10–12 find the sum of the angles in the polygon and the measure of ∠ *y*. 540°; 113°   360°; 70°   720°; 70°

10.

11.

12.

For Exercises 13–15 find the measure of each angle of the polygon.

80°, 140°, 40°, 100°   105°, 150°, 145°, 65°, 155°, 100°   108°, 60°, 90°, 132°, 150°

C **13.**   **14.** **15.**

13-3 *Similar, Congruent Polygons*

You know from Chapter 11 that if two triangles are similar, their corresponding angles are equal and their corresponding sides are in proportion. They are the same shape but not necessarily the same size. This relationship is true for all similar polygons. We use the symbol ~ to mean "is similar to."

$ABCDE \approx FGHIJ$

← *Just think of* FGHIJ *as being upside down. Imagine flipping it over. Then it's easier to find the corresponding sides and angles.*

Corresponding Angles		Corresponding Sides	
$\angle A$ and $\angle F$	$\angle D$ and $\angle I$	$\overline{AB}$ and $\overline{FG}$	$\overline{DE}$ and $\overline{IJ}$
$\angle B$ and $\angle G$	$\angle E$ and $\angle J$	$\overline{BC}$ and $\overline{GH}$	$\overline{EA}$ and $\overline{JF}$
$\angle C$ and $\angle H$		$\overline{CD}$ and $\overline{HI}$	

Since the sides of similar polygons are in proportion, you can solve a proportion to find the length of a missing side.

Example 1 $QRSTU \sim ABCDE$
Find the length of $\overline{AE}$.

Solution $\dfrac{QR}{AB} = \dfrac{QU}{AE}$ ← *When you want to refer to the length of a segment, just write the letters without a bar above them.*

$$\frac{16}{8} = \frac{12}{n}$$

$(12)(8) = 16n$

$96 = 16n$

$6 = n$ ← $\overline{AE}$ *is 6 units long.*

Your Turn • $\triangle ABC \sim \triangle XYZ$. Find the length of side AC. 27

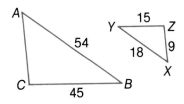

Two polygons are **congruent** if they have the same size and the same shape. We use the symbol $\cong$ to mean "is congruent to." In congruent polygons, corresponding sides are equal and corresponding angles are equal. To show congruence, corresponding parts are marked in the same way. In referring to congruent polygons it is important to pair corresponding sides in order and to list corresponding vertices in order. For the polygons on the right, the corresponding angles and sides are listed below.

Corresponding Angles

$\angle A = \angle W$
$\angle B = \angle X$
$\angle C = \angle Y$
$\angle D = \angle Z$

Corresponding Sides

$\overline{AB} \cong \overline{WX}$
$\overline{BC} \cong \overline{XY}$
$\overline{CD} \cong \overline{YZ}$
$\overline{DA} \cong \overline{ZW}$

To show that two polygons are congruent, you must show that corresponding parts are equal. When the polygons in question are triangles, it is only necessary to show that certain parts are equal to prove that the triangles are congruent.

Side-Side-Side (SSS)

If the three sides of one triangle are equal to the corresponding sides in another triangle, the triangles are congruent.

Side-Angle-Side (SAS)

If two sides and the angle between them in one triangle are equal to the corresponding parts in another triangle, the triangles are congruent.

Angle-Side-Angle (ASA)

If two angles and the side included between them in one triangle are equal to the corresponding parts in another triangle, the triangles are congruent.

If two triangles share a common segment, the segment is congruent to itself.

Example 2 Are triangles *MAD* and *HDA* congruent? Give a reason for your answer.

Solution

$\angle 1 = \angle 4$
$\angle 2 = \angle 3$
$AD = AD$ ← *Notice that $\overline{AD}$ is included between angles 1 and 3, and 2 and 4.*

The triangles are congruent by ASA ← *Angle-side-angle*

Class Exercises

Complete. Assume *MNOP* ~ *EFGH*.

1. $\dfrac{MN}{EF} = \dfrac{MP}{\_?\_}$ *EH*   2. $\dfrac{PM}{HE} = \dfrac{\_?\_}{GF}$ *ON*

3. $\dfrac{\_?\_}{PM} = \dfrac{GH}{HE}$ *OP*   4. $\dfrac{MP}{\_?\_} = \dfrac{EH}{HG}$ *PO*

Complete. Assume $\triangle ABC \cong \triangle XYZ$.

5. $AC = \_?\_$ *XZ*   6. $\angle B = \_?\_$ *∠Y*   7. $XY = \_?\_$ *AB*

8. $BC = 15$, so $YZ = \_?\_$ 15

9. $\angle C = 85°$ so $\angle \_?\_ = 85°$ *Z*

Exercises

Write *Yes* or *No* to tell if the two polygons are similar, and give a reason for your answer.

yes; corresp. sides are in proportion.   yes; corresp. sides are in proportion

A 1.

2. no

3.

The figure shown is made up of congruent polygons. Write *Yes* or *No* to tell if the statements correctly name congruent polygons.

4. $ABKL \cong EFGH$ yes   5. $BMK \cong EHM$ no

6. $ABMKL \cong FEMHG$ no 7. $EFGH \cong KHIJ$ yes

8. $BEM \cong KHM$ no   9. $KEDC \cong KEIJ$ no

10. $AFGL \cong CDIJ$ no   11. $CDEB \cong EFHG$ no

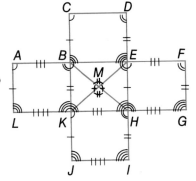

In Exercises 12-14 the pairs of polygons are similar. Find the lengths of the missing sides.

12.

10; 31.25

13.

5; 1.75

14.

2.4; 5

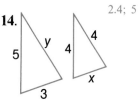

In Exercises 15-17 the pairs of polygons are congruent. List the corresponding sides and angles.

B 15.

16.

17.

Are the triangles congruent? Give a reason for your answer.

18. yes; ASA

19. yes; SSS

20. no

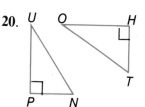

15. $\angle DAB$, $\angle BEF$; $\angle ABC$, $\angle EBC$; $\angle BCD$, $\angle BCF$; $\angle CDA$, $\angle CFE$;
$\overline{AB}$, $\overline{BE}$; $\overline{BC}$, $\overline{BC}$; $\overline{DC}$, $\overline{CF}$; $\overline{AD}$, $\overline{EF}$

16. $\angle MNP$, $\angle ONP$; $\angle NPM$, $\angle NPO$; $\angle PMN$, $\angle PON$; $\overline{MN}$, $\overline{NO}$; $\overline{NP}$, $\overline{NP}$; $\overline{PM}$, $\overline{PO}$

17. $\angle EMO$, $\angle ETR$; $\angle MOU$, $\angle TRA$; $\angle OUS$, $\angle RAP$; $\angle USE$, $\angle APE$; $\angle SEM$, $\angle PET$;
$\overline{MO}$, $\overline{TR}$; $\overline{OU}$, $\overline{RA}$; $\overline{US}$, $\overline{AP}$; $\overline{SE}$, $\overline{PE}$; $\overline{EM}$, $\overline{ET}$

13-4 Problem Solving

Many problems are difficult to solve because the words are unfamiliar, the numbers are intimidating, or because they are long and therefore just look hard.

It sometimes helps to rewrite a problem in your own words.

Example 1 On the average, the earth's temperature increases 25°C for every kilometer of depth below the earth's surface. If an oil well were drilled to a depth of 9160 m, about how much hotter would you expect the temperature at the bottom to be than at the surface?

Solution Rewrite the problem in your own words. Then change the measures of depth to the same units.
Simpler Problem—An oil well is 9.16 km deep. The temperature in it rises 25°C per 1 km of depth. How much hotter is it at the bottom of the well?
Computation—25° × 9.16 = 229°

You might also choose to reorganize the information to make it easier to use.

Example 2 Four of the elements of which the human body is made up are present in the following amounts: oxygen—65%, carbon—18%, hydrogen—10%, nitrogen—3%. What would the weight be of each in a 178 lb person?

Solution Reorganize the information to make it easier to use.

Element	Oxygen	Carbon	Hydrogen	Nitrogen
Percentage	65	18	10	3
Decimal	0.65	0.18	0.10	0.03
178 lb × %	115.7 lb	32.0 lb	17.8 lb	5.3 lb

Your Turn • Some elements are present in the body in very small amounts. They include potassium—0.35%, sulfur—0.25%, sodium—0.15%, chlorine—0.15%, magnesium—0.05% and iron—0.004%. What would be the weight of each element in a 122 lb person?

<small>potassium, 0.427 lb; sulfur, 0.305 lb; sodium, 0.183 lb; chlorine, 0.183 lb; magnesium, 0.061 lb; iron, 0.00488 lb</small>

Class Exercises

Rewrite the problem in your own words. Write *add, subtract, multiply,* or *divide* to tell how you would solve the problem.

1. The lowest land spot on earth lies 8100 ft below sea level in Marie Byrd, Antarctica. The lowest known spot in the ocean is 36,198 ft below sea level in the Pacific Ocean's Marianas Trench. About how many times deeper is the Marianas Trench? <small>divide; $4\frac{1}{2}$ times deeper</small>

2. The Helena's hummingbird, at about $2\frac{1}{4}$ in. from bill tip to tail, is the smallest bird on earth. A North African ostrich, the largest bird in the world, can reach a height of 9 ft. How many hummingbirds would it take lined up from bill tip to tail to reach the height of a 9 ft ostrich? <small>divide; 48 hummingbirds</small>

Exercises

Write a simpler problem in your own words; then solve the problem.

A 1. A chameleon can extend its tongue to a distance equal to its body length. If Cammie the chameleon is $7\frac{5}{8}$ in. long, how long would he be from tongue tip to tail, if his tongue were fully extended? <small>15.25 in.</small>

2. Though the name centipede means "100 feet", these creatures may actually have from 28 to 354 legs. Each body segment has one pair of legs and the number depends on the species. Suppose a centipede had 37 body segments. How many legs would it have? <small>74 legs</small>

B 3. Automobiles contribute heavily to pollution of the atmosphere. For every liter of gas burned, a car traveling at 40 km/h might give off many substances. They include 284.9 g of carbon monoxide, 22.2 g of nitrogen oxides, 14.8 g of hydrocarbons, 1.3 g of solid particles, and 1.0 g of sulfur oxides. If a car uses 76 L of gas in a week, how much of each type of pollutant is released into the atmosphere?

<small>carbon monoxide: 21,652.4 g; nitrogen: 1687.2 g; hydrocarbons: 1124.8 g; solid particles: 98.8 g; sulfur: 76 g</small>

423

4. In a sample of 1,000,000 parts of seawater the following dissolved minerals were found: 25,416 parts of sodium chloride, 3986 parts of magnesium chloride, 1475 parts of magnesium sulfate, and 1282 parts of calcium sulfate. What percent of the seawater does each substance account for?

sodium chloride, 2.54%; magnesium chloride, 0.40%; magnesium sulfate, 0.15%; calcium sulfate, 0.13%

Self Test 1

For Exercises 1–3 refer to the figure on the right. $\overleftrightarrow{AB} \parallel \overleftrightarrow{CD}$.

1. Name two pairs of alternate interior angles. ∠4, ∠6; ∠3, ∠5

2. ∠4 = 146° so ∠6 = __?__. 146°

3. ∠3 = 34° so ∠7 = __?__. 34°

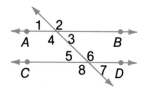

13-1

For Exercises 4 and 5 find the sum of the angles in the polygon and the measure of ∠x.

4.
   115° 540°; 43°
   130°
   x
   126°   126°

5. 108° 720°; 119°
   125° 137°
   x 103°
   —128°

13-2

In Exercises 6 and 7 the pairs of polygons are similar. Find the length of the missing side.

6.

   | 5 |
   | 16 16 |
   | 5 |

   $2\frac{1}{2}$ *b*

   8 | *b* | 8

7. 20   16   5   4   3
   8 8 12   2 2 *a*

13-3

Solve.

8. A water truck holds 650 gal of water. Due to a leak, it loses about 18 gal of water each time it makes a trip from the hydrant to a construction site. About how much water is delivered in 8 trips? 5056 gal

13-4

13-5 *Triangles*

Triangles can be classified by their angles or by their sides.

Triangles Classified by Angles

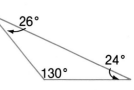

Acute Triangle   **Right Triangle**   **Equiangular Triangle**   **Obtuse Triangle**
All angles acute   One right angle   All angles equal   One angle obtuse

Triangles Classified by Sides.

Scalene Triangle   **Isosceles Triangle**   **Equilateral Triangle**
No two sides equal   At least two sides equal   All three sides equal

If a triangle is equiangular it is also equilateral.

Example 1   Name an acute, an isosceles, and a scalene triangle in the figure.

Solution

Acute triangle—*BCD* ⟵ *All angles are less than 90°.*
Isosceles triangle—*BCD* ⟵ *Sides* BC *and* BD *are equal.*
Scalene triangle—*ABD* ⟵ *No two sides are equal.*

Your Turn   Use the figure in Example 1.
- Name a right triangle. △*ACD*
- Name an obtuse triangle. △*BAD*
- Name an equilateral triangle. △*BCD*

You can use the properties of special triangles to solve problems.

Example 2   The perimeter of the triangle is 30.
Find the length of each side.

Solution   Write an equation to show that the perimeter is the
sum of the lengths of the sides.
$$x + x + 1.75x = 30 \longleftarrow \boxed{\textit{The two sides marked are equal.}}$$
$$3.75x = 30$$
$$x = 8$$
The lengths of the sides are:
$$AB = 8, \ BC = 8, \ AC = (1.75)(8) = 14$$

Your Turn   • The perimeter of $\triangle XYZ$ is 23.
Find the length of each side. 5, 11, 7

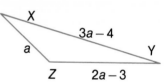

   • $\triangle MTA \cong \triangle BUS$. Is $\triangle BUS$ an
acute or obtuse triangle? acute

Class Exercises

True or false? Write *T* or *F*.

1. A right triangle can also be an obtuse triangle. F
2. An isosceles triangle can also be an equilateral triangle. T
3. An isosceles triangle can also be a right triangle. T
4. An obtuse triangle can have more than one obtuse angle. F
5. A scalene triangle can also be an equilateral triangle. F
6. If $\triangle RUN \cong \triangle HOP$, both triangles must be right triangles. F
7. If isosceles $\triangle SAM \cong \triangle TED$ and side $SA = 17$, then side
$ED = 17$. F
8. In right $\triangle SAP$, $SP = AP$. $\triangle SAP$ is an isosceles triangle. T

Exercises

Classify the triangle as acute, right, obtuse, or equiangular.

A **1.** acute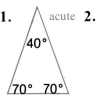
40°
70° 70°

2. right
30°
60°

3. equiangular
60°
60° 60°

4. obtuse
120° 37°
23°

Classify the triangle as scalene, isosceles, or equilateral.

5. isosceles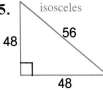
48 56
48

6. scalene
55 77
66

7. equilateral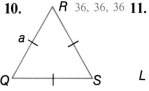
25 25
25

8. scalene
17
21 11

Find the lengths of the sides of the triangle.

9. B 9, 21, 14
$2x-5$ $3x$
A $x+7$ C

The perimeter is 44.

10. R 36, 36, 36
a
Q S

The perimeter is 108.

11. S 20, 20, 26
y
L $2y-14$ T

The perimeter is 66.

12. 6, 6, 6
60°
$2x$
60°   60°

The perimeter is 18.

13. $\triangle QED \cong \triangle MLS$. What is the measure of $\angle SML$?   70°

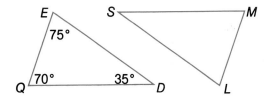

E S M
75°
70°   35°
Q D L

14. $\triangle MOP \cong \triangle BRD$. Is $\angle DBR$ acute, obtuse, or right?   obtuse

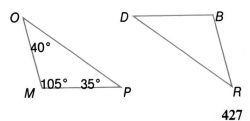

O D B
40°
105°   35°
M P R

13-6 Quadrilaterals

Many convex quadrilaterals have special properties. Some of the most common are described below.

Parallelogram— Quadrilateral with opposite sides parallel.

Rectangle— Parallelogram with four right angles.

Square— Parallelogram with four right angles and all sides equal.

Rhombus— Parallelogram with all sides equal in length

Trapezoid— Quadrilateral with exactly one pair of opposite sides parallel.

You can use what you know about congruent triangles and alternate interior angles to show that opposite sides and opposite angles of a parallelogram must be equal.

Quadrilateral *ABCD* is a parallelogram. To show that $AB = CD$ and $AD = CB$ you can go through a simple proof. Though many of the steps seem obvious, they are all necessary to form a logical conclusion.

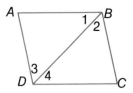

Proof: You can prove that $AB = CD$ and $AD = CB$ by showing that $\triangle ABD \cong \triangle CDB$.

Step 1. $\overline{AB} \parallel \overline{CD}$ and $\overline{BD}$ is a transversal. Therefore, $\angle 1 = \angle 4$.
Step 2. $\overline{BC} \parallel \overline{AD}$ and $\overline{BD}$ is a transversal. Therefore, $\angle 2 = \angle 3$.
Step 3. $BD = BD$
Step 4. Therefore, $\triangle ABD \cong \triangle CDB$ by ASA.

Quadrilateral *PORK* is a parallelogram.
Show that ∠*KPO* ≅ ∠*ORK* and ∠*POR* ≅ ∠*RKP*.

Proof: Step 1. $\overline{KO}$ is a diagonal that forms congruent triangles *KPO* and *ORK*.

Step 2. ∠*KPO* ≅ ∠*ORK* since corresponding parts of congruent triangles are congruent.

Step 3. $\overline{PR}$ is a diagonal that forms congruent triangles *POR* and *RKP*.

Step 4. ∠*POR* ≅ ∠*RKP* since corresponding parts of congruent triangles are congruent.

The preceding proofs allow us to make some statements about parallelograms.

A diagonal of a parallelogram divides the parallelogram into congruent triangles.

Opposite sides of a parallelogram are congruent.

If both pairs of opposite sides of a quadrilateral are congruent, the quadrilateral is a parallelogram.

Opposite angles of a parallelogram are congruent.

If two sides of a quadrilateral are both parallel and congruent, the quadrilateral is a parallelogram.

Class Exercises

True or false? Write *T* or *F*.

1. A rhombus can never be a square. F
2. All squares are rectangles. T
3. A trapezoid always has one pair of equal opposite sides. F
4. A parallelogram always has at least one right angle. F
5. Opposite sides of a parallelogram are equal. T
6. A trapezoid can be a parallelogram. F
7. A rhombus is a regular polygon. F

429

Exercises

For Exercises 1–9 refer to parallelogram *TUNA*.

A   **1.** $\triangle TUA \cong \triangle \underline{\ ?\ }$ *NAU*   **2.** $\triangle ANT \cong \triangle \underline{\ ?\ }$ *UTN*

    3. $TA = 50$ so $NU = \underline{\ ?\ }$ 50   **4.** $AN = 78$ so $UT = \underline{\ ?\ }$ 78

    5. $\angle 3 = 40°$ so $\angle 2 = \underline{\ ?\ }$ 40°

    6. $\angle TUN = 85°$ so $\angle NAT = \underline{\ ?\ }$ 85°

    7. $\angle 1 = 45°$, $\angle 3 = 40°$, so $\angle TAN = \underline{\ ?\ }$ 85°

    8. $\angle 2 = 50°$, $\angle 4 = 55°$, so $\angle ANU = \underline{\ ?\ }$ 75°

    9. $AT = 16$, $TU = 33$, so the perimeter of *TUNA* is $\underline{\ ?\ }$ 98

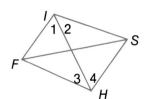

For Exercises 10–12 refer to parallelogram *FISH*. Find the value of *x*.

B   **10.** $FI = 3x + 7$, $HS = 16$ 3

    11. $FH = \dfrac{26}{x}$, $IS = 13$ 2

    12. $\angle 3 = (x - 4)°$, $\angle 2 = 48°$ 52

Self Test 2

Find the lengths of the sides of the triangle.

1.   15, 5, 15   **2.**   17, 17, 17   **3.**   6a   21, 30, 37   **13-5**

The perimeter   The perimeter   The perimeter
is 35.   is 51.   is 88.

Exercises 4–6 refer to parallelogram *LAMP*.

    4. $\triangle PAM \cong \triangle \underline{\ ?\ }$ *APL*   **13-6**

    5. $\angle 2 = 60°$ so $\angle 3 = \underline{\ ?\ }$ 60°

    6. $LP = 15$ so $AM = \underline{\ ?\ }$ 15

Algebra Practice

Write an equation. Solve.

1. 1,336,064 divided by 136 is p. $1{,}336{,}064 \div 136 = p;\ 9824$

2. 3462 multiplied by 863 is f. $3462(863) = f;\ 2{,}987{,}706$

3. The difference between 152 and 107.98 is z. $152 - 107.98 = z;\ 44.02$

4. The quotient of 0.1716 and 0.33 is b. $0.1716 \div 0.33 = b;\ 0.52$

5. The sum of $6\frac{1}{4}$ and $1\frac{2}{3}$ is m. $6\frac{1}{4} + 1\frac{2}{3} = m;\ 7\frac{11}{12}$

6. $\frac{1}{6}$ of $7\frac{1}{8}$ is equal to g. $\frac{1}{6} \cdot 7\frac{1}{8} = g;\ 1\frac{9}{48}$

7. The circumference of a circle with a radius of 5.2 m is c. $3.14(10.4) = c;\ 32.656$ m

8. The surface area of a cylinder with a radius of 3 in. and a height of 10 in. is s. $2(3.14)(3^2) + 3.14(6)(10) = s;\ 244.92$ in.^{2}

Write the LCM of each set of expressions.

9. $4x$ and y^2 $4xy^2$

10. 7, gh, and h^2 $7gh^2$

11. a^2, 10, and $4b^2$ $20a^2b^2$

Solve.

12. $\frac{1}{4}n = {}^-8$ $^-32$

13. $\frac{2}{5}x - 1 = 3$ 10

14. $1.4m = 0.4m - 3$ $^-3$

15. 30% of 72 is f. 21.6

16. 0.75% of 1000 is t. 7.5

17. 2.9 is 116% of c. 2.5

18. $\frac{^-3}{8}a - 2 = \frac{1}{4}$ $^-6$

19. $6 - 3p > \frac{^-3}{4}$ $p < \frac{9}{4}$

20. $7 < {}^-5w + 3$ $\frac{^-4}{5} > w$

What is the slope and y-intercept of the equation?

21. $y = 2x + 7$ $2;\ 7$

22. $y = 4x - 3$ $4;\ ^-3$

23. $y = 12 - 5x$ $^-5;\ 12$

Find the lengths of the sides of the triangle.

24. Perimeter 70, sides $3m - 4$, $2m + 2$, $4m$ $20,\ 18,\ 32$

25. Perimeter 82, sides $6d - 14$, $4d$, $3d + 5$ $28,\ 28,\ 26$

26. Perimeter 59, sides $j + 12$, $3j - 7$, $2j$ $21,\ 20,\ 18$

Write an equation and solve the problem.

27. Last year Riverside Motors sold 815 cars and trucks. They sold 129 more cars than trucks. How many trucks did they sell last year? How many cars did they sell last year? $(x + 129) + x = 815;\ 343$ trucks, 472 cars

Problem Solving on the Job

Insurance Broker

An insurance broker may help you choose your car insurance. There are four basic types of car insurance that most people buy.

1. *Bodily injury*—insures against accidental injuries to people.
2. *Property Damage*—insures against damage to the property of others.
3. *Collision*—insures against damage to your car.
4. *Comprehensive*—insures against loss due to fire, vandalism, or theft of property.

```
INSURANCE BROKER

DESCRIPTION: Helps individuals and
businesses choose best insurance to
suit their needs.
QUALIFICATIONS: College work is
very desirable but many agencies
will train qualified high school
graduates. Must pass a written test
to obtain a license.
JOB OUTLOOK: Demand expected to
grow as fast as the average for all
jobs.
```

The rating group depends on the make and model of the car.

If you choose a $50 deductible, you must pay the first $50 of each loss.

The age group depends on the age of the car.

		Insurance Rating Group				
		1–5	**6**	**7**	**8**	**9**	**10**
AGE		Full comprehensive					
	A	$19.60	$22.00	$26.00	$32.40	$45.60	$58.40
	B	16.40	18.40	22.00	27.60	38.80	49.60
	C	14.80	16.40	19.60	24.40	34.40	44.00
	D	12.80	14.40	16.80	21.20	29.60	38.00
		Comprehensive $50 deductible					
	A	$12.80	$15.60	$19.60	$26.40	$39.20	$52.00
	B	10.80	13.20	16.80	22.40	33.20	44.40
	C	9.60	11.60	14.80	20.00	29.60	39.20
	D	8.40	10.00	12.80	17.20	25.60	34.00
		Collision $50 deductible					
	A	$92.00	$97.20	$108.00	$124.40	$140.40	$156.80
	B	78.40	82.80	92.00	105.60	129.20	133.20
	C	69.20	72.80	81.20	93.20	10.20	117.60
	D	55.20	58.40	64.80	74.80	84.40	94.00
		Collision $100 deductible					
	A	$74.00	$83.20	$92.40	$106.30	$124.80	$143.20
	B	62.80	70.80	78.40	90.40	106.00	121.60
	C	55.60	62.40	69.20	80.00	93.60	109.60
	D	44.40	50.00	55.60	64.00	76.80	86.00

PROPERTY DAMAGE LIMITS	BODILY INJURY LIMITS			
	15/30	**25/100**	**50/100**	**100/300**
$10,000	$ 93.20	$104.00	$109.20	$120.00
$25,000	$ 97.20	$108.00	$113.20	$124.00
$50,000	$100.00	$111.20	$116.00	$127.20

A choice of 15/30 limits means the insurance company would pay a maximum of $15,000 for injuries to one person in an accident or $30,000 maximum for injuries to several people.

Complete the table.

	Customer Name / Car	Age Group	Rating Group	Limits — Bodily Injury	Limits — Property Damage	Comprehensive	Collision	Total
1. Plan 1	Smith Pronto	B	7	25/100	25,000	full	$ 50 ded.	
	Premium			$108		$ 22	$92	? $222
2. Plan 2	Smith Pronto	B	7	100/300	50,000	$ 50 ded.	$ 50 ded.	
	Premium			? $127.20		$16.80	$92	? $236
3. Plan 1	Barkley Excella	A	10	25/100	10,000	full	$ 100 ded.	
	Premium			? $104		? $58.40	? $143.20	? $305.60
4. Plan 2	Barkley Excella	A	10	50/100	50,000	$ 50 ded.	$ 100 ded.	
	Premium			? $116		? $52	? $143.20	? $311.20
5. Plan 1	Chou Mesa	D	3	15/30	10,000	$50 ded.	$ 50 ded.	
	Premium			? $93.20		? $8.40	? $55.20	? $156.80
6. Plan 2	Chou Mesa	D	3	100/300	50,000	$ 50 ded.	$ 100 ded.	
	Premium			? $127.20		? $8.40	? $44.40	? $180

Use the completed table to solve.

7. The owner of the Pronto decided to purchase Plan 1. The broker asked for a 25% deposit. How much was the deposit? $55.50

8. The owner of the Excella chose Plan 2. The broker informed her that she was entitled to a good driver discount of 15% on the BI/PD portion of her insurance. What was her total premium? $293.80

9. The owner of the Mesa chose Plan 2. He also chose to pay in 12 monthly installments. The broker told him that with interest, his monthly payments would be $17.35. How much interest is he paying? $28.20

Enrichment

Arrangements

Peaches, Muffy, and Buster are finalists in the competition for best behaved dog at the Tip Top Dog Training Center. In how many different ways can the three places be chosen?

You could list all the possibilities, but that would be pretty tedious. Instead, let's make a tree diagram to show the possible choices.

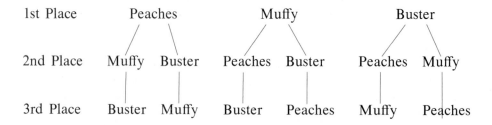

There are three possible choices for first place. Once that has been decided there are two possible choices left for second place and then one choice for third place. So there are $3 \times 2 \times 1 = 6$ possible ways to choose the three places.

1. Five contestants are entered in the Broadway Bowl-a-thon. In how many orders can the bowling lineup be chosen? 120
2. The Quincy High School Essay Contest attracted 22 entrants. In how many ways can the three prizes be awarded? 9240
3. Suppose you are buying a system of stereo components. You can choose from three different turntables, four sets of speakers, four cassette players, and five tuners. How many different four-piece systems are possible? 240
4. You just installed an electronic burglar alarm system that can only be disarmed by punching in a 4-digit code. You can choose any 4-digit code using the numerals from 0 through 9 with no repetitions. How many choices do you have? 5040
5. If 8 runners compete in a race, in how many ways can prizes be awarded for first, second, and third place? 336
6. In some states automobile license plates consist of 3 letters followed by 2 or 3 digits. How many possibilities are there for those plates with 2 digits? for those with 3 digits? 1,757,600; 17,576,000

Chapter Review

True or false? Write *T* or *F*.

1. The sum of the angles of a polygon is always 180°. F
2. A transversal intersects two lines in two different points. T
3. A diagonal of a parallelogram cuts the parallelogram into two congruent triangles. T
4. Parallel lines can also be skew lines. F
5. When two planes do not intersect they are parallel. T
6. An equilateral triangle is a regular, three-sided polygon. T
7. If you know that the three sides of △*ARK* are equal to the corresponding sides of △*RED*, you know the two triangles are congruent. T
8. You can use a compass to measure an angle. F

The triangles are congruent. Write a, b, or c to indicate the correct reason.

9.
  a. ASS
  b. SSS
  c. SAS

10. b
  a. ASA
  b. SSS
  c. SAS

The polygons are congruent. Complete to show the corresponding parts.

11. $AB = $? FE
12. $\angle BCD = \angle$? EHG
13. $BC = $? EH

Complete.
Polygon *MIST* is a rhombus.

14. $\overline{MI} \cong$? $\overline{IS}, \overline{ST},$ or $\overline{TM}$
15. $\overline{MT} \cong$? $\overline{MI}, \overline{ST},$ or $\overline{IS}$
16. $\angle T \cong \angle$? I
17. $\angle I = $? T

T ⟍105°⟍ S

Polygon *MINK* is a parallelogram.

18. $\angle IMN \cong \angle$? KNM
19. $\angle IMN = $? $\angle KNM$
20. $\angle MKN = $? $\angle MIN$
21. $\angle MIN = $? $\angle MKN$

M 55° I
K 50° N

Chapter Test

For Exercises 1–3 refer to the ∠4, ∠8; ∠3, ∠7;
figure on the right. $\overleftrightarrow{WX} \parallel \overleftrightarrow{YZ}$. ∠1, ∠5; ∠2, ∠6

1. Name four pairs of corresponding angles.   **13-1**

2. ∠2 = 50° so ∠8 = __?__ 50° and ∠4 = __?__. 50°

3. ∠1 = 130° so ∠5 = __?__ 130° and ∠3 = __?__. 130°

For Exercises 4 and 5 find the sum of the angles in the polygon and the measure of ∠t.

4. 180°; 45°   **13-2**

47°
88° t

5. 360°; 140°
75°
t
65° 80°

In Exercises 6 and 7 the polygons are similar. Find the length of the missing side.

6. 7.5   **13-3**

9   7.5
12
6

x   6.25
5   10

7. 10.5

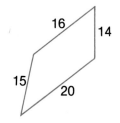
9.8 11.2
14   w
16   14
15   20

Solve.

8. In a recent year it cost 39.59¢ per mile to run a compact car. The next   **13-4**
year the cost rose 1.09¢. What percent increase was that? 2.75%

Find the lengths of the sides of the triangle.

9.   27, 45, 36   **10.**   68, 100, 100   **11.**   **13-5**
5x   y − 32   y   z + 9   25, 34, 20
3x   z
4x   2z − 30
Perimeter: 108   Perimeter 268   Perimeter 79

Exercises 12–13 refer to parallelogram
MATH.

12. $\overline{MA} \parallel$ __?__ $\overline{HT}$ 13. MH = 25, so AT = __?__ 25   **13-6**

Cumulative Review (Chapters 1–13)

Choose the best estimate.

1. The difference between 7648 and 895 c   **a.** 5000   **b.** 7500   **c.** 6700

2. The product of 38 and 195 a   **a.** 8000   **b.** 6000   **c.** 6500

3. The sum of $4.85 and $9.25 b   **a.** $13.50   **b.** $14.00   **c.** $15.00

4. $2250 minus $1105 c   **a.** 1300   **b.** 1000   **c.** 1100

5. The difference between $16\frac{3}{5}$ and $3\frac{1}{2}$ a   **a.** 13   **b.** 10   **c.** 14

6. The sum of 8427, 3592, and 1600 c   **a.** 13,000   **b.** 12,000   **c.** 14,000

For each pair of similar triangles, find n.

7.

8.

The lengths of the sides of a triangle are a, b, and c. Use the **Pythagorean Theorem to check to see if the triangle is a right triangle or not. Write *Yes* or *No*.**

9. $a = 2$ no   10. $a = 3$ yes   11. $a = 5$ no
    $b = 4$ $b = 4$ $b = 7$
    $c = 6$ $c = 5$ $c = 8$

State the probability as a fraction in lowest terms and as a percent. $\frac{1}{5}$; 20%

12. $P(A) = \frac{6}{24}$ $\frac{1}{4}$; 25%   13. $P(B) = \frac{18}{36}$ $\frac{1}{2}$; 50%   14. $P(X) = \frac{8}{40}$

Write an equation for the problem. Solve it.

15. A coach ordered jerseys for the field hockey team. She ordered twice as many size M as size S, and four more size L than size S. Altogether she ordered 16 jerseys. Let $n =$ the number of size S jerseys. How many of each size did she order? 3 small, 6 medium, 7 large

16. When you double a number and add 35, the result is 23. What is the original number? −6

14
Programming in BASIC

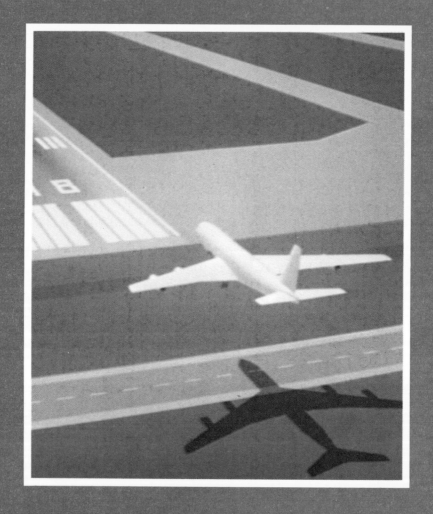

Fasten your seatbelts! Though this picture looks real, it was actually generated by a computer without a single pen stroke by an artist.

14-1 Symbols and Line Numbers

Sets of instructions called programs are used to communicate with computers. You will be learning a language called BASIC. There are many similar though distinctly different versions of BASIC. The language demonstrated in this chapter covers many common statements and uses common punctuation.

The BASIC symbols for arithmetic operations are given below.

Operation	BASIC Symbol	Expression	BASIC Expression
Addition	+	$4 + 3$	$4+3$
Subtraction	−	$10 - 6$	$10-6$
Multiplication	*	$8 \cdot 8$	$8*8$
Division	/	$12 \div 4$ or $\frac{12}{4}$	$12/4$
Exponentiation	↑, or ∧, or **	5^2	$5↑2$, or $5∧2$, or $5**2$

Programs are written one line at a time. Each line is numbered and usually contains only one instruction. Line numbers can be any number from 1 to 99999. PRINT commands are used to tell the computer to perform calculations and print the results.

Example 1   Write the output for the program.
```
10  PRINT  13.4*17.5
20  END
```
This statement tells the computer to multiply two numbers.
This statement tells the computer that the program is over.

Solution   When you type RUN, the computer will execute the program. The output will be 234.5.

Your Turn   Write a program to compute the following:

- $26.7 \div 15.25$ ● 4^6
```
10  PRINT 26.7/15.25        10  PRINT 4↑6
20  END                     20  END
```
Programs usually have many lines of instructions. They are usually numbered in multiples of 10 or 100 to allow the programmer to insert new lines in the correct sequence without renumbering the lines.

Example 2 Write the output for the program.
```
10  PRINT  1+2+3
20  PRINT  2*57
30  END
15  PRINT  1.75/25
```

Solution 6

0.07 ◄――――― *The computer calculates line 15 in order between lines 10 and 20.*

114

Your Turn Write the output for the program. 48
- `10  PRINT  15-9`   6
- `20  END`   1.8
- `15  PRINT  18/10`
- `5  PRINT  16*3`

When a statement contains more than one operation a computer follows these rules:
1. Perform all operations within parentheses.
2. Perform all exponentiations.
3. Do all multiplications and divisions in order from left to right.
4. Do all additions and subtractions in order from left to right.

Example 3 Write the output for the program.   **Solution** 3
```
10  PRINT  5-6/3
20  PRINT  3*(8-5)
30  PRINT  (2+3)/(4*5)
40  END
```
9

0.25

Class Exercises

Write the expression using BASIC symbols.

(17−2)*3

1. 3×4 3*4   **2.** 16^3 16↑3   **3.** $a \div 6$ a/6   **4.** $(17 - 2) \times 3$

Write the output for the program.

5. 10 PRINT 15+32+61 108
   20 PRINT 18/6   330
   30 END   3
   15 PRINT 11*3*10

6. 10 PRINT 48−29 141
   20 END   19
    5 PRINT 47*3   70
   15 PRINT 19+51 512
   16 PRINT 8↑3

Exercises

Write the expression using BASIC symbols.

A 1. $2x - 7$ 2*x−7   2. $\dfrac{2}{a^3}$ 2/a↑3   3. $\dfrac{1}{2}bh$ 1/2*b*h

   4. $\dfrac{a}{2} + b^5$ a/2+b↑5

5. $\dfrac{a}{2} + \dfrac{b}{3}$ a/2+b/3   6. $3.14r^2$ 3.14*r↑2   7. $\dfrac{xy}{z}$ x*y/z

   8. $\dfrac{1}{2} + 4\dfrac{1}{5}y$ 1/2+(4+1/5)*y

Write the output for the program.

9. 10 PRINT 3+6/2   6
   20 PRINT 3+5*6.1   33.5
   30 PRINT 1−7/28+4*2   8.75
   40 PRINT −5+9*4   31
   50 END

10. 10 PRINT (3+6)/2   4.5
    20 PRINT (3+5)*6.1   48.8
    30 PRINT (9−1)/(28+4)*2 0.5
    40 PRINT −(5+9)*4   −56
    50 END

Write a BASIC program to compute the value of the expression.

B 11. $1 \times 2 \times 3$ 10 PRINT 1*2*3   20 END
  12. $\dfrac{18}{36}$ 10 PRINT 18/36   20 END
  13. $512 - 367$ 10 PRINT 512−367   20 END
  14. $396 + 405 + 271$ 10 PRINT 396+405+271   20 END

15. Write a program that computes the circumference of a circle with
a radius of 7.2. Use 3.14 to approximate π.   10 PRINT 3.14*2*7.2   20 END

Challenge

Write the output for the following program.

10 PRINT 8+4↑2/2*3−5 27
20 END

10 PRINT (8+4)↑2/2*3−5
10 PRINT 8+4↑2/2*(3−5)
10 PRINT 8+4↑2/(2*3−5)

Show the different ways in which one set of parenthesis could be
added to line 10 to produce the following outputs: 211, −8, 24

14-2 REM, LET, and PRINT

You can use a REMARK (REM) statement to state what a program or part of a program is supposed to do. These statements are numbered within the program and are printed only when the program is listed. They do not interfere with or have any effect on the execution of the program. LET statements are used to assign a value to a variable.

Example 1 Write a program to calculate the circumference of a circle with a radius of 2.75.

Solution
```
10  REM CALCULATE THE CIRCUMFERENCE OF A CIRCLE
15  REM FORMULA FOR CIRCUMFERENCE IS C=2*PI*R
20  LET P = 3.14  ←——— P stands for π.
30  LET R = 2.75  ←——— R stands for radius.
40  PRINT 2*P*R
50  END
```

You may use any letter to stand for a variable. Always be sure that the assigned value of a variable is on the right of the equal sign. The statement LET A + B = C is not valid, but LET C = A + B is.

You can use quotation marks around any group of words, numbers, or symbols that you want printed exactly as they appear.

Example 2 Write the output for the program.
```
10  REM CALCULATE THE AREA OF A RECTANGLE
20  LET L = 12.5
30  LET W = 5.7
40  LET A = L*W
50  PRINT "THE AREA OF THE RECTANGLE IS" A
60  END
```

Solution
```
The area of the rectangle   ←——— The computer prints
is 71.25.                          what is in the quotes
                                   and the value of A.
```

If a program contains an error or "bug" the computer cannot complete execution. Some type of error message will be printed to tell you at which line and why execution was halted.

Example 3 Debug the program.

```
10  REM CALCULATE INTEREST
20  LET P = 100
30  LET R = 0.15
40  LET 2 = T
50  PRINT "INTEREST IS $" P*R*T
60  END
```

Solution Line 40 is incorrect. It should read

```
40  LET T = 2
```

Your Turn Write the output for the program.

THE AREA IS 70.56

```
•  5   REM AREA OF A SQUARE
   10  LET S = 8.4
   20  LET A = S↑2
   30  PRINT "THE AREA IS" A
   40  END
```

```
10  LET A=50
30  LET C=35
```

Debug the program.

```
•  10  LET 50 = A
   20  LET B = 65
   30  LET 35 = C
   40  PRINT A+B+C
   50  END
```

Use a comma or a semicolon to separate variables in a PRINT statement when you want more than one calculation printed on the same line.

Example 4 Write the output for the program.

```
 5   REM CIRCUMFERENCE AND AREA OF A CIRCLE
10   LET P = 3.14
20   LET R = 7.2
30   LET C = 2*P*R
40   LET A = P*R↑2
50   PRINT C, A
60   END
```

Solution 45.216   162.7776

Class Exercises

Write the output for the program.

THE PERIMETER IS 25.2

1. 5 REM PERIMETER OF A SQUARE
10 LET S = 6.3
20 LET P = 4*S
30 PRINT "THE PERIMETER IS" P
40 END

THE AREA IS 134.56

2. 5 REM AREA OF A SQUARE
10 LET S = 11.6
20 LET A = S↑2
30 PRINT "THE AREA IS" A
40 END

Exercises

Write the output for the program.

A

1. 10 LET X = 5.7+4.8 10.5
20 LET Y = X/5   2.1
30 LET Z = Y-1.5 0.6
40 PRINT X, Y, Z
50 END

THE SUM IS 220.6

2. 10 LET X = 12.3-9.7
20 LET Y = 4.36/0.02
30 LET Z = X+Y
40 PRINT "THE SUM IS" Z
50 END

3. 10 LET E = 7.8 3.3
20 LET F = 4.5 35.1
30 LET X = E-F 38.4
40 LET Y = E*F
50 PRINT X, Y, X+Y
60 END

THE AVERAGE IS 75

4. 10 LET X = 51
20 LET Y = 78
30 LET Z = 96
40 LET M = (X+Y+Z)/3
50 PRINT "THE AVERAGE IS" M
60 END

B

THE VOLUME IS 301.44

5. 10 LET P = 3.14
20 LET R = 4
30 LET B = P*R↑2
40 LET H = 6
50 LET V = B*H
60 PRINT "THE VOLUME IS" V
70 END

6. 10 LET N = 125   PURCHASE PRICE IS 1622.50
20 LET P = 12.98 TAX IS 64.90
30 LET C = N*P   TOTAL COST IS 1687.40
40 LET T = 0.04*C
50 PRINT "PURCHASE PRICE IS" C
60 PRINT "TAX IS" T
70 PRINT "TOTAL COST IS" T+C
80 END

7. Change the program in Exercise 5 so that it computes the volume of a cone. Use the same values for R and H. Change line 50 to 50 LET V=B*H/3

8. Change the program in Exercise 6 so that a 25% discount is deducted from the purchase price before the tax is computed. Change line 30 to 30 LET C=N*P*0.75

Debug the program.

9.
```
 5  REM AVERAGE SCORE
10  LET A = 96
20  LET B = 85
30  LET C = 73
40  LET AVG = A+B+C/3
50  PRINT "THE AVERAGE SCORE IS" AVG
60  END
```
40 LET M=(A+B+C)/3
50 PRINT "THE AVERAGE SCORE IS" M

10.
```
 5  REM DISTANCE FORMULA
10  LET R = 85
20  LET T = 17
30  LET R*T = D
40  PRINT "THE DISTANCE IS"
45  PRINT D, "MI"
50  END
```
Delete 45
30 LET D=R*T
40 PRINT "THE DISTANCE IS"; D

Write the BASIC program. Check students' programs.

C 11. Write a program to compute the area of a circle with a radius of 2.6. Use at least one REM statement and one LET statement and one PRINT statement with quotation marks.

12. Write a program to compute the area of a triangle with a base of 8.2 and a height of 3.5. Use at least one REM statement and one LET statement and one PRINT statement with quotation marks.

13. Write a program to compute the area and perimeter of a rectangle with length 9.4 and width 6.2. Have the values of the area and perimeter printed on one line.

14. Write a program that prints the sum, difference, product, and quotient of two numbers A and B. Use A = 17.2 and B = 12.5. Have the values printed on one line.

Using the Calculator

To find the square root of a number, make a guess and divide the number by your guess. If the quotient is more than your guess, then guess higher. If the quotient is less than your guess, guess lower.

Use this method to find the square root of each of the following perfect squares.

1. 529 23
2. 1156 34
3. 2304 48
4. 11236 106
5. 5329 73
6. 4489 67

14-3 FOR-NEXT

You can use a FOR-NEXT statement when you want the computer to repeat an operation for a certain number of times using the same or different values for a variable.

Example 1 Write the output for the program.

```
10  FOR X = 1 TO 3
20  PRINT "MATH IS FUN"
30  NEXT X
40  END
```

This statement combined with line 30 creates a loop. It tells the computer to loop back and repeat line 20 three times.

Solution
```
MATH IS FUN
MATH IS FUN
MATH IS FUN
```

Example 2 Write the output for the program.

```
10  FOR A = 1 TO 5
20  PRINT "3 PLUS" A "=" 3+A
30  NEXT A
40  END
```

This FOR-NEXT statement uses the changing value of the variable as a counter.

Solution
```
3 PLUS 1 = 4
3 PLUS 2 = 5
3 PLUS 3 = 6
3 PLUS 4 = 7
3 PLUS 5 = 8
```

Your Turn Write the output for the program.

- ```
  10  FOR N = 1 TO 4
  20  PRINT 5*N
  30  NEXT N
  40  END
  ```
  ```
   5
  10
  15
  20
  ```

- ```
  10  FOR N = 6 TO 11
  20  PRINT N "TIMES 2 =" N*2
  30  NEXT N
  40  END
  ```
  ```
   6 TIMES 2 = 12
   7 TIMES 2 = 14
   8 TIMES 2 = 16
   9 TIMES 2 = 18
  10 TIMES 2 = 20
  11 TIMES 2 = 22
  ```

You can also use a FOR-NEXT statement to count by numbers other than 1.

Example 3 Write the output for the program.

```
 5  REM RAISE NUMBERS TO THE THIRD POWER
10  FOR N = 1 TO 10 STEP 3 ←— The STEP 3 command tells
20  PRINT N, N↑3                the computer to add 3 to
30  NEXT N                      the previous value of N, to
40  END                        a maximum of 10, each time
                                a loop is made.
```

Solution

1	1
4	64
7	343
10	1000

At each step the computer adds 3 to the variable before raising to the third power.

Your Turn Write the output for the program.

*
```
10  FOR N = 10 TO 20 STEP 2
20  PRINT N, N-6
30  NEXT N
40  END
```

10	4
12	6
14	8
16	10
18	12
20	14

*
```
10  FOR X = 10 TO 40 STEP 10
20  PRINT X, X/5
30  NEXT X
40  END
```

10	2
20	4
30	6
40	8

Class Exercises

For each program tell how many loops the computer will make.

1.
```
10  FOR N = 1 TO 25   25
20  PRINT N+3
30  NEXT N
40  END
```

2.
```
10  FOR N = 15 TO 19   5
20  PRINT N*6
30  NEXT N
40  END
```

3.
```
10  FOR N = 1 TO 20 STEP 5   4
20  PRINT N/2
30  NEXT N
40  END
```

4.
```
10  FOR N = 50 TO 100 STEP 5   11
20  PRINT (N/10)*6
30  NEXT N
40  END
```

Exercises

Write the output for the program.

A 1.
```
10  FOR A = 1 TO 6
20  PRINT A+5
30  NEXT A
40  END
```
6
7
8
9
10
11

B 3.
```
10  FOR Y = 7 TO 14 STEP 2
20  PRINT Y
30  NEXT Y
40  END
```
7
9
11
13

5.
```
10  FOR L = 5 TO 10
20  LET W = 15
30  LET A = L*W
40  PRINT A
50  NEXT L
60  END
```
75
90
105
120
135
150

2. 5 squared = 25   6 squared = 36
7 squared = 49   8 squared = 64
9 squared = 81   10 squared = 100

2.
```
10  FOR M = 5 TO 10
20  PRINT M "SQUARED =" M↑2
30  NEXT M
40  END
```

4.
```
10  FOR N = 20 TO 32 STEP 4
20  PRINT N/4
30  NEXT N
40  END
```
5
6
7
8

6.
```
10  FOR R = 8 TO 20 STEP 4
20  LET P = 3.14
30  LET A = P*R↑2
40  PRINT A
50  NEXT R
60  END
```
200.96
452.16
803.84
1256

7. Change the program in Exercise 5 so that the value of L varies from 20 to 30. 10 FOR L=20 to 30

8. Change the program in Exercise 6 so that the values of R are 5, 10, 15, and 20. 10 FOR R=5 to 20 STEP 5   Check students' programs for Exercises 9–11.

C 9. Write a program to print out the multiples of 6 from six to ninety.

10. Write a program to calculate the cubes of the first ten odd integers.

11. Write a program to calculate the distance traveled at a constant rate of 55 mph for 3, 6, 9, and 12 hours. Use the formula *d = rt*.

14-4 *Problem Solving*

Flowcharts are frequently used by computer programmers to set forth the logical steps involved in completing a program. Flowcharts are also useful in laying out the logical process needed to solve many types of problems.

Example   Suppose you want to write a program to have the computer read the lengths and widths of several rectangles and print out the perimeters if they are greater than 50. Draw a flowchart to show the steps needed to write the program.

Solution

Your Turn   • Draw a flowchart for a program that reads the length of the side of a square and prints the area if it is greater than 45. Check students' flowcharts.

Class Exercises

Correct the flowcharts. Check students' flowcharts.

1.

2.

Exercises

Draw a flowchart to show the steps needed to complete the activity or solve the problem. Check students' flowcharts.

A
1. Get ready for school.
2. Read a number *N* and compare it to 100. Then print *N is greater than 100, N equals 100,* or *N is less than 100* depending on the results of the comparison.
3. Read a temperature *T* (in Fahrenheit degrees). Print *no jacket* if *T* is greater than 60, *light jacket* if *T* is between 40 and 60, and *bundle up* if *T* is less than 40.

B
4. Read the measures of the three angles of a triangle and print acute or obtuse.
5. Compute the interest *I* for a loan with principal *P* and rate of interest *R*.
6. Read three numbers and print the greatest of the three.
7. Read a test score T and print *excellent* if T is greater than 90, *good* if T is from 80 to 90, *fair* if T is from 70 to 80, and *work harder* if T is less than 70.

Write a program for the flowchart. Check students' programs.

C 8.

9.

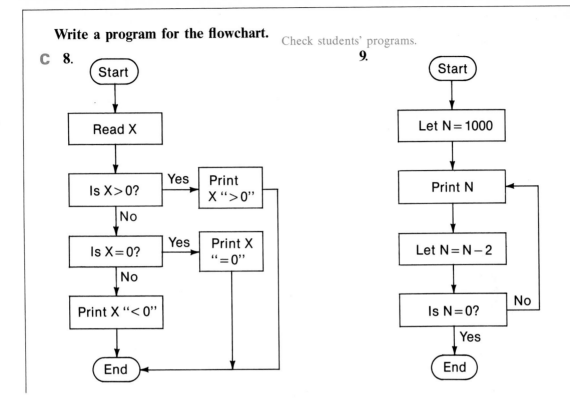

Self Test 1

Write a BASIC program to compute the value of the expression. 10   PRINT 4↑2+5↑3
    20   END

1. 48 ÷ 6   10   PRINT 48/6   **2.** (3 + 7) ÷ 2   10   PRINT (3+7)/2   **3.** $4^2 + 5^3$ **14-1**
    20   END   20   END

Write the output for the program.

4.
```
10  LET A = 3.5
20  LET B = 6.8
30  LET C = A*B
40  PRINT A, B, C
50  END
```
3.5
6.8
23.8

5.
```
10  REM CALCULATE PERIMETER
20  LET L = 25
30  LET W = 50
40  LET P = 2*L+2*W
50  PRINT L, W, P
60  END
```
25
50
150

14-2

6. Write a BASIC program to print the even numbers from 20 to 30. Check students' programs. **14-3**

7. Make a flowchart to show the steps involved in computing a total purchase price for items that qualify for a 20% discount and are subject to a 3% sales tax. Check students' flowcharts. **14-4**

Self Test answers and Extra Practice are at the back of the book.

14-5 READ . . . DATA, GOTO

In addition to LET statements you can use a combination of READ and DATA statements to assign values to variables. Whenever a READ statement appears, the computer looks for a DATA statement to determine the value of the variables. It then sequentially assigns one data value to each variable until it runs out of variables or data.

Example 1   Write the output for the program.

```
10   READ X, Y, Z
20   LET A = (X+Y+Z)/3
30   PRINT "YOUR AVERAGE IS" A
40   DATA 126,153,162
50   END
```

The computer assigns 126 to X, 153 to Y, and 162 to Z.

Solution   YOUR AVERAGE IS 147

You can use a GOTO statement to form a loop and have the computer repeat the same calculations on several items of data.

Example 2   Write a program using READ . . . DATA, and GOTO statements that calculates and prints the average of three bowling scores for each of 3 bowlers. The bowling scores are:

Bowler 1: 126, 153, 162   Bowler 2: 215, 189, 196
Bowler 3: 143, 165, 170

Solution

```
10   READ X, Y, Z
20   LET A = (X+Y+Z)/3
30   PRINT "THE AVERAGE SCORE IS" A
40   GOTO 10
50  DATA 126,153,162
55  DATA 215,189,196
60  DATA 143,165,170
70  END
```

The computer will continue to loop back to line 10 as long as DATA values are available.

Example 3 Write the output for the program in Example 2.

Solution
```
THE AVERAGE IS 147
THE AVERAGE IS 200
THE AVERAGE IS 159.3333
OUT OF DATA IN LINE 10
```

Your Turn Write the output for the program.
```
• 10  READ L, W
  15  REM FORMULA FOR PERIMETER IS 2L+2W
  20  LET P = 2*L+2*W
  30  PRINT "PERIMETER IS" P
  40  DATA 15,8
  50  END
```
PERIMETER IS 46

Class Exercises

Write the output for the program.

PERIMETER IS 120
1.
```
10  READ L, W
20  LET P = 2*L+2*W
30  PRINT "PERIMETER IS" P
40  DATA 15, 8
50  END
```

AREA IS 78.5
2.
```
10  READ P, R
20  LET A = P*R↑2
30  PRINT "AREA IS" A
40  DATA 3.14, 5
50  END
```

Exercises

Delete lines 10 and 20   Delete lines 10 and 20

Rewrite the program so that it uses READ . . . DATA to assign values
to variables.

5 READ A, B   5 READ L, W
35 DATA 15, 12.7   45 DATA 10.5, 7.28

A **1.**
```
10  LET A = 15
20  LET B = 12.7
30  PRINT B-A, B/A, A↑2
40  END
```

2.
```
10  LET L = 10.5
20  LET W = 7.28
30  LET A = L*W
40  PRINT "AREA IS" A
50  END
```

Write the output for the program.

3.
```
10   READ S
20   LET P = 4*S
30   LET A = S↑2
40   PRINT "PERIMETER IS" P
50   PRINT "AREA IS" A
60   GOTO 10
70   DATA 5,13,7.3
80   END
```

PERIMETER IS 20
AREA IS 25
PERIMETER IS 52
AREA IS 169

PERIMETER IS 29.2
AREA IS 53.29
OUT OF DATA IN LINE 10

4.
```
10   READ L, W
20   LET P = 2*L+2*W
30   PRINT "PERIMETER IS" P
40   GOTO 10
50   DATA 10,7.1,18,12
60   DATA 100,82.5
70   END
```

4. PERIMETER IS 34.2
PERIMETER IS 60
PERIMETER IS 365
OUT OF DATA IN LINE 10

B **5.** Write a program using READ . . . DATA and GOTO that computes the area of four rectangles. Use the following dimensions:

Length	5.2	92.3	17	2.25
Width	3.9	80	11	1.4

```
10   READ L, W     50   DATA 5.2, 3.9, 92
20   LET A=L*W     60   DATA 17, 11, 2.25
30   PRINT "AREA IS"; A
40   GOTO 10          70   END
```

6. Write a program using READ . . . DATA AND GOTO that computes the squares of the integers from 1 to 30. Each line of the output should show the integer and its square. Check students' programs.

Example The fifth line should be   5   25

C **7.** Avon Rental Company rents panel trucks for $45.95 per day plus $.29 per mile. Write a program using READ . . . DATA AND GOTO statements to find the cost for each rental: Check students' programs.

Number of days	2	1	1	3	4
Miles	350	120	85	645	2120

14-6 More READ . . . DATA, GOTO

You can use the statements you have learned thus far to write many programs.

Example   The following program finds a certain percent of a given number. What is the output?
```
10  READ P, N
20  LET X = P/100*N
30  PRINT P "PERCENT OF" N "IS" X
40  GOTO 10
50  DATA 54,65,125,80,16,40,4.5,152,0.08,1386
60  END
```

Solution
```
54 PERCENT OF 65 IS 35.1
125 PERCENT OF 80 IS 100
16 PERCENT OF 40 IS 6.4
4.5 PERCENT OF 152 IS 6.84
0.08 PERCENT OF 1386 IS 1.1088
OUT OF DATA IN LINE 10
```

Your Turn   Write the output for the above program if line 50 is replaced with the following:
```
50  DATA 45,90,12,150,6.8,200
```
45 PERCENT OF 90 IS 40.5
12 PERCENT OF 150 IS 18
6.8 PERCENT OF 200 IS 13.6

Class Exercises

Solve.

1. 58 is what percent of 80?   72.5%

2. 4.5 is 15% of what number?   30

3. 3 is what percent of 450? $0.66\frac{2}{3}\%$

4. 90 is 225% of what number?   40

5. 18 is what percent of 24?   75%

6. 375 is 40% of what number?   937.5

Exercises

Write the output for the program.

A **1.**
```
10   READ N, D
20   LET P = N/D*100
30   PRINT N "IS" P "PERCENT OF" D
40   GOTO 10
50   DATA 72,48,35,70,75,150,90,120
60   END
```
72 IS 150 PERCENT OF 48
35 IS 50 PERCENT OF 70
75 IS 50 PERCENT OF 150
90 IS 75 PERCENT OF 120
OUT OF DATA IN LINE 10

2.
```
10   READ A, B
20   LET N = A/B*100
30   PRINT A "IS" B "PERCENT OF" N
40   GOTO 10
50   DATA 18,0.15,16,0.25,26.88,0.56
60   END
```
18 IS 0.15 PERCENT OF 12000
16 IS 0.25 PERCENT OF 6400
26.88 IS 0.56 PERCENT OF 4800
OUT OF DATA IN LINE 10

In BASIC, the square root of a number x may be written SQR(x).

Example   If $x = 9$, then $SQR(x) = 3$.

Write the output for the program.

B **3.**
```
10   READ X
20   PRINT X, SQR(X)
30   GOTO 10
40   DATA 1,4,9,16,25,36,49
50   END
```
1	1
4	2
9	3
16	4
25	5
36	6
49	7

OUT OF DATA IN LINE 10

4.
```
10   READ A, B
20   LET Y = A*B
30   PRINT SQR(Y)
40   GOTO 10
50   DATA 4,9,27,3,5,125,2,8
60   END
```
6
9
25
4

OUT OF DATA IN LINE 10

The following program approximates the length of the hypotenuse, C, for a right triangle with legs of lengths A and B. Partial answer is given.

5.
```
10   READ A, B
20   LET C = SQR (A↑2+B↑2)
30   PRINT "THE LEG LENGTHS ARE" A, B
40   PRINT "THE LENGTH OF THE HYPOTENUSE IS" C
50   GOTO 10
60   DATA 12,5,8,6,8,15,2,2,15,20
70   END
```
THE LEG LENGTHS ARE 12 5
THE LENGTH OF THE HYPOTENUSE IS 13
THE LEG LENGTHS ARE 8 6
THE HYPOTENUSE IS 10

For exercises 6, 7 use the figure and DATA from Exercise 5. You may wish to refer to Chapter 11 to review the trigonometric functions.

Check students' programs.

C **6.** Write a program to compute tan D. What is the output?

7. Write a program to compute sin D. What is the output?

14-7 Branching: IF . . . THEN

It is possible to tell the computer to jump to some other line in the program under certain conditions. This is called branching. The GOTO statement is one type of branching statement. An example of another kind of branching instruction, IF . . . THEN, is shown below.

Example 1   What is the output for the program?
```
10  READ X, Y, Z
20  LET A = (X+Y+Z)/3
30  PRINT "YOUR AVERAGE TEST SCORE IS" A
40  IF A<60 THEN 70
50  PRINT "YOU ARE PASSING"
60  DATA 80,71,65
70  END
```

When A < 60 is true, the computer will go to line 70; otherwise it will execute the next line in the program.

Solution   YOUR AVERAGE TEST SCORE IS 72
YOU ARE PASSING.

Your Turn   Write the output for the program in Example 1 if line 60 is changed to the following: YOUR AVERAGE TEST SCORE IS 55
```
60  DATA 53,70,42
```

You can use IF . . . THEN statements to compare data by using any of the following relations.

Symbol	Meaning
$<$	less than
$>$	greater than
$<=$	less than or equal to
$>=$	greater than or equal to
$=$	equal to
$<>$	not equal to

Example 2 Any three numbers *a*, *b*, and *c* that satisfy the equation
$a^2 + b^2 = c^2$, are called Pythagorean Triples.
Write the output for the program.
```
10  READ A, B, C
20  IF C↑2 = A↑2+B↑2 THEN 40
30  GOTO 10
40  PRINT A, B, C "ARE PYTHAGOREAN TRIPLES"
50  GOTO 10
60  DATA 3,4,5,5,12,14,6,9,10,8,15,17
70  END
```

Solution
```
3, 4, 5 ARE PYTHAGOREAN TRIPLES
8, 15, 17 ARE PYTHAGOREAN TRIPLES
OUT OF DATA IN LINE 10
```

Your Turn What would be the output above if line 60 had the following data? 60 DATA 6,8,10,9,10,20
6, 8, 10 ARE PYTHAGOREAN TRIPLES
OUT OF DATA IN LINE 10

Class Exercises

Let *A* = 5 and *B* = 8. **Write the line number that will be executed
after the IF . . . THEN statement.**

1. 20 IF A>6 THEN 40 ³⁰
    30 PRINT A

2. 30 IF A+B>=12 THEN 60 ⁶⁰
    40 PRINT A+B

Exercises

Write the output for the program.

A 1.
```
10  READ X
20  IF X<=0 THEN 40
30  PRINT X
40  GOTO 10
50  DATA −1.5,0,7.1,−2,4.7,6,−3.2,−4.5,3.9,17.2
60  END
```
7.1
4.7
6
3.9
17.2

2.
```
10   READ A, B
20   IF A>B THEN 60
30   IF A<B THEN 80
40   PRINT A "=", B
50   GOTO 10
60   PRINT A ">", B
70   GOTO 10
80   PRINT A "<", B
90   GOTO 10
100  DATA ⁻5,4,2,2,12,1,9,10,⁻12,15.2,4,18.6,⁻12
110  END
```

-5<4
2=2
12>1
9<10
-12<15.2
4<18
6>-12

Rewrite the program to include an IF . . . THEN statement to accomplish the desired result.

B **3.** Have the computer print "Great Bowling" if the average score is above 220.

```
10   READ X, Y, Z
20   LET A = (X+Y+Z)/3
30   PRINT "AVERAGE IS" A
40   GOTO 10
50   DATA 126,153,162,240,215,232,203,218,239
60   END
```

```
35   IF A<=220 THEN 40
36   PRINT "GREAT BOWLING"
```

4. Have the computer print only negative numbers.

```
10   READ N
20   PRINT N
30   GOTO 10
40   DATA −4,9,0,11.3,−9.7,−0.5,8.7
50   END
```

```
15   IF N>=O THEN 30
```

14-8 More Uses of IF . . . THEN

The IF . . . THEN statement can be used in programs to compute weekly payrolls.

Example   This program computes the weekly wages for four workers. The rate of pay is $4.95 per hour for the first 40 hours and $7.40 per hour for any hours over 40. What is the output for the program?

```
 5  REM COMPUTE WEEKLY PAY, H = HOURS, P=PAY
10  READ H
20  IF H>40 THEN 50  ◄─────────────
30  LET P = H*4.95
40  GOTO 60
50  LET P = 40*4.95+(H-40)*7.40
60  PRINT "WEEKLY PAY IS $" P
70  GOTO 10
80  DATA 38, 42, 49, 40
90  END
```

The IF . . . THEN statement separates hours greater than 40 from hours less than or equal to 40.

Solution

WEEKLY PAY IS $188.10 ◄─────── *Since H is less than 40, the*
WEEKLY PAY IS $212.80   *computer goes to line 30.*
WEEKLY PAY IS $264.60 ◄─────── *Since H is greater than 40,*
WEEKLY PAY IS $198   *the computer goes to line 50.*

Your Turn   Write the output for the program in the Example using the following data.

80 DATA 35, 39, 48, 50

WEEKLY PAY IS $173.25
WEEKLY PAY IS $193.05
WEEKLY PAY IS $257.20
WEEKLY PAY IS $272.00
OUT OF DATA IN LINE 10

Class Exercises

Use the program that follows to answer the question.

1. What will the computer do at   END
   line 40 if A is equal to 10?

2. How many numbers and their squares will the computer print? 9

3. What would happen if line 40 were changed to read 40 IF A < 100 THEN 20?

The computer will print the numbers from 1 to 99 and their squares.

```
10  READ A
20  PRINT A, A↑2
30  LET A = A+1
40  IF A<10 THEN 20
50  DATA 1
60  END
```

Exercises

Write the output for the program.

RED RIBBON   OUT OF DATA
BLUE RIBBON   IN LINE 10
RED RIBBON

A 1.
```
 10  READ X, Y, Z
 20  LET A = (X+Y+Z)/3
 30  IF A>=90 THEN 70
 40  IF A>=80 THEN 90
 50  IF A>=70 THEN 110
 60  PRINT "TRY AGAIN NEXT YEAR"
 65  GOTO 10
 70  PRINT "BLUE RIBBON"
 80  GOTO 10
 90  PRINT "RED RIBBON"
100  GOTO 10
110  PRINT "YELLOW RIBBON"
120  GOTO 10
130  DATA 71,83,90,85,95,92
135  DATA 64,87,91
140  END
```

Solve. Check students' programs.

2. Sample telephone rates from Detroit to Los Angeles are $2.35 for the first three minutes and $.40 for each additional minute. Write a program that will print out the charges for each phone call listed. 2 min, 7 min, 11 min, 3 min, 23 min, 16 min

3. Write a program that READS two numbers at a time from DATA, and prints whether they are equal or unequal (for example, 3 = 3, 4.2 <> 40.2). Use DATA 7.5, 7.5, −1, 1, −16, −16, −18.1, 18.1, 0.62, 6.02.

B 4. A Freight Company's rules for shipping a package state that width plus height can total no more than 72 in. Write a program that determines if packages with the following dimensions can be carried by air freight. Print "PACKAGE CANNOT BE MAILED" if the package does not meet the requirements. Print nothing if the dimensions are satisfactory. Use READ . . . DATA, GOTO, IF . . . THEN.

Package	Width	Height
1	20 in.	4 in.
2	48 in.	23 in.
3	59 in.	15 in.
4	36 in.	10 in.

Self Test 2

Write the output for the program.

1.
```
10  READ X, Y
20  PRINT X*Y, X/Y
30  GOTO 10
40  DATA 20, 10, 4.8, 2.4, 15, 5
50  END
```
200   2
11.52   2
75   3

14-5

2.
```
10  READ A, B, C
20  PRINT (A+B)/C
30  GOTO 10
40  DATA 4, 8, 2, 17.5, 15.8, 3
50  END
```
6
11.1

14-6

3. Change the program in Exercise 1 to print the sum of X^2 and Y^2. Write the output for the program.

20 PRINT X↑2+Y↑2

500
28.8
250

14-7

4.
```
10  READ A, B, C
20  LET D = (A+B+C)/3
30  PRINT "YOUR AVERAGE IS" D
40  IF D>=90 THEN 50
45  GOTO 10
50  PRINT "CONGRATULATIONS. YOU'VE MADE HONOR ROLL"
60  GOTO 10
70  DATA 85, 90, 68, 100, 100, 78
80  END
```
YOUR AVERAGE IS 81
YOUR AVERAGE IS 92.6667;
CONGRATULATIONS. YOU'VE MADE HONOR ROLL

14-8

40 IF D<90 THEN 50
50 PRINT "SORRY, YOU MISSED HONOR ROLL"

5. Change the program in Exercise 4 to print "SORRY, YOU MISSED HONOR ROLL" if D is less than 90.

14-9

Algebra Practice

Write an equation. Solve.

1. 2803 times 318 is equal to *d*. $2803 \cdot 318 = d$; 891,354

2. The quotient of 5,324,670 and 738 is *w*. $5{,}324{,}670 \div 738 = w$; 7215

3. The sum of 12.087, 3.494, and 28.513 is *h*. $12.087 + 3.494 + 28.513 = h$; 44.094

4. The product of 0.018 and 0.62 is *a*. $(0.018)(0.62) = a$; 0.01116

5. $7\frac{7}{15}$ minus $2\frac{4}{5}$ is equal to *n*. $7\frac{7}{15} - 2\frac{4}{5} = n$; $4\frac{2}{3}$

6. $\frac{7}{8}$ divided by $\frac{21}{32}$ is equal to *y*. $\frac{7}{8} \div \frac{21}{32} = y$; $1\frac{1}{3}$

7. The area of a triangle with a base of $3\frac{1}{2}$ in. and a height of 2 in. is *A*. $\left(3\frac{1}{2}\right)(2) \div 2 = A$; $3\frac{1}{2}$ in.²

8. The volume of a cone with a radius of 5 cm and a height of 9 cm is *V*. $(3.14)(5^2)(9) \div 3 = V$; 235.5 cm³

Use the distributive property to factor each expression.

9. $12a^3b - 15ab^2$ $3ab(4a^2 - 5b)$

10. $10p^2q - 5p^2q^2 + 15pq^3$ $5pq(2p - pq + 3q^2)$

11. $2j^3 + 16j^3k - 14j^2k^2$ $2j^2(j + 8jk - 7k^2)$

Solve.

12. $\frac{-5}{6}s = 15$ -18

13. $\frac{3}{7}z + 1 = 10$ 21

14. $^-0.2n = 1.8n - 8$ 4

15. 6.5% of 120 is *g*.   7.8

16. $8\frac{1}{2}\%$ of 75 is *v*. $6\frac{3}{8}$

17. 55 is 62.5% of *m*.   88

18. $\frac{2}{3}d + {}^-4 = 24$ 42

19. $20 > \frac{5}{6}k - 4$ $28\frac{4}{5} > k$

20. $12 - \frac{7}{8}q > \frac{-5}{6}$ $q < 14\frac{2}{3}$

Is the ordered pair a solution of the linear inequality?

21. $(8, 7)$, $x - 3 \leq y$ yes

22. $(6, 4)$, $y < x - 2$ no

23. $(2, 10)$, $y \geq 3x + 5$ no

Find the lengths of the sides of the triangle.

24. Perimeter 90, sides $3j$, $2j + 6$, $4j - 15$ 33, 28, 29

25. Perimeter 59, sides $6f - 13$, $5f + 2$, $3f$ 17, 27, 15

Write the expression using BASIC symbols.

26. $3a^2 - 5$ 3*a↑2−5

27. $\frac{2r}{s}$ 2*r/s

28. $g^2 + \frac{h}{5}$ g↑2+h/5

Problem Solving for the Consumer

Evaluating Consumer Purchases

When making large purchases it's a good idea to compare the features and prices of several brands. You can start your research by reading consumer magazines, talking to people who already own the item, and visiting stores to have the various options explained and prices quoted.

Michael developed a system of weights to measure the features of several personal computers that met his basic needs for record-keeping, game playing, and word processing.

Here's how his system worked:

1. He chose eight features and weighted each from 1 (not too important) to 5 (very important).

2. He rated each computer (the Essex, Supra, and Whiz) on each feature using the following ratings: 0 = none, 1 = poor, 2 = fair, 3 = good, 4 = very good, 5 = excellent.

3. To get a score for each feature he multiplied the feature weight by the rating.

Complete the table.

	Feature	Weight	Essex Rating	Essex Score	Supra Rating	Supra Score	Whiz Rating	Whiz Score
1.	Cost	3	2	6	5	? 15	3	? 9
2.	Memory	4	5	20	3	? 12	4	? 16
3.	Software	5	5	25	3	? 15	1	? 5
4.	Display	2	3	? 6	3	? 6	3	? 6
5.	Add-ons	4	5	? 20	3	? 12	3	? 12
6.	Service	3	4	? 12	3	? 9	3	? 9
7.	Keyboard	4	3	? 12	4	? 16	4	? 16
8.	Color	3	3	? 9	0	? 0	5	? 15
9.	Total			? 110		? 85		? 88

Use the information in the table to answer the questions.

10. Which feature was most important? software

11. Which feature was least important? display

12. The Essex memory score is 20 and the keyboard score is 12, yet both features are weighted 4. Explain the difference in scores.
Memory score has a 5 rating and the keyboard a 3 rating. Both have the same weight of 4.

When visiting the computer store, Michael saw the following ads.

Whiz
Personal Computer $299.95
Graphic Printer $395.00
Single Disk Drive $695.00

Essex
Personal Computer $399.00
Thermal Printer $299.95
Disk Drive $599.95

Supra
710 Computer $459.95
Disk Drive $799.00
Modem $279.00
Printer $350.00

$1389.95 (Whiz), $1298.90 (Essex), $1887.95 (Supra)

Use the information in the ads to solve.

13. What is the total cost for each system as described in the ad?

14. If a sales tax of 7% is applied, what would be the final cost of the Supra system? $2020.11

15. Suppose you want to buy the Essex System described. You want to put 25% down and pay the rest in twelve monthly installments. If you pay $90.25 per month, how much is the service charge? $108.83

16. Suppose you buy a computer system and receive a $100 gift certificate for software. Can you buy a Bouncer game for $24.88, a budgeting program for $37.59, a Cat and Mouse game for $19.95, and an Algebra Program for $23.88? If you owe money, how much? If you get change, how much? owe $6.30

Enrichment

Greatest Integer Function

You can use the integer (INT) command to program a computer to round a decimal to any place.

INT (X) is the greatest integer less than or equal to the number X. The examples below show how this works for various values of X.

INT (2.5) = 2   INT (0.99) = 0   INT (⁻2.2) = ⁻3   INT (4) = 4

To round a decimal X to the nearest whole number, you first add 0.5 to X and then find INT (X + 0.5). The examples below show how this works.

X	X + 0.5	INT (X + 0.5)
2.6	3.1	3
5.1	5.6	5

When you want to round a decimal to the nearest tenth, you first multiply the number by 10, then add 0.5, and then divide by 10. The command would look like this: INT(X*10+0.5)/10. For the decimal 2.47 the computer would follow these steps:

X	X * 10	X * 10 + 0.5	INT (X * 10 + 0.5)	INT (X * 10 + 0.5)/10
2.47	24.7	25.2	25	2.5

Evaluate the expression.

1. INT (5.2) 5   2. INT (71.78) 71   3. INT (−6.1) ⁻7   4. INT (0.137) 0

Write the output for the program. 6.781 ROUNDED TO . . . IS 7
3.925 ROUNDED TO . . . IS 4
4.617 ROUNDED TO . . . IS 5
86.138 ROUNDED TO . . . IS 86

```
5. 10  READ D
   20  LET Y = INT(D+0.5)
   30  PRINT D" ROUNDED TO THE NEAREST"
   40  PRINT "WHOLE NUMBER IS" Y
   50  DATA 6.781, 3.925, 4.617, 86.138
   60  GOTO 10
   70  END
```

6. Change line 20 in Exercise 5 so that numbers are rounded to the nearest tenth, the nearest hundredth. Write the output for each new program. 20 LET Y=INT(D*10+0.5)/10   Check new output.
   20 LET Y=INT(D*100+0.5)/100

Chapter Review

True or false? Write *T* or *F*.

1. A PRINT statement is used in a BASIC program to tell a computer to perform operations in a loop. F
2. In the statement IF X > = 40 THEN 50 the computer will go to line 50 if X = 40. T
3. A computer will execute instructions in numerical order even if a program is written with the steps out of order. T
4. REM statements tell the computer to add two numbers. F
5. The statement FOR A = 2 TO STEP 2 combined with a NEXT A statement will tell the computer use 2, 4, 6, and 8 for values of A. F

What will be the output? Write *a*, *b*, or *c*.

6.
```
10  LET A = 5
20  PRINT A, A↑3
30  END
```
b
    a. 125
    b. 5 125
    c. 5 15

7.
```
10  LET A = 20
20  LET B = 30
30  LET C = (A+B)/2
40  PRINT C
50  END
```
a
    a. 25
    b. 20 30 25
    c. 35

Write the output for the program.

8.
```
10  FOR N = 0 TO 25 STEP 5
20  LET M = N*2
30  PRINT M "=" N "TIMES TWO"
40  NEXT N
50  END
```
    0=0 TIMES TWO
    10=5 TIMES TWO
    20=10 TIMES TWO
    30=15 TIMES TWO
    40=20 TIMES TWO
    50=25 TIMES TWO

9.
```
10  READ X, Y, Z
20  LET W = X/Y
30  LET R = W↑Z
40  PRINT R
50  DATA 100,10,3,45,15,2
60  END
```
    1000
    9
    OUT OF DATA IN LINE 10

10.
```
10  READ S
20  LET A = S↑2
30  PRINT "THE AREA OF THE SQUARE IS" A
40  GOTO 10
50  DATA 6,18,32
60  END
```
    THE AREA OF THE SQUARE IS 36
    THE AREA OF THE SQUARE IS 324
    THE AREA OF THE SQUARE IS 1024
    OUT OF DATA IN LINE 10

11. Write a BASIC program to print your name, street address, city, and phone number. Make sure the printout is on four lines. Check students' programs.

Chapter Test

Write the expression using BASIC symbols.

1. $3x^2 + 5$ 3*x↑2+5   **2.** $(25 + a^2) \div 2$ (25+a↑2)/2   **3.** $(14 + 6)^2 \div a$ (14+6)↑2/a   **14-1**

Write the output for the program.

4.
```
10   LET A = 5
20   PRINT A "SQUARED =" A↑2
30   END
```
5 SQUARED=25   **14-2**

5.
```
20   LET C = 598
30   LET E = 150
40   LET P = C-E
50   PRINT "PROFIT IS" P
60   END
```
PROFIT IS 448

6. Change the program in Exercise 4 to print the squares of the first   **14-3**
five multiples of 2. 10 FOR A=2 TO 10 STEP 2
                      25 NEXT A

7. Make a flowchart to show the steps involved in solving a problem   **14-4**
to calculate an average of 5 grades. Check students' flowcharts.

Write the output for the program. THE AREA OF THE TRIANGLE IS 24
                                      THE AREA OF THE TRIANGLE IS 30   **14-5**

8.
```
10   READ B, H
20   LET A = (B*H)/2
30   PRINT "THE AREA OF THE TRIANGLE IS" A
40   GOTO 10
50   DATA 6,8,12,5,100,60
60   END
```
THE AREA OF THE TRIANGLE IS 3000

9. Change the program in Exercise 8 to calculate the area of a rec-   **14-6**
tangle. 20 LET A=B*H
         30 PRINT "THE AREA OF THE RECTANGLE IS" A

10. Change the program in Exercise 8 so that it includes an   **14-7**
IF—THEN statement and prints "THE AREA IS TOO LARGE"
if A is greater than 100.   35 IF A>100 THEN 45
                            45 PRINT "THE AREA IS TOO LARGE"
Write the output for the program. 46 GOTO 10

11.
```
10   READ M, N
20   IF M>N THEN 40
30   PRINT "CONGRATULATIONS, NED. YOU WIN"
35   GOTO 10
40   PRINT "CONGRATULATIONS MILT. YOU WIN"
50   GOTO 10
60   DATA 70,65,108,120,88,87
70   END
```
14-8

CONGRATULATIONS MILT. YOU WIN
CONGRATULATIONS, NED. YOU WIN
CONGRATULATIONS MILT. YOU WIN

Cumulative Review (Chapters 1–14)

Add, subtract, multiply, or divide.

1. $2007 - 14 \cdot 6$ 1923

2. $2(4.7 + 0.29)$ 9.98

3. $10^3 \times 13.7$ 13,700

4. $2\frac{1}{2} + \frac{5}{8}$ $3\frac{1}{8}$

5. $\frac{3}{5} + \frac{7}{9}$ $1\frac{17}{45}$

6. $4\frac{1}{9} - 3\frac{3}{4}$ $3\frac{13}{36}$

7. $\frac{5}{6} \times 1\frac{1}{15}$ $\frac{8}{9}$

8. $\frac{2}{9} \times 3\frac{3}{8}$ $\frac{3}{4}$

9. $1\frac{1}{2} \div \frac{4}{5}$ $1\frac{7}{8}$

Solve.

10. 30 out of 250 is what percent? 12%

11. 37% of 80 is what number? 29.6

12. What is 99% of 350? 346.5

13. What percent of 200 is 46? 23%

14. 4% of $350 is what amount? $14

15. 120% of what amount is $504? $420

16. What is the simple interest paid on a loan of $2000 for 6 months at a rate of $9\frac{1}{2}$%? $95

17. When an item in a store is reduced from $56 to $42, what is the percent of decrease? 25%

Draw a circle graph to show the information. Check students' graphs.

18. The average American uses 60 gal of water per day in the home. Here is the breakdown of the usage: 40% flushing toilets; 35% washing and bathing; 10% kitchen use; 5% washing clothes; 10% other.

Find the probability.

19. A contest has 5 second prizes and 1 first prize. There are 500 entry blanks in a box. Five are drawn for second prizes, and are not returned to the box again. Then one entry is drawn for the first prize. Rosie has one entry blank in the box. If she doesn't win second prize, what is the probability she'll win first prize? $\frac{1}{495}$

Write an equation and solve the problem.

20. Bottles of a brand of vitamins are available two ways—with a regular cap and with a child-proof cap. One store has 36 bottles of the vitamins in stock. There are 16 more in child-proof caps than in regular caps. How many bottles of each type are there? 10 regular; 26 child-proof

Table of Square Roots of Integers from 1 to 100

Number	Positive Square Root	Number	Positive Square Root	Number	Positive Square Root	Number	Positive Square Root
N	$\sqrt{N}$	N	$\sqrt{N}$	N	$\sqrt{N}$	N	$\sqrt{N}$
1	1	26	5.099	51	7.141	76	8.718
2	1.414	27	5.196	52	7.211	77	8.775
3	1.732	28	5.292	53	7.280	78	8.832
4	2	29	5.385	54	7.348	79	8.888
5	2.236	30	5.477	55	7.416	80	8.944
6	2.449	31	5.568	56	7.483	81	9
7	2.646	32	5.657	57	7.550	82	9.055
8	2.828	33	5.745	58	7.616	83	9.110
9	3	34	5.831	59	7.681	84	9.165
10	3.162	35	5.916	60	7.746	85	9.220
11	3.317	36	6	61	7.810	86	9.274
12	3.464	37	6.083	62	7.874	87	9.327
13	3.606	38	6.164	63	7.937	88	9.381
14	3.742	39	6.245	64	8	89	9.434
15	3.873	40	6.325	65	8.062	90	9.487
16	4	41	6.403	66	8.124	91	9.539
17	4.123	42	6.481	67	8.185	92	9.592
18	4.243	43	6.557	68	8.246	93	9.644
19	4.359	44	6.633	69	8.307	94	9.695
20	4.472	45	6.708	70	8.367	95	9.747
21	4.583	46	6.782	71	8.426	96	9.798
22	4.690	47	6.856	72	8.485	97	9.849
23	4.796	48	6.928	73	8.544	98	9.899
24	4.899	49	7	74	8.602	99	9.950
25	5	50	7.071	75	8.660	100	10

Exact square roots are shown in red. For the others, rational approximations are given correct to three decimal places.

Table of Trigonometric Ratios

Angle	Sine	Cosine	Tangent	Angle	Sine	Cosine	Tangent
1°	.0175	.9998	.0175	46°	.7193	.6947	1.0355
2°	.0349	.9994	.0349	47°	.7314	.6820	1.0724
3°	.0523	.9986	.0524	48°	.7431	.6691	1.1106
4°	.0698	.9976	.0699	49°	.7547	.6561	1.1504
5°	.0872	.9962	.0875	50°	.7660	.6428	1.1918
6°	.1045	.9945	.1051	51°	.7771	.6293	1.2349
7°	.1219	.9925	.1228	52°	.7880	.6157	1.2799
8°	.1392	.9903	.1405	53°	.7986	.6018	1.3270
9°	.1564	.9877	.1584	54°	.8090	.5878	1.3764
10°	.1736	.9848	.1763	55°	.8192	.5736	1.4281
11°	.1908	.9816	.1944	56°	.8290	.5592	1.4826
12°	.2079	.9781	.2126	57°	.8387	.5446	1.5399
13°	.2250	.9744	.2309	58°	.8480	.5299	1.6003
14°	.2419	.9703	.2493	59°	.8572	.5150	1.6643
15°	.2588	.9659	.2679	60°	.8660	.5000	1.7321
16°	.2756	.9613	.2867	61°	.8746	.4848	1.8040
17°	.2924	.9563	.3057	62°	.8829	.4695	1.8807
18°	.3090	.9511	.3249	63°	.8910	.4540	1.9626
19°	.3256	.9455	.3443	64°	.8988	.4384	2.0503
20°	.3420	.9397	.3640	65°	.9063	.4226	2.1445
21°	.3584	.9336	.3839	66°	.9135	.4067	2.2460
22°	.3746	.9272	.4040	67°	.9205	.3907	2.3559
23°	.3907	.9205	.4245	68°	.9272	.3746	2.4751
24°	.4067	.9135	.4452	69°	.9336	.3584	2.6051
25°	.4226	.9063	.4663	70°	.9397	.3420	2.7475
26°	.4384	.8988	.4877	71°	.9455	.3256	2.9042
27°	.4540	.8910	.5095	72°	.9511	.3090	3.0777
28°	.4695	.8829	.5317	73°	.9563	.2924	3.2709
29°	.4848	.8746	.5543	74°	.9613	.2756	3.4874
30°	.5000	.8660	.5774	75°	.9659	.2588	3.7321
31°	.5150	.8572	.6009	76°	.9703	.2419	4.0108
32°	.5299	.8480	.6249	77°	.9744	.2250	4.3315
33°	.5446	.8387	.6494	78°	.9781	.2079	4.7046
34°	.5592	.8290	.6745	79°	.9816	.1908	5.1446
35°	.5736	.8192	.7002	80°	.9848	.1736	5.6713
36°	.5878	.8090	.7265	81°	.9877	.1564	6.3138
37°	.6018	.7986	.7536	82°	.9903	.1392	7.1154
38°	.6157	.7880	.7813	83°	.9925	.1219	8.1443
39°	.6293	.7771	.8098	84°	.9945	.1045	9.5144
40°	.6428	.7660	.8391	85°	.9962	.0872	11.4301
41°	.6561	.7547	.8693	86°	.9976	.0698	14.3007
42°	.6691	.7431	.9004	87°	.9986	.0523	19.0811
43°	.6820	.7314	.9325	88°	.9994	.0349	28.6363
44°	.6947	.7193	.9657	89°	.9998	.0175	57.2900
45°	.7071	.7071	1.0000	90°	1.0000	0.0000	Undefined

Extra Practice – Chapter 1

Evaluate the expression using the given value for the variable.

1. $5x + 7$; $x = 3$ 22 **2.** $2n - 9$; $n = 5$ 1 **3.** $y \div 3$; $y = 27$ 9

4. $14 - 3s$; $s = 4$ 2 **5.** $28 \div y$; $y = 4$ 7 **6.** $m \div 9$; $m = 72$ 8

Solve the equation.

7. $450 + 35 = t$ 485 **8.** $9007 - 138 = c$ 8869 **9.** $f = 19 + 189$ 208

10. $k = 370 - 174$ 196 **11.** $28 + 347 + 6 = r$ 381 **12.** $d = 4 + 89 + 275$ 368

Solve the equation.

13. $n = 43 \cdot 9$ 387 **14.** $9^2 = x$ 81 **15.** $p = 38 \cdot 16$ 608

16. $s = 4(6 \cdot 21)$ 504 **17.** $6(5 + 2) = y$ 42 **18.** $n = 18(4 - 1)$ 54

19. $a = 640 \div 4$ 160 **20.** $96 \div 4 = w$ 24 **21.** $121 \div 11 = f$ 11

22. $\dfrac{384}{24} = d$ 16 **23.** $g = \dfrac{156}{13}$ 12 **24.** $\dfrac{1288}{56} = y$ 23

Solve the equation.

25. $5 + 3 \cdot 2 = b$ 11 **26.** $21 \div 7 + 6 = d$ 9 **27.** $(9 - 3)6 = g$ 36

28. $h = 4 + 12 \div 6$ 6 **29.** $0(5 + 18) \div 6 = j$ 0 **30.** $16 \div (5 - 3) - 1 = k$ 7

Combine like terms.

31. $n + 5n$ $6n$ **32.** $7c - 2 + 4c$ $11c - 2$ **33.** $12x + 3y - x$ $11x + 3y$

34. $25t - 16t - t$ $8t$ **35.** $13k + 7 - 12k$ $k + 7$ **36.** $28 + 5j + 2$ $5j + 30$

37. $8a + 4c - 3c$ $8a + c$ **38.** $16 + 7r + 8r - 4$ $15r + 12$ **39.** $9x + 2y + y - 5x$ $4x + 3y$

Write an expression for the phrase.

40. 36 less than a number r $r - 36$ **41.** x decreased by 15 $x - 15$

42. 45 more than a number x $x + 45$ **43.** 42 greater than p $p + 42$

44. w used as a factor 4 times w^4 **45.** the sum of x and y $x + y$

Complete.

46. Lisa is 8 lb lighter than her dog Dynamo.
Let w = weight of Dynamo. Then ___?___ = Lisa's weight. $w - 8$

Extra Practice – Chapter 2

Write the decimals in order from greatest to least.

1. 4.7, 4.82, 4.16 4.82, 4.7, 4.16

2. 0.61, 0.35, 0.109 0.61, 0.35, 0.109

3. 6.2, 4.863, 9.7 9.7, 6.2, 4.863

4. 3.01, 3.018, 3.1 3.1, 3.018, 3.01

5. 6.2, 6.22, 6.02 6.22, 6.2, 6.02

6. 9.56, 8.98, 9.01 9.56, 9.01, 8.98

Round the number to the place of the underlined digit.

7. 0.8   1

8. 6.3   6

9. 12.71   13

10. 35.67   35.7

11. 1.265   1.3

12. 16.049   16.05

13. 0.553   0.6

14. 14.256   14.26

15. 249.9   250

16. 39.9   40

Add, subtract, multiply, or divide.

17. $2.04 + 0.07$ 2.11

18. $36.21 - 0.46$ 35.75

19. $21.09 - 0.672$ 20.418

20. $5.63 - 0.7$ 4.93

21. 4×0.7 2.8

22. 0.63×7 4.41

23. 5.1×0.6 3.06

24. 3.2×0.004 0.0128

25. 27.2×10 272

26. 100×6.24 624

27. 9.6×100 960

28. 4.7×10^2 470

29. $14.4 \div 12$ 1.2

30. $84 \div 2.1$ 40

31. $1008 \div 5.6$ 180

32. $2.313 \div 0.9$ 2.57

33. $49.14 \div 2.1$ 23.4

34. $47.1 \div 10$ 4.71

35. $3.62 \div 100$ 0.0362

36. $5.084 \div 1000$ 0.005084

37. $6.4 \div 100$ 0.064

Complete.

38. $4 \text{ cm} = \underline{\ ?\ } \text{ mm}$ 40

39. $12 \text{ mm} = \underline{\ ?\ } \text{ cm}$ 1.2

40. $46 \text{ cm} = \underline{\ ?\ } \text{ m}$ 0.46

41. $200 \text{ km} = \underline{\ ?\ } \text{ m}$ 200,000

42. $15 \text{ L} = \underline{\ ?\ } \text{ mL}$ 15,000

43. $2.4 \text{ g} = \underline{\ ?\ } \text{ mg}$ 2400

Write an expression for the phrase.

44. 6.4 decreased by y $6.4 - y$

45. r greater than 3.401 $3.401 + r$

46. c multiplied by 4.6 $4.6c$

47. 17.4 divided by n $17.4 \div n$

48. p used as a factor 6 times p^6

49. 3.07 increased by c $3.07 + c$

Solve.

50. A traveling salesperson figures her daily driving distance ranges from 60 mi to 130 mi. In the last 7 working days she drove 1085 mi. Did she drive within her estimated range each day?   no

Extra Practice – Chapter 3

Is the first number divisible by the second number? Write *Yes* or *No*.

1. 480 by 2 yes

2. 634 by 4 no

3. 259 by 3 no

4. 260 by 5 yes

5. 1355 by 5 yes

6. 432 by 6 yes

7. 870 by 3 yes

8. 246 by 4 no

Use exponents to write the prime factorization of the number.

9. 120 $2^3 \cdot 3 \cdot 5$

10. 72 $2^3 \cdot 3^2$

11. 625 5^4

12. 250 $2 \cdot 5^3$

13. 68 $2^2 \cdot 17$

14. 450 $2 \cdot 3^2 \cdot 5^2$

15. 155 $5 \cdot 31$

16. 270 $2 \cdot 3^3 \cdot 5$

Write the GCF of the pair of numbers.

17. 8 and 10 2

18. 9 and 6 3

19. 24 and 15 3

20. 25 and 40 5

21. 12 and 32 4

22. 21 and 35 7

Write the GCF of the set of expressions.

23. n^2 and n n

24. $2k$ and 10 2

25. $2r^2$ and $2r$ $2r$

26. $5m$ and $10m^2$ $5m$

27. $6f$ and f^2 f

28. $2c^2$ and $14c$ $2c$

Use the distributive property to factor the expression.

29. $2a - a$ $a(2 - 1)$

30. $5x + 10y$ $5(x + 2y)$

31. $2h^2 - 6$ $2(h^2 - 3)$

32. $12e^2 + 6e$ $6e(2e + 1)$

33. $25r + r^2$ $r(25 + r)$

34. $4ab + 8a$ $4a(b + 2)$

35. $9b^2 + 3b + 15$ $3(3b^2 + b + 5)$

36. $ay^2 - a^2y$ $ay(y - a)$

37. $10n + 16n^2 + 4$ $2(5n + 8n^2 + 2)$

38. $7n - 21 - 14n^2$ $7(n - 3 - 2n^2)$

39. $xy^2 + xy - 3x^2y$ $xy(y + 1 - 3x)$

40. $5ab^2 - a^2b + 2ab^2x$ $ab(5b - a + 2bx)$

Write the LCM of the numbers.

41. 6 and 7   42

42. 4 and 16 16

43. 6 and 9   18

44. 10 and 4 20

45. 8 and 12 24

46. 18 and 12 36

Solve.

47. Quality control workers in a factory must inspect every 20th item off the manufacturing line to see if it has any imperfections. The first item to be tested will be the 20th item manufactured, the second item to be tested will be the 40th item manufactured, and so on. How many items must be manufactured in order for the workers to test 15 items? 300 items

Extra Practice – Chapter 4

Write the fraction in lowest terms.

1. $\dfrac{16}{20}$ $\dfrac{4}{5}$ **2.** $\dfrac{4}{8}$ $\dfrac{1}{2}$ **3.** $\dfrac{18}{24}$ $\dfrac{3}{4}$ **4.** $\dfrac{20}{35}$ $\dfrac{4}{7}$ **5.** $\dfrac{5h}{h}$ 5

6. $\dfrac{x^2}{x}$ x **7.** $\dfrac{2x}{x}$ 2 **8.** $\dfrac{3a^2}{a}$ $3a$ **9.** $\dfrac{2a}{2a^2}$ $\dfrac{1}{a}$ **10.** $\dfrac{15cx}{5c}$ $3x$

Add or subtract. Write the answer in lowest terms.

11. $\dfrac{3}{8}+\dfrac{3}{8}$ $\dfrac{3}{4}$ **12.** $\dfrac{2}{3}+7$ $7\dfrac{2}{3}$ **13.** $\dfrac{11}{12}+\dfrac{8}{12}$ $1\dfrac{7}{12}$ **14.** $\dfrac{4}{9}+\dfrac{2}{3}$ $1\dfrac{1}{9}$

15. $\dfrac{5}{7}+\dfrac{3}{4}$ $1\dfrac{13}{28}$ **16.** $1\dfrac{1}{2}+2\dfrac{3}{5}$ $4\dfrac{1}{10}$ **17.** $\dfrac{4}{7}+3\dfrac{5}{8}$ $4\dfrac{11}{56}$ **18.** $\dfrac{6}{7}-\dfrac{1}{3}$ $\dfrac{11}{21}$

19. $\dfrac{7}{9}-\dfrac{3}{4}$ $\dfrac{1}{36}$ **20.** $\dfrac{9}{10}-\dfrac{1}{2}$ $\dfrac{2}{5}$ **21.** $7\dfrac{3}{4}-1\dfrac{1}{3}$ $6\dfrac{5}{12}$ **22.** $4\dfrac{1}{8}-\dfrac{9}{10}$ $3\dfrac{9}{40}$

23. $\dfrac{4}{a}-\dfrac{3}{a}$ $\dfrac{1}{a}$ **24.** $\dfrac{6}{c}+\dfrac{4}{c}$ $\dfrac{10}{c}$ **25.** $\dfrac{2a}{7}+\dfrac{3a}{7}$ $\dfrac{5a}{7}$ **26.** $\dfrac{4n}{10}+\dfrac{n}{10}$ $\dfrac{n}{2}$

Multiply or divide. Write the answer in lowest terms.

27. $\dfrac{3}{4}\cdot\dfrac{4}{5}$ $\dfrac{3}{5}$ **28.** $\dfrac{1}{2}\cdot\dfrac{1}{2}$ $\dfrac{1}{4}$ **29.** $1\dfrac{1}{2}\cdot\dfrac{2}{3}$ 1 **30.** $6\cdot\dfrac{5}{12}$ $2\dfrac{1}{2}$

31. $\dfrac{5}{9}\div5$ $\dfrac{1}{9}$ **32.** $\dfrac{6}{7}\div\dfrac{3}{5}$ $1\dfrac{3}{7}$ **33.** $\dfrac{1}{c}\cdot8$ $\dfrac{8}{c}$ **34.** $\dfrac{3}{4}\cdot a$ $\dfrac{3a}{4}$

35. $\dfrac{3n}{7}\cdot\dfrac{21}{9}$ n **36.** $\dfrac{2a}{7}\cdot\dfrac{a}{12}$ $\dfrac{a^2}{42}$ **37.** $\dfrac{x}{6}\div\dfrac{x}{4}$ $\dfrac{2}{3}$ **38.** $\dfrac{6}{5r^2}\div\dfrac{3}{r}$ $\dfrac{2}{5r}$

Write the fraction as a terminating or a repeating decimal.

39. $\dfrac{4}{5}$ 0.8 **40.** $\dfrac{5}{8}$ 0.625 **41.** $\dfrac{1}{3}$ $0.\overline{3}$ **42.** $\dfrac{5}{9}$ $0.\overline{5}$ **43.** $\dfrac{4}{11}$ $0.\overline{36}$

44. $\dfrac{3}{8}$ 0.375 **45.** $\dfrac{1}{6}$ $0.1\overline{6}$ **46.** $\dfrac{5}{3}$ $1.\overline{6}$ **47.** $\dfrac{9}{2}$ 4.5 **48.** $\dfrac{12}{11}$ $1.\overline{09}$

Solve.

49. Suppose you and your family are on a cross-country trip and you want to cover 2500 mi in seven days. The first day you intend to drive 300 mi to visit a special spot. How far must you drive each of the other days? Round your answer to the nearest ten miles. 370 mi

475

Extra Practice – Chapter 5

Solve the equation.

1. $n + 9 = 14$ ₅   **2.** $4 + s = 12$ ₈   **3.** $52 = x + 19$ ₃₃

1. $n + 9 = 14$ 5   **2.** $4 + s = 12$ 8   **3.** $52 = x + 19$ 33

4. $k - 16 = 30$ 46   **5.** $m - 20 = 42$ 62   **6.** $35 = t - 16$ 51

7. $f - 28 = 7$ 35   **8.** $61 = y - 52$ 113   **9.** $n + 16 = 51$ 35

10. $5a = 40$ 8   **11.** $8c = 48$ 6   **12.** $15g = 105$ 7

13. $20r = 100$ 5   **14.** $4t = 76$ 19   **15.** $\dfrac{n}{4} = 5$ 20

16. $\dfrac{a}{7} = 12$ 84   **17.** $\dfrac{1}{2}c = 18$ 36   **18.** $\dfrac{3}{5}n = 6$ 10

Solve the equation.

19. $2a + 5 = 25$ 10   **20.** $6n + 2 = 20$ 3   **21.** $3y - 7 = 14$ 7

22. $2(x + 1) = 16$ 7   **23.** $5(y - 1) = 15$ 4   **24.** $6(c - 4) = 12$ 6

25. $68 = 4(f + 5)$ 12   **26.** $45 = 9(g + 2)$ 3   **27.** $6r = 2r + 12$ 3

28. $7h = 2h + 15$ 3   **29.** $2a + 1 = a + 17$ 16   **30.** $5p - 2 = 2p + 7$ 3

31. $14 - s = 7s - 2$ 2   **32.** $9n + 4 = 5n + 20$ 4   **33.** $8w - 1 = w + 13$ 2

Complete by writing an algebraic expression.

34. Claire has twice as much money as Cindy.
Emily has $20 more than Claire.
Let m = the amount of money Cindy has.
Then __?__ = the amount of money Claire has, $2m$
and __?__ = the amount of money Emily has. $2m + 20$

35. Chip scored four more points than Kevin in the game.
Kevin scored twice as many points as Mike.
Let p = the number of points Kevin scored.
Then __?__ = the number of points Chip scored, $p + 4$
and __?__ = the number of points Mike scored. $\dfrac{1}{2}p$

Write an equation. Solve.

36. Franny's brother Jeff is half Franny's age. Jeff is 9 years old. How
old is Franny? $\dfrac{1}{2}x = 9$; 18 years

37. Pearl has twice as much money this week as she had last week.
She has $25. How much money did she have last week? $2n = 25$; $12.50

Extra Practice – Chapter 6

Find the perimeter or circumference. Use 3.14 for π.

1. rectangle 16.8 cm
l = 4.6 cm
w = 3.8 cm

2. square 48 in.
s = 12 in.

3. circle 25.12
r = 4

**The measure of an angle is given below. Tell whether the angle
is an acute, obtuse, or a right angle.**

4. 160° obtuse **5.** 90° right **6.** 35° acute **7.** 85° acute **8.** 110° obtuse

Find the area. Use 3.14 for π.

9. rectangle 42 ft²
b = 5 ft
h = 8.4 ft

10. triangle 21 cm²
b = 12 cm
h = 3.5 cm

11. circle 12.56 m²
d = 4 m

Find the volume.

12. rectangular prism 216 cm³
B = 27 cm²
h = 8 cm

13. triangular prism 151.2 m³
B = 56 m²
h = 2.7 m

14. cube 1728 mm³
l = 12 mm

15. cylinder 188.4 cm³
r = 2 cm
h = 15 cm

16. rectangular pyramid 275 in.³
B = 150 in.²
h = 5.5 in.

17. cone 200.96 mm³
r = 4 mm
h = 12 mm

Find the surface area.

18. 724 cm²

12 cm
11 cm
10 cm

19. 5 ft 471 ft²
10 ft

20. 144 m²

10 m
4 m
6 m
8 m

**A formula for determining distance traveled is $D = rt$. D = distance,
r = rate, t = time. Use the formula to solve the problems.**

21. A van is traveling down the road at 55 mi per hour. How far will it
travel in 4 hours? 220 mi

22. A truck driver plans to drive 440 mi at a speed of 55 mi per hour.
How long will the trip take if the driver takes two breaks, each 15
minutes long? $8\frac{1}{2}$ h

Extra Practice – Chapter 7

Write the ratio as a fraction in lowest terms.

1. 24 books out of 250 books $\frac{12}{125}$

2. 70 students absent to 450 total $\frac{7}{45}$

3. 18 hatchback cars to 50 cars $\frac{9}{25}$

4. 21 solar heated houses out of 35 houses $\frac{3}{5}$

Solve the proportion. Round the number to the nearest tenth.

5. $\frac{12}{18} = \frac{x}{28}$ 18.7

6. $\frac{25}{80} = \frac{n}{120}$ 37.5

7. $\frac{65}{90} = \frac{80}{a}$ 110.8

8. $\frac{9}{11} = \frac{c}{85}$ 69.5

Write the percent.

9. 7 out of 10   70%

10. 35 out of 50   70%

11. 17 out of 340 5%

12. 288 out of 480 60%

13. What percent of 90 is 45? 50%

14. What percent of 650 is 156? 24%

Solve.

15. 26% of 45 is what number? 11.7

16. 35% of 600 is what number? 210

17. What is 80% of 25? 20

18. $2\frac{1}{2}$% of $700 is what amount? $17.50

19. What is $\frac{1}{2}$% of 90? 0.45

20. What is 200% of $875? $1750

21. 126 is 20% of what number? 630

22. 11.55 is 5.5% of what number? 210

23. 65% of what number is 140? $215\frac{5}{13}$

24. 86% of what number is 172? 200

Find the percent of increase or decrease.

25. old price: $350 10%
increase: $35

26. from: $700 35%
to: $455

27. from: 1500 20%
to: 1800

Write an equation. Solve.

28. In the quality control department in a TV factory, workers found that 6 out of 40 TV sets had problems with the on-off switch. How many TV sets out of 250 might be expected to have the same problem? Round your answer to the nearest whole number. 38 sets

29. A bus pass used to cost $17 per month. The price went up to $22. What percent of increase is this? Round the answer to the nearest tenth of a percent. 29.4%

Extra Practice – Chapter 8

Compare. Write $<$ or $>$.

1. $^-7$ _?_ 0 $<$ **2.** 3 _?_ $^-2$ $>$ **3.** $^-4$ _?_ $^-7$ $>$ **4.** $^-8$ _?_ 5 $<$

5. 9 _?_ $^-2$ $>$ **6.** $^-7$ _?_ $^-10$ $>$ **7.** $^-8$ _?_ $^-1$ $<$ **8.** 12 _?_ $^-17$ $>$

Add or subtract.

9. $4 + {}^-6$ $^-2$ **10.** $0 + {}^-9$ $^-9$ **11.** $^-1 + {}^-3$ $^-4$ **12.** $^-10 + {}^-8$ $^-18$

13. $^-12 - 5$ $^-17$ **14.** $^-6 - {}^-2$ $^-4$ **15.** $^-9 - {}^-11$ 2 **16.** $8 - {}^-4$ 12

17. $^-6 - {}^-8$ 2 **18.** $^-9 + {}^-3$ $^-12$ **19.** $^-4 - {}^-1$ $^-3$ **20.** $16 + {}^-8$ 8

21. $^-20 + {}^-12$ $^-32$ **22.** $^-35 - {}^-6$ $^-29$ **23.** $8 - {}^-15$ 23 **24.** $^-6 - {}^-19$ 13

Multiply or divide.

25. $6(^-4)$ $^-24$ **26.** $^-8(^-6)$ 48 **27.** $^-5(4)$ $^-20$ **28.** $^-6 \cdot {}^-3$ 18

29. $7 \cdot {}^-8$ $^-56$ **30.** $7(^-3)$ $^-21$ **31.** $^-9 \cdot {}^-8$ 72 **32.** $4 \cdot {}^-9$ $^-36$

33. $^-21 \div 3$ $^-7$ **34.** $35 \div {}^-5$ $^-7$ **35.** $^-42 \div {}^-6$ 7 **36.** $^-56 \div {}^-8$ 7

37. $100 \div {}^-25$ $^-4$ **38.** $^-36 \div 9$ $^-4$ **39.** $^-81 \div {}^-9$ 9 **40.** $72 \div {}^-8$ $^-9$

Add, subtract, multiply, or divide.

41. $4.6 - {}^-2.3$ 6.9 **42.** $8.6 + {}^-9$ $^-0.4$ **43.** $^-6.3 \times {}^-5$ 31.5 **44.** $^-7.6 \div {}^-2$ 3.8

45. $2.5 + {}^-3.7$ $^-1.2$ **46.** $^-8.2 \times {}^-3.1$ 25.42 **47.** $^-8.4 \div 0.6$ $^-14$ **48.** $^-0.76 - {}^-0.235$ $^-0.525$

49. $1\frac{1}{3} + {}^-4\frac{3}{5}$ $^-3\frac{4}{15}$ **50.** $2\frac{7}{8} - \frac{^-1}{6}$ $3\frac{1}{24}$ **51.** $\frac{6}{8} \times {}^-1\frac{3}{4}$ $^-1\frac{5}{16}$ **52.** $^-1\frac{2}{3} \div {}^-4\frac{1}{6}$ $\frac{2}{5}$

53. $8\frac{1}{2} + {}^-2\frac{1}{2}$ 6 **54.** $^-6\frac{2}{3} - {}^-1\frac{1}{3}$ $^-5\frac{1}{3}$ **55.** $\frac{^-4}{5} \times {}^-1\frac{1}{2}$ $1\frac{1}{5}$ **56.** $12\frac{1}{4} \div {}^-1\frac{3}{4}$ $^-7$

Solve the equation or inequality.

57. $x - {}^-2 = 7$ 5 **58.** $y + {}^-3 = 9$ 12 **59.** $^-2a = 12$ $^-6$ **60.** $\frac{b}{^-4} = {}^-10$ 40

61. $^-6h = 5.4$ $^-0.9$ **62.** $^-8k = {}^-6.4$ 0.8 **63.** $c + \frac{^-1}{2} = 7$ $7\frac{1}{2}$ **64.** $m - \frac{^-2}{3} = 8$ $7\frac{1}{3}$

65. $t + 6 > 2t$ $>{}^-4$**66.** $x - 5 < 3$ $x < 8$ **67.** $y - 6 > {}^-8$ $y > {}^-2$**68.** $^-8y < 2$ $y > \frac{^-1}{4}$

69. $^-5n < {}^-2$ $n > \frac{2}{5}$**70.** $\frac{n}{7} < {}^-1$ $n < {}^-7$ **71.** $\frac{a}{^-4} > 10$ $a < {}^-40$ **72.** $j - 6 \leq 15$ $j \leq 21$

Extra Practice – Chapter 9

Find the next three terms of the sequence.

1. 0, 4, 8, 12, 16   20, 24, 28

2. 5, 11, 17, 23, 29   35, 41, 47

3. ⁻5, 0, 5, 10, 15   20, 25, 30

4. 8, 13, 18, 23, 28   33, 38, 43

5. ⁻15, ⁻9, ⁻3, 3, 9   15, 21, 27

6. 8, 3, ⁻2, ⁻7, ⁻12   ⁻17, ⁻22, ⁻27

Graph the ordered pairs on a coordinate plane. Label the point with the given letter. Check students' graphs.

7. $A(4, 0)$ **8.** $B(7, {}^-5)$ **9.** $C({}^-3, 0)$ **10.** $D({}^-1, {}^-6)$

11. $E(0, 6)$ **12.** $F(0, {}^-4)$ **13.** $G({}^-3, {}^-2)$ **14.** $H({}^-4, 3)$

Graph the following data. Use the graph to find the 6th term. Check students' graphs.

15. No. of term	Sequence	**16.** No. of term	Sequence	**17.** No. of term	Sequence
	35		25		16
1	0	1	5	1	⁻9
2	7	2	9	2	⁻4
3	14	3	13	3	1
4	21	4	17	4	6

Find three ordered pairs that are solutions of the given equation. Then graph them and draw the line for the equation. Check students' graphs.

18. $y = x + 1$ **19.** $y = x - 2$ **20.** $y = x + 5$

21. $y = 2x + 2$ **22.** $y = 3x - 1$ **23.** $y = {}^-x + 4$

24. $y = {}^-4x + 2$ **25.** $y = 5x - 5$ **26.** $y = \dfrac{1}{2}x + 6$

What are the slope and *y*-intercept of the equation?

27. $y = 2x - 9$ 2; ⁻9   **28.** $y = 8x + 7$ 8; 7   **29.** $y = {}^-x - 2$ ⁻1; ⁻2

30. $y = \dfrac{1}{4}x + 5$ $\frac{1}{4}$; 5   **31.** $y = \dfrac{2}{3}x - 6$ $\frac{2}{3}$; ⁻6   **32.** $y = \dfrac{3}{2}x + 8$ $\frac{3}{2}$; 8

33. $y = {}^-8x + \dfrac{5}{3}$ ⁻8; $\frac{5}{3}$ **34.** $y = \dfrac{3}{4}x + \dfrac{3}{5}$ $\frac{3}{4}$; $\frac{3}{5}$ **35.** $y = \dfrac{{}^-1}{3}x - \dfrac{1}{4}$ $\frac{{}^-1}{3}$; $\frac{{}^-1}{4}$

Is the ordered pair a solution of the linear inequality?

36. $(2, 5)$; $y > x + 2$ yes   **37.** $({}^-1, 7)$; $y > 2x + 10$ no

38. $(0, 4)$; $y < x + 7$ yes   **39.** $({}^-5, {}^-12)$; $y < 3x + 5$ yes

Extra Practice – Chapter 10

1. Find the range, mode, median and mean of the given data: 3.1; 8.4; 5.1; 3.1; 0.8; 1.1; 3.6. 7.6; 3.1; 3.1; 3.6

Use the circle graph.

2. There are 2450 students attending the college. How many are in each age group?

STUDENTS, EAST SIDE COMMUNITY COLLEGE

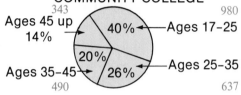

343
Ages 45 up
14%
40% — Ages 17–25
980
20%
Ages 35–45 → 26% — Ages 25–35
490
637

Use the bar graph.

3. About what percent of the total sales were red? 33%

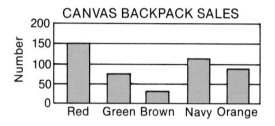

Use the line graph.

4. Traffic at __?__ is the 5:45 P.M. heaviest.

5. The decline in traffic after __?__ (time) is sharper than after __?__. 6 P.M.; 8 A.M.

TRAFFIC AT ONE INTERSECTION

Use the histogram.

6. About __?__ watched television 40–59 hours per week. 320

7. There were approximately __?__ viewers surveyed in all. 800

Use the scattergram.

8. Using the trend line, how much time would you expect a 17-mile commute to take? a 5-mile commute? 70 min; 40 min

Extra Practice – Chapter 11

For each pair of similar triangles, find *n*.

1. 4

n 6

 12

2. 8

5 4.6

7 n

3. 6.44 12.8

8 n

10 16

Use the Pythagorean Theorem to find the length of the hypotenuse to the nearest hundredth. Use the table on page 470.

4. 6.40

5

4

5. 7 9.22

6

6. 8.60

5

7

For the triangle, find tan *A*, sin *B*, and cos *A*. Write as a ratio in lowest terms.

$\dfrac{4}{3}; \dfrac{3}{5}; \dfrac{3}{5}$

7. 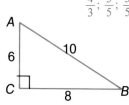 A

6 10

C 8 B

8. A 1 C

1.41 1

B

$1; \dfrac{100}{141}; \dfrac{100}{141}$

9. B

13 5

A 12 C

$\dfrac{5}{12}; \dfrac{12}{13}; \dfrac{12}{13}$

10–12. For Exercises 7–9, use the table on page 471 to find the measures of ∠*A* and ∠*B* to the nearest degree. 10. 53°; 37° 11. 45°; 45° 12. 23°; 67°

Find the measure of ∠*A* and ∠*B* to the nearest degree. Use the table on page 471.

13. 60°; 30°

A

4

C 7 B

14. 45°; 45°

B

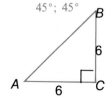 6

A 6 C

15. 49°; 41°

A

13

C 15 B

Extra Practice — Chapter 12

The following words are written on individual cards. Words are picked at random. Use this information for Exercises 1–7.

TO	**SLOWLY**	**THE**	**APPLE**	**ON**
BALLOON	**MEOWS**	**A**	**MY**	**RUNNING**
WALK	**UNDER**	**KITTEN**	**CHAIR**	**WEATHER**

1. What is P(CHAIR)? $\frac{1}{15}$

2. What is P(WALK or APPLE)? $\frac{2}{15}$

3. What is P(not WEATHER)? $\frac{14}{15}$

4. What is P(SIDEWALK)? 0

5. Suppose three words are picked and each time replaced. What is the probability that the words THE KITTEN MEOWS are picked in any order? $\frac{2}{1125}$

6. If three words are picked, what is the probability that THE is picked first, KITTEN next, and MEOWS third? The cards are not replaced as they are picked. $\frac{1}{2730}$

7. The words BARKS, BIG, and DOG are written on a spinner. What is the probability of picking KITTEN from the cards and spinning BARKS on the spinner? $\frac{1}{45}$

There are 5 yellow cards, 4 blue cards, and 6 green ones in a box. One card is picked at random. Use this information for Exercises 8–9.

CARDS	
yellow	5
blue	4
green	6

8. What are the odds in favor of picking a yellow card? $\frac{1}{2}$

9. What are the odds against picking a green card? $\frac{3}{2}$

Chip and his friends each took a random sample of 15 marbles from a bag containing 360 marbles, some red, some white, and some blue, with the following results.

	Red	White	Blue
Chip	4	6	5
Roberto	3	5	7
Peg	5	4	6

10. How many marbles of each color would you predict to be in the bag based on the combined data? red, 96; white, 120; blue, 144

Extra Practice – Chapter 13

$\overleftrightarrow{AB}$ and $\overleftrightarrow{CD}$ are parallel. Complete.

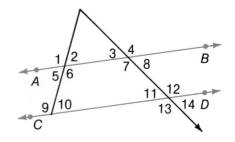

1. $\angle 1 = 120°$ so $\angle 9 = \underline{}$ 120°

2. $\angle 8 = 75°$ so $\angle 11 = \underline{}$ 75°

3. $\angle 2 = 60°$ so $\angle 10 = \underline{}$ 60° and $\angle 5 = \underline{}$ 60°

Find the missing measure of the angle in triangle ABC.

4. $\angle A = 45°,\ \angle B = 60°$ 75° 5. $\angle C = 90°,\ \angle A = 35°$ 55° 6. $\angle B = 110°,\ \angle A = 22°$ 48°

The pairs of polygons are similar. Find the length of the missing side.

7.

6.5   4.5 c $2\frac{10}{13}$

8.

x $4\frac{1}{6}$

Find the lengths of the sides of the triangle.

9. perimeter 30 6, 12, 12   10. perimeter 36 9, 12, 15   11. perimeter 54 12, 27, 15

Look at the parallelogram. Complete.

12. $\overline{AB} \parallel \underline{}$, so $\angle 2 = \angle \underline{}$. $\overline{DC}$; 3

13. $\overline{AD} \parallel \underline{}$. If $AD = 8$ cm, then
   $CB = \underline{}$ cm. $\overline{BC}$; 8

14. $\triangle ABC \cong \underline{}$, so $\angle 5 = \angle \underline{}$. $\triangle CDA$; 6

15. $\angle 1 + \angle 2 = \angle \underline{} + \angle \underline{}$ 3; 4

16. $\angle 5 + \angle 3 = \angle \underline{} + \angle \underline{}$ 6; 2

Extra Practice – Chapter 14

Write the output for the program.

15% OF 10 IS 1.5 15% OF 11 IS 1.65
15% OF 12 IS 1.8 15% OF 13 IS 1.95

AREA IS 18

1.
```
5   REM AREA OF TRIANGLE
10  LET B = 4
20  LET H = 9
30  PRINT "AREA IS" 1/2*B*H
40  END
```

2.
```
10  FOR A = 10 TO 20
20  PRINT "15% OF" A "IS" .15*A
30  NEXT A
40  END
```
15% OF 14 IS 2.1 15% OF 15 IS 2.25
15% OF 16 IS 2.4 15% OF 17 IS 2.55
15% OF 18 IS 2.7 15% OF 19 IS 2.85
15% OF 20 IS 3

3. Change the program in Exercise 2 so that the computer will print 15% of 10, 15, 20, and 25. 10 FOR A = 10 TO 25 STEP 5

4. Make a flowchart to show the steps to follow when you want to compare two numbers X and Y and write the numbers in order, the greater number second. Check students' flowcharts.

Write the output for the program.

YOU'VE SPENT 48.56 SO FAR

5.
```
5   REM BUDGET CHECK
10  READ A, B, C
20  LET N = A+B+C
30  PRINT "YOU'VE SPENT" N
    "SO FAR"
40  DATA 24.98, 6.59, 16.99
50  END
```

6.
```
5   REM FIGURING TOTAL COST
10  READ P
20  LET C = P*.29
30  PRINT "THE TOTAL COST IS" C
40  GOTO 10
50  DATA 5, 6, 7, 8, 9
60  END
```
THE TOTAL COST IS 1.45
THE TOTAL COST IS 1.74
THE TOTAL COST IS 2.03
THE TOTAL COST IS 2.32
THE TOTAL COST IS 2.61

7.
```
5    REM TRIANGLE CHECK
10   READ A, B, C
20   LET S = A+B+C
30   IF S < > 180 THEN 70
40   PRINT "THE SUM OF THE MEASURES OF THE ANGLES IS 180"
50   PRINT "SO THE POLYGON IS A TRIANGLE"
60   GOTO 10
70   PRINT "NOT A TRIANGLE"
80   GOTO 10
90   DATA 40, 50, 90, 62, 75, 30, 25, 82, 90
100  END
```
THE SUM OF THE MEASURES OF THE ANGLES IS 180
SO THE POLYGON IS A TRIANGLE
NOT A TRIANGLE   NOT A TRIANGLE

8. Change the program in Exercise 7 so that the computer will read data for four angles and determine whether the figure can be a quadrilateral or not. Check students' programs.

Glossary

absolute value (p. 274) The distance of a number from 0 on the number line.

acute angle (p. 179) An angle with a measure between 0° and 90°.

additive inverse (p. 241) *See under* opposite of a number.

algebraic factorization (p. 81) An algebraic expression written as the product of its factors.

alternate interior angles (p. 413) *See under* parallel lines.

associative properties (pp. 5, 14)
$(a + b) + c = a + (b + c)$
$(ab)c = a(bc)$

base, in a percent (p. 228) The number represented by 100% to which other quantities are compared.

certain event (p. 376) An event with probability 1, or 100%.

circumference (p. 176) The distance around a circle.

coefficient (p. 24) A number multiplied by a variable in an expression.

collinear points (p. 411) Points that lie on the same line.

commutative properties (pp. 5, 14)
$a + b = b + a$
$ab = ba$

composite number (p. 75) A number with more than two factors.

congruent polygons (p. 419) Polygons that have the same size and the same shape.

consecutive integers (pp. 72, 294) Integers that differ by 1.

coordinates (p. 285) The number paired with a point on the number line; an ordered pair of numbers assigned to a point on the coordinate plane.

corresponding angles (p. 413) *See under* parallel lines.

cosine ratio (p. 358) The cosine of an acute angle of a right triangle is the ratio of the length of the side adjacent to the angle to the length of the hypotenuse.

dependent events (p. 390) Events in which the outcome of one event affects the outcome of the other events.

diagonal (p. 415) A line segment that joins two non-consecutive vertices of a polygon.

diameter (p. 176) A line segment that passes through the center of a circle and whose endpoints are on the circle. Also, the length of such a segment.

distributive properties (p. 14)
$a(b + c) = ab + ac$
$a(b - c) = ab - ac$

equally likely outcomes (p. 375) Two or more outcomes are equally likely if each outcome is as likely to occur as the others.

equiangular triangle (p. 425) A triangle in which the three angles have the same measure.

equilateral triangle (p. 425) A triangle with three equal sides.

equation (p. 4, 135) A statement that two numbers or expressions are equal.

event (p. 375) A set of one or more outcomes in a probability problem.

experimental probability (p. 396) The ratio of the number of favorable outcomes of an experiment to the number of experiments.

exponent (p. 15) A raised number that indicates the number of times a factor is used.

expression (p. 1) An expression represents a number. $x + 2$ and $3d - 4$ are expressions.

factor (p. 75) Any of two or more numbers that are multiplied to obtain a product.

favorable outcome (p. 375) A desired outcome.

flowchart (p. 449) A diagram of the logical steps needed to solve a problem or to write a computer program.

frequency distribution (p. 329) A summary of the number of items in each interval of a tally.

frequency polygon (p. 330) A broken line connecting the midpoint of the top of each bar of a histogram.

graph of a number (p. 241) The point on the number line paired with a number.

greatest common factor (GCF) (p. 79) The greatest number that is a factor of each of two or more numbers or expressions.

histogram (p. 330) A graph used to show a frequency distribution.

hypotenuse (p. 351) The side of a right triangle that is opposite the right angle.

identity number for addition (p. 21) Zero. $0 + a = a$.

identity number for multiplication (p. 21) One. $1 \cdot a = a$.

impossible event (p. 376) An event with probability 0.

independent events (p. 386) Events in which the outcome of one event in no way affects the outcome of the other events.

inequality (p. 267) A statement that two quantities are unequal.

integers (p. 241) The numbers 1, 2, 3, 4, . . ., together with their opposites $^-1$, $^-2$, $^-3$, $^-4$, . . ., and 0.

isosceles triangle (p. 425) A triangle with at least two sides equal.

least common denominator (LCD) (p. 109) The least common multiple of the denominators of two or more fractions.

least common multiple (LCM) (p. 87) The least positive number that is a multiple of two of more given numbers.

leg of a right triangle (p. 351) One of the two sides which form the right angle of a right triangle.

like terms (p. 24) Terms with the same variables.

linear equation (p. 295) An equation whose graph is a straight line.

linear inequality (p. 298) An inequality whose graph is a region above or below a straight line.

mean (p. 309) The sum of a set of numbers divided by the total number of addends.

median (p. 309) In a set of numbers arranged in increasing order, the middle number.

mode (p. 309) The number that occurs most frequently in a set of data. Sometimes a set of data has no mode.

multiple (p. 87) A multiple of a number is any product of that number and a natural number.

natural numbers The numbers 1, 2, 3, 4, and so on.

obtuse angle (p. 179) An angle with a measure greater than 90° and less than 180°.

487

odds (p. 393) A ratio that compares favorable outcomes to unfavorable outcomes.

opposite of a number (p. 241) A number and its opposite are the same distance from 0 on the number line but on opposite sides. The opposite of 3 is ⁻3. Also called *additive inverse*.

outcome (p. 375) One possible result in a probability problem.

parallel lines (p. 180) Lines in a plane that do not intersect. ∠1 and ∠5 are corresponding angles; ∠3 and ∠5 are alternate interior angles; ∠2 and ∠8 are alternate exterior angles.

parallelogram (p. 428) A quadrilateral with opposite sides parallel.

percent (p. 216) A notation for a ratio with the denominator 100.

perimeter (p. 173) The distance around a geometric figure.

perpendicular lines (p. 180) Lines that meet to form right angles.

power (p. 15) A product of equal factors. The third power of 7 is 7^3 or $7 \cdot 7 \cdot 7$.

prime number (p. 75) A number greater than 1 whose only factors are itself and 1.

prism (p. 192) A solid figure with two identical bases.

probability (p. 375) The ratio of the number of favorable outcomes to the total number of outcomes.

proportion (p. 212) An equation that shows two equal ratios.

Pythagorean theorem (p. 351) In a right triangle, the square of the length of the hypotenuse (*c*) equals the sum of the squares of the lengths of the two other sides (*a* and *b*); $c^2 = a^2 + b^2$.

radius (p. 177) A segment drawn from the center of a circle to any point on the circle. Also, the length of such a segment.

random sample (p. 399) A sample in which each possible outcome is equally likely to appear.

range (p. 309) The difference between the greatest and least numbers in a set of data.

ratio (p. 209) The ratio of one number to another (not zero) is the quotient of the first number divided by the second.

reciprocals (p. 118) Two numbers whose product is 1.

rhombus (p. 428) A parallelogram with all sides equal in length.

right angle (p. 179) An angle with a measure of 90°.

right prism A prism in which the edges joining the bases are perpendicular to the bases; that is, each edge is perpendicular to all the lines it intersects in the bases.

sample space (p. 379) The set of all possible outcomes in a probability problem.

scalene triangle (p. 425) A triangle with no two sides equal.

scattergram (p. 333) A graph of individual points that shows the relationship between two sets of data. Each point represents an ordered pair with one coordinate from each set of data.

scientific notation (p. 90) The system of writing a number as the product of two factors in which the first factor is a number between 1 and 10 and the second factor is a power of 10. For example, $210{,}000 = 2.1 \times 10^5$.

segment (p. 411) A part of a line consisting of two endpoints and all the points between them.

sequence (p. 85) An ordered list of terms in which each term can be obtained by applying a rule.

similar polygons (p. 345) Polygons in which corresponding angles have equal measures and corresponding sides are in proportion.

sine ratio (p. 358) The sine of an acute angle of a right triangle is the ratio of the length of the side opposite the angle to the length of the hypotenuse.

skew lines (p. 412) Lines that do not intersect and do not lie in the same plane.

slope (p. 294) The steepness of a nonvertical line; the ratio

$$\text{slope} = \frac{\text{difference of } y\text{-coordinates}}{\text{difference of } x\text{-coordinates}}.$$

solution (pp. 135, 292) Replacement values for variables that make the equation true.

square root (p. 352) If $a^2 = n$ then a is a square root of n. The positive square root of n is shown by the symbol $\sqrt{n}$ and the negative square root by $-\sqrt{n}$.

statistics (p. 309) The study of the collection, organization, and interpretation of data.

straight angle (p. 179) An angle with a measure of 180°.

system of equations (p. 304) Two or more equations in the same variables.

term (p. 24) An expression using numerals or variables or both to indicate a product or a quotient.

term of a sequence (p. 85) One of the entries in a sequence.

transversal (p. 413) A line that intersects two other lines.

trapezoid (p. 428) A quadrilateral with exactly one pair of opposite sides parallel.

trend line (p. 333) The line to which the points of a scattergram is closest.

variable (p. 1) A symbol used to represent one or more numbers.

vertex of an angle (p. 180) The common endpoint of the sides of an angle.

vertex of a polygon (p. 415) A point where two adjacent sides of a polygon intersect.

y-intercept (p. 294) The y-coordinate of the point where a line intersects the y-axis.

Index

Credits

Book design by Ligature Publishing Services, Inc.

Cover and title page photo: "Tiered Orbits" by Jerome Kirk, at the Phoenix Civic Plaza. Photo by Nick Nicholson/Image Bank.

Technical art by ANCO/Boston

Diagrams on pages *173, 234, 235* and *308 - 343* by William DePippo.

Photographs

facing page 1 Carl Frank/Photo Researchers, Inc. **1** Eunice Harris/Photo Researchers, Inc. **8** Australian Information Service. **11** David F. Hughes/The Picture Cube. **13** Gillian Harper. **20** Adelheid Heine-Stillmark/The Image Bank. **29** Milton Feinberg/The Picture Cube. **30** Len DeMunde/The Image Bank. **34** James Ballard. **41** Anthony Howarth/Woodfin Camp. **45** Burton McNeely/The Image Bank. **48** Janeart Ltd./The Image Bank. **60** F. Fontana/The Image Bank. **65** Hank Morgan/Rainbow. **70** Bill Gallery/Stock, Boston. **85** Betty and Dennis Milon. **87** Lou Jones. **95** B. Cole/The Picture Cube. **100** Bill Gallery/Stock, Boston. **108** Owen Franken/Stock, Boston. **115** Lewis Trusty/Animals Animals. **120** Katherine Baldwin. **123** Russell Abraham/Stock, Boston. **129** Barbara Alper/The Picture Group. **134** © Joel Gordon. **140** Edith G. Haun/Stock, Boston. **145** ©Joel Gordon. **161** Bohdan Hrynewych/Stock, Boston. **162** Lou Jones. **167** Lou Jones. **168** G. L. Kooyman/Animals Animals. **172** Timothy Eagan/Woodfin Camp. **185** Focus on Sports. **191** Brett H. Froomer/The Image Bank. **194** Luis Villota/The Stock Market. **202** Katherine Baldwin. **203** Jonathon Rawle/Stock, Boston. **208** Ken Lax/The Stock Shop. **214** courtesy of Megatek Corp. **219** Mike Mazzaschi/Stock, Boston. **220** Stephen Comeau. **225** G. Gladstone/The Image Bank. **230** Michal Heron. **234** Ken Lax/The Stock Shop. **240** Thomas Ives. **243** Joe DiMaggio & JoAnne Kalish/Focus on Sports. **245** Phil Ellin/The Picture Cube. **256** NASA. **259** Michal Heron. **263** Alan G. Nelson/Animals Animals. **273** Marc Romanelli/The Image Bank. **278** Bernard P. Wolff/Photo Researchers, Inc. **284** Stephen Comeau. **297** Michal Heron. **302** Stanley Rowin/The Picture Cube. **308** Focus on Sports. **315** Stephen Comeau. **321** Rick Browne/The Picture Group. **328** Stanley Rowin/The Picture Cube. **338** R. Terry Walker/The Picture Cube. **344** Gary Cralle/The Image Bank. **348** C. T. Seymour/The Picture Cube. **351** Stephen Comeau. **363** Niki Mareschal/The Image Bank. **368** Tom Tracy/The Stock Shop. **374** David Frazier/Photo Researchers, Inc. **375** Michal Heron. **382** Bill Galler/Stock, Boston. **393** Michal Heron. **404** Michal Heron/Monkmeyer Press. **410** Michael James. **411** Michael James. **424** Dave Britzius/The Stock Shop. **438** courtesy of Evans & Sutherland and Rediffusion Simulation. **448** Harald Sund/The Image Bank. **454** Katherine Baldwin. **459** Bill Gallery/Stock, Boston. **461** Cara Moore/The Image Bank. **465** Michal Heron.

Answers to Your Turn Exercises

CHAPTER 1 WHOLE NUMBERS AND VARIABLES
Page 1 •24 •36 **Page 2** •$a + 7$
•$n \div 3$ **Page 4** •$482 + 59 = x$; $x = 541$
•$1535 + 496 = b$; $b = 2031$ **Page 5**
(Example 2) •$35 + 37 = n$; $n = 72$
•$40 + 39 = n$, $n = 79$ •$256 + 460 = n$;
$n = 716$ **(Example 3)** •147 •166 •396
Page 9 •$1500 - 685 = y$; $y = 815$
•$365 - 87 = n$; $n = 278$ **Page 11**
•$75 - 69 = w$; 6; lost 6 kg **Page 15**
•$x = 970$ •$n = 7700$ •$y = 8600$
•$a = 342$ **Page 16** •y^5 •16 •48
Page 18 •$276 \div 3 = 92$ or $276 \div 92 = 3$
•$87 \times 8 = 696$ •$6111 \div 9 = 679$ or
$6111 \div 679 = 9$ **Page 19** •$68 \div 5 = n$;
$n = 13R3$ •$160 \div 12 = g$; $g = 13R4$
Page 24 (Example 3) •$a = 14$ •$b = 18$
•$m = 148$ •$n = 100$ **(Example 4)** •$10a$
•$22n + 2x$ •$6z + y$

CHAPTER 2 DECIMALS
Page 36 •five hundred seventy-four and four
hundred five thousandths •7005.2002
Page 38 •$4.1 < 4.16$ •$30.72 > 30.62$
Page 42 (Example 3) •7.0 •18.786
(Example 4) •0.60 **Page 45** •40
Page 46 •$y = 25.908$ **Page 49**
(Example 2) •38 **(Example 3)**
•$m = 7.89$ •$d = 15.66$ **Page 51** •Yes
•\$210 **Page 53 (Example 1)** •$y = 0.0084$
•$x = 0.0186$ **(Example 2)** •$a = 4892.1$
$s = 3700.6$ **Page 54** •15,000 **Page 57**
•7.42 **Page 58 (Example 3)** •8
(Example 4) •$d = 0.2378$ **Page 61**
•7000 mL •0.0095 hL

CHAPTER 3 NUMBER THEORY
Page 72 (Example 2) •2, 3, 4, 6, yes; 5, 10,
no **(Example 3)** •odd •17 •18
Page 76 •$54 = 2 \times 3^3$ •$126 = 2 \times 3^2 \times 7$
Page 77 •$2^3 \times 13$ •$2^2 \times 5 \times 11$
•$2 \times 3^3 \times 5^2$ **Page 79** •GCF of 8 and 12
is 4 •GCF of 15 and 20 is 5 •GCF of 12
and 32 is 4 •GCF of 12 and 18 is 6 •GCF
of 9 and 30 is 3 •GCF of 16 and 24 is 8
Page 81 •$5m$ •3 **Page 82** •$4(2x - 1)$
•$y(5y + 1)$ •$7(a + 2b - c)$ **Page 85**
•12:15 P.M. **Page 87** •24 •180 **Page 88**

•24 •225 •$16x^2$ **Page 90** •Yes •No
•No •120,000 •61,000,000,000
•750,000,000 **Page 91** •5.4×10^4
•2.038×10^9 •3.1×10^6

CHAPTER 4 FRACTIONS
Page 102 (Example 1) •$4\frac{3}{8}$, $2\frac{8}{9}$ **(Example 2)**
•$\frac{44}{7}$, $\frac{49}{6}$ **Page 106** •y •$\frac{1}{2b}$ •$\frac{c}{2}$
Page 109 •$6\frac{5}{12}$ •$\frac{12}{d}$ •$\frac{e}{3}$ **Page 112**
(Example 2) •$\frac{9}{x}$ •$\frac{3}{xy}$ •$\frac{3a}{10}$ **(Example 3)**
•$\frac{b}{6}$ •$\frac{3}{5}$ •$1\frac{9}{10}$ **Page 116** •$\frac{2}{5}$ •$\frac{7a}{20}$
Page 119 •$\frac{1}{7}$ •$\frac{1}{6}$ •$\frac{1}{2m}$ **Page 122**
•\$2666.67 **Page 125** •$\frac{1}{4}$ •$0.\overline{6}$ •$0.8\overline{3}$

CHAPTER 5 SOLVING EQUATIONS
Page 136 (Example 2) •Yes •No •Yes
(Example 4) •$h = 5$ •$y = 14$ •$z = 40$
Page 139 •$c = 40$ •$d = 52$ •$e = 9$
Page 141 (Example 2) •$b = 6$ •$c = 9$
•$d = 16\frac{8}{9}$ **(Example 3)** •Divide by 5;
$p = 4$ •Subtract 10; $s = 6$ **Page 143**
•$a = 26$ •$c = 36$ **Page 146** •$w = 35$
•$v = 20$ •$n = 15$ **Page 150 (Example 3)**
•$d = 6$ •$x = 5$ •$e = 39$ **(Example 4)**
•$x = 8$ •$x = 4$ **Page 154** •$d = 3$
•$f = 6$ **Page 155** •$3s$, $3s + 1$ **Page 156**
•$2x + 2$ •$2n$, $2n + 1$ **Page 159** •60 in.
Page 163 •$x + 29 = 57$; 28 people

CHAPTER 6 FORMULAS
Page 173 •84 ft **Page 174** •65
Page 177 •28.26 yd •34.54 in. •66 m
Page 181 •JH •AB **Page 184** •10 in.²
•26 cm² **Page 186** •113.04 cm² **Page 187**
•34.54 sq. units •226.08 sq. units
Page 189 •45 lb **Page 193** •60 cm³
Page 195 •4019.2 in.³ •1339.73 in.³
Page 198 •552 in.² **Page 199** •253 in.²

CHAPTER 7 RATIO, PROPORTION, PERCENT
Page 210 •$\frac{3}{1}$ •$\frac{8}{5}$ •$\frac{9}{10}$ **Page 213** •$7\frac{1}{2}$ h
•280 km **Page 217 (Example 1)** •7%

•15% •14% **(Example 2)** •$\frac{37}{100}$; 0.37
•$\frac{9}{100}$; 0.09 •$\frac{83}{100}$; 0.83 **Page 219** •$7.14
Page 220 •$18.75 •$266.00 **Page 223**
•Diamond Bank **Page 225** •1.5 •3.96
Page 226 (Example 2) •Office supplies, $60;
salaries, $6000 (Foot of page) •116.1
•150 **Page 228** •2212 •4288 books
Page 231 •37.5% •20%

CHAPTER 8 INTEGERS AND RATIONAL NUMBERS
Page 242 •$^-12 < ^-2$ **Page 243** •$^-9$
Page 246 •$y = ^-4$ **Page 248** •$^-3$ •14
•$^-7$ •11 **Page 250** •$y = ^-56$
•$p = ^-30$ **Page 251** •$p = ^-27$ •$g = ^-56$
Page 253 •$y = ^-6$ **Page 257 (Example 2)**
•$t = ^-8.69$ •$n = \frac{^-5}{8}$ **(Example 4)**
•$h = ^-9\frac{5}{8}$ **Page 265** •$n = ^-7$ •$k = 2$
•$m = ^-24.8$ •$a = ^-21.7$ **Page 268**
•$t < 4$ •$x > 7$ **Page 269** •$x \geq ^-1$

CHAPTER 9 GRAPHING IN THE COORDINATE PLANE
Page 279 •32 •300 •2984 •4002
Page 280 •26 •32 •152 •302
Page 282 •$2n + 3$ **Page 286** •$E(^-5, ^-3)$
•$F(1, 2)$ •$G(^-4, 2)$ •$H(1, ^-5)$ **Page 292**
•Yes **Page 295 (Example 1)** •slope, 4; y-
intercept, $^-2$; $y = 4x - 2$ **(Example 2)**
•slope, 6; y-intercept, 9 •slope, 4; y-
intercept, $^-3$ •slope, $^-7$; y-intercept, $^-2$
Page 299 •Not a solution •Not a solution

CHAPTER 10 STATISTICS
Page 310 •mean = 14 L, range = 5 L,
mode = 12 L, median = 13 L **Page 312**
•6336 **Page 315** •$30,000 •$15,000
•$55,000 •$$$$ $$$$ $$ •$$$$ $$$$ $$$$
$$$ •$$$$ $$$$ $$$$ $$$$ $$$$ $
Page 318 •$425 **Page 319** •345
Page 322 •Television **Page 326** •What is
the latest I can leave home and get to the
concert before 7:30 P.M.? 6.50 P.M.
Page 330 •1 **Page 333** •67 in. **Page
334** •About 5

CHAPTER 11 SPECIAL TRIANGLES
Page 346 •6 **Page 348** •45 ft
Page 352 •2.236 **Page 356** •0.6634

Page 359 •$\sin P = \frac{3}{5}$, $\cos P = \frac{4}{5}$
•$\sin M = 0.6$, $\cos M = 0.8$ **Page 362**
•2.3096 •6 **Page 364** •$\angle A = 37°$,
$\angle B = 53°$

CHAPTER 12 PROBABILITY
Page 376 •$\frac{1}{2}$, 0.5, 50% •$\frac{1}{2}$, 0.5, 50% •1, 1,
100% •0, 0, 0% **Page 380** •$\frac{5}{6}$
Page 383 •$\frac{1}{24}$ **Page 386** •$\frac{6}{25}$ •$\frac{4}{25}$
Page 387 •$\frac{1}{216}$ •$\frac{1}{24}$ **Page 390** •$\frac{2}{7}$ •$\frac{2}{7}$
Page 394 •$\frac{5}{992}$ •$\frac{992}{5}$ **Page 396** •$0.\overline{6}$
•$0.\overline{13}$ •0.2 **Page 397** •0.225 **Page 399**
•$\frac{7}{20}$ •$\frac{1}{5}$ **Page 400** •2750 •4250 •750

CHAPTER 13 GEOMETRY
Page 412 •$\overrightarrow{NB}$ **Page 413 (Example 3)**
•parallel •skew **(Example 4)** •50°; 50°;
50° **Page 419** •27 **Page 423** •Potassium,
0.427 lb; sulfur, 0.305 lb; sodium, 0.183 lb;
chlorine, 0.183 lb; magnesium, 0.061 lb; iron,
0.00488 lb **Page 425** •$\triangle ACD$ •$\triangle BAD$
•$\triangle BCD$ **Page 426** •$XZ = 5$, $ZY = 7$,
$XY = 11$ •Acute

CHAPTER 14 PROGRAMMING IN BASIC
Page 439 •10 PRINT 26.7/15.25, 20 END
•10 PRINT 4↑6, 20 END **Page 440** •48,
6, 1.8 **Page 443** •THE AREA IS 70.56
•10 LET A = 50, 30 LET C = 35
Page 446 •5, 10, 15, 20 •6 TIMES 2 = 12,
7 TIMES 2 = 14, 8 TIMES 2 = 16, 9 TIMES
2 = 18, 10 TIMES 2 = 20, 11 TIMES
2 = 22 **Page 447** •10, 4; 12, 6; 14, 8; 16,
10; 18, 12; 20, 14 •10, 2; 20, 4; 30, 6; 40,
8 **Page 453** •PERIMETER IS 46.
Page 455 •45 PERCENT OF 90 IS 40.5,
12 PERCENT OF 150 IS 18, 6.8 PERCENT
OF 200 IS 13.6 **Page 457** •YOUR
AVERAGE TEST SCORE IS 55. **Page
458** •6, 8, 10 ARE PYTHAGOREAN
TRIPLES. OUT OF DATA IN LINE 10
Page 460 •WEEKLY PAY IS $173.25,
WEEKLY PAY IS $193.05, WEEKLY PAY IS
$257.20, WEEKLY PAY IS $272

APPENDIX SIMPLIFYING POLYNOMIALS
Page 516 •$5a^2 + 3a$ •$6x^2 - 3xy$

Answers to Self Tests

CHAPTER 1 WHOLE NUMBERS AND VARIABLES

Self Test 1, p. 10 **1.** 42 n **2.** 33 **3.** 2 **4.** 53 **5.** 178 **6.** 112 **7.** 3625 **8.** 63 **9.** 62
Self Test 2, p. 26 **1.** 14.4 mi/gal **2.** 1428 **3.** 2530 **4.** 405 **5.** 13 **6.** 78 **7.** 27 **8.** 872 **9.** 475 **10.** 1006 **11.** 45 **12.** 34 **13.** 60

CHAPTER 2 DECIMALS

Self Test 1, p. 44 **1.** 28.07 **2.** 7013.0062 **3.** 600.004 **4.** 5.000014 **5.** 7.56, 7.66, 7.67, 8.66 **6.** 82.29, 92.28, 92.29, 92.92 **7.** 0.7, 0.75, 0.756, 0.76 **8.** 8.3, 8.34, 8.341, 8.44 **9.** 1 **10.** 4 **11.** 36 **12.** 130 **13.** 0.5 **14.** 8.4 **15.** 41.0 **16.** 112.7
Self Test 2, p. 62 **1.** 74.3 **2.** 30.65 **3.** 123.095 **4.** 4.58 **5.** 7.96 **6.** 298.15 **7.** Yes **8.** 174.64 **9.** 0.0086 **10.** 8650 **11.** 2.3 **12.** 2.4 **13.** 0.362 **14.** 4.562 **15.** 841 **16.** 0.724

CHAPTER 3 NUMBER THEORY

Self Test 1, p. 83 **1.** Yes **2.** No **3.** No **4.** Yes **5.** $2^2 \times 3 \times 7$ **6.** $2^3 \times 5 \times 23$ **7.** 3×7^2 **8.** $2^3 \times 5 \times 47$ **9.** 2 **10.** 5 **11.** 1 **12.** $3(a - 4)$ **13.** $5b(b + 2)$ **14.** $2(1 + 3c - 2c^2)$
Self Test 2, p. 92 **1.** Monday **2.** 360 **3.** $6a$ **4.** $24b^2$ **5.** 8000 **6.** 170,000 **7.** 940,000,000 **8.** 2.8×10^6 **9.** 9.6×10^4 **10.** 5.4×10^7

CHAPTER 4 FRACTIONS

Self Test 1, p. 114 **1.** $\frac{23}{3}$ **2.** $\frac{29}{6}$ **3.** $\frac{49}{9}$ **4.** $\frac{71}{7}$ **5.** $2\frac{1}{10}$ **6.** 3 **7.** 2 **8.** $3x^2$ **9.** $\frac{c}{2}$ **10.** $\frac{5a}{8b}$ **11.** $\frac{3x}{4}$ **12.** $\frac{13}{b}$ **13.** $\frac{11}{c}$ **14.** $10\frac{1}{15}$ **15.** $8\frac{17}{28}$ **16.** $\frac{3n}{r}$ **17.** $\frac{31s}{24}$ **18.** $1\frac{29}{48}$

Self Test 2, p. 126 **1.** $\frac{7p}{13}$ **2.** $2x$ **3.** $\frac{2d}{5}$ **4.** $\frac{5n^2}{108}$ **5.** $\frac{18b}{121}$ **6.** $\frac{1}{9}$ **7.** $\frac{2}{3}c$ **8.** $0.0\overline{6}$ **9.** 0.175 **10.** 0.5625 **11.** $\frac{59}{100}$ **12.** $\frac{1}{100}$ **13.** $5\frac{13}{20}$

CHAPTER 5 SOLVING EQUATIONS

Self Test 1, p. 148 **1.** Yes **2.** Yes **3.** 58 **4.** 25 **5.** 18 **6.** 13 **7.** 50 **8.** 231 **9.** 91 **10.** 123 **11.** 55 **12.** 525 **13.** 39 **14.** 40
Self Test 2, p. 164 **1.** 15 **2.** 5 **3.** 9 **4.** 11 **5.** 2 **6.** 3 **7.** $j + 5$ **8.** $j + 2$ **9.** $2n = 16;\ \$8$ **10.** $(x + 7)3 = 54;\ 11$

CHAPTER 6 FORMULAS

Self Test 1, p. 182 **1.** 44 ft **2.** 68 in. **3.** 53.8 cm **4.** 65.94 yd **5.** 20.096 m **6.** 6.908 mi **7.** right **8.** obtuse **9.** straight **10.** acute **11.** acute
Self Test 2, p. 191 **1.** 16 ft^2 **2.** 150.96 in.^{2} **3.** 120.36 yd^2 **4.** 19.625 ft^2 **5.** 379.94 yd^2 **6.** 243.1616 cm^2 **7.** 625 mi/h
Self-Test 3, p. 200 **1.** 1200 cm^3 **2.** 360 mm^3 **3.** 2260.8 in.^{2} **4.** 615.44 cm^3 **5.** 72 m^2 **6.** 18,463.2 mm^2

CHAPTER 7 RATIO, PROPORTION, PERCENT

Self Test 1, p. 224 **1.** Glisten: $\frac{11}{17}$; $\frac{22}{85}$; $\frac{8}{85}$. Pearly White: $\frac{63}{88}$, $\frac{9}{44}$, $\frac{7}{88}$. Shine'n Smile: $\frac{19}{96}$, $\frac{25}{32}$, $\frac{1}{48}$ **2.** 4 **3.** 18 **4.** 11 **5.** 21 **6.** 16% **7.** 25% **8.** 20% **9.** 25% **10.** \$7.65 **11.** \$4.12 **12.** \$10.63 **13.** \$2.60, \$5.20, \$7.80, \$10.40, \$13, \$15.60, \$18.20, \$23.40, \$26. You save \$1.56
Self Test 2, p. 232 **1.** 1.5 **2.** 675 **3.** 3.8 **4.** 150 **5.** 350 **6.** 75% **7.** 65% **8.** 6.9%

CHAPTER 8 INTEGERS AND RATIONAL NUMBERS

Self Test 1, p. 255 **1.** $5 > {}^-6$ **2.** $3 > {}^-8$ **3.** $20 > {}^-12$ **4.** $18 > {}^-4$ **5.** $^-11$ **6.** $^-22$ **7.** $^-29$ **8.** 3 **9.** $^-6$ **10.** $^-8$ **11.** $^-8$ **12.** $^-18$ **13.** $^-3$ **14.** $^-56$ **15.** $^-40$ **16.** 66 **17.** $^-8$ **18.** $^-5$ **19.** 4
Self Test 2, p. 270 **1.** 0.4 **2.** $^-3.7$ **3.** 5.9 **4.** $^-6.3$ **5.** $^-1.44$ **6.** 1.3 **7.** 8 ways **8.** 7.7 **9.** 7.6 **10.** $^-2.1$ **11.** $y > 2$ **12.** $x < 3$ **13.** $b < {}^-3$

CHAPTER 9 GRAPHING IN THE COORDINATE PLANE

Self Test 1, p. 291 **1.** $^-1$, 0, 1, 2, 3 **2.** 8, 11, 14, 17, 20 **3.** $^-6$, $^-8$, $^-10$, $^-12$, $^-14$ **4.** 4, 3, 2, 1, 0 **5.** $3n - 2$; 28; 148 **6.** $3n - 6$; 24; 144 **7.** $^-4n + 13$; $^-27$; $^-187$ **8.** $5n + 6$; 56; 256 **9.** Move 3 right and up 5. **10.** Move 4 left. **11.** Move 6 right and down 2. **12.** Move 5 left and down 1. **13.** 31 **14.** $^-13$
Self Test 2, p. 300 **1.** The graph passes through (0, 1), ($^-1$, 0). **2.** The graph passes through (0, $^-5$), (2, 1). **3.** The graph passes through (0, 4), (2, 0). **4.** Slope, 4; y-intercept, $^-1$. **5.** Slope, $^-1$; y-intercept, 2 **6.** Slope, 3; y-intercept, 4 **7.** Yes **8.** Yes **9.** No

CHAPTER 10 STATISTICS

Self Test 1, p. 317 **1.** 30.5 mi, 36 mi, 31 mi, 12 mi **2.** 9.525 km, 9.4 km, 9.4 km, 0.9 km **3.** \$79 **4.** \$144 **5.** 200 **6.** 160
Self Test 2, p. 325 **1.** 10 **2.** 70 **3.** Kim **4.** June to July
Self Test 3, p. 336 **1.** 18–21 **2.** 2 **3.** \$30,000/y **4.** 10 years

CHAPTER 11 SPECIAL TRIANGLES

Self Test 1, p. 354 **1.** 4 **2.** 5.6 **3.** 9 m **4.** 11.2 m **5.** 7.8 in. **6.** 7.2 cm **7.** 9.9 in.
Self Test 2, p. 366 **1.** $\frac{3}{5}$ **2.** $\frac{3}{4}$ **3.** 1.6639 **4.** 0.4472 **5.** 0.8945 **6.** 0.4472 **7.** 0.8945 **8.** 4.2 **9.** 5.1 **10.** 14.0 **11.** 53°; 37° **12.** 53°: 37°

CHAPTER 12 PROBABILITY

Self Test 1, p. 389 **1.** $\frac{1}{5}$ **2.** $\frac{2}{5}$ **3.** $\frac{4}{5}$ **4.** $\frac{2}{5}$ **7.** 60 **8.** 24 **9.** $\frac{1}{10}$ **10.** $\frac{1}{5}$ **11.** $\frac{1}{5}$
Self Test 2, p. 402 **1.** $\frac{5}{92}$ **2.** $\frac{3}{46}$ **3.** $\frac{2}{23}$ **4.** $\frac{1}{3}$ **5.** $\frac{7}{5}$ **6.** $\frac{5}{1}$ **7.** 0.3 **8.** 0.2 **9.** 3600 **10.** 2400

CHAPTER 13 GEOMETRY

Self Test 1, p. 424 **1.** $\angle 4$, $\angle 6$; $\angle 3$, $\angle 5$ **2.** 146° **3.** 34° **4.** 540°; 43° **5.** 720°; 119° **6.** $2\frac{1}{2}$ **7.** 3 **8.** 5056 gal
Self Test 2, p. 430 **1.** 15, 5, 15 **2.** 17, 17, 17 **3.** 21, 30, 37 **4.** *APL* **5.** 60° **6.** 15

CHAPTER 14 PROGRAMMING IN BASIC

Self Test 1, p. 451 **1.** 10 PRINT 48/6, 20 END **2.** 10 PRINT (3+7)/2, 20 END **3.** 10 PRINT 4↑2+5↑3, 20 END **4.** 3.5, 6.8, 23.8 **5.** 25, 50, 150 **6.** 10 FOR N=20 TO 30 STEP 2, 20 PRINT N, 30 NEXT N, 40 END **7.** Answers will vary
Self Test 2, p. 462 **1.** 200, 2; 11.52, 2; 75, 3 **2.** 6, 11.1 **3.** 20 PRINT X↑2+Y↑2; 500, 28.8, 250 **4.** YOUR AVERAGE IS 81; YOUR AVERAGE IS 92.6667; CONGRATULATIONS. YOU'VE MADE HONOR ROLL **5.** 40 IF D<90 THEN 50, 50 PRINT "SORRY, YOU MISSED HONOR ROLL"

Answers to Selected Exercises

CHAPTER 1. WHOLE NUMBERS AND VARIABLES

Page 3 Exercises   1. 18   **3.** 11   **5.** 50   **7.** 8
9. 6   **11.** 11   **13.** 16   **15.** 15   **17.** 57
19. $x + 15$ **21.** $y - 65$ **23.** $r \div 26$ **25.** $24n$
27. $s \div 8$ **29.** $n + 52$ **31.** $y + 8$
33. $125 - t$ **35.** $\$19.35 \div n$

Page 3 Problems   1. $20b$

Pages 6–7 Exercises   1. 55   **3.** 189   **5.** 456
7. 589   **9.** 1397   **11.** 1562   **13.** 1662
15. 4785   **17.** $598 + 63 = x$; 661
19. $886 + 749 = v$; 1635
21. $158 + 6839 = z$; 6997   **23.** 89   **25.** 256
27. 1881   **29.** $15 + 26 + 56 + 46 = d$;
$d = 143$ **31.** $56 + 26 + 15 + 15 + 10 = d$;
$d = 122$ **33.** 274

Pages 9–10 Exercises   1. 1689   **3.** 1002
5. $3.41   **7.** 22,148   **9.** 92   **11.** 1230
13. 389   **15.** 2715   **17.** 5542
19. $4080 - 67 = x$ **21.** $x = 6000 - 87$
23. $a = 75 + 46$ **25.** 18   **27.** 374   **29.** 259
31. 97   **33.** $897 - 255 = n$; 642
35. $426 - 399 = n$; 27   **37.** No; for example,
$(6 - 4) - 2 \neq 6 - (4 - 2)$

Pages 12–13 Exercises
1. $480 + 521 + 511 + 609 = t$; 2121
students   **3.** $94 - 72 = t$; 22 seconds
5. $(350 + 158) - 198 = m$; $310
7. $(475 - 298) + 965 = b$; $1142

Pages 16–17 Exercises   1. 988   **3.** 26,169
5. 3,047,404   **7.** 1728   **9.** 9   **11.** 7161
13. 24,320   **15.** 54   **17.** 238   **19.** 406
21. 343   **23.** 360   **25.** 86   **27.** $5086b$
29. $r + 3000$ **31.** $a + 7215$ **33.** $9n$

Page 17 Problems   1. $132   **3.** 3 tickets; 2nd
balcony matinee; $5

Pages 19–20 Exercises   1. 12   **3.** 128
5. 1559R1   **7.** 92R34   **9.** 16   **11.** 9
13. 364R10   **15.** 11   **17.** 15   **19.** 11   **21.** 15
23. 58   **25.** $468 \div x$ **27.** $r + 76$
29. $w \div 339$ **31.** $21 \div n$ **33.** No, for

example $6 \div 3 \neq 3 \div 6$

Page 20 Problems   1. $25.50

Page 22 Exercises   1. 1   **3.** 23   **5.** 76   **7.** 0
9. 9865   **11.** 675   **13.** 96   **15.** 9   **17.** 50
19. 1000   **21.** 0   **23.** 0   **25.** 1   **27.** 1   **29.** 1
31. 1   **33.** 37   **35.** 76   **37.** Yes, 0; $n - 0 = n$

Page 22 Using the Calculator   1. 732,323
3. 6761   **5.** 22,761

Page 25 Exercises   1. a. 22   **b.** 26   **3. a.** 26
b. 42   **5. a.** 39   **b.** 114   **7. a.** 31   **b.** 72
9. a. 210   **b.** 1728   **11.** 4; b **13.** 87; c
15. 963; z **17.** 4, 7; p, q **19.** $4n$ **21.** $16x$
23. $47r - 17x$ **25.** $30s - 5t$ **27.** $11e - 27b$
29. 60   **31.** 20   **33.** 1   **35.** 72   **37.** 2
39. 438   **41.** $19a + 6b$ **43.** $6b - 4y + 75$

Page 27 Algebra Practice   1. 14   **3.** 9   **5.** 60
7. $406 + 97 = s$; 503   **9.** $89 + 19 = l$; 108
11. $623 + 94 = f$; 717   **13.** $42h$
15. $6273 \div n$ **17.** $c + 50$ **19.** 42   **21.** 683
23. 1   **25.** 4   **27.** 6   **29.** 25   **31.** 16   **33.** 0
35. 0   **37.** $2n$ **39.** $5s + t$ **41.** $8x + y$
43. $10a + 8$ **45.** $3x + y$

Pages 28–29 Problem Solving on the Job
1. $228   **3.** 42   **5.** $8.75   **7.** $285
9. 7500 bricks   **11.** $14,280   **13.** $4140
15. $2745

Page 30 Enrichment   1. 1, 1, 2, 3, 5, 8, 13,
21, 34, 55, 89, 144, 233, 377, 610, 987, 1597,
2584, 4181, 6765   **3.** 54; 143; 1596

Page 31 Chapter Review   1. c   **3.** a   **5.** d
7. c   **9.** a   **11.** a   **13.** b   **15.** T   **17.** T
19. F   **21.** F   **23.** T   **25.** T   **27.** T   **29.** T

Page 33 Cumulative Review (Ch. 1)   1. 486
3. 7267   **5.** 2232   **7.** 35   **9.** 80   **11.** 133
13. 15   **15.** 1   **17.** 9   **19.** 16   **21.** 43   **23.** 40
25. 2   **27.** 3   **29.** $4x + 4$ **31.** $7x$ **33.** y
35. $6p + 6$ **37.** $7b$ **39.** $14c + 21$ **41.** 0
43. $7g + 9h$ **45.** $x - 16$ **47.** $54 + 16 + w$
49. $12c$

CHAPTER 2. DECIMALS

Pages 36–37 Exercises 1. 24.45 **3.** 24.22
5. 24.61 **7.** 86.79; 86.790 **9.** 86.77; 86.770
11. c **13.** b **15.** b **17.** 0.7 **19.** 0.2401
21. 17.006 **23.** 4001.0023 **25.** 0.009
27. 4.0006 **29.** 640.050201 **31.** 0.1 **33.** 0.1
35. 0.1 **37.** 0.01

Pages 39–40 Exercises 1. 3.7, 5.2, 6.8
3. 3.2, 3.3, 4.2 **5.** 52.2, 52.3, 53.3 **7.** 87.77,
87.78, 87.87 **9.** 9.013, 9.103, 9.301
11. 413.12, 413.23, 413.32, 431.32 **13.** 2.1349,
21.349, 213.49, 2134.9 **15.** 0.8, 0.08, 0.008
17. 39.954, 29.95, 29.9 **19.** 71.455, 71.45, 71.4
21. 7.2913, 7.291, 7.29, 7.28 **23.** 190.9,
190.099, 190.09, 19.009 **25.** 610.8, 61.0813,
61.081, 61.008 **27.** $>$ **29.** $>$ **31.** $>$
33. $>$ **35.** $>$ **37.** $<$

Page 40 Problems 1. $a > 4.1$ **3.** $s = 5.21$
5. $7.45 < c$ **7.** $h > 7.04$ **9.** $7.6 < f$

Page 40 Challenge 4 dimes, 1 quarter, 1 half
dollar

Pages 43–44 Exercises 1. 5 cm **3.** 10 cm
5. 12 cm **7.** 0 **9.** 47 **11.** 89 **13.** 493
15. 470 **17.** 0.3 **19.** 38.1 **21.** 69.0
23. 863.0 **25.** 766.3 **27.** 0.57 **29.** 31.21
31. 38.49 **33.** 840.40 **35.** 590.01 **37.** 0.131
39. 18.579 **41.** 86.005 **43.** 877.056
45. 440.321 **47.** 99.5, 100.4 **49.** 108.5, 109.4
51. 501.5, 502.4

Pages 46–47 Exercises 1. 47.06 **3.** 84.05
5. 57.44 **7.** 701.72 **9.** 807.71 **11.** 40
13. 770 **15.** 80 **17.** 99 **19.** 7.89
21. 32.343 **23.** 117.257 **25.** 36.38
27. 31.278 **29.** 17.742 **31.** $12b$ **33.** $33.84a$
35. $25.797g$ **37.** $36.2406m$ **39.** $193.51t$
41. $22.31g + 3.77h$ **43.** $24.91s + 57t$
45. $7.94j + 3.9k$

Page 47 Problems 1. $x + 3.7$ **3.** $b + 0.92$
5. $5.61 + a$ **7.** $b + 2.3$ **9.** $4.85 + 31.7 = b$;
36.55 **11.** $71.6 + 2.13 = g$; 73.73
13. $n = 3.074 + 12.62$; 15.694

Pages 49–50 Exercises 1. 0.242 **3.** 4.17
5. 244.87 **7.** 18.75 **9.** 475.7514 **11.** 2
13. 537 **15.** 246 **17.** 6 **19.** 1.91 **21.** 0.661
23. 29.92 **25.** 0.287 **27.** 4.738 **29.** 220.69
31. $2.2a$ **33.** $7.68x$ **35.** $51.74b$ **37.** $3.6v$

39. $168.108z$ **41.** 13.93 **43.** 23.93 **45.** 73.15
47. 826.531 **49.** $388.596 - 68.079 = 320.517$
51. $17.0036 - 8.2462 = 8.7574$

Page 50 Problems 1. $8.3 - t$ **3.** $x - 18.4$
5. $b + 7.41$ **7.** $21.073 - 4.68 = r$; 16.393
9. $40.61 + 321.7 = a$; 362.31

Page 52 Exercises 1. 2.66 **3.** 0.91, 0.9
5. 0.91, 0.1 **7.** 4:15 P.M.; 5:00 P.M.

Page 55 Exercises 1. 20.8 **3.** 84.36 **5.** 6.84
7. 0.007 **9.** 0.3609 **11.** 150 **13.** 32
15. 240 **17.** 320 **19.** 42.91 **21.** 22.32
23. 2299.18 **25.** 591.2 **27.** 36.82 **29.** 0.006
31. 4 **33.** 36.8 **35.** 746.3 **37.** 63 **39.** 963.4
41. 640 **43.** 571 **45.** 9812.4 **47.** 29,340
49. 2.108 **51.** 79.19 **53.** 22.03

Page 56 Problems 1. $3.7b$ **3.** $4.82d$
5. $3.712 + m$ **7.** $2h$ **9.** $3.02 **11.** $3.80
13. $.65 **15.** $2.69 **17.** $12.05

Pages 59–60 Exercises 1. 4.5 **3.** 0.2
5. 182 **7.** 0.68 **9.** 0.04 **11.** 12.4 **13.** 4
15. 42 **17.** 30 **19.** 60 **21.** 2 **23.** 2
25. 45.236 **27.** 0.623 **29.** 0.055 **31.** 0.06486
33. 5.8861 **35.** 0.8216 **37.** 0.004312
39. 0.000921 **41.** 1.5308 **43.** 1.46 **45.** 2.18
47. 3.5 **49.** 40 **51.** 25 **53.** 32 **55.** 29

Page 60 Problems 1. $7.3a$ **3.** $81.1b$ **5.** $3.8s$
7. $47.2 - d$ **9.** $5.18 \div b$ **11.** $(2.13)(1.5) = z$;
3.195 **13.** $80.08 - 14.7 = v$; 65.38

Page 62 Exercises 1. 1000 **3.** 10 **5.** 0.01
7. 600 **9.** 2.4 **11.** 86 **13.** 85 **15.** 0.0743
17. 0.304 **19.** 8.342 **21.** 45 **23.** 724.3

Page 63 Algebra Practice 1. 12 **3.** 3 **5.** 1
7. $16.18r$ **9.** $13c + 6.2f$ **11.** $13.177b$
13. 7.436 **15.** $a^2 + 4a$ **17.** h^4 **19.** $g - 2.6$
21. $7.5 \div v$ **23.** $196 + 505 = n$; 701
25. $36.409 - 19.7 = h$; 16.709
27. $18 \div 3.6 = b$; 5
29. $11.097 + 230.28 + 1.973 = s$; 243.35
31. $21 + 804 = y$; 825 **33.** $37 + 27.4 = q$;
64.4 **35.** $j = 6^2$; 36 **37.** $86 - 2.71 = h$;
83.29 **39.** $n = (2.01)(0.009)$; 0.01809

**Pages 64–65 Problem Solving for the
Consumer 1.** $9125.60 **3.** $6042.60
5. $1396.90 **7.** $575.82; $164.22 **9.** $7218.66,
$415.80, $8257, $7634.46, $622.54
11. $304.23 **13.** $466.93, $504.28 **15.** 10

503

Page 66 Enrichment **1.** 100101 110100 100100 010010 010101 101001 101001 **3.** 010010 011001 100101 010001 101001 111000 **5.** 100100 110100 100011 110011 011001 100111 100011 111000 **7.** 011000 100110 100100 010011 110110 100110 101001 100010 **9.** John von Neumann

Page 67 Chapter Review **1.** C **3.** A **5.** F **7.** B **9.** No **11.** Yes **13.** Yes **15.** b **17.** a

19. c **21.** 27.15 **23.** 0.42 **25.** 219.75 **27.** 731.235 **29.** 0.423 **31.** 76.2 **33.** 0.0058

Page 69 Cumulative Review (Chapters 1–2)
1. 87,019 **3.** 0 **5.** 35 **7.** 74 **9.** 480.7
11. 84.213 **13.** 4 **15.** 81 **17.** 5290 **19.** 322
21. 30,000 **23.** 5300 **25.** 4.0 **27.** a **29.** b
31. a^2 **33.** $5a^3$ **35.** $5xyz$ **37.** $4t^2w$ **39.** 1
41. $7j + j^2$ **43.** $83 - 47.1 = g$; 35.9
45. $d = 55(2)$; 110 mi

CHAPTER 3. NUMBER THEORY

Pages 73–74 Exercises **1.** Yes **3.** Yes
5. Yes **7.** Yes **9.** No **11.** No **13.** Yes
15. No **17.** Divisible by 2, 3, 4, 5, 6, 8, and
10 **19.** Divisible by 2, 3, 4, 5, 6, 9, and 10
21. Divisible by 2, 3, 6, 9 **23.** Divisible by 2,
3, 6 **25.** Divisible by 2, 3, 4, 6, 9
27. Divisible by 2, 3, 6 **29.** Divisible by all
31. Divisible by 2, 4, 8 **33.** Divisible by 2, 4,
8 **35.** Divisible by 2, 3, 4, 6, 9, **37.** T
39. T **41.** T **43.** 2 **45.** 4, 6 **47.** $2n + 1$
49. $n + 2$ **51.** Yes **53.** No **55.** Yes

Page 74 Problems **1.** Yes **3.** 8 teams of 9, 9
teams of 8, 2 teams of 36, 3 teams of 24, 4
teams of 18, 6 teams of 12

Page 74 Using the Calculator **1.** 6
3. 3,628,800 **5.** 29,030,400

Page 78 Exercises **1.** $90 = 3 \times 3 \times 2 \times 5$
3. $2^3 \times 3$ **5.** $3^2 \times 7$ **7.** $2 \times 3 \times 5$
9. $2 \times 3 \times 11$ **11.** 2^7 **13.** $2 \times 5 \times 13$
15. $2^3 \times 3^2 \times 5^2 \times 7$ **17.** $2^4 \times 11$
19. $2 \times 3^3 \times 7$ **21.** $2^2 \times 3 \times 5 \times 11$
23. $2^6 \times 5^2$ **25.** $2^4 \times 7^2$ **27.** $5^2 \times 7^2$
29. 15, 6

Page 78 Problems **1.** 6; 3, 5; 5, 7; 11, 13;
17, 19; 29, 31; 41, 43

Page 80 Exercises **1.** 1, 2, 3, 6 **3.** 1, 3,
5, 15 **5.** 1, 2, 3, 4, 6, 8, 12, 24 **7.** 3 **9.** 6
11. 14 **13.** 4 **15.** 6 **17.** 4 **19.** 3 **21.** 18
23. 6 **25.** 16 **27.** 9 **29.** 12 **31.** 36
33. Yes **35.** No

Page 83 Exercises **1.** h **3.** 2 **5.** n **7.** q
9. $3(s^2 - 1)$ **11.** $5(v^2 - 2)$ **13.** $4(3x^3 - 1)$

15. $a(a + 2)$ **17.** $c(c - 2)$ **19.** $e(1 - 2e)$
21. $3g(2g - 1)$ **23.** $5j(3 + 4j)$
25. $5m(6 + 5m)$ **27.** $pq(6 + pq)$
29. $4uv(3u - 2v)$ **31.** $a(y^2 + y + 1)$
33. $2(6 + 4a - 3a^2)$ **35.** $4c(3c - 2 - d)$

Page 86 Exercises **1.** 10 **3.** 4 **5.** 204

Page 89 Exercises **1.** 8, 16, 24, 32
3. 12, 16 **5.** 30, 60, 90; LCM = 30
7. 14, 28, 42, 56, 70, 84, 98; LCM = 14
9. 30, 60, 90; LCM = 30 **11.** 60;
LCM = 60 **13.** 4 **15.** 9 **17.** 36 **19.** 20
21. 30 **23.** 30 **25.** 90 **27.** 240 **29.** $2a^2$
31. $8c^2$ **33.** $30e^3$ **35.** hj **37.** 100 **39.** 360
41. 300 **43.** $75d^3$ **45.** $24x^2y^2$

Pages 91–92 Exercises **1. a.** 1000 **b.** 3000
c. 3100 **3. a.** 100,000 **b.** 200,000
c. 210,000 **5. a.** 1.0×10^4 **b.** 5.0×10^4
c. 5.1×10^4 **7. a.** 1.0×10^6 **b.** 7.0×10^6
c. 7.2×10^6 **9.** 9300 **11.** 17,000 **13.** 180
15. 380,000 **17.** 3,900,000,000,000
19. 7,100,000,000 **21.** 300,000,000
23. 1,230,000 **25.** 7.6×10^4

Page 93 Algebra Practice
1. $2398 + 9746 = r$; 12,144 **3.** $780(67) = m$;
52,260 **5.** $2784 \div 87 = f$; 32
7. $1986.21 + 8.005 + 497.6 = d$; 2491.815
9. $(0.41)(0.25) = y$; 0.1025 **11.** $11.1a + 5.2b$
13. $6.9p - 4.8q$ **15.** 5.356 **17.** $2r^2$ **19.** $4m$
21. $2y$ **23.** $2s(s^2 - 3st + 5)$ **25.** $5b(b^2 - 3)$
27. $fg(fg + f - g)$ **29.** $4x(2xy - x + y^2)$
31. $3w^2$ **33.** $15q^2$ **35.** $3k^2n$ **37.** $60d^2$
39. $20r^2s$ **41.** $48a^2b^2$

Pages 94–95 Problem Solving on the Job
1. 10 days **3.** 9 days **5.** $9\frac{1}{2}$ days **7.** 9 days

9. 9 days **11.** $24.45 **13.** $30.30 **15.** $443
17. $447.50

Page 96 Enrichment **1.** 50 **3.** 400 **5.** 199

Page 97 Chapter Review **1.** c **3.** c **5.** c
7. d **9.** d **11.** e **13.** $2(3a + 1)$
15. $2(c - 2c^2 + 3)$ **17.** F **19.** T
21. 9:35 P.M.

Page 99 Cumulative Review (Chapters 1–3)
1. 670 **3.** 8 **5.** 100,000 **7.** 125 **9.** 143
11. 10 **13.** $8a + 4$ **15.** $p + 14y - 2$
17. $5a - b$ **19.** $3(x + 1)$ **21.** $2(4 - c)$
23. $5(y^2 + 2)$ **25.** $3(2s^2 - s + 5)$
27. $5(2f^2 + f - 5)$ **29.** $35 - n$ **31.** $12 + 5y$
33. $3d$

CHAPTER 4. FRACTIONS

Pages 103–104 Exercises **1.** $\frac{6}{1}$ **3.** $\frac{8}{1}$ **5.** $\frac{10}{1}$
7. $\frac{12}{1}$ **9.** $\frac{14}{1}$ **11.** $\frac{16}{1}$ **13.** $\frac{4}{1}$ **15.** $\frac{7}{2}$ **17.** $\frac{9}{4}$
19. $\frac{8}{11}$ **21.** $\frac{5}{13}$ **23.** $\frac{3}{2}$ **25.** $\frac{5}{4}$ **27.** $\frac{5}{4}$ **29.** $\frac{7}{4}$
31. $\frac{7}{2}$ **33.** $1\frac{1}{2}$ **35.** $1\frac{1}{5}$ **37.** 2 **39.** 7 **41.** 8
43. $\frac{21}{4}$ **45.** $\frac{49}{6}$ **47.** $\frac{44}{7}$ **49.** $\frac{53}{5}$ **51.** $\frac{129}{10}$
53. $1\frac{1}{4}$ **55.** $2\frac{2}{5}$ **57.** $3\frac{3}{7}$ **59.** 2 **61.** $1\frac{11}{20}$

Page 104 Problems **1.** $\frac{n}{21}$ **3.** $\frac{m}{30}$ **5.** $\frac{28}{81}$
7. $\frac{65}{81}$ **9.** $\frac{81}{81}$

Page 107 Exercises **1.** 6 **3.** 49 **5.** 42 **7.** 3
9. $\frac{2}{3}$ **11.** $\frac{1}{2}$ **13.** $\frac{1}{4}$ **15.** $\frac{3}{2}$ **17.** 1 **19.** b
21. $\frac{1}{2c}$ **23.** $\frac{1}{2}$ **25.** y **27.** $\frac{a}{3}$ **29.** $\frac{2}{3}$ **31.** $\frac{2c}{3}$
33. $\frac{3}{4t}$ **35.** $\frac{3mb}{2}$ **37.** $x + 1$ **39.** 8 **41.** 3
43. $\frac{1}{3}$ **45.** $\frac{3r}{5r + 2}$ **47.** $\frac{3e + 1}{2}$

Page 110 Exercises **1.** $9\frac{43}{72}$ **3.** $6\frac{17}{24}$ **5.** $10\frac{73}{88}$
7. $13\frac{3}{7}$ **9.** $10\frac{25}{33}$ **11.** Yes **13.** No
15. $\frac{8w + 2c}{cw}$ **17.** $\frac{3c + 2b}{bc}$ **19.** $\frac{3b}{8}$
21. $\frac{m + 2f}{10}$

Page 110 Problems **1.** $4\frac{1}{2} + \frac{3}{5} = n$; $5\frac{1}{10}$
3. $\frac{3}{4} + \frac{1}{2} = p$; $1\frac{1}{4}$ lb **5.** $\frac{5}{8} + \frac{5}{6} + \frac{2}{3} + \frac{1}{4} = m$;
$2\frac{3}{8}$ mi

Pages 113 Exercises **1.** $\frac{1}{3}$ **3.** $\frac{1}{10}$ **5.** $\frac{2}{5}$ **7.** $\frac{2}{3}$
9. $\frac{9}{20}$ **11.** $\frac{5}{14}$ **13.** $\frac{5}{y}$ **15.** $\frac{10}{s}$ **17.** $\frac{a}{n}$ **19.** 0
21. $\frac{2b}{9}$ **23.** $\frac{m}{24}$ **25.** $\frac{3}{4}$ **27.** $\frac{9}{20}$ **29.** $\frac{4}{9}$
31. $1\frac{7}{12}$ **33.** $2\frac{1}{36}$ **35.** $4\frac{8}{15}$ **37.** $\frac{7a + 4}{8}$

39. $\frac{7c + 5}{12}$ **41.** $2a - 2b$

Page 114 Problems **1.** $4\frac{2}{3} - 1\frac{1}{3} = n$; $3\frac{1}{3}$
3. $\frac{5}{8} - \frac{1}{3} = n$; $\frac{7}{24}$ **5.** $\frac{7}{8} - \frac{7}{10} = n$; $\frac{7}{40}$ mi

Page 117 Exercises **1.** $2\frac{1}{2}$ **3.** $3\frac{1}{2}$ **5.** 4 **7.** 1
9. $\frac{1}{3}$ **11.** $\frac{1}{4}$ **13.** $\frac{8}{b}$ **15.** $\frac{7f}{13}$ **17.** $\frac{1}{3}$ **19.** 8
21. $\frac{22m}{21}$ **23.** $\frac{2b}{3}$ **25.** $\frac{b}{3}$ **27.** $\frac{g}{6}$ **29.** $\frac{q}{8}$

Page 117 Problems **1.** $2 \cdot \frac{3}{4} = n$; $1\frac{1}{2}$
3. $25 \cdot \frac{4}{5} = n$; 20 **5.** $25 \cdot \frac{2}{3} = n$; $16\frac{2}{3}$ lb

Pages 119–120 Exercises **1.** $\frac{1}{6}$ **3.** $\frac{1}{20}$ **5.** $3\frac{1}{3}$
7. $5\frac{1}{4}$ **9.** 1 **11.** $1\frac{1}{2}$ **13.** $\frac{x}{2}$ **15.** $\frac{17c}{64}$ **17.** $\frac{5e}{3}$
19. $\frac{17g}{13}$ **21.** $\frac{11}{35r}$ **23.** $\frac{11}{12e}$ **25.** $\frac{4}{5}b$ **27.** $\frac{3}{8}m$
29. $\frac{1}{3}m$ **31.** $\frac{4}{7}r$

Page 120 Problems **1.** $\frac{24}{x}$ **3.** $4\frac{5}{8}$ ft **5.** 4
7. $8\frac{1}{3}$ yd

Pages 122–123 Exercises **1.** $1\frac{9}{16}c$ **3.** $60;
$80 **5.** yes **7.** $368 **9.** 3 mi

Page 125 Exercises **1.** 2.5 **3.** 0.24 **5.** 0.625
7. $0.\overline{5}$ **9.** 1.25 **11.** 0.875 **13.** 0.2 **15.** $0.4\overline{6}$
17. $\frac{24}{25}$ **19.** $\frac{11}{50}$ **21.** $\frac{37}{100}$ **23.** $2\frac{7}{10}$ **25.** $1\frac{1}{8}$
27. $1\frac{4}{5}$ **29.** $7\frac{3}{125}$ **31.** 3.2 **33.** $1.\overline{72}$ **35.** $3.41\overline{6}$
37. 4.35 **39.** 1.54 **41.** $0.\overline{6}$ **43.** $0.\overline{3}$ **45.** 0.2

Page 127 Algebra Practice **1.** 1 **3.** 13 **5.** 1
7. $3b(b^2 + 2c + 5)$ **9.** $jk(3k + jk + 2j)$
11. $12a^2b$ **13.** 2 **15.** $\frac{6}{b}$ **17.** $\frac{d}{e}$
19. $4073 - 2981 = a$; 1092

505

21. $9632 \div 112 = u$; 86
23. $86.28 + 100.5 + 1.097 = t$; 187.877
25. $n = 2\frac{1}{3} + 1\frac{1}{4}$; $3\frac{7}{12}$ **27.** $\frac{3}{4} \cdot 18 = n$; $13\frac{1}{2}$
29. $2\frac{2}{5} \cdot 1\frac{7}{8} = n$; $4\frac{1}{2}$

Pages 128–129 Problem Solving for the Consumer 1. $98\frac{1}{8}$ **3.** $64\frac{3}{8}$ **5.** $1\frac{1}{8}$
7. $1055 **9.** 11 shares **11** $250 **13.** $980

Page 130 Enrichment 1. $\frac{1}{3}$ **3.** $\frac{11}{9}$ **5.** $\frac{233}{99}$
7. $\frac{62}{99}$ **9.** $\frac{711}{333}$

Pages 131 Chapter Review 1. f **3.** e **5.** c

7. d **9.** b **11.** c **13.** $\frac{c}{2}$ **15.** $\frac{11r}{24}$ **17.** 16
19. $\frac{m}{r}$ **21.** $2\frac{1}{3}$ **23.** $1\frac{5}{14}$ **25.** $9\frac{7}{20}$

Page 133 Cumulative Review 1. 1.74 **3.** 18
5. 21 **7.** 1 **9.** $\frac{1}{5}$ **11.** $8\frac{1}{4}$ **13.** $1\frac{2}{5}$ **15.** $\frac{5}{9}$
17. $\frac{1}{3}$ **19.** $2y + 11x$ **21.** 12 **23.** $6n$
25. $4x^2 + 4x$ **27.** $9x - 18$ **29.** $\frac{d}{8}$ **31.** $24x$
33. $\frac{1}{4a}$ **35.** $17t$ **37.** $18; $22

CHAPTER 5. SOLVING EQUATIONS

Page 137 Exercises 1. yes **3.** no **5.** no
7. no **9.** *no* **11.** 16 **13.** 12 **15.** 20 **17.** 10
19. 82 **21.** 160 **23.** 3 **25.** 2 **27.** 5 **29.** 23
31. 96 **33.** 13 **35.** 30 **37.** 7 **39.** 85
41. 2.2 **43.** 1.6 **45.** $\frac{1}{2}$ **47.** 3
49. $e + 36 = 60$ **51.** $d + 7 = 8$

Page 139 Exercises 1. 9 **3.** 5 **5.** 4 **7.** 6
9. 2 **11.** 1 **13.** 4 **15.** 11 **17.** 3 **19.** 39
21. 16 **23.** 18 **25.** 197 **27.** 843 **29.** 19
31. 13 **33.** 5.5 **35.** 0.1 **37.** $5\frac{1}{4}$ **39.** 3
41. 3.24

Page 142 Exercises 1. 3 **3.** 6 **5.** 9 **7.** 4
9. 7 **11.** 6.5 **13.** 30 **15.** 5 **17.** 61 **19.** 30
21. 7 **23.** 32 **25.** 2 **27.** 20 **29.** 1.2
31. 200 **33.** 9 **35.** 20 **37.** 16 **39.** 12
41. 40 **43.** 13 **45.** 8 **47.** 0 **49.** $247\frac{1}{2}$
51. 9 **53.** $1\frac{1}{3}$

Page 144 Exercises 1. 6 **3.** 5 **5.** 14 **7.** 18
9. 13 **11.** 17 **13.** 20 **15.** 20 **17.** 46
19. 211 **21.** 60 **23.** 100 **25.** 126 **27.** 141
29. 1 **31.** $5\frac{1}{4}$ **33.** 5 **35.** 5 **37.** 16 **39.** 74
41. 94 **43.** 73 **45.** 11 **47.** 0.7

Page 144 Problems 1. $5n$ **3.** $x + 5$ **5.** 55

Page 147 Exercises 1. 2 **3.** 4 **5.** 2 **7.** 4
9. 8 **11.** 24 **13.** 10 **15.** 28 **17.** 24
19. 300 **21.** 16 **23.** 120 **25.** 36 **27.** 76
29. 17.5 **31.** 7.4 **33.** 3 **35.** 5.1 **37.** 60
39. 38 **41.** 62 **43.** 180 **45.** 159 **47.** 12
49. 3 **51.** 3

Pages 151–152 Exercises 1. $a = 6$
3. $x = 6$ **5.** $d = 20$ **7.** $f = 5$ **9.** 36 **11.** 4
13. 18 **15.** 5 **17.** 5 **19.** 3 **21.** 16 **23.** 2
25. 9 **27.** 1 **29.** 4 **31.** 24 **33.** 32 **35.** 0
37. 5 **39.** 9 **41.** 5 **43.** 7 **45.** 7 **47.** 5
49. $1\frac{2}{3}$ **51.** $3\frac{5}{6}$ **53.** Yes **55.** No **57.** Yes

Page 152 Challenge Plan B

Page 154 Exercises 1. $e = 4$ **3.** $g = 2$
5. 11 **7.** 4 **9.** 9 **11.** $1\frac{4}{5}$ **13.** 4 **15.** 1
17. 16 **19.** 2 **21.** 6 **23.** 7 **25.** 25 **27.** 2
29. 2 **31.** 4 **33.** 1 **35.** 1 **37.** 1 **39.** 11
41. 5 **43.** 6

Pages 157–158 Exercises 1. d **3.** k **5.** c
7. g **9.** b **11. a.** $n + 1$; **b.** $2x + 1$;
c. $3p + 1$; **d.** $2r + 1$ **13. a.** $50 - 10$;
b. $m - 10$; **c.** $2x - 10$ **15. a.** $s + 3$;
b. $s + 2$ **17. a.** $\frac{1}{2}a$; **b.** $\frac{1}{2}a + 3$ **19. a.** $2c$;
b. $2c + 5$ **21.** $0.1d$ **23.** $\frac{h}{10}$

Pages 160–161 Exercises 1. a; 16 years
3. d; 192 in. **5.** $s + 13 = 35$; 22
7. $t - 3 = 62$; 65 in. **9.** $x + x + 5 = 27$;
16 games **11.** $3s = 18$; 6 tickets
13. $x + x + 38 = 952$; 457 boys, 495 girls

Pages 163–164 Exercises 1. $x - 14 = 29$;
43 people **3.** $2n = 54$; 27 computers
5. $6x = 486$; 81 **7.** $2t + t = 687$; 229,458
9. $c + c + 20 = 78$; 49 customers;
29 customers **11.** $\frac{1}{2}x + x = 1272$; 424 pets;
106 pets

Page 165 Algebra Practice **1.** $308 \cdot 280 = k$; 86,240 **3.** $56.07 - 9.806 = w$; 46.264 **5.** $52.635 \div 8.7 = f$; 6.05 **7.** $7\frac{1}{2} - 3\frac{5}{6} = k$; $3\frac{2}{3}$ **9.** $3\frac{1}{2} + 1\frac{1}{8} + 4\frac{3}{4} = h$; $9\frac{3}{8}$ **11.** $uv(8v + 2uv + u^2)$ **13.** $qr(7 + qr + r)$ **15.** $12gh^2$ **17.** 7 **19.** 23.7 **21.** 1.8 **23.** 6.7 **25.** $\frac{5}{6}$ **27.** 24 **29.** 7 **31.** 11

Pages 166–167 Problem Solving on the Job **1.** \$37.43 **2.** \$37.80 **5.** \$43.37 **7.** \$241.36 **9.** \$3952 **11.** \$697.24

Page 169 Chapter Review **1.** a **3.** 19 **5.** 4 **7.** 26 **9.** 94 **11.** 150 **13.** 42 **15.** 12 **17.** 16 **19.** 3 **21.** c **23.** e **25.** d **27.** f **29.** $6n + 9 = 345$; 56

Page 171 Cumulative Review **1.** 388.2 **3.** 157 **5.** 7965.79 **7.** 81 **9.** 16 **11.** $\frac{1}{4}$ **13.** 68 **15.** 0 **17.** 1670 **19.** $\frac{1}{2}(a + b + c)$ **21.** $5y(y - 2)$ **23.** $5(n^2 - 5)$ **25.** $n - 47$ **27.** $(9.50)(8) + (9.50)(1.5)(4) = x$; \$133 **29.** $56 - 24 = x$; 32

CHAPTER 6. FORMULAS

Page 175 Exercises **1.** 44 **3.** 28.4 **5.** 16.8 mi **7.** 64.5 **9.** $28\,s$ **11.** $78.9\,m$ **13.** 16

Page 178 Exercises **1.** 31.4 **3.** 15.7 **5.** $238.64\,m$ **7.** $94.2\,m$ **9.** 19.5936 km **11.** 132 **13.** $2\frac{2}{3}$ **15.** 3

Page 178 Problems **1.** Neither.

Pages 181–182 Exercises **1.** Yes **3.** No **5.** No **7.** acute **9.** straight **11.** obtuse **13.** obtuse **15.** obtuse **17.** *ST, TV* **19.** 180° **21.** 270° **23.** 180° **25.** No. They do not form right angles.

Page 185 Exercises **1.** 17.5 ft² **3.** 110.25 m² **5.** $43\frac{1}{20}$ in. **7.** 72 cm² **9.** 288 square units

Page 185 Problems **1.** 9 yd **3.** 20 yd **5.** 9 ft

Page 188 Exercises **1.** 200.96 in.² **3.** 5538.96 yd² **5.** 38.465 in.² **7.** 254.34 yd² **9.** 314 mi² **11.** circle; 481.5 in.² **13.** circle; 15.94 ft² **15.** 18.84 sq. units **17.** 100.48 sq. units **19.** 1316.16 yd²

Pages 190–191 Exercises **1.** 132 **3.** 104.5 **5.** 52.25 **7.** $6.\overline{6}$ ft **9.** 595 mi/h

Pages 193–194 Exercises **1.** 154 in.³ **3.** 330 yd³ **5.** 200 ft³ **7.** 6331.625 yd³ **9.** 29.75 m³ **11.** 7644 in.³ **13.** 1521 ft³

Page 194 Problems **1.** 16 yd² **3.** 6 m **5.** 11 **7.** $47,282\frac{2}{3}$ ft³

Pages 196–197 Exercises **1.** 2769.48 in.³ **3.** 2207.8125 m³ **5.** 4521.6 m³ **7.** 1959.36 cm³ **9.** 221.37 ft³ **11.** 602.88 cm³

Page 200 Exercises **1.** 384 sq. units **3.** 533.8 sq. units **5.** 465 ft² **7.** 468 cm² **9.** 1628 cm²

Page 201 Algebra Practice **1.** $r = 355 \times 982$; 348,610 **3.** $0.0861 \div 0.07 = x$; 1.23 **5.** $(\frac{1}{8})(4\frac{4}{5}) = q$; $\frac{3}{5}$ **7.** $2b(3c + b + 2bc)$ **9.** $\frac{3}{8}$ **11.** $\frac{7}{8}$ **13.** 6 **15.** $P = (2)(4.8) + (2)(3.6)$; 16.8 m **17.** $C = (3.14)(28)$; 87.92 yd **19.** $A = (3.14)(5^2)$; 78.5 m² **21.** $V = (10)(6) \div 3$; 20 m³ **23.** $S = 2(5 \times 3) + 2(5 \times 10) + 2(3 \times 10)$; 190 cm²

Pages 202–203 Problem Solving for the Consumer **1.** 130 ft² **3.** 2 qt; 4 qt **5.** \$15.50 **7.** \$47.21; Yes **9.** \$19.81

Page 204 Enrichment **1.** 9, 13, 17, 21, 25, 29, 33 **3.** 7, 12, 19, 28, 39, 52, 67 **5.** $n \to n^2 + 2n$; 24, 35, 48, 63, 80

Page 205 Chapter Review **1.** d **3.** h **5.** l **7.** j **9.** o **11.** n **13.** c **15.** m **17.** c **19.** a

Page 207 Cumulative Review **1.** 2608 **3.** 62 **5.** 213 **7.** 44.4 **9.** 31 **11.** 67 **13.** 46 **15.** 8920 **17.** 56 **19.** 165 **21.** 4000 **23.** 16 **25.** 16 **27.** 486 **29.** 6.6 **31.** $n \cdot 10 = 4.6$; 0.46 **33.** $(\frac{2}{3})(63) = n$; 42 **35.** $\frac{1}{4}n = 35$; 140 **37.** 64K

CHAPTER 7. RATIO, PROPORTION, PERCENT

Pages 210–211 Exercises 1. $\frac{7}{2}$ **3.** $\frac{4}{1}$ **5.** $\frac{9}{1}$
7. $\frac{3}{1}$ **9.** $2:3$ **11.** $19:20$ **13.** $47:92$
15. $x:y$ **17.** $23:40$ **19.** $\frac{7}{15}; \frac{2}{5}; \frac{2}{15}$

Page 211 Problems 1. a. $48:120$, $72:48$
b. $\frac{2}{5}$, $2:5$; $\frac{3}{2}$, $3:2$ **3.** $\frac{2325}{4481}$; $\frac{4481}{1192}$; $\frac{2325}{1192}$

Page 214 Exercises 1. 3 **3.** 1 **5.** 27 **7.** 18
9. 45 **11.** 70 **13.** 720 **15.** 54.125 **17.** 123
19. The perimeter is doubled.

Page 215 Problems 1. 800 mi **3.** $133.33
5. 12 runs **7.** 48 games

Page 215 Using the Calculator 1. 120 cm
3. 153.6 cm **5.** 140 cm **7.** 179.2 cm

Page 218 Exercises 1. 7% **3.** 99% **5.** 12%
7. 3% **9.** 15% **11.** 90% **13.** $\frac{1}{20}$; 0.05 **15.** $\frac{9}{20}$;
0.45 **17.** $\frac{2}{25}$; 0.08 **19.** $\frac{91}{100}$; 0.91 **21.** $\frac{1}{2}$; 0.50
23. 20% **25.** 90% **27.** 38% **29.** 12%
31. 33% **33.** 14% **35.** 24% **37.** 50%
39. 75% **41.** 43% **43.** 45%

Page 221 Exercises 1. 288 **3.** 18 **5.** 140
7. 1064 **9.** 138 **11.** 12 **13.** $31.98
15. $510.00 **17.** $111.18 **19.** $38.95
21. $25.66 **23.** $135.75

Page 221 Problems 1. $1200; $1000; $720;
$520; $400; $320; $240; $120; The total
amount is more than $4000 because the sum
of the percents is greater than 100%.

Page 227 Exercises 1. 8% **3.** 750%
5. 512.5% **7.** 0.3% **9.** 362% **11.** 1.25%
13. 0.8% **15.** 0.5% **17.** 2 **19.** 1241.25
21. 45.10

Page 227 Problems 1. 4786 mixers **3.** 8090

Page 229 Exercises 1. 1500 **3.** 79,300
5. 1200 **7.** 1200 **9.** 10,000 **11.** 52 **13.** 263

Page 229 Problems 1. $2300 **3.** 5000
transmissions

Pages 231–232 Exercises 1. 26% **3.** 18%
5. 10% **7.** 15% **9.** 20% **11.** 15% **13.** 13%
15. 16% **17.** 133.3% **19.** 40.7% **21.** 28.2%
23. 17.4% **25.** 27.6% **27.** 11.8%

Page 232 Problems 1. $11.\overline{1}\%$ **3.** 20%

Page 233 Algebra Practice 1. $487 \cdot 503 = s$;
244,961 **3.** $20 - 5.683 = d$; 14.317
5. $\frac{2}{15} + \frac{29}{30} = w$; $1\frac{1}{10}$ **7.** $2(2\frac{5}{8}) + 2(1\frac{7}{8}) = p$;
$7\frac{3}{4}$ in. **9.** $(4\frac{1}{2})(2\frac{1}{4})(\frac{1}{2}) = a$; $5\frac{1}{16}$ in.^{2}
11. $(2)(2^2)(3.14) + (4)(4)(3.14) = s$; 75.36 ft^2
13. $6rs^2$ **15.** $\frac{3}{14}$ **17.** 3.5 **19.** 576 **21.** 4
23. 1.6 **25.** 200 **27.** 72 **29.** 2.5

Pages 234–235 Problem Solving on the Job
1. $13,500 **3.** $200; $5200 **5.** $4044
7. $400 **9.** $13,229 **11.** $55.00, $170.00

Page 236 Enrichment 1. 3, 15, 75, 375
3. direct; inverse

Page 237 Chapter Review 1. T **3.** F **5.** T
7. a **9.** e **11.** c **13.** b

Page 239 Cumulative Review 1. $3\frac{2}{3}$ **3.** $7\frac{11}{24}$
5. 0 **7.** 20 **9.** 5.3 **11.** $5\frac{5}{8}$ **13.** 0 **15.** 8340
17. 33 ft^2 **19.** 28.08 m^2 **21.** 28.26 m^2 **23.** 4
seconds **25.** $58.00

CHAPTER 8. INTEGERS AND RATIONAL NUMBERS

Page 242 Exercises 1. $^-8$ **3.** 23 **5.** 17
7. $^-3$ **9.** 4 **15.** $12 > 0$ **17.** $67 > ^-57$
19. 7 units to left **21.** 9 units to left **23.** 9
units to left **25.** True **27.** False

Page 244 Exercises 1. $^-7$ **3.** $^-12$ **5.** $^-12$
7. $^-14$ **9.** $^-13$ **11.** $^-14$ **13.** $^-20$ **15.** $^-34$

17. $^-20$ **19.** $^-35$ **21.** $^-44$ **23.** $^-51$ **25.** $^-81$
27. $^-73$ **29.** ^-7x **31.** ^-20t **33.** ^-25g
35. ^-20y **37.** $^-9n + ^-12p$ **39.** $^-20a + ^-18x$

Page 247 Exercises 1. 6 **3.** $^-2$ **5.** 0 **7.** $^-3$
9. 1 **11.** $^-5$ **13.** 0 **15.** 2 **17.** $^-4$ **19.** 2
21. 11 **23.** $^-5$ **25.** 15 **27.** 27 **29.** $^-8$
31. 4 **33.** a **35.** ^-y **37.** $4x$ **39.** $6m$
41. ^-p **43.** $30n$ **45.** $x + 7y + 6$
47. $^-2t + 6p + 10$ **49.** $3g + ^-3n + ^-8$

Page 249 Exercises 1. $12 + {}^-3 = 9$
3. $4 + 10 = 14$ **5.** ${}^-9 + {}^-6 = {}^-15$
7. $17 + 8 = 25$ **9.** ${}^-8 + 19 = 11$
11. $16 + 23 = 39$ **13.** 10 **15.** ${}^-10$ **17.** ${}^-27$
19. ${}^-18$ **21.** 0 **23.** 42 **25.** ${}^-12$ **27.** 22
29. 0 **31.** 47 **33.** ${}^-47$ **35.** ${}^-9d$ **37.** $18x$
39. ${}^-11h$ **41.** $2p$ **43.** $10x + 7y$
45. $19g + {}^-3n$

Page 252 Exercises 1. ${}^-88$ **3.** ${}^-48$ **5.** 42
7. 30 **9.** ${}^-32$ **11.** 15 **13.** ${}^-120x$ **15.** ${}^-28h$
17. 88 **19.** ${}^-120$ **21.** ${}^-48$ **23.** ${}^-12$ **25.** ${}^-30$
27. 35 **29.** ${}^-28$ **31.** 8 **33.** ${}^-18$ **35.** 30
37. ${}^-40$ **39.** 12 **41.** ${}^-120$ **43.** 120
45. ${}^-16x + 28$ **47.** $15d + 12$
49. ${}^-24k + {}^-32$ **51.** ${}^-66t + 28$

Pages 254-255 Exercises 1. ${}^-7$ **3.** 11
5. ${}^-7$ **7.** ${}^-7$ **9.** ${}^-3$ **11.** ${}^-11$ **13.** $2x$
15. ${}^-2d$ **17.** ${}^-2m$ **19.** ${}^-13k$ **21.** ${}^-2x$
23. ${}^-20y$ **25.** $9h$ **27.** ${}^-8n$ **29.** ${}^-8$ **31.** ${}^-12$
33. ${}^-10$ **35.** ${}^-8$ **37.** ${}^-35$ **39.** 3 **41.** 11
43. ${}^-32$ **45.** 20 **47.** ${}^-39$ **49.** ${}^-24$ **51.** 0

Page 255 Problems 1. ${}^-7°C$ **3.** All; $1641
profit

Page 258 Exercises 1. Negative **3.** Positive
5. Negative **7.** Positive **9.** 0.6 **11.** 8.3
13. 12.3 **15.** 1.51 **17.** 0 **19.** 6.42 **21.** $1\frac{1}{3}$
23. ${}^-1\frac{1}{4}$ **25.** ${}^-14$ **27.** $1\frac{1}{2}$ **29.** ${}^-9\frac{5}{8}$ **31.** ${}^-26\frac{1}{9}$
33. ${}^-11.2$

Page 258 Using the Calculator Final
balance = $61.48. The club has lost money.

Pages 260-261 Exercises 1. ${}^-9.2$ **3.** 17.36
5. ${}^-\frac{1}{4}$ **7.** ${}^-\frac{2}{5}$ **9.** ${}^-1.9$ **11.** ${}^-4.6$ **13.** ${}^-\frac{4}{5}$
15. $1\frac{1}{6}$ **17.** 50.22 **19.** 42.78 **21.** 15.61
23. ${}^-\frac{1}{2}$ **25.** ${}^-\frac{1}{8}$ **27.** ${}^-\frac{3}{16}$ **29.** ${}^-4$ **31.** ${}^-4$
33. $1\frac{1}{4}$ **35.** $3a$ **37.** ${}^-15n$

Page 264 Problems 1. 10 handshakes **3.** 6
ways **5.** 16 ways **7.** $\frac{1}{2}$ ft; $46\frac{1}{2}$ ft **9.** $5\frac{5}{9}$ ft,
$16\frac{2}{9}$ ft, $27\frac{7}{9}$ ft

Page 266 Exercises 1. ${}^-1$ **3.** ${}^-12$ **5.** ${}^-12$
7. 7 **9.** ${}^-12$ **11.** 15 **13.** ${}^-\frac{3}{10}$ **15.** 7 **17.** 7.9

19. ${}^-1.1$ **21.** 12.6 **23.** 10 **25.** ${}^-4.8$ **27.** 6.6
29. ${}^-2.5$ **31.** 0.9 **33.** $\frac{1}{2}$ **35.** ${}^-\frac{5}{6}$ **37.** ${}^-1\frac{1}{2}$
39. $1\frac{1}{2}$ **41.** ${}^-1$ **43.** ${}^-3$

Pages 269-270 Exercises 1. Add 7
3. Divide by 6 **5.** No **7.** No **9.** Yes
11. Yes **13.** $a < {}^-3$ **15.** $p > 6$ **17.** $b < {}^-4$
19. $n < 27$ **21.** $n > {}^-10$ **23.** $y > \frac{3}{5}$
25. $a \geq {}^-20$ **27.** $x \leq 5$ **29.** $d < {}^-30$
31. $h \leq 4$ **33.** $x > {}^-2$ **35.** $x \geq 3$
37. $x > 4$ **39.** $m < \frac{13}{3}$

Page 271 Algebra Practice 1. $761(1002) = r$;
762,522 **3.** $364.8 + 1.065 + 98.37 = d$;
464.235 **5.** $17\frac{8}{9} - 5\frac{3}{8} = m$; $12\frac{37}{72}$
7. $2\frac{1}{2} + 3\frac{5}{8} + 5\frac{3}{4} = P$; $11\frac{7}{8}$
9. $(3.14)(2^2)4 = V$; $50.24 \ m^3$
11. $5q(r^2 + rq + 2q)$ **13.** $\frac{4}{9}$ **15.** 1.2
17. 8.75 **19.** ${}^-9$ **21.** ${}^-11$ **23.** 12 **25.** 27
27. ${}^-63$ **29.** ${}^-14$ **31.** ${}^-13.31$ **33.** $5\frac{2}{3}$ **35.** $1\frac{5}{9}$
37. $x > 4$ **39.** $m < 20$

**Pages 272-273 Problem Solving for the
Consumer 1.** $198 **3.** $354, one way
5. $481.85 **7.** $1201

Page 274 Enrichment 1. ${}^-7$ **3.** ${}^-12$ **5.** ${}^-\frac{7}{10}$
7. $|{}^-8|$ **9.** $|{}^-15|$ **11.** $|{}^-50|$ **13.** $|{}^-24|$ **15.** $|{}^-4|$,
$|0|, |{}^-3|, |{}^-4|, |5|$ **17.** ${}^-|3.8|, |{}^-4.3|, |5.6|, |{}^-6.2|$,
$|7.1|$ **19.** 3 **21.** 15 **23.** 39 **25.** 17
27. $a = \pm b$ **29.** $|a| > |b|$, $a \geq 0$ and $b \leq 0$,
or $|a| > |b|$, $a \leq 0$ and $b \geq 0$

Page 275 Chapter Review 1. $<$ **3.** $>$ **5.** c
7. b **9.** No **11.** Yes **13.** No **15.** No
17. No **19.** Yes **21.** ${}^-10$ **23.** 10 **25.** ${}^-35$
27. 10.7 **29.** ${}^-10$ **31.** 1.2 **33.** $y < 3$
35. $g > {}^-14$ **37.** $a < {}^-54$ **39.** $x > {}^-20$
41. $y > {}^-3$

Page 277 Cumulative Review (Chapters 1-8)
1. 5.735 **3.** 13.167 **5.** 120 **7.** $\frac{8}{15}$ **9.** 160
11. $27\frac{1}{2}$ **13.** $1\frac{3}{5}$ **15.** $1\frac{1}{4}$ **17.** 50.5 **19.** 38
21. 24 **23.** 8.1 **25.** 250 **27.** 48
29. $120 \ in.^3$ **31.** $50.24 \ cm^3$ **33.** 4.9 points, 9.8
points

CHAPTER 9. GRAPHING IN THE COORDINATE PLANE

Page 281 Exercises   1. 24; 132, 156, 180, 204, 228 **3.** 127; 638, 765, 892, 1019, 1146 **5.** $^-$24; 444, 420, 396, 372, 348 **7.** 9, 10, 11, 12, 13 **9.** 0, 5, 10, 15, 20 **11.** 10, 8, 6, 4, 2 **13.** $^-$7, $^-$20, $^-$33, $^-$46, $^-$59 **15.** 258, 758 **17.** 1215, 825

Page 283 Exercises   1. $4n$; 40; 60 **3.** $3n + 4$; 34; 49 **5.** $7n + 3$; 73; 108 **7.** $^-$1; 2, 1, 0, $^-$1, $^-$2 **9.** 5; 0, 5, 10, 15, 20 **11.** 3; 6, 9, 12, 15, 18 **13.** $-n + 11$; 1; $^-$39 **15.** $4a - 9$; 31; 191 **17.** $5n - 2$; 48; 248 **19.** $\frac{5}{2}a + \frac{11}{2}$; $30\frac{1}{2}$; $130\frac{1}{2}$ **21.** $^-\frac{8}{5}n + \frac{88}{5}$; $1\frac{3}{5}$; $^-62\frac{2}{5}$

Page 284 Problems   1. a. $1.75; $3; $13 **b.** 78 weeks **3.** 6 **5.** 10 **7.** 22 **9.** 7 tables

Page 287 Exercises   13. $(^-6, 3)$ **15.** $(5, ^-3)$ **17.** $(0, ^-3)$ **19.** $(^-4, 0)$ **21.** square **23.** triangle **25.** square **27.** parallelogram

Page 290 Exercises   1. 11 **3.** 15 **5.** 14 **7.** 23 **9.** $^-$1 **11.** 16 **13.** $15\frac{1}{2}$ **15.** $^-5\frac{3}{4}$

Page 291 Problems   1. $70 h$

Page 293 Exercises   1. $(^-2, ^-5)$ **3.** $(3, 5)$ **5.** $^-$18; $(^-5, ^-18)$ **7.** 2; $(0, 2)$

Pages 296–297 Exercises   1. 1; 3; $y = x + 3$ **3.** $^-$4; 20; $y = ^-4x + 20$ **5.** $\frac{3}{5}$; $^-$4; upward

7. 1.5; 7.2; upward **9.** 7.3; $^-$12.6; upward **11.** same; parallel **13.** product is $^-1$; perpendicular **15.** horizontal **17.** vertical

Page 297 Problems   1. $\frac{3}{16}$

Pages 299–300 Exercises   1. No **3.** Yes **5.** No **7.** Yes **9.** Yes **11.** Yes **13.** Yes

Page 301 Algebra Practice
1. $49,452 \div 78 = c$; 634 **3.** $103 + 99.44 = v$; 202.44 **5.** $4\frac{2}{3} + 4\frac{7}{16} = t$; $9\frac{5}{48}$ **7.** $4(6\frac{7}{8}) = P$; $27\frac{1}{2}$ in. **9.** $(20)(6) = V$; 120 ft^3 **11.** $st(3t + st + 2s)$ **13.** $^-$2 **15.** $^-$4 **17.** $^-$2 **19.** 6, 7, 8, 9, 10 **21.** 1, $^-$3, $^-$7, $^-$11, $^-$15 **23.** $^-\frac{16}{7}n + 15$; $^-12\frac{4}{7}$; $^-30\frac{4}{7}$ **25** Answers vary **27.** 5; 3 **29.** $^-$3; 6 **31.** Yes

Pages 302–303 Problem Solving on the Job
1. d **3.** d **5.** c **7.** d **9.** d

Page 304 Enrichment   1. Yes **3.** Yes **5.** $(10, ^-3)$ **7.** $(1, 1)$ **9.** $(^-1, ^-6)$

Page 305 Chapter Review   1. d **3.** c **5.** a **7.** $5n - 4$; 71; 96 **9.** $3n - 8$; 37; 52 **15.** Yes **17.** No **19.** No **25.** 4; $^-$5 **27.** No **29.** No **31.** No

Page 307 Cumulative Review (Chapters 1–9)
1. $3\frac{15}{16}$ **3.** $\frac{1}{6}$ **5.** 1.96 **7.** 21 **9.** 190 **11.** $^-$10 **13.** $^-$27 **15.** 2 **17.** 24 **19.** $^-$8 **21.** $^-$12 **23.** 11 **25.** 9 **27.** 36 **29.** 10 **31.** 4 **33.** 3 **35.** 1 **37.** 864 cm^2

CHAPTER 10. STATISTICS

Page 311 Exercises   1. 19.25, 18 **3.** $\frac{5}{12}$, $\frac{1}{8}$ **5.** 3.9, 1.3 **7.** 71°, 72°, 72°, 5° **9.** $57.45, $49.95, $49.95, $100

Page 311 Problems   1. 62,612 **3.** $4

Page 313 Exercises   1. $4000 **3.** $1000 **5.** $4350 **7.** $100 **9.** WROQ, 45%; WCLS, 5%; WCAW, 20%; WANY, 30%

Pages 316–317 Exercises   1. $400 **3.** $100, $50 **5.** $2\frac{1}{2}$; $250 **7.** $2\frac{1}{4}$, $225 **9.** $150 **11.** 3 **13.** $5\frac{1}{2}$

Pages 319–320 Exercises   1. 90 **3.** 615 **5.** 300 **7.** 60 **9.** 25% **11.** Political action **13.** $15,000 **15.** $13,000

Pages 323–324 Exercises   1. Decrease **3.** 1960 to 1980 **5.** Magazine **7.** 35% **9.** 15% **11.** West **13.** After **15.** 41 million

Pages 327–328 Exercises (Answers may vary) **1.** How long will it be before rental charges equal the cost of buying the TV? 12 months **3.** What is the greatest amount of milk and detergent you can buy for $4? $\frac{3}{4}$ gal milk, 32 oz detergent **5.** When would you start

dinner so that it would be ready at 6:30?
4:20 **7.** How long will it be before the cost
of buying batteries equals the cost of buying
a charger and rechargeable batteries?
13 months

Pages 331–332 Exercises 1. 76–79, 3; 80–83,
1; 84–87, 2; 88–91, 1; 92–95, 2; 96–99, 3
3. $1\frac{3}{4}$ times greater **5.** 15 **7.** Between 8–9
and 10–11 **9.** 2 **11.** 7 **13.** 3

Page 335 Exercises 1. *L, R, P* **3.** *R*
5. Negative **7.** 150 lb **9.** Negative
11. Under 3:40

Page 337 Algebra Practice 1. $385(124) = y$;
47,740 **3.** $70.54 + 8.346 + 21.43 = n$;
100.316 **5.** $5\frac{1}{2} - 3\frac{4}{5} = s$; $1\frac{7}{10}$
7. $C = 2(3.14)(6.2)$; 38.936 cm **9.** $2r^3s$
11. $12j^3k^2$ **13.** 2 **15.** 128 **7.** 75

19. $n < {}^-7$ **21.** 6, 7, 8, 9, 10 **23.** 9, 12, 15,
18, 21

**Pages 338–339 Problem Solving for the
Consumer 1.** $65 **3.** $183.50 **5.** E **7.** A, B,
E, F **9.** 4 **11.** C

Page 340 Enrichment 1. 2 **3.** 14 **5.** 12
7. 82 **9.** 10 at or below; 61 **11.** 30 at or
below; 91 **13.** 24 at or below; 84

Page 341 Chapter Review 1. B, 30 jeans
3. A, $30 **5.** D, 136 **7.** C; 600

Page 343 Cumulative Review (Chapters 1–10)
1. 25 **3.** 56 **5.** 0.27263 **7.** $1\frac{7}{20}$ **9.** $5\frac{1}{6}$
11. $18\frac{13}{36}$ **13.** 3 **15.** 0 **17.** 5 **19.** 4 **21.** 2
23. 64.35 **25.** 46.2 **27.** 81.25% **29.** ${}^-12$
31. ${}^-210$ **33.** ${}^-22$ **35.** ${}^-5$ **37.** ${}^-5$; 0 **39.** $\frac{1}{2}$;
8 **41.** ${}^-16$; 4 **43.** 63

CHAPTER 11. SPECIAL TRIANGLES

Page 347 Exercises 1. 4.5 **3.** 3 **5.** 14
7. 6 **9.** 12

Page 349 Exercises 1. 7.5 ft **3.** 69 ft
5. 21.8 ft

Page 350 Problems 1. 200 m **3.** 10 ft 4 in.

Page 353 Exercises 1. 6 **3.** 9 **5.** 1
7. 2.449 **9.** 3.606 **11.** Yes **13.** No **15.** Yes
17. 3.606 km **19.** 10 cm **21.** 8.602 m
23. 6.325 **25.** 7.483 **27.** 8.062

Page 354 Problems 1. 5.4 ft **3.** 6.7 mi
5. 7 ft

Pages 356–357 Exercises 1. $\frac{1}{2}$; 2 **3.** $\frac{3}{2}$; $\frac{2}{3}$
5. 4; $\frac{1}{4}$ **7.** 0.8 **9.** 0.9 **11.** 1.9 **13.** 1.8
15. 4.4 **17.** 1.3 **19.** 0.9

Page 357 Using the Calculator 1. 3 **3.** 15
5. 49

Pages 359–360 Exercises 1. $\frac{5}{13}$; $\frac{12}{13}$; $\frac{12}{13}$; $\frac{5}{13}$
3. $\frac{3}{5}$; $\frac{4}{5}$; $\frac{4}{5}$; $\frac{3}{5}$ **5.** $\frac{70}{99}$; $\frac{70}{99}$; $\frac{70}{99}$; $\frac{70}{99}$ **7.** 40; $\frac{40}{41}$ **9.** 8;
$\frac{8}{17}$ **11.** 8.602; 0.8138 **13.** $\frac{4}{5}$ **15.** 0.7071

17. 0.7071 **19.** $\frac{4}{5}$ **21.** $\frac{3}{4}$ **23.** $\frac{3}{5}$ **25.** $\frac{3}{5}$ **27.** $\frac{3}{5}$;
$\frac{3}{5}$; $\sin M = \cos N$; Yes

Page 360 Challenge 1. $\dfrac{\sqrt{6}}{6}$ **3.** $\dfrac{2\sqrt{5}}{5}$
5. $\dfrac{7\sqrt{3}}{3}$

Page 362 Exercises 1. 6 **3.** 4.6 **5.** 13.0
7. 5.7 **9.** 18.1

Page 363 Problems 1. 477 m **3.** 55 mi

Page 365 Exercises 1. 34° **3.** 64° **5.** 61°
7. 63°; 27° **9.** 48°; 42° **11.** 34°; 56°
13. 66°; 24° **15.** 30°; 60° **17.** 37° **19.** 53°
21. 26°; 64°; 8

Page 366 Problems 1. 23°

Page 367 Algebra Practice
1. $293,675 \div 425 = m$; 691
3. $700 - 469.89 = C$; 230.11
5. $12\frac{3}{5} + 5\frac{9}{10} = g$; $18\frac{1}{2}$ **7.** $(3.14)(4.2)^2 = A$;
55.3896 in.^{2} **9.** $2g(g - 1 + 3g)$
11. $3cd(4c + cd - d^2)$ **13.** ${}^-6$ **15.** 9
17. 312 **19.** $V > {}^-3$ **21.** $5n - 12$; 63; 138
23. $5.3 + 2.8 = b$; 8.1 cm

511

Pages 368–369 Problem Solving on the Job
1. 43.75%; 51.43%; 48.84%; 46.55%; 43.75%
3. 24% **5.** 51.06% **7.** 5d **9.** 14d
11. $15,500; $20,133.33 **13.** 30 h; 67.5 h;
60 h; 22.5 h

Page 370 Enrichment 1. $3\sqrt{2}$ **3.** 5; 5
5. 2; 4

Page 371 Chapter Review 1. b **3.** 7.2 m

5. a **7.** a **9.** 16 **11.** 37°; 53° **13.** 41°;
49° **15.** $\frac{4}{5}$ **17.** $\frac{3}{5}$

Page 373 Cumulative Review 1. $\frac{2}{9}$ **3.** $\frac{1}{4}$
5. $\frac{9}{16}$ **7.** $\frac{14}{27}$ **9.** $\frac{2}{5}$ **11.** $\frac{7}{9}$ **13.** $\frac{7}{8}$ **15.** $\frac{1}{3}$
17. 60% **19.** 55.04 **21.** 35 **23.** $150
25. ⁻2 **27.** ⁻7 **29.** ⁻11 **31.** 8 **33.** ⁻48
35. ⁻5 **37–41.** Check students' graphs.
43. $24.75; $54.75

CHAPTER 12. PROBABILITY

Pages 377–378 Exercises 1. $\frac{1}{2}$ **3.** $\frac{100}{500} = \frac{1}{5}$
5. (Ex. 1) 50% **7.** (Ex. 3) 20% **9.** $\frac{1}{4}$ **11.** $\frac{1}{2}$
13. $\frac{1}{4}$ **15.** $\frac{1}{2}$ **17.** $\frac{3}{4}$ **19.** $\frac{3}{4}$ **21.** 30% **23.** 0%
25. 80% **27.** $\frac{1}{4}$ **29.** $\frac{2}{3}$

Page 378 Problems 1. 50% **3.** 48%

Pages 380–381 Exercises 1. $\frac{1}{8}$ **3.** $\frac{1}{4}$ **5.** $\frac{1}{8}$
7. $\frac{1}{6}$ **9.** 0 **11.** $\frac{1}{3}$ **13.** $\frac{1}{12}$ **15.** 0 **17.** $\frac{1}{6}$ **19.** $\frac{1}{4}$
21. $\frac{1}{6}$ **23.** $\frac{1}{2}$ **25.** $\frac{2}{3}$

Page 381 Problems 1. $\frac{1}{8}$

Pages 384–385 Exercises 1. 10
3. $2 \times 2 \times 5 = 20$ **5.** 125 **7.** 90 **9.** $\frac{1}{15}$
11. $\frac{2}{15}$ **13.** $\frac{1}{18}$ **15.** $\frac{1}{90}$ **17.** $\frac{1}{30}$ **19.** $\frac{1}{90}$ **21.** 16
23. $\frac{1}{4}$

Page 385 Problems 1. 60 **3.** 150 **5.** 240

Pages 387–388 1. $\frac{1}{36}$ **3.** $\frac{1}{12}$ **5.** $\frac{5}{36}$ **7.** $\frac{1}{32}$
9. $\frac{1}{15}$ **11.** $\frac{21}{32}$ **13.** $\frac{8}{15}$ **15.** $\frac{1}{720}$ **17.** $\frac{7}{18}$
19. $\frac{1}{288,000}$ **21.** Freshman

Page 388 Problems 1. 0.64

Page 389 Using the Calculator 1. 0.512
3. 0.250 **5.** 0.062

Pages 391–392 Exercises 1. $\frac{2}{3}$ **3.** 0.02
5. $\frac{4}{11}$ **7.** $\frac{5}{22}$ **9.** $\frac{1}{66}$ **11.** $\frac{2}{11}$ **13.** $\frac{3}{28}$ **15.** $\frac{15}{56}$
17. $\frac{1}{56}$ **19.** $\frac{1}{56}$ **21.** $\frac{1}{132}$ **23.** $\frac{1}{12}$ **25.** $\frac{5}{22}$

Page 392 Problems 1. $\dfrac{9 \cdot 8 \cdot 7 \cdot 6 \cdot 5}{10^5}$ **3.** $\dfrac{1}{10^5}$
5. 0

Pages 394–395 Exercises 1. $\frac{1}{1}$ **3.** $\frac{1}{5}$ **5.** $\frac{1}{2}$
7. $\frac{2}{1}$ **9.** $\frac{2}{1}$ **11.** $\frac{1}{1}$ **13.** $\frac{2}{1}$ **15.** $\frac{3}{2}$ **17.** $\frac{5}{4}$ **19.** $\dfrac{n}{1}$
21. $\frac{3}{7}$ **23.** $\frac{4}{1}$ **25.** $\dfrac{n}{100 - n}$ **27.** A **29.** $\frac{4}{1}$
31. $\frac{1}{2}$ **33.** $\dfrac{1}{n - 1}$ **35.** 16; $\frac{3}{8}$

Page 398 Exercises 1. 0.105 **3.** 0.215
5. 0.075 **7.** $0.1\overline{6}$ **9.** 0.2 **11.** 0.25 **13.** 0.3
15. $0.58\overline{3}$ **17.** 0.5 **19.** $\frac{23}{82}$

Page 398 Problems 1. 0.400 **3.** Season.
Greater number of times at bat gives a better
approximation.

Page 401 Exercises 1. 0.3 **3.** 0.6 **5.** 0.42
7. 360 **9.** 336 **11.** 1333 **13.** 162 **15.** 1160

Page 403 Algebra Practice 1. $(304)(465) = b$;
141,360 **3.** $5.84 + 9.473 + 6.958 = j$;
22.271 **5.** $20\frac{3}{8} - 12\frac{5}{6} = h$; $7\frac{13}{24}$
7. $2(6.2) + 2(5.9) = P$; 24.2 m
9. $6x^2(8x - 7)$ **11.** $2r(r^2 - 3rs + 2s^3)$
13. ⁻2 **15.** 3.84 **17.** 78 **19.** $k < 6$
21. (⁻1, ⁻7), (0, ⁻6), (1, ⁻5). (Answers will
vary.) **23.** (⁻1, 13), (0, 8); (1, 3). (Answers will
vary.) **25.** $g - 18.79 = 58.42$; $77.21

**Pages 404–405 Problem Solving for the
Consumer 1.** $\frac{1}{4}$ **3.** 800 **5.** Sum of the
results from Polls 1–4. **7.** Telephone book

Page 406 Enrichment 1. It is cold. **3.** 13 is
a prime number. **5.** 48 is a multiple of 4
7. You will receive $1000. You will be on TV.
You will be a celebrity.

Page 407 Chapter Review 1. $\frac{3}{5}$ **3.** 0 **5.** $\frac{9}{25}$
7. $\frac{4}{25}$ **9.** $\frac{12}{49}$ **11.** $\frac{87}{245}$ **15.** $\frac{3}{5}$ **17.** 720 **19.** $\frac{3}{10}$

Page 409 Cumulative Review 1. $4\frac{5}{12}$ **3.** $1\frac{23}{45}$
5. 83 **7.** 3196 **9.** 17 **11.** 7 **13.** 112°

CHAPTER 13. GEOMETRY

Page 414 Exercises 1. F **3.** T **5.** T **7.** F
9. T **11.** Alternate interior
13. Corresponding **15.** $\angle 7$, $\angle 13$; $\angle 6$, $\angle 16$;
$\angle 3$, $\angle 9$; $\angle 2$, $\angle 12$ **17.** 125° **19.** Yes
21. No **23.** No

Page 417 Exercises 1. F **3.** F **5.** T
7. No **9.** Yes. No. **11.** 360°; 70° **13.** 80°,
140°, 40°, 100° **15.** 108°, 60°, 90°, 132°,
150°

Pages 420–421 Exercises 1. Yes.
Corresponding sides are in proportion.
3. Yes. Corresponding sides are in
proportion. **5.** No **7.** Yes **9.** No **11.** No
13. 5; 1.75 **15.** $\angle DAB$, $\angle BEF$; $\angle ABC$,
$\angle EBC$; $\angle BCD$, $\angle BCF$; $\angle CDA$, $\angle CFE$;
$\overline{AB}$, $\overline{BE}$; $\overline{BC}$, $\overline{BC}$; $\overline{CD}$, $\overline{CF}$; $\overline{AD}$, $\overline{EF}$.
17. $\angle EMO$, $\angle ETR$; $\angle MOU$, $\angle TRA$;
$\angle OUS$, $\angle RAP$; $\angle USE$, $\angle APE$; $\angle SEM$,
$\angle PET$; $\overline{MO}$, $\overline{TR}$; $\overline{OU}$, $\overline{RA}$; $\overline{US}$, $\overline{AP}$; $\overline{SE}$,
$\overline{PE}$; $\overline{EM}$, $\overline{ET}$ **19.** Yes; SSS

Pages 423–424 Exercises 1. 15.25 in.
3. Carbon monoxide, 21.652.4 g; nitrogen,
1687.2 g; hydrocarbons, 1124.8 g; solid
particles, 98.8 g; sulfur, 76 g

15. 50° **17.** 99° **19.** 32.4 cm²
21. 17.64 m² **23.** 28.26 ft³
25. $420 + m = 725$; 305 mi
27. $x + x + 160 + x - 70 = 1860$; Team A,
$750; Team B, $590; Team C, $520

Page 427 1. Acute **3.** Equiangular
5. Isosceles **7.** Equilateral **9.** 9, 21, 14
11. 20, 20, 26 **13.** 70°

Page 430 Exercises 1. NAU **3.** 50 **5.** 40°
7. 85° **9.** 98 **11.** 2

Page 431 Algebra Practice
1. $1{,}336{,}064 \div 136 = p$; 9824
3. $152 - 107.98 = z$; 44.02 **5.** $6\frac{1}{4} + 1\frac{2}{3} = m$;
$7\frac{11}{12}$ **7.** $3.14(10.4) = c$; 32.656 m **9.** $4xy^2$
11. $20a^2b^2$ **13.** 10 **15.** 21.6 **17.** 2.5
19. $p < 2\frac{1}{4}$ **21.** 2; 7 **23.** $^-5$; 12 **25.** 28, 28,
26 **27.** $(x + 129) + x = 815$; 343 trucks, 472
cars

Pages 432–433 Problem Solving on the Job
1. $222 **3.** $104, $58.40, $143.20, $305.60
5. $93.20, $8.40, $55.20, $156.80 **7.** $55.50
9. $28.20

Page 434 Enrichment 1. 120 **3.** 240 **5.** 336

Page 435 Chapter Review 1. F **3.** T **5.** T
7. T **9.** c **11.** FE **13.** EH **15.** $\overline{MI}$, $\overline{ST}$, or
$\overline{IS}$ **17.** T **19.** $\angle KNM$ **21.** $\angle NKM$

Page 437 Cumulative Review (Chapters 1–13)
1. c **3.** b **5.** a **7.** 3.75 **9.** No **11.** No
13. $\frac{1}{2}$; 50% **15.** 3 small, 6 medium, 7 large

CHAPTER 14. PROGRAMMING IN BASIC

Page 441 Exercises 1. $2*x - 7$ **3.** $1/2*b*h$
5. $a/2 + b/3$ **7.** $x*y/z$ **9.** 6; 33.5; 8.75; 31
11. 10 PRINT 1*2*3, 20 END **13.** 10
PRINT 512 − 367, 20 END **15.** 10 PRINT
3.14*2*7.2, 20 END

Page 441 Challenge Output = 27; 10 PRINT
(8 + 4)↑2/2*3 − 5; 10 PRINT
8 + 4↑2/2*(3 − 5); 10 PRINT 8 + 4↑2/(2*3 − 5)

Pages 444–445 Exercises 1. 10.5; 2.1; 0.6
3. 3.3; 35.1; 38.4 **5.** THE VOLUME IS
301.44 **7.** Change line 50 to 50 LET
V = B*H/3 **9.** 40 LET M = (A + B + C)/3
50 PRINT "THE AVERAGE SCORE IS" M

Page 445 Using the Calculator 1. 23 **3.** 48
5. 73

Page 448 Exercises 1. 6, 7, 8, 9, 10, 11
3. 7, 9, 11, 13 **5.** 75, 90, 105, 120, 135, 150
7. 10 FOR L = 20 TO 30

Pages 453–454 Exercises 1. Delete lines 10 and 20; 5 READ A B; 35 DATA 15, 12.7 **3.** PERIMETER IS 20; AREA IS 25; PERIMETER IS 52; AREA IS 169; PERIMETER IS 29.2; AREA IS 53.29; OUT OF DATA IN LINE 10 **5.** 10 READ L, W; 20 LET A=L*W; 30 PRINT "AREA IS" A; 40 GO TO 10; 50 DATA 5.2, 3.9, 92.3, 80, 60 DATA 17, 11, 2.25, 1.4 70 END **7.** 10 READ D, M; 20 LET T=45.95*D+0.29*M; 30 PRINT "TOTAL COST IS" T; 40 GOTO 10; 50 DATA 2, 350, 1, 120, 1, 85; 60 DATA 3, 645, 4, 2120; 70 END

Page 456 Exercises 1. 72 IS 150 PERCENT OF 48; 35 IS 50 PERCENT OF 70; 75 IS 50 PERCENT OF 150; 90 IS 75 PERCENT OF 120; OUT OF DATA IN LINE 10 **3.** 1, 1; 4, 2; 9, 3; 16, 4; 25, 5; 36, 6; 49, 7, OUT OF DATA IN LINE 10 **5.** THE LEG LENGTHS ARE 12, 5; THE LENGTH OF THE HYPOTENUSE IS 13; THE LEG LENGTHS ARE 8, 6; THE LENGTH OF THE HYPOTENUSE IS 10; THE LEG LENGTHS ARE 8, 15; THE LENGTH OF THE HYPOTENUSE IS 17; THE LEG LENGTHS ARE 2, 2; THE LENGTH OF THE HYPOTENUSE IS 2.82843; THE LEG LENGTHS ARE 15, 20; THE LENGTH OF THE HYPOTENUSE IS 25 **7.** 10 READ A, B; 20 LET C = SQR(A↑2 + B↑2); 30 LET S = A/C; 40 PRINT "SIN D IS" S; 50 GOTO 10; 60 DATA 12, 5, 8, 6, 8, 15, 2, 2, 15, 20; 70 END

Pages 458–459 Exercises 1. 7.1, 4.7, 6, 3.9, 17.2 **3.** 35 IF $A<=220$ THEN 40; 36 PRINT "GREAT BOWLING"

EXTRA PRACTICE

Page 472 Extra Practice—Chapter 1 1. 22 **3.** 9 **5.** 7 **7.** 485 **9.** 208 **11.** 381 **13.** 387 **15.** 608 **17.** 42 **19.** 160 **21.** 11 **23.** 12 **25.** 11 **27.** 36 **29.** 0 **31.** $6n$ **33.** $11x + 3y$ **35.** $k + 7$ **37.** $8a + c$ **39.** $4x + 3y$ **41.** $x - 15$ **43.** $p + 42$ **45.** $x + y$

Page 473 Extra Practice—Chapter 2 1. 4.82, 4.7, 4.16 **3.** 9.7, 6.2, 4.863 **5.** 6.22, 6.2, 6.02 **7.** 1 **9.** 13 **11.** 1.3 **13.** 0.6 **15.** 250 **17.** 2.11 **19.** 20.418 **21.** 2.8 **23.** 3.06

Pages 461–462 Exercises 1. RED RIBBON; BLUE RIBBON; RED RIBBON **3.** 10 READ X, Y 20 IF X=Y THEN 40 30 IF X<>Y THEN 60 40 PRINT X; "="; Y 50 GO TO 10 60 PRINT X; "<>"; Y 70 GO TO 10 80 DATA 7.5, 7.5, ⁻1, 1, ⁻16, ⁻16, ⁻18.1, 18.1, 0.62, 6.02 90 END

Page 463 Algebra Practice 1. $2803(318) = d$; 891,354 **3.** $12.087 + 3.494 + 28.513 = h$; 44.094 **5.** $7\frac{7}{15} - 2\frac{4}{5} = n$; $4\frac{2}{3}$ **7.** A $= \frac{1}{2}(3\frac{1}{2})(2)$; $3\frac{1}{2}$ in.² **9.** $3ab(4a^2 - 5b)$ **11.** $2j^2(j + 8jk - 7k^2)$ **13.** 21 **15.** 7.8 **17.** 88 **19.** $28\frac{4}{5} > k$ **21.** Yes **23.** No **25.** 17, 27, 15 **27.** $2*r/s$

Page 464 Problem Solving for the Consumer 1. 15, 9 **3.** 15, 5 **5.** 20, 12, 12 **7.** 12, 16, 16 **9.** 110, 85, 88 **11.** Display **13.** Whiz, $1389.95; Essex, $1298.90; Supra, $1887.95 **15.** $108.83

Page 466 Enrichment 1. 5 **3.** ⁻7 **5.** 6.781 ROUNDED TO THE NEAREST WHOLE NUMBER IS 7; 3.925 ROUNDED TO THE NEAREST WHOLE NUMBER IS 4; 4.617 ROUNDED TO THE NEAREST WHOLE NUMBER IS 5; 86.138 ROUNDED TO THE NEAREST WHOLE NUMBER IS 86

Page 467 Chapter Review 1. F **3.** T **5.** F **7.** a **9.** 1000, 9

Page 469 Cumulative Review (Chapters 1–14) 1. 1923 **3.** 13,700 **5.** $1\frac{17}{45}$ **7.** $\frac{8}{9}$ **9.** $1\frac{7}{8}$ **11.** 29.6 **13.** 23% **15.** $420 **17.** 25% **19.** $\frac{1}{495}$

25. 272 **27.** 960 **29.** 1.2 **31.** 180 **33.** 23.4 **35.** 0.0362 **37.** 0.064 **39.** 1.2 **41.** 200,000 **43.** 2400 **45.** $3.401 + r$ **47.** $17.4 \div n$ **49.** $3.07 + c$

Page 474 Extra Practice—Chapter 3 1. Yes **3.** No **5.** Yes **7.** Yes **9.** $2^3 \cdot 3 \cdot 5$ **11.** 5^4 **13.** $2^2 \cdot 17$ **15.** $5 \cdot 31$ **17.** 2 **19.** 3 **21.** 4 **23.** n **25.** $2r$ **27.** f **29.** $a(2 - 1)$ **31.** $2(h^2 - 3)$ **33.** $r(25 + r)$ **35.** $3(3b^2 + b + 5)$ **37.** $2(5n + 8n^2 + 2)$ **39.** $xy(y + 1 - 3x)$ **41.** 42 **43.** 18 **45.** 24 **47.** 300 items

Page 475 Extra Practice—Chapter 4 1. $\frac{4}{5}$
3. $\frac{3}{4}$ **5.** 5 **7.** 2 **9.** $\frac{1}{a}$ **11.** $\frac{3}{4}$ **13.** $1\frac{7}{12}$

15. $1\frac{13}{28}$ **17.** $4\frac{11}{56}$ **19.** $\frac{1}{36}$ **21.** $6\frac{5}{12}$ **23.** $\frac{1}{a}$

25. $\frac{5a}{7}$ **27.** $\frac{3}{5}$ **29.** 1 **31.** $\frac{1}{9}$ **33.** $\frac{8}{c}$ **35.** n

37. $\frac{2}{3}$ **39.** 0.8 **41.** $0.\overline{3}$ **43.** $0.\overline{36}$ **45.** $0.1\overline{6}$
47. 4.5 **49.** 370 mi

Page 476 Extra Practice—Chapter 5 1. 5
3. 33 **5.** 62 **7.** 35 **9.** 35 **11.** 6 **13.** 5
15. 20 **17.** 36 **19.** 10 **21.** 7 **23.** 4 **25.** 12
27. 3 **29.** 16 **31.** 2 **33.** 2 **35.** $p + 4$; $\frac{1}{2}p$
37. $2n = 25$; \$12.50

Page 477 Extra Practice—Chapter 6
1. 16.8 cm **3.** 25.12 **5.** Right **7.** Acute
9. 42 ft^2 **11.** 12.56 m^2 **13.** 151.2 m^3
15. 188.4 cm^3 **17.** 200.96 mm^3 **19.** 471 ft^2
21. 220 mi

Page 478 Extra Practice—Chapter 7 1. $\frac{12}{125}$
3. $\frac{9}{25}$ **5.** 18.7 **7.** 110.8 **9.** 70% **11.** 5%
13. 50% **15.** 11.7 **17.** 20 **19.** 0.45 **21.** 630
23. $215\frac{5}{13}$ **25.** 10% **27.** 20% **29.** 29.4%

Page 479 Extra Practice—Chapter 8 1. $<$
3. $>$ **5.** $>$ **7.** $<$ **9.** $^-2$ **11.** $^-4$ **13.** $^-17$
15. 2 **17.** 2 **19.** $^-3$ **21.** $^-32$ **23.** 23
25. $^-24$ **27.** $^-20$ **29.** $^-56$ **31.** 72 **33.** $^-7$
35. 7 **37.** $^-4$ **39.** 9 **41.** 6.9 **43.** 31.5
45. $^-1.2$ **47.** $^-14$ **49.** $^-3\frac{4}{15}$ **51.** $^-1\frac{5}{16}$ **53.** 6

55. $1\frac{1}{5}$ **57.** 5 **59.** $^-6$ **61.** $^-0.9$ **63.** $7\frac{1}{2}$
65. $t > ^-4$ **67.** $y > ^-2$ **69.** $n > \frac{2}{5}$
71. $a < ^-40$

Page 480 Extra Practice—Chapter 9 1. 20,
24, 28 **3.** 20, 25, 30 **5.** 15, 21, 27 **15.** 35
17. 16 **27.** 2; $^-9$ **29.** $^-1$; $^-2$ **31.** $\frac{2}{3}$; $^-6$
33. $^-8$; $\frac{5}{3}$ **35.** $\frac{^-1}{3}$; $\frac{^-1}{4}$ **37.** No **39.** Yes

Page 481 Extra Practice—Chapter 10 1. 7.6;
3.1; 3.1; 3.6 **3.** 33% **5.** 6 P.M.; 8 A.M.
7. 800

Page 482 Extra Practice—Chapter 11 1. 8
3. 12.8 **5.** 9.22 **7.** $\frac{4}{3}, \frac{3}{3}, \frac{3}{3}$ **9.** $\frac{5}{12}, \frac{12}{13}, \frac{12}{13}$
11. 45°, 45° **13.** 60°, 30° **15.** 49°, 41°

Page 483 Extra Practice—Chapter 12 1. $\frac{1}{15}$
3. $\frac{14}{15}$ **5.** $\frac{2}{1125}$ **7.** $\frac{1}{45}$ **9.** $\frac{3}{2}$

Page 484 Extra Practice—Chapter 13
1. 120° **3.** 60°; 60° **5.** 55° **7.** $2\frac{10}{13}$ **9.** 6,
12, 12 **11.** 12, 27, 15 **13.** $\overline{BC}$; 8 **15.** 3; 4

Page 485 Extra Practice—Chapter 14
1. AREA IS 18 **3.** 10 FOR A=10 TO 25
STEP 5 **5.** YOU'VE SPENT 48.56 SO FAR
7. THE SUM OF THE MEASURES OF
THE ANGLES IS 180 SO THE POLYGON
IS A TRIANGLE; NOT A TRIANGLE;
NOT A TRIANGLE

APPENDIX

Page 516 Exercises 1. $6a$ **3.** $8y$
5. $3c + 4d - 5c^3$ **7.** $m + 4n$
9. $5c^4 + 2c - c^2$ **11.** $x + y + 2z$
13. $3a^2b - 3ab^2 + b^2$
15. $r^4 - 4r^2 + 2r + r^3$ **17.** $9w + 6 - 4wz$
19. $^-x^2y^2 + x^2y - 2x^2$

Simplifying Polynomials

The expressions below are called **monomials.**

$$6x \quad z^2 \quad 10 \quad {}^-4m^3n$$

The number 6 in the monomial $6x$ is called the **coefficient.** In the monomial z^2, the coefficient is understood to be 1.

An expression whose terms are monomials is called a **polynomial.** For example, $4x^2 + 3xy + y^2$ is a polynomial whose terms are $4x^2$, $3xy$, and y^2. Polynomials with two and three terms have special names.

Binomials (two terms): $4y + 9$ $2x^2 - 5y$
Trinomials (three terms): $x^2 + 7x + 12$ $3a^2 - 2ab^2 + b^2$

You have learned that two or more terms are called **like terms** if their variable parts are the same. Like terms can be added or subtracted by adding or subtracting their numerical coefficients. Unlike terms cannot be added or subtracted.

$$2x + 6x = 8x \qquad\qquad x^2 + x$$

| like terms | | unlike terms |

We say that a polynomial is **simplified** when none of its terms are like terms. To simplify a polynomial, rearrange its terms so that like terms are next to each other. Then combine like terms.

Example 1   Simplify $4y^2 + 7y - 2y^2$.

Solution
$$\begin{aligned}
4y^2 + 7y - 2y^2 &= 4y^2 + 7y + {}^-2y^2 \\
&= 4y^2 + {}^-2y^2 + 7y \longleftarrow \textit{Rearrange the terms.} \\
&= 2y^2 + 7y \longleftarrow \textit{Combine like terms.}
\end{aligned}$$

In practice, we usually do not write the difference as a sum as in Example 1. Instead, we rearrange the terms and subtract coefficients as shown in the example on the next page.

Example 2 Simplify $2x^2 + 9x - 8x^2$.

Solution $2x^2 + 9x - 8x^2 = 2x^2 - 8x^2 + 9x$ ←——— *Rearrange the terms.*
$$= -6x^2 + 9x \leftarrow \text{\textit{Combine like terms.}}$$

Example 3 Simplify $4a^2 + 5ab - 4a^2 - 7ab$.

Rearrange the terms.

Solution $4a^2 + 5ab - 4a^2 - 7ab = 4a^2 - 4a^2 + 5ab - 7ab$ ←———
$$= 0a^2 - 2ab \leftarrow \text{\textit{Combine like terms.}}$$
$$= {}^-2ab$$

Your Turn Simplify.
- $a^2 + 3a + 4a^2$
  $5a^2 + 3a$
- $2xy^2 - 3xy + 4xy^2$
  $6xy^2 - 3xy$

Exercises

Simplify.

A **1.** $2a + 5a - a$ $6a$

2. $^-7c + 5c + 4c$ $2c$

3. $5y + 6y - 3y$ $8y$

4. $4x - 3x^2 + 7x$ $11x - 3x^2$

5. $3c + 4d - 5c^3$ $3c + 4d - 5c^3$

6. $^-m^3 - 6m + 3m^3$ $2m^3 - 6m$

7. $^-2m + 4n + 7m - 4m$ $m + 4n$

8. $3r^3 + 4r^2 + 2r^3 + r$ $5r^3 + 4r^2 + r$

9. $4c^4 + 2c + c^4 - c^2$ $5c^4 + 2c - c^2$

10. $m^3 + 3m - 4m^2 + m^3$ $2m^3 + 3m - 4m^2$

11. $x + 3y + 2z - 2y$ $x + y + 2z$

12. $3a^3 - 7 - 2a^2 - 6a^2$ $3a^3 - 7 - 8a^2$

B **13.** $2a^2b - 3ab^2 + a^2b + b^2$
$3a^2b - 3ab + b^2$

14. $9x^2y + 5y + 5x^2y - 10x^2y$ $4x^2y + 5y$

15. $r^4 - 3r^2 + 2r - r^2 + r^3$
$r^4 - 4r^2 + 2r + r^3$

16. $a^3 + 3a^2b - 6ab^2 + 3a^3 - 2a^2b$
$4a^3 + a^2b - 6ab^2$

17. $3w + 6 + 2w - 5wz + 4w + wz$
$9w + 6 - 4wz$

18. $xy - 5y + 7 - 6xy + y + 9$
$-5xy - 4y + 16$

19. $^-2x^2y^2 + x^2y + 3x^2 + x^2y^2 - 5x^2$
$-x^2y^2 + x^2y - 2x^2$

20. $^-7a^3 + a + 5a^2 - 3a + a^3 + a^2$
$-6a^3 - 2a + 6a^2$

517

Algebra Readiness Test

Evaluate the expression using the given value for the variable.

1. $n + 6$; $n = 11$ $_{17}$

2. $x - 9$; $x = 20$ $_{11}$

3. $4y$; $y = 9$ $_{36}$

4. $3 + n^2$; $n = 5$ $_{28}$

5. $m \div 6$; $m = 54$ $_9$

6. $10 - 2c$; $c = 4$ $_2$

7. $12r^2$; $r = 4$ $_{192}$

8. $z^2 - 14$; $z = 9$ $_{67}$

Review work: pages 1–20

Combine like terms

9. $a + 4a$ $_{5a}$

10. $3x + 7 + 4x$ $_{7x + 7}$

11. $c + 25x - c$ $_{25x}$

12. $3n + 4n + n$ $_{8n}$

13. $5h - 2.4h + 6$ $_{2.6h + 6}$

14. $6.3y + 4x + y - x$ $_{7.3y + 3x}$

15. $0.3p + 21p - 6 + n$ $_{21.3p - 6 + n}$

16. $1.1s + 5t - 0.1s + t$ $_{s + 6t}$

pages 23–25, pages 45–50

Write an expression for the given phrase.

17. 7 added to x $_{x + 7}$

18. n decreased by 9 $_{n - 9}$

19. c more than 17 $_{17 + c}$

20. the product of m and 35 $_{35m}$

21. n used as a factor 4 times $_{n^4}$

22. 54 divided by r $_{54 \div r}$

23. 26.4 subtracted from g $_{g - 26.4}$

pages 1–3

Write an equation for the given sentence. Solve the equation.

24. The sum of 8247 and 16 is x. $_{8247 + 16 = x; \ 8263}$

25. The product of 14 and 35 is c. $_{14 \times 35 = c; \ 490}$

26. 86 increased by 135 is y. $_{86 + 135 = y; \ 221}$

27. 4.7 decreased by 3.9 is equal to t. $_{4.7 - 3.9 = t; \ 0.8}$

28. n is equal to 4.92 greater than 6.5. $_{n = 6.5 + 4.92; \ 11.42}$

pages 4–10, pages 18–20, pages 45–50

Use the distributive property to factor the expression.

29. $c^2 + 4c$ $c(c + 4)$

30. $4m + 3m^2$ $m(4 + 3m)$

31. $5t + 7t^2$ $t(5 + 7t)$

32. $k - 5k^2$ $k(1 - 5k)$

33. $4mn + 4n$ $4n(m + 1)$

34. $3y^2 - 6y + 9yz$
$3y(y - 2 + 3z)$

Write the fraction in lowest terms.

35. $\dfrac{5}{10}$ $\dfrac{1}{2}$

36. $\dfrac{6}{18}$ $\dfrac{1}{3}$

37. $\dfrac{8}{24}$ $\dfrac{1}{3}$

38. $\dfrac{x}{x}$ 1

39. $\dfrac{2x}{4}$ $\dfrac{x}{2}$

40. $\dfrac{10a}{5a}$ 2

41. $\dfrac{21cd}{7c}$ $3d$

42. $\dfrac{9m^2}{3m}$ $3m$

43. $\dfrac{8ab}{4ab^2}$ $\dfrac{2}{b}$

Add, subtract, multiply, or divide.

44. $\dfrac{2}{8} + \dfrac{1}{8}$ $\dfrac{3}{8}$

45. $\dfrac{a}{9} + \dfrac{3a}{9}$ $\dfrac{4a}{9}$

46. $\dfrac{8}{6} - \dfrac{3}{6}$ $\dfrac{5}{6}$

47. $\dfrac{10}{x} - \dfrac{3}{x}$ $\dfrac{7}{x}$

48. $\dfrac{m}{2} - \dfrac{m}{4}$ $\dfrac{m}{4}$

49. $\dfrac{1}{3} \cdot \dfrac{7}{8}$ $\dfrac{7}{24}$

50. $\dfrac{1}{2} \cdot n$ $\dfrac{1}{2}n$, or $\dfrac{n}{2}$

51. $\dfrac{3}{c} \cdot \dfrac{x}{7}$ $\dfrac{3x}{7c}$

52. $\dfrac{6}{n} \div 11$ $\dfrac{6}{11n}$

Solve the equation.

53. $c + 7 = 12$ 5

54. $5 + x = 9$ 4

55. $21 = p + 16$ 5

56. $9 + d = 25$ 16

57. $6x = 24$ 4

58. $40e = 1200$ 30

59. $0.2f = 8$ 40

60. $12g = 48$ 4

61. $d - 9 = 12$ 21

62. $m - 12 = 52$ 64

63. $\dfrac{a}{10} = 5$ 50

64. $\dfrac{e}{9} = 7$ 63

Solve the multi-step equation.

65. $2a + 5 = 21$ 8

66. $4c - 2 = 14$ 4

67. $5f - 9 = 21$ 6

68. $6m - 1 = 35$ 6

69. $6 + 8d = 62$ 7

70. $9j - 7 = 65$ 8

71. $2x = x + 8$ 8

72. $5r = 7 - 2r$ 1

73. $3y = y + 18$ 9

Write an expression.

pages 155–158

74. Emily is 4 in. taller than Carl.
    Let h = Carl's height in inches.
    Emily's height is __?__ in. $h + 4$
75. Fred has twice as much money as Al.
    Let m = amount of money Al has.
    Amount of money Fred has = __?__. $2m$
76. Jean's term paper has 7 fewer pages than Don's.
    Let p = number of pages in Don's term paper.
    Number of pages in Jean's term paper = __?__. $p - 7$

Write an equation. Solve.

pages 159–164

77. The length of a picture frame is 14 in.
    The length is 2 times the width.
    What is the width? $2n = 14$; 7 in.
78. Mark is 2 in. taller than Bob.
    Mark is 70 in. tall.
    How tall is Bob? $n + 2 = 70$; 68 in.
79. In Houston, Texas, the average yearly rainfall
    is 15.8 in. greater than in Dallas. Houston's $n + 15.8 = 48.2$;
    average rainfall is 48.2 in. What is Dallas'? 32.4 in.
80. One number is three times another.
    The sum of the numbers is 36.
    What are the two numbers? $n + 3n = 36$; 9 and 27

Add, subtract, multiply, or divide.

pages 243–257

81. $^-8 + {}^-6$ $^-14$ 82. $6 + {}^-11$ $^-5$ 83. $^-4 + 9$ 5

84. $^-6 + 2$ $^-4$ 85. $^-12 - 3$ $^-15$ 86. $^-18 - {}^-4$ $^-14$

87. $^-20 - {}^-9$ $^-11$ 88. $^-5(^-8)$ 40   89. $^-9 \cdot 6$ $^-54$

90. $^-3 \cdot 2d$ ^-6d 91. $^-21 \div {}^-3$ 7   92. $^-40 \div 10$ $^-4$

Find three ordered pairs that are solutions of the given equation, then graph them and draw the line for the equation. Check students' graphs.

pages 292–297

93. $y = x - 4$ (0, $^-4$), (4, 0), (2, $^-2$)

94. $y = x + 8$ (0, 8), ($^-8$, 0), ($^-4$, 4)

95. $y = 2x + 1$ (0, 1), $\left(\frac{^-1}{2}, 0\right)$, (1, 3)

96. $y = 3x - 4$ (0, $^-4$), $\left(\frac{4}{3}, 0\right)$, (2, 2)

520